THE COLLEGE WRITER
BRIEF

A Guide to Thinking, Writing, and Researching
Third Edition

Randall VanderMey
Westmont College

Verne Meyer
Dordt College

John Van Rys
Redeemer University College

Pat Sebranek

WADSWORTH
CENGAGE Learning™

Australia • Brazil • Japan • Korea • Mexico • Singapore • Spain • United Kingdom • United States

WADSWORTH
CENGAGE Learning™

The College Writer Brief: A Guide to Thinking, Writing, and Researching, with the 2009 MLA Update, Third Edition

Randall VanderMey, Verne Meyer, John Van Rys, and Pat Sebranek

Executive Publisher: Patricia Coryell

Senior Marketing Manager: Tom Ziolkowski

Discipline Product Manager: Pina Daniel

Development Manager, English: Judith Fifer

Senior Project Editor: Aileen Mason

Senior Media Producer: Philip Lanza

Content Manager: Janet Edmonds

Cover Design Manager: Anne S. Katzeff

Senior Photo Editor: Jennifer Meyer Dare

Senior New Title Project Manager: Patricia O'Neill

Editorial Associate: Daisuke Yasutake

Marketing Associate, English and Student Success: Bettina Chiu

Editorial Assistant, Editorial Production: Anne Finley

Sebranek, Inc.: Steve Augustyn, Laura Bachman, Ron Bachman, April Barrons, Colleen Belmont, Chris Erickson, Mark Fairweather, Mariellen Hanrahan, Tammy Hintz, Rob King, Lois Krenzke, Mark Lalumondier, Kevin Nelson, Mike Ramczyk, Janae Sebranek, Lester Smith, Jean Varley

For product information and technology assistance, contact us at **Cengage Learning Customer & Sales Support, 1-800-354-9706**

For permission to use material from this text or product, submit all requests online at **cengage.com/permissions**
Further permissions questions can be emailed to **permissionrequest@cengage.com**

Library of Congress Control Number: 2009927219

ISBN-13: 978-0-495-80342-3

ISBN-10: 0-495-80342-1

Wadsworth
20 Channel Center Street
Boston, MA 02210
USA

Cengage Learning is a leading provider of customized learning solutions with office locations around the globe, including Singapore, the United Kingdom, Australia, Mexico, Brazil, and Japan. Locate your local office at: **international.cengage.com/region**

Cengage Learning products are represented in Canada by Nelson Education, Ltd.

For your course and learning solutions, visit **www.cengage.com**

Purchase any of our products at your local college store or at our preferred online store **www.ichapters.com**.

Credits begin on page 567, which constitutes an extension of this copyright page.

Printed in Canada.
1 2 3 4 5 6 7 13 12 11 10 09

Preface

The College Writer Brief, third edition, offers students thorough yet accessible coverage of the writing process; the book's visual format helps them quickly grasp the big picture and easily locate supporting details. In response to reviewers' requests, the authors added new student and professional samples, including new MLA and APA papers, to help students achieve a formal academic voice. In addition, the entire book, as well as audio, video, exercises, models, and weblinks, is available as an e-book or with a separate passkey that permits students to access additional online features.

Key Features of *The College Writer Brief,* Third Edition

- Unique "at-a-glance" format presents each concept in one or two pages.
- Colorful design and visuals reinforce the concepts and aid retention.
- Tabbed sections enable students to find topics quickly.
- Coverage of planning, drafting, revising, editing, and proofreading is thorough, with sample paragraphs and visuals that walk students through the rhetorical situation (identifying purpose, audience, and context).
- Instruction on "Writing with Sources" is integrated into the writing-process chapters in page spreads that explain how to use sources during a given step (e.g., pages 40–41 and 68–69).
- Both student and professional samples of each type of writing are included to offer students writing models appropriate for their needs.
- Coverage of research methods, such as electronic research, includes extensive instruction on how to work with and evaluate sources, integrate them effectively, and document them so as to avoid plagiarism.
- New model MLA and APA papers illustrate a wide variety of research-writing practices, including accessing and documenting online sources.
- A friendly "coaching" tone develops students' self-confidence as learners.
- Cross-curricular writing instruction is offered throughout the text: chapters 2–7 give research-writing tips called "Cross-Curricular Connections"; chapter 9 identifies writing forms and skills emphasized in each discipline; chapters 10–23 include sample papers written in a variety of courses; and chapters 28–33 address research skills.
- Coverage of critical thinking and critical viewing throughout the text helps students learn to analyze and evaluate both written and visual "arguments," such as advertisements and political campaign coverage.

 A thematic table of contents supports instructors who employ themes such as community and conscience or ethics and equity.

New to This Edition

Critical Thinking and Reading From cover to cover, *The College Writer Brief* helps students develop and apply critical-thinking skills. For example, chapter 1 explains how to think critically when reading, studying, taking tests, or viewing; chapters 2–8 show how to think critically while working through the writing process; and chapters 10–32 explain how to apply critical-thinking strategies when reading or writing a broad range of literary forms.

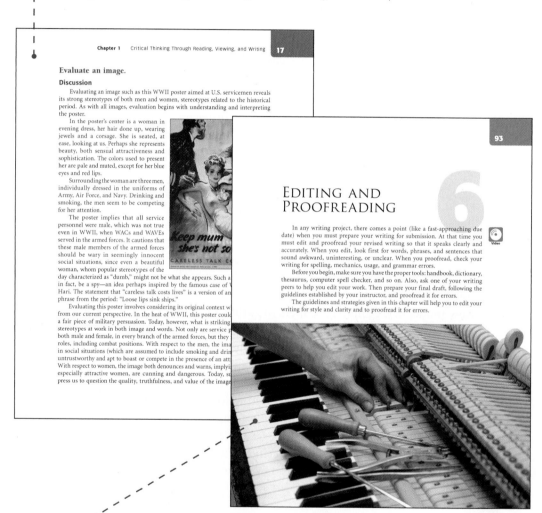

New Visuals and Thinking Prompts Each of the first thirty-two chapters begins with a visual that introduces the chapter and concludes with a prompt (called "Visually Speaking") that challenges students to think critically about the nature and function of the visual.

Additional Third-Person Essays Third-person essays, both student and professional, have been added to this edition of the text. Additional student models are available in a new print supplement, *Student Voices: A Sampling of College Writing,* and on the text's companion website.

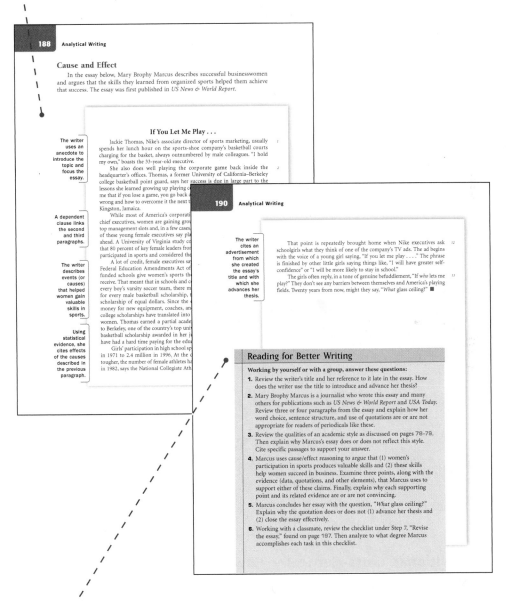

188   Analytical Writing

Cause and Effect
In the essay below, Mary Brophy Marcus describes successful businesswomen and argues that the skills they learned from organized sports helped them achieve that success. The essay was first published in *US News & World Report.*

If You Let Me Play . . .

The writer uses an anecdote to introduce the topic and focus the essay.

Jackie Thomas, Nike's associate director of sports marketing, usually spends her lunch hour on the sports-shoe company's basketball courts charging for the basket, always outnumbered by male colleagues. "I hold my own," boasts the 33-year-old executive.

She also does well playing the corporate game back inside the headquarter's offices. Thomas, a former University of California–Berkeley college basketball point guard, says her success is due in large part to the lessons she learned growing up playing c...

A dependent clause links the second and third paragraphs.

me that if you lose a game, you go back a... wrong and how to overcome it the next t... Kingston, Jamaica.

While most of America's corporati... chief executives, women are gaining gro... top management slots and, in a few cases,...

The writer describes events (or causes) that helped women gain valuable skills in sports.

of these young female executives say pla... ahead. A University of Virginia study co... that 80 percent of key female leaders fro... participated in sports and considered the...

A lot of credit, female executives sa... Federal Education Amendments Act of... funded schools give women's sports th... receive. That meant that in schools and c... every boy's varsity soccer team, there m... for every male basketball scholarship, t... scholarship of equal dollars. Since the...

Using statistical evidence, she cites effects of the causes described in the previous paragraph.

money for new equipment, coaches, an... college scholarships have translated into... women. Thomas earned a partial acade... basketball scholarship awarded in her j... have had a hard time paying for the edu...

Girls' participation in high school sp... in 1971 to 2.4 million in 1996. At the... tougher, the number of female athletes ha... in 1982, says the National Collegiate Ath...

190   Analytical Writing

The writer cites an advertisement from which she created the essay's title and with which she advances her thesis.

That point is repeatedly brought home when Nike executives ask schoolgirls what they think of one of the company's TV ads. The ad begins with the voice of a young girl saying, "If you let me play . . . ." The phrase is finished by other little girls saying things like, "I will have greater self-confidence" or "I will be more likely to stay in school."

The girls often reply, in a tone of genuine befuddlement, "If *who* lets me play?" They don't see any barriers between themselves and America's playing fields. Twenty years from now, might they say, "*What* glass ceiling?" ■

Reading for Better Writing

Working by yourself or with a group, answer these questions:

1. Review the writer's title and her reference to it late in the essay. How does the writer use the title to introduce and advance her thesis?

2. Mary Brophy Marcus is a journalist who wrote this essay and many others for publications such as *US News & World Report* and *USA Today.* Review three or four paragraphs from the essay and explain how her word choice, sentence structure, and use of quotations are or are not appropriate for readers of periodicals like these.

3. Review the qualities of an academic style as discussed on pages 78–79. Then explain why Marcus's essay does or does not reflect this style. Cite specific passages to support your answer.

4. Marcus uses cause/effect reasoning to argue that (1) women's participation in sports produces valuable skills and (2) these skills help women succeed in business. Examine three points, along with the evidence (data, quotations, and other elements), that Marcus uses to support either of these claims. Finally, explain why each supporting point and its related evidence are or are not convincing.

5. Marcus concludes her essay with the question, "*What* glass ceiling?" Explain why the quotation does or does not (1) advance her thesis and (2) close the essay effectively.

6. Working with a classmate, review the checklist under Step 7, "Revise the essay," found on page 197. Then analyze to what degree Marcus accomplishes each task in this checklist.

Collaborative Work In addition to providing activities for individual thinking and writing, each chapter also features response topics that promote group discussion and projects that facilitate collaborative learning.

More on Integrating Sources Chapters 2–7 each include a new two-page spread called "Writing with Sources." This feature offers tips on how to work with researched information at each step in the writing process. For example, chapter 2 presents and explains how to do the following:

- Track resources in a working bibliography.
- Use a note-taking system that respects sources.
- Distinguish summaries, paraphrases, and quotations.

Additional coverage of integrating sources is included in section 3, "Research and Writing." (More on avoiding plagiarism and integrating sources can also be found on the student website.)

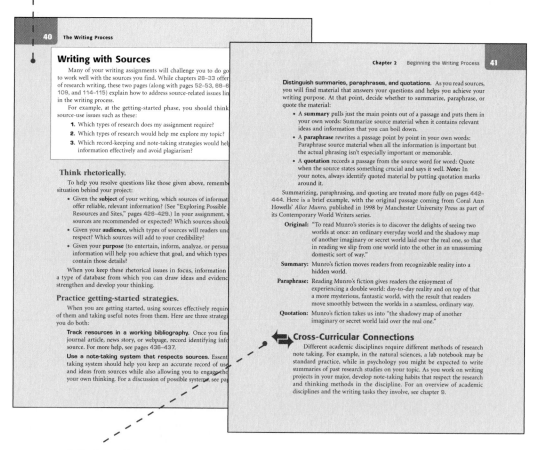

40   The Writing Process

Writing with Sources

Many of your writing assignments will challenge you to do go to work well with the sources you find. While chapters 28–33 offer of research writing, these two pages (along with pages 52–53, 68–6 109, and 114–115) explain how to address source-related issues lin in the writing process.

For example, at the getting-started phase, you should think source-use issues such as these:

1. Which types of research does my assignment require?
2. Which types of research would help me explore my topic?
3. Which record-keeping and note-taking strategies would hel information effectively and avoid plagiarism?

Think rhetorically.

To help you resolve questions like those given above, rememb situation behind your project:

- Given the **subject** of your writing, which sources of informat offer reliable, relevant information? (See "Exploring Possible Resources and Sites," pages 428–429.) In your assignment, v sources are recommended or expected? Which sources shoul
- Given your **audience**, which types of sources will readers respect? Which sources will add to your credibility?
- Given your **purpose** (to entertain, inform, analyze, or persua information will help you achieve that goal, and which types contain those details?

When you keep these rhetorical issues in focus, information a type of database from which you can draw ideas and evidenc strengthen and develop your thinking.

Practice getting-started strategies.

When you are getting started, using sources effectively requir of them and taking useful notes from them. Here are three strategi you do both:

Track resources in a working bibliography. Once you fine journal article, news story, or webpage, record identifying info source. For more help, see pages 436–437.

Use a note-taking system that respects sources. Essent taking system should help you keep an accurate record of use and ideas from sources while also allowing you to engage tho your own thinking. For a discussion of possible systems, see pa

---

Chapter 2   Beginning the Writing Process   **41**

Distinguish summaries, paraphrases, and quotations. As you read sources, you will find material that answers your questions and helps you achieve your writing purpose. At that point, decide whether to summarize, paraphrase, or quote the material:

- A **summary** pulls just the main points out of a passage and puts them in your own words: Summarize source material when it contains relevant ideas and information that you can boil down.
- A **paraphrase** rewrites a passage point by point in your own words: Paraphrase source material when all the information is important but the actual phrasing isn't especially important or memorable.
- A **quotation** records a passage from the source word for word: Quote when the source states something crucial and says it well. *Note:* In your notes, always identify quoted material by putting quotation marks around it.

Summarizing, paraphrasing, and quoting are treated more fully on pages 442–444. Here is a brief example, with the original passage coming from Coral Ann Howells' *Alice Munro*, published in 1998 by Manchester University Press as part of its Contemporary World Writers series.

Original: "To read Munro's stories is to discover the delights of seeing two worlds at once: an ordinary everyday world and the shadowy map of another imaginary or secret world laid over the real one, so that in reading we slip from one world into the other in an unassuming domestic sort of way."

Summary: Munro's fiction moves readers from recognizable reality into a hidden world.

Paraphrase: Reading Munro's fiction gives readers the enjoyment of experiencing a double world: day-to-day reality and on top of that a more mysterious, fantastic world, with the result that readers move smoothly between the worlds in a seamless, ordinary way.

Quotation: Munro's fiction takes us into "the shadowy map of another imaginary or secret world laid over the real one."

Cross-Curricular Connections

Different academic disciplines require different methods of research note taking. For example, in the natural sciences, a lab notebook may be standard practice, while in psychology you might be expected to write summaries of past research studies on your topic. As you work on writing projects in your major, develop note-taking habits that respect the research and thinking methods in the discipline. For an overview of academic disciplines and the writing tasks they involve, see chapter 9.

Additional Cross-Curricular Coverage Chapters 2–7 each include a new feature called "Cross-Curricular Connections," an insert explaining research-writing strategies required or emphasized in specific disciplines. Chapter 9, "Forms of College Writing," lists the types of writing and thinking skills emphasized across the curriculum. In addition, chapters 10–23 include instructions for and models of writing done in a variety of courses.

New MLA and APA Papers The third edition of *The College Writer Brief* includes new MLA and APA student sample papers and reflects updates to electronic citation for the APA system. The MLA citations in this text follow the sixth edition of the *MLA Handbook for Writers of Research Papers* pending publication of the seventh edition; visit mla.org for more information.

More Online Supplementation for the Student

The College Writer Brief E-book *The College Writer Brief* is now available as an e-book (electronic book), which offers students online access to the entire text, along with video and audio explanations that enhance the text, writing tutorials, grammar exercises, additional writing models, and links to carefully selected websites.

Student Website Students can go to **www.thecollegewriter.com/3e** to find weblinks, visual activities, games, annotated readings, writing assignments, grammar exercises, and more.

Student Voices: A Sampling of College Writing This new 64-page supplement of student papers illustrates each of the modes and provides additional writing formats. This resource can be packaged with the text for only $5.00.

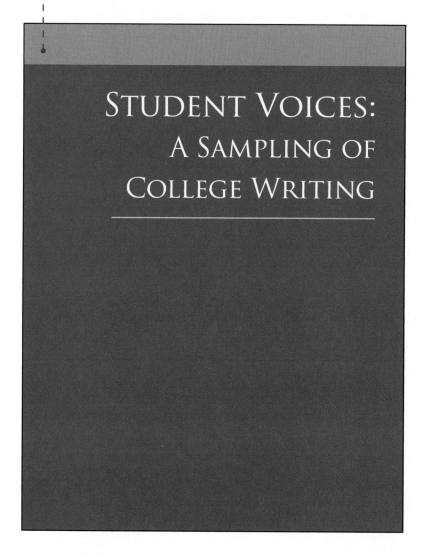

STUDENT VOICES: A SAMPLING OF COLLEGE WRITING

WriteSPACE offers additional premium content that is passkey-protected and is available to be packaged with the text. This content includes all of the features of WriteSPACE with Eduspace, Cengage Learning's signature Classroom Management System, but can be used with any CMS. This premium content includes tutorials, grammar exercises, writing assignments, interactive proofreading practice, additional readings, visual activities, games, and music activities.

More Online Supplementation for the Instructor

Instructor's Resource Manual is available in a print version or is downloadable from the instructor's website; the document contains an overview of the course, sample syllabi, chapter summaries, and teaching suggestions.

Instructor's Website, a password-protected site accessed at **www .thecollegewriter.com/3e,** provides the downloadable version of the *Instructor's Resource Manual,* assessment rubrics, learning objectives, and access to all materials in the student website.

WriteSPACE with Eduspace, Cengage Learning's Classroom Management System, provides an integrated, customizable system with a wide variety of content that can be administered as self-paced exercises or gradable exams. WriteSPACE delivers exercises, diagnostic tests, assignments, and learning modules, as well as access to CL Assess, a personalized assessment tool that can pinpoint a student's writing problems and track his or her progress.

Acknowledgments

The authors express their gratitude to the following people, who have contributed to the development of this edition of the text or to prior editions and supplements.

Reviewers: Alena Balmforth, *Salt Lake Community College;* Cherrie Bergandi, *Chippewa Valley Technical College;* Michael D. Cook, *Everest College—Phoenix;* Tamera Davis, *Northern Oklahoma College— Stillwater;* Mary Etter, *Davenport University;* Patrick L. Green, *Aiken Technical College;* Jennifer Haber, *St. Petersburg College;* Patricia A. Herb, *North Central State College;* David Jacobsen, *Westmont College;* John L. Liffiton, *Scottsdale Community College;* Molly Luby, *Central Carolina Community College;* Kelly B. McCalla, *Central Lakes College;* Christine A. Miller, *Davenport University;* Nancy W. Noel, *Germanna Community College;* Francie Quaas-Berryman, *Cerritos College;* Christine A. Saxlid, *Wisconsin Indianhead Technical College;* Vicki Scheurer, *Palm Beach Community College;* Catherine Scudder Wolf, *Susssex County Community College;* Susan M. Smith, *Tompkins Cortland Community College;* Donald Stinson, *Northern Oklahoma College;* Christine Szymczak, *Erie Community College*

Instructors: Mary Adams, *Peru State College;* Jim Addison, *Western Carolina University;* Susan Aguila, *Palm Beach Community College;* Cathryn Amdahl, *Harrisburg Area Community College;* Edmund August, *McKendree College;* Richard Baker, *Adams State College;* Thomas G. Beverage, *Coastal Carolina Community College;* Patricia Blaine, *Paducah Community College;* Tammie Bob, *College of DuPage;* Candace Boeck, *San Diego State University;* Charley Boyd, *Genesee Community College;* Deborah Bradford, *Bridgewater State College;* Linda Brender, *Macomb Community College;* Colleen M. Burke, *Rasmussen College;* Vicki Byard, *Northeastern Illinois University;* Susan Callender, *Sinclair Community College;* Sandra Camillo, *Finger Lakes Community College;* Sandy Cavanah, *Hopkinsville Community College;* Annette Cedarholm, *Snead State Community College;* James William Chichetto, *Stonehill College;* Sandra Clark, *Anderson University;* Beth Conomos, *Erie Community College, SUNY;* Keith Coplin, *Colby Community College;* Sue Cornett, *St. Petersburg College;* Debra Cumberland, *Winona State University;* David Daniel,

Newbury College; Sarah Dangelantonio, *Franklin Pierce College;* Rachelle L. Darabi, *Indiana University, Purdue University Fort Wayne;* Judy C. Davidson, *University of Texas, Pan American;* Helen Deese, *University of California, Riverside;* Darren DeFrain, *Wichita State University;* Sarah Dengler, *Franklin Pierce College;* Linda Dethloff, *Prairie State College;* Steven Dolgin, *Schoolcraft College;* Carol Jean Dudley, *Eastern Illinois University;* Chris Ellery, *Angelo State University;* Ernest J. Enchelmayer, *Louisiana State University;* Anne K. Erickson, *Atlantic Cape Community College;* Kelly A. Foth, *University of Dubuque;* Julie Foust, *Utah State University;* Lyneé Lewis Gaillet, *Georgia State University;* Gregory R. Glau, *Arizona State University;* Patricia Glynn, *Middlesex Community College;* Samuel J. Goldstein, *Daytona Beach Community College;* Kim Grewe, *Wor-Wic Community College;* Loren C. Gruber, *Missouri Valley College;* Michael Hammond, *Northeastern Illinois University;* Katona Hargrave, *Troy State University;* Dick Harrington, *Piedmont Virginia Community College;* Karla Hayashi, *University of Hawaii, Hilo;* Anne Christine Helms, *Alamance Community College;* Stan Hitron, *Middlesex Community College;* Karen Holleran, *Kaplan College;* Barbara Dondiego Holmes, *University of Charleston;* Maurice Hunt, *Baylor University;* Barbara Jacobskind, *University of Massachusetts, Dartmouth;* Linda G. Johnson, *Southeast Technical Institute;* Alex M. Joncas, *Estrella Mountain Community College;* Nina B. Keery, *Massachusetts Bay Community College;* Sandra Keneda, *Rose State College;* Margo LaGattuta, *University of Michigan, Flint;* Richard Larschan, *University of Massachusetts, Dartmouth;* Dusty Maddox, *DeVry University;* Bonnie J. Marshall, *Grand Valley State University;* Daphne Matthews, *Mississippi Delta Community College;* Claudia Milstead, *Missouri Valley College;* Kate Mohler, *Mesa Community College;* Meghan Monroe, *Central Michigan University;* Ed Moritz, *Indiana University, Purdue University Fort Wayne;* Linda Morrison, *Niagara University;* Deborah Naquin, *Northern Virginia Community College;* Julie Nichols, *Okaloosa-Walton Community College;* Robert H. Nordell, *Des Moines Area Community College;* Christine Pavesic, *University of Wisconsin, Waukesha;* Sherry Rankin, *Abilene Christian University;* Laura Robbins, *Portland Community College;* Matthew Roudané, *Georgia State University;* Robert E. Rubin, *Wright State University;* Nancy Ruff, *Southern Illinois University, Edwardsville;* Christine M. Ryan, *Middlesex Community College;* Larry W. Severeid, *College of Eastern Utah;* Donna K. Speeker, *Wallace State Community College;* Talbot Spivak, *Edison College;* Joyce Swofford, *Clayton College & State University;* Terry Thacker, *Coastline Community College;* Diane Thompson, *Northern Virginia Community College;* Monica Parrish Trent, *Montgomery College;* Dori Wagner, *Austin Community College;* Shonda Wilson, *Suffolk County Community College;* Frances J. Winter, *Massachusetts Bay Community College;* Kelly Wonder, *University of Wisconsin, Eau Claire;* Benjamin Worth, *Bluegrass Community and Technical College;* Deanna L. Yameen, *Quincy College.*

Students: Lindsi Bittner, *St. Petersburg College;* Danielle Brown, *Oakton Community College;* Marie Burns, *University of Tampa;* Will Buttner, *University of Tampa;* Debra Cotton, *St. Petersburg College;* Jessica de Olivera, *Northeastern Illinois University;* Petra Hickman, *St. Petersburg College;* Anne Hsiao, *Oakton Community College;* Cassie Hull, *St. Petersburg College;* Courtney Langford, *St. Petersburg College;* Sandy Lehrke, *Hillsborough Community College;* Michael Pistorio, *Oakton Community College;* Crystal Smuk, *Triton Junior College;* Marc Sordja, *St. Petersburg College;* Johnny Velez, *Hillsborough Community College;* Anthony Zalud, *Harper Community College;* Omar Zamora, *Northeastern Illinois University.*

Special Thanks: A special thanks goes to Sarah Dangelantonio and Sarah Dengler of *Franklin Pierce College* for their work on the *Instructor's Resource Manual.* Also, thanks to Mark Gallaher, Kelly McGuire, Julie Nash, Dee Seligman, and Janet Young.

Randall VanderMey • Verne Meyer • John Van Rys • Pat Sebranek

Contents

Preface, **iii**

I. Rhetoric: A College Student's Guide to Writing

Reading, Thinking, Viewing, and Writing

1 Critical Thinking Through Reading, Viewing, and Writing **3**

Critical Thinking Through Reading, **4**
  Use a reading strategy: SQ3R, **4**
Reading Actively, **6**
  Take thoughtful notes, **6**
  Annotate the text, **6**
  Map the text, **8**
  Outline the text, **8**
  Evaluate the text, **9**
Responding to a Text, **10**
  Follow these guidelines for response writing, **10**
Summarizing a Text, **11**
  Use these guidelines for summary writing, **11**
Critical Thinking Through Viewing, **12**
  Consider these guidelines for actively viewing images, **12**
  View an image, **13**
Interpreting an Image, **14**
  Understand the elements of interpretation, **14**
  Understand the complications in interpretation, **14**
  Interpret an image, **15**
Evaluating an Image, **16**
  Consider the purpose, **16**
  Evaluate the quality, **16**
  Determine the value, **16**
  Evaluate an image, **17**
Critical Thinking Through Writing, **18**
  Develop sound critical-thinking habits, **18**
  Ask probing questions, **19**
  Practice inductive and deductive logic, **20**
Practicing Modes of Thinking in Your Writing, **21**
  Think by using analysis, **22**
  Think by using synthesis, **23**
  Think by using evaluation, **24**
  Think by using application, **25**
Critical-Thinking Checklist, **26**
Writing Activities, **26**

The Writing Process

2 Beginning the Writing Process **27**

The Writing Process: From Start to Finish, **28**
  An overview of the writing process, **28**
  Adapting the process to your project, **29**
Understanding the Rhetorical Situation: Subject, Audience, and Purpose, **30**
  Understand your subject, **30**
  Understand your audience, **30**
  Understand your purpose, **30**
Understanding the Assignment, **31**
  Read the assignment, **31**
  Relate the assignment, **32**
  Reflect on the assignment, **32**
Selecting a Subject, **33**
  Limit the subject area, **33**
  Conduct your search, **33**
  Explore for possible topics, **34**
Freewriting Quick Guide, **35**
Collecting Information, **37**
  Find out what you already know, **37**
  Ask questions, **38**
  Identify possible sources, **39**
  Explore different sources of information, **39**
  Carry out your research, **39**
Writing with Sources, **40**
Beginning the Process Checklist, **42**
Writing Activities, **42**

3 Planning   **43**

Taking Inventory of Your Thoughts, **44**
  Revisit your rhetorical situation, **44**
  Continue the process, **44**
Forming Your Thesis Statement, **45**
  Find a focus, **45**
  State your thesis, **45**
Using Methods of Development, **46**
  Let your thesis guide you, **46**
Developing a Plan or an Outline, **48**
  Choose an organization method, **48**
Types of Graphic Organizers, **50**
Writing with Sources, **52**
Planning Checklist, **54**
Writing Activities, **54**

4 Drafting   **55**

Writing Your First Draft, **56**
  Reconsider your audience, **56**
  Reconsider your purpose, **56**
  Focus on your subject, **56**
Basic Essay Structure: Major Moves, **57**
Opening Your Draft, **58**
  Engage your reader, **58**
  Establish your direction, **58**
  Get to the point, **59**
Developing the Middle, **60**
  Advance your thesis, **60**
  Test your ideas, **60**
  Build a coherent structure, **61**
  Arrange supporting details, **62**
Ending Your Draft, **66**
  Reassert the main point, **66**
  Urge the reader, **66**
  Complete and unify your message, **67**
Writing with Sources, **68**
Drafting Checklist, **70**
Writing Activities, **70**

5 Revising   **71**

Addressing Whole-Paper Issues, **72**
  Revisit your rhetorical situation, **72**
  Consider your overall approach, **72**
Revising Your First Draft, **73**
  Prepare to revise, **73**
  Think globally, **73**
Revising for Ideas and Organization, **74**
  Examine your ideas, **74**
  Examine your organization, **75**
Revising for Voice and Style, **77**
  Check the level of commitment, **77**
  Check the intensity of your writing, **77**
  Develop an academic style, **78**
  Know when to use the passive voice, **80**
Addressing Paragraph Issues, **81**
  Remember the basics, **81**
  Keep the purpose in mind, **81**
  Check for unity, **82**
  Check for coherence, **84**
Transitions and Linking Words, **85**
  Check for completeness, **86**
Revising Collaboratively, **87**
  Know your role, **87**
  Provide appropriate feedback, **87**
  Respond according to a plan, **88**
Using the Writing Center, **89**
Writing with Sources, **90**
Revising Checklist, **92**
Writing Activities, **92**

6 **Editing and Proofreading 93**

Editing Your Revised Draft, **94**
 *Review the overall style of your
  writing,* **94**
 Consider word choice, **94**
Combining Sentences, **95**
 Edit short, simplistic sentences, **95**
Expanding Sentences, **96**
 Use cumulative sentences, **96**
 Expand with details, **96**
Checking for Sentence Style, **97**
 Avoid these sentence problems, **97**
 *Review your writing for
  sentence variety,* **97**
 Vary sentence structures, **98**
 Use parallel structure, **100**
 Avoid weak constructions, **101**
Avoiding Imprecise, Misleading, and
 Biased Words, **102**
 Substitute specific words, **102**
 Replace jargon and clichés, **103**
 Change biased words, **104**
Proofreading Your Writing, **107**
 *Review punctuation and
  mechanics,* **107**
 *Look for usage and grammar
  errors,* **107**

 Check for spelling errors, **107**
 *Check the writing for form and
  presentation,* **107**
Writing with Sources, **108**
Editing and Proofreading
 Checklist, **110**
Writing Activities, **110**

7 **Submitting Writing and
Creating Portfolios 111**

Formatting Your Writing, **112**
 *Strive for clarity in page
  design,* **112**
Submitting Writing and
 Creating Portfolios, **113**
 Consider potential audiences, **113**
 *Select appropriate
  submission methods,* **113**
 Use a writing portfolio, **113**
Writing with Sources, **114**
Submissions and Portfolio
 Checklist, **116**
Writing Activities, **116**

The College Essay

8 **One Writer's Process 117**

Angela's Assignment and
 Response, **118**
 Angela examined the assignment, **118**
 *Angela explored and narrowed her
  assignment,* **119**
Angela's Planning, **120**
 Angela focused her topic, **120**
 Angela researched the topic, **120**
 *Angela decided how to organize her
  writing,* **121**
Angela's First Draft, **122**
 *Angela kept a working
  bibliography,* **123**
Angela's First Revision, **124**
Angela's Second Revision, **126**
Angela's Edited Draft, **128**
Angela's Proofread Draft, **129**
Angela's Finished Essay, **130**
Writing Activities, **133**
Effective Writing Checklist, **134**

II. Reader: Strategies and Models

Writing Across the Curriculum

9 **Forms of College Writing**   **137**

Three Curricular Divisions, **138**
Types of Writing in Each
Division, **139**
Traits of Writing Across the
Curriculum, **140**

Narrative, Descriptive, and Reflective Writing

10 **Narration and Description**   **145**

Overview: Writing Narration and
Description, **146**
Personal Narrative, **147**
Anecdote introducing a topic, **147**
Anecdote illustrating a point, **147**
*Anecdote illustrating character
traits,* **148**
Narration and Description, **149**
Student Model: "Mzee Owitti,"
Jacqui Nyangi Owitti, **149**
Model: "That Morning on the
Prairie," *James C. Schaap,* **152**
Model: "A Hanging," *George
Orwell,* **154**
Model: "Sunday in the Park,"
Bel Kaufman, **158**
Guidelines: Writing Narration and
Description, **162**
Writing Checklist, **164**
Writing Activities, **164**

11 **Description and
Reflection**   **165**

Overview: Writing Description and
Reflection, **166**
Student Model: "The Stream in
the Ravine," *Nicole Suurdt,* **167**
Model: "Scab!" *Randall
VanderMey,* **169**
Model: "Call Me Crazy, But I
Have to Be Myself," *Mary
Seymour,* **171**
Model: "American Dream Boat,"
K. Oanh Ha, **173**
Guidelines: Writing Description
and Reflection, **178**
Writing Checklist, **180**
Writing Activities, **180**

Analytical Writing

12 **Cause and Effect**   **183**

Overview: Writing a Cause-Effect
Essay, **184**
Student Model: "Life-Threatening
Stress," *Tiffany Boyett,* **185**
Model: "If You Let Me Play . . . ,"
Mary Brophy Marcus, **188**
Model: "The Legacy of
Generation Ñ," *Christy
Haubegger,* **191**
Model: "Our Tired, Our Poor,
Our Kids," *Anna Quindlen,* **193**
Guidelines: Writing a Cause-Effect
Essay, **196**
Writing Checklist, **198**
Writing Activities, **198**

13 Comparison and Contrast **199**

Overview: Writing a Comparison-
Contrast Essay, **200**
  Student Model: **"Beyond Control,"**
  Janae Sebranek, **201**
  Model: **"Two Views of the River,"**
  Mark Twain, **203**
  Model: **"Shrouded in Contra-
  diction,"** *Gelareh Asayesh,* **205**
  Model: **"Like Mexicans,"** *Gary
  Soto,* **208**
Guidelines: Writing a Comparison-
Contrast Essay, **212**
Writing Checklist, **214**
Writing Activities, **214**

14 Classification **215**

Overview: Writing a Classification
Essay, **216**
  Student Model: **"Three Family
  Cancers,"** *Kim Brouwer,* **217**
  Model: **"Four Ways to Talk About
  Literature,"** *John Van Rys,* **220**
  Model: **"No Wonder They Call Me
  a Bitch,"** *Ann Hodgman,* **222**
Guidelines: Writing a Classification
Essay, **226**
Writing Checklist, **228**
Writing Activities, **228**

15 Process Writing **229**

Overview: Writing About a
Process, **230**
  Student Model: **"Wayward Cells,"**
  Kerri Mertz, **231**
  Model: **"Downloading
  Photographs from the MC-150
  Digital Camera,"** **233**
  Model: **"Campus Racism 101,"**
  Nikki Giovanni, **234**
  Model: **"Love and Race,"**
  Nicholas D. Kristof, **238**
Guidelines: Writing About a
Process, **240**
Writing Checklist, **242**
Writing Activities, **242**

16 Definition **243**

Overview: Writing a Definition
Essay, **244**
  Student Model: **"Economic
  Disparities Fuel Human
  Trafficking,"** *Shon Bogar,* **245**
  Student Model: **"Understanding
  Dementia,"** *Sarah Anne
  Morelos,* **247**
  Model: **"Deft or Daft,"** *David
  Schelhaas,* **250**
  Model: **"On *Excellence*,"** *Cynthia
  Ozick,* **251**
Guidelines: Writing a Definition
Essay, **254**
Writing Checklist, **256**
Writing Activities, **256**

Persuasive Writing

17 Strategies for
Argumentation
and Persuasion **259**

Building Persuasive Arguments, **260**
Preparing Your Argument, **261**
  Consider the situation, **261**
  Develop a line of reasoning, **261**
Making and Qualifying Claims, **262**
  *Distinguish claims from facts and
  opinions,* **262**
  *Distinguish three types of
  claims,* **262**
  Develop a supportable claim, **263**
Supporting Your Claims, **264**
  Gather evidence, **264**
  Use evidence, **265**
Identifying Logical Fallacies, **267**
Engaging the Opposition, **271**
  Make concessions, **271**
  Develop rebuttals, **271**
  Consolidate your claim, **271**
Using Appropriate Appeals, **272**
  Build credibility, **272**
  Make logical appeals, **272**
  Focus on readers' needs, **273**
Writing Activities, **274**

18 Taking a Position 275

Overview: Taking a Position, **276**
  Student Model: "An Apology for
    the Life of Ms. Barbie D. Doll,"
    Rita Isakson, **277**
  Model, "Apostles of Hatred
    Find It Easy to Spread Their
    Message," *Leonard Pitts, Jr.,* **279**
  Model: "Pornography," *Margaret
    Atwood,* **281**
  Model: "Fatherless America,"
    David Blankenhorn, **287**
Guidelines: Taking a Position, **292**
Writing Checklist, **294**
Writing Activities, **294**

**19 Persuading Readers
   to Act 295**

Overview: Persuading Readers
  to Act, **296**
  Student Model: "To Drill or Not
    to Drill," *Rebecca Pasok,* **297**
  Model: "I Have a Dream,"
    Dr. Martin Luther King, Jr., **300**
  Model, "The Media's Image of
    Arabs," *Jack G. Shaheen,* **304**
  Model, "In Africa, AIDS Has
    a Woman's Face," *Kofi A.
    Annan,* **307**
Guidelines: Persuading Readers to
  Act, **310**
Writing Checklist, **312**
Writing Activities, **312**

20 Proposing a Solution 313

Overview: Proposing a Solution, **314**
  Student Model: "Preparing for
    Agroterror," *Brian Ley,* **315**
  Model: "Uncle Sam and Aunt
    Samantha," *Anna Quindlen,* **318**
  Model: "The Media and the Ethics
    of Cloning," *Leigh Turner,* **321**
Guidelines: Proposing a Solution, **326**
Writing Checklist, **328**
Writing Activities, **328**

Report Writing

21 Interview Report 331

Overview: Writing an Interview
  Report, **332**
  Student Model: "The Dead
    Business," *Benjamin Meyer,* **333**
Guidelines: Writing an Interview
  Report, **336**
Writing Checklist, **338**
Writing Activities, **338**

**22 Lab, Experiment,
   and Field Reports 339**

Overview: Writing Lab, Experiment,
  and Field Reports, **340**
  Student Model Lab Report:
    "Working with Hydrochloric
    Acid," *Coby Williams,* **341**
  Student Model Experiment Report:
    "The Effects of Temperature
    and Inhibitors on the
    Fermentation Process for
    Ethanol," *Andrea Pizano,* **343**
  Model Field Report, **347**
Guidelines: Writing Lab, Experiment,
  and Field Reports, **350**
Writing Checklist, **352**
Writing Activities, **352**

Special Forms of Writing

23 **Writing About Literature and the Arts** **355**

Overview: Writing About Literature and the Arts, **356**
Writing About a Short Story, **357**
  Student Model: " 'Good Country People': Broken Body, Broken Soul," *Anya Terekhina,* **357**
Writing About a Poem, **361**
  Student Model: " 'Let Evening Come': An Invitation to the Inevitable," *Sherry Van Egdom,* **362**
Writing About a Performance, **364**
  Student Model: "Sigur Ros, Agaetis Byrjun," *Annie Moore,* **364**
Writing About a Film, **365**
  Student Model, "Terror on the Silver Screen: Who Are the Aliens?" *David Schaap,* **365**
Guidelines: Writing About Literature and the Arts, **366**
Literary Terms, **368**
  Poetry Terms, **371**
Writing Checklist, **372**
Writing Activities, **372**

24 **Taking Essay Tests** **373**

Reviewing for Tests, **374**
  Perform daily reviews, **374**
  Perform weekly reviews, **374**
Forming a Study Group, **375**
Using Mnemonics and Other Memory Guides, **376**
Taking the Essay Test, **377**
  Look for key words, **377**
  Plan and write the essay-test answer, **379**
Writing Under Pressure: The Essay Test Quick Guide, **382**
Taking an Objective Test, **383**
Tips for Coping with Test Anxiety, **384**

25 **Writing for the Workplace** **385**

Writing the Business Letter, **386**
  Parts of the Business Letter, **386**
  Model Letter, **387**
Writing Memos and E-mail, **388**
  Sending E-mail, **389**
Applying for a Job, **390**
  The Letter of Application, **390**
  The Recommendation Request Letter, **391**
  The Application Essay, **392**
  Model Application Essay, **393**
Preparing a Resumé, **394**
  Tips for resumé writing, **394**
  Sample Resumé, **395**
  Sample Electronic Resumé, **396**

26 **Writing and Designing for the Web** **397**

Webpage Elements and Functions, **398**
  Page Elements, **398**
  Sample Webpage, **399**
  Page Functions, **400**
Developing a Website and Webpages, **400**
  Get focused, **400**
  Establish your central message, **401**
  Create a site map, **401**
  Study similar sites, **402**
  Gather and prioritize content, **402**
  Think about support materials, **402**
  Design and develop individual pages, **403**
  Test, refine, and post your site, **404**
  Sample Webpages, **405**
Writing for Different Internet Environments, **407**
Writing Checklist, **408**
Writing Activities, **408**

**27 Preparing Oral
Presentations   409**

Organizing Your Presentation, **410**
   Prepare an introduction, **410**
   Develop the body, **411**
   Come to a conclusion, **412**
   Hold a Q & A session, **412**
Writing Your Presentation, **413**
   Student Model: **"Save Now or Pay
      Later,"** *Burnette Sawyer,* **414**
   Use visual aids, **416**
Developing Computer
   Presentations, **417**
Overcoming Stage
   Fright Checklist, **418**

III. Research and Writing

Research and Writing

**28 Getting Started:
From Planning Research
to Evaluating Sources   421**

Papers with Documented Research
   Quick Guide, **422**
The Research Process: A
   Flowchart, **423**
Getting Started: Getting Focused, **424**
   *Establish a narrow, manageable
      topic,* **424**
   Brainstorm research questions, **424**
   Develop a working thesis, **425**
Developing a Research Plan, **426**
   Choose research methods, **426**
   Get organized to do research, **427**

Exploring Possible Information
   Resources and Sites, **428**
   *Consider different information
      resources,* **428**
   *Consider different information
      sites,* **429**
Conducting Effective Keyword
   Searches, **430**
   Choose keywords carefully, **430**
   Use keyword strategies, **431**
Engaging and Evaluating
   Sources, **432**
   Engage your sources, **432**
   *Rate source reliability and
      depth,* **433**
   *Evaluate print and online
      sources,* **434**
Creating a Working Bibliography, **436**
   Choose an orderly method, **436**
Developing a Note-Taking
   System, **438**
   Develop note-taking strategies, **438**
Summarizing, Paraphrasing, and
   Quoting Source Material, **442**
   Summarize useful passages, **443**
   Paraphrase key passages, **443**
   *Quote crucial phrases, sentences,
      and passages,* **444**
Avoiding Unintentional
   Plagiarism, **445**
   *Practice the principles of ethical
      research,* **445**
Checklist for Research, **446**
Writing Activities, **446**

29 Conducting Primary and Library Research **447**

Primary and Secondary Sources, **448**
  Consider primary sources, **448**
  Consider secondary sources, **448**
Conducting Primary Research, **449**
  Conduct primary research, **449**
  Conduct surveys, **450**
  Sample Survey, **451**
  Analyze texts, documents, records, and artifacts, **452**
  Conduct interviews, **454**
Using the Library, **455**
  Become familiar with the library, **455**
  Search the catalog, **456**
Using Books in Research, **458**
  Approach the book systematically, **458**
Finding Periodical Articles, **460**
  Search online databases, **460**
  Generate citation lists of promising articles, **461**
  Study citations and capture identifying information, **462**
  Find and retrieve the full text of the article, **462**
Checklist for Research, **464**
Writing Activities, **464**

30 Conducting Research on the Internet **465**

Understanding Internet Basics: A Primer, **466**
  What is the Internet? **466**
  What is the World Wide Web? **466**
  What does an Internet address mean? **467**

How can you save Internet information? **467**
Locating Reliable Information, **468**
  Proceed with caution, **468**
  Use your library's website, **468**
  Work with URLs, **469**
  Follow helpful links, **469**
  Follow the branches of a "subject tree," **469**
  Use search engines and metasearch tools, **472**
Checklist for Internet Research, **474**
Writing Activities, **474**

31 Drafting a Paper with Documented Research **475**

Avoiding Plagiarism, **476**
  What is plagiarism? **476**
  Why is plagiarism serious? **478**
  How do I avoid plagiarism? **479**
Avoiding Other Source Abuses, **480**
Organizing and Synthesizing Your Findings, **482**
  Develop your ideas, **482**
  Develop a structure for delivering research results, **483**
Developing Your First Draft, **484**
  Choose a drafting method, **484**
  Shape your first draft, **484**
Using Source Material in Your Writing, **486**
  Integrate source material carefully, **486**
  Effectively document your sources, **488**
Writing Checklist, **490**
Writing Activities, **490**

Documentation and Format Styles

32 MLA Documentation Format   **493**

MLA Research Paper Guidelines
  Questions & Answers, **494**
Guidelines for In-Text Citations, **496**
Sample In-Text Citations, **498**
MLA Works Cited Quick Guide, **504**
Works-Cited Entries: Books and
  Other Documents, **505**
Works-Cited Entries: Print Periodical
  Articles, **511**
Works-Cited Entries: Online
  Sources, **514**
Works-Cited Entries: Other Sources
  (Primary, Personal, and
  Multimedia), **520**
Sample MLA Paper, **522**
  Sample Paper, **523**
  *Sample Paper: Works-Cited
  List,* **532**
Checklist for MLA Format, **534**
Writing Activities, **534**

33 APA Documentation Format   **535**

APA Research Paper Guidelines
  Questions & Answers, **536**
Guidelines for In-Text Citations, **538**
Sample In-Text Citations, **538**
APA References Quick Guide, **542**
Reference Entries: Books and Other
  Documents, **543**
Reference Entries: Print Periodical
  Articles, **546**
Reference Entries: Online
  Sources, **548**
Reference Entries: Other Sources
  (Primary, Personal, and
  Multimedia), **551**
Sample APA Paper, **553**
  Sample Title Page, **553**
  Sample Abstract, **554**
  APA Research Paper: The Body,
  555
  Sample Paper: References List, **564**
Checklist for APA Format, **565**
Writing Activities, **565**
Research Paper Abbreviations, **566**

Credits, **567**
Index, **568**

Thematic Table of Contents for Readings

Character and Conscience

"Apostles of Hatred Find It Easy to Spread Their Message" by Leonard Pitts, Jr., **279**
"Call Me Crazy, But I Have to Be Myself" by Mary Seymour, **171**
"Campus Racism 101" by Nikki Giovanni, **234**
"Fatherless America" by David Blankenhorn, **287**
"If You Let Me Play . . ." by Mary Brophy Marcus, **188**
"I Have a Dream" by Dr. Martin Luther King, Jr., **300**
"In Africa, AIDS Has a Woman's Face" by Kofi A. Annan, **307**
"On *Excellence*" by Cynthia Ozick, **251**
"Our Tired, Our Poor, Our Kids" by Anna Quindlen, **193**
"Pornography" by Margaret Atwood, **281**
"Sunday in the Park" by Bel Kaufman, **158**
"To Drill or Not to Drill" by Rebecca Pasok, **297**
"Uncle Sam and Aunt Samantha" by Anna Quindlen, **318**

Community and Culture

"American Dream Boat" by K. Oanh Ha, **173**
"An American Hybrid" by Katie Hughey, **523**
"An Apology for the Life of Ms. Barbie D. Doll" by Rita Isakson, **277**
"Fatherless America" by David Blankenhorn, **287**
"I Have a Dream" by Dr. Martin Luther King, Jr., **300**
"Like Mexicans" by Gary Soto, **208**
"Love and Race" by Nicholas D. Kristof, **238**
"Mzee Owitti" by Jacqui Nyangi Owitti, **149**
"Our Roots Go Back to Roanoke: Investigating . . ." by Renee Danielle Singh, **555**
"Shrouded in Contradiction" by Gelareh Asayesh, **205**
"The Legacy of Generation Ñ" by Christy Haubegger, **191**
"The Media's Image of Arabs" by Jack G. Shaheen, **304**

Disease, Death, and Coping

"A Hanging" by George Orwell, **154**
"In Africa, AIDS Has a Woman's Face" by Kofi A. Annan, **307**
" 'Let Evening Come': An Invitation to the Inevitable" by Sherry Van Egdom, **362**
"Life-Threatening Stress" by Tiffany Boyett, **185**
"Mzee Owitti" by Jacqui Nyangi Owitti, **149**
"The Dead Business" by Benjamin Meyer, **333**
"Three Family Cancers" by Kim Brouwer, **217**
"Understanding Dementia" by Sarah Anne Morelos, **247**
"Wayward Cells" by Kerri Mertz, **231**

Diversity and Equity

"American Dream Boat" by K. Oanh Ha, **173**
"Campus Racism 101" by Nikki Giovanni, **234**
"I Have a Dream" by Dr. Martin Luther King, Jr., **300**
"If You Let Me Play . . ." by Mary Brophy Marcus, **188**
"Like Mexicans" by Gary Soto, **208**
"Love and Race" by Nicholas D. Kristof, **238**
"Our Tired, Our Poor, Our Kids" by Anna Quindlen, **193**

"Shrouded in Contradiction" by Gelareh Asayesh, **205**
"The Legacy of Generation Ñ" by Christy Haubegger, **191**
"The Media's Image of Arabs" by Jack G. Shaheen, **304**
"Uncle Sam and Aunt Samantha" by Anna Quindlen, **318**

Education and Learning

"An American Hybrid" by Katie Hughey, **523**
"Apostles of Hatred Find It Easy to Spread Their Message" by Leonard Pitts, Jr., **279**
"Beyond Control" by Janae Sebranek, **201**
"Campus Racism 101" by Nikki Giovanni, **234**
"Deft or Daft" by David Schelhaas, **250**
"Four Ways to Talk About Literature" by John Van Rys, **220**
" 'Let Evening Come': An Invitation to the Inevitable" by Sherry Van Egdom, **362**
"Love and Race" by Nicholas D. Kristof, **238**
"No Wonder They Call Me a Bitch" by Ann Hodgman, **222**
"On *Excellence*" by Cynthia Ozick, **251**
"Terror on the Silver Screen" by David Schaap, **365**
"The Media's Image of Arabs" by Jack G. Shaheen, **304**
"That Morning on the Prairie" by James C. Schaap, **152**
"Two Views of the River" by Mark Twain, **203**

Environment and Nature

"Investigation of Cockroach Infestation at 5690 Cherryhill" by Hue Nguyen, **347**
"No Wonder They Call Me a Bitch" by Ann Hodgman, **222**
"That Morning on the Prairie" by James C. Schaap, **152**
"The Stream in the Ravine" by Nicole Suurdt, **167**
"To Drill or Not to Drill" by Rebecca Pasok, **297**
"Two Views of the River" by Mark Twain, **203**
"Wayward Cells" by Kerri Mertz, **231**

Ethics and Ideology

"A Hanging" by George Orwell, **154**
"Apostles of Hatred Find It Easy to Spread Their Message" by Leonard Pitts, Jr., **279**
"Beyond Control" by Janae Sebranek, **201**
"Campus Racism 101" by Nikki Giovanni, **234**
"Fatherless America" by David Blankenhorn, **287**
"If You Let Me Play . . ." by Mary Brophy Marcus, **188**
"I Have a Dream" by Dr. Martin Luther King, Jr., **300**
"In Africa, AIDS Has a Woman's Face" by Kofi A. Annan **307**
"Love and Race" by Nicholas D. Kristof, **238**
"Our Tired, Our Poor, Our Kids" by Anna Quindlen, **193**
"Pornography" by Margaret Atwood, **281**
"Scab!" by Randall VanderMey, **169**
"Shrouded in Contradiction" by Gelareh Asayesh, **205**
"Sunday in the Park" by Bel Kaufman, **158**
"The Legacy of Generation Ñ" by Christy Haubegger, **191**
"The Media and the Ethics of Cloning" by Leigh Turner, **321**
"The Media's Image of Arabs" by Jack G. Shaheen, **304**
"To Drill or Not to Drill" by Rebecca Pasok, **297**
"Uncle Sam and Aunt Samantha" by Anna Quindlen, **318**

Ethnicity and Identity

"American Dream Boat" by K. Oanh Ha, **173**
"Apostles of Hatred Find It Easy to Spread Their Message" by Leonard Pitts, Jr., **279**
"I Have a Dream" by Dr. Martin Luther King, Jr., **300**
"Like Mexicans" by Gary Soto, **208**
"Love and Race" by Nicholas D. Kristof, **238**
"Mzee Owitti" by Jacqui Nyangi Owitti, **149**
"On *Excellence*" by Cynthia Ozick, **251**
"Shrouded in Contradiction" by Gelareh Asayesh, **205**
"The Legacy of Generation Ñ" by Christy Haubegger, **191**
"The Media's Image of Arabs" by Jack G. Shaheen, **304**

Family and Friends

"American Dream Boat" by K. Oanh Ha, **173**
"Fatherless America" by David Blankenhorn, **287**
"In Africa, AIDS Has a Woman's Face" by Kofi A. Annan **307**
"Like Mexicans" by Gary Soto, **208**
"Love and Race" by Nicholas D. Kristof, **238**
"Mzee Owitti" by Jacqui Nyangi Owitti, **149**
"On *Excellence*" by Cynthia Ozick, **251**
"Sunday in the Park" by Bel Kaufman, **158**
"The Stream in the Ravine" by Nicole Suurdt, **167**
"Three Family Cancers" by Kim Brouwer, **217**

Fashion and Lifestyle

"American Dream Boat" by K. Oanh Ha, **173**
"Call Me Crazy, But I Have to Be Myself" by Mary Seymour, **171**
"Fatherless America" by David Blankenhorn, **287**
"If You Let Me Play . . . " by Mary Brophy Marcus, **188**
"Life-Threatening Stress" by Tiffany Boyett, **185**
"Love and Race" by Nicholas D. Kristof, **238**
"On *Excellence*" by Cynthia Ozick, **251**
"Our Tired, Our Poor, Our Kids" by Anna Quindlen, **193**
"The Legacy of Generation Ñ" by Christy Haubegger, **191**
"Uncle Sam and Aunt Samantha" by Anna Quindlen, **318**

Gender and Integrity

"An Apology for the Life of Ms. Barbie D. Doll" by Rita Isakson, **277**
" 'Good Country People': Broken Body, Broken Soul" by Anya Terekhina, **357**
"If You Let Me Play . . . " by Mary Brophy Marcus, **188**
"In Africa, AIDS Has a Woman's Face" by Kofi A. Annan, **307**
"Pornography" by Margaret Atwood, **281**
"Shrouded in Contradiction" by Gelareh Asayesh, **205**
"Sunday in the Park" by Bel Kaufman, **158**
"Uncle Sam and Aunt Samantha" by Anna Quindlen, **318**

Language and Literature

"Beyond Control" by Janae Sebranek, **201**
"Deft or Daft" by David Schelhaas, **250**
"Four Ways to Talk About Literature" by John Van Rys, **220**

"Let Evening Come" by Jane Kenyon, **361**
" 'Let Evening Come': An Invitation to the Inevitable" by Sherry Van Egdom, **362**
" 'Good Country People': Broken Body, Broken Soul" by Anya Terekhina, **357**
"On *Excellence*" by Cynthia Ozick, **251**
"Sigur Ros, *Agaetis Byrjun*" by Annie Moore, **364**
"Terror on the Silver Screen" by David Schaap, **365**
"That Morning on the Prairie" by James C. Schaap, **152**

Memory and Tradition

"American Dream Boat" by K. Oanh Ha, **173**
"An Apology for the Life of Ms. Barbie D. Doll" by Rita Isakson, **277**
"Like Mexicans" by Gary Soto, **208**
"Love and Race" by Nicholas D. Kristof, **238**
"Mzee Owitti" by Jacqui Nyangi Owitti, **149**
"On *Excellence*" by Cynthia Ozick, **251**
"Sunday in the Park" by Bel Kaufman, **158**
"That Morning on the Prairie" by James C. Schaap, **152**
"The Stream in the Ravine" by Nicole Suurdt, **167**

Science and Health

"Call Me Crazy, But I Have to Be Myself" by Mary Seymour, **171**
"Clean Water Is Everyone's Business" by Angela Franco, **130**
"If You Let Me Play . . ." by Mary Brophy Marcus, **188**
"In Africa, AIDS Has a Woman's Face" by Kofi A. Annan, **307**
"Investigation of Cockroach Infestation at 5690 Cherryhill" by Hue Nguyen, **347**
"Let Evening Come" by Jane Kenyon, **361**
"Life-Threatening Stress" by Tiffany Boyett, **185**
"Seeing the Light" by David Zupp, **61**
"The Effects of Temperature and Inhibitors . . ." by Andrea Pizano, **343**
"The Media and the Ethics of Cloning" by Leigh Turner, **321**
"Three Family Cancers" by Kim Brouwer, **217**
"To Drill or Not to Drill" by Rebecca Pasok, **297**
"Understanding Dementia" by Sarah Anne Morelos, **247**
"Wayward Cells" by Kerri Mertz, **231**
"Working with Hydrochloric Acid" by Coby Williams, **341**

Terror and Our Time

"A Hanging" by George Orwell, **154**
"Apostles of Hatred Find It Easy to Spread Their Message" by Leonard Pitts, Jr., **279**
"Campus Racism 101" by Nikki Giovanni, **234**
"Pornography" by Margaret Atwood, **281**
"Preparing for Agroterror" by Brian Ley, **315**
"Shrouded in Contradiction" by Gelareh Asayesh, **205**
"Sunday in the Park" by Bel Kaufman, **158**
"Terror on the Silver Screen" by David Schaap, **365**
"That Morning on the Prairie" by James C. Schaap, **152**
"The Media's Image of Arabs" by Jack G. Shaheen, **304**

Rhetoric:
A College Student's
Guide to Writing

CONTENTS

■ Reading, Thinking, Viewing, and Writing

1 Critical Thinking Through Reading, Viewing, and Writing

Critical Thinking Through Reading	4	Interpreting an Image	14
Reading Actively	6	Evaluating an Image	16
Responding to a Text	10	Critical Thinking Through Writing	18
Summarizing a Text	11	Practicing Modes of Thinking in Your Writing	21
Critical Thinking Through Viewing	12	Critical-Thinking Checklist/Writing Activities	26

■ The Writing Process

2 Beginning the Writing Process

The Writing Process	28	Collecting Information	37
Understanding the Rhetorical Situation	30	Writing with Sources	40
Understanding the Assignment	31	Beginning the Process Checklist	
Selecting a Subject	33	and Writing Activities	42

3 Planning

Taking Inventory of Your Thoughts	44	Developing a Plan or an Outline	48
Forming Your Thesis Statement	45	Writing with Sources	52
Using Methods of Development	46	Planning Checklist and Writing Activities	54

4 Drafting

Writing Your First Draft	56	Ending Your Draft	66
Basic Essay Structure	57	Writing with Sources	68
Opening Your Draft	58	Drafting Checklist and Writing Activities	70
Developing the Middle	60		

5 Revising

Addressing Whole-Paper Issues	72	Addressing Paragraph Issues	81
Revising Your First Draft	73	Revising Collaboratively	87
Revising for Ideas and Organization	74	Using the Writing Center	89
Revising for Voice and Style	77	Writing with Sources	90
		Revising Checklist and Writing Activities	92

6 Editing and Proofreading

Editing Your Revised Draft	94	Avoiding Misleading and Biased Words	102
Combining Sentences	95	Proofreading Your Writing	107
Expanding Sentences	96	Writing with Sources	108
Checking for Sentence Style	97	Editing and Proofreading Checklist	
		and Writing Activities	110

7 Submitting Writing and Creating Portfolios

Formatting Your Writing	112	Writing with Sources	114
Submitting Writing and Creating Portfolios	113	Submissions and Portfolio Checklist	
		and Writing Activities	116

■ The College Essay

8 One Writer's Process

Angela's Assignment and Response	118	Angela's Edited Draft	128
Angela's Planning	120	Angela's Proofread Draft	129
Angela's First Draft	122	Angela's Finished Essay	130
Angela's First Revision	124	Critical-Thinking and Writing Activities	133
Angela's Second Revision	126	Effective Writing Checklist	134

CRITICAL THINKING THROUGH READING, VIEWING, AND WRITING

Audio

In many respects, critical thinking defines your college work. When you think critically, you examine ideas fully and logically, weigh multiple perspectives on issues, and draw reasonable conclusions. In the process, you carry on an in-depth dialogue with information and evidence.

In many of your courses, your instructors will ask you to undertake critical thinking through reading, viewing, and writing. You might have to analyze Flannery O'Connor's short story "Good Country People," identify the comic conventions in the film *Sideways*, or analyze data gathered about the fermentation of ethanol. In all of these assignments, you are being pressed to think critically, using reading, viewing, and writing—connected as they are—to make sense of things. And one goal is that your training in critical thinking will prepare you for work in your profession and in the public square.

Thoughtful reading and viewing, then, lie at the heart of critical thinking and feed into thoughtful writing. These natural reading-viewing-thinking-writing connections are this chapter's focus.

Video

Critical Thinking Through Reading

Reading is basic to writing the way that eating is basic to cooking. Just as creating food worth tasting and digesting is at the heart of cooking, so is making words worth reading at the heart of writing. And while the cook must plan the meal around the tastes of his or her guests, the writer must always develop his or her text with awareness of the readers' perspectives. To appeal to a reader, in other words, the writer must know firsthand what good reading is.

Use a reading strategy: SQ3R.

Obviously, reading a novel, a textbook, and a webpage are all different activities. Nevertheless, all college reading assignments can be approached systematically, especially when your goal is to absorb and engage the text. One such strategy for critical reading, especially of information-rich texts, is called **SQ3R: Survey, Question, Read, Recite,** and **Review.** Here is how SQ3R works.

Survey

The first step in SQ3R is to preview the material. Try to spot main ideas. They will serve as reference points during the reading that follows. Perhaps you've been given questions or a study guide. Read those first. Then read the introductory and concluding paragraphs and glance at each page in between. Pay special attention to headings, chapter titles, illustrations, and boldfaced type. Also check out any graphics—charts, maps, diagrams, illustrations—that visually reinforce key points.

Benefits: Surveying serves three important purposes: (1) It gives you the big picture, (2) it stabilizes and directs your thoughts, and (3) it gets you over the starting hump.

Question

As you survey, begin to ask questions that you hope to answer as you read.

- Turn the headings and subheadings into questions. For example, if the subhead says "Methods," ask, "What methods did the researcher use?"
- Imagine a specific test question covering each major point in your reading. For example, if the reading addresses the media and the ethics of cloning, as shown on page **7**, you might imagine this test question: "What can the media do to foster productive public debate on cloning?"
- Be thorough by asking the journalist's questions: *who, what, when, where, why,* and *how.* Examples: *Who are the media? What's the popular understanding of cloning? How have the media presented cloning? Why does the author see the media's treatment of cloning as an ethical issue?*
- Look over any questions found at the end of the text or the chapter.

Benefits: Asking questions will keep you actively thinking about what is coming up and will help you to maintain an appropriate critical distance.

Read

As you encounter facts and ideas, ask these questions: What does this mean? How do the ideas relate to each other and to what I know? What's coming next?

Keep track of your answers by taking notes, annotating the text, mapping, or outlining. (See pages 6–9 for more on these active-reading techniques.) Read difficult parts slowly; reread them if necessary. Look up unfamiliar words or ideas, and use your senses to imagine the events, people, places, or things you are reading about. Imagine talking with the writer. Express agreement, lodge complaints, ask for proof—and imagine the writer's response or look for it in the text.

Benefits: Engaging actively with the text in this way will draw you deeper into the world of the writing. You'll trigger memories and make surprising connections.

Recite

After finishing a page, section, or chapter, recite the key points aloud. Answering *Who? What? When? Where? Why?* and *How?* questions is a quick way of testing yourself on how well you understood what you read. You can also recite the key points by listing them or writing a summary (see page 11).

Benefits: Reciting tests your comprehension, drives the material deeper into your long-term memory, and helps you connect the content with what you already know.

Review

As soon as you finish reading the material, double-check the questions you posed in the "question" stage of SQ3R. Can you answer them? Glance over any notes you made as well. But don't stop there if the reading is especially important. You will remember the material much better by spacing out your reviews; spend a few minutes reviewing each text over the next few days. Consider the following helpful memory techniques:

- Visualize the concepts in concrete ways. *Example:* If a text discusses media sound bites about cloning, imagine a television panel discussing the topic.
- Draw diagrams or develop clusters. *Example:* See the cluster on page 36.
- Put the material in your own words. *Example:* See the summary on page 11.
- Teach it to someone. *Example:* For a text on cloning, explain the main points to a friend or relative—in person, on the phone, or by e-mail.
- Use acronyms or rhymes. *Example:* "*i* before *e* except after *c*."

Benefits: Research shows that reviewing within 24 hours helps considerably to move information from your short-term memory to your long-term memory. You will also improve your memory if you create a network of associations with the information you want to remember, if you link the memory to two or more senses, or if you reorganize the material while still retaining the substance with accuracy.

Reading Actively

Truly active reading requires more than highlighting every line in yellow or pink. Active reading is really *inter*-active, a kind of mental dialogue with the writer. Certain practical techniques will help you stay alert for active reading:

- **Pace yourself.** Read in stretches of thirty to forty-five minutes, followed by short breaks. As you read, slow down in tough spots, respond to the text, ask questions, and note your reactions.
- **Project.** Based on where you've been and where you are in the text, anticipate what will come next and why.
- **Speak the text.** Read difficult parts out loud, or take turns reading aloud with a partner.
- **Track the text.** Record your dialogue with the text through writing strategies such as note taking, annotating, mapping, and outlining (all of which are explored on the following pages).

Take thoughtful notes.

Find a note-taking system that suits you, using legal tablets, note cards, laptop software, or a handheld device. Your system should allow you to distinguish clearly among facts, quotations, paraphrases, summaries, and personal remarks. It is a good idea to include a reference number or topic word at the top of each note to help you organize your notes later.

 Although effective note taking is crucial for typical reading assignments in your courses, it's especially important for any research-based writing. On pages 438–441 you'll find more instruction on note-taking systems.

Annotate the text.

Annotating involves marking up the text itself. If you own the book you're reading or if you are reading a photocopy, write notes in the margins. Writing activates your thinking and records your insights. Try these techniques, shown in the sample passage on the next page:

- Write a question—or a simple "?"—next to anything that concerns or puzzles you. See if the text eventually answers your question.
- Link related passages by drawing circles, lines, or arrows, or by making notes such as "see page 36."
- Add personal observations. Keep track of your reactions without worrying about them initially. You can analyze these reactions later.
- Create a marginal index. Write key words in the margin or at the top of the page to identify important themes, names, or patterns. For books, list these key words, with page numbers, on a blank page at the end. By doing so, you'll create an index for future use.

Annotating in Action

The excerpt below is from an article written by Leigh Turner, an academic and medical professional who has studied, worked, and taught in both the United States and Canada. Written in the wake of the first successful animal cloning, of Dolly the sheep, this reading might be assigned in a communication, philosophy, biology, environmental studies, political science, or agriculture course for class discussion, a written response, a test, or a research project. This excerpt shows how a student reader engages the text and comments on key ideas. (The full essay appears on pages 321–325.)

What's the connection?

The Media and the Ethics of Cloning

Who is he? check

If the contemporary debate on cloning has a patron saint, surely it is Andy Warhol. Not only did Warhol assert that everyone would have fifteen minutes of fame—witness the lawyers, philosophers, theologians, and bioethicists who found their expertise in hot demand on the nightly morality plays of network television following Ian Wilmut's cloning of the sheep Dolly—but he also placed "clones," multiple copies of the same phenomenon, at the heart of popular culture. Instead of multiple images of Marilyn Monroe and Campbell's soup cans, we now have cloned sheep. Regrettably, it is Warhol's capacity for hyperbole rather than his intelligence and ironic vision that permeates the current debate on cloning.

see textbook p. 375

good definition of cloning

means extreme exaggeration

It would be unfair to judge hastily written op-ed pieces, popular talk shows, and late-night radio programs by the same standards that one would apply to a sustained piece of philosophical or legal analysis. But the popular media could do more to foster thoughtful public debate on the legal, moral, political, medical, and scientific dimensions of the cloning of humans and nonhuman animals.

media needs to consider cloning thoughtfully

As did many of my colleagues at the Hastings Center, I participated in several interviews with the media following Ian Wilmut's announcement in *Nature* that he had succeeded in cloning Dolly from a mammary cell of an adult sheep. After clearly stating to one Los Angeles radio broadcaster before our interview that I was not a theologian and did not represent a religious organization, I was rather breathlessly asked during the taping what God's view on cloning is and whether cloning is "against creation." Predictably, the broadcaster didn't want to discuss how religious ethicists are contributing to the nascent public discourse about the ethics of cloning. Instead, he . . .

INSIGHT: Underlining or highlighting key words or phrases can be helpful, but don't overdo it. If you're not careful, too much highlighting or underlining becomes a means of evading rather than engaging the text. Excessive highlighting might be your brain saying "I'll learn this later." Moreover, excessive highlighting can make the text difficult to reread and hence tough to review.

Map the text.

If you are visually oriented, you may understand a text best by mapping out its important parts. One way to do so is by "clustering." Start by naming the main topic in a circle at the center of the page. Then branch out using lines and "balloons," where each balloon contains a word or phrase for one major subtopic. Branch out in further layers of balloons to show even more subpoints. If you wish, add graphics, arrows, drawings—anything that helps you visualize the relationships among ideas.

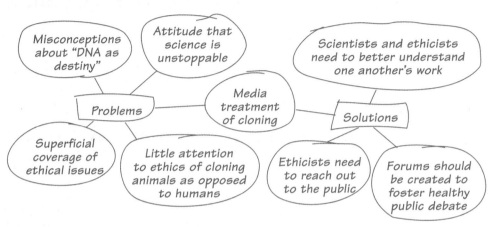

Outline the text.

Outlining is the traditional way of showing all the major parts, points, and subpoints in a text. An outline uses parallel structure to show main points and subordinate points. See pages **48–49** for more on outlines.

SAMPLE OUTLINE FOR "THE MEDIA AND THE ETHICS OF CLONING"

1. Introduction: The debate about cloning is filled with exaggeration.
2. The mass media have confused the debate:
   - Bombarding the public with sound bites
   - Focusing on human cloning and ignoring animal cloning
   - Wrongly stressing that people are products of their genes
   - Promoting the idea that scientific "progress" can't be stopped
3. Thesis: The discussion can be improved in three ways:
   - Scientists and ethicists must learn to understand one another's work.
   - Ethicists need to improve how they communicate to the mass media.
   - Public debate about scientific topics must be expanded to forums and outreach programs.
4. Conclusion: We need more intelligent discussion so that the public is not misled by the mass media.

Evaluate the text.

Critical reading does not mean disproving the text or disapproving of it. It means thoughtfully inspecting, weighing, and evaluating the writer's ideas. To strengthen your reading skills, learn to evaluate texts using the criteria below.

1. **Judge the reading's credibility.** Where was it published? How reliable is the author? How current is the information? How accurate and complete does it seem to be? In addition, consider the author's tone of voice, attitude, and apparent biases.

   Discussion: Leigh Turner, the author of "The Media and the Ethics of Cloning" on pages **321–325**, tells us that he was a member of the Hastings Center, a nonprofit research institute. How does this information build or break his credibility? Within the article, how does he build credibility?

2. **Put the reading in a larger context.** How do the text's ideas match what you know from other sources? Which details of background, history, and social context help you understand this text's perspective? How have things changed or remained the same since the text's publication? Which allusions (references to people, events, and so on) does the writer use? Why?

   Discussion: The topic of cloning belongs to the broader subjects of genetic research and ethics. In addition, the topic relates to debates over the nature of human identity, and cloning research has advanced and expanded dramatically since the article's publication. As for allusions, Turner refers to the artist Andy Warhol and the cloning of the sheep Dolly. What else is part of this context?

3. **Evaluate the reasoning and support.** Is the reasoning clear and logical? Are the examples and other supporting details appropriate and enlightening? Are inferences (what the text implies) consistent with the tone and message? (Look especially for hidden logic and irony that undercut what is said explicitly.)

   Discussion: Turner uses examples and illustrations extensively in his article. He analyzes the problem by breaking it down, and he systematically presents a three-part solution. Is his reasoning sound?

4. **Reflect on how the reading challenges you.** Which of your beliefs and values does the reading call into question? What discomfort does it create? Does your own perspective skew your evaluation?

   Discussion: The article may make us feel uncomfortable about several issues: our lack of concern for animals, our inability to see past the media's treatment of cloning, and the application of cloning to several areas of life (including replication of ourselves). What other challenges does the article raise?

 For additional help evaluating texts, see pages **432–435**. For information on detecting logical fallacies often used in texts by writers, see pages **267–270**.

Responding to a Text

In a sense, when you read a text, you enter into a dialogue with it. Your response expresses your turn in the dialogue. Such a response can take varied forms, from a journal entry to a blog to a discussion-group posting.

Follow these guidelines for response writing.

On the surface, responding to a text seems perfectly natural—just let it happen. But it can be a bit more complicated. A written response typically is not the same as a private diary entry but is instead shared with other readers, whether your instructor or a class. You develop your response keeping in mind your instructor's requirements and the response's role in the course. Therefore, follow these guidelines:

1. **Be honest.** Although you want to remain sensitive to the context in which you will share your response, be bold enough to be honest about your reaction to the text—what it makes you think, feel, and question. To that end, a response usually allows you to express yourself directly using the pronoun "I."

2. **Be fluid.** Let the flow of your thoughts guide you in what you write. Don't stop to worry about grammar, punctuation, mechanics, and spelling. These can be quickly cleaned up before you share or submit your response.

3. **Be reflective.** Generally, the goal of a response is to offer thoughtful reflection as opposed to knee-jerk reaction. Show, then, that you are engaging the text's ideas, relating them to your own experience, looking both inward and outward. Avoid a shallow reaction that comes from skimming the text or misreading it.

4. **Be selective.** By nature, a response must limit its focus; it cannot exhaust all your reactions to the text. So zero in on one or two elements of your response, and run with those to see where they take you in your dialogue with the text.

Sample Response

Here is part of a student's response to Leigh Turner's "The Media and the Ethics of Cloning," on pages **321–325**. Note the informality and exploratory tone.

Turner seems dead right about the treatment of cloning in the media, based on some news stories I've recently heard about food from cloned cows. The media just don't go very deep, especially on science issues, which most people find too tough to understand anyway.

Like most people, I've focused on the (scary?) idea of human cloning, afraid of what it could lead to, but I'm also curious about it. Cloning animals is an issue that hasn't been on my radar screen much. Cloning animals just for the benefit of people, is that right? Would I approve of human cloning if it benefited me, if it helped someone I loved or saved my own life?

INSIGHT: A response does not simply summarize the text. See the next page to understand the difference between a response and a summary.

Summarizing a Text

Writing a summary disciplines you by making you pull only essentials from a reading—the main points, the thread of the argument. By doing so, you not only create a brief record of the text's contents but also exercise your ability to comprehend, analyze, and synthesize information.

Use these guidelines for summary writing.

Writing a summary requires sifting out the least important points, sorting the essential ones to show their logical relationships, and putting those points in your own words. Follow these guidelines:

1. **Skim first; then read closely.** First, get a sense of the whole, including the main idea and strategies for support. Then read carefully, taking notes as you do.

2. **Capture the text's argument.** Review your notes and annotations, looking for main points and clear connections. State these briefly and clearly, in your own words. Include only what is essential, excluding most examples and details. Don't say simply that the text talks about its subject; tell *what it says* about that subject.

3. **Test your summary.** Aim to objectively provide the heart of the text; avoid interjecting your own opinions and presence as a writer. Similarly, don't confuse an objective summary of a text with a response to it (shown on the previous page). Finally, check your summary against the original text for accuracy and consistency.

Sample Summary

Below is a student's summary of Leigh Turner's article, "The Media and the Ethics of Cloning," on pages 321–325. Note how the summary writer includes only main points and phrases them in terms she understands. She departs from the precise order of ideas in the original but communicates their sense accurately.

> Popular media cover the topic of cloning inadequately. They offer unfocused and one-sided coverage, typically ignoring animal cloning, especially the ethics of cloning animals to create "pharmaceutical factories." By stressing "genetic essentialism," the idea that people are simply products of their genes, they ignore the complexity of growth. And last, the media make it sound as though the advance of cloning is unstoppable. How can this problem be resolved? First, through training, scientists and ethicists need to understand one another's work better. Second, ethicists need to be better communicators in the media, especially by publishing in journals that nonscientists can understand. Finally, public institutions need to sponsor debates so that views can be expressed at the grassroots level.

INSIGHT: Writing formal summaries—whether as part of literature reviews or as abstracts—is an important skill, especially in the social and natural sciences. For help, go to **www.thecollegewriter.com/3e.**

Video

Critical Thinking Through Viewing

A flood of visual images—on magazine covers, movie trailers, webpages, and cell phones with flip-up video screens—affect the way we think. Images quicken our work, provoke ideas, and often trigger our emotions. Images convey persuasive ideas, simplify complex concepts, and dramatize important points.

But images have drawbacks, too. They can distort facts, manipulate emotions, and cut reasoning short. As a writer, you must learn to think critically through viewing—to "read" images actively; to interpret what is meant by an image, not just what is shown; and to evaluate the quality and value of an image. These challenges are addressed on the following pages.

Consider these guidelines for actively viewing images.

View with a purpose. Your viewing of an image needs to be guided by your own reading goals. Are you a student seeking to learn something, a citizen seeking insight into social and political issues, or a consumer seeking guidance on a purchase? Also, given where the image has been published and by whom, what is the image meant to do?

- **Arouse curiosity?** Open your imagination, but stay on guard.
- **Entertain?** Look for the pleasure or the joke, but be wary of excess or of ethically questionable material in the image.
- **Inform or educate?** Search for key instruction, noting what's left out.
- **Illustrate?** Relate the image to the words or concept being illustrated: Does the image clarify or distort the meaning?
- **Persuade?** Examine how the image appeals to the viewer's needs, from safety and satisfaction to self-worth. Are the appeals manipulative, clichéd, or fallacious? Do they play on emotions to bypass reason?
- **Summarize?** Look for the essential message in the image: Does that main idea correspond with the written text?

View with a plan. Give your active attention by following this process:

1. **Survey the image.** See the image as a whole so that you can absorb its overall idea. Look for the image's focal point—what your eye is drawn to. Also consider the relationship between the image's foreground and background, its left content and right content, and its various colors.

2. **Inspect the image.** Let your "sight" touch every part of the image, as if you were reading Braille. Hints of its meaning may lurk in the tiny details as well as in the relationship between the image's parts.

3. **Question the image.** Who made the image? What does it show? When was it made? Where does it appear? Why was it placed there?

4. **Relate the image.** Put the image in context by connecting it to surrounding text, to other images, and to your own experience.

View an image.

The use of *minors* **as** *miners* **is no** *minor* **problem.**

Discussion

The illustration and caption above by Chris Krenzke effectively combine humor with instruction. Originally published in a high school writing handbook, the image's aim is to teach students about a specific word-usage problem while also entertaining them. The image is line art in the "comic" genre, using a humorous scene to convey a serious message. Here are some thoughts on how you might actively view this image:

1. **Survey.** The image tells a story of heavily burdened children working under the heavy supervision of an authoritarian male. That story moves from left to right, from breaking rocks to loading rocks to carrying rocks toward a likely distant destination, the destination pointed to by the man. The black-and-white medium accentuates the starkness.

2. **Inspect.** In terms of the illustration's details, each figure is striking. The individual children share a thinness in their bodies and a strain in their faces. The four children in the line are pictured as beasts of burden bent over by bags that dwarf them. The repetition of figures emphasizes the trudging repetition of their work, and each child in line is pressed farther toward the ground. As for the man, his back is straight and his posture tall. His enormous chin, large nose, overly long but skinny arm, and sharply pointed finger suggest a negative authority. His stubbly face and his caveman clothing add to this figure's prehistoric character.

3. **Question.** Who is the artist Chris Krenzke? When did he first create this image? In what book was it published? When? Why did Krenzke use this caveman style? Who or what do "minors," "miners," and "minor" refer to in the illustration?

4. **Relate.** The connection between the sentence and the image becomes clear when the viewer realizes that "minors" are children not of a legal age to work, "miners" refers to an occupation, and "minor" means insignificant. But the image prompts other connections: the history of horrific child-labor practices during the Industrial Revolution as well as continuing child-labor issues in today's global economy. With these allusions, Krenzke succeeds in deepening the instruction offered by his art.

Interpreting an Image

Interpreting an image follows naturally from viewing or "reading" the image. Interpreting means figuring out what the image or design is meant to do, say, or show. If the meaning were fixed, like the number of jellybeans in a jar, interpreting would be easy. But the meaning is something you have to gather for yourself by considering all the evidence.

Understand the elements of interpretation.

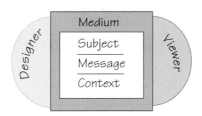

Keep in mind the following elements as you interpret an image. The **designer** of the image (for example, a cartoonist or webpage editor) uses an **image** to get some kind of **message** across to a **viewer**. The **image** offers a certain view of a certain **subject** in a certain **medium**. All of this is set in a certain **context**—a page of a textbook, an annual report, or a webpage. When you interpret the image, you consider each of these elements to arrive at an overall sense of meaning.

Understand the complications in interpretation.

Each element in the diagram above may offer special challenges to the reader:

Image: It might be strange, deceiving, very detailed, or highly technical.

Designer: He or she might be unknown or representing someone else, or the image might be designed by a team of people.

Viewer: You might be uninterested in the subject, unfamiliar with the visual "language" used by the designer, or biased toward the subject.

Subject: It might be vague, unfamiliar, complex, or disturbing.

Message: It might be mixed, implied, ironic, unwelcome, or distorted. The content could be literal, stylized, numeric, symbolic, and so on.

Context: It might be disconnected from the image, changing, or multilayered.

Medium: It might be multiple, awkward, or "the message."

INSIGHT: Like words, visuals can be clichés—trite, misleading, or worn-out expressions of concepts or ideas. For example, TV ads for weight-loss drugs commonly picture scantily clad, fit young people, incorrectly suggesting that using the drugs will produce fit, youthful bodies.

Interpret an image.

Discussion

This color photograph shows a multireligious commemoration of the 229,000 victims of the Indian Ocean tsunami of December 26, 2004.

The symbolism is clearly rooted in the points of light created by the candle balloons, where light itself is a cross-cultural symbol of hope, endurance, the human spirit, and God's presence. The skyward angle of the photograph, with the clusters of candle balloons floating up and the people in the lower right of the frame, creates this sense of vertical longing and release, emphasizing perhaps humanity's longing to solve life's mysteries, including death and disaster. Although the large, just-released candle balloons are most prominent, the viewer's eyes are also drawn upward, where clusters of far-off candles become constellations of starlike lights. The mourners in the right of the frame, forming a loose circle, are all gazing skyward, like the viewer. Ordinary people in ordinary clothes, they appear to be clapping and, for some, the clapping shows their hands virtually in a posture of prayer. In this way, the image both mourns the dead and celebrates life.

Designer:	Photographer Bazuki Muhammad.
Medium:	Digital color photograph.
Subject:	Thais release candle balloons during mass prayer for tsunami victims.
Message:	Remember those who died; move forward with hope.
Context:	Part of a series of photographs provided by Reuters, for inclusion in global newspapers with news stories about the commemoration on January 19, 2005.
Viewer:	Anyone around the globe reading a newspaper, magazine article, or web article on this story.

Evaluating an Image

When you encounter an image, you must do more than understand and interpret it: You must assess its quality, truthfulness, and value. In other words, you must evaluate it. When you have done that well, you can fairly say you have thought it through. The following questions will guide your assessment.

Consider the purpose.

What purpose does the visual image best seem to serve?

- **Ornamentation:** Makes the page more pleasing to the eye
- **Illustration:** Supports points made in the accompanying text
- **Revelation:** Gives an inside look at something or presents new data
- **Explanation:** Uses imagery or graphics to clarify a complex subject
- **Instruction:** Guides the viewer through a complex process
- **Persuasion:** Influences feelings or beliefs
- **Entertainment:** Amuses the reader

Evaluate the quality.

Essentially, how good is the image?

- Is the image done with skill? A map, for example, should be accurately and attractively drawn, should use color effectively, and should be complete enough to serve its purpose.
- Does the image measure up to standards of quality? See **www.thecollegewriter.com/3e** for design tips for a variety of visuals.
- Is it backed by authority? Does the designer have a good reputation? Does the publication or institution have good credentials?
- How does the image compare to other images like it? Are clearer or more accurate images available?
- What are its shortcomings? Are there gaps in its coverage? Does it twist the evidence? Does it convey clichéd or fallacious information? (See pages 267–270 for a discussion of logical fallacies.)
- Could you think of a better way to approach the image's subject? If you were to produce the visual, what might you improve?

Determine the value.

What is the image's tangible and intangible worth? Its benefits and drawbacks?

- Is the visual worth viewing? Does it enrich the document by clarifying or otherwise enhancing its message?
- Does the visual appeal to you? Listen to authorities and peers, but also consider your own perspective.

Evaluate an image.

Discussion

Evaluating an image such as this WWII poster aimed at U.S. servicemen reveals its strong stereotypes of both men and women, stereotypes related to the historical period. As with all images, evaluation begins with understanding and interpreting the poster.

In the poster's center is a woman in evening dress, her hair done up, wearing jewels and a corsage. She is seated, at ease, looking at us. Perhaps she represents beauty, both sensual attractiveness and sophistication. The colors used to present her are pale and muted, except for her blue eyes and red lips.

Surrounding the woman are three men, individually dressed in the uniforms of Army, Air Force, and Navy. Drinking and smoking, the men seem to be competing for her attention.

The poster implies that all service personnel were male, which was not true even in WWII, when WACs and WAVEs served in the armed forces. It cautions that these male members of the armed forces should be wary in seemingly innocent social situations, since even a beautiful woman, whom popular stereotypes of the day characterized as "dumb," might not be what she appears. Such a woman might, in fact, be a spy—an idea perhaps inspired by the famous case of WWI spy Mata Hari. The statement that "careless talk costs lives" is a version of another common phrase from the period: "Loose lips sink ships."

Evaluating this poster involves considering its original context while assessing it from our current perspective. In the heat of WWII, this poster could be considered a fair piece of military persuasion. Today, however, what is striking are the gender stereotypes at work in both image and words. Not only are service personnel today both male and female, in every branch of the armed forces, but they fulfill the same roles, including combat positions. With respect to the men, the image implies that in social situations (which are assumed to include smoking and drinking), they are untrustworthy and apt to boast or compete in the presence of an attractive woman. With respect to women, the image both denounces and warns, implying that women, especially attractive women, are cunning and dangerous. Today, such stereotypes press us to question the quality, truthfulness, and value of the image.

Critical Thinking Through Writing

In college, your writing often must show your ability to think critically about topics and issues by analyzing complex processes, synthesizing distinct concepts, weighing the value of opposing perspectives, and practicing new applications of existing principles. To hone your critical-thinking skills, you need to develop sound critical-thinking habits, sharpen your reasoning skills, and distinguish inductive and deductive logic.

Develop sound critical-thinking habits.

Like everything worthwhile, improving your critical-thinking skills takes time and practice. But cultivating the habits below will pay off in sound, thoughtful writing.

1. **Be curious.** Ask "Why?" Cultivate your ability to wonder; question what you see, hear, and read—both inside and outside the classroom.

2. **Be creative.** Don't settle for obvious answers. Look at things in a fresh way, asking "what-if" questions such as "What if Ophelia didn't die in *Hamlet?* How would the play be different?"

3. **Be open to new ideas.** Approach thinking as you would approach a road trip—looking for the unexpected and musing over mysteries.

4. **Value others' points of view.** Look at issues from another person's perspective and weigh that against your own. Honestly examine how the core of her or his perspective compares to the core of your perspective, and how each basis for thought might lead to different conclusions.

5. **Get involved.** Read books, journals, and newspapers. Watch documentaries. Join book clubs, film clubs, or political and social-action activities.

6. **Focus.** Sharpen your concentration, looking for details that distinguish a topic and reveal key questions related to its nature, function, and impact.

7. **Be rational.** Choose logical thinking patterns like those discussed in this chapter, and then work through the steps to deepen and develop your understanding of a topic.

8. **Make connections.** Use writing to explore how and why topics or issues are related. Use comparisons to identify and name these relationships.

9. **Tolerate ambiguity.** Respectfully analyze issues not readily resolved—and acknowledge when your position requires further research or thought.

10. **Test the evidence.** Be properly skeptical about all claims (see pages 262–263). Look for corroboration (or verification) in other sources.

11. **Develop research-based conclusions.** Focus on understanding issues, assessing their history, development, function, and impact. During the process, gather details that lead to and support a reasonable conclusion.

12. Expect results. Consider each paper to be a benchmark that reflects your progress in developing your thinking and writing skills. Save your papers for periodic analyses of your progress and revision of the writing.

 For more help with critical-thinking skills such as making and supporting claims, recognizing logical fallacies, and dealing with opposition, see "Strategies for Argumentation and Persuasion," pages **259–274.**

Ask probing questions.

Every field uses questions to trigger critical thinking. For example, scientific questions generate hypotheses, sociological questions lead to studies, mathematical questions call for proofs, and literary criticism questions call for interpretations. A good question opens up a problem and guides you all the way to its solution. But not all questions are created equal. Consider the differences:

- "Rhetorical" questions aren't meant to be answered. They're asked for effect. *Example:* Who would want to be caught in an earthquake?
- Closed questions seek a limited response and can be answered with "yes," "no," or a simple fact. *Example:* Would I feel an earthquake measuring 3.0 on the Richter scale?
- Open questions invite brainstorming and discussion. *Example:* How might a major earthquake affect this urban area?
- Theoretical questions call for organization and explanation of an entire field of knowledge. *Example:* What might cause a sudden fracturing of Earth's crust along fault lines?

To improve the critical thinking in your writing, ask better questions. The strategies below will help you think freely, respond to reading, study for a test, or collect your thoughts for an essay.

Ask open questions. Closed questions sometimes choke off thinking. Use open questions to trigger a flow of ideas.

Ask "educated" questions. Compare these questions: (A) What's wrong with television? (B) Does the 16.3 percent rise in televised acts of violence during the past three years signal a rising tolerance for violence in the viewing audience? You have a better chance of expanding the "educated" question—question B—into an essay because the question is clearer and suggests debatable issues.

Keep a question journal. Divide a blank notebook page or split a computer screen. On one side, write down any questions that come to mind regarding the topic that you want to explore. On the other side, write down answers and any thoughts that flow from them.

Write Q & A drafts. To write a thoughtful first draft, write quickly, then look it over. Turn the main idea into a question and write again, answering your question. For example, if your main idea is that TV viewers watch far more violence than they did ten years ago, ask *Which viewers? Why?* and *What's the result?* Go on that way until you find a key idea to serve as the main point of your next draft.

Practice inductive and deductive logic.

Questions invite thinking; reasoning responds to that challenge in an organized way. Will the organization of your thoughts be inductive or deductive? **Inductive logic** reasons from specific information toward general conclusions. **Deductive logic** reasons from general principles toward specific applications. Notice in the diagram below that inductive reasoning starts with specific details or observations (as shown at the base) and then moves "up" to broader ideas and eventually to a concluding generalization. In contrast, deduction starts with general principles at the top and works down, applying the principles to explain particular instances.

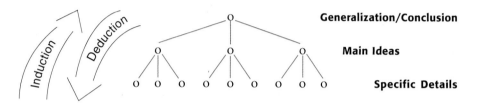

Sentences, paragraphs, and entire essays can be organized either inductively or deductively. Use induction when you want to postpone your conclusions. Use deduction for logical clarity, directness, and strength, or to apply what is already agreed on to what is still under dispute. Narrative or personal essays tend toward inductive organization, whereas analytical essays (particularly those written in the social or natural sciences) typically use both induction and deduction.

Example: Read through the paragraphs below from the student essay "If We Are What We Wear, What Are We?" by Allison Young (**www.thecollegewriter.com/3e**). The first paragraph works deductively, the second paragraph inductively. Note how each approach affects the message.

Deduction:
generalization to specific details

The American excuse for owning multiples is that clothing styles change so rapidly. At the end of the '80s, trends in high fashion changed every two and a half months (During 95). Even for those of us who don't keep up with high fashion, styles change often enough that our clothing itself lasts much longer than the current trend. Perhaps this is one of the reasons the average American spent $997 on clothing in 1996 (U.S. Department of Commerce).

Induction:
specific details to generalization

While Americans are spending a thousand dollars on clothing a year, people in Ethiopia make an average of only $96 a year, those in Bangladesh $280, and the average Filipino worker makes $1,052 (United Nations Statistics Division). I, on the other hand, made over $5,000 last year, and that job was only part-time. When an American college student can earn more money at her part-time job than three billion people each make for a living, it's time to question our culture and ask, as Alan During did, "How much is enough?"

Practicing Modes of
Thinking in Your Writing

In your various writing assignments, you will need to practice specific modes of thinking. The table below maps out these modes (from elementary to complex) and the tasks each requires. The more complex modes are then fleshed out on the following pages.

When you are asked to _____ *, be ready to* _____ *.*

Know
define	memorize
identify	name
list	recall
match	recognize

Call to mind what you have learned
- Recall information
- List details
- Define key terms
- Identify main points

Understand
comprehend	interpret
connect	restate
explain	summarize
grasp	

Show what you have learned
- Connect related examples
- Summarize important details
- Explain how something works
- Interpret what something means

Analyze
characterize	contrast
classify	divide
compare	examine

Break down information
- Divide a whole into its parts
- Group things into categories
- Analyze causes and effects
- Examine similarities and differences

Synthesize
assemble	imagine
combine	invent
construct	link
formulate	

Shape information into a new form
- Bring together a body of evidence
- Blend the old with the new
- Predict or hypothesize
- Construct a new way of looking at something

Evaluate
assess	measure
check	monitor
critique	rank
judge	rate

Determine the worth of information
- Point out a subject's strengths and weaknesses
- Evaluate its clarity, accuracy, logic, value, and so on
- Convince others of its value/worth

Apply
anticipate	propose
choose	select
generate	

Use what you have learned
- Propose a better way of doing something
- Generate a plan of action
- Offer solutions to a problem

Think by using analysis.

The word *analyze* literally means "to loosen or undo." When you analyze something, you break it down into parts and examine each part separately. You classify information, compare objects, trace a process, or explain causes.

As you analyze, think about the questions listed below. Note that each type of thinking answers certain kinds of questions. Remember, too, that thinking tasks often require two or more kinds of analysis that support one another.

Composition: What elements does it contain? What is not part of it?

Categories: How are things grouped, divided, or classified?

Structures: What are the parts or elements? How are they related?

Comparisons/ contrasts: How are things similar? How are they different?

Causes/effects: Why did this happen? What are the results?

Processes: How does it work or happen? What are the stages?

Example: Read through the passage below, from "Wayward Cells." In the full essay on pages 231–232, student writer Kerri Mertz explains the process by which healthy body cells become cancerous cells. Note how in this excerpt, the writer develops an overall analysis based on a process but also uses compare-contrast and cause-effect thinking within that structure, as well as informal definition.

The writer explains a cellular process and contrasts healthy and cancerous versions.	Most healthy cells reproduce rather quickly, but their reproduction rate is controlled. For example, your blood cells completely die off and replace themselves within a matter of weeks, but existing cells make only as many new cells as the body needs. The DNA codes in healthy cells tell them how many new cells to produce. However, cancer cells don't have this control, so they reproduce quickly with no stopping point, a characteristic called "autonomy" (Braun 3). What's more, all their "offspring" have the same qualities as their messed-up parent, and the resulting overpopulation produces growths called tumors.
The writer explains the three harmful effects of tumor cells (the cause).	Tumor cells can hurt the body in a number of ways. First, a tumor can grow so big that it takes up space needed by other organs. Second, some cells may detach from the original tumor and spread throughout the body, creating new tumors elsewhere. This happens with lymphatic cancer—a cancer that's hard to control because it spreads so quickly. A third way that tumor cells can hurt the body is by doing work not called for in their DNA. For example, a gland cell's DNA code may tell the cell to produce a necessary hormone in the endocrine system. However, if cancer damages or distorts
Examples illustrate the analysis.	that code, sick cells may produce more of the hormone than the body can use—or even tolerate (Braun 4). Cancer cells seem to have minds of their own, and this is why cancer is such a serious disease.

Think by using synthesis.

Synthesis is the opposite of analysis. Where analysis breaks things down into parts, synthesis combines elements into a new whole. In your writing, when you pull together things that are normally separate, you are synthesizing. Common ways of synthesizing include predicting, inventing, redesigning, and imagining a whole new way of looking at something.

Working with synthesis involves both reason and imagination. Start by looking closely at two or more items that you want to synthesize, and then think of fresh ways they can be related. Don't be afraid to see your subjects in a new way. In other words, think "sideways" rather than straight ahead. Ask the following questions:

Applying: What can I do with both? What will be the outcome?

Bridging: How can I build a connection between the two?

Combining: How can I connect, associate, or blend the two?

Conflicting: Which is good, better, or best? What strength does each offer the other?

Inventing: What parts could these two play in a drama?

Proposing: What do I suggest doing with both?

Sequencing: Which comes first? Is one an extension of the other?

Projecting: Based on current information, what is the best forecast for what will happen in the near future or the long term?

Example: Read through the passage below, from "In Africa, AIDS Has a Woman's Face," by former United Nations Secretary-General Kofi Annan (see pages 307–309). In the full article, Annan argues that resolving the AIDS crisis in Africa must begin by saving the familial, social, and economic backbones of African cultures—women. In the following passage, Annan synthesizes his discussion by projecting what is necessary for successful solutions.

Pulling together his discussion of the twin tragedies of AIDS and famine in Africa, the writer calls for imaginative, multifaceted solutions.

Because this crisis is different from past famines, we must look beyond relief measures of the past. Merely shipping in food is not enough. Our effort will have to combine food assistance and new approaches to farming with treatment and prevention of H.I.V. and AIDS. It will require creating early-warning and analysis systems that monitor both H.I.V. infection rates and famine indicators. It will require new agricultural techniques, appropriate to a depleted work force. It will require a renewed effort to wipe out H.I.V.-related stigma and silence.

It will require innovative, large-scale ways to care for orphans, with specific measures that enable children in AIDS-affected communities to stay in school. Education and prevention are still the most powerful weapons against the spread of H.I.V. Above all, this new international effort must put women at the center of our strategy to fight AIDS.

Think by using evaluation.

Movies, proposals, arguments—anything can be evaluated. Evaluation measures the value or worth of things. For example, when you express your judgment about an issue or discuss the weak and strong points of what someone else has said, you are evaluating. Many kinds of writing are evaluative.

To evaluate a topic, start by learning as much about it as possible. Then consider which criteria or standards are appropriate. Next, judge how the topic measures up based on those criteria. Support your judgment with concrete details, examples, illustrations, and comparisons. Ask questions like these:

Aspects: What elements of the topic will I evaluate?

Vantage point: What are my experience and my point of view?

Criteria: On which standards will I base my judgment?

Assessment: How does the topic measure up by those standards?

Comparison: How does it compare to and contrast with similar things?

Recommendation: Based on my evaluation, what do I advise?

Example: The passage below is taken from David Blankenhorn's "Fatherless America," on pages **287–291**. In the full essay, Blankenhorn examines the causes and effects of the increased fatherlessness within U.S. families—that is, the absence of fathers in many homes. In the following excerpt, he assesses the failures of a society that is losing a healthy sense of fatherhood.

The writer establishes a criterion for evaluating a culture's fatherhood models and practices.

. . . Margaret Mead and others have observed that the supreme test of any civilization is whether it can socialize men by teaching them to be fathers—creating a culture in which men acknowledge their paternity and willingly nurture their offspring. Indeed, if we can equate the essence of the antisocial male with violence, we can equate the essence of the socialized male with being a good father. Thus, at the center of our most important cultural imperative, we find the fatherhood script: the story that describes what it ought to mean for a man to have a child. . . .

After exploring this criterion in depth (not shown), the writer measures U.S. culture and assesses its failures with respect to fatherhood.

The stakes on this issue could hardly be higher. Our society's conspicuous failure to sustain or create compelling norms of fatherhood amounts to a social and personal disaster. Today's story of fatherhood features one-dimensional characters, an unbelievable plot, and an unhappy ending. It reveals in our society both a failure of collective memory and a collapse of moral imagination. It undermines families, neglects children, causes or aggravates our worst social problems, and makes individual adult happiness—both male and female—harder to achieve.

Ultimately, this failure reflects nothing less than a culture gone awry: a culture increasingly unable to establish the boundaries, erect the signposts, and fashion the stories that can harmonize individual happiness with collective well-being. In short, it reflects a culture that increasingly fails to "enculture" individual men and women, mothers and fathers.

Think by using application.

Thinking by using application defines the practical implications of something. It involves using what you know to demonstrate, show, relate, or extend ideas in view of their outcomes. For example, using what you have learned about the ecology of forest fires to examine the effects of a particular fire—that's application in action.

Applying involves moving from ideas to possible action. First, understand the information you have. Second, relate this information to a given situation. Third, select those facts and details that clarify and support the application. Fourth, test the application to see whether it has been reasonable.

When applying ideas, let questions like these guide your writing:

Purpose: What is something designed to be or do?

Benefits: What would this idea make clearer, better, or more complete?

Solutions: What problems are solved by application of this idea?

Outcomes: What results can be expected? Where could we go from there?

Example: Read the paragraphs below, from Anna Quindlen's "Uncle Sam and Aunt Samantha" (pages 318–320). In this essay, Quindlen argues that in the United States, women— as well as men—should be eligible to be drafted for military service. In the passage below, she applies the concept of equal rights to this specific situation.

Using the word "egalitarian" to refer to a key principle, the writer points out the real inequality and argues for a change.	Parents face a series of unique new challenges in this more egalitarian world, not the least of which would be sending a daughter off to war. But parents all over this country are doing that right now, with daughters who enlisted; some have even expressed surprise that young women, in this day and age, are not required to register alongside their brothers and friends. While all involved in this debate over the years have invoked the assumed opposition of the people, even 10 years ago more than half of all Americans polled believed women should be made eligible for the draft. Besides, this is not about comfort but about fairness. My son has to register with the Selective Service this year, and if his sister does not when she turns 18, it makes a mockery not only of the standards of this household but of the standards of this nation.
She backs up her conclusion with historical context and presses readers to agree.	It is possible in Afghanistan for women to be treated like little more than fecund pack animals precisely because gender fear and ignorance and hatred have been codified and permitted to hold sway. In this country, largely because of the concerted efforts of those allied with the women's movement over a century of struggle, much of that bigotry has been beaten back, even buried. Yet in improbable places the creaky old ways surface, the ways suggesting that we women were made of finer stuff. The finer stuff was usually porcelain, decorative and on the shelf, suitable for meals and show. Happily, the finer stuff has been transmuted into the right stuff. But with rights come responsibilities, as teachers like to tell their students . . .

Critical-Thinking Checklist

Use the checklist below to track improvements in critical thinking.

_____ I regularly and effectively practice the SQ3R reading method for important reading assignments for my courses and research projects.

_____ I read actively rather than passively by taking thoughtful notes, annotating texts, mapping, and outlining.

_____ I evaluate the credibility, context, reasoning, and challenges of texts.

_____ As needed, I can generate thoughtful responses to texts and/or objective summaries of textual content.

_____ I can effectively "read" visual images by carefully viewing, interpreting, and evaluating their content and design.

_____ I am developing advanced critical-thinking skills that include curiosity, creativity, reason, and tolerance of complexity and ambiguity—all rooted in asking probing questions.

_____ I can effectively reason using inductive and/or deductive logic.

_____ I am improving my ability to write out of advanced thinking modes: analysis, synthesis, evaluation, and application.

Critical-Thinking and Writing Activities

As directed by your instructor, complete the following critical-thinking and writing activities by yourself or with classmates.

1. Northrop Frye has argued that "[n]obody is capable of free speech unless he [or she] knows how to use language, and such knowledge is not a gift: It has to be learned and worked at." How does Frye's claim relate to the discussions of critical reading, viewing, and writing in this chapter?

2. What thinking, reading, viewing, and writing skills are required in your field of study? Reflect on those possibilities.

3. Choose a subject you know something about. Practice thinking about that subject both inductively and deductively. Then write two paragraphs—one developed inductively and the other developed deductively.

4. Select a sample essay from the "Strategies and Models" section. Read the piece carefully and identify where and how the writer uses different thinking modes. Do the same analysis on a recent sample of your own writing, rating your analysis, synthesis, evaluation, and application.

◀ VISUALLY SPEAKING:

Review the image on page 3 and explain what is suggests about critical thinking and critical viewing. Note: You will find additional visual-literacy activities in each chapter, as well as at **www.thecollegewriter.com/3e**.

BEGINNING THE WRITING PROCESS

College instructors assign writing projects for a variety of reasons. Often they want to encourage you to think more deeply about a topic. For example, writing a paper on climate change helps you sort out the issues, digging into a topic only briefly introduced in class or in a textbook. Your writing helps you get at the complex truth of a topic.

Your instructors may have additional reasons for assigning writing. They may want you to practice the specific thinking habits and forms of writing used in their disciplines. For these reasons, you might be assigned a lab report in biology, a case study in business, or a literary analysis in English.

Finally, your instructors may assign writing so that you learn how to contribute to a learning community. Submitting your paper for graded feedback is a basic contribution, but you might also share your writing with other members of your class or a broader online audience. By sharing your writing, you contribute to research and discussion on your topic.

Video

Web Link

Video

The Writing Process:
From Start to Finish

It's easy to feel overwhelmed by a writing project—especially if the form of writing is new to you, the topic is complex, or the paper must be long. However, using the writing process will relieve some of that pressure by breaking down the task into manageable steps. An overview of those steps is shown below, and key principles are addressed on the next page.

An Overview of the Writing Process

The following flowchart maps out the basic steps in the writing process. As you work on your writing project, periodically review this diagram to keep yourself on task.

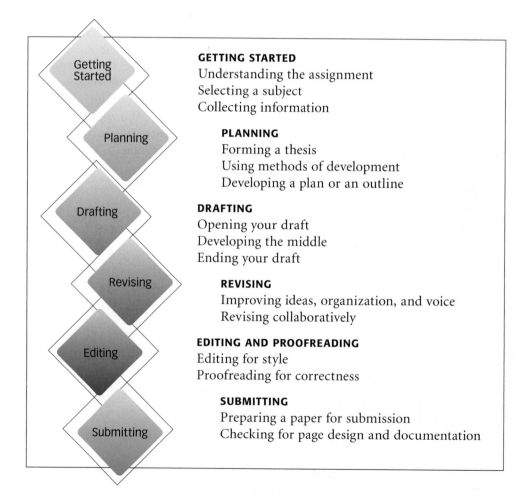

GETTING STARTED
Understanding the assignment
Selecting a subject
Collecting information

PLANNING
Forming a thesis
Using methods of development
Developing a plan or an outline

DRAFTING
Opening your draft
Developing the middle
Ending your draft

REVISING
Improving ideas, organization, and voice
Revising collaboratively

EDITING AND PROOFREADING
Editing for style
Proofreading for correctness

SUBMITTING
Preparing a paper for submission
Checking for page design and documentation

Adapting the Process to Your Project

The writing process shown on the previous page is flexible, not rigid. As a writer, you need to adapt the process to your situation and assignment. To do so, consider these essential principles.

Writing tends not to follow a straight path. While writing begins with an assignment or a need and ends with a reader, the journey in between is often indirect. The steps in the flowchart overlap to show that when you write, you sometimes move back and forth between steps, meaning that the process is recursive. For example, during the revision phase, you may discover that you need to draft a new paragraph or do more research.

Each assignment presents distinct challenges. A personal essay may develop best through clustering or freewriting; a literary analysis through close reading of a story; a lab report through the experimental method; and a position paper through reading of books and journal articles, as well as through careful and balanced reasoning.

Writing can involve collaboration. From using your roommate as a sounding board for your topic choice to working with a group to produce a major report, college writing is not solitary writing. In fact, many colleges have a writing center to help you refine your writing assignments. (See page 89 for more.)

Each writer works differently. Some writers do extensive prewriting before drafting, while others do not. You might develop a detailed outline, whereas someone else might draft a brief list of topics. Experiment with the strategies introduced in chapters 2–7, adopting those that help you.

Good writing can't be rushed. Although some students regard pulling an all-nighter as a badge of honor, good writing takes time. A steady, disciplined approach will generally produce the best results. For example, by brainstorming or reading early in a project, you stimulate your subconscious mind to mull over issues, identify problems, and project solutions—even while your conscious mind is working on other things. Similarly, completing a first draft early enough gives you time to revise objectively.

Different steps call for attention to different writing issues. As you use the writing process, at each stage keep your focus where it belongs:

1. While getting started, planning, and drafting, focus on global issues: ideas, structure, voice, format, and design.

2. During revising, fix big content problems by cutting, adding, and thoroughly reworking material. (Our experience is that students benefit the most from revising—but spend the least time doing it!)

3. While editing and proofreading, pay attention to small, local issues— word choice, sentence smoothness, and grammatical correctness. Worrying about these issues early in the writing process interrupts the flow of drafting and wastes time on material that later is deleted.

Understanding the Rhetorical Situation:
Subject, Audience, and Purpose

Rhetoric is the art of using language effectively. As Aristotle, Quintilian, and others have explained, your language is effective when all aspects of your message (including content and style) fit your **subject,** address the needs of your **audience,** and fulfill your **purpose.** For these reasons, before you put fingers to the keyboard, you must think carefully about all three. By doing so you're analyzing your *rhetorical situation*—the conditions or issues that affect writing decisions, including choosing the best *form* (such as essay or report), the best *medium* (paper or electronic), and the best *organizational strategy* (such as cause/effect or chronological process).

Understand your subject.

Ideas—and the information that relates to them—are the substance of all good writing. Without informative ideas, your writing cannot fulfill the needs of your audience and will not achieve your purpose. Understanding your subject involves gathering and assimilating all relevant details, including its history, makeup, function, and impact on people and culture. Knowing these details will help you decide issues such as what to include in your writing and how to organize it.

Understand your audience.

For any writing task, you must understand your audience in order to develop writing that meets their needs. To assess your audience, answer questions like these:

- Who are my readers: instructor? classmates? web surfers?
- What do they know about my topic, and what do they need to know?
- How well do they understand the terminology, procedures, and technology?
- What are their attitudes toward the topic and toward me?
- How well do they read written English—or visuals such as graphs and charts?
- How will they use my writing (as entertainment or to complete a task)?

Note: Answers to such questions will help you develop meaningful sentences (pages **95–101**), choose appropriate words (pages **102–106**), and select relevant visuals (page **416**).

Understand your purpose.

Knowing your purpose—*why* you are writing—will help you make decisions, such as choosing an organizational strategy. In assignments, key words (especially verbs) either hint at or specify your purpose. For example, an assignment asking you to *analyze* a topic requires that you break the subject into subparts and then explain the relationships among those subparts. Organizational patterns useful for analyzing a topic include classification, definition, and process (pages **62–65**).

Understanding the Assignment

Each college instructor has a way of personalizing a writing assignment, but most assignments will spell out (1) the objective, (2) the task, (3) the formal requirements, and (4) suggested approaches and topics. Your first step, therefore, is to read the assignment carefully, noting the options and restrictions that are part of it. The suggestions below will help you do that. (Also see pages **117–121** for one writer's approach.)

Read the assignment.

Certain words in the assignment explain what main action you must perform. Here are some words that signal what you are to do:

Key Words

Analyze:	Break down a topic into subparts, showing how those parts relate.
Argue:	Defend a claim with logical arguments.
Classify:	Divide a large group into well-defined subgroups.
Compare/contrast:	Point out similarities and/or differences.
Define:	Give a clear, thoughtful definition or meaning of something.
Describe:	Show in detail what something is like.
Evaluate:	Weigh the truth, quality, or usefulness of something.
Explain:	Give reasons, list steps, or discuss the causes of something.
Interpret:	Tell in your own words what something means.
Reflect:	Share your well-considered thoughts about a subject.
Summarize:	Restate someone else's ideas very briefly in your own words.
Synthesize:	Connect facts or ideas to create something new.

Options and Restrictions

The assignment often gives you some choice of your topic or approach but may restrict your options to suit the instructor's purpose. Note the options and restrictions in the following short sample assignment:

Reflect on the way a natural disaster or major historical event has altered your understanding of the past, the present, or the future.

Options:	(1) You may choose any natural disaster or historical event.
	(2) You may focus on the past, present, or future.
	(3) You may examine any kind of alteration.
Restrictions:	(1) You must reflect on a change in your understanding.
	(2) The disaster must be natural.
	(3) The historical event must be major.

Relate the assignment to the goals of the course.

1. How much value does the instructor give the assignment? (The value is often expressed as a percentage of the course grade.)
2. What benefit does your instructor want you to receive?
   - Strengthen your comprehension?
   - Improve your research skills?
   - Deepen your ability to explain, prove, or persuade?
   - Expand your style?
   - Increase your creativity?
3. How will this assignment contribute to your overall performance in the course? What course goals (often listed in the syllabus) does it address?

Relate the assignment to other assignments.

1. Does it build on previous assignments?
2. Does it prepare you for the next assignment?

Relate the assignment to your own interests.

1. Does it connect with a topic that already interests you?
2. Does it connect with work in your other courses?
3. Does it connect with the work you may do in your chosen field?
4. Does it connect with life outside school?

Reflect on the assignment.

1. **First impulses:** How did you feel when you first read the assignment?
2. **Approaches:** What's the usual approach for an assignment like this? What's a better way of tackling it?
3. **Quality of performance:** What would it take to produce an excellent piece of writing?
4. **Benefits:** What are the benefits to your education? to you personally? to the class? to society?
5. **Features:** Reflect further on four key features of any writing assignment.
   Purpose: What is the overall purpose of the assignment—to inform, to explain, to analyze, to entertain? What is the desired outcome?
   Audience: Should you address your instructor? your classmates? a general reader? How much does the reader already know about the topic? What type of language should you use?
   Form: What are the requirements concerning length, format, and due date?
   Assessment: How will the assignment be evaluated? How can you be sure that you are completing the assignment correctly?

Selecting a Subject

For some assignments, finding a suitable subject (or topic) may require little thinking on your part. If an instructor asks you to summarize an article in a professional journal, you know what you will write about—the article in question. But suppose the instructor asks you to analyze a feature of popular culture in terms of its impact on society. You won't be sure of a specific writing topic until you explore the possibilities. Keep the following points in mind when you conduct a topic search. Your topic must . . .

- meet the requirements of the assignment.
- be limited in scope.
- seem reasonable (that is, be within your means to research).
- genuinely interest you.

Limit the subject area.

Many of your writing assignments may relate to general subject areas you are currently studying. Your task, then, is to select a specific topic related to the general area of study—a topic limited enough that you can treat it with some depth in the length allowed for the assignment. The following examples show the difference between general subjects and limited topics:

General Subject Area: Popular culture
       Limited Topic: *The Simpsons* TV show

General Subject Area: Energy sources
       Limited Topic: Using wind power

Conduct your search.

Finding a writing idea that meets the requirements of the assignment should not be difficult, if you know how and where to look. Follow these steps:

1. Check your class notes and handouts for ideas related to the assignment.

2. Search the Internet. Type in a keyword or phrase (the general subject stated in the assignment) and see what you can find. You could also follow a subject tree to narrow a subject. (See pages **469–471**.)

3. Consult indexes, guides, and other library references. *The Readers' Guide to Periodical Literature*, for example, lists current articles published on specific topics and where to find them. (See pages **458–463**.)

4. Discuss the assignment with your instructor or an information specialist.

5. Use one or more of the prewriting strategies described on the following pages to generate possible writing ideas.

Explore for possible topics.

You can generate possible writing ideas by using the following strategies. These same strategies can be used when you've chosen a topic and want to develop it further.

Journal Writing

Write in a journal on a regular basis. Reflect on your personal feelings, develop your thoughts, and record the happenings of each day. Periodically go back and underline ideas that you would like to explore in writing assignments. In the following journal-writing samples, the writer came up with an idea for a writing assignment about the societal impacts of popular culture.

> I read a really disturbing news story this morning. I've been thinking about it all day. In California a little girl was killed when she was struck by a car driven by a man distracted by a billboard ad for lingerie featuring a scantily clothed woman. Not only is it a horrifying thing to happen, but it also seems to me all too symbolic of the way that sexually charged images in the media are putting children, and especially girls, in danger. That reminds me of another news story I read this week about preteen girls wanting to wear the kinds of revealing outfits that they see in music videos, TV shows, and magazines aimed at teenagers. <u>Too many of today's media images give young people the impression that sexuality should begin at an early age. This is definitely a dangerous message.</u>

Freewriting

Write nonstop for ten minutes or longer to discover possible writing ideas. Use a key concept related to the assignment as a starting point. You'll soon discover potential writing ideas that might otherwise have never entered your mind. Note in the following example that the writer doesn't stop writing even when he can't think of anything to say. Note also that he doesn't stop to correct typos and other mistakes.

> Popular culture. What does that include? Television obviously but thats a pretty boring subject. What else? Movies, pop music, video games. Is there a connection between playing violent video games and acting out violent behavior? Most video players I know would say no but sometimes news reports suggest a connection. Is this something I'd want to write about? Not really. What then? Maybe I could think about this a different way and focus on the positive effects of playing video games. They release tension for one thing and they can really be challenging. Other benefits? They help to kill time, that's for sure, but maybe that's not such a good thing. I would definitely read more if it weren't for video games, tv, etc. Maybe I could write about how all the electronic entertainment that surrounds us today is creating a generation of nonreaders. Or maybe I could focus on whether people aren't getting much physical exercise because of the time they spend with electronic media. Maybe both. At least I have some possibilities to work with.

QUICK GUIDE
▬ Freewriting ▬▬▬▬▬▬▬▬▬▬▬▬▬▬▬▬▬

Freewriting is the writing you do without having a specific outcome in mind. You simply write down whatever pops into your head as you explore your topic. Freewriting can serve as a starting point for your writing, or it can be combined with any of the other prewriting strategies to help you select, explore, focus, or organize your writing. If you get stuck at any point during the composing process, you can return to freewriting as a way of generating new ideas.

▬ Reminders

- **Freewriting helps you get your thoughts down on paper.** (Thoughts are constantly passing through your mind.)
- **Freewriting helps you develop and organize these thoughts.**
- **Freewriting helps you make sense out of things** that you may be studying or researching.
- **Freewriting may seem awkward at times,** but just stick with it.

▬ The Process

- **Write nonstop and record whatever comes into your mind.** Follow your thoughts instead of trying to direct them.
- **If you have a particular topic or assignment to complete, use it as a starting point.** Otherwise, begin with anything that comes to mind.
- **Don't stop to judge, edit, or correct your writing;** that will come later.
- **Keep writing even when you think you have exhausted all of your ideas.** Switch to another angle or voice, but keep writing.
- **Watch for a promising writing idea to emerge.** Learn to recognize the beginnings of a good idea, and then expand that idea by recording as many specific details as possible.

▬ The Result

- **Review your writing and underline the ideas you like.** These ideas will often serve as the basis for future writings.
- **Determine exactly what you need to write about.** Once you've figured out what you are required to do, you may then decide to do a second freewriting exercise.
- **Listen to and read the freewriting of others;** learn from your peers.

Listing

Freely list ideas as they come to mind, beginning with a key concept related to the assignment. (Brainstorming—listing ideas in conjunction with members of a group—is often an effective way to extend your lists.) The following is an example of a student's list of ideas for possible topics on the subject of news reporting:

Aspect of popular culture: News reporting

Sensationalism
Sound bites rather than in-depth analysis
Focus on the negative
Shock radio
Shouting matches pretending to be debates
Press leaks that damage national security, etc.
Lack of observation of people's privacy
Bias
Contradictory health news confusing to readers
Little focus on "unappealing" issues like poverty
Celebration of "celebrity"

Clustering

To begin the clustering process, write a key word or phrase related to the assignment in the center of your paper. Circle it, and then cluster ideas around it. Circle each idea as you record it, and draw a line connecting it to the closest related idea. Keep going until you run out of ideas and connections. The following is a student's cluster on the subject of sports:

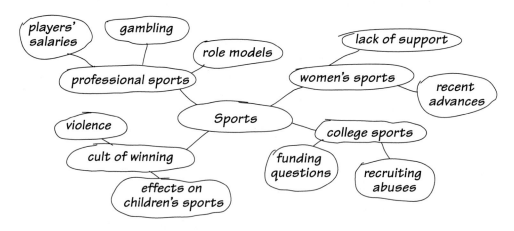

TIP: After four or five minutes of listing or clustering, scan your work for an idea to explore in a freewriting. A writing idea should begin to emerge during this freewriting session. (See pages **34–35**.)

Collecting Information

Writer and instructor Donald Murray said that "writers write with information. If there is no information, there will be no effective writing." How true! Before you can develop a thoughtful piece of writing, you must gain a thorough understanding of your topic; to do so, you must carry out the necessary reading, reflecting, and researching. Writing becomes a satisfying experience once you can speak with authority about your topic. Use the following guidelines when you start collecting information. (Also see "Research and Writing" in this book.)

- Determine what you already know about your topic. (Use the strategies below this bulleted list.)
- Consider listing questions you would like to answer during your research. (See page **38**.)
- Identify and explore possible sources of information. (See page **39**.)
- Carry out your research following a logical plan. (See page **48–51**.)

Find out what you already know.

Use one or more of the following strategies to determine what you already know about a writing topic.

1. **Focused freewriting:** At this point, you can focus your freewriting by (1) exploring your limited topic from different angles or (2) approaching your freewriting as if it were a quick draft of the actual paper. A quick version will tell you how much you know about your topic and what you need to find out.

2. **Clustering:** Try clustering with your topic serving as the nucleus word. Your clustering should focus on what you already know. (See page **36**.)

3. **Five W's of writing:** Answer the five W's—*Who? What? When? Where?* and *Why?*—to identify basic information on your subject. Add *How?* to the list for better coverage.

4. **Directed writing:** Write whatever comes to mind about your topic, using one of the modes listed below. (Repeat the process as often as you need to, selecting a different mode each time.)

   Describe it: What do you see, hear, feel, smell, and taste?

   Compare it: What is it similar to? What is it different from?

   Associate it: What connections between this topic and others come to mind?

   Analyze it: What parts does it have? How do they work together?

   Argue it: What do you like about the topic? What you do not like about it? What are its strengths and weaknesses?

   Apply it: What can you do with it? How can you use it?

Ask questions.

To guide your collecting and researching, you may find it helpful to list questions about your topic that you would like to answer. Alternatively, you can refer to the questions below. These questions address problems, policies, and concepts. Most topics will fall under one of these categories. Use those questions that seem helpful as a guide to your research.

	DESCRIPTION	FUNCTION	HISTORY	VALUE
P R O B L E M S	What is the problem? What type of problem is it? What are its parts? What are the signs of the problem?	Who or what is affected by it? What new problems might it cause in the future?	What is the current status of the problem? What or who caused it? What or who contributed to it?	What is its significance? Why? Why is it more (or less) important than other problems? What does it symbolize or illustrate?
P O L I C I E S	What is the policy? How broad is it? What are its parts? What are its most important features?	What is the policy designed to do? What is needed to make it work? What are or will be its effects?	What brought about this policy? What are the alternatives?	Is the policy workable? What are its advantages and disadvantages? Is it practical? Is it a good policy? Why or why not?
C O N C E P T S	What is the concept? What are its parts? What is its main feature? Whom or what is it related to?	Who has been influenced by this concept? Why is it important? How does it work?	When did it originate? How has it changed over the years? How might it change in the future?	What practical value does it have? Why is it superior (or inferior) to similar concepts? What is its social worth?

Identify possible sources.

Finding meaningful sources is one of the most important steps you will take as you prepare to write. Listed below are tips that will help you identify good sources:

1. **Give yourself enough time.** Finding good sources of information may be time-consuming. Books and periodicals you need may be checked out, your computer service may be down, and so on.

2. **Be aware of the limits of your resources.** Print material may be out-of-date. Online information may be more current, but it may not always be reliable. (See pages **432–435** for ways to help you evaluate information.)

3. **Use your existing resources to find additional sources of information.** Pay attention to books, articles, and individuals mentioned in reliable initial sources of information.

4. **Ask for help.** The specialists in your school library can help you find information that is reliable and relevant. These people are trained to find information; don't hesitate to ask for their help. (See page **455**.)

5. **Bookmark useful websites.** Include reference works and academic resources related to your major.

Explore different sources of information.

Of course, books and websites are not the only possible sources of information. Primary sources such as interviews, observations, and surveys may lead you to a more thorough and meaningful understanding of a topic. (See pages **449–451**.)

PRIMARY SOURCES	SECONDARY SOURCES
Interviews	Articles
Observations	Reference book entries
Participation	Books
Surveys	Websites

Carry out your research.

As you conduct your research, try to use a variety of reliable sources. It's also a good idea to choose an efficient note-taking method before you start. You will want to take good notes on the information you find and record all the publishing information necessary for citing your sources. (See pages **438–441**.)

Reserve a special part of a notebook to question, evaluate, and reflect on your research as it develops. The record of your thoughts and actions created during this process will mean a great deal to you—as much as or more than the actual information you uncover. Reflection helps you make sense of new ideas, refocus your thinking, and evaluate your progress.

Writing with Sources

Many of your writing assignments will challenge you to do good research and to work well with the sources you find. While chapters 28–33 offer a full treatment of research writing, these two pages (along with pages 52–53, 68–69, 90–91, 108–109, and 114–115) explain how to address source-related issues linked to each step in the writing process.

For example, at the getting-started phase, you should think through broad source-use issues such as these:

1. Which types of research does my assignment require?

2. Which types of research would help me explore my topic?

3. Which record-keeping and note-taking strategies would help me use source information effectively and avoid plagiarism?

Think rhetorically.

To help you resolve questions like those given above, remember the rhetorical situation behind your project:

- Given the **subject** of your writing, which sources of information would offer reliable, relevant information? (See "Exploring Possible Information Resources and Sites," pages 428–429.) In your assignment, which types of sources are recommended or expected? Which sources should be avoided?
- Given your **audience,** which types of sources will readers understand and respect? Which sources will add to your credibility?
- Given your **purpose** (to entertain, inform, analyze, or persuade), which information will help you achieve that goal, and which types of sources contain those details?

When you keep these rhetorical issues in focus, information sources become a type of database from which you can draw ideas and evidence that help you strengthen and develop your thinking.

Practice getting-started strategies.

When you are getting started, using sources effectively requires keeping track of them and taking useful notes from them. Here are three strategies that will help you do both:

Track resources in a working bibliography. Once you find a useful book, journal article, news story, or webpage, record identifying information for the source. For more help, see pages 436–437.

Use a note-taking system that respects sources. Essentially, your note-taking system should help you keep an accurate record of useful information and ideas from sources while also allowing you to engage those sources with your own thinking. For a discussion of possible systems, see pages 438–441.

Distinguish summaries, paraphrases, and quotations. As you read sources, you will find material that answers your questions and helps you achieve your writing purpose. At that point, decide whether to summarize, paraphrase, or quote the material:

- A **summary** pulls just the main points out of a passage and puts them in your own words: Summarize source material when it contains relevant ideas and information that you can boil down.

- A **paraphrase** rewrites a passage point by point in your own words: Paraphrase source material when all the information is important but the actual phrasing isn't especially important or memorable.

- A **quotation** records a passage from the source word for word: Quote when the source states something crucial and says it well. *Note:* In your notes, always identify quoted material by putting quotation marks around it.

Summarizing, paraphrasing, and quoting are treated more fully on pages 442–444. Here is a brief example, with the original passage coming from Coral Ann Howells' *Alice Munro,* published in 1998 by Manchester University Press as part of its Contemporary World Writers series.

Original: "To read Munro's stories is to discover the delights of seeing two worlds at once: an ordinary everyday world and the shadowy map of another imaginary or secret world laid over the real one, so that in reading we slip from one world into the other in an unassuming domestic sort of way."

Summary: Munro's fiction moves readers from recognizable reality into a hidden world.

Paraphrase: Reading Munro's fiction gives readers the enjoyment of experiencing a double world: day-to-day reality and on top of that a more mysterious, fantastic world, with the result that readers move smoothly between the worlds in a seamless, ordinary way.

Quotation: Munro's fiction takes us into "the shadowy map of another imaginary or secret world laid over the real one."

Cross-Curricular Connections

Different academic disciplines require different methods of research note taking. For example, in the natural sciences, a lab notebook may be standard practice, while in psychology you might be expected to write summaries of past research studies on your topic. As you work on writing projects in your major, develop note-taking habits that respect the research and thinking methods in the discipline. For an overview of academic disciplines and the writing tasks they involve, see chapter 9.

Beginning the Process Checklist

Use this checklist as a guide to help you plan your writing.

The Situation and Assignment *I know the . . .*

_____ subject and form—essay, narrative, or research paper.

_____ audience—who they are, what they know, and what they need.

_____ purpose of the writing—to inform, explain, analyze, or persuade.

_____ main action (key words), restrictions, and options.

_____ connection to personal and course goals.

_____ requirements for length, format, research, and documentation.

_____ assessment method that will be used.

The Topic *I have . . .*

_____ explored possible topics through journal writing, freewriting, listing, clustering, or dialogue.

_____ chosen a limited topic that fits the assignment and spurs my interest.

_____ recorded what I already know and what I need to learn.

_____ developed a research plan and collected information about the topic.

Critical-Thinking and Writing Activities

As directed by your instructor, complete the following critical-thinking and writing activities by yourself or with classmates.

1. Writer Ralph Fletcher shares, "When I write, I am always struck at how magical and unexpected the process turns out to be." Would you describe the writing process you follow as "magical" and "unexpected"? Why or why not? What would it take to make writing this kind of experience for you?

2. Reread one of your recent essays. Does the writing show that you thoroughly understood your *subject*, met the needs of your *audience*, and achieved your writing *purpose*?

3. Below is a list of general subject areas. Select one that interests you and do the following: Using the strategies on pages 33–36, brainstorm possible topics and select one. Then use the strategies on pages 37–39 to explore what you know about that topic and what you need to learn.

Arts/music	Environment	Exercise
Health/medicine	Housing	Work/occupation

◀ VISUALLY SPEAKING

Consider the photo on page 27. In a one- to two-page double-spaced response, reflect on what that image suggests about beginning the writing process.

PLANNING

Video

Planning of almost any type requires careful thinking. When you plan an essay, you have two basic thinking objectives: (1) establish a thesis or focus for your writing, and (2) organize the supporting information. The amount of organization time required depends on the type of writing. For narratives, very little organizing may be required. For most academic essays, however, you will need to identify the method of development—comparison, cause/effect, classification—that best supports your thesis, and then organize your details accordingly. (See pages **46–47**.) At this point, your goal is to establish the general structure of your writing.

Writer and instructor Ken Macrorie offers this important insight about planning: "Good writing is formed partly through plan and partly through accident." In other words, too much early planning can get in the way. Writing at its best is a process of discovery. You never know what new insights or ideas will spring to mind until you put pen to paper or fingers to keyboard.

Taking Inventory of Your Thoughts

Suppose you've done some searching, and you've succeeded in discovering some interesting information and perspectives about your subject. Now may be a good time to see how well your findings match up with your topic.

Revisit your rhetorical situation.

After considering the following questions, you should be able to decide whether to move ahead with your planning or reconsider your topic.

Subject

- How much do I already know about this topic?
- Do I need to know more? Is additional information available? Where?
- Have I tried any of the collecting strategies? (See pages **37–39**.)
- What help would I need to find information, schedule an interview with a source, and so on?

Audience

- How much does my audience already know about this subject?
- How can I get my audience interested in my idea?
- How can I help them understand related technical terms and concepts?

Purpose

- What are the specific requirements of this assignment?
- Do I have enough time to do a good job with this topic?
- Am I writing to entertain, to inform, to explain, to analyze, or to persuade?
- How important is this assignment, and how will it be assessed?

Continue the process.

Assess whether you need additional information. If you think you do, go back to researching.

Research more deeply. If you need to know more about your topic, continue collecting your own thoughts and/or investigating other sources of information. Remember that it is important to investigate secondary and primary sources of information. (See pages **448–463**.)

Review your material. If you are ready to move ahead, carefully review your initial notes. As you read through this material, circle or underline ideas that seem important enough to include in your writing. Then look for ways in which these ideas connect or relate. The activities on the following pages will help you focus your thoughts for writing.

Forming Your Thesis Statement

Web Link

After you have completed enough research and collecting, you may begin to develop a more focused interest in your topic. If all goes well, this narrowed focus will give rise to a thesis for your writing. A thesis statement identifies your central idea. It usually highlights a special condition or feature of the topic, expresses a specific claim about it, or takes a stand.

State your thesis in a sentence that effectively expresses what you want to explore or explain in your essay. Sometimes a thesis statement develops early and easily; at other times, the true focus of your writing emerges only after you've written your first draft.

Find a focus.

A general subject area is typically built into your writing assignments. Your task, then, is to find a limited writing topic and examine it from a particular angle or perspective. (You will use this focus to form your thesis statement.)

FOCUSING A TOPIC

GENERAL SUBJECT	LIMITED TOPIC	SPECIFIC FOCUS
(Alternative energy sources)	(Wind power)	(Wind power as a viable energy source in the Plains states)

State your thesis.

You can use the following formula to write a thesis statement for your essay. A thesis statement sets the tone and direction for your writing. Keep in mind that at this point you're writing a *working thesis statement*—a statement in progress, so to speak. You may change it as your thinking on the topic evolves.

A manageable or limited topic (wind power)
+ a specific claim (provides a viable energy source in the Plains states)
= an effective thesis statement

Thesis Statement: Wind power provides a viable energy source in the Plains states.

THESIS CHECKLIST

_____ Does the thesis statement reflect a limited topic?
_____ Does it clearly state the specific idea you plan to develop?
_____ Is the thesis supported by the information you have gathered?
_____ Does the thesis suggest a pattern of organization for your essay?

Using Methods of Development

An organizing pattern for your essay may be built into your assignment. For example, you may be asked to develop an argument or to write a process paper. When a pattern is not apparent, one may still evolve naturally during the research and information-collecting steps. If this doesn't happen, take a careful look at your thesis statement.

Let your thesis guide you.

An effective thesis will often suggest an organizing pattern. Notice how the thesis statements below provide direction and shape for the writing to follow. (Also see page 21.)

Thesis (Focus) for a Personal Narrative

What began as a simple prank ended up having serious consequences for all of us who were involved.

Discussion: This statement identifies the focus of a personal narrative. It suggests that the essay will recount a personal experience and will most likely be arranged chronologically, beginning with the planning and execution of the prank and then going on to relate the consequences that followed. Writers of personal narratives do not always state a thesis directly, but they will generally have in mind an implied theme or main idea that governs the way they develop their writing.

Thesis for a Descriptive Essay

Although it was no more than an overgrown lot, as children we imagined the property next to my boyhood home to be a forest full of danger and adventure.

Discussion: This statement indicates that the writer will describe a special place from childhood. This description might be organized spatially, moving from the edges of the wooded lot to its interior. A description may be organized thematically, in this case by describing the specific features of the lot through the adventures the children imagined having there.

Thesis for a Cause-and-Effect Essay

Some stress is inescapable, but for their own health and for the well-being of others, people must understand what stress is, as well as its causes and effects.

Discussion: This thesis indicates that the writer is developing a cause-and-effect essay. Essays following this pattern usually begin with one or more causes followed by an explanation of the effects, or they begin with a primary effect followed by an explanation of the causes. To develop this thesis, the writer will follow the first route, exploring the causes of stress before examining its effects. (See pages 185–187 for this essay.)

Thesis for an Essay of Comparison

Bigger in *Native Son* and Alan in *Equus* are both entering adulthood and have come to realize that they are controlled by work, religion, and the media.

Discussion: Comparisons are patterned in two ways: Either you discuss one of the subjects completely and then the other (whole versus whole), or you discuss both subjects at the same time (point by point). The writer of this thesis is comparing two literary characters point by point. (See pages 201–202 for this essay.)

Thesis for an Essay of Classification

There are four main perspectives, or approaches, that readers can use to converse about literature.

Discussion: The writer is writing an essay of classification. Essays following this pattern identify the main parts or categories of a topic and then examine each one. In this thesis, the writer identifies four ways to discuss literature, and he examines each one in turn. (See pages 220–221 for this essay.)

Thesis for a Process Essay

When a cell begins to function abnormally, it can initiate a process that results in cancer.

Discussion: As indicated in this thesis, the writer of this essay will explain how cancer cells multiply and affect the body. Process essays, such as this one, are organized chronologically. Each step is examined in turn to help readers understand the complete process. (See pages 231–232 for this essay.)

Thesis for an Essay of Definition

Strangely, the word *gullible* connects people and birds, relating them to each other by their willingness to "swallow."

Discussion: This essay of definition explores the root meaning of the word *gullible*. To do so, the writer explains the word's meaning by analyzing its etymology (history) and identifying its lingual associations.

Thesis for an Essay Proposing a Solution

The best solution to controlling deer populations is to stay as close to nature's ways as possible, and game management by hunting meets this criterion.

Discussion: The writer of this thesis is developing a problem/solution essay. Essays following this pattern usually begin with a discussion of the problem and its causes and then examine possible solutions. In this essay, the writer presents a problem's history, causes, and effects. He then identifies and dismisses some solutions before arguing for one solution in particular.

Developing a Plan or an Outline

After writing a working thesis and reviewing the methods of development (pages 46–47), you should be ready to organize the information you have collected. A simple listing of main points may work for you, or you may need to outline the information or use a graphic organizer.

- **Basic list:** a brief listing of main points
- **Topic outline:** a more formal arrangement, including main points and essential details (See below.)
- **Sentence outline:** a formal arrangement, including main points and essential details, written as complete sentences (See page 49.)
- **Graphic organizer:** an arrangement of main points and essential details in an appropriate chart or diagram (See pages 49–51.)

Choose an organization method.

If you have a good deal of information to sort and arrange, you may want to use a topic or sentence outline for your planning.

Topic Outline

In a topic outline, you state each main point and essential detail as a word or phrase. Before you start constructing your outline, write your working thesis statement at the top of your paper to help keep you focused on the subject. (Do not attempt to outline your opening and closing paragraphs unless you are specifically asked to do so.)

SAMPLE TOPIC OUTLINE

Thesis: There are four main perspectives, or approaches, that readers can use to converse about literature.
  I. Text-centered approaches
    A. Also called formalist criticism
    B. Emphasis on structure of text and rules of genre
    C. Importance placed on key literary elements
  II. Audience-centered approaches
    A. Also called rhetorical or reader-response criticism
    B. Emphasis on interaction between reader and text
  III. Author-centered approaches
    A. Emphasis on writer's life
    B. Importance placed on historical perspective
    C. Connections made between texts
  IV. Ideological approaches
    A. Psychological analysis of text
    B. Myth or archetype criticism
    C. Moral criticism
    D. Sociological analysis

Sentence Outline

The sample outline below uses complete sentences to explain the main points and essential details that will be covered in the main part of the essay.

SAMPLE SENTENCE OUTLINE

Thesis: There are four main perspectives, or approaches, that readers can use to converse about literature.

   I. A text-centered approach focuses on the literary piece itself.
     A. This approach is often called formalist criticism.
     B. This method of criticism examines text structure and the rules of the genre.
     C. A formalist critic determines how key literary elements reinforce meaning.
  II. An audience-centered approach focuses on the "transaction" between text and reader.
     A. This approach is often called rhetorical or reader-response criticism.
     B. A rhetorical critic sees the text as an activity that is different for each reader.
 III. An author-centered approach focuses on the origin of a text.
     A. An author-centered critic examines the writer's life.
     B. This method of criticism may include a historical look at a text.
     C. Connections may be made between the text and related works.
 IV. The ideological approach applies ideas outside of literature.
     A. Some critics apply psychological theories to a literary work.
     B. Myth or archetype criticism applies anthropology and classical studies to a text.
     C. Moral criticism explores the moral dilemmas in literature.
     D. Sociological approaches include Marxist, feminist, and minority criticism.

Graphic Organizers

If you are a visual person, you might prefer a graphic organizer when it comes to arranging your ideas for an essay or a report. Graphic organizers can help you map out ideas and illustrate relationships among them. Here is a graphic organizer—a line diagram—that was used to organize the ideas for the essay. (Also see pages 50–51.)

SAMPLE GRAPHIC ORGANIZER

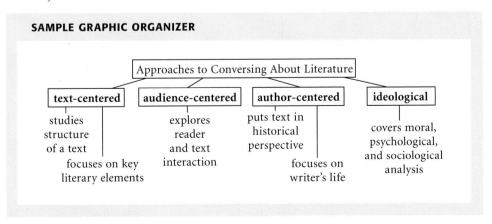

Types of Graphic Organizers

The following organizers are related to some of the methods of development discussed on pages **46–47**. Each will help you collect and organize your information. Adapt the organizers as necessary to fit your particular needs or personal style.

CAUSE/EFFECT

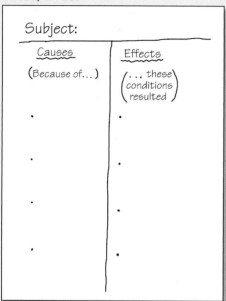

COMPARISON/CONTRAST

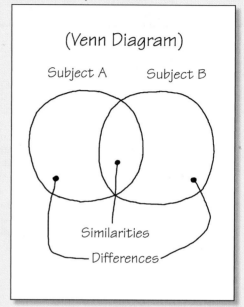

COMPARISON

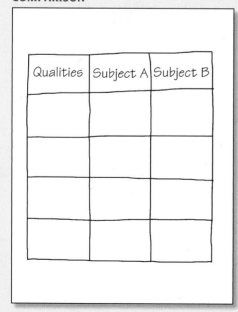

CLASSIFICATION

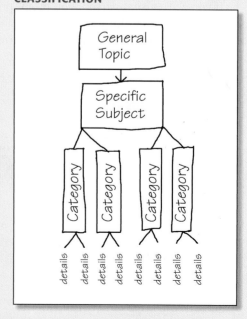

PROCESS ANALYSIS

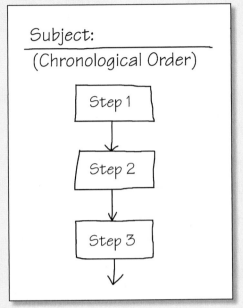

Subject: _____
(Chronological Order)

Step 1 → Step 2 → Step 3

PROBLEM/SOLUTION

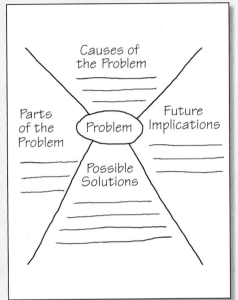

Causes of the Problem

Parts of the Problem   Problem   Future Implications

Possible Solutions

DEFINITION

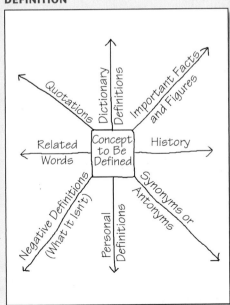

Quotations
Dictionary Definitions
Important Facts and Figures
Related Words
Concept to Be Defined
History
Negative Definitions (What It Isn't)
Personal Definitions
Synonyms or Antonyms

EVALUATION

Subject: _____

Points to Evaluate	Supporting Details
1.	
2.	
3.	
4.	
5.	

Writing with Sources

When your writing project involves working with sources, the planning phase will involve a great deal of sorting through and sorting out sources as they relate to your own thinking. To advance your writing toward a first draft, thoughtfully review and order your source notes, using them to stimulate your thinking and planning.

Think rhetorically.

At the beginning of this chapter, you were encouraged to review your subject, audience, and purpose when planning your first draft. For projects that involve research, consider how all three might guide your use of sources:

1. For your **subject,** which sources offer reliable information and analysis that has shaped your thinking and pointed you toward a working thesis?

2. Given your **audience,** which resources will help you create credibility with readers and clarify the topic for them?

3. To achieve your **purpose** (to entertain, inform, analyze, and/or persuade), which resources should be featured in your writing?

When you keep these rhetorical questions in mind, your own thinking will control the sources rather than being controlled by them.

Practice planning strategies.

When you plan your first draft, use the following source-focused strategies to develop a working thesis, choose a method of development, and form an outline. (For more on planning research writing, see pages 424–427.)

Let your research notes speak to you. Read and reread your research notes to let key ideas develop. What discoveries have you made? What conclusions have you reached? What questions have you answered? Those discoveries, conclusions, and answers will point toward a thesis and supporting details.

Consider where to position primary and secondary sources. Different writing projects require different approaches to integrating and balancing primary and secondary sources. (See page 448 for the distinction.) Ask these questions:

- Where and how should I work with primary sources—interviews, surveys, analyses, observations, experiments, and other data I have collected?

- Where and how should I bring in secondary sources—scholarly books, journal articles, and the like?

Example: In a literary analysis, you may rely on primary textual analysis of a novel throughout your paper but support that analysis with secondary-source information from biographical research placed early in your paper.

Order your writing around key sources. Sometimes your writing can take direction specifically from your sources. Consider these options:

- **Make your thesis a response to a specific source.** Did a particular source stand out as especially strong or especially contrary to your own thinking? Shape your thesis as an affirmation of the strong source's authority or as a rebuttal to the contrary source's claims.

- **Structure your paper around a dialogue with sources.** Do your sources offer multiple, divergent, or even contradictory perspectives on your topic? If they do, consider organizing your paper around a dialogue with these sources. This approach works especially well with complex or controversial topics or in papers that need to present multiple dimensions or views.

Put your discussion in context. Often, the early part of your paper establishes a context for your topic. Use sources to present background, explain terms, describe the big picture, or establish a theoretical framework for your discussion.

Example: If your paper will explore the problem of teen homelessness in Atlanta, you might put that analysis in context by supplying information on national trends, general causes of homelessness, or sociological definitions of homelessness.

Clump source material under your supporting points. Once you have developed a thesis and sketched out some supporting points, arrange source material under those points. Depending on the note-taking method you have used, try the following:

- Reorder your notes: For electronic notes, try copy-and-paste. For notes on paper, cut and paste using scissors.

- Code your notes using numbers or letters matching points in your outline.

- With books, articles, and other resources, apply sticky notes to key pages.

Caution: Whatever method you use, make sure that you can still identify source material so as to avoid plagiarism when you draft your paper.

Cross-Curricular Connections

In most disciplines, it is common practice early in the paper to "survey the literature" on the topic. In a literary analysis, you might survey common interpretations of a key concept before you relay your view. In a botany field report, you might situate your own study by first reviewing other studies done on the topic. To conduct such a review, do the following:

1. Based on whether your review must be comprehensive or representative, identify the studies that should be included in the review.

2. Order these studies logically by (1) categorizing them according to their approach, perspective, or essential argument, or (2) arranging them chronologically from earliest to most recent publication (if you need to convey the history of research on your topic).

Planning Checklist

Use this checklist as a guide to help you plan your writing.

Thesis *I have . . .*

_____ reviewed information I've collected up to this point.

_____ identified a specific focus or feature of my topic to develop.

_____ stated a focus in a working thesis statement.

_____ tested the thesis to make sure it is supportable.

Development *I have . . .*

_____ identified a pattern of organization to develop my thesis.

_____ organized my support in a list, an outline, or a graphic organizer.

_____ prepared to write the first draft.

Critical-Thinking and Writing Activities

As directed by your instructor, complete the following critical-thinking and writing activities by yourself or with classmates.

1. Author Ken Macrorie claims that "good writing is formed partly through plan and partly through accident." Do you agree? Why or why not? Relate Macrorie's idea to your own writing experiences. How carefully do you plan? How much do you leave to accident?

2. A number of organizational patterns are discussed on pages **46–47**. Choose one of these patterns and select a model essay from chapters 10–20 that follows the pattern. Read the essay, note the thesis, and explain how the writer develops it.

3. Listed below are general subject areas. Do the following for three of these subjects: (1) identify a limited topic, (2) write a working thesis statement, and (3) identify a pattern of organization you could use to develop the thesis.

Afghanistan	Education	Iraq
Agriculture	Entertainment	Medicine
Careers	Exercise	Natural Resources
Communications	Family	Olympics
Community	Freedom	U.S. Courts

◄ VISUALLY SPEAKING ━━━━━━━━━━━━

Consider the photo on page **43**. Then explain in writing how the photo's "story" parallels the planning stage in writing.

DRAFTING

Video

The early twentieth-century French novelist Anatole France is reported to have said that one of his first drafts could have been written by any schoolboy, his next draft by a bright upper-level student, his third draft by a superior graduate, his fourth draft by a seasoned professional, and his final draft "only by Anatole France." Even if that report is exaggerated, the point is well taken: The first draft is not the one that will distinguish you as a writer. It's a way of getting material together, starting out, connecting your ideas. A first draft gives you something to work with—verbal wet clay—that will later, through revising and editing, result in a polished piece of writing.

This section provides information and advice about drafting a college-level essay. Our special focus is on the sorts of "moves" that may occur at each major stage of the draft. If you know in advance what moves to make, you'll be in a better position to develop a thoughtful and complete draft.

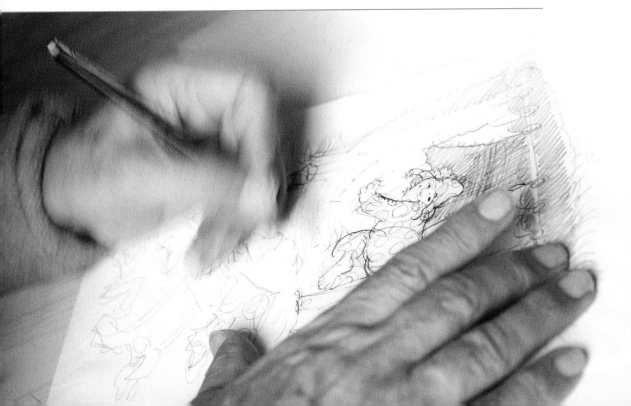

Writing Your First Draft

The American novelist Kurt Vonnegut once laughingly divided writers into two categories: swoopers and bashers. Swoopers write seventeen drafts at high speed before they're done; bashers won't move to sentence number two until they have polished sentence number one. When you draft your next paper, you'll strike a better balance between carelessness and care if you focus on the essentials of your rhetorical situation: audience, purpose, and subject.

Reconsider your audience.

Review who your readers are, including their knowledge of and attitude toward your topic. Then get ready to talk with them, person to person.

Reconsider your purpose.

Briefly review (1) what you want your writing to do (your task), (2) what you want it to say (your thesis), and (3) how you want to say it (list of ideas or outline).

Focus on your subject.

As you develop your first draft, these strategies can help you keep your subject in focus.

- Use your outline or writing plan as a general guide. Try to develop your main points, but allow new ideas to emerge naturally.
- Write freely without being too concerned about neatness and correctness. Concentrate on developing your ideas, not on producing a final copy.
- Include as much detail as possible, continuing until you reach a logical stopping point.
- Use your writing plan or any charts, lists, or diagrams you've produced, but don't feel absolutely bound by them.
- Complete your first draft in one or two sittings.
- Use the most natural voice you can so that the writing will flow smoothly. If your voice is too formal during drafting, you'll be tempted to stop and edit your words.
- Quote sources accurately by using your word-processing program's copy-and-paste features or by handwriting or typing quotations carefully.

INSIGHT: If you have trouble getting started, think of your writing as half of a conversation with a reader you invent. Talk to your silent partner. Think about what you've already said and let that help you decide what you should say next.

Basic Essay Structure:
Major Moves

The following chart lists the main writing moves that occur during the development of a piece of writing. Use it as a general guide for all of your drafting. Remember to keep your purpose and audience in mind throughout the drafting process.

Opening

Engage your reader.
Stimulate and direct the reader's attention.

Establish your direction.
Identify the topic and put it in perspective.

Get to the point.
Narrow your focus and state your thesis.

Middle

Advance your thesis.
Provide background information and cover your main points.

Test your ideas.
Raise questions and consider alternatives.

Support your main points.
Add substance and build interest.

Build a coherent structure.
Start new paragraphs and arrange the support.

Use different levels of detail.
Clarify and complete each main point.

Ending

Reassert the main point.
Remind the reader of the purpose and rephrase the thesis.

Urge the reader.
Gain the reader's acceptance and look ahead.

Opening Your Draft

The opening paragraph is one of the most important elements in any composition. It should accomplish at least three essential things: (1) engage the reader; (2) establish your direction, tone, and level of language; and (3) introduce your line of thought.

Advice: The conventional way of approaching the first paragraph is to view it as a kind of "funnel" that draws a reader in and narrows to a main point. Often, the final sentence explicitly states your thesis.

Cautions: • Don't feel bound by the conventional pattern, which may sound stale if not handled well.

• Don't let the importance of the first paragraph paralyze you. Relax and write.

The information on the next two pages will help you develop your opening. You can refer to the sample essays in the handbook for ideas.

Engage your reader.

Your reader will be preoccupied with other thoughts until you seize, stimulate, and direct his or her attention. Here are some effective ways to "hook" the reader:

• Mention little-known facts about the topic.
• Pose a challenging question.
• Offer a thought-provoking quotation.
• Tell a brief, illuminating story.
• Introduce your angle or focus on the topic.

Establish your direction.

The direction of your line of thought should become clear in the opening part of your writing. Here are some moves you might make to set the right course:

• **Identify the topic (issue).** Show a problem, a need, or an opportunity.
• **Deepen the issue.** Connect the topic, showing its importance.
• **Acknowledge other views.** Tell what others say or think about the topic.

Web Link

INSIGHT: Your opening affects the direction and line of thinking of your entire piece of writing. If you don't like the first or second attempt, keep trying. You'll know when you hit the right version because it will help you visualize the rest of your draft.

Get to the point.

You may choose to state your main point up front, or you may wait until later to introduce your thesis. For example, you could work inductively by establishing an issue, a problem, or a question in your opening and then build toward the answer—your thesis—in your conclusion. (See page 20 for more on inductive reasoning.) Sometimes, in fact, your thesis may simply be implied. In any case, the opening should at least hint at the central issue or thesis of your paper. Here are three ways to get to the point:

1. **Narrow your focus.** Point to what interests you about the topic.

2. **Raise a question.** Answer the question in the rest of the essay.

3. **State your thesis.** If appropriate, craft a sentence that boils down your thinking to a central claim. You can use the thesis sentence as a "map" for the organization of the rest of the essay. (See pages 45–47, 118–121, and 424–425.)

Weak Opening

Although the opening below introduces the topic, the writing lacks interesting details and establishes no clear focus for the essay.

> I would like to tell you about the TV show *The Simpsons*. It's about this weird family of five people who look kind of strange and act even stranger. In fact, the characters aren't even real—they're just cartoons.

Strong Opening

In the essay opener below, the writer uses his first paragraph to get his readers' attention and describe his subject. He uses the second paragraph to raise a question that leads him to a statement of his thesis (underlined).

> The Simpsons, stars of the TV show by the same name, are a typical American family, or at least a parody of one. Homer, Marge, Bart, Lisa, and Maggie Simpson live in Springfield, U.S.A. Homer, the father, is a boorish, obese oaf who works in a nuclear power plant. Marge is an overprotective, nagging mother with an outrageous blue hairdo. Ten-year-old Bart is an obnoxious, "spiky-haired demon." Lisa is eight and a prodigy on the tenor saxophone and in class. The infant Maggie never speaks but only sucks on her pacifier.
>
> What is the attraction of this yellow-skinned family that stars on a show in which all of the characters have pronounced overbites and only four fingers on each hand? Viewers see a little bit of themselves in everything the Simpsons do. The world of Springfield is a parody of the viewer's world, and Americans can't get enough of it. Viewers experience this parody in the show's explanations of family, education, workplace, and politics.

INSIGHT: Note how, after stating the thesis, the writer forecasts the method of supporting that thesis.

Developing the Middle

The middle of an essay is where you do the "heavy lifting." In this part you develop the main points that support your thesis statement.

Advice: As you write, you will likely make choices that were unforeseen when you began. Use "scratch outlines" (temporary jottings) along the way to show where your new ideas may take you.

Cautions: • Writing that lacks effective detail gives only a vague image of the writer's intent.

• Writing that wanders loses its hold on the essay's purpose.

For both of these reasons, always keep your thesis in mind when you develop the main part of your writing. Refer to the guidelines on the next two pages for help. You can refer to the sample essays in this book for ideas.

Advance your thesis.

If you stated a thesis in the opening, you can advance it in the middle paragraphs by covering your main points and supporting them in these ways.

Explain: Provide important facts, details, and examples.

Narrate: Share a brief story or re-create an experience to illustrate an idea.

Describe: Tell in detail how someone appears or how something works.

Define: Identify or clarify the meaning of a specific term or idea.

Analyze: Examine the parts of something to better understand the whole.

Compare: Provide examples to show how two things are alike or different.

Argue: Use logic and evidence to prove that something is true.

Reflect: Express your thoughts or feelings about something.

Cite authorities: Add expert analysis or personal commentary.

Test your ideas.

When you write a first draft, you're testing your initial thinking about your topic. You're determining whether your thesis is valid and whether you have enough compelling information to support it. Here are ways to test your line of thinking as you write:

Raise questions. Try to anticipate your readers' questions.

Consider alternatives. Look at your ideas from different angles; weigh various options; reevaluate your thesis.

Answer objections. Directly or indirectly deal with possible problems that a skeptical reader might point out.

Build a coherent structure.

Design paragraphs as units of thought that develop and advance your thesis clearly and logically. For example, look at the brief essay below, noting how each body paragraph presents ideas with supporting details that build on and deepen the main idea.

The writer introduces the topic, suggests his organizational pattern (comparison/contrast), and states his thesis.

Making a transition into his discussion, the writer starts with a basic explanation of how the two types of lightbulbs function differently; details show how.

The writer shifts his attention to weaknesses of compact bulbs.

Using "On the other hand" as a transition, he next explains the strengths of compacts.

He acknowledges that compacts cost more, but he then justifies the cost.

The writer rephrases his thesis as a challenge.

Seeing the Light

All lightbulbs make light, so they're all the same, right? Not quite. You have many choices regarding how to light up your life. Two types of bulbs are the traditional incandescent and the newer, more compact fluorescent. <u>By checking out how they're different, you can better choose which one to buy.</u>

While either incandescent or compact fluorescent bulbs can help you read or find the bathroom at night, each bulb makes light differently. In an incandescent bulb, electricity heats up a tungsten filament (thin wire) to 450 degrees, causing it to glow with a warm, yellow light. A compact fluorescent is a glass tube filled with mercury vapor and argon gas. Electricity causes the mercury to give off ultraviolet radiation. That radiation then causes phosphors coating the inside of the tube to give off light.

Both types of bulbs come in many shapes, sizes, and brightnesses, but compacts have some restrictions. Because of their odd shape, compacts may not fit in a lamp well. Compacts also may not work well in very cold temperatures, and they can't be used with a dimmer switch.

On the other hand, while compact fluorescents are less flexible than incandescents, compacts are four times more efficient. For example, a 15-watt compact produces as many lumens of light as a 60-watt incandescent! Why? Incandescents turn only about 5 percent of electricity into light and give off the other 95 percent as heat.

But are compacts less expensive than incandescents? In the short run, no. A compact costs about $15 while an incandescent costs only a dollar. However, because compacts burn less electricity—and last 7 to 10 times longer—in the long run, compacts are less expensive.

Now that you're no longer in the dark about lightbulbs, take a look at the lamp you're using to read this essay. Think about the watts (electricity used), lumens (light produced), efficiency, purchase price, and lamplife. Then decide how to light up your life in the future.

Arrange supporting details.

Organizing information in a logical pattern within a paragraph strengthens its coherence. The following pages explain and illustrate ten organizational strategies. (See also page **483**.)

Analogy

An analogy is a comparison that a writer uses to explain a complex or unfamiliar phenomenon (how the immune system works) in terms of a familiar one (how mall security works).

> The human body is like a mall, and the immune system is like mall security. Because the mall has hundreds of employees and thousands of customers, security guards must rely on photo IDs, name tags, and uniforms to decide who should be allowed to open cash registers and who should have access to the vault. In the same way, white blood cells and antibodies need to use DNA cues to recognize which cells belong in a body and which do not. Occasionally security guards make mistakes, wrestling Kookie the Klown to the ground while DVD players "walk" out of the service entrance, but these problems amount only to allergic reactions or little infections. If security guards become hypervigilant, detaining every customer and employee, the situation is akin to leukemia, in which white blood cells attack healthy cells. If security guards become corrupt, letting thieves take a "five-finger discount," the situation is akin to AIDS. Both systems—mall security and human immunity—work by correctly differentiating friend from foe.
>
> —Rob King

Cause and Effect

Cause-and-effect organization shows how events are linked to their results. If you start with effects, follow with specific causes; if you begin with causes, follow with specific effects. The example below discusses the effects of hypothermia on the human body.

> Even a slight drop in the normal human body temperature of 98.6 degrees Fahrenheit causes hypothermia. Often produced by accidental or prolonged exposure to cold, the condition forces all bodily functions to slow down. The heart rate and blood pressure decrease. Breathing becomes slower and shallower. As the body temperature drops, these effects become even more dramatic until it reaches somewhere between 86 and 82 degrees Fahrenheit and the person lapses into unconsciousness. When the temperature reaches between 65 and 59 degrees Fahrenheit, heart action, blood flow, and electrical brain activity stop. Normally such a condition would be fatal. However, as the body cools down, the need for oxygen also slows down. A person can survive in a deep hypothermic state for an hour or longer and be revived without serious complications.
>
> —Laura Black

Chronological Order

Chronological (time) order helps you tell a story or present steps in a process. For example, the following paragraph describes how cement is made. Notice how the writer explains every step and uses transitional words to lead readers through the process.

> The production of cement is a complicated process. The raw materials that go into cement consist of about 60 percent lime, 25 percent silica, and 5 percent alumina. The remaining 10 percent is a varying combination of gypsum and iron oxide (because the amount of gypsum determines the drying time of the cement). First, this mixture is ground up into very fine particles and fed into a kiln. Cement kilns, the largest pieces of moving machinery used by any industry, are colossal steel cylinders lined with firebricks. They can be 25 feet in diameter and up to 750 feet long. The kiln is built at a slant and turns slowly as the cement mix makes its way down from the top end. A flame at the bottom heats the kiln to temperatures of up to 3,000 degrees Fahrenheit. When the melted cement compound emerges from the kiln, it cools into little marble-like balls called clinker. Finally, the clinker is ground to a consistency finer than flour and packaged as cement.
>
> —Kevin Maas

Classification

When classifying a subject, place the subject in its appropriate category and then show how this subject is different from other subjects in the same category. In the following paragraph, a student writer uses classification to describe the theory of temperament.

> Medieval doctors believed that "four temperaments rule man kind wholly." According to this theory, each person has a distinctive temperament or personality (sanguine, phlegmatic, melancholy, or choleric) based on the balance of four elements in the body, a balance peculiar to the individual. The theory was built on Galen's and Hippocrates' notion of "humors," which stated that the body contains blood, phlegm, black bile, and yellow bile—four fluids that maintain the balance within the body. The sanguine person was dominated by blood, associated with fire: Blood was hot and moist, and the person was fat and prone to laughter. The phlegmatic person was dominated by phlegm (associated with earth) and was squarish and slothful—a sleepy type. The melancholy person was dominated by cold, black bile (connected with the element of water) and as a result was pensive, peevish, and solitary. The choleric person was dominated by hot, yellow bile (air) and thus was inclined to anger.
>
> —Jessica Radsma

Compare-Contrast

To compare and contrast, show how two or more subjects are similar and different. See models on pages **201–211**.

Climax

Climax is a method in which you first present details and then provide a general climactic statement or conclusion drawn from the details.

> The cockroach is unhonored and unsung. It walks about with downcast eyes. Its head hangs dejectedly between its knees. It lives on modest fare and in humble circumstances. It is drab-colored and inconspicuous. But don't let that Uriah Heep exterior fool you. For there you have Superbug, himself!
>
> —Edwin Way Teale, *The Lost Woods*

Definition

A definition provides the denotation (dictionary meaning) and connotation (feeling) of a given term. It often provides examples, gives anecdotes, and offers negative definitions—what the thing is not. In the paragraph below, the writer begins his definition by posing a question.

> First of all, what is the grotesque—in visual art and in literature? A term originally applied to Roman cave art that distorted the normal, the grotesque presents the body and mind so that they appear abnormal— different from the bodies and minds that we think belong in our world. Both spiritual and physical, bizarre and familiar, ugly and alluring, the grotesque shocks us, and we respond with laughter and fear. We laugh because the grotesque seems bizarre enough to belong only outside our world; we fear because it feels familiar enough to be part of it. Seeing the grotesque version of life as it is portrayed in art stretches our vision of reality. As Bernard McElroy argues, "The grotesque transforms the world from what we 'know' it to be to what we fear it might be. It distorts and exaggerates the surface of reality in order to tell a qualitative truth about it."
>
> —John Van Rys

Illustration

An illustration supports a general idea with specific reasons, facts, and details.

> As the years passed, my obsession grew. Every fiber and cell of my body was obsessed with the number on the scale and how much fat I could pinch on my thigh. No matter how thin I was, I thought I could never be thin enough. I fought my sisters for control of the TV and VCR to do my exercise programs and videos. The cupboards were stacked with cans of diet mixes, the refrigerator full of diet drinks. Hidden in my underwear drawer were stacks of diet pills that I popped along with my vitamins. At my worst, I would quietly excuse myself from family activities to turn on the bathroom faucet full blast and vomit into the toilet. Every day I stood in front of the mirror, a ritual not unlike brushing my teeth, and scrutinized my body. My face, arms, stomach, buttocks, hips, and thighs could never be small enough.
>
> —Paula Treick

Narration

In the paragraph below, the writer uses narration and chronological order to relate an anecdote—a short, illustrative story.

> When I was six or seven years old, growing up in Pittsburgh, I used to take a precious penny of my own and hide it for someone else to find. It was a curious compulsion; sadly, I've never been seized by it since. For some reason I always "hid" the penny along the same stretch of sidewalk up the street. I would cradle it at the roots of a sycamore, say, or in a hole left by a chipped-off piece of sidewalk. Then I would take a piece of chalk, and, starting at either end of the block, draw huge arrows leading up to the penny from both directions. After I learned to write I labeled the arrows: surprise ahead or money this way. I was greatly excited, during all this arrow-drawing, at the thought of the first lucky passer-by who would receive in this way, regardless of merit, a free gift from the universe. But I never lurked about. I would go straight home and not give the matter another thought, until, some months later, I would be gripped again by the impulse to hide another penny.
>
> —Annie Dillard, *Pilgrim at Tinker Creek*

Process

In the paragraph that follows, a student writer describes the process of entering the "tube," or "green room," while surfing.

> At this point you are slightly ahead of the barreling part of the wave, and you need to "stall," or slow yourself, to get into the tube. There are three methods of stalling used in different situations. If you are slightly ahead of the tube, you can drag your inside hand along the water to stall. If you are a couple of feet in front of the barrel, apply all your weight onto your back foot and sink the tail of the board into the water. This is known as a "tail stall" for obvious reasons, and its purpose is to decrease your board speed. If you are moving faster than the wave is breaking, you need to do what is called a "wrap-around." To accomplish this maneuver, lean back away from the wave while applying pressure on the tail. This shifts your forward momentum away from the wave and slows you down. When the wave comes, turn toward the wave and place yourself in the barrel.
>
> —Luke Sunukjian, "Entering the Green Room"

TIP: Choose an organizational pattern that most clearly advances your thesis for your specific audience. For example, to explain anorexia to readers unfamiliar with the condition, Paula Treick illustrates its effects (see page 64).

Web Link

Ending Your Draft

Closing paragraphs can be important for tying up loose ends, clarifying key points, or signing off with the reader. In a sense, the entire essay is a preparation for an effective ending; the ending helps the reader look back over the essay with new understanding and appreciation. Many endings leave the reader with fresh food for thought.

Advice: Because the ending can be so important, draft a variety of possible endings. Choose the one that flows best from a sense of the whole.

Cautions: • If your thesis is weak or unclear, you will have a difficult time writing a satisfactory ending. To strengthen the ending, strengthen the thesis.

• You may have heard this formula for writing an essay: "Say what you're going to say, say it, then say what you've just said." Remember, though, if you need to "say what you've just said," say it in new words.

The information on the next two pages will help you develop your ending. You can refer to the sample essays elsewhere in this book for ideas.

Reassert the main point.

If an essay is complicated, the reader may need reclarification at the end. Show that you are fulfilling the promises you made in the beginning.

Remind the reader. Recall what you first set out to do; check off the key points you've covered; or answer any questions left unanswered.

Rephrase the thesis. Restate your thesis in light of the most important support you've given. Deepen and expand your original thesis.

Urge the reader.

Your reader may still be reluctant to accept your ideas or argument. The ending is your last chance to gain the reader's acceptance. Here are some possible strategies:

Show the implications. Follow further possibilities raised by your train of thought; be reasonable and convincing.

Look ahead. Suggest other possible connections.

List the benefits. Show the reader the benefits of accepting or applying the things you've said.

INSIGHT: When your writing comes to an effective stopping point, conclude the essay. Don't tack on another idea.

Complete and unify your message.

Your final paragraphs are your last opportunity to refocus, unify, and otherwise reinforce your message. Draft the closing carefully, not merely to finish the essay but to further advance your purpose and thesis.

Weak Ending

The ending below does not focus on and show commitment to the essay's main idea. Rather than reinforcing this idea, the writing leads off in a new direction.

> So the bottom line is that Mom's photo showed how much I liked my little stream. Of course, I have lots of other good childhood memories as well, like the times Dad would read to me before bedtime. I loved those books. How about you? Do you have good childhood memories?

Strong Endings

Below are final paragraphs from two essays in this book. Listen to their tone, watch how they reconsider the essay's ideas, and note how they offer further food for thought. (The first example is a revision of the weak paragraph above.)

> Sometimes, I want to go back there, back into that photo. I want to step into a time when life seemed safe, and a tiny stream gave us all that we needed. In that picture, our smiles last, our hearts are calm, and we hear only quiet voices, forest sounds, and my bubbling stream. Bitter words are silenced and tears held back by the click and whir of a camera.
>
> I've been thinking about making the journey again past the hunter's fort, under the stand of cedars, through the muck and mire, and over the rocky rise. But it's been a long summer, and the small seasonal stream running out of the overflow of the pond has probably dried up.

(See the full essay on pages 167–168.)

> I still wish I could cure cancer with a magic miracle liquid in a medicine bottle. But today I understand that cancer is a complicated disease. My grandparents died from three types of the disease—multiple myeloma, prostate cancer, and lung cancer. If it hadn't been for cancerous tumors taking over their bodies, my grandparents might still be alive, and I'd have many more memories of them. Maybe I'd even be sharing with them stories about my first year at college. On the other hand, perhaps this paper is a cure of a different type—while it can't change what happened, it can help me understand it.

(See the full essay on pages 217–219.)

INSIGHT: Think about your document's opening and closing as a type of contract that you make with your reader. Whereas the opening explains what you intend to do, the closing reviews and confirms what you have done.

Writing with Sources

Writing a first draft often involves exploring your own thinking in relation to the ideas and information you have discovered through research. Use creativity and care—the creativity to see connections and to trace lines of thinking, and the care to respect ideas and information from sources. (See pages **484–487** for drafting strategies for research papers.)

Think rhetorically.

Decide which sources aid your *purpose* (to entertain, to inform, to persuade) and help you connect with your *audience*. Also focus on your role as the writer. In a research paper, you are not only using sources to support your own ideas, but are also conversing with those sources. While showing respect for your sources, you want to avoid being intimidated by them.

Practice drafting strategies.

To work with sources during your drafting, try these strategies:

Keep your sources handy. While drafting, keep source material at your fingertips, whether in paper or electronic form, so that you can integrate summaries, paraphrases, and quotations without disrupting the flow of your drafting.

Start your draft with a strong source reference. Could something from a source get your paper off to an engaging start? Consider these powerful beginnings:

- A pithy, thought-provoking, or startling quotation
- A problematic or controversial statement or fact from a source
- An anecdote (a brief example, story, or case study) that makes the issue concrete

Take care not to overwhelm your draft with source material. As you draft, keep the focus on your own ideas:

- Avoid strings of references and chunks of source material with no discussion, explanation, or interpretation on your part in between.
- Don't offer entire paragraphs of material from a source (whether paraphrased or quoted) with a single in-text citation at the end. When you do so, your thinking disappears.
- Be careful not to overload your draft with complex information and dense data lacking explanation.
- Resist the urge to simply copy and paste big chunks from sources. Even if you document the sources, your paper will quickly become a patchwork of source material with a few weak stitches (your contribution) holding it together.

Advance and deepen your thesis with reliable reasons and evidence. A typical supporting paragraph starts with a topic sentence and elaborates it with detailed evidence and careful reasoning. Note this pattern in the paragraph below:

SAMPLE PARAGRAPH SHOWING INTEGRATION OF SOURCE MATERIAL

Topic sentence: idea elaborating and supporting thesis **Development of idea through reasoning** **Support of idea through reference to source material** **Concluding statement of idea**	Antibiotics are effective only against infections caused by bacteria and should never be used against infections caused by viruses. Using an antibiotic against a viral infection is like throwing water on a grease fire—water may normally put out fires but will only worsen the situation for a grease fire. In the same way, antibiotics fight infections, but they cause the body harm only when they are used to fight infections caused by viruses. Viruses cause the common cold, the flu, and most sore throats, sinus infections, coughs, and bronchitis. Yet antibiotics are commonly prescribed for these viral infections. The *New England Journal of Medicine* reports that 22.7 million kilograms (25,000 tons) of antibiotics is prescribed each year in the United States alone (Wenzel and Edmond, 1962). Meanwhile, the CDC reports that approximately 50 percent of those prescriptions are completely unnecessary ("Antibiotic Overuse" 25). "Every year, tens of millions of prescriptions for antibiotics are written to treat viral illnesses for which these antibiotics offer no benefits," says the CDC's antimicrobial resistance director David Bell, M.D. (qtd. in Bren 30). Such mis-prescribing is simply bad medical practice that contributes to the problem of growing bacterial infection.

Save the best for last. Consider using an especially thought-provoking or summarizing statement, quotation, or detail in your conclusion. Doing so clinches your point and leaves your reader with provocative food for thought.

Track borrowed material in your draft. As you bring source material into your draft, track those summaries, paraphrases, and quotations by marking them clearly with codes, highlighting, brackets, or other symbols that will allow you to identify that material as you revise, edit, and polish your paper.

Cross-Curricular Connections

Referring to sources is handled differently from one discipline to the next. In humanities disciplines, a reference might give the author's name and credentials and the source's title; by contrast, a reference in the social or natural sciences might give the year that the study was done or published.

Drafting Checklist

Use this checklist as a guide when you develop a first draft for an essay. (To see drafting in action, turn to pages 122–129.)

Opening *The opening of my paper . . .*

_____ engages the reader.

_____ establishes a focus and states a main point.

Middle *The middle of my paper . . .*

_____ advances my thesis by developing and testing my ideas.

_____ has a clear, logical order and includes needed supporting details.

Closing *The closing of my paper . . .*

_____ reasserts the main point and emphasizes the topic's relevance.

_____ completes and unifies the message.

Critical-Thinking and Writing Activities

As directed by your instructor, complete the following critical-thinking and writing activities by yourself or with classmates.

1. Patricia T. O'Connor says, "All writing begins life as a first draft, and first drafts are never any good. They're not supposed to be." Is this claim true? Why or why not? What do you hope to accomplish with a first draft?

2. Study the chart on page 57. Based on other material you have read or written, add another writing move for each of the three main parts of the essay: opening, middle, and ending. Name the move, explain it, and tell what types of writing it might appear in.

3. Read the final paragraphs of any three essays included in this book. Write a brief analysis of each ending based on the information on pages 66–67.

4. Imagine that you are a journalist who has been asked to write an article about a wedding, a funeral, or another significant event you have experienced. Choose an event and sketch out a plan for your article. Include the main writing moves and the type of information at each stage of your writing.

◀ VISUALLY SPEAKING

Consider the photo on page 55. In a one- to two-page double-spaced response, reflect on what the photo suggests about drafting a piece of writing.

REVISING

Revising takes courage. Once you have your first draft on paper, the piece may feel finished. The temptation then is to be satisfied with a quick "spell check" before turning in the paper. A word to the wise: Avoid this temptation.

Video

Good writing almost always requires revising and, in some cases, substantial rework. During this step in the writing process, you make changes in the content of your first draft until it says exactly what you mean. To get started, assess the overall quality of the ideas, organization, and voice in your writing. Then be prepared to tinker with your writing until it effectively carries your message. It's also a good idea to share your draft with your instructor, a peer, or a tutor. All writers benefit from sincere, constructive advice during the revision process. This chapter will introduce you to valuable revising guidelines and strategies to use in all of your writing.

Addressing Whole-Paper Issues

When revising, first look at the big picture. Take it all in. Determine whether the content is interesting, informative, and worth sharing. Note any gaps or soft spots in your line of thinking. Ask yourself how you can improve what you have done so far. The information that follows will help you address whole-paper issues such as these.

Revisit your rhetorical situation.

Remember why you are writing—your purpose. Are you entertaining readers, sharing information, recalling an experience, explaining a process, or arguing a point? Does your writing achieve that purpose? Also, consider your readers. How much do they know about the subject? What else do they need to know? Finally, revisit the subject. Has your draft addressed the topic fully and clearly?

Consider your overall approach.

Sometimes it's better to start fresh if your writing contains stretches of uninspired ideas. Consider a fresh start if your first draft shows one of these problems:

The topic is worn-out. An essay titled "Lead Poisoning" may not sound very interesting. Unless you can approach it with a new twist ("Get the Lead Out!"), consider cutting your losses and finding a fresh topic.

The approach is stale. If you've been writing primarily to get a good grade, finish the assignment, or sound cool, start again. Try writing to learn something, prompt real thinking in readers, or touch a chord.

Your voice is predictable or fake. Avoid the bland "A good time was had by all" or the phony academic "When one studies this significant problem in considerable depth . . . " Be real. Be honest.

The draft sounds boring. Maybe it's boring because you pay an equal amount of attention to everything and hence stress nothing. Try condensing less important material and expanding what's important.

The essay is formulaic. In other words, it follows the "five-paragraph" format. This handy organizing frame may prevent you from doing justice to your topic and thinking. If your draft is dragged down by rigid adherence to a formula, try a more original approach.

TIP: To energize your writing, try these strategies:
- Freewrite to find a new angle or approach to the topic.
- Review your research notes for additional interesting details.
- List and respond to arguments opposed to your thesis.

Revising Your First Draft

Revising helps you turn your first draft into a more complete, thoughtful piece of writing. The following information will help you do that.

Prepare to revise.

Once you've finished a first draft, set it aside (ideally for a few days) until you can look at the draft objectively and make needed changes. If you drafted on paper, photocopy the draft. If you drafted on a computer, print your paper (double-spaced). Then make changes with a good pencil or colored pen. If you prefer revising on the computer, consider using your software editing program. In all cases, save your first draft for reference.

Think globally.

When revising, focus on the big picture—the overall strength of the ideas, organization, and voice.

Ideas: Check your thesis, focus, or theme. Has your thinking on your topic changed? Also think about your readers' most pressing questions concerning this topic. Have you answered these questions? Finally, consider your reasoning and support. Are both complete and sound?

Organization: Check the overall design of your writing, making sure that ideas move smoothly and logically from one point to the next. Does your essay build effectively? Do you shift directions cleanly? Fix structural problems in one of these ways:

- Reorder material to improve the sequence.
- Cut information that doesn't support the thesis.
- Add details where the draft is thin.
- Rewrite parts that seem unclear.
- Improve links between points by using transitions.

Voice: Voice is your personal presence on the page, the tone and attitude that others hear when reading your work. In other words, voice is the between-the-lines message your readers get (whether you want them to or not). When revising, make sure that the tone of your message matches your purpose, whether it is serious, playful, or satiric.

INSIGHT: Don't pay undue attention to spelling, grammar, and punctuation at this early stage in the process. Otherwise, you may become distracted from the task at hand: improving the content of your writing. Editing and proofreading come later.

Web Link

Revising for Ideas and Organization

As you review your draft for content, make sure the ideas are fully developed and the organization is clear. From your main claim or thesis to your reasoning and your evidence, strengthen your thinking and sequencing.

Examine your ideas.

Review the ideas in your writing, making sure that each point is logical, complete, and clear. To test the logic in your writing, see pages 267–270.

Complete Thinking

Have you answered readers' basic questions? Have you supported the thesis? The original passage below is too general; the revision is clearly more complete.

Original Passage (Too general)

As soon as you receive a minor cut, the body's healing process begins to work. Blood from tiny vessels fills the wound and begins to clot. In less than 24 hours, a scab forms.

Revised Version (More specific)

As soon as you receive a minor cut, the body's healing process begins to work. In a simple wound, the first and second layers of skin are severed along with tiny blood vessels called capillaries. As these vessels bleed into the wound, minute structures called platelets help stop the bleeding by sticking to the edges of the cut and to one another, forming a plug. The platelets then release chemicals that react with certain proteins in the blood to form a clot. The blood clot, with its fiber network, begins to join the edges of the wound together. As the clot dries out, a scab forms, usually in less than 24 hours.

Clear Thesis

Make sure that your writing centers on one main issue or thesis. Although this next original passage lacks a thesis, the revision has a clear one.

Original Passage (Lacks a thesis)

Teen magazines are popular with young girls. These magazines contain a lot of how-to articles about self-image, fashion, and boy-girl relationships. Girls read them to get advice on how to act and how to look. Girls who don't really know what they want are the most eager readers.

Revised Version (Identifies a specific thesis statement)

Adolescent girls often see teen magazines as handbooks on how to be teenagers. These magazines influence the ways they act and the ways they look. For girls who are unsure of themselves, these magazines can exert an enormous amount of influence. Unfortunately, the advice these magazines give about self-image, fashion, and boys may do more harm than good.

Examine your organization.

Good writing has structure. It leads readers logically and clearly from one point to the next. When revising for organization, consider four areas: the overall plan, the opening, the flow of ideas, and the closing.

Overall Plan

Look closely at the sequence of ideas or events that you share. Does that sequence advance your thesis? Do the points build effectively? Are there gaps in the support or points that stray from your original purpose? If you find such problems, consider the following actions:

- Refine the focus or emphasis by rearranging material within the text.
- Fill in the gaps with new material. Go back to your planning notes.
- Delete material that wanders away from your purpose.
- Use an additional (or different) method of organization. For example, if you are comparing two subjects, add depth to your analysis by contrasting them as well. If you are describing a complex subject, show the subject more clearly and fully by distinguishing and classifying its parts. (See pages 62–65 for more on organizational methods.)

INSIGHT: What is the best method of organization for your essay? The writing you are doing will usually determine the choice. As you know, a personal narrative is often organized by time. Typically, however, you combine and customize methods to develop a writing idea. For example, within a comparison essay you may do some describing or classifying. See pages 46–47 and 118 for more on the common methods of development.

Opening Ideas

Reread your opening paragraph(s). Is the opening organized effectively? Does it engage readers, establish a direction for your writing, and express your thesis or focus? The original opening below doesn't build to a compelling thesis statement, but the revised version engages the reader and leads to the thesis.

Original Opening (Lacks interest and direction)

The lack of student motivation is a common subject in the news. Educators want to know how to get students to learn. Today's higher standards mean that students will be expected to learn even more. Another problem in urban areas is that large numbers of students are dropping out. How to interest students is a challenge.

Revised Version (Effectively leads readers into the essay)

How can we motivate students to learn? How can we get them to meet today's rising standards of excellence? How can we, in fact, keep students in school long enough to learn? The answer to these problems is quite simple. Give them money. Pay students to study and learn and stay in school.

Flow of Ideas

Look closely at the beginnings and endings of each paragraph. Have you connected your thoughts clearly? (See page 85 for a list of transition words.) The original opening words of the paragraph sequence below, from an essay of description, offer no links for readers. The revised versions use strong transitions indicating spatial organization (order by location).

Original First Words in the Four Middle Paragraphs
There was a huge, steep hill . . .
Buffalo Creek ran . . .
A dense "jungle" covering . . .
Within walking distance from my house . . .

Revised Versions (Words and phrases connect ideas)
Behind the house, there was a huge, steep hill . . .
Across the road from the house, Buffalo Creek ran . . .
On the far side of the creek bank was a dense "jungle" covering . . .
Up the road, within walking distance from my house . . .

INSIGHT: Review "Supporting Your Claims" (pages 264–266) and use those strategies to strengthen weak or unconvincing passages.

Closing Ideas

Reread your closing paragraph(s). Do you offer an effective summary, reassert your main point in a fresh way, and provide readers with food for thought as they leave your writing? Or is your ending abrupt, repetitive, or directionless? The original ending below is uninspiring; it adds little to the main part of the writing. The revision summarizes the main points in the essay and then urges the reader to think again about the overall point of writing.

Original Ending (Sketchy and flat)
Native Son deals with a young man's struggle against racism. It shows the effects of prejudice. Everyone should read this book.

Revised Version (Effectively ends the writing)
Native Son deals with a young man's struggle in a racist society, but also with so much more. It shows how prejudice affects people, how it closes in on them, and what some people will do to find a way out. Anyone who wants to better understand racism in the United States should read this book.

> **TIP:** To generate fresh ideas for your closing, freewrite answers to questions like these: Why is the topic important to me? What should my readers have learned? Why should this issue matter to readers? What evidence or appeal (pages 272–273) will help readers remember my message and act on it? How does the topic relate to broader issues in society, history, or life?

Revising for Voice and Style

Generally, readers more fully trust writing that speaks in an informed voice and a clear, natural style. To develop an informed voice, make sure that your details are correct and complete; to develop a clear style, make sure that your writing is well organized and unpretentious. Check the issues below. (For a definition of voice, see page **73**.)

Web Link

Check the level of commitment.

Consider how and to what degree your writing shows that you care about the topic and reader. For example, note how the original passage below lacks a personal voice, revealing nothing about the writer's connection to—or interest in—the topic. In contrast, the revision shows that the writer cares about the topic.

Original Passage (Lacks voice)

Cemeteries can teach us a lot about history. They make history seem more real. There is an old grave of a Revolutionary War veteran in the Union Grove Cemetery. . . .

Revised Version (Personal, sincere voice)

I've always had a special feeling for cemeteries. It's hard to explain any further than that, except to say history never seems quite as real as it does when I walk among many old gravestones. One day I discovered the grave of a Revolutionary War veteran. . . .

Check the intensity of your writing.

All writing—including academic writing—is enriched by an appropriate level of intensity, or even passion. In the original passage below, the writer's concern for the topic is unclear because the piece sounds neutral. In contrast, the revised version exudes energy.

Original Passage (Lacks feeling and energy)

Motz blames Barbie dolls for all the problems that women face today. Instead, one should look to romance novels, fashion magazines, and parental training for causes of these societal problems.

Revised Version (Expresses real feelings)

In other words, Motz uses Barbie as a scapegoat for problems that have complex causes. However, a girl's interest in romance is no more Barbie's fault than the fault of books like *On the Shores of Silver Lake*. Fashion magazines targeted at adolescents are the cause of far more anorexia than is Barbie. And mothers who encourage daughters to find security in men teach female dependency, but Barbie doesn't.

INSIGHT: To develop your personal writing voice, begin each writing assignment by freely recording your thoughts and feelings about the topic.

Develop an academic style.

Most college writing requires an academic style. Such a style isn't stuffy; you're not trying to impress readers with ten-dollar words. Rather, you are using language that facilitates a thoughtful, engaged discussion of the topic. To choose the best words for such a conversation, consider the issues that follow.

Personal Pronouns

In some academic writing, personal pronouns are acceptable. Such is the case in informal writing, such as reading responses, and in personal essays involving narration, description, and reflection. In addition, *I* is correctly used in academic writing rooted in personal research, sometimes called an *I-search paper.*

Generally, however, avoid using *I, we,* and *you* in traditional academic writing. The concept, instead, is to focus on the topic itself and let your attitude be revealed indirectly. As E. B. White puts it, "To achieve style, begin by affecting none—that is, begin by placing yourself in the background."

No: I really think that the problem of the homeless in Chicago is serious, given the number of people who are dying, as I know from my experience where I grew up.

Yes: Homelessness in Chicago often leads to death. This fact demands the attention of more than lawmakers and social workers; all citizens must address the problems of their suffering neighbors.

> **TIP:** Use the pronoun *one* carefully in academic prose. When it means "a person," *one* can lead to a stilted style if overused. In addition, the pronoun *their* (a plural pronoun) should not be used with *one* (a singular pronoun).

Technical Terms and Jargon

Technical terms and jargon—"insider" words—can be the specialized vocabulary of a subject, a discipline, a profession, or a social group. As such, jargon can be difficult to read for "outsiders." Follow these guidelines:

- Use technical terms to communicate with people within the profession or discipline as a kind of shorthand. However, be careful that such jargon doesn't devolve into meaningless buzzwords and catchphrases.
- Avoid jargon when writing for readers outside the profession or discipline. Use simpler terms and define technical terms that must be used.

Technical: Bin's Douser power washer delivers 2200 psi p.r., runs off standard a.c. lines, comes with 100 ft. h.d. synthetic-rubber tubing, and features variable pulsation options through three adjustable s.s. tips.

Simple: Bin's Douser power washer has a pressure rating of 2200 psi (pounds per square inch), runs off a common 200-volt electrical circuit, comes with 100 feet of hose, and includes three nozzles.

Level of Formality

Most academic writing (especially research papers, literary analyses, lab reports, and argumentative essays) should meet the standards of formal English. **Formal English** is characterized by a serious tone; careful attention to word choice; longer and more complex sentences reflecting complex thinking; strict adherence to traditional conventions of grammar, mechanics, and punctuation; and avoidance of contractions.

> Formal English, modeled in this sentence, is worded correctly and carefully so that it can withstand repeated readings without seeming tiresome, sloppy, or cute.

You may write other papers (personal essays, commentaries, journals, and reviews) in which informal English is appropriate. **Informal English** is characterized by a personal tone, the occasional use of popular expressions, shorter sentences with slightly looser syntax, contractions, and personal references (*I, we, you*), but it still adheres to basic conventions.

> Informal English sounds like one person talking to another person (in a somewhat relaxed setting). It's the type of language you are reading now. It sounds comfortable and real, not affected or breezy.

TIP: In academic writing, generally avoid slang—words considered outside standard English because they are faddish, familiar to few people, and sometimes insulting.

Unnecessary Qualifiers

Using qualifiers (such as *mostly, often, likely,* or *tends to*) is an appropriate strategy for developing defendable claims in argumentative writing. (See pages 262–263.) However, when you "overqualify" your ideas or add intensifiers (*really, truly*), the result is insecurity—the impression that you lack confidence in your ideas. The cure? Say what you mean, and mean what you say.

> **Insecure:** I totally and completely agree with the new security measures at sporting events, but that's only my opinion.
>
> **Secure:** I agree with the new security measures at sporting events.

 Each academic discipline has its own vocabulary and its own vocabulary resources. Such resources include dictionaries, glossaries, or handbooks. Check your library for the vocabulary resources in your discipline. Use them regularly to deepen your grasp of that vocabulary.

Know when to use the passive voice.

Most verbs can be in either the active or the passive voice. When a verb is active, the sentence's subject performs the action. When the verb is passive, the subject is acted upon.

Active: If you *can't attend* the meeting, *notify* Richard by Thursday.

Passive: If a meeting *can't be attended* by you, Richard *must be notified* by Thursday.

Weaknesses of Passive Voice: The passive voice tends to be wordy and sluggish because the verb's action is directed backward, not ahead. In addition, passive constructions tend to be impersonal, making people disappear.

Passive: The sound system *can* now *be used* to listen in on sessions in the therapy room. Parents *can be helped* by having constructive one-on-one communication methods with children modeled by therapists.

Active: Parents *can* now *use* the sound system to listen in on sessions in the therapy room. Therapists *can help* parents by modeling constructive one-on-one communication methods with children.

Strengths of Passive Voice: Using the passive voice isn't wrong. In fact, the passive voice has some important uses: (1) when you need to be tactful (say, in a bad-news letter), (2) if you wish to stress the object or person acted upon, and (3) if the actual actor is understood, unknown, or unimportant.

Active: Our engineers determined that you *bent* the bar at the midpoint.

Passive: Our engineers determined that the bar *had been bent* at the midpoint. (tactful)

Active: Congratulations! We *have approved* your scholarship for $2,500.

Passive: Congratulations! Your scholarship for $2,500 *has been approved*. (emphasis on receiver; actor understood)

TIP: Avoid using the passive voice unethically to hide responsibility. For example, an instructor who says, "Your assignments could not be graded because of scheduling difficulties," might be trying to evade the truth: "I did not finish grading your assignments because I was watching *CSI*."

Addressing Paragraph Issues

While drafting, you may have constructed paragraphs that are loosely held together, poorly developed, or unclear. When you revise, take a close look at your paragraphs for focus, unity, and coherence (pages **82–84**).

Remember the basics.

A paragraph should be a concise unit of thought. Revise a paragraph until it . . .

- Is organized around a controlling idea—often stated in a topic sentence.
- Consists of supporting sentences that develop the controlling idea.
- Concludes with a sentence that summarizes the main point and prepares readers for the next paragraph or main point.
- Serves a specific function in a piece of writing—opening, supporting, developing, illustrating, countering, describing, or closing.

SAMPLE PARAGRAPH

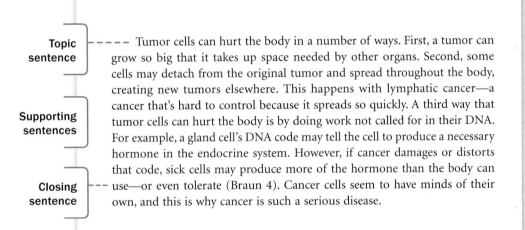

Topic sentence ----- Tumor cells can hurt the body in a number of ways. First, a tumor can grow so big that it takes up space needed by other organs. Second, some cells may detach from the original tumor and spread throughout the body, creating new tumors elsewhere. This happens with lymphatic cancer—a cancer that's hard to control because it spreads so quickly. A third way that **Supporting sentences** tumor cells can hurt the body is by doing work not called for in their DNA. For example, a gland cell's DNA code may tell the cell to produce a necessary hormone in the endocrine system. However, if cancer damages or distorts that code, sick cells may produce more of the hormone than the body can **Closing sentence** --- use—or even tolerate (Braun 4). Cancer cells seem to have minds of their own, and this is why cancer is such a serious disease.

Keep the purpose in mind.

Use these questions to evaluate the purpose and function of each paragraph:

- What function does the paragraph fulfill? How does it add to your line of reasoning or the development of your thesis?
- Would the paragraph work better if it were divided in two—or combined with another paragraph?
- Does the paragraph flow smoothly from the previous paragraph, and does it lead effectively into the next one?

Check for unity.

A unified paragraph is one in which all the details help to develop a single main topic or achieve a single main effect. Test for unity by following these guidelines.

Topic Sentence

Very often the topic of a paragraph is stated in a single sentence called a "topic sentence." Check whether your paragraph needs a topic sentence. If the paragraph has a topic sentence, determine whether it is clear, specific, and well focused. Here is a formula for writing good topic sentences:

Formula: A topic sentence = a limited topic + a specific feeling or thought about it.

Example: The fear that Americans feel (limited topic) comes partly from the uncertainty related to this attack (a specific thought).

Placement of the Topic Sentence

Normally the topic sentence is the first sentence in the paragraph. However, it can appear elsewhere in a paragraph.

Middle Placement: Place a topic sentence in the middle when you want to build up to and then lead away from the key idea.

During the making of *Apocalypse Now,* Eleanor Coppola created a documentary about the filming called *Hearts of Darkness: A Filmmaker's Apocalypse.* In the first film, the insane Colonel Kurtz has disappeared into the Cambodian jungle. As Captain Willard searches for Kurtz, the screen fills with horror. **However, as *Hearts of Darkness* relates, the horror portrayed in the fictional movie was being lived out by the production company.** For example, in the documentary, actor Larry Fishburne shockingly says, "War is fun. . . . Vietnam must have been so much fun." Then toward the end of the filming, actor Martin Sheen suffered a heart attack. When an assistant informed investors, the director exploded, "He's not dead unless I say he's dead."

End Placement: Place a topic sentence at the end when you want to build to a climax, as in a passage of narration or persuasion.

When sportsmen stop to reflect on why they find fishing so enjoyable, most realize that what they love is the feel of a fish on the end of the line, not necessarily the weight of the fillets in their coolers. Fishing has undergone a slow evolution over the last century. While fishing used to be a way of putting food on the table, most of today's fishermen do so only for the relaxation that it provides. The barbed hook was invented to increase the quantity of fish a man could land so that he could better feed his family. **This need no longer exists, so barbed hooks are no longer necessary.**

Supporting Sentences

All the sentences in the body of a paragraph should support the topic sentence. The closing sentence, for instance, will often summarize the paragraph's main point or emphasize a key detail. If any sentences shift the focus away from the topic, revise the paragraph in one of the following ways:

- Delete the material from the paragraph.
- Rewrite the material so that it clearly supports the topic sentence.
- Create a separate paragraph based on the odd-man-out material.
- Revise the topic sentence so that it relates more closely to the support.

Consistent Focus

Examine the following paragraph about fishing hooks. The original topic sentence focuses on the point that some anglers prefer smooth hooks. However, the writer leaves this initial idea unfinished and turns to the issue of the cost of new hooks. In the revised version, unity is restored: The first paragraph completes the point about anglers who prefer smooth hooks; the second paragraph addresses the issue of replacement costs.

Original Paragraph (Lacks unity)

According to some anglers who do use smooth hooks, their lures perform better than barbed lures as long as they maintain a constant tension on the line. Smooth hooks can bite deeper than barbed hooks, actually providing a stronger hold on the fish. Some people have argued that replacing all of the barbed hooks in their tackle would be a costly operation.

Revised Version (Unified)

According to some anglers who do use smooth hooks, their lures perform better than barbed lures as long as the anglers maintain a constant tension on the line. Smooth hooks can bite deeper than barbed hooks, actually providing a stronger hold on the fish. These anglers testify that switching from barbed hooks has not noticeably reduced the number of fish that they are able to land. In their experience, and in my own, enjoyment of the sport is actually heightened by adding another challenge to playing the fish (maintaining line tension).

Some people have argued that replacing all of the barbed hooks in their tackle would be a costly operation. While this is certainly a concern, barbed hooks do not necessarily require replacement. With a simple set of pliers, the barbs on most conventional hooks can be bent down, providing a cost-free method of modifying one's existing tackle. . . .

 Paragraphs that contain unrelated ideas lack unity and are hard to follow. As you review each paragraph for unity, ask yourself these questions: Is the topic of the paragraph clear? Does each sentence relate to the topic? Are the sentences organized in the best possible order?

Check for coherence.

When a paragraph is coherent, the parts stay together. A coherent paragraph flows smoothly because each sentence is connected to others by patterns in the language such as repetition and transitions. To strengthen the coherence in your paragraphs, check for the issues discussed below.

Effective Repetition

To achieve coherence in your paragraphs, consider using repetition—repeating words or synonyms where necessary to remind readers of what you have already said. You can also use parallelism—repeating phrase or sentence structures to show the relationships among ideas. At the same time, you will add a unifying rhythm to your writing.

Ineffective: The floor was littered with discarded soda cans, newspapers that were crumpled, and wrinkled clothes.

Effective: **The floor was littered with discarded soda cans, crumpled newspapers, and wrinkled clothes.** (Three parallel phrases are used.)

Ineffective: Reading the book was enjoyable; to write the critique was difficult.

Effective: **Reading the book was enjoyable; writing the critique was difficult.** (Two similar structures are repeated.)

Clear Transitions

Linking words and phrases like "next," "on the other hand," and "in addition" connect ideas by showing the relationship among them. There are transitions that show location and time, compare and contrast things, emphasize a point, conclude or summarize, and add or clarify information. (See page **85** for a list of linking words and phrases.) Note the use of transitions in the following examples:

- The paradox of Scotland is that violence had long been the norm in this now-peaceful land. In fact, the country was born, bred, and came of age in war. (The transition is used to emphasize a point.)

- The production of cement is a complicated process. First, the mixture of lime, silica, alumina, and gypsum is ground into very fine particles. (The transition is used to show time or order.)

INSIGHT: Another way to achieve coherence in your paragraphs is to use pronouns effectively. A pronoun forms a link to the noun it replaces and ties that noun (idea) to the ideas that follow. As always, don't overuse pronouns or rely too heavily on them in establishing coherence in your paragraphs.

Transitions and Linking Words

The words and phrases below can help you tie together words, phrases, sentences, and paragraphs.

WORDS USED TO SHOW LOCATION:

above	behind	down	on top of
across	below	in back of	onto
against	beneath	in front of	outside
along	beside	inside	over
among	between	into	throughout
around	beyond	near	to the right
away from	by	off	under

WORDS USED TO SHOW TIME:

about	during	next	today
after	finally	next week	tomorrow
afterward	first	second	until
as soon as	immediately	soon	when
at	later	then	yesterday
before	meanwhile	third	

WORDS USED TO COMPARE THINGS (SHOW SIMILARITIES):

also	in the same way	likewise
as	like	similarly

WORDS USED TO CONTRAST THINGS (SHOW DIFFERENCES):

although	even though	on the other hand	still
but	however	otherwise	yet

WORDS USED TO EMPHASIZE A POINT:

again	for this reason	particularly	to repeat
even	in fact	to emphasize	truly

WORDS USED TO CONCLUDE OR SUMMARIZE:

all in all	finally	in summary	therefore
as a result	in conclusion	last	to sum up

WORDS USED TO ADD INFORMATION:

additionally	and	equally important	in addition
again	another	finally	likewise
along with	as well	for example	next
also	besides	for instance	second

WORDS USED TO CLARIFY:

for instance	in other words	put another way	that is

Note: Use transitions to link, expand, or intensify an idea, but don't add elements carelessly, creating run-on or rambling sentences.

Check for completeness.

The sentences in a paragraph should support and expand on the main point. If your paragraph does not seem complete, you will need to add information.

Supporting Details

If some of your paragraphs are incomplete, they may lack details. There are numerous kinds of details, including the following:

facts	anecdotes	analyses	paraphrases
statistics	quotations	explanations	comparisons
examples	definitions	summaries	analogies

Add details based on the type of writing you are engaged in.

Describing: Add details that help readers see, smell, taste, touch, or hear it.

Narrating: Add details that help readers understand the events and actions.

Explaining: Add details that help readers understand what it means, how it works, or what it does.

Persuading: Add details that strengthen the logic of your argument.

Specific Details

The original paragraph below fails to answer fully the question posed by the topic sentence. In the revised paragraph, the writer uses an anecdote to answer the question.

Original Paragraph (Lacks completeness)

So what is stress? Actually, the physiological characteristics of stress are some of the body's potentially good self-defense mechanisms. People experience stress when they are in danger. In fact, stress can be healthy.

Revised Version (Full development)

So what is stress? Actually, the physiological characteristics of stress are some of the body's potentially good self-defense mechanisms. Take, for example, a man who is crossing a busy intersection when he spots an oncoming car. Immediately his brain releases a flood of adrenaline into his bloodstream. As a result, his muscles contract, his eyes dilate, his heart pounds faster, his breathing quickens, and his blood clots more readily. Each one of these responses helps the man leap out of the car's path. His muscles contract to give him exceptional strength. His eyes dilate so that he can see more clearly. His heart pumps more blood and his lungs exchange more air—both to increase his metabolism. If the man were injured, his blood would clot faster, ensuring a smaller amount of blood loss. In this situation and many more like it, stress symptoms are good (Curtis 25–26).

INSIGHT: If a paragraph is getting long, divide it at a natural stopping point. The topic sentence can then function as the thesis for that part of your essay or paper.

Web Link

Revising Collaboratively

Every writer can benefit from feedback from an interested audience, especially one that offers constructive and honest advice during a writing project. Members of an existing writing group already know how valuable it is for writers to share their work. Others might want to start a writing group to experience the benefits. Your group might collaborate online or in person. In either case, the information on the next two pages will help you get started.

Know your role.

Writers and reviewers should know their roles and fulfill their responsibilities during revising sessions. Essentially, the writer should briefly introduce the draft and solicit honest responses. Reviewers should make constructive comments in response to the writing.

Provide appropriate feedback.

Feedback can take many forms, including the three approaches described here.

Basic Description: In this simple response, the reviewer listens or reads attentively and then simply describes what she or he hears or sees happening in the piece. The reviewer offers no criticism of the writing.

Ineffective: "That was interesting. The piece was informative."

Effective: "First, the essay introduced the challenge of your birth defect and how you have had to cope with it. Then in the next part you . . ."

Summary Evaluation: Here the reviewer reads or listens to the piece and then provides a specific evaluation of the draft.

Ineffective: "Gee, I really liked it!" or "It was boring."

Effective: "Your story at the beginning really pulled me in, and the middle explained the issue strongly, but the ending felt a bit flat."

Thorough Critique: The reviewer assesses the ideas, organization, and voice in the writing. Feedback should be detailed and constructive. Such a critique may also be completed with the aid of a review sheet or checklist. As a reviewer, be prepared to share specific responses, suggestions, and questions. But also be sure to focus your comments on the writing, rather than the writer.

Ineffective: "You really need to fix that opening! What were you thinking?"

Effective: "Let's look closely at the opening. Could you rewrite the first sentence so it grabs the reader's attention? Also, I'm somewhat confused about the thesis statement. Could you rephrase it so it states your position more clearly?"

Respond according to a plan.

Using a specific plan or scheme like the following will help you give clear, helpful, and complete feedback.

OAQS Method: Use this simple four-step scheme—**Observe, Appreciate, Question,** and **Suggest**—to respond to your peers' writing.

1. **Observe** means to notice what another person's essay is designed to do and say something about its design or purpose. For example, you might say, "Even though you are writing about your boyfriend, it appears that you are trying to get a message across to your parents."

2. **Appreciate** means to praise something in the writing that impresses or pleases you. You can find something to appreciate in any piece of writing. For example, you might say, "You make a very convincing point" or "With your description, I can actually see his broken tooth."

3. **Question** means to ask whatever you want to know after you've read the essay. You might ask for background information, a definition, an interpretation, or an explanation. For example, you might say, "Can you tell us what happened when you got to the emergency room?"

4. **Suggest** means to give helpful advice about possible changes. For example, you might say, "With a little more physical detail—especially more sounds and smells—your third paragraph could be the highlight of the whole essay. What do you think?"

ASKING THE WRITER QUESTIONS

Reviewers should ask the following types of questions while reviewing a piece of writing:

- **To help writers reflect on their purpose and audience . . .**
  Why are you writing this?
  Who will read this, and what do they need to know?

- **To help writers focus their thoughts . . .**
  What message are you trying to get across?
  Do you have more than one main point?
  What are the most important examples?

- **To help writers think about their information . . .**
  What do you know about the subject?
  Does this part say enough?
  Does your writing cover all of the basics (*Who? What? Where? When? Why?* and *How?*)?

- **To help writers with their openings and closings . . .**
  What are you trying to say in the opening?
  How else could you start your writing?
  How do you want your readers to feel at the end?

Using the Writing Center

A college writing center or lab is a place where a trained adviser will help you develop and strengthen a piece of writing. You can expect the writing center adviser to do certain things; other things only you can do. For quick reference, refer to the chart below.

Web Link

ADVISER'S JOB	YOUR JOB
Make you feel at home	Be respectful
Discuss your needs	Be ready to work
Help you choose a topic.	Decide on a topic
Discuss your purpose and audience.	Know your purpose and audience
Help you generate ideas.	Embrace the best ideas
Help you develop your logic	Consider other points of view; stretch your own perspective
Help you understand how to research your material	Do the research
Read your draft.	Share your writing
Identify problems in organization, logic, expression, and format	Recognize and fix problems
Teach ways to correct weaknesses	Learn important principles
Help you with grammar, usage, diction, vocabulary, and mechanics	Correct all errors

---

TIPS for getting the most out of the writing center
- Visit the center at least several days before your paper is due.
- Take your assignment sheet with you to each advising session.
- Read your work aloud, slowly.
- Expect to rethink your writing from scratch.
- Do not defend your wording—if it needs defense, it needs revision.
- Ask questions. (No question is "too dumb.")
- Request clarification of anything you don't understand.
- Ask for examples or illustrations of important points.
- Write down all practical suggestions.
- Ask the adviser to summarize his or her remarks.
- Rewrite as soon as possible after—or even during—the advising session.
- Return to the writing center for a response to your revisions.

Writing with Sources

When your writing project involves working with sources, test your first draft for effective use of researched material. You can do this by examining how well references to sources advance your thesis and enrich your ideas.

Think rhetorically.

At the beginning of this chapter, you were instructed to revisit your project's rhetorical situation: your purpose, your audience, and your subject. When revising your paper, consider how well your sources help you achieve that purpose, reach that audience, and thoroughly address that subject. Specifically, assess your first draft by asking questions like these:

- Will readers accept my sources and how I used them, or will they question my reasoning and evidence? What alternatives, objections, or questions might they raise?

- Does my writing encourage readers to think thoroughly about my topic? Do I need to add more background details, definitions, and contextual information?

- Do my sources get at essential, deep truths about my subject, or do they simply offer basic data or common knowledge?

Depending on your answers to these questions, you may have to reread your notes and sources, or you may have to look for additional information.

Practice revising strategies.

To improve source use in your paper as you revise, try strategies like these:

Test the balance of reasoning and support. Examine the big picture of how you have used source material—summaries, paraphrases, and quotations—in relation to your own discussion of the issue. If your draft is thin on the support side (filled with big claims that lack adequate support), you need to either scale back your claims or beef up the support with more information and evidence.

Conversely, your draft may be dominated by source material, not your own thinking. If your paper reads like a series of source summaries or loosely stitched together quotations, if it contains big patches of copy-and-paste material, if your paragraphs all seem to start and end with source material, or if your writing is dense with detailed but almost incomprehensible data, you may need to deepen your own contribution to the paper. Do so by trying the following:

1. Before diving into source material within a paragraph or section of your paper, flesh out your thinking more fully. Offer reasoning that elaborates the claim and effectively leads into the evidence.

2. As you present evidence from source material, build on it by explaining what it means. Evidence doesn't typically speak for itself: through

analysis, synthesis, illustration, contrast, and other means, you need to show how or why your sources advance your thesis.

3. After you have presented evidence that elaborates on and supports your idea, extend your thoughts by addressing the reader's "So what?" or "Why does this matter?" skepticism.

Test your evidence. Review your draft by examining how well your researched information expands on and backs up your points or claims. That evidence should be solid enough to encourage readers to accept your ideas; weak evidence will lead readers to reject your analysis or argument. Specifically, the evidence should be

- **accurate:** The information is all correct.
- **precise:** The data are concrete and specific, not vague and general.
- **substantial:** The amount of evidence reaches a critical mass—enough to convey the idea and convince readers of its validity.
- **authoritative:** The evidence comes from a reliable source. Moreover, the information is as close to the origin as possible; it is not a report conveying thirdhand or fourthhand information.
- **representative:** The information fairly represents the range of data on the issue. Your presentation of evidence is balanced.
- **fitting:** Given your purpose, the topic, and your reader, the evidence is appropriate and relevant for the question or issue you are discussing.

Test the flow of information. Generally, your writing with source material should follow the known/new principle. Because readers "build" meaning as they proceed through your writing, your paper's overall structure, its sections, and its paragraphs should all be built so that new information emerges gradually and is linked to information the reader already knows. Make sure your draft unfolds this way.

Test for plagiarism. Going back to your notes and sources as needed, check that you have clearly indicated which material in your draft is summarized, paraphrased, or quoted from a source. In particular, check that your attributive phrases and citations set off all source material except for common knowledge. (For more help with this issue, see pages 486–489.)

Cross-Curricular Connections

Different disciplines treat evidence differently; in fact, each field values certain types of evidence and reasoning more highly than other types. For example, humanities disciplines might value close interpretations of texts and documents, social sciences might prefer statistics and case studies, and natural sciences would value quantitative evidence gathered through the scientific method in lab experiments and in field work. As you write papers for your major, make sure that you use types of evidence and methods of analysis that this research community accepts and respects.

Revising Checklist

Use this checklist as a guide when you revise your writing. (To see revising in action, turn to pages 124–127.)

Ideas

_____ My writing has a clear thesis, focus, or theme.

_____ I have fully developed and supported that thesis with relevant, accurate, well-researched details.

Organization

_____ My writing follows a clear pattern of organization that advances the main idea.

_____ I have added, cut, reordered, and rewritten material as needed.

_____ All of the paragraphs are unified, coherent, and complete.

Voice

_____ The tone is matched to the assignment, the reader, and the purpose.

_____ The style is clear, genuine, and appropriately academic.

_____ My voice sounds energetic and interested.

Critical-Thinking and Writing Activities

As directed by your instructor, complete the following critical-thinking and writing activities by yourself or with classmates.

1. Doris Lessing has stated that when it comes to writing, "The more a thing cooks, the better." In what sense is revision a crucial stage in that cooking process? Using Lessing's cooking metaphor as a starting point, explore how revision should function in your own writing.

2. Review the opening and closing paragraphs of one of your essays. Then come up with fresh and different approaches for those paragraphs using the information on pages 75–76 as a guide.

3. For your current writing assignment, ask a peer to provide detailed feedback using the information in this chapter as a guide. Then take a fresh copy of your paper to the writing center and work through your draft with an adviser. Revise the draft as needed.

◀ VISUALLY SPEAKING

Review the photograph on page 71. Then explain in writing how the potter's work shown in the picture might be similar to (or different from) your work when revising an essay.

EDITING AND PROOFREADING

Video

In any writing project, there comes a point (like a fast-approaching due date) when you must prepare your writing for submission. At that time you must edit and proofread your revised writing so that it speaks clearly and accurately. When you edit, look first for words, phrases, and sentences that sound awkward, uninteresting, or unclear. When you proofread, check your writing for spelling, mechanics, usage, and grammar errors.

Before you begin, make sure you have the proper tools: handbook, dictionary, thesaurus, computer spell checker, and so on. Also, ask one of your writing peers to help you edit your work. Then prepare your final draft, following the guidelines established by your instructor, and proofread it for errors.

The guidelines and strategies given in this chapter will help you to edit your writing for style and clarity and to proofread it for errors.

Editing Your Revised Draft

When you have thoroughly revised your writing, you need to edit it so as to make it clear and concise enough to present to readers. Use the editing guidelines below to check your revised draft.

Review the overall style of your writing.

1. Read your revised writing aloud. Better yet, have a writing peer read it aloud to you. Highlight any writing that doesn't read smoothly and naturally.

2. Check that your style fits the rhetorical situation.

    Goal: Does your writing sound as if you wrote it with a clear aim in mind? Do the sentence style and word choice match the goal?

    Reader: Is the tone sincere? Does the writing sound authentic and honest?

    Subject: Does the writing suit the subject and your treatment of it in terms of seriousness or playfulness, complexity or simplicity?

3. Examine your sentences. Check them for clarity, conciseness, and variety. Replace sentences that are wordy or rambling; combine or expand sentences that are short and choppy. Also, vary the beginnings of your sentences and avoid sentence patterns that are too predictable. (See pages **95–101**.)

Consider word choice.

1. Avoid redundancy. Be alert for words or phrases that are used together but mean nearly the same thing.

    repeat again   red in color   refer back

2. Watch for repetition. When used appropriately, repetition can add rhythm and coherence to your writing. When used ineffectively, however, it can be a real distraction.

    The man looked as if he were in his late seventies. **The man** was dressed in an old suit. I soon realized that **the man** was homeless. . . .

3. Look for general nouns, verbs, and modifiers. Specific words are much more effective than general ones. (See page **102**.)

    The girl moved on the bench. (general)

    Rosie slid quietly to the end of the park bench. (specific)

4. Avoid highly technical terms. Check for jargon or technical terms that your readers will not know or that you haven't adequately explained. (See page **103**.)

    As the **capillaries** bleed, **platelets** work with **fibrinogens** to form a clot.

5. Use fair language. Replace words or phrases that are biased or demeaning. (See pages **104–106**.)

Combining Sentences

Effective sentences often contain several basic ideas that work together to show relationships and make connections. Here are five basic ideas followed by seven examples of how they can be combined into effective sentences.

1. The longest and largest construction project in history was the Great Wall of China.

2. The project took 1,700 years to complete.

3. The Great Wall of China is 1,400 miles long.

4. It is between 18 and 30 feet high.

5. It is up to 32 feet wide.

Edit short, simplistic sentences.

Combine your short, simplistic sentences into longer, more detailed sentences. Sentence combining is generally carried out in the following ways:

- Use a **series** to combine three or more similar ideas.

  The Great Wall of China is **1,400 miles long,** between **18 and 30 feet high,** and up to **32 feet wide.**

- Use a **relative pronoun** (*who, whose, that, which*) to introduce subordinate (less important) ideas.

  The Great Wall of China, **which is 1,400 miles long and between 18 and 30 feet high,** took 1,700 years to complete.

- Use an **introductory phrase** or **clause**.

  Having taken 1,700 years to complete, the Great Wall of China was the longest construction project in history.

- Use a **semicolon** (and a conjunctive adverb if appropriate).

  The Great Wall took 1,700 years to complete**;** it is 1,400 miles long and up to 30 feet high and 32 feet wide.

- Repeat a **key word** or phrase to emphasize an idea.

  The Great Wall of China was the longest construction **project** in history, a **project** that took 1,700 years to complete.

- Use **correlative conjunctions** (*either, or; not only, but also*) to compare or contrast two ideas in a sentence.

  The Great Wall of China is **not only** up to 30 feet high and 32 feet wide, **but also** 1,400 miles long.

- Use an **appositive** (a word or phrase that renames) to emphasize an idea.

  The Great Wall of China—**the largest construction project in history**—is 1,400 miles long, 32 feet wide, and up to 30 feet high.

Expanding Sentences

Expand sentences when you edit so as to connect related ideas and make room for new information. Length has no value in and of itself: The best sentence is still the shortest one that says all it has to say. An expanded sentence, however, is capable of saying more—and saying it more expressively.

Use cumulative sentences.

Modern writers often use an expressive sentence form called the cumulative sentence. A cumulative sentence is made of a general "base clause" that is expanded by adding modifying words, phrases, or clauses. In such a sentence, details are added before and after the main clause, creating an image-rich thought. Here's an example of a cumulative sentence, with the base clause or main idea in boldface:

> In preparation for her Spanish exam, **Julie was studying** at the kitchen table, completely focused, memorizing a list of vocabulary words.

Discussion: Notice how each new modifier adds to the richness of the final sentence. Also notice that each of these modifying phrases is set off by a comma. Here's another sample sentence:

> With his hands on his face, **Tony was laughing** half-heartedly, looking puzzled and embarrassed.

Discussion: Such a cumulative sentence provides a way to write description that is rich in detail, without rambling. Notice how each modifier changes the flow or rhythm of the sentence.

Expand with details.

Here are seven basic ways to expand a main idea:

1. with **adjectives and adverbs:** *half-heartedly, once again*
2. with **prepositional phrases:** *with his hands on his face*
3. with **absolute phrases:** *his head tilted to one side*
4. with **participial (-*ing* or -*ed*) phrases:** *looking puzzled*
5. with **infinitive phrases:** *to hide his embarrassment*
6. with **subordinate clauses:** *while his friend talks*
7. with **relative clauses:** *who isn't laughing at all*

INSIGHT: To edit sentences for more expressive style, it is best to (1) know your grammar and punctuation (especially commas); (2) practice tightening, combining, and expanding sentences using the guidelines in this chapter; and (3) read carefully, looking for models of well-constructed sentences.

Checking for Sentence Style

Writer E. B. White advised young writers to "approach sentence style by way of simplicity, plainness, orderliness, and sincerity." That's good advice from a writer steeped in style. It's also important to know what to look for when editing your sentences. The information on this page and the following four pages will help you edit your sentences for style and correctness.

Avoid these sentence problems.

Always check for and correct the following types of sentence problems. Turn to the pages listed below for guidelines and examples when attempting to fix problems in your sentences.

Short, Choppy Sentences: Combine or expand any short, choppy sentences; use the examples and guidelines on page 95.

Flat, Predictable Sentences: Rewrite any sentences that sound predictable and uninteresting by varying their structures and expanding them with modifying words, phrases, and clauses. (See pages 98–100.)

Incorrect Sentences: Look carefully for fragments, run-ons, and comma splices and correct them accordingly.

Unclear Sentences: Edit any sentences that contain unclear wording, misplaced modifiers, dangling modifiers, or incomplete comparisons.

Unacceptable Sentences: Change sentences that include nonstandard language, double negatives, or unparallel construction.

Unnatural Sentences: Rewrite sentences that contain jargon, clichés, or flowery language. (See page 103.)

Review your writing for sentence variety.

Use the following strategy to review your writing for variety in terms of sentence beginnings, lengths, and types.

- In one column on a piece of paper, list the opening words in each of your sentences. Then decide if you need to vary some of your sentence beginnings.
- In another column, identify the number of words in each sentence. Then decide if you need to change the lengths of some of your sentences.
- In a third column, list the kinds of sentences used (exclamatory, declarative, interrogative, and so on). Then, based on your analysis, use the instructions on the next two pages to edit your sentences as needed.

Vary sentence structures.

To energize your sentences, vary their structures using one or more of the methods shown on this page and the next.

1. Vary sentence openings. Move a modifying word, phrase, or clause to the front of the sentence to stress that modifier. However, avoid creating dangling or misplaced modifiers.

> **The norm:**   We apologize for the inconvenience this may have caused you.
>
> **Variation:**   For the inconvenience this may have caused you, we apologize.

2. Vary sentence lengths. Short sentences (ten words or fewer) are ideal for making points crisply. Medium sentences (ten to twenty words) should carry the bulk of your information. When well crafted, occasional long sentences (more than twenty words) can develop and expand your ideas.

> **Short:**   Welcome back to Magnolia Suites!
>
> **Medium:**   Unfortunately, your confirmed room was unavailable last night when you arrived. For the inconvenience this may have caused you, we apologize.
>
> **Long:**   Because several guests did not depart as scheduled, we were forced to provide you with accommodations elsewhere; however, for your trouble, we were happy to cover the cost of last night's lodging.

3. Vary sentence kinds. The most common sentence is declarative—it states a point. For variety, try exclamatory, imperative, interrogative, and conditional statements.

> **Exclamatory:**   Our goal is providing you with outstanding service!
>
> **Declarative:**   To that end, we have upgraded your room at no expense.
>
> **Imperative:**   Please accept, as well, this box of chocolates as a gift to sweeten your stay.
>
> **Interrogative:**   Do you need further assistance?
>
> **Conditional:**   If you do, we are ready to fulfill your requests.

INSIGHT: In creative writing (stories, novels, plays), writers occasionally use fragments to vary the rhythm of their prose, emphasize a point, or create dialogue. Avoid fragments in academic or business writing.

4. Vary sentence arrangements. Where do you want to place the main point of your sentence? You make that choice by arranging sentence parts into loose, periodic, balanced, or cumulative patterns. Each pattern creates a specific effect.

Loose Sentence

The Travel Center offers an attractive flight-reservation plan for students, one that allows you to collect bonus miles and receive $150,000 in life insurance per flight.

Analysis: This pattern is direct. It states the main point immediately (bold), and then tacks on extra information.

Periodic Sentence

Although this plan requires that you join the Travel Center's Student-Flight Club and pay the $10 admission fee, **in the long run you will save money!**

Analysis: This pattern postpones the main point (bold) until the end. The sentence builds to the point, creating an indirect, dramatic effect.

Balanced Sentence

Joining the club in your freshman year will save you money over your entire college career; in addition, **accruing bonus miles over four years will earn you a free trip to Europe!**

Analysis: This pattern gives equal weight to complementary or contrasting points (bold); the balance is often signaled by a comma and a conjunction (*and, but*) or by a semicolon. Often a conjunctive adverb (*however, nevertheless*) or a transitional phrase (*in addition, even so*) will follow the semicolon to further clarify the relationship.

Cumulative Sentence

Because the club membership is in your name, **you can retain its benefits** as long as you are a student, even if you transfer to a different college or go on to graduate school.

Analysis: This pattern puts the main idea (bold) in the middle of the sentence, surrounding it with modifying words, phrases, and clauses.

5. Use positive repetition. Although you should avoid needless repetition, you might use emphatic repetition to repeat a key word to stress a point.

Repetitive Sentence

Each year, more than a million young people who read poorly leave high school unable to read well, functionally illiterate.

Emphatic Sentence

Each year, more than a million young people leave high school functionally illiterate, so **illiterate** that they can't read daily newspapers, job ads, or safety instructions.

Use parallel structure.

Coordinated sentence elements should be parallel—that is, they should be written in the same grammatical forms. Parallel structures save words, clarify relationships, and present the information in the correct sequence. Follow these guidelines.

1. For words, phrases, or clauses in a series, keep elements consistent.

> **Not parallel:** I have tutored students in Biology 101, also Chemistry 102, not to mention my familiarity with Physics 200.
>
> **Parallel:** I have tutored students in *Biology 101*, *Chemistry 102*, and *Physics 200*.
>
> **Not parallel:** I have volunteered as a hospital receptionist, have been a hospice volunteer, and as an emergency medical technician.
>
> **Parallel:** I have done volunteer work as *a hospital receptionist*, *a hospice counselor*, and *an emergency medical technician*.

2. Use both parts of correlative conjunctions *(either, or; neither, nor; not only, but also; as, so; whether, so; both, and)* so that both segments of the sentence are balanced.

> **Not parallel:** *Not only* did Blake College turn 20 this year. Its enrollment grew by 16 percent.
>
> **Parallel:** *Not only* did Blake College turn 20 this year, *but* its enrollment *also* grew by 16 percent.

3. Place a modifier correctly so that it clearly indicates the word or words to which it refers.

> **Confusing:** MADD promotes *severely* punishing and eliminating drunk driving because this offense leads to a *great number* of deaths and sorrow.
>
> **Parallel:** MADD promotes eliminating and *severely* punishing drunk driving because this offense leads to *many* deaths and *untold* sorrow.

4. Place contrasting details in parallel structures (words, phrases, or clauses) to stress a contrast.

> **Weak contrast:** The average child watches 24 hours of television a week and reads for 36 minutes.
>
> **Strong contrast:** Each week, the average child *watches television for 24 hours but reads for only about half an hour.*

Avoid weak constructions.

Avoid constructions (like those below) that weaken your writing.

Nominal Constructions

The nominal construction is both sluggish and wordy. Avoid it by changing the noun form of a verb (*description or instructions*) to a verb (*describe or instruct*). At the same time, delete the weak verb that preceded the noun.

NOMINAL CONSTRUCTIONS (NOUN FORM UNDERLINED)	STRONG VERBS
Tim gave a <u>description</u> . . . Lydia provided <u>instructions</u> . . .	Tim *described* . . . Lydia *instructed* . . .

Sluggish: John *had a discussion* with the tutors regarding the incident. They gave him their *confirmation* that similar developments had occurred before, but they had not *provided* submissions of their reports.

Energetic: John *discussed* the incident with the tutors. They *confirmed* that similar problems had developed before, but they hadn't *submitted* their reports.

Expletives

Expletives such as "it is" and "there is" are fillers that serve no purpose in most sentences—except to make them wordy and unnatural.

Sluggish: *It is* likely that Nathan will attend the Communication Department's Honors Banquet. *There is* a journalism scholarship that he might win.

Energetic: Nathan will likely attend the Communication Department's Honors Banquet and might win a journalism scholarship.

Negative Constructions

Sentences constructed upon the negatives *no, not, neither/nor* can be wordy and difficult to understand. It's simpler to state what *is* the case.

Negative: During my four years on the newspaper staff, *I have not been* behind in making significant contributions. My editorial skills *have* certainly *not deteriorated*, as I have *never failed* to tackle challenging assignments.

Positive: During my four years on the newspaper staff, *I have made* significant contributions. My editorial skills have steadily *developed* as I *have tackled* difficult assignments.

Web Link

Avoiding Imprecise, Misleading, and Biased Words

As you edit your writing, check your choice of words carefully. The information on the next five pages will help you edit for word choice.

Substitute specific words.

Replace vague nouns and verbs with words that generate clarity and energy.

Specific Nouns

Make it a habit to use specific nouns for subjects. General nouns *(woman, school)* give the reader a vague, uninteresting picture. More specific nouns *(actress, university)* give the reader a better picture. Finally, very specific nouns *(Meryl Streep, Notre Dame)* are the type that can make your writing clear and colorful.

GENERAL TO SPECIFIC NOUNS

Person	Place	Thing	Idea
woman	school	book	theory
actor	university	novel	scientific theory
Meryl Streep	Notre Dame	*Pride and Prejudice*	relativity

Vivid Verbs

Like nouns, verbs can be too general to create a vivid word picture. For example, the verb *looked* does not say the same thing as *stared, glared, glanced,* or *peeked.*

- Whenever possible, use a verb that is strong enough to stand alone without the help of an adverb.

  Verb and adverb: John fell down in the student lounge.
  Vivid verb: John **collapsed** in the student lounge.

- Avoid overusing the "be" verbs *(is, are, was, were)* and helping verbs. Often a main verb can be made from another word in the same sentence.

  A "be" verb: Cole is someone who follows international news.
  A stronger verb: Cole **follows** international news.

- Use active rather than passive verbs. (Use passive verbs only if you want to downplay who is performing the action in a sentence. See page 80.)

  Passive verb: Another provocative essay was submitted by Kim.
  Active verb: Kim **submitted** another provocative essay.

- Use verbs that show rather than tell.

  A verb that tells: Dr. Lewis is very thorough.
  A verb that shows: Dr. Lewis **prepares** detailed, interactive lectures.

Replace jargon and clichés.

Replace language that is overly technical or difficult to understand. Also replace overused, worn-out words.

Understandable Language

Jargon is language used in a certain profession or by a particular group of people. It may be acceptable to use if your audience is that group of people, but to most ears jargon will sound technical and unnatural.

Jargon: The bottom line is that our output is not within our game plan.

Clear: Production is not on schedule.

Jargon: I'm having conceptual difficulty with these academic queries.

Clear: I don't understand these review questions.

Jargon: Pursuant to our conversation, I have forwarded you a remittance attached herewith.

Clear: As we discussed, I am mailing you the check.

Fresh and Original Writing

Clichés are overused words or phrases. They give the reader no fresh view and no concrete picture. Because clichés spring quickly to mind (for both the writer and the reader), they are easy to write and often slip by.

an axe to grind	piece of cake
as good as dead	planting the seed
beat around the bush	rearing its ugly head
between a rock and a hard place	stick your neck out
burning bridges	throwing your weight around
easy as pie	up a creek

Purpose and Voice

Other aspects of your writing may also be tired and overworked. Be alert to the two types of clichés described below.

Clichés of Purpose:

- Sentimental papers gushing about an ideal friend or family member, or droning on about a moving experience
- Overused topics with recycled information and predictable examples

Clichés of Voice:

- Writing that assumes a false sense of authority: "I have determined that there are three basic types of newspapers. My preference is for the third."
- Writing that speaks with little or no sense of authority: "I flipped when I saw *Viewpoints*."

Change biased words.

When depicting individuals or groups according to their differences, you must use language that implies equal value and respect for all people.

Words Referring to Ethnicity

Acceptable General Terms	*Acceptable Specific Terms*
American Indians, Native Americans	**Cherokee people, Inuit people,** and so forth
Asian Americans (not *Orientals*)	**Chinese Americans, Japanese Americans,** and so forth
Latinos, Latinas, Hispanics	**Mexican Americans, Cuban Americans,** and so forth

African Americans, blacks
"African American" has come into wide acceptance, though the term "black" is preferred by some individuals.

Anglo Americans (English ancestry), **European Americans**
Use these terms to avoid the notion that "American," used alone, means "white."

ADDITIONAL REFERENCES

Not Recommended	*Preferred*
Eurasian, mulatto	**person of mixed ancestry**
nonwhite	**person of color**
Caucasian	**white**
American (to mean U.S. citizen)	**U.S. citizen**

Words Referring to Age

Age Group	*Acceptable Terms*
up to age 13 or 14	**boys, girls**
between 13 and 19	**youth, young people, young men, young women**
late teens and 20s	**young adults, young women, young men**
30s to age 60	**adults, men, women**
60 and older	**older adults, older people** (not *elderly*)
65 and older	**seniors** (**senior citizens** also acceptable)

INSIGHT: Whenever you write about a person with a disability, an impairment, or other special condition, give the person and your readers the utmost respect. Nothing is more distracting to a reader than an insensitive or outdated reference.

Words Referring to Disabilities or Impairments

In the recent past, some writers were choosing alternatives to the term *disabled*, including *physically challenged, exceptional,* or *special.* However, it is not generally held that these new terms are precise enough to serve those who live with disabilities. Of course, degrading labels such as *crippled, invalid,* and *maimed,* as well as overly negative terminology, must be avoided.

Not Recommended	*Preferred*
handicapped	disabled
birth defect	congenital disability
stutter, stammer, lisp	speech impairment
an AIDS victim	person with AIDS
suffering from cancer	person who has cancer
mechanical foot	prosthetic foot
false teeth	dentures

Words Referring to Conditions

People with various disabilities and conditions have sometimes been referred to as though they *were* their condition (*quadriplegics, depressives, epileptics*) instead of people who simply happen to have a particular disability. As much as possible, remember to refer to the person first, the disability second.

Not Recommended	*Preferred*
the disabled	people with disabilities
cripples	people who have difficulty walking
the retarded	people with a developmental disability
dyslexics	students with dyslexia
neurotics	patients with neuroses
subjects, cases	participants, patients
quadriplegics	people who are quadriplegic
wheelchair users	people who use wheelchairs

Additional Terms

Make sure you understand the following terms that address specific impairments:

hearing impairment	=	partial hearing loss, hard of hearing (not *deaf*, which is total loss of hearing)
visual impairment	=	partially sighted (not *blind*, which is total loss of vision)
communicative disorder	=	speech, hearing, and learning disabilities affecting communication

Words Referring to Gender

- Use parallel language for both sexes:

  The **men** and the **women** rebuilt the school together.

  Hank and **Marie**

  Mr. Robert Gumble, Mrs. Joy Gumble

  Note: The courtesy titles *Mr., Ms., Mrs.,* and *Miss* ought to be used according to the person's preference.

- Use nonsexist alternatives to words with masculine connotations:

  humanity (not *mankind*)   **synthetic** (not *man-made*)

  artisan (not *craftsman*)

- Do not use masculine-only or feminine-only pronouns *(he, she, his, her)* when you want to refer to a human being in general:

  A politician can kiss privacy good-bye when **he** runs for office. (not recommended)

  Instead, use *he or she,* change the sentence to plural, or eliminate the pronoun:

  A politician can kiss privacy good-bye when **he or she** runs for office.

  Politicians can kiss privacy good-bye when **they** run for office.

  A politician can kiss privacy good-bye when running for office.

- Do not use gender-specific references in the salutation of a business letter when you don't know the person's name:

  Dear Sir: Dear Gentlemen: (neither is recommended)

  Instead, address a position:

  Dear Personnel Officer:

  Dear Members of the Economic Committee:

Occupational Issues

Not Recommended	*Preferred*
chairman	**chair, presiding officer, moderator**
salesman	**sales representative, salesperson**
mailman	**mail carrier, postal worker, letter carrier**
insurance man	**insurance agent**
fireman	**firefighter**
businessman	**executive, manager, businessperson**
congressman	**member of Congress, representative, senator**
steward, stewardess	**flight attendant**
policeman, policewoman	**police officer**

Proofreading Your Writing

The following guidelines will help you check your revised writing for spelling, mechanics, usage, grammar, and form.

Web Link

Review punctuation and mechanics.

1. **Check for proper use of commas** before coordinating conjunctions in compound sentences, after introductory clauses and long introductory phrases, between items in a series, and so on.
2. **Look for apostrophes** in contractions, plurals, and possessive nouns.
3. **Examine quotation marks** in quoted information, titles, or dialogue.
4. **Watch for proper use of capital letters** for first words in written conversation and for proper names of people, places, and things.

Look for usage and grammar errors.

1. **Look for misuse of any commonly mixed-up words:** *there/their/they're; accept/except.*
2. **Check for verb use.** Subjects and verbs should agree in number: Singular subjects go with singular verbs; plural subjects go with plural verbs. Verb tenses should be consistent throughout.
3. **Review for pronoun/antecedent agreement problems.** A pronoun and its antecedent must agree in number.

Check for spelling errors.

1. **Use a spell checker.** Your spell checker will catch most errors.
2. **Check each spelling you are unsure of.** Especially check those proper names and other special words your spell checker won't know.

Check the writing for form and presentation.

1. **Note the title.** A title should be appropriate and lead into the writing.
2. **Examine any quoted or cited material.** Are all sources of information properly presented and documented? (See pages **493–534** and **535–566**.)
3. **Look over the finished copy of your writing.** Does it meet the requirements for a final manuscript? (See page **134**.)

Writing with Sources

When you edit and proofread your writing, you sweat the small stuff—sentence style and word choice, grammatical correctness and punctuation, usage and spelling. When you are writing with sources, you need to sweat additional stuff—documentation, for example. For help, follow the guidelines below.

Think rhetorically.

As noted on page 30, when editing you need to consider the rhetorical situation: your writing's goal, your audience, and your subject. Correctly cited sources smoothly integrated into your writing establish your authority with the *subject*, build credibility with your *reader*, and help you achieve your writing *goal*.

Practice editing and proofreading strategies.

For a full treatment of editing issues related to sources, see chapters 32 and 33. However, to get started on a close edit for proper treatment of sources in your writing, check your paper for these issues.

Respect for Sources: Your draft needs to show respect for sources and for your reader. Test your writing for lapses, especially when you disagree with a source or press your reader to accept a position. And when the evidence itself is contradictory, incomplete, or uncertain, signal those limits with qualifiers such as *possibly, usually,* and *might.* (See pages 262–263 for more.)

Weak: The arguments that such slaves of the oil companies use to attack climate change are completely ignorant of the overwhelming evidence.

Strong: While researchers are right to be cautious about interpreting the climate-change evidence, the arguments used to question climate change are flawed.

Correct Summaries, Paraphrases, and Quotations: Check your use of sources for accuracy. Are summaries and paraphrases true to the original? Are your quotations word-for-word the same as the original? Have you attributed source material to the right source, with the author's name spelled correctly? Is the page number correct?

Correct Use of Historical Present Tense: Even though the sources you are using were written in the past, in a sense they still "speak" in the present. That's the logic behind what's called the historical present tense. Unless you are emphasizing the pastness of a source or its publication date in relation to other sources, use the present tense when conveying what an author says in the source.

Example: In his review of Alice Munro's 1996 *Selected Stories,* John Updike **offers** [not *offered*] the following assessment of the composite heroine at the heart of Munro's work: "She is neither virtuous nor a victim; what she is is vital" (11).

Correct Grammar with Quotations and Citations: Quotations need to be integrated into your sentences so that the syntax and punctuation are correct. Check especially for these issues:

- Proper use of commas and colons before source material, as well as end punctuation after source material
- Proper pronoun reference (When using a quotation in a sentence, make sure the pronouns in the quotation match the nouns and pronouns in the rest of the sentence.)
- Proper content, format, and punctuation for citations (For MLA rules, see pages **496–497**; for APA rules, see page **538**.)

Incorrect: As she explores her spiritual attraction to monasteries, Kathleen Norris clarifies that: "I am not a monk, although I have a formal relationship with the Benedictines as an oblate." (page 17)

Correct: As she explores her spiritual attraction to monasteries, Kathleen Norris states, "I am not a monk, although I have a formal relationship with the Benedictines as an oblate" (17).

Acknowledgment of Changes to and Errors in Quotations: Sometimes, you need to signal changes that you have made to quotations, changes that do not seriously change the meaning of the original but may be needed for clarity and conciseness. Brackets [] signal changes to words and letters; ellipses [. . .] signal that you have omitted words from the original; and the Latin [sic] signals that the preceding word contains an error (e.g., spelling) that was in the original source, not in your own writing. See page **489** for more details.

Example: As she explores her spiritual attraction to monasteries, Kathleen Norris clarifies that "[she is] not a monk, although [she has] a formal relationship with the Benedictines as an oblate . . . of a community of about sixty-five monks" (17).

Cross-Curricular Connections

Some editing issues related to writing with sources are discipline-specific. That is, different disciplines and their preferred documentation systems refer to sources differently, using different conventions, formats, and punctuation practices. For example, note the differences between the MLA and APA in-text citations below:

MLA: Some child prodigies "are not necessarily retarded or autistic—there have been itinerant calculators of normal intelligence as well" (Sacks 191).

APA: Some child prodigies "are not necessarily retarded or autistic—there have been itinerant calculators of normal intelligence as well" (Sacks, 1995, p. 191).

Editing and Proofreading Checklist

Use this checklist as a guide when you edit and proofread your writing. To see editing and proofreading in action, turn to pages 128–129.

Sentence Structure

_____ Sentences are clear, complete, and correct.

_____ Sentences flow smoothly and vary in terms of their lengths, beginnings, kinds (exclamatory, declarative), and arrangements (loose, periodic).

Word Choice

_____ The writing is free of vague words, jargon, and clichés.

_____ The language is unbiased and fair.

Correctness

_____ Spelling, punctuation, and mechanics are correct.

_____ Verb tenses are correct.

_____ Subjects agree with their verbs; pronouns agree with their antecedents.

_____ Research documentation is punctuated correctly.

_____ Formatting and design follow assigned instructions.

Critical-Thinking and Writing Activities

As directed by your instructor, complete the following activities.

1. The nineteenth-century British writer Matthew Arnold offers this advice to writers about refining their writing: "Have something to say and say it as clearly as you can. That is the only secret of style." Does your own writing clearly communicate a meaningful message? Explain why or why not.

2. Choose a writing assignment that you have recently completed. Edit the sentences in this writing for style and correctness using pages 94–101 as a guide. Then use pages 102–107 in this chapter to edit the piece of writing for vague words, jargon, clichés, and biased language.

3. Combine some of the following ideas into longer, more mature sentences. Write at least four sentences, using page 95 as a guide.

Dogs can be difficult to train. The necessary supplies include a leash and treats. Patience is also a necessity. Dogs like to please their owners. Training is not a chore for dogs. A well-trained dog is a pleasure to its owner.

◀ VISUALLY SPEAKING

The photograph on page 93 represents editing and proofreading. Reflect in writing on that image, relating it to the writing process and your own practices.

SUBMITTING WRITING AND CREATING PORTFOLIOS

Video

Submitting a final paper is the driving force behind writing. Doing so explains why you may have spent so much time planning, drafting, revising, and editing an essay or a paper in the first place—to share a finished piece of writing that effectively expresses your thoughts and feelings. Often, the most immediate and important form of submitting is sharing a finished piece of writing with your instructor and writing peers. As writer Tom Liner states, "You learn ways to improve your writing by seeing its effect on others."

You can also submit a piece of writing to a newspaper, journal, or website—or simply place it in your writing portfolio. This chapter will help you prepare your writing for virtually any audience or publication.

Formatting Your Writing

A good page design makes your writing clear and easy to follow. Keep that in mind when you produce a final copy of your writing.

Strive for clarity in page design.

Examine the following design elements, making sure that each is appropriate and clear in your project and in your writing.

Format and Documentation

Keep the design clear and uncluttered. Aim for a sharp, polished look in all your assigned writing.

Use the designated documentation form. Follow all the requirements outlined in the MLA (pages **493–534**) or APA (pages **535–566**) style guides.

Typography

Use an easy-to-read serif font for the main text. *Serif* type, like this, has "tails" at the tops and bottoms of the letters. For most types of writing, use a 10- or 12-point type size.

Consider using a sans serif font for the title and headings. Sans serif type, like this, does not have "tails." Use larger, perhaps 18-point, type for your title and 14-point type for any headings. You can also use boldface for headings if they seem to get lost on the page. (Follow your instructor's formatting guidelines.)

Because most people find a sans serif font easier to read on screen, consider a sans serif font for the body and a serif font for the titles and headings in any writing you publish online.

Spacing

Follow all requirements for indents and margins. This usually means indenting the first line of each paragraph five spaces, maintaining a one-inch margin around each page, and double-spacing throughout the paper.

Avoid widows and orphans. Avoid leaving headings, hyphenated words, or single lines of new paragraphs alone at the bottom of a page. Also avoid single words at the bottom of a page or carried over to the top of a new page.

Graphic Devices

Create bulleted or numbered lists to highlight important points. But, be selective; your writing should not include too many lists.

Include charts or other graphics. Graphics should neither be so small that they get lost on the page, nor so large that they overpower the page.

Submitting Writing and Creating Portfolios

Once you have formatted and proofread your final draft, you should be ready to share your writing. For college assignments, you will often simply turn in your paper to your instructor. However, you should also think about sharing your writing with other audiences, including those who will want to see your writing portfolio.

Consider potential audiences.

You could receive helpful feedback by taking any of the following steps:

- Share your writing with peers or family members.
- Submit your work to a local publication or an online journal.
- Post your writing on an appropriate website, including your own.
- Turn in your writing to your instructor.

Select appropriate submission methods.

There are two basic methods for submitting your work.

- **Paper submission:** Print an error-free copy on quality paper.
- **Electronic submission:** If allowed, send your writing as an e-mail attachment.

Use a writing portfolio.

There are two basic types of writing portfolios: (1) a *working portfolio* in which you store documents at various stages of development, and (2) a *showcase portfolio* with which you share appropriate finished work. For example, you could submit a portfolio to complete course requirements or to apply for a scholarship, graduate program, or job. The documents below are commonly included in a showcase portfolio:

- A table of contents listing the pieces included in your portfolio
- An opening essay or letter detailing the story behind your portfolio (how you compiled it and why it features the qualities expected by the intended reader)
- A specified number of—and types of—finished pieces
- A cover sheet attached to each piece of writing, discussing the reason for its selection, the amount of work that went into it, and so on
- Evaluation sheets or checklists charting the progress or experience you want to show related to issues of interest to the reader

Writing with Sources

For your writing project, submitting your paper and adding it to your portfolio clearly mark the end of the writing process. However, in a larger sense, these steps are simply mile markers on your writing journey. This is also the case when you are writing with sources: Sharing and collecting your writing signals your deepening participation in the world of research and research writing. To make this process productive, follow the guidelines below.

Think rhetorically.

Sharing your writing and building your portfolio are activities closely related to your rhetorical situation: your goals, your readers, and your subjects. For example, getting feedback from real *readers* helps you know whether you have achieved your *goals,* whether those goals are to entertain, to inform, to analyze, or to persuade. Similarly, adding a paper to your portfolio helps you see the range of *subjects* that you have addressed. When your writing is research-based, you should think about the following issues:

- **Your Goals:** How have submitting this paper and adding it to your portfolio helped you achieve specific aims as a researcher and a writer? Have you strengthened certain research skills, become familiar with important research tools, or learned about key resources? Have you improved your ability to think and write with researched information? Have you become more familiar with a specific form of research writing (e.g., literary interpretation, historical analysis, field report)?

- **Your Readers:** How has sharing your research writing deepened your participation in your major? How have you entered into or continued a dialogue with a specific research community (e.g., others in the discipline, experts on your topic, students on your campus, people looking for information on the web)?

- **Your Subjects:** How has writing on your topic added to the range of subjects on which you have written? How has researching this topic modified your understanding of other topics you have researched? Has this research project piqued your interest in conducting further research into this topic? Did you come across other interesting topics during research—topics you might research and write about in the future?

Practice submission and portfolio strategies.

When you submit research papers and add them to your writing portfolio, pay attention to helpful strategies such as these.

Follow submission guidelines. Double-check your assignment description to make sure that your paper meets your instructor's expectations. Have you followed all the format and citation rules of the system you are using (e.g., MLA, APA)? For example, are all of your in-text citations or notes properly keyed to entries in your bibliography? Finally, turn in print and/or electronic copies as directed by your instructor, and, if required, run your paper through a plagiarism detector such as www.Turnitin.com.

Analyze feedback on your paper. Your writing doesn't stop with submitting the paper and placing it in a portfolio. Study all the feedback you can get: your instructor's marginal notes and concluding comments, peer discussion of your research and thinking, responses to your online posting or website. What do these responses tell you about what you did well, what you need to work on, and what it means to participate in this research community?

Reflect on your research in a cover sheet. Instead of just placing a final copy of your paper in your portfolio, take time to reflect on what went well in your research and writing and what needs to be improved. Reflect on the project as a process of discovery and dialogue. Save these reflections and revisit them at the start of your next research project.

Save and track resources you used. Keep more of your research project than just the final copy of the paper. For comparison purposes, hold onto the first draft: That way, you can revisit which major changes you had to make. Moreover, keep a full bibliography of resources on the topic, including key reference works, books, journal articles, and web pages. In fact, if you have hard copies, printouts, and electronic copies of sources, collect them in folders (paper and/or electronic). You can use such bibliographies and folders not only to create a record of your research, but also to establish a resource that might prove useful for future research and writing.

Cross-Curricular Connections

When you turn in research writing in your major and when you add that writing to a portfolio, you achieve important goals in your discipline.

1. By writing a paper that carefully follows the format and documentation guidelines used in your major (e.g., MLA or APA style, business case study or chemistry lab report), you
   - work within your role as a scholar in the discipline.
   - show respect for your discipline's research methods.
   - participate in your discipline's research community.

2. When you add your paper to a portfolio, you
   - show the range of discipline-specific subjects with which you are becoming familiar through in-depth research and analysis.
   - generate a foundation of research writing on which to build in future projects, such as a senior thesis.
   - add to the writing samples that you can use for professional preparation, for an application for advanced training, or for a job search.

Submissions and Portfolio Checklist

Use the checklist below to review details regarding submitting your writing and building your portfolio.

_____ The submission method (such as an essay given to an instructor or posted on a website) is appropriate for my assignment, program, and career goals.

_____ The publishing process tests and develops my skills as a writer and scholar.

_____ The document's format (e.g., parts, headings, layout, margins, typography, and documentation) conforms to all of the instructor's guidelines.

_____ My portfolio documents address the types of topics and show the level of research and scholarship expected by my readers.

_____ The voice and style of my portfolio documents are appropriate for the kinds of writing done in the program or job for which I am applying.

_____ The portfolio includes an engaging essay or cover letter that clearly explains the portfolio's design, purpose, and focus.

Critical-Thinking and Writing Activities

As directed by your instructor, complete the following critical-thinking and writing activities by yourself or with classmates.

1. Catherine Drinker Bowen has argued the following: "Writing is not apart from living. Writing is a kind of double living." As you think about sharing your own writing and adding it to your writing portfolio, does this claim ring true? Why or why not?

2. Choose one of your recent writing assignments and use the instructions on page 112 to assess the quality of your formatting and page design. Edit and redesign the paper as needed.

3. For the class in which you are using this book, begin two working portfolios: (1) an electronic portfolio on your computer and (2) a paper portfolio in a sturdy folder or binder. In the electronic portfolio, store all drafts of your assignments, as well as all related electronic correspondence with your instructor. In your paper portfolio, store all printed drafts of your work, including copies that show your instructor's notations and grades.

◖ VISUALLY SPEAKING

The photograph on page 111 pictures a writer's sharing his or her writing in book form. How is this sharing similar to your submitting an assigned essay or portfolio?

ONE WRITER'S PROCESS 8

Audio

An essay is an attempt to understand a topic more deeply and clearly. That's one of the reasons this basic form of writing is essential in many college courses. It's a tool for both discovering and communicating.

How do you move from an assignment to a finished, polished essay? The best strategy is to take matters one step at a time, from understanding the assignment to submitting the final draft. Don't try to churn out the essay the night before it's due.

This chapter shows up close how student writer Angela Franco followed the writing process outlined in chapters 2 through 7.

Video

Audio

Angela's Assignment and Response

In this chapter you will follow student Angela Franco as she writes an assigned essay for her Environmental Policies class. Start by carefully reading the assignment and discussion below, noting how she thinks through the assignment's purpose, audience, form, and assessment method.

Angela examined the assignment.

Angela carefully read her assignment and responded with the notes below.

"Explain in a two- to three-page essay how a recent environmental issue is relevant to the world community. Using *The College Writer* as your guide, format the paper and document sources in APA style, but omit the title page and abstract. You may seek revising help from a classmate or from the writing center."

Subject

- *The subject is a recent environmental issue.*

Purpose

- *My purpose is to explain how the issue is relevant to all people. That means I must show how this issue affects my audience— both positively and negatively.*

Audience

- *My audience will be people like me—neighbors, classmates, and community members.*
- *I'll need to keep in mind what they already know and what they need to know.*

Form

- *I need to write a two- to three-page essay—that sounds formal.*
- *I'll need to include a thesis statement, as well as references to my sources using APA style.*

Assessment

- *I'll use the guidelines and checklists in the handbook to evaluate and revise my writing.*
- *I'll get editing feedback from Jeanie and from the writing center.*

TIP: For each step in the writing process, choose strategies that fit your writing situation. For example, a personal essay in an English class might require significant time getting started, whereas a lab report in a chemistry class might require little or none.

Angela explored and narrowed her assignment.

Video

Angela explored her assignment and narrowed its focus by clustering and freewriting.

Angela's Cluster

When she considered environmental issues, Angela first thought of water pollution as a possible topic for her essay. After writing the phrase in the center of her page, she drew from memories, experiences, and readings to list related ideas and details. Notice how she used three different-colored inks to distinguish the topic (blue) from ideas (red) and details (green).

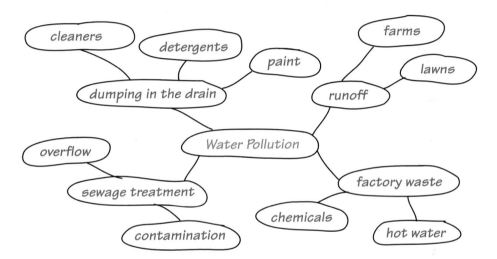

Angela's Freewriting

Angela decided to freewrite about the water pollution caused a few years earlier by improper sewage treatment in a small Canadian town.

I remember reading an article about problems in a small Canadian town. People actually died. The water they drank was contaminated. This is becoming a problem in developed countries like ours. I thought for a long time this was a problem only in developing countries. So who is responsible for sewage treatment? Who guarantees the safety of our drinking water? How does water get contaminated? Are there solutions for every kind of contamination: mercury, PCBs, sewage?

Angela's Narrowed Assignment

Based on her freewriting, Angela rephrased her assignment to narrow its focus.

Explain in a two- to three-page essay how a recent water pollution problem in a small Canadian town is relevant to the world community.

Audio

Angela's Planning

Angela reviewed her narrowed assignment and reassessed her topic.

Narrowed Writing Assignment

Explain in a two- to three-page essay how a recent water pollution problem in a small Canadian town is relevant to the world community.

Video

Angela focused her topic.

To focus her topic, Angela answered the journalistic questions (five Ws and H).

Topic: Water pollution in a small Canadian town

Who?	*- Farm operators, wastewater officials, Walkerton residents*
What?	*- Water supply contaminated*
	- Spread bacteria (E. coli)
	- Caused disease
	- Clean, fresh water depleted
Where?	*- Walkerton, Ontario*
When?	*- May 2000*
Why?	*- Improper regulation; human error*
How?	*- Groundwater from irrigation, untreated sewage, and runoff*

Angela researched the topic.

Angela then did some research to check her information and collect more details for her paper. She recorded all the essential data on each source and then listed the specific details related to her topic. Here's one source:

Nikiforuk, Andrew. (2000, June 12) "When Water Kills." <u>Maclean's</u>. pp. 18–21.

- *Factory farms hold as many as 25,000 cattle*
- *Manure contains things like heavy metals (from mineral-rich feed), nutrients, and pathogens (E. coli)*
- *8,000 hogs can produce as much waste as 240,000 people*
- *Six rural Ontario counties had high E. coli O157 levels in 1990 and 1995*

TIP: During your research, take time to create or copy visuals (charts, graphs, or photos) that clarify details about which you're writing. If you copy an item, be sure to correctly record the source as well. To create your own graphic, gather the data that you want to present, and then choose the type of graphic (table, pie graph, bar graph) that best displays your point.

Angela decided how to organize her writing.

With a focus selected, Angela used the three guidelines below to choose the best organizational pattern for her writing.

Guidelines

1. **Review your assignment and record your response.**

Assignment: Explain in a two- to three-page essay how a recent environmental issue is relevant to the world community.

Response: *My assignment clearly states that I need to explain my topic, so I have a general idea of how my paper will be organized.*

2. **Decide on your thesis statement and think about your essay's possible content and organization.**

Thesis Statement: The water pollution incident in Walkerton, Ontario, had a devastating effect that every town should learn from.

Reflection: *After reading my thesis statement, it's obvious that I'm going to be writing about a problem and its causes.*

3. **Choose an overall method and reflect on its potential effectiveness.**

Reflection: *Looking at the list of methods, I see that I can use cause/ effect or problem/solution. After making two quick lists of my main points using both approaches, I decided to use a problem/ solution approach. I will still talk about causes and effects in my essay—they just won't be front and center.*

With problem/solution, I need to first present the problem clearly so that readers can fully understand it and see why it's important. Then I need to explore solutions to the problem—maybe what they did in Walkerton and what we all need to do to make water safe.

TIP: Many essays you write will be organized according to one basic method or approach. However, within that basic structure you may want to include other methods. For example, while developing a comparison essay you may do some describing or classifying. In other words, you should choose methods of development that (1) help you understand the topic and (2) help your readers understand your message.

Audio

Angela's First Draft

After composing her opening, middle, and closing paragraphs, Angela put together her first draft. She then added a working title.

Video

The writer uses a series of images to get the reader's attention.

The thesis statement (boldfaced) introduces the subject.

Video

The writer describes the cause of the problem.

The writer indicates some of her source material with a citation.

Water Woes

It's a hot day. Several people just finished mowing their lawns. A group of bicyclists—more than 3,000—have been passing through your picturesque town all afternoon. Dozens of Little Leaguers are batting, running, and sweating. What do all these people have in common? They all drinks lots of tap water, especially on hot summer days. They also take for granted that the water is clean and safe. But in reality, the water they drink could be contaminated and pose a serious health risk. **That's just what happened in Walkerton, Ontario, where a water pollution incident had a devastating effect that every town can learn from.**   *1*

What happened in Walkerton Ontario? Heavy rains fell on May 12. It wasn't until May 21 that the townspeople were advised to boil their drinking water. The rains washed cattle manure into the town well. The manure contained E coli, a type of bacteria. E coli is harmless to cattle. It can make people sick. Seven days after the heavy rains, people began calling public health officials. The warning came too late. Two people had already died (Wickens, 2000).   *2*

Once Walkerton's problem was identified, the solutions were known. The government acted quickly to help the community and to clean the water supply. One Canadian newspaper reported that a $100,000 emergency fund was set up to help families with expenses. Bottled water for drinking and containers of bleach for sanitizing and cleaning were donated by local businesses.   *3*

So what messed up Walkerton? Basically, people screwed up! According to one news story, a flaw in the water treatment system allowed the bacteria-infested water to enter the well. The manure washed into the well, but the chlorine should have killed the deadly bacteria. In Walkerton, the PUC group fell asleep at the wheel.

4

The writer covers the solutions that were used to resolve the problem.

At last, the Provincial Clean Water Agency restored the main water and sewage systems by flushing out all of the town's pipes and wells. The ban on drinking Walkerton's water was finally lifted seven months after the water became contaminated.

5

The concluding paragraph stresses the importance of public awareness.

Could any good come from Walkerton's tragedy? Does it have a silver lining? It is possible that more people are aware that water may be contaminated. Today people are beginning to take responsibility for the purity of the water they and their families drink. In the end, more and more people will know about the dangers of contaminated water—without learning it the hard way.

6

Video

Angela kept a working bibliography.

As she researched her topic, Angela kept a working bibliography—a list of resources that she thought might offer information helpful to her essay. During the writing process, she deleted some resources, added others, and edited the document that became the references page on page 133.

Working References

Wickens, Barbara. (2000, June 5), Tragedy in Walkerton.
   Macleans' 113 (23): 34–36.
Phone interview with Alex Johnson, Walkerton Police
   Department, 23 September 2007.
Blackwell, Thomas (2001, January 9). Walkerton doctor defends
   response. *The Edmonton Journal*.
   http://edmontonjournal.com.

Video

Audio

Angela's First Revision

After finishing the first draft, Angela set it aside. When she was ready to revise it, she looked carefully at global issues—ideas, organization, and voice. She wrote notes to herself to help keep her thoughts together.

Angela's comments

Water Woes

an unusually Saturday afternoon ☺

It's ᴧa̶ hot ~~day.~~ Several people just finished mowing their
                                pedal up the street
lawns. A group of bicyclists ~~—more than 3,000—have been~~
~~passing through your picturesque town all afternoon.~~ Dozens of
Little Leaguers are batting, running, and sweating. What do all
these people have in common? They all drink lots of tap water,
especially on hot summer days. They also take for granted that
the water is clean and safe. But in reality, the water they drink
could be contaminated and pose a serious health risk. That's just
what happened in Walkerton, Ontario, where a water pollution
incident had a devastating effect that every town can learn from.

What happened in Walkerton, Ontario? Heavy rains fell on
May 12. [It wasn't until May 21 that the townspeople were
advised to boil their drinking water.] The rains washed cattle
manure into the town well. The manure contained E coli, a type
of bacteria. E coli is harmless to cattle. It can make people sick.
Seven days after the heavy rains, people began calling public
health officials. The warning came too late. Two people had
already died (Wickens, 2000).

Once Walkerton's problem was identified, the solutions were
known. The government acted quickly to help the community
and to clean the water supply. One Canadian newspaper reported
that a $100,000 emergency fund was set up to help families
with expenses. Bottled water for drinking and containers of
bleach for sanitizing and cleaning were donated
by local businesses.

Side notes:

- I need to give my opening more energy.
- Does my thesis still fit the paper?— Yes.
- Using time sequence, put this paragraph in better order.
- Move this paragraph—it interrupts the discussion of causes.

1

2

3

My voice here is too informal.

went wrong in   Human error was a critical factor.
So what ~~messed up~~ Walkerton? ~~Basically, people screwed~~ 4
~~up!~~ First, According to one news story, a flaw in the water treatment
system allowed the bacteria-infested water to enter the well. *Even after* The
manure washed into the well, ~~but~~ the chlorine should have killed
the deadly bacteria. In Walkerton, the ~~PUC group fell asleep at~~
~~the wheel.~~

Explain "fell asleep." Move paragraph three here and combine.

In addition,
~~At last~~ the Provincial Clean Water Agency restored the 5
main water and sewage systems by flushing out all of the
town's pipes and wells. The ban on drinking Walkerton's
water was finally lifted seven months after the water became
contaminated.

Could any good come from Walkerton's tragedy? ~~Does it~~ 6
Cut the clichés.
~~have a silver lining?~~ It is possible that more people are aware
that water may be contaminated. Today people are beginning to
take responsibility for the purity of the water they and their
families drink. In the end, more and more people will know
about the dangers of contaminated water—without learning it
the hard way.

*Public Utilities Commission was responsible for overseeing
the testing and treating of the town's water, but they
failed to monitor it properly. Apparently, shortcuts were
taken when tracking the water's chlorine level, and as a
result, some of the water samples were mislabeled. There
was also a significant delay between the time that the
contamination was identified and the time it was reported.*

Video

Angela's Second Revision

Next, Angela asked a peer to review her work. His comments are in the margin. Angela used them to make additional changes, including writing a new opening and closing.

Water Woes

WARNING: City tap water is polluted with animal waste. Using the water for drinking, cooking, or bathing could cause sickness or death.   *1*

Could you make the opening more relevant and urgent?

According to the Seirra Club, run-off pollutants from farm cites are steadily seeping into our streams, lakes, reservoirs and wells. Because much of our drinking water comes from these resources, warnings like the one above are already posted in a number of U.S. and Canadian communities, and many more postings will be needed (Sierra Club, 2005).   *2*

Could you clarify your focus on the topic?

As the Seirra Club argues, the pollution and related warnings are serious, and failure to take them seriously could be deadly. For example, a few years ago the citizens of Walkerton Ontario learned that the water that they believed to be clean was actually poisoned.

The events ~~What happened~~ *began* in Walkerton, ~~Ontario? Heavy rains fell~~ *2000, when heavy rains* on May 12, ~~The rains~~ washed cattle manure into the town well. The manure contained E coli, a type of bacteria. E coli is harmless to cattle. It can make people sick. Seven days after   *3*

Add the year and other specific details.

to complain of nausea and diarrhea ⊙ the heavy rains, people began calling public health officials. It wasn't until May 21 that the townspeople were advised to boil their drinking water. The warning came too late. Two people had *, and more than 2,000 were ill* already died (Wickens, 2000).

Make sure you document all source material— you have just one citation in your draft.

Several factors contributed to the terrible tragedy in Walkerton, ~~So what went wrong in Walkerton? Human error was a~~ *including human error.*   *The Edmonton Journal* ~~critical factor.~~ First, according to ~~one news story,~~ a flaw in the water treatment system allowed the bacteria-infested water to *(Blackwell, 2001)* ⊙ enter the well. Even after the manure washed into the well, the chlorine should have killed the deadly bacteria. In Walkerton, the Public Utilities Commission was responsible for overseeing   *4* the testing and treating of the town's water, but it failed to monitor it properly. Apparently, shortcuts were taken when tracking the water's chlorine level, and as a result, some of the water samples were mislabeled. There was also a significant delay between the time that the contamination was identified and the time it was reported.

Once Walkerton's problem was identified, the ~~solutions were known.~~ The government acted quickly to help the community ~~and to clean the water supply.~~ One Canadian newspaper, *The Edmonton Journal*, reported a $100,000 emergency fund was set up to help families with expenses. *Local businesses donated* Bottled water for drinking and containers of bleach for basic sanitizing and cleaning ~~were donated by local businesses.~~ In addition, the Provincial Clean Water Agency restored the main water and sewage systems by flushing out all of the town's pipes and wells. The ban on drinking Walkerton's water was finally lifted seven months after the water became contaminated.

Use active voice.

As the Sierra Club warned and the citizens of Walkerton learned, water purity is a life-and-death issue. Fortunately, both the United States and Canada have been addressing the problem. For example, since 2001, more states and provinces are tightening their clean-water standards, more communities have begun monitoring their water quality, and more individuals have been using water-filtration systems, bottled water, or boiled tap water. However, a tragedy like that in Walkerton could happen again. To avoid such horror, all of us must get involved by demanding clean tap water in our communities and by promoting the polices and procedures needed to achieve that goal.

Consider adding details— maybe an entire paragraph— calling readers to action, and stating your thesis clearly.

4

5

Video

Audio

Angela's Edited Draft

When Angela began editing, she read each of her sentences aloud to check for clarity and smoothness. **The first page of Angela's edited copy is shown below.**

The writer revises the title.

Water Woes *in Walkerton*

> *Warning: City tap water is polluted with animal waste. Using the water for drinking, cooking, or bathing could cause sickness or death.*

According to the Seirra Club, run-off pollutants from farm cites are steadily seeping into our streams, lakes, reservoirs, and wells. Because much of our drinking water comes from these resources, warnings like the one above are already posted in a number of U.S. and Canadian communities, and many more postings *might* ~~will~~ be needed *in the future* (Sierra Club, 2005). As the Seirra Club argues, the pollution and related warnings are serious, and failure to take them seriously could be deadly. For example, a few years ago the citizens of Walkerton Ontario learned that the water that they believed to be clean was *tragically* ~~actually~~ poisoned.

She qualifies her statement, replacing "will" with "might"

The events in Walkerton began on May 12, 2000, when heavy rains washed cattle manure into the town well. The manure contained ~~E coli,~~ a bacteria. *commonly called* E coli *While E coli* is harmless to cattle. It can make people sick. Seven days after the heavy rains, people began calling public health officials to complain of nausea and diarrhea. It wasn't until May 21 that the townspeople were advised to boil their drinking water. The warning came too late. Two people had already died, and more than 2,000 were ill (Wickens, 2000).

She rewrites and combines several choppy sentences.

Several factors contributed to the ~~terrible~~ tragedy in Walkerton, including human error. First, according to *The Edmonton Journal*, a flaw in the water treatment system allowed the ~~bacteria~~-infested water to enter the well (Blackwell, 2001). Even after the manure washed into the well, the chlorine . . .

Angela deletes unnecessary words.

1

2

3

Angela's Proofread Draft

Angela reviewed her edited copy for punctuation, agreement issues, and spelling. **The first page of Angela's proofread essay is shown below.**

Video

Water Woes in Walkerton

> *Warning: City tap water is polluted with animal waste. Using the water for drinking, cooking, or bathing could cause sickness or death.*

The writer corrects errors that the spell checker did not pick up.

According to the Sierra Club, run-off pollutants from farm sites are steadily seeping into our streams, lakes, reservoirs, and wells. Because much of our drinking water comes from these resources, warnings like the one above are already posted in a number of U.S. and Canadian communities, and many more postings might be needed in the future (Sierra Club, 2005). As the Sierra Club argues, the pollution and related warnings are serious, and failure to take them seriously could be deadly.

She adds a comma between the city and province.

For example, a few years ago the citizens of Walkerton, Ontario, learned that the water that they believed to be clean was tragically poisoned.

She adds periods and italicizes "E. coli" to show that it is a scientific term.

The events in Walkerton began on May 12, 2000, when heavy rains washed cattle manure into the town well. The manure contained bacteria commonly called *E. coli*. While *E. coli* is harmless to cattle, it can make people sick. Seven days after the heavy rains, people began calling public health officials to complain of nausea and diarrhea. It wasn't until May 21 that the townspeople were advised to boil their drinking water. The warning came too late. Two people had already died, and more than 2,000 were ill (Wickens, 2000).

She adds a word for clarity.

Several factors contributed to the tragedy in Walkerton, including human error. First, according to *The Edmonton Journal*, a flaw in the water treatment system allowed the infested water to enter Walkerton's well (Blackwell, 2001). Even after the manure washed ~~into the well,~~ *into Walkerton's well* the chlorine should have . . .

1

2

3

Angela's Finished Essay

After proofreading and formatting her essay, Angela added a heading and page numbers. She also added more documentation and a references page at the end. As assigned, she omitted the title page and abstract.

Clean Water Is Everyone's Business 1

Angela Franco

Professor Kim Van Es

English 101

October 10, 2008

Clean Water Is Everyone's Business

> Warning: City tap water is polluted with animal waste. Using the water for drinking, cooking, or bathing could cause sickness or death.

According to the Sierra Club, run-off pollutants from farm sites are steadily seeping into our streams, lakes, reservoirs, and wells. Because much of our drinking water comes from these resources, warnings like the one above are already posted in a number of U.S. and Canadian communities, and many more postings might be needed in the future (Sierra Club, 2005). As the Sierra Club argues, the pollution and related warnings are serious, and failure to take them seriously could be deadly. For example, a few years ago the citizens of Walkerton, Ontario, learned that the water that they believed to be clean was tragically poisoned.

The events in Walkerton began on May 12, 2000, when heavy rains washed cattle manure into the town well. The

Complete details are supplied in the heading.

The title is changed. The warning is emphasized with red print.

An appropriate font and type size are used.

1

2

Clean Water Is Everyone's Business 2

Title and page number are used on each page.

manure contained the bacteria commonly called *E. coli*. While *E. coli* is harmless to cattle, it can make people sick. Seven days after the heavy rains, people began calling public health officials to complain of nausea and diarrhea. It wasn't until May 21 that the townspeople were advised to boil their drinking water. The warning came too late. Two people had already died, and more than 2,000 were ill (Wickens, 2000).

Each claim or supporting point is backed up with reasoning and evidence.

Several factors contributed to the tragedy in Walkerton, including human error. First, according to *The Edmonton Journal*, a flaw in the water treatment system allowed the infested water to enter Walkerton's well (Blackwell, 2001). Even after the manure washed into Walkerton's well, the chlorine should have killed the deadly bacteria. In Walkerton, the Public Utilities Commission was responsible for overseeing the testing and treating of the town's water, but it failed to monitor the procedure properly ("Walkerton's water-safety," 2000). Apparently, shortcuts were taken when tracking the water's chlorine level, and as a result, some of the water samples were mislabeled. There was also a significant delay between the time that the contamination was identified and the time it was reported.

The writer continues to give credit throughout the essay.

Once Walkerton's problem was identified, the government acted quickly to help the community. In its December 7, 2000, edition, *The Edmonton Journal* reported that a $100,000 emergency fund was set up to help families with expenses. Local businesses donated bottled water for drinking and containers of bleach for basic sanitizing and cleaning. In addition, the Provincial

Clean Water Is Everyone's Business 3

Clean Water Agency restored the main water and sewage systems by flushing out all of the town's pipes and wells. Seven months after the water became contaminated, the ban on drinking Walkerton's water was finally lifted.

As the Sierra Club warns and the citizens of Walkerton   5 learned, water purity is a life-and-death issue. Fortunately, both the United States and Canada have been addressing the problem. For example, since 2001, more states and provinces have been tightening their clean-water standards, more communities have been monitoring their water quality, and more individuals have been using water-filtration sytems, bottled water, or boiled tap water. However, a tragedy like that in Walkerton could happen again. To avoid such horror, all of us must get involved by demanding clean tap water in our communities and by promoting the policies and procedures needed to achieve that goal.

The writer restates her thesis in the last sentence.

Clean Water Is Everyone's Business 4

References

Blackwell, T. (2001, January 9). Walkerton doctor defends response. *The Edmonton Journal*. Retrieved September 22, 2008, from <http://edmontonjournal.com>.

Sierra Club. (n.d.) Water sentinels: Keeping it clean around the U.S.A. Retrieved September 24, 2008, from <http://sierraclub.org/watersentinels/>.

Walkerton's water-safety tests falsified regularly, utility official admits. (2000, December 7). *The Edmonton Journal*. Retrieved April 2, 2005, from <http://edmontonjournal.com>.

Wickens, B. (2000, June 5). Tragedy in Walkerton. *Maclean's*, *113*(23), 34–36.

Sources used are listed correctly, in alphabetical order.

Each entry follows APA rules for content, format, and punctuation.

Critical-Thinking and Writing Activities

Complete these activities by yourself or with classmates.

1. Scott Russell Sanders suggests that "essays are experiments in making sense of things." Does Sanders' statement ring true? What makes such experiments flop or succeed? What kinds of "sense" do essays create?

2. Review Angela's writing process. How does it compare with your own writing process on a recent assignment?

3. Review the peer-editing instructions in "Revising Collaboratively" (pages 87–88). Then reread the reviewer's comments in the margins of Angela's second revision (pages 126–127). Do the comments reflect the instructions? Explain.

◆ VISUALLY SPEAKING

Revisit the photograph on page 117. Then explain what the picture suggests about Angela's writing process shown in this chapter—and your own writing process.

Effective Writing Checklist

Check your finished work using these traits or standards as a guide.

Stimulating Ideas *The writing . . .*

_____ presents interesting and important information.

_____ maintains a clear focus or purpose—centered on a thesis, theme, concern, or question.

_____ develops the focus through a line of thought or reasoning elaborated with sufficient details or evidence.

_____ holds the reader's attention (and answers her or his questions).

Logical Organization

_____ includes a clear beginning, middle, and ending.

_____ contains specific details, arranged in an order that builds understanding with readers.

_____ uses transitions to link sentences and paragraphs.

Engaging Voice

_____ speaks in a sincere, natural way that fits the writing situation.

_____ shows that the writer really cares about the subject.

Appropriate Word Choice

_____ contains specific, clear words.

_____ uses a level of language appropriate for the type of writing and the audience.

Overall Fluency

_____ flows smoothly from sentence to sentence.

_____ displays varied sentence beginnings and lengths.

_____ follows a style that fits the situation (e.g., familiar versus academic).

Correct, Accurate Copy

_____ adheres to the rules of grammar, spelling, and punctuation.

_____ follows established documentation guidelines.

Reader-Friendly Design

_____ exhibits a polished, professional design in terms of overall format, page layout, and typographical choices.

_____ makes the document attractive and easy to read.

_____ is formatted correctly in MLA or APA style.

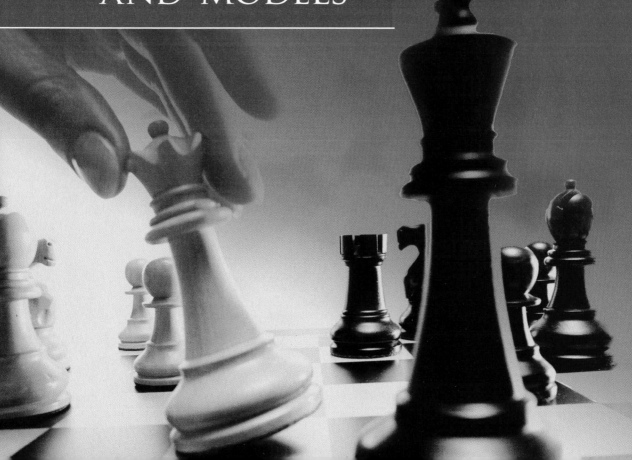

II

Reader:
STRATEGIES
AND MODELS

CONTENTS

Writing Across the Curriculum

9 Forms of College Writing

Three Curricular Divisions — **138**

Types of Writing in Each Division — **139**

Traits of Writing Across the Curriculum — **140**

FORMS OF
COLLEGE WRITING

9

Video

In college, professors in nearly all departments give writing assignments. Why? Because they know that writing helps you in two ways: (1) to learn course content and (2) to learn how to carry on a written dialogue with others in your field. In other words, writing will help you learn course material today, but it will also help you use that information in subsequent college courses and in the workplace.

The purpose of this chapter is to show you three important things about writing across the curriculum:

- How a college curriculum and faculty are organized
- What kinds of writing you can expect to do in your courses
- How writing and thinking skills required in one class are linked to writing and thinking skills required in another class

The chapter begins by showing the big picture: the three divisions into which most college curricula are divided, and the academic departments that constitute each division. The chapter then presents more specific information about academic departments, including the topics students study, the forms of writing teachers assign, and the traits of those forms.

Three Curricular Divisions

Based on each department's area of study and focus, the college curriculum is generally divided into three groups: humanities, social sciences, and natural and applied sciences. These groups are then subdivided into specific departments, such as biology, chemistry, and physics. Below you will find an explanation of each division, along with its more common departments.

Humanities

Scholars within this division study human culture, both past and present. They examine topics such as the history of civilization, cultural institutions and trends, religious beliefs and practices, languages and their use, and artwork and performance skills. Some departments in this division include the following:

Archeology	Ethnic Studies	Modern Languages	Theater Arts
Asian Studies	Film Studies	Music	Theology
Dance	Graphic Design	Philosophy	Visual Arts
English	History	Religion	Women's Studies

Social Sciences

Scholars in this division study human behavior and societies using research strategies adapted from the natural sciences. For example, a researcher may develop a hypothesis regarding a topic or phenomenon, and then devise an experiment to test that hypothesis. Students study economic systems, correctional programs, and personality disorders. Departments in this division include the following:

Anthropology	Economics	Geophysics	Psychology
Business	Education	Government	Social Work
Communication	Genetics	Health & Phys. Ed.	Sociology
Criminology	Geography	Political Science	Urban Planning

Natural and Applied Sciences

The natural sciences (such as biology, zoology, and chemistry) focus on specific aspects of nature, such as animal life, plant life, and molecular structures. In contrast, the applied sciences (such as mathematics, computer science, and engineering) consider how to use science-based information to understand concepts and develop artifacts. Here are some of the departments in this division:

Agriculture	Biology	Environment	Physics
Agronomy	Botany	Forestry	Physiology
Anatomy	Chemistry	Mathematics	Public Health
Architecture	Computer Science	Nutrition	Space Science
Astronomy	Engineering	Oceanography	Zoology

Types of Writing in Each Division

Listed below are the types of writing commonly assigned in the three academic divisions. Often instructors in different divisions will assign the same type of essay—but with a different purpose, audience, or focus. When an assigned form differs from the one shown in the book, adapt the guidelines in the book to the form stated in the assignment.

Humanities

Anecdotes (147–148)
Application Writing (390–396)
Cause and Effect (183–198)
Classification (215–228)
Comparison and Contrast (199–214)
Definition (243–256)
Describing a Process (229–242)
Description and Reflection (165–180)
Essay Test (377–382)
Interview Report (331–338)

Literary Analysis (355–372)
Narration and Description (145–164)
Oral Presentations (409–418)
Personal Essay (145–180)
Persuading Readers to Act (295–312)
Proposing a Solution (313–328)
Research Paper (493–534)
Taking a Position (275–294)
Test Taking (383–384)
Web Writing (397–408)

Social Sciences

Abstracts/Summaries (442–444)
Application Writing (390–396)
Cause and Effect (183–198)
Classification (215–228)
Comparison and Contrast (199–214)
Definition (243–256)
Describing a Process (229–242)
Description and Reflection (165–180)
Field Report (347–352)
Interview Report (331–338)

Literary Analysis (355–372)
Oral Presentations (409–418)
Personal Essay (145–180)
Persuading Readers to Act (295–312)
Proposing a Solution (313–328)
Surveys (449–451)
Taking a Position (275–294)
Test Taking (383–384)
Web Writing (397–408)

Natural and Applied Sciences

Abstracts/Summaries (442–444)
Application Writing (390–396)
Cause and Effect (183–198)
Classification (215–228)
Comparison and Contrast (199–214)
Definition (243–256)
Describing a Process (229–242)
Experiment Report (343–346)
Field Report (347–352)
Interview Report (331–338)

Lab Report (340–342)
Personal Essay (145–180)
Persuading Readers to Act (295–312)
Proposing a Solution (313–328)
Research Paper (475–490)
Surveys (449–451)
Test Taking (383–384)
Web Writing (397–408)

Traits of Writing Across the Curriculum

Listed below are the more common writing tasks in each of the three divisions, along with seven traits that distinguish good writing for each task.

Humanities

Idea: **Personal writing:** Explores the writer's ideas, experiences, and feelings

Organization: Usually chronological

Voice: Engaging, fits the story, honest, direct

Word Choice: Words are precise and fit the writer's topic, purpose, audience, and characters

Sentences: Appropriate for dialogue and description; others use varied forms

Correctness: Documentation (where necessary) follows MLA or CMS style

Design: Designed as an essay with proper formatting and typeface

---

Idea: **Analysis of a work of art:** Describes the work and analyzes its parts and how they function

Organization: Appropriate for the work and the writer's focus

Voice: Objective appraisal and analysis, supported by evidence

Word Choice: Appropriate for the art form; technical terms explained

Sentences: Varied in length and structure, with clear transitions

Correctness: Documentation follows MLA or CMS style

Design: Designed as an essay with proper formatting and typeface

---

Idea: **Argument supporting a claim:** Persuades reader regarding the point's meaning, importance, and truth

Organization: Order fits the topic and purpose: cause/effect, compare/contrast, and so on

Voice: Informed, impartial, inviting

Word Choice: Precise, with scholarly terms used in the discipline

Sentences: Tend to be longer; complexity fits the topic and audience

Correctness: Documentation follows MLA or CMS style

Design: Designed as an essay with proper formatting and typeface

---

Idea: **Analysis of a phenomenon:** Explains its meaning in relation to its historical, social, and/or natural context (e.g., Marxism)

Organization: Often combines cause/effect, compare/contrast, and examples

Voice: Scholarly, fair, informed, balanced

Word Choice: Precise, often including scholarly terms used in the discipline

Sentences: Tend to be longer; complexity fits the topic and audience

Correctness: Documentation follows MLA or CMS style

Design: Designed as an essay with proper formatting, typeface, and graphics

Social Sciences

Idea: **Case study:** Describes and analyzes the topic, identifies methodology, gives results

Organization: Gives overview, presents steps chronologically, analyzes outcome

Voice: Impartial reporting; respectful, thoughtful analysis

Word Choice: Precise statistics and discipline-related terms

Sentences: Medium-length sentences with clear transitions

Correctness: Documentation follows APA or CMS style

Design: Formatted as a report for easy reading and in accordance with the discipline's or department's style guide

---

Idea: **Literature review:** Summarizes and evaluates journal articles (usually research based) on a topic

Organization: Each article discussed separately followed by conclusions

Voice: Unbiased reporting, formal tone, logical analysis

Word Choice: Includes precise technical terms and statistics

Sentences: Shorter sentences and paragraphs with clear transitions

Correctness: Documentation follows APA or CMS style

Design: Formatted as a report for easy reading and in accordance with the discipline's or department's style guide

---

Idea: **Policy or project analysis:** Analyzes the topic, its history, and its effects

Organization: Analysis often uses cause/effect, classification, and compare/contrast

Voice: Impartial, informed, concerned, thoughtful

Word Choice: Includes precise technical terms and statistics

Sentences: Sentences are varied in length and structure, with clear transitions

Correctness: Documentation follows APA or CMS style

Design: Formatted as a report for easy reading and in accordance with the discipline's or department's style guide

---

Idea: **Process description:** Describes materials, steps in the process, and the importance of the process

Organization: Usually states topic and outcome, gives steps chronologically

Voice: Objective, yet concerned about effectiveness and safety

Word Choice: Precise, often including technical terms

Sentences: Description of a process—sentences tend to be short, direct, and in parallel form

Correctness: Documentation follows APA or CMS style

Design: Formatted as a report for easy reading and in accordance with the discipline's or department's style guide, or as workplace instructions with numbered steps and graphics

Natural and Applied Sciences

Idea: **Lab or experiment report:** Includes clear data, logical analysis, unbiased reporting

Organization: States issues and hypothesis, methods with procedure, results with data, discusses results

Voice: Interested, curious, impartial, logical, meticulous

Word Choice: Precise, often including scientific and technical terms

Sentences: Medium length, logical, passive voice only when needed

Correctness: Documentation and format follow CSE or APA style

Design: Formatted as a report in accordance with the discipline's style guide; graphics (such as tables, charts) are clear

---

Idea: **Field report:** Includes clear data and unbiased reporting

Organization: States focus and issues, methods with procedure, results with data, discusses results

Voice: Interested, curious, logical, meticulous

Word Choice: Precise, often including scientific and technical terms

Sentences: Medium length, logical, passive voice only when needed

Correctness: Documentation and format follow CSE or APA style

Design: Formatted as a report in accordance with the discipline's style guide; graphics (such as tables, photos) are strong

---

Idea: **Literature review:** Summarizes and compares journal articles (usually research based)

Organization: Each article discussed separately, followed by conclusions

Voice: Equitable reporting, formal tone, logical, clear analysis

Word Choice: Includes technical scientific words and concepts; first person rarely used

Sentences: Shorter sentences and paragraphs with clear transitions

Correctness: Documentation and format follow CSE or APA style

Design: Formatted as a report with proper spacing and typeface

---

Idea: **Process explanation:** Describes each step in a process

Organization: Usually states topic, gives steps chronologically, closes

Voice: Impartial, concerned about effectiveness and safety

Word Choice: Precise, often including scientific and technical terms

Sentences: Description of a process—sentences vary depending on the form; instructions—short, direct

Correctness: Description follows CSE or APA style

Design: Formatted as an essay or workplace instructions

Research and Documentation Websites
MLA Modern Language Association **www.mla.org**
APA American Psychological Association **www.apa.org**
CMS Chicago Manual of Style **www.press.uchicago.edu**
CSE Council of Science Editors **councilscienceeditors.org**

Note: CSE has replaced CBE *(Council of Biology Editors)*

NARRATIVE, DESCRIPTIVE, AND REFLECTIVE WRITING

Chapters 10 and 11 offer instruction in writing personal essays, pieces that focus on experience, especially the writer's experience—whether of places, people, or events—with the goal of vividly sharing that experience with readers. To that end, personal essays tend to be informal in voice and style, freely using personal pronouns such as "I" and "we." Note, too, that such writing depends on strategies of narration, description, and reflection. While virtually all personal essays blend the three techniques, chapter 10 focuses on the combination of narration and description, and chapter 11 focuses on the combination of description and reflection.

As with all forms of writing, you should develop your personal essays using whatever strategies fit your writing situation: your subject, audience, and purpose. For examples, watch how the authors of the essays in chapters 10 and 11 use not only the strategies narration, description, and reflection (commonly associated with personal writing), but also the strategies cause/effect, compare/contrast, and definition (often associated with analytical writing).

CONTENTS

Narrative, Descriptive, and Reflective Writing

10 Narration and Description ———————————————————————

Overview: Writing Narration and Description   **146**
   Student Model   **149**
   Professional Models   **152**
Guidelines   **162**
Writing Checklist and Activities   **164**

11 Description and Reflection ———————————————————————

Overview: Writing Description and Reflection   **166**
   Student Model   **167**
   Professional Models   **169**
Guidelines   **178**
Writing Checklist and Activities   **180**

NARRATION AND DESCRIPTION

10

A personal narrative is a story—a story that mirrors you and your experiences. In a narrative, you may tell about a time when you were afraid, lost something (or someone), found joy, learned a tough lesson, or discovered some secret. Whatever the topic, your story should help readers see, hear, touch, and taste those details that make your experience come alive. To do that, you must carefully describe key aspects of the experience.

As you prepare to share your story with others, get ready to relive it yourself— to reexperience all that you felt, thought, or sensed during the original event. But get ready also to learn something new about the event, about others, and even about yourself. That's what writing a personal narrative can do.

Audio

Video

Video

Web Link

Overview
Writing Narration and Description

Writer's Goal

Your goal is to write a personal narrative about something significant that has happened to you. Write in a way that allows your readers to vividly relive the experience and to learn something about you and about themselves.

Keys for Success

Be passionate. Choose an experience from your life, anchored in your memory, that still makes you feel happy, angry, humble, afraid, or some other strong emotion.

Include characters. Make the people in your narrative come to life. Let your story unfold through their actions and words. Above all, show how you—and these other people—react to the experience.

Create memorable descriptions. Choose details that create pictures in your readers' minds. First, use your senses to trigger the readers' senses. What did you see? What did you hear? Next, choose strong nouns and active verbs. Finally, show what happened—don't tell about it.

Topics to Consider

Memorable experiences can be categorized in a number of ways. Understanding these categories may help you identify possible subjects for your narratives. *Remember:* Your personal narratives should show something significant about you and about human nature in general.

- **Initiation:** Think of a time when you had to prove yourself, test your abilities, or "grow up." Share this "test" with your readers.
- **Loss:** Explore a time when you lost someone or something that was important to you.
- **Run-In:** Consider an unavoidable confrontation with another person. How did you react to the situation? What did you learn about yourself?
- **Arrival:** Recall when you were the new kid on the block or in school. How did the experience change your life? Or remember a time when someone new arrived in your life. How did this person affect you?
- **Occasion:** Focus on a revealing get-together, celebration, holiday, party, or vacation experience. What did you learn from the experience?

> **Next Step** Read the model essays and perform the activities that follow. As you read, think of "defining experiences" in your life. How did each shape you? Would your readers find something of value for themselves in your experiences? Would they sense the importance of your experience?

Personal Narrative

A common personal narrative is the anecdote—a short, direct story that adds spark to your writing while introducing a topic or illustrating an idea. Below and on the following page are three anecdotes taken from essays in this book.

Anecdote introducing a topic:

The story gets our attention and shows some causes and effects of stress.

It was 8:00 a.m.; her husband, Lance, had left for work without filling the tank on the Mazda; and her daughter, Gina, had gotten on the school bus without her show-and-tell bunny. "Great!" thought Jan, "now I have to get gas at Demler's, stop by Gina's school, and drop Alex off at day care—all before my 9:30 class!" Quickly she grabbed the diaper bag, picked up the baby, and headed for the door. At 9:35, with her heart pounding and hands sweating, she scrambled into the classroom, found an open seat, and was hurriedly pulling out her psych notes when the prof asked, "So . . . precisely what does Jung mean by 'collective unconscious'—Jan?"

"Uh . . . what was the question?" she responded.

The transition links the anecdote and the thesis.

Does the scene sound familiar—too much work, too little time, and too much stress?

From "Life-Threatening Stress," page **185**

Anecdote illustrating a point:

The transition tells why the anecdote is used.

Steve is a good example. When he entered the nursing home just six months ago, he was experiencing the early stages of dementia. Today, however, his illness is much more advanced. The stress of moving into this new environment and leaving his wife at home alone affected Steve deeply. When he first arrived, Steve often cried and begged to be taken home. "I'll give you $20—please just take me home," he'd plead.

The quote and description show how a dementia patient feels.

Painfully, I would explain, "Steve, this is your home." After some time, the situation got so bad that he would not sleep or eat. He was depressed, and he cried often, thinking that no one cared about him. Eventually, Steve was given stronger drugs to help with the depression. For a few months, the medication seemed to work—he laughed at jokes and occasionally told one himself. But then Steve's dementia returned. Soon he was asking his same sad questions: "Where am I?" and "Do you know what I'm doing here?"

The transition shifts the focus.

So what is the best "medication" for people with dementia?

From "Understanding Dementia," page **247**

The writer describes how Jackie Thomas's competitive drive helps her excel in both basketball and business.

The writer then argues that the same trait is helping other women succeed in business.

Anecdote illustrating character traits:

Jackie Thomas, Nike's associate director of sports marketing, usually spends her lunch hour on the sports-shoe company's basketball courts charging for the basket, always outnumbered by male colleagues. "I hold my own," boasts the 33-year-old executive.

She also does well playing the corporate game back inside the headquarter's offices. Thomas, a former University of California-Berkeley college basketball point guard, says her success is due in large part to the lessons she learned growing up playing competitive team sports. "It's taught me that if you lose a game, you go back afterward and figure out what went wrong and how to overcome it the next time," says the former tomboy from Kingston, Jamaica.

While most of America's corporations are still commanded by male chief executives, women are gaining ground, winning vice-presidential and top management slots and, in a few cases, the highest leadership roles. Many of these young female executives say playing team sports helped them get ahead. A University of Virginia study conducted in the late 1980s showed that 80 percent of key female leaders from *Fortune* 500 companies said they participated in sports and considered themselves tomboys.

From "If You Let Me Play . . . ," page **188**

Reading for Better Writing

Working by yourself or with a group, answer these questions:

1. Reread the three models and explain the qualities of an effective anecdote.

2. How does each transitional sentence link the story to the rest of the essay?

3. Find the introductory anecdotes on pages **185**, **188**, and **247**; explain why each does or does not effectively introduce the topic and focus the essay.

Audio

Narration and Description

In this essay, student writer Jacqui Nyangi Owitti recalls an important personal experience in her life that taught her the pain of loss.

Mzee Owitti

The opening sets the scene and gives background information.

I am about 12 years old. We are en route from Nairobi, the capital city, to the rural area of Kisumu on the eastern shores of Lake Victoria in western Kenya, where my grandparents live. My five brothers and I are traveling with Mum on the overnight train. I am not particularly sad, though I know what has happened. I base my reactions on my mother's, and since she appears to be handling the whole thing well, I am determined to do the same. You see, my grandfather has died. My dad's dad.   *1*

The narrator describes what she sees and how she feels.

We reach the town of my ancestry just as dawn lazily turns into early morning. We buy snacks and hire a car for the last leg of the journey. We then meander through a bewildering maze of mud huts, sisal scrub, and sandy clay grassland, until we come within sight of my grandfather's land, the place where my father grew up.   *2*

The first thing I notice is a crude "tent" made by sticking four poles in the ground, crisscrossing the top with long branches, and covering that with thatch. Despite the early hour, the place is filled with dignitaries, guests, and people like my mother's parents, who have traveled far to honor our family. I am struck by the stillness and all-pervading silence. Everything seems frozen. Time itself seems to mourn, and even the wind is still. The car stops a short distance from the property, and we sit motionless and quiet.   *3*

Verbs in present tense describe the action.

I turn to my mother, questioning. But she has drawn a handkerchief from somewhere and is climbing out of the car. Almost as an actor on the stage, she releases a sound I have never heard before. It is a moan, a scream, and a sob that is deep-throated, guttural, and high-pitched all at the same time. This sudden transformation from a calm, chipper person to a stricken stranger strikes in me a fear that I will long remember. Holding her handkerchief to her face, she breaks into a shuffling run. I sit in the car petrified, watching the drama unfold.   *4*

Out of seemingly nowhere, wailing answers my mother's cry. Other women appear at a run, heading for my mother, hands fluttering from the tops of their heads, to their waists, to their feet. Their heads are thrown back and from side to side in restless anguish. Their bodies are half-bent forward, and their feet are in constant motion even though no distance is covered. My aunts and close female relatives weep, letting loose high-pitched, ululating moaning in support of my mother. As the wife of the first child and only son, she commands a high place, and she must not grieve alone.   *5*

The last sentence explains the women's actions.

In the confusion, one lady is knocked down, and she seems to rock with her legs separated in a way that in other circumstances would be inappropriate and humiliating. Oddly, the people in the tent, mostly male,   *6* appear to have seen and heard nothing. They continue silent and still. The whole scene seems unreal. Seeing my fear and confusion, the driver talks soothingly, explaining what is going on.

7   The wailing and mourning continue intermittently for a couple of days. Then the time comes for my grandfather to be taken from the mortuary in Kisumu to his final resting place. We all travel to the mortuary. He is dressed in his best suit and then taken to church, where his soul is committed to God. Afterward, the procession starts for home. On the way we are met by the other mourners, who, according to tradition, will accompany the hearse on foot, driving along the cows that are a symbol of wealth in life and a testament to a good life, respectability, and honor in death. Being city kids unable to jog for an hour with the mourners and cows, we ride in a car.

8   Finally, we are back at the homestead. My grandfather is put in the house where he spent the latter part of his life. The crying and mourning are now nearly at a feverish pitch, and the sense of loss is palpable. However, before people may enter the house to pay their last respects, one—they call him "Ratego"—must lead the way to say his good-byes. Suddenly, there is a commotion, and I stare in disbelief as a big bull, taller than my tall-for-my-age twelve-year-old height and wider than the doorway, is led toward my grandfather's house. Long, thick horns stick out of the colossal head. The body, pungent with an ammonia-laced, grassy smell, is a mosaic of black and brown—an odorous, pulsing mountain.

9   The bull's wild, staring eyes seem fixed on me. An old, barefoot man, dressed in a worn, too-short jacket and dusty black pants, leads this bull with a frayed rope. He waves his rod, yelling and leaping in syncopation with the bull's snorting and pawing. Dust puffs dance around their feet. The bull is a symbol of high honor for my grandfather, and only the largest bull in the land can embody this deep respect. Although I do not fully comprehend its significance, I know that it is the biggest animal I have ever seen. I step back as people try to get the bull into the house to pay its respects to my grandfather. After much yelling, shoving, and cries of pain from those whose feet the bull steps on, the effort is abandoned. Ratego is much too big.

10   As the bull is led away into the *boma*, people enter the room that has been emptied of furniture. I squeeze through the heaving, weeping mass, almost suffocating in the process. The room is surprisingly cool and dim, unlike the hot and bright sun outside. I approach curiously and cautiously, not knowing what to expect. At last I stand before the casket and look at my grandfather. He does not look dead. In fact, he is smiling! He looks like the person I remember, who always had a smile and an unshared secret lurking in the depths of his eyes.

A flashback adds depth to the present.

I peer into his face, recalling a time when I was four and he caught me *11* doing something that deserved a reprimand. I had thought no one had seen me. However, my grandfather, on one of his rare visits to the city, had seen. Standing in front of his casket, I again hear him laugh. I remember how his kind, brown eyes had twinkled, and his white mustache, white teeth, and rich bitter-chocolate face had broken into an all-knowing, but-you-can-trust-me smile. I remember how the deep love that radiated from him assured me that I was his no matter what. And I remember how I had responded to his love by laughing happily and then skipping away, his answering laugh reverberating in my ears.

The narrator describes a pivotal point in the story.

That is my grandfather. Death cannot possibly touch him! Then I look *12* closer and realize that the white streak breaking up his face is not the white teeth I remember. It is, instead, cotton stuffed into his mouth, as white as his teeth had been, making a mockery of my memories. At that moment, my granddaddy dies.

Until this point, the whole has been a drama played out before my *13* stunned, wide-eyed gaze. Rich in ancestry and tradition, its very nature and continuity are a celebration of life rather than death, fostering in me a keen sense of identity and a strong desire to keep the ancestral torch burning brightly, fiercely, and with pride. Now, however, Grandpa is dead. It is now that I cry. I am grieving. My granddaddy is gone, and the weighted arrow of sorrow pierces home. The pain is personal, unrelenting, and merciless. I stare at him and cannot tear myself away. I weep, saying over and over that he is smiling, he is smiling. My heartbreak and tears echo the refrain. He is smiling—a radiant, unforgettable smile. ■

The last sentence offers a powerful image.

Reading for Better Writing

Working by yourself or with a group, answer these questions:

1. The writer uses verbs in the present tense to tell her story. How does this choice affect (a) the clarity of the plot, (b) the tension in the episode about the bull, and (c) your empathy with the narrator in the closing?

2. Choose a paragraph containing a particularly vivid description. How do the word choice, sentence structure, and punctuation affect your ability to sense the action?

3. In a conversation with an editor of this book, Jacqui Nyangi Owitti described her love for her grandfather and her pride in her heritage. Does the story reflect that love and pride? Explain.

Narration and Description

James C. Schaap is a writer and college professor. In this essay he describes the place that he took his writing students on a particularly memorable day. The essay was first published in the *Des Moines Register*.

That Morning on the Prairie

The writer introduces the setting.

On some beautiful early fall days out here on the emerald cusp of the Great Plains, it's hard to believe that we are where we are. Warm southern breezes swing up from Texas, the sun smiles with a gentleness not seen since June, and the spacious sky reigns over everything in azure glory.

Early on exactly that kind of fall morning, I like to take my writing classes to a ghost town, Highland, Iowa, ten miles west and two south, as they say out here on the square-cut prairie. Likely as not, Highland fell victim to a century-old phenomenon in the Upper Midwest: 100 years ago, land was cut into 160-acre chunks, most had homesteads, and small towns thrived. Today, when the portions are ten times bigger, fewer people live out here, and many towns have died out.

He details the location.

What's left of Highland is a stand of pines circled around no more than twenty gravestones, and an old carved sign with hand-drawn figures detailing what was home for some people—a couple of Protestant churches, a couple of horse barns, and a blacksmith shop, little else. The town of Highland once flourished atop this swell of land at the confluence of a pair of nondescript gravel roads that still float out in four distinct directions like dusky ribbons over undulating prairie. But mostly, today, it's gone.

He explains why he takes students to Highland— and how they respond.

I like to take my students to Highland because what's not there never fails to silence them. Maybe it's the emaciated cemetery; maybe it's the south wind's low moan through that stand of pines, a sound you don't hear often on the plains; maybe it's some variant of culture shock—they stumble sleepily out of their cubicle dorm rooms and wake up suddenly in a place with no walls.

I'm lying. I know why they fall into psychic shock. It's the sheer immensity of the land that unfurls before them, the horizon only seemingly there where earth weaves effortlessly into sky; it's the vastness of rolling landscape William Cullen Bryant once claimed looked like an ocean stopped in time. It seems as if there's nothing here, and everything, and that's what stuns them into silence. That September morning, on those gravel roads, no cars passed. We were alone—twenty of us, all alone and vulnerable on a high-ground swath of prairie once called Highland, surrounded by nothing but startling openness.

The topic sentence indicates a transition.

That's where I was—and that's where they were—on September 11, 2001. We left for Highland about the same time Mohamed Atta and his friends were commandeering American Airlines Flight 11 into the north tower of the World Trade Center, so we knew absolutely nothing about what had happened until we returned. While the rest of the world watched in horror, my students, notebooks and pens in hand, looked over a landscape so immense only God could live there—and were silent.

They found it hard to leave, but then no one can stay on retreat forever, so when we returned we heard the horrible news. All over campus and all over town, TVs blared.   *7*

I like to think that maybe on our campus that morning my students were best prepared for the horror everyone felt—prepared, not by having been warned, but by having been awed.   *8*

Every year it's a joy for me to sit at Highland with a new group of students, all of us trying to define and describe the beauty of what seems characterless prairie. But this year our being there on the morning of September 11 was more than a joy—it was also a kind of blessing. ■   *9*

The writer reflects on the trip's impact on students.

Reading for Better Writing

Working by yourself or with a group, answer these questions:

1. In the first three paragraphs of his essay, the writer describes Highland. Cite passages that do or do not help you see the setting. What mood or feeling does the description evoke?

2. James C. Schaap, himself a writer, takes his students to Highland, where he asks them to use the setting as a writing prompt. What could students learn from the experience? Why?

3. Schaap concludes the essay by saying that his students' presence in Highland on September 11 was "a kind of blessing." What does he mean?

4. What do you think the writer is trying to say in the last several lines?

Narration and Description

Eric Arthur Blair, better known as George Orwell, was a British author who wrote political and cultural commentary in the 1930s and 1940s. Some of his best-known works include the novels *Animal Farm* and *1984* and essays such as this one.

A Hanging

The writer starts in the middle of the scene so that we have to keep reading to learn what is happening.

It was in Burma, a sodden morning of the rains. A sickly light, like yellow tinfoil, was slanting over the high walls into the jail yard. We were waiting outside the condemned cells, a row of sheds fronted with double bars, like small animal cages. Each cell measured about ten feet by ten and was quite bare within except for a plank bed and a pot for drinking water. In some of them brown, silent men were squatting at the inner bars, with their blankets draped round them. These were the condemned men, due to be hanged within the next week or two. [1]

One prisoner had been brought out of his cell. He was a Hindu, a puny wisp of a man, with a shaven head and vague liquid eyes. He had a thick sprouting mustache, absurdly too big for his body, rather like the mustache of a comic man on the films. Six tall Indian warders were guarding him and getting him ready for the gallows. Two of them stood by with rifles and fixed bayonets, while the others handcuffed him, passed a chain through his handcuffs and fixed it to their belts, and lashed his arms tight to his sides. They crowded very close about him, with their hands always on him in a careful, caressing grip, as though all the while feeling him to make sure he was there. It was like men handling a fish which is still alive and may jump back into the water. But he stood quite unresisting, yielding his arms limply to the ropes, as though he hardly noticed what was happening. [2]

The word *caressing* is an unexpected choice to describe the handling of the prisoner.

Eight o'clock struck and a bugle call, desolately thin in the wet air, floated from the distant barracks. The superintendent of the jail, who was standing apart from the rest of us, moodily prodding the gravel with his stick, raised his head at the sound. He was an army doctor, with a grey toothbrush mustache and a gruff voice. "For God's sake, hurry up, Francis," he said irritably. "The man ought to have been dead by this time. Aren't you ready yet?" [3]

The writer offers few details about the characters and event, building our curiosity.

Francis, the head jailer, a fat Dravidian in a white drill suit and gold spectacles, waved his black hand. "Yes sir, yes sir," he bubbled. "All iss satisfactorily prepared. The hangman iss waiting. We shall proceed." [4]

"Well, quick march, then. The prisoners can't get their breakfast till this job's over." [5]

We set out for the gallows. Two warders marched on either side of the prisoner, with their rifles at the slope; two others marched close against him, gripping him by arm and shoulder, as though at once pushing and [6]

> **A surprise adds interest and contrast.**

supporting him. The rest of us, magistrates and the like, followed behind. Suddenly, when we had gone ten yards, the procession stopped short without any order or warning. A dreadful thing had happened—a dog, come goodness knows whence, had appeared in the yard. It came bounding among us with a loud volley of barks and leapt round us wagging its whole body, wild with glee at finding so many human beings together. It was a large woolly dog, half Airedale, half pariah. For a moment it pranced around us, and then, before anyone could stop it, it had made a dash for the prisoner, and jumping up tried to lick his face. Everybody stood aghast, too taken aback even to grab the dog.

> **The quotation enlivens the scene.**

"Who let that bloody brute in here?" said the superintendent angrily. "Catch it, someone!"   7

A warder detached from the escort, charged clumsily after the dog, but   8
it danced and gambolled just out of his reach, taking everything as part of the game. A young Eurasian jailer picked up a handful of gravel and tried to stone the dog away, but it dodged the stones and came after us again. Its yaps echoed from the jail walls. The prisoner, in the grasp of the two warders, looked on incuriously, as though this was another

> **The writer offers a specific detail.**

formality of the hanging. It was several minutes before someone managed to catch the dog. Then we put my handkerchief through its collar and moved off once more, with the dog still straining and whimpering.

> *This man was not dying, he was alive . . .*   9

It was about forty yards to the gallows. I watched the bare brown back of the prisoner marching in front of me. He walked clumsily with his bound arms, but quite steadily, with that bobbing gait of the Indian who never straightens his knees. At each step his muscles slid neatly into place, the lock of hair on his scalp danced up and down, his feet printed themselves on the wet gravel. And once, in spite of the men who gripped him by each shoulder, he stepped lightly aside to avoid a puddle on the path.

> **Multiple details show that the man "was alive just as we are alive."**

It is curious; but till that moment I had never realized what it means   10
to destroy a healthy, conscious man. When I saw the prisoner step aside to avoid the puddle, I saw the mystery, the unspeakable wrongness, of cutting a life short when it is in full tide. This man was not dying, he was alive just as we are alive. All the organs of this body were working—bowels digesting food, skin renewing itself, nails growing, tissues forming—all toiling away in solemn foolery. His nails would still be growing when he stood on the drop, when he was falling through the air with a tenth-of-a-second to live. His eyes saw the yellow gravel and the grey walls, and his brain still remembered, foresaw, reasoned—even about puddles. He and we were a party of men walking together, seeing, hearing, feeling, understanding the same world; and in two minutes, with a sudden snap, one of us would be gone—one mind less, one world less.

Details help us to picture the scene.

The gallows stood in a small yard, separate from the main grounds of the prison, and overgrown with tall prickly weeds. It was a brick erection like three sides of a shed, with planking on top, and above that two beams and a crossbar with the rope dangling. The hangman, a greyhaired convict in the white uniform of the prison, was waiting beside his machine. He greeted us with a servile crouch as we entered. At a word from Francis the two warders, gripping the prisoner more closely than ever, half led, half pushed him to the gallows and helped him clumsily up the ladder. Then the hangman climbed up and fixed the rope around the prisoner's neck. 11

Details about sounds and sights add tension and suspense.

We stood waiting, five yards away. The warders had formed in a rough circle round the gallows. And then, when the noose was fixed, the prisoner began crying out to his god. It was a high, reiterated cry of "Ram! Ram! Ram! Ram!" not urgent and fearful like a prayer or cry for help, but steady, rhythmical, almost like the tolling of a bell. The dog answered the sound with a whine. The hangman, still standing on the gallows, produced a small cotton bag like a flour bag and drew it down over the prisoner's face. But the sound, muffled by the cloth, still persisted, over and over again: "Ram! Ram! Ram! Ram!" 12

The writer contrasts the super-intendent's musings with the spectators' desire that the man die quickly so order can be restored.

The hangman climbed down and stood ready, holding the lever. Minutes seemed to pass. The steady, muffled crying from the prisoner went on and on, "Ram! Ram! Ram!" never faltering for an instant. The superintendent, his head on his chest, was slowly poking the ground with his stick; perhaps he was counting the cries, allowing the prisoner a fixed number—fifty, perhaps, or a hundred. Everyone had changed colour. The Indians had gone grey like bad coffee, and one or two of the bayonets were wavering. We looked at the lashed, hooded man on the drop, and listened to his cries—each cry another second of life; the same thought was in all our minds; oh, kill him quickly, get it over, stop that abominable noise! 13

> *The Indians had gone grey like bad coffee . . .*

Suddenly the superintendent made up his mind. Throwing up his head he made a swift motion with his stick. "Chalo!" he shouted almost fiercely. 14

There was a clanking noise, and then dead silence. The prisoner had vanished, and the rope was twisting on itself. I let go of the dog, and it galloped immediately to the back of the gallows; but when it got there it stopped short, barked, and then retreated into a corner of the yard, where it stood among the weeds, looking timorously out at us. We went round the gallows to inspect the prisoner's body. He was dangling with his toes pointed straight downwards, very slowly revolving, as dead as a stone. 15

"*He's* all right" is an unexpected, ironic remark.

The superintendent reached out with his stick and poked the bare brown body; it oscillated slightly. "*He's* all right," said the superintendent. He backed out from under the gallows, and blew out a deep breath. The moody look had gone out of his face quite suddenly. He glanced at his 16 wrist-watch. "Eight minutes past eight. Well, that's all for this morning, thank God."

> The closing describes an orderly, upbeat scene.

The warders unfixed bayonets and marched away. The dog, sobered and conscious of having misbehaved itself, slipped after them. We walked out of the gallows yard, past the condemned cells with their waiting prisoners, into the big central yard of the prison. The convicts, under the command of warders armed with lathis, were already receiving their breakfast. They squatted in long rows, each man holding a tin pannikin, while two warders with buckets marched around ladling out rice; it seemed quite a homely, jolly scene, after the hanging. An enormous relief had come upon us now that the job was done. One felt an impulse to sing, to break into a run, to snigger. All at once everyone began chattering gaily. ■   *17*

Reading for Better Writing

Working by yourself or with a group, answer these questions:

1. Orwell's title, "A Hanging," summarizes the plot and forecasts the closing. Would the climax of the piece shift if the hanging were a surprise? How and why?

2. What effect does the writer create by beginning the essay in the middle of the action, without explaining what led up to the hanging?

3. We anticipate that a hanging will take place, so the event itself is no surprise. However, some characters' actions do surprise us. Cite examples and explain their effects.

4. What do we learn about the narrator by what is—and is not—included in his retelling of events? For example, how do you respond to his summary of the hanging as a "job" and a "relief"? Why do you think the prisoner "vanishes" from the narrative after the hanging?

5. Throughout the piece, the narrator carefully describes the setting while offering few details about characters' emotional responses to the hanging. Why?

Narration and Description

Bel Kaufman is known as the author of *Up the Down Staircase* and as a scholar and a teacher. In this piece she explores what happens when an academic couple encounters a bully in the park.

In the essay, highlight narrative passages. In the margin, note how each passage distinguishes a character or develops the essay's ideas.

Sunday in the Park

It was still warm in the late-afternoon sun, and the city noises came muffled through the trees in the park. She put her book down on the bench, removed her sunglasses, and sighed contentedly. Morton was reading the *Times Magazine* section, one arm flung around her shoulder; their three-year-old son, Larry, was playing in the sandbox; a faint breeze fanned her hair softly against her cheek. It was five-thirty of a Sunday afternoon, and the small playground, tucked away in a corner of the park, was all but deserted. The swings and seesaws stood motionless and abandoned, the slides were empty, and only in the sandbox two little boys squatted diligently side by side. *How good this is*, she thought, and almost smiled at her sense of well-being. They must go out in the sun more often; Morton was so city-pale, cooped up all week inside the gray factorylike university. She squeezed his arm affectionately and glanced at Larry, delighting in the pointed little face frowning in concentration over the tunnel he was digging. The other boy suddenly stood up and with a quick, deliberate swing of his chubby arm threw a spadeful of sand at Larry. It just missed his head. Larry continued digging; the boy remained standing, shovel raised, stolid and impassive. 1

"No, no, little boy." She shook her finger at him, her eyes searching for the child's mother or nurse. "We mustn't throw sand. It may get in someone's eyes and hurt. We must play nicely in the nice sandbox." The boy looked at her in unblinking expectancy. He was about Larry's age but perhaps ten pounds heavier, a husky little boy with none of Larry's quickness and sensitivity in his face. Where was his mother? The only other people left in the playground were two women and a little girl on roller skates leaving now through the gate, and a man on a bench a few feet away. He was a big man, and he seemed to be taking up the whole bench as he held the Sunday comics close to his face. She supposed he was the child's father. He did not look up from his comics, but spat once deftly out of the corner of his mouth. She turned her eyes away. 2

At that moment, as swiftly as before, the fat little boy threw another spadeful of sand at Larry. This time some of it landed on his hair and forehead. Larry looked up at his mother, his mouth tentative; her expression would tell him whether to cry or not. 3

Her first instinct was to rush to her son, brush the sand out of his hair, and punish the other child, but she controlled it. She always said that she wanted Larry to learn to fight his own battles. 4

"Don't *do* that, little boy," she said sharply, leaning forward on the   *5*
bench. "You mustn't throw sand!"

The man on the bench moved his mouth as if to spit again, but instead   *6*
he spoke. He did not look at her, but at the boy only.

"You go right ahead, Joe," he said loudly. "Throw all you want. This   *7*
here is a *public* sandbox."

She felt a sudden weakness in her knees as she glanced at Morton. He   *8*
had become aware of what was happening. He put his *Times* down carefully
on his lap and turned his fine, lean face toward the man, smiling the shy,
apologetic smile he might have offered a student in pointing out an error
in his thinking. When he spoke to the man, it was with his usual
reasonableness.

"You're quite right," he said pleasantly,   *9*
"but just because this is a public place. . . ."

The man lowered his funnies and looked   *10*
at Morton. He looked at him from head to foot,
slowly and deliberately. "Yeah?" His insolent
voice was edged with menace. "My kid's got
just as good right here as yours, and if he feels
like throwing sand, he'll throw it, and if you
don't like it, you can take your kid the hell out of here."

> *His insolent voice was edged with menace.*

The children were listening, their eyes and mouths wide open, their   *11*
spades forgotten in small fists. She noticed the muscle in Morton's jaw
tighten. He was rarely angry; he seldom lost his temper. She was suffused
with a tenderness for her husband and an impotent rage against the man for
involving him in a situation so alien and so distasteful to him.

"Now, just a minute," Morton said courteously, "you must realize. . . ."   *12*

"Aw, shut up," said the man.   *13*

Her heart began to pound. Morton half rose; the *Times* slid to the   *14*
ground. Slowly the other man stood up. He took a couple of steps toward
Morton, then stopped. He flexed his great arms, waiting. She pressed her
trembling knees together. Would there be violence, fighting? How dreadful,
how incredible. . . . She must do something, stop them, call for help. She
wanted to put her hand on her husband's sleeve, to pull him down, but for
some reason she didn't.

Morton adjusted his glasses. He was very pale. "This is ridiculous,"   *15*
he said unevenly. "I must ask you. . . ."

"Oh, yeah?" said the man. He stood with his legs spread apart, rocking   *16*
a little, looking at Morton with utter scorn. "You and who else?"

For a moment the two men looked at each other nakedly. Then Morton   *17*
turned his back on the man and said quietly, "Come on, let's get out of
here." He walked awkwardly, almost limping with self-consciousness, to the
sandbox. He stooped and lifted Larry and his shovel out.

At once Larry came to life; his face lost its rapt expression and he began to kick and cry. "I don't *want* to go home, I want to play better, I don't want any supper, I don't *like* supper. . . ." It became a chant as they walked, pulling their child between them, his feet dragging on the ground. In order to get to the exit gate they had to pass the bench where the man sat sprawling again. She was careful not to look at him. With all the dignity she could summon, she pulled Larry's sandy, perspiring little hand, while Morton pulled the other. Slowly and with head high she walked with her husband and child out of the playground.   18

Her first feeling was one of relief that a fight had been avoided, that no one was hurt. Yet beneath it there was a layer of something else, something heavy and inescapable. She sensed that it was more than just an unpleasant incident, more than defeat of reason by force. She felt dimly it had something to do with her and Morton, something acutely personal, familiar, and important.   19

> *Yet beneath it there was a layer of something else . . .*

Suddenly Morton spoke. "It wouldn't have proved anything."   20

"What?" she asked.   21

"A fight. It wouldn't have proved anything beyond the fact that he's bigger than I am."   22

"Of course," she said.   23

"The only possible outcome," he continued reasonably, "would have been—what? My glasses broken, perhaps a tooth or two replaced, a couple of days' work missed—and for what? For justice? For truth?"   24

"Of course," she repeated. She quickened her step. She wanted only to get home and to busy herself with her familiar tasks; perhaps then the feeling, glued like heavy plaster on her heart, would be gone. *Of all the stupid, despicable bullies,* she thought, pulling harder on Larry's hand. The child was still crying. Always before she had felt a tender pity for his defenseless little body, the frail arms, the narrow shoulders with sharp, winglike shoulder blades, the thin legs, unsure, but now her mouth tightened in resentment.   25

"Stop crying," she said sharply. "I'm ashamed of you!" She felt as if all three of them were tracking mud along the street. The child cried louder.   26

If there had been an issue involved, she thought, *if there had been something to fight for. . . . But what else could he possibly have done? Allow himself to be beaten? Attempt to educate the man? Call a policeman? "Officer, there's a man in the park who won't stop his child from throwing sand on mine. . . ."* The whole thing was as silly as that, and not worth thinking about.   27

"Can't you keep him quiet, for Pete's sake?" Morton asked irritably.   28

"What do you suppose I've been trying to do?" she said. Larry pulled   29
back, dragging his feet.

"If you can't discipline this child, I will," Morton snapped, making   30
a move toward the boy.

But her voice stopped him. She was shocked to hear it, thin and cold   31
and penetrating with contempt. "Indeed?" she heard herself say. "You and
who else?" ■

Reading for Better Writing

Working by yourself or with a group, answer these questions:

1. Reread the first paragraph. How does Kaufman's description make the
setting seem first idyllic and then suddenly menacing?

2. Why isn't the woman given a name?

3. Notice that Morton is reading the *Times* whereas the other man is
reading the "funnies." What does Kaufman suggest about each man by
noting what he is reading?

4. How might the overall effect of the essay differ if it were told from
Morton's perspective?

5. Notice the use of contrast and repetition in this piece: repeated
references to the contrasting newspapers; repeated contrasts between
the way the woman had previously felt and the way she feels now;
repeated physical contrasts between Morton and the man, or Larry and
the boy; and repeated contrasts in the tone and diction of Morton and
the man. In what ways does this contrast and repetition accentuate the
significance of the woman's final question?

Model

Guidelines
Writing Narration and Description

1. **Select a topic.** Think about your own experiences. Sort through the stories you recall and choose one that is important enough to share with others. Think of a way to approach this experience in a personal narrative.

   > **TIP:** If you can't think of an interesting story, try writing in response to the following statement: *Remember a time when you first discovered that the world was (a) stranger, (b) more wonderful, or (c) more complex than you had thought as a child.* Think about how that experience prepared you to be who you are today.

2. **Narrow your focus.** Once you have chosen an experience to write about, begin to narrow your topic by focusing on a specific moment or outcome. The following questions can help you find a clear focus:
   - What is the key moment—the significant point or climax— in the story?
   - What led up to this key moment? What resulted from it?
   - What was really going on?
   - How did others experience the event?
   - What has time taught you about this experience?
   - What would you have changed?

3. **Determine your purpose and audience.** After you have a specific focus, decide why you are telling your story and who might read the story. Personal narratives can serve one of many purposes and appeal to many audiences. Consider these purposes:
   - To entertain
   - To warn
   - To challenge
   - To celebrate
   - To illustrate
   - To persuade
   - To remind
   - To gain sympathy
   - To encourage

4. **Gather details.** Gather material that will serve your purpose. Try sorting through photo albums, home videos, and letters. Interview someone who shared your experience or saw you through it. Consult your journal or diary.

5. **Collaborate.** Tell someone your story; then ask for comments and questions. Based on the feedback you receive, create a basic writing plan. Your plan can be anything from a simple list to a detailed outline.

6. **Write your first draft.** As you write, keep in mind your specific focus and your overall purpose for telling this story. Use the following strategies as you create your first draft:

   - **Set the stage.** Show where things happened. Describe the atmosphere, the people, and the events by using precise details that appeal to the five senses. If appropriate, use comparisons and metaphors to make the descriptions vivid.
   - **Include dialogue.** To infuse your narrative with a sense of reality, recall and create conversations between the people in your story.

   > **TIP:** Use dialogue to enhance a key scene or to explain the relationship between people. But be selective—don't let dialogue dribble on for its own sake.

   - **Build the plot.** Arouse and sustain interest by establishing conflict, building suspense, highlighting the main point, and showing the outcome.
   - **Express your feelings.** It may help to include both past and present thoughts and feelings—those you had during the experience and those you have now, looking back on the past.
   - **Use transitions.** Words like *as, before, meanwhile,* and *later* show where your story is leading. (See page 85.)
   - **Select verbs carefully.** Verbs affect the movement and voice of your story. Choose strong, active verbs, and make sure tenses accurately reflect time sequences and relationships.

7. **Share your story.** Show your draft to someone. What main point does this reader see in your story? What suggestions or questions does the reader have?

8. **Revise your writing.** Carefully review and revise your writing. Remember that your goal is to re-create an interesting incident or event for your readers. Ask yourself the following questions:

   - Does the writing focus on a specific incident or event?
   - Does the writing contain effective details, descriptions, and dialogue?
   - Does the narrative effectively state or imply a theme, thesis, or point of significance?
   - Does the writing sound sincere and natural?
   - Will readers appreciate the way the story is told?

9. **Edit and proofread.** (See the checklist on page 110.)

10. **Prepare your final copy.** Use an appropriate type font and size. Leave the right margin ragged (uneven). Place photographs or drawings close to the text they illustrate. Print your final copy on quality paper.

Writing Checklist

Use these seven traits to check the quality of your writing; then revise as needed:

_____ The **ideas** focus on a specific experience or event and present an engaging picture of the action and people involved.

_____ The **organization** pattern adds to the clarity of the piece and includes a clear beginning that pulls readers in.

_____ The **voice** shows that the writer is truly interested in the subject by speaking knowledgeably and enthusiastically.

_____ The **words** *show* instead of *tell about*; they appeal to the senses and evoke pictures in the reader's mind.

_____ The **sentences** are clear, varied in structure, and smooth.

_____ The **copy** includes no errors in spelling, mechanics, punctuation, or grammar.

_____ The **design** follows assigned guidelines for format. Photographs and drawings are clear and well placed.

Interactive

Critical-Thinking and Writing Activities

As directed by your instructor, complete the following activities alone or with a group.

1. Review "Mzee Owitti" and "Sunday in the Park," observing how the writers help you share their experiences by presenting vivid details in an open, honest way. List a few of your own experiences that you would like to explore and share. Then choose one that would be an appropriate subject for a personal narrative. Write the narrative, perhaps using some of the same organizational strategies employed in these models.

2. Review the ways in which Bel Kaufman uses dialogue, physical description, and personal objects/possessions to contrast two characters in "Sunday in the Park." Draft or revise a narrative in which you shape characters through distinctive dialogue, physical description, and personal possessions.

3. Review "A Hanging" and "Sunday in the Park," noting how the authors of both essays portray certain characters in a negative light without making direct comments to that effect. Draft or revise a portrayal of a person in which you show (rather than tell) your feelings about the individual.

◀ VISUALLY SPEAKING ━━━━━━━━━━━━━━

Review the image on page **145**, looking for its "story." Imagine what has happened and what is happening. Then write a brief narrative relating what happens next.

DESCRIPTION AND REFLECTION

Audio

Video

It is human nature to reflect. On this score, eighteenth-century poet Robert Burns thought mice luckier than people. In his poem "To a Mouse," Burns noted that mice worry only about the present, whereas humans worry about past, present, and future woes. Whether or not reflecting on the past is unique to humans, we do know that this trait brings joy, regret, and a thousand variations of those feelings to humans both young and old.

A personal reflection is often written to draw wisdom from past experiences. Accordingly, you may want to explore an earlier time in your life and reflect on why you felt as you did when you suffered a stinging setback or won a glorious victory.

In this chapter, you'll find topics to consider, model essays, and guidelines that will help you describe and reflect on a memorable experience. In the process, you will likely gain insight not only into your past experience, but also into its links to your present and future.

Overview
Writing Description and Reflection

Writer's Goal

Your goal is to write an essay in which you carefully describe one or more past experiences and reflect on their importance in your life.

Keys for Success

Recall precise details. To understand and appreciate your reflections, readers first have to grasp exactly what you experienced. For that reason, you must describe those key details (sights, smells, tastes) that make the experience memorable to you—and worth reflecting on. Often you will find these details in the hardly-noticed-at-the-time part of your memory.

Probe the topic. The mind-searching aspect of writing this essay happens while asking *so-why* questions: *So why does this picture still make me smile?* or *Why does his comment still hurt?* or *Why did I do that when I knew better?*—or *Did I know better?* Your answers will help explain why this memory is important to you.

Reveal what you find. Your readers need to experience what you experienced, so don't hide what's embarrassing, painful, or still unclear. Show them the details clearly, explain your insights honestly, and then trust readers to respond with sensitivity, appreciation, and respect.

Topics to Consider

The most promising topics are experiences that gave you insights into yourself, and possibly into others as well. Often such an experience will have led you or others to change patterns of thinking, feeling, or behavior. To identify such topics, consider the categories below and then list whatever experiences come to mind:

- Times when you felt *secure, hopeful, distraught, appreciated, confident, frightened, exploited,* or *misunderstood.*
- Times when you made a decision about *lifestyles, careers, education, politics, religion, leaving home,* or *getting an education.*
- Events that tested your *will, patience, self-concept,* or *goals.*
- Events that changed or confirmed your assessment of a *person,* a *group,* an *institution,* a *religious belief,* a *political conviction,* or a *philosophical worldview.*

> **Next Step** Read the model essays and perform the activities that follow. As you read, note how the writers help you grasp what they experienced and why their experiences are important.

Description and Reflection

Audio

Nicole Suurdt is a student from Ontario, Canada. In this essay, she describes a time and place that she loved as a child and yearns for as an adult.

The Stream in the Ravine

The writer introduces the topic and then gives background information.

Behind my childhood home is a small ravine, and through it runs the seasonal overflow of a little pond deep within the woods. It's a noisy stream, just narrow enough for an eight-year-old to take one stretching step across and reach the other side with dry shoes. And when I was eight, this stream was everything to me.   *1*

You see, for most of my childhood, I lived on a small hobby farm in Ontario, Canada, where rolling pasture and croplands surrounded my home. The pasture fenced in Scottish Highland cattle with terrifying horns, unbroken horses with skittish hooves, and one half-blind, unpredictable donkey. These creatures separated me from the woods just beyond the pasture. But when I was little, it wasn't simply my fear of these fitful animals that penned me in on my side of the fence—it was a fear of what lay beyond the shadowy barrier of maples and pines.   *2*

Description of the visits builds tension.

It's not that I'd never been to the woods before. I had, twice. The first time, my brother took me in search of the tallest tree in the forest and got us lost for a couple of hours. My second visit was a dark winter journey. Dad dragged the family into the woods late one night in search of a missing cow. We found her half-devoured body lying in bloodstained snow, packed down by wolves' paws.   *3*

A transition signals a shift in the action.

But eventually, curiosity overpowered my fears. One spring day when I was eight, armed with a staff, I skirted the pasture and headed for the forest. I approached the fence that my dad had put up to ward off the woods. Quickly I scaled the fence, but then stood some time holding on to its boards, figuring that if a wolf came along, I could scramble back to the other side. However, after five minutes passed and no wolf appeared, I calmed down, let go of the fence, and stepped into the forest—lured on by the sound of chipmunks, birds, wind through trees, and snapping twigs.   *4*

Drawn forward, I discovered rocky burrows of unknown creatures. I chased chipmunks. I sang. I passed a hunter's fort perched high in a pine, deserted after last fall's deer-hunting season. I passed under an archway of tall cedars. I waded through the muck and mire surrounding a small swamp and plodded my mud-caked shoes up a small rise, thick with the faded, crumbled leaves of last year's fall. One particular sound kept pulling me forward—the gurgle of running water.   *5*

The writer describes the stream and shares its personal importance.

Standing at the peak of the rise, with brown leaves stuck to my muddy sneakers, I found the source. Below me, within its shallow bed, ran a tiny stream, little more than a trickle, really. But to me it was a beautiful, rushing   *6* brook, my own source of clear, cold water protected by oak, maple, and pine sentries. That day I spent hours scooping decaying leaves out of my stream's bed and sitting by her side to watch the water spill over the rocks and roots. She was my own discovery, my own territory, my own secret place. From that day on, the little stream past the hunter's fort, under the cedar archway, through the muck and the mire, and over the rocky rise became my quiet, private place.

The picture shows the father, the daughter, and their bridge.

But I never could keep a secret for long. During dinner one Sunday, I told my parents about my stream. I figured that it needed a bridge, something only Dad could help me build. And so, that afternoon, I led Mom and Dad over the fence, into the woods, and up to my secret stream. Together, we built a bridge using the fallen branches lying about. Mom took a picture of Dad and me sitting on our homemade, lopsided bridge, the water washing over the toes of the big rubber boots that she had insisted we wear. 7

My parents separated eight years after that picture was taken, and I haven't gone back to my stream since, though I think of it often. Somewhere, tucked away in Mom's photo albums, is the picture of a little girl in her dreamland, her dad beside her, his big feet hanging near her small ones. Her mom stands in the water just a few feet away behind the camera lens. 8

The writer yearns for life as shown in the photo.

Sometimes, I want to go back there, back into that photo. I want to step into a time when life seemed safe, and a tiny stream gave us all that we needed. In that picture, our smiles last, our hearts are calm, and we hear only quiet voices, forest sounds, and my bubbling stream. Bitter words are silenced and tears held back by the click and whir of a camera. 9

I've been thinking about making the journey again past the hunter's fort, under the stand of cedars, through the muck and mire, and over the rocky rise. But it's been a long summer, and the small, seasonal stream running out of the overflow of the pond has probably dried up. ■ 10

Reading for Better Writing

Working by yourself or with a group, answer these questions:

1. Three times in the essay, the writer mentions four sites (hunter's fort, cedar archway, muck and mire, rocky rise) along her route. What do the references to these sites contribute to the description?

2. How does the writer organize her description? Identify the strategies used and discuss their effectiveness.

3. Review the references to the photograph taken by the mother, and describe what the photo shows. What does the writer mean when she says, "Sometimes, I want to go back there, back into that photo"?

4. Reread the opening and closing paragraphs, comparing how the writer describes the stream in each paragraph. Are the details and voices of the two passages different? Give examples.

Description and Reflection

Randall VanderMey is a college professor and writer who based this essay on the observations he recorded while waiting for a bus in a Greyhound station. As you will see, the essay is much more than an as-it-happened record of what the writer saw and heard. It is also a brief documentary of a particular slice of American life.

"Scab!"

1

The opening establishes a tense context and tone.

The driver of the airport shuttle bus had to drop me off on the street so as not to cross the line of Greyhound drivers marching with their picket signs in the dusk. The picketers were angry. Had he turned in at the driveway to the terminal, they would have spat on him and yelled "Scab!" or "Strikebreaker!" Newspapers and TV had carried stories of rocks and bottles being thrown at passenger-filled buses by disgruntled Greyhound drivers whose demands for decent wages had not been heard. Most of the drivers in other unions were honoring the picket lines. Someday, they knew, they might be in the same fix.

2

The writer locates himself in the scene.

Inside the terminal I sat with my feet on my suitcase. I didn't want to pay four quarters for a storage box and didn't want to turn my back on my belongings. In the strange, tense atmosphere of the bus depot, I wondered if I was better off there or on a bus. Writing notes became my shield.

3

Switching to present tense, he describes what he senses.

A Hispanic couple behind me plays Spanish music for everyone in the terminal to hear. Men go in the men's room and stay there for a strangely long time, punching the button on the electric blow dryer over and over as if to cover up their talk. Near me an old man in a blue baseball cap and blue nylon jacket mumbles to himself as he paces the floor slowly. I hear him say, "My children is all grown up." Another man in a white yachting cap strides around the terminal making a sliding, streaking sound with a metal heel protector that's working its way loose. He seems to like the sound because he keeps walking around on the hard tile floors, over to the video-game room, over to the cafeteria, over to the bathroom, over to the ticket window, around and around in the open spaces in front of the nuns, college kids, young black girls with children, and Texas farmers waiting for their bus to Dallas. I know where the man in the yachting cap is without even looking up.

4

He describes the terminal and the people, including snippets of dialogue.

A tiny boy, curiosity in a red sweater, is twirling around. Everybody who sees him smiles. A while ago I saw an older man teasing him, saying "Hey, I'm gonna get you" and trying to slip a ten-gallon straw cowboy hat over his ears.

5

A policeman with his hair shaved off all over his round, bumpy head takes his drawn nightstick into the men's room and brings out, by the elbow, a young black man who doesn't seem to know where he is. He cradles a radio in his arm that blasts its music to everyone's discomfort. The cop says,

"Didn't I throw you out of here last night? Come on with me."

The guy looks dazed and says, "Where we going?"   6

The cop says, "We're just going to have a little talk." Turning off the   7
blaring radio, he walks the young man toward the entrance.

He records what he sees, hears, and smells.

Something weird is in the air, as if drugs are being dealt in the   8
bathrooms, though the place remains calm and well lit. The odor of french
fries and cleaning solutions fills the air.

The Hispanic music plays much more softly now, and I hear the dyed-   9
blond lady break out of her Spanish to say to her husband or boyfriend,
"Thang you very mush."

The writer briefly reflects on the scene.

The iron screen benches are starting to lay a print in my back and rear   10
end, so I shift and squirm. When I bought my ticket at the front counter, I
asked the lady who took my money what I'd have to do for two hours and a
half. She had laughed and said, "Look at the walls," and she had been right.

The man in the blue baseball cap is mumbling again. But now I see   11
that he's reading the newspaper and seems not to be able to read unless he
pronounces the words aloud. I hear him say, "That's a liquidation sale."

Contrasting details create rich impressions.

The man with the metal heel protector is back again, clicking and   12
shrieking across the tile floor, carrying a blue nylon satchel. Out of the
video-game room come noises like echoes in a long hollow pipe. A kid
behind the cash register in the cafeteria has neatly combed hair and glasses.
He keeps smiling all the time, looking comfortingly sane. Overhead in there,
the ceiling-fan blades turn hardly faster than the second hand on a clock.

Reflecting on his experience, the writer relates it to crossing a picket line.

It has taken me some time to realize fully how I felt on that hard metal   13
bench for two and a half hours among so many different kinds of people
harboring so many different purposes. I said not a word to anyone. Only
wrote and wrote. With my eyes and ears I broke into their lives while giving
nothing of myself. I got in and got away without any real contact.

I hope the drivers get their money. But I'm not sure my being there   14
helped. I felt like a scab. ■

Reading for Better Writing

Working by yourself or with a group, answer these questions:

1. This personal essay is filled with tension. What is the source of this tension,
and how does it create a theme for the essay?

2. Locate where the writer shifts verb tenses from past to present, and then
to past again. What is the effect of these shifts?

3. How does the writer make his observations vivid? Trace sights, sounds,
smells, textures, and tastes. Do these details create patterns or themes?

4. The writer is both present in and separate from the scene. Explore the
strengths and limitations of the writer's uneasy position.

Description and Reflection

Mary Seymour reflects on her experiences with bipolar disorder, which is sometimes called manic depression.

Call Me Crazy, But I Have to Be Myself

The writer labels herself "mentally ill."

Nearly every day, without thinking, I say things like "So-and-so is driving me crazy" or "That's nuts!" Sometimes I catch myself and realize that I'm not being sensitive toward people with mental illness. Then I remember I'm one of the mentally ill. If I can't throw those words around, who can? 1

Being a functional member of society and having a mental disorder is an intricate balancing act. Every morning I send my son to junior high school, put on professional garb, and drive off to my job as alumni-magazine editor at a prep school, where I've worked for six years. Only a few people at work know I'm manic-depressive, or bipolar, as it's sometimes called. 2

An example illustrates the extent of the illness.

Sometimes I'm not sure myself what I am. I blend in easily with "normal" people. You'd never know that seven years ago, fueled by the stress of a failing marriage and fanned by the genetic inheritance of a manic-depressive grandfather, I had a psychotic break. To look at me, you'd never guess I once ran naked through my yard or shuffled down the hallways of a psychiatric ward. To hear me, you'd never guess God channeled messages to me through my computer. After my breakdown at 36, I was diagnosed as bipolar, a condition marked by moods that swing between elation and despair. 3

More examples show the difficulties the writer faces.

It took a second, less-severe psychotic episode in 1997, followed by a period of deep depression, to convince me I truly was bipolar. Admitting I had a disorder that I'd have to manage for life was the hardest thing I've ever done. Since then, a combination of therapy, visits to a psychiatrist, medication, and inner calibration have helped me find an even keel. Now I manage my moods with the vigilance of a mother hen, nudging them back to center whenever they wander too far. Eating wisely, sleeping well, and exercising regularly keep me balanced from day to day. Ironically, my disorder has taught me to be healthier and happier than I was before. 4

Most of the time, I feel lucky to blend in with the crowd. Things that most people grumble about—paying bills, maintaining a car, working 9 to 5—strike me as incredible privileges. I'll never forget gazing through the barred windows of the psychiatric ward into the parking lot, watching people come and go effortlessly, wondering if I'd ever be like them again. There's nothing like a stint in a locked ward to make one grateful for the freedoms and burdens of full citizenship. 5

Yet sometimes I feel like an impostor. Sometimes I wish I could sit at the lunch table and talk about lithium and Celexa instead of *Will & Grace*. 6

Each sentence begins with a similar phrase that reveals the writer's feelings.

While everyone talks about her fitness routine, I want to brag how it took five orderlies to hold me down and shoot me full of sedatives when I was admitted to the hospital, and how for a brief moment I knew the answers to every infinite mystery of the blazingly bright universe. I yearn for people to know me—the real me—in all my complexity, but I'm afraid it would scare the bejesus out of them.

Every now and then, I feel like I'm truly being myself. Like the time the school chaplain, in whom I'd confided my past, asked me to help counsel a severely bipolar student. This young woman had tried to commit suicide, had been hospitalized many times, and sometimes locked herself in her dorm room to keep the "voices" from overwhelming her. I walked and talked with her, sharing stories about medication and psychosis. I hoped to show by example that manic-depression did not necessarily mean a diminished life. At commencement, I watched her proudly accept her diploma; despite ongoing struggles with her illness, she's continuing her education. 7

An extended example illustrates the point.

I'm able to be fully myself with my closest friends, all of whom have similar schisms between private and public selves. We didn't set out to befriend each other—we just all speak the same language, of hardship and spiritual discovery and psychological awareness. 8

The final line echoes the title.

What I yearn for most is to integrate both sides of myself. I want to be part of the normal world but I also want to own my identity as bipolar. I want people to know what I've been through so I can help those traveling a similar path. Fear has kept me from telling my story: fear of being stigmatized, of making people uncomfortable, of being reduced to a label. But hiding the truth has become more uncomfortable than letting it out. It's time for me to own up to who I am, complicated psychiatric history and all. Call me crazy, but I think it's the right thing to do. ■ 9

Reading for Better Writing

Working by yourself or with a group, answer these questions:

1. What purpose does Seymour identify for writing the essay? What other purposes might be served by publishing this piece for *Newsweek*'s readers?

2. The writer starts with one category label for herself ("mentally ill") and then quickly adds another ("functional member of society"). How does the second label redefine the first?

3. Description is used to support many other kinds of writing, including the types of analytical and persuasive writing outlined here in *The College Writer*. In what other chapters could this essay have been included, and how do you know?

4. Review the "Editing and Proofreading" section of this book (pages 93–110), especially the portion on biased words. Why does Seymour use the phrase "call me crazy"? Is her use of the word biased or insulting? Explain.

Description and Reflection

At the age of six, K. Oanh Ha fled Vietnam as a refugee and came to the United States, where she has become an accomplished journalist. In this essay, Ha reflects on experiences through which she developed her Asian American identity. (Note: By typing the writer's name in your browser, you can peruse her website, blog, and sample publications.)

American Dream Boat

As you read this essay, highlight key descriptive and reflective passages. Then, in the margin, note what each contributes to the essay.

The wedding day was only two weeks away when my parents called with yet another request. In accordance with Vietnamese custom, they fully expected Scott Harris, my fiancé, and his family to visit our family on the morning of the wedding, bearing dowry gifts of fruit, candies, jewelry, and a pig, in an elaborate procession. 1

"But it's not going to mean anything to Scott or his family. They're not Vietnamese!" I protested. My parents were adamant: "Scott's marrying a Vietnamese. If he wants to marry you, he'll honor our traditions." 2

Maybe there's no such thing as a stress-free wedding. Small or large, there's bound to be pressure. But our February 12 wedding was a large do-it-yourselfer that required a fusion of Vietnamese and American traditions—a wedding that forced me and my parents to wrestle with questions about our identities, culture, and place in America. After nearly twenty years here, my family, and my parents in particular, were determined to have a traditional Vietnamese wedding of sorts, even if their son-in-law and Vietnam-born, California-raised daughter are as American as they can be. 3

And so I grudgingly called Scott that night to describe the wedding procession and explain the significance of the ritual. It's a good thing that he is a patient, easygoing man. "I'll bring the pig," he said, "but I'm worried it'll make a mess in the car." 4

"Oh! It's a roasted pig," I told him, laughing. 5

I was six years old when my family fled Vietnam in July 1979, just one family among the thousands who collectively became known as the "boat people," families who decided it was better to risk the very real possibility of death at sea than to live under Communist rule. But, of course, I never understood the politics then. I was just a child following my parents. 6

My memories are sketchy. There was the time that Thai pirates wielding saber-like machetes raided our boat. Two years ago, I told my mother, Kim Hanh Nguyen, how I remembered a woman dropping a handful of jewelry into my porridge during the raid with the instruction to keep eating. "That was no woman," my mother said. "That was me!" When we reached the refugee camp in Kuala Lumpur, my mother used the wedding ring and necklace to buy our shelter. 7

In September 1980, we arrived in Santa Ana, California, in Orange *8* County, now home to the largest Vietnamese community outside of Vietnam. Those who had left in 1975, right after the end of the war and the American withdrawal, had been well educated, wealthy, and connected with military. My family was part of the wave of boat people—mostly middle-class and with little education—who sought refuge in America.

For nearly a year after we arrived, *9* we crowded into the same three-bedroom apartment—all thirteen of us: brothers, sisters, cousins, uncles, aunts, sisters-in-law, and my father's mother. There were only four of us children in my immediate family then, three born in Vietnam and one born shortly after our resettlement in the U.S.

> *We started school and watched Mr. Rogers on PBS in the afternoons, grew to love hamburgers and ketchup, and longed to lose our accents.*

We started school and watched Mr. *10* Rogers on PBS in the afternoons, grew to love hamburgers and ketchup, and longed to lose our accents. We older kids did lose our accents—and those who came later never had accents to begin with because they were born here. When we first came, I was the oldest of three children, all born in Vietnam. Now I have seven siblings, twenty-two years separating me from my youngest brother, who will start kindergarten in the fall.

In some ways, I was the stereotypical Asian nerd. I took honors classes, *11* received good grades, played the violin and cello. But there was a part of me that also yearned to be as American as my blond-haired neighbors across the street. I joined the school's swim and tennis teams, participated in speech competitions (which were attended by mostly white students) and worshipped Esprit and Guess. My first serious boyfriend was white, but most of my friends were Asians who were either born in the U.S. or immigrated when they were very young. None of us had accents, and we rarely spoke our native languages around one another. The last thing we wanted was to be mistaken for FOBs—fresh off the boat. I even changed my name to Kyrstin, unaware of its Nordic roots.

I wanted so badly to be a full-fledged American, whatever that meant. *12* At home, though, my parents pushed traditional Vietnamese values. I spent most of my teenage years babysitting and had to plead with my then overly strict parents to let me out of the house. "Please, please. I just want to be like any other American kid."

My parents didn't understand. "You'll always be Vietnamese. No one's *13* going to look at you and say you're an American," was mother's often-heard refrain.

I saw college as my escape, the beginning of the trip I would undertake on my own. We had come to America as a family but it was time I navigated alone. College was my flight from the house that always smelled of fish sauce and jasmine tea.

At UCLA, I dated the man who would become my husband. Though he's seventeen years older than I am, my parents seemed to be more concerned with the cultural barriers than our age difference. "White Americans are fickle. They don't understand commitment and family responsibility like we Asians do," I was told.

Soon after I announced my engagement, my father, Minh Phu Ha, and I had a rare and intimate conversation. "I'm just worried for you," he said. "All the Vietnamese women I know who have married whites are divorced from them. Our cultures are too far apart."

My father, I think, is worried that none of his kids will marry Vietnamese. My sisters are dating non-Vietnamese Asians while my brother is dating a white American. "It's just that with a Vietnamese son-in-law, I can talk to him," my father explained to me one day. "A Vietnamese son-in-law would call me 'Ba' and not by my first name."

Although my parents have come to terms with having Scott as their son-in-law and to the prospect of grandchildren who will be racially mixed, there are still times when Scott comes to visit that there are awkward silences. There are still many cultural barriers.

I still think of what it all means to marry a white American. I worry that my children won't be able to speak Vietnamese and won't appreciate that part of their heritage. I also wonder if somehow this is the ultimate fulfillment of a latent desire to be "American."

Vietnamese-Americans, like Chinese-Americans, Indian-Americans, and other assimilated immigrants, often speak of leading hyphenated lives, of feet that straddle both cultures. I've always been proud of being Vietnamese. As my family and I discussed and heatedly debated what the wedding event was going to look like, I began to realize just how "American" I had become.

And yet there was no denying the pull of my Vietnamese roots. Four months before the wedding, I traveled back to Vietnam for the second time since our family's escape. It was a trip I planned for more than a year. I was

> *Vietnamese-Americans, like Chinese-Americans, Indian-Americans, and other assimilated immigrants, often speak of leading hyphenated lives, of feet that straddle both cultures.*

14
15
16
17
18
19
20
21

in Saigon, the city of my birth, to research and write a novel that loosely mirrors the story of my own family and our journey from Vietnam. The novel is my tribute to my family and our past. I'm writing it for myself as much as for my younger siblings, so they'll know what our family's been through.

I returned to Vietnam to connect with something I can't really name but know I lost when we left twenty years ago. I was about to start a new journey with the marriage ahead, but I needed to come back to the place where my family's journey began.

I returned to Vietnam to connect with something I can't really name but know I lost when we left twenty years ago.

22

23

Scott came along for the first two weeks and met my extended family. They all seemed to approve, especially when he showed he could eat pungent fish and shrimp sauce like other Vietnamese.

During my time there I visited often with family members and talked about the past. I saw the hospital where I was born, took a walk through our old house, chatted with my father's old friends. The gaps in the circle of my hyphenated life came closer together with every new Vietnamese word that I learned, with every Vietnamese friend that I made.

24

I also chose the fabric for the tailoring of the ao dai, the traditional Vietnamese dress of a long tunic over flowing pants, which I would change into at the reception. I had my sisters' bridesmaid gowns made. And I had a velvet ao dai made for my eighty-eight-year-old maternal grandmother, B Ngoai, to wear to the wedding of her oldest grandchild. "My dream is to see you on your wedding day and eat at your wedding feast," she had told me several times.

25

B Ngoai came to the U.S. in 1983, three years after my family landed in Orange County as war refugees. As soon as we got to the United States, my mother filed immigration papers for her. B Ngoai nurtured and helped raise her grandchildren.

26

I had extended my stay in Vietnam. Several days after my original departure date, I received a phone call. B Ngoai had died. I flew home carrying her ao dai. We buried her in it.

27

In Vietnamese tradition, one is in mourning for three years after the loss of a parent or grandparent. Out of respect and love for the deceased, or hieu, decorum dictates that close family members can't get married until after the mourning period is over. But my wedding was only a month and a half away.

28

On the day we buried my grandmother, my family advised me to burn the white cloth headband that symbolized my grief. By burning it, I ended my official mourning.

29

Through my tears I watched the white cloth become wispy ashes. My   *30*
family was supportive. "It's your duty to remember and honor her," my
father told me. "But you also need to move forward with your life."

On the morning of our wedding, Scott's family stood outside our house   *31*
in a line bearing dowry gifts. Inside the house, Scott and I lighted incense in
front of the family altar. Holding the incense between our palms, we bowed
to my ancestors and asked for their blessings. I looked at the photo of B
Ngoai and knew she had to be smiling. ■

Reading for Better Writing

Working by yourself or with a group, answer these questions:

1. What is the writer's thesis or main idea? Explain why you do or do not
find the idea relevant to your history, culture, or identity.

2. Identify all passages in the essay in which the writer describes or reflects
on her wedding. How does she use those passages to develop her main
idea? How are the early references different from the later references?
Which passages include more description or reflection? Why?

3. In the opening of the essay, the writer and her parents disagree
regarding a specific wedding tradition. What are their arguments? Do
the details regarding the family's history help you understand why they
have different views? Explain.

4. In paragraph 22, the writer says, "I returned to Vietnam to connect
with something I can't really name but know I lost when we left twenty
years ago." What does she mean? Review what she does and learns on
this trip, and then explain how her research and writing might help her
identify and regain what she lost.

5. Review the writer's description of her grandmother's funeral (paragraphs
29–30). Explain how the wedding and funeral ceremonies affect the
family. In what ways are the impacts of both similar or different?

6. How do the wedding and the funeral help the writer "connect with
something I can't really name but know I lost when we left [Vietnam]
twenty years ago"?

7. If you were to describe and reflect upon your own cultural heritage,
which images, elements, moments, conflicts, and/or themes would come
to mind?

Model

Guidelines
Writing Description and Reflection

1. **Select a topic.** Choose an experience or experiences that influenced you in some key way—either confirming what you thought or planned at that time or changing those thoughts or plans. (Revisit "Topics to Consider" on page 166 for additional ideas.)

    > **TIP:** If you can't think of any experiences, try listing topics in response to the following statement: *Reflect on times when you first discovered that the world was one of the following—strange, wonderful, complex, frightening, boring, small, uncaring, like you, unlike you, full, or empty.* How did these experiences affect who you are today?

2. **Get the big picture.** Once you have chosen one or more experiences to write about, gather your thoughts by reflecting on the questions below through brainstorming or by freewriting.
    - What are the key moments—the pivotal points—in your experiences?
    - What led to those key moments? Why? What resulted from them?
    - What was going on from your perspective?
    - How did others experience the events?
    - What did you learn from these experiences?
    - Did these experiences end as you had hoped? Why or why not?
    - What themes, conflicts, and insights arose from these experiences?
    - How do your feelings now differ from your feelings then?

    > **TIP:** To find out more details about the event or people involved, sort through photo albums and home videos to trigger memories; talk to someone who shared your experiences or saw you through them; or consult your journal, diary, old letters, and saved e-mail.

3. **Get organized.**
    - Review your brainstorming or freewriting, and highlight key details, quotations, or episodes that you want to include in your writing.
    - Draft a brief outline that shows where key information fits into the big picture.
    - List the main events in chronological order, or use a cluster to help you gather details related to your experiences.

    > **TIP:** To help you decide which details to include and how to organize your information, consider what your audience needs to understand and appreciate your story.

4. **Write the first draft.** Review your outline and rough out the first draft in one sitting. Then test your reflection for its significance. Does it answer these questions: What happened? How did the experience affect you? How do you feel about it now?

5. **Review and revise.** After drafting the essay, take a break. Then read your paper again for accuracy and completeness. Look first at the entire piece. Does it say what you wanted to say? Does it include any gaps or weak spots? Check your outline to make sure all key details are covered and in the right sequence. (See the checklist on page 92.)

6. **Test your reflection.** Review what you say about the experiences:
   - Does the tone—whether sarcastic, humorous, regretful, or meditative—fit the content of the reflection?
   - Have you established a viewpoint, and is the reflection built on this point of view?
   - Will the intended readers appreciate the treatment of the subject?

7. **Get feedback.** Ask a classmate or someone in the writing center to read your paper, looking for the following:
   - An opening that pulls the reader into the reflection
   - Experiences that are portrayed clearly and vividly
   - An explanation of how you've changed that is woven naturally into the experiences
   - Transitions that connect paragraphs effectively
   - A conclusion that restates the point of the reflection clearly and succinctly

8. **Edit and proofread your essay.** Once you have revised the content, organization, and voice of your personal reflection, polish it. Carefully check your choice of words; the clarity of your sentences; and your grammar, usage, and mechanics.

9. **Publish your writing by doing one or more of the following:**
   - Share your essay with friends and family.
   - Publish it in a journal or on a website.
   - Make copies of your writing, read it to your class, and discuss their responses.
   - Place a copy in your professional portfolio.
   - Submit a copy to your instructor.

Writing Checklist

Use these seven traits to check the quality of your writing; then revise as needed:

_____ The **ideas** (the topic being reflected on) provide the reader with an interesting look at your experience.

_____ The **organization** pattern effectively blends description and reflection.

_____ The **voice** is thoughtful, and characters and events are treated respectfully.

_____ The **words** are precise and clear; descriptions help the reader experience what you experienced.

_____ The **sentences** are smooth and natural.

_____ The **copy** is free of errors in grammar, punctuation, and mechanics.

_____ The **design** uses a format, page layout, and typography fitting for your assignment.

Interactive

Critical-Thinking and Writing Activities

As directed by your instructor, complete the following activities.

1. Writing reflectively requires sharing personal thoughts and feelings about experiences and events—a task that can be difficult to do effectively. Review Mary Seymour's piece, "Call Me Crazy, But I Have To Be Myself" noting the places where she uses phrases similar to "I think" and "I feel," along with an example or comparison to make her perspective clear to her readers. Draft or revise a reflection in which you use these strategies to clarify your own point of view.

2. In "American Dream Boat," K. Oanh Ha describes and reflects on a time in her life during which she sought clarity regarding who she was as a Vietnamese American. Think about a time in your life when you needed clarity regarding an issue related to your identity: nationality, cultural heritage, family legacy, faith life, career path, health challenge, and so forth. Then describe that time in your life, probe its impact on you, and reflect on its value.

◀ Visually Speaking

Review the photograph at the opening of this chapter. What thoughts or feelings does the picture elicit? What does the picture suggest about the relationship between descriptive details and reflective thought?

ANALYTICAL WRITING

Chapters 12 through 16 introduce the traditional modes of analytical writing: cause-effect, comparison-contrast, classification, process, and definition. All of these modes are analytical in the sense that they involve mentally "breaking down" a topic in an effort to reveal structures and logical relationships. Often called expository writing, such modes seek to clearly explain to readers the logical workings of a given topic—from stress to dog food to dementia.

Note, however, that virtually any piece of analytical writing blends these distinctive modes. For example, you might use compare-contrast as the primary organizational strategy for an entire essay, but you also might use another mode (such as definition) to organize a specific paragraph within that essay. In all of your writing, you should choose the writing strategy that best fits your subject, audience, and purpose.

CONTENTS
Analytical Writing

12 Cause and Effect

Overview: Writing a Cause-Effect Essay	184
Student Model	185
Professional Models	188
Guidelines	196
Writing Checklist and Activities	198

13 Comparison and Contrast

Overview: Writing a Comparison-Contrast Essay	200
Student Model	201
Professional Models	203
Guidelines	212
Writing Checklist and Activities	214

14 Classification

Overview: Writing a Classification Essay	216
Student Model	217
Professional Models	220
Guidelines	226
Writing Checklist and Activities	228

15 Process Writing

Overview: Writing About a Process	230
Student Model	231
Professional Models	234
Guidelines	240
Writing Checklist and Activities	242

16 Definition

Overview: Writing a Definition Essay	244
Student Models	245
Professional Models	250
Guidelines	254
Writing Checklist and Activities	256

CAUSE AND EFFECT

12

Now, why did that happen? We ask this question every day at home, in college, and on the job. But why do we ask, "Why?"

Audio

Video

We ask it to understand and cope with things that happen in our lives. For example, knowing why our car overheated will help us avoid that problem in the future. Knowing what causes a disease such as diabetes—or knowing its effects—helps us understand and control the condition. In other words, cause-effect reasoning helps us deal with everyday issues.

In a cause-effect essay, the writer develops the thesis through cause-effect reasoning. That is, he or she analyzes and explains the causes, the effects, or both the causes and the effects of a phenomenon.

Are you ready to write—to analyze and explain the causes and/or effects of one of life's "happenings"? This chapter will help you do so.

Web Link

Overview
Writing a Cause-Effect Essay

Writer's Goal

Your goal is to analyze and explain the causes, the effects, or both the causes and the effects of some phenomenon (fact, occurrence, or circumstance).

Keys for Success

Know your readers. Consider what your readers know and think about your subject. Are they aware of the cause-effect connection associated with it? Do they accept it? Why or why not? If they deny that the connection exists or is relevant, which arguments support their position? Are these arguments strong?

Think logically. Linking cause to effect, or vice versa, requires clear, logical thinking supported by strong evidence. To practice this kind of reasoning, (1) research the topic for evidence connecting a specific cause and/or effect to a specific phenomenon, (2) draft a working thesis stating that connection, and (3) explain the connection in language that your readers will understand.

Test your thinking. Check your main points for clarity, your supporting points for relevance, and your overall argument for logic. Use the list of logical fallacies to identify common weaknesses. (See pages **267–270**, especially "False Cause" on page **269**.)

Topics to Consider

Choose a topic that you care about. Begin by thinking about categories such as those listed below. Then brainstorm a list of phenomena related to each category. From this list, choose a topic and prove its causes, its effects, or both.

- **Family life:** adult children living with parents, increasing number of stay-at-home dads, families choosing to simplify their lifestyles, more people squeezed by needs of children and parents, older women having babies
- **Politics:** decreasing number of student voters, increasing support for oil exploration, increased interest in third-party politics, tension between political action groups
- **Society:** nursing shortage, security concerns, nursing-care facilities, immigrant-advocacy groups, shifting ethnic balances
- **Environment:** common water pollutants, new water-purification technology, effects of a community's recycling program
- **Workplace:** decreasing power of unions, more businesses providing child-care services, need for on-the-job training in technology

> **Next Step** Read the model essays and do the activities that follow. As you read, note how the writers develop their theses using cause-effect reasoning.

Cause and Effect

In the essay below, student writer Tiffany Boyett analyzes the causes and effects of stress in our lives.

Life-Threatening Stress

The writer uses an anecdote to introduce the topic.

It was 8:00 a.m.; her husband, Lance, had left for work without filling the tank on the Mazda, and her daughter, Gina, had gotten on the school bus without her show-and-tell bunny. "Great," thought Jan, "now I have to get gas at Demler's, stop by Gina's school, and drop Alex off at day care—all before my 9:30 class!" Quickly she grabbed the diaper bag, picked up the baby, and headed for the door. At 9:35, with her heart pounding and hands sweating, she scrambled into the classroom, found an open seat, and was hurriedly pulling out her psych notes when the prof asked, "So . . . precisely what does Jung mean by 'collective unconscious'—Jan?" 1

"Uh . . . what was the question?" she responded. 2

Does the scene sound familiar—too much work, too little time, and too much stress? Actually, periods of excessive stress are just part of life in college—or out of college, for that matter. Normally, stress (the response to a perceived threat) is a powerful, life-saving force, but when stress becomes excessive, it is a life-threatening condition. So what should people do— simply accept stress as one more cost of living? 3

She states the thesis.

While accepting some stress is inescapable, for their own health and for the well-being of others, people must do more. They have to understand what stress is—both its causes and its effects. In addition, to avoid the negative effects, they have to learn how to manage the stress in their lives. 4

She explains the symptoms of stress with an example.

So what is stress? Actually, the physiological characteristics of stress are some of the body's potentially good self-defense mechanisms. Take, for example, a man who is crossing a street when he spots an oncoming car. Immediately his brain signals his adrenal glands to release a flood of adrenaline into his bloodstream. As a result, his muscles contract, his eyes dilate, his heart pounds faster, his breathing quickens, and his blood clots more readily. Each one of these responses helps the man leap out of the car's path. His muscles contract to give him exceptional strength. His eyes dilate so that he can see more clearly. His heart pumps more blood and his lungs exchange more air—both to increase his metabolism. If the man were injured, his blood would clot faster, ensuring a smaller amount of blood loss. In this situation and many more like it, stress symptoms are good (Curtis 25–26). 5

A question indicates a transition.

So when is stress dangerous? The danger comes when stress responses are triggered too frequently in a short period of time, or when they are triggered constantly over a longer period of time. While everyday stressors are not life-threatening by themselves, when these stressors happen so 6 frequently that the body lacks time to relax, the normal effects of stress become compounded. One result is that certain body hormones, such as adrenaline and cortisol, are elevated. If the levels of these two hormones are elevated over an extended period of time, several life-threatening conditions can result.

One of the most immediate results of prolonged stress is a decrease   *7*
in the body's natural immune function. The release of cortisol into the bloodstream inhibits a protective hormone released during the immune response and thereby suppresses immune reactions. During periods of stress, the immune system becomes compromised, and the body experiences increased susceptibility to disease (Dombrowski 128). For example, some studies have proven that when medical students prepare for board exams, they experience more stress and get sick more often than when they prepare for less stressful exams.

How do elevated stress levels affect one's health? According to the U.S.   *8*
Census Bureau, the most common cause of death in the United States is heart disease (90). Elevated levels of adrenaline and cortisol in the bloodstream trigger the release of fatty acids, triglycerides, and cholesterol. These substances contribute to the blockage of arteries in the heart, and the blockages lead to heart attacks (Dombrowski 126). Excessive production of cortisol also produces a sustained level of elevated blood pressure or hypertension. If a person is under stress for a long period of time, his or her blood pressure will remain high, forcing the heart to work harder and, consequently, wear out sooner (Wickrama 527).

But stress-induced illnesses include more than head colds, flu, and   *9*
heart disease. The U.S. Census Bureau reports that the second most common cause of death in the United States is cancer (90). Recent studies have linked stress with an increased risk of developing cancer. Increased levels of cortisol associated with stress reduce the efficacy of the immune system, allowing cancer cells to multiply more easily and, therefore, lead to full-blown cancer (Eysenck 223).

According to the U.S. Census Bureau, the third most common cause   *10*
of death in the United States is stroke (90). A new study released by the University of Michigan claims that stress is linked to increased risk of stroke in middle-aged white men (Chande 1771). Increased blood pressure from higher adrenaline levels, along with the blood's increased clotting ability associated with stress, results in a higher risk that blood clots will develop in the brain and cause a stroke.

Diabetes is another illness that has recently been linked to stress.   *11*
Adrenaline in the bloodstream causes the liver to release glucose, the increased glucose raises the level of blood sugar, and increased blood sugar causes the pancreas to secrete insulin. In addition, because cortisol released into the bloodstream actually decreases the effectiveness of insulin, the pancreas must release even greater amounts of insulin. As a result of the high insulin levels, the insulin receptors become less sensitive to insulin,

---

An effect of prolonged stress is described.

The writer explains the effects of elevated stress.

She shows that stress is linked to specific illnesses.

Another example is given.

making it harder for the cells to take up sugar, even when there are no stressors. This decrease in the receptors' sensitivity is the basis for type II diabetes (Dombrowski 127).

12

The writer inserts a qualifier to refine the focus of the sentence.

Excessive stress is dangerous not only because of its link to serious illnesses, but also because of its very nature. In other words, stress is a nonspecific response: Although stress may vary in degree, its nature is the same no matter what sort of threat is perceived. In fact, the threat doesn't even have to be real! As long as a person perceives a threat, he or she will experience stress. For example, someone who is afraid of poisonous spiders may undergo great stress even when in the presence of a harmless spider. In addition, the nonspecific nature of stress works the other way: Someone who is in real danger, but doesn't perceive the danger, will experience no stress. Finally, stress's nonspecific nature makes stress particularly dangerous for those people who perceive threats very readily. These individuals experience stress more commonly—and often more intensely—than others.

13

She reuses her opening illustration to close and unify the essay.

Because stress is so common, many people fail to recognize its potential danger. For example, Jan, the student described earlier, was certainly aware that she experienced stress while bustling through her busy morning. However, if she is like most college students, she wasn't aware that excessive stress could lead to serious illness and early death. Learning about stress's causes and effects is an important first step that they must take. After that, they will be ready for the second step—learning how to manage life-threatening stress. ■

Note: The Works Cited page is not shown. For sample pages, see MLA (pages **532–533**) and APA (page **564**).

Reading for Better Writing

Working by yourself or with a group, answer these questions:

1. The writer uses an anecdote to open and close the essay. Explain why the illustration is or is not effective.

2. List the causes of stress described in the essay. Are they described objectively? Cite examples to support your answer.

3. The writer distinguishes between—and describes the effects of—three forms of stress: normal stress, prolonged stress, and elevated (or excessive) stress. Examine the thinking she uses to link each form to specific effects. Is the logic clear? Is it believable? Why or why not?

4. The writer states her purpose as follows: "They have to understand what stress is—both its causes and its effects." Does she convince you that understanding and managing stress are important? Cite examples to support your answer.

Cause and Effect

In the essay below, Mary Brophy Marcus describes successful businesswomen and argues that the skills they learned from organized sports helped them achieve that success. The essay was first published in *US News & World Report.*

If You Let Me Play . . .

The writer uses an anecdote to introduce the topic and focus the essay.

1. Jackie Thomas, Nike's associate director of sports marketing, usually spends her lunch hour on the sports-shoe company's basketball courts charging for the basket, always outnumbered by male colleagues. "I hold my own," boasts the 33-year-old executive.

2. She also does well playing the corporate game back inside the headquarter's offices. Thomas, a former University of California–Berkeley college basketball point guard, says her success is due in large part to the lessons she learned growing up playing competitive team sports. "It's taught me that if you lose a game, you go back afterward and figure out what went wrong and how to overcome it the next time," says the former tomboy from Kingston, Jamaica.

A dependent clause links the second and third paragraphs.

3. While most of America's corporations are still commanded by male chief executives, women are gaining ground, winning vice-presidential and top management slots and, in a few cases, the highest leadership roles. Many of these young female executives say playing team sports helped them get ahead. A University of Virginia study conducted in the late 1980s showed that 80 percent of key female leaders from *Fortune* 500 companies said they participated in sports and considered themselves tomboys.

The writer describes events (or causes) that helped women gain valuable skills in sports.

4. A lot of credit, female executives say, has to go to Title IX, part of the Federal Education Amendments Act of 1972. It mandated that federally funded schools give women's sports the same treatment as men's games receive. That meant that in schools and colleges across the United States, for every boy's varsity soccer team, there must be a girl's varsity soccer team; for every male basketball scholarship, there must be a female basketball scholarship of equal dollars. Since the early 1970s, the law has increased money for new equipment, coaches, and travel for women's teams. More college scholarships have translated into more diplomas and better jobs for women. Thomas earned a partial academic scholarship when she applied to Berkeley, one of the country's top universities, but without an additional basketball scholarship awarded in her junior and senior years, she would have had a hard time paying for the education.

Using statistical evidence, she cites effects of the causes described in the previous paragraph.

5. Girls' participation in high school sports has spiked from about 300,000 in 1971 to 2.4 million in 1996. At the college level, where competition is tougher, the number of female athletes has increased to 123,832 from 80,040 in 1982, says the National Collegiate Athletic Association.

A quotation supports the writer's thesis: Skills learned in sports help one succeed in business.

"No other experience I know of can prepare you for the high-level competition of business," says Anh Ngyuen, 25, a former Carnegie Mellon University varsity soccer star. She should know. Now she battles Microsoft as a product manager for Netscape Communications. "My colleagues can't believe how aggressive I am," she says.   6

Sports helped these women master the interpersonal skills, like teamwork, that many men take for granted. "I've seen firsthand hundreds and hundreds of times that one person can't win a soccer or softball game," says Maria Murnane, a 28-year-old senior account executive for a San Francisco public-relations firm. "Same goes for work. You have to learn to trust the people on your team, let them run with projects," the former Northwestern soccer center midfielder says. Her boss, William Harris, the president of Strategy Associates, agrees: "We don't want Lone Rangers. She's a team player—a captain and cheerleader."   7

Playing team sports helps with the little things, too. Women learn to speak in sports metaphors as many men do. Lisa Delpy, professor of sports management at George Washington University in Washington, D.C., also notes that in many companies a lot of business is conducted on the golf course, at ballgames, or at other sports events. Women who know the difference between a slide tackle and a sweeper at a World Cup soccer match can fit right in.   8

The writer supports her thesis with an anecdote.

Stephanie Delaney, now 31, captained the varsity soccer team at Franklin and Marshall College in Lancaster, Pennsylvania, when it won the Mid-Atlantic Conference championship her senior year. Now the sales manager for the Caribbean and Latin American division of ConAgra's Lamb-Weston, one of the world's largest frozen-French-fry producers, she was the only woman to play a game of basketball with potential clients at a big food conference last year in Jamaica. "I was the high scorer," she notes.   9

A lively quotation offers interesting details.

And yes, it helped sell french fries. "I didn't close the deal on the court, but afterward when we were hanging out drinking water and shooting the breeze, they agreed to test my product. Now we have Kentucky Fried Chicken's business in Jamaica," says Delaney.   10

Female executives say that Title IX had another subtle, but important, effect. For the first time, many boys, coaches, and parents opened their eyes to the fact that their sisters and daughters could be just as strong, fast, and nimble on the field as their brothers and sons. Likewise, girls whose talents had formerly gone unnoticed under driveway basketball nets and on back lots began realizing their own power—that they could compete with boys and win. "When my girlfriends and I formed a softball team back in college, we were dreadful—like the Keystone Kops," recalls Penny Cate, 45, now a vice president at Quaker Oats. "There'd be four of us in the outfield and the ball would go through our legs. But after a few years, we became very good. It built my confidence, made me realize I could accomplish anything in sports or out," she says.   11

The dash links the word *power* to the defining clause that follows.

The writer cites an advertisement from which she created the essay's title and with which she advances her thesis.

That point is repeatedly brought home when Nike executives ask   *12*
schoolgirls what they think of one of the company's TV ads. The ad begins
with the voice of a young girl saying, "If you let me play . . . ." The phrase
is finished by other little girls saying things like, "I will have greater self-
confidence" or "I will be more likely to stay in school."

The girls often reply, in a tone of genuine befuddlement, "If *who* lets me   *13*
play?" They don't see any barriers between themselves and America's playing
fields. Twenty years from now, might they say, "*What* glass ceiling?" ■

Reading for Better Writing

Working by yourself or with a group, answer these questions:

1. Review the writer's title and her reference to it late in the essay. How
does the writer use the title to introduce and advance her thesis?

2. Mary Brophy Marcus is a journalist who wrote this essay and many
others for publications such as *US News & World Report* and *USA Today*.
Review three or four paragraphs from the essay and explain how her
word choice, sentence structure, and use of quotations are or are not
appropriate for readers of periodicals like these.

3. Review the qualities of an academic style as discussed on pages 78–79.
Then explain why Marcus's essay does or does not reflect this style.
Cite specific passages to support your answer.

4. Marcus uses cause-effect reasoning to argue that (1) women's
participation in sports produces valuable skills and (2) these skills
help women succeed in business. Examine three points, along with the
evidence (data, quotations, and other elements), that Marcus uses to
support either of these claims. Finally, explain why each supporting
point and its related evidence are or are not convincing.

5. Marcus concludes her essay with the question, "*What* glass ceiling?"
Explain why the quotation does or does not (1) advance her thesis and
(2) close the essay effectively.

6. Working with a classmate, review the checklist under Step 7, "Revise
the essay," found on page 197. Then analyze to what degree Marcus
accomplishes each task in this checklist.

Cause and Effect

Christy Haubegger is the founder of *Latina* magazine. This essay was originally published in the July 12, 1999, issue of *Newsweek* magazine.

The Legacy of Generation Ñ

About 20 years ago, some mainstream observers declared the 1980s the "decade of the Hispanic." The Latino population was nearing 15 million! (It's since doubled.) However, our decade was postponed—a managerial oversight, no doubt—and eventually rescheduled for the '90s. What happens to a decade deferred? It earns compounded interest and becomes the next hundred years. The United States of the 21st century will be undeniably ours. Again.

A metaphor helps to make the writer's point.

It's Manifest *Destino*. After all, Latinos are true Americans, some of the original residents of the *Américas*. Spanish was the first European language spoken on this continent. Which is why we live in places like *Los Angeles*, *Colorado*, and *Florida* rather than The Angels, Colored, and Flowered. Now my generation is about to put a Latin stamp on the rest of the culture—and that will ultimately be the Ñ legacy.

The writer lists examples that illustrate her claim.

We are not only numerous; we are also growing at a rate seven times that of the general population. Conservative political ads notwithstanding, this growth is driven by natural increase (births over deaths) rather than immigration. At 30, I may be the oldest childless Latina in the United States. More important, however, while our preceding generation felt pressure to assimilate, America has now generously agreed to meet us in the middle. Just as we become more American, America is simultaneously becoming more Latino.

Examples from pop culture connect with readers and help to make the writer's ideas memorable.

This quiet *revolución* can perhaps be traced back to the bloodless coup of 1992, when salsa outsold ketchup for the first time. Having toppled the leadership in the condiment category, we set our sights even higher. Fairly soon, there was a congresswoman named Sanchez representing Orange County, a taco-shilling Chihuahua became a national icon, and now everyone is *loca* for Ricky Martin.

We are just getting started. Our geographic concentration and reputation for family values are making us every politician's dream constituency. How long can New Hampshire, with just four Electoral College votes—and probably an equal number of Hispanic residents—continue to get so much attention from presidential candidates? Advertisers will also soon be begging for our attention. With a median age of 26 (eight years younger than the general market), Latinos hardly exist outside their coveted 18–34 demographic. Remember, we may only be 11 percent of the country, but we buy 16 percent of the lipliner.

The writer transitions to the anticipated effects of the population growth she has described.

The media will change as well, especially television, where we now appear to be rapidly approaching extinction. Of the 26 new comedies and dramas appearing this fall [1999] on the four major networks, not one has a Latino in a leading role. The Screen Actors Guild released employment statistics for 1998 showing that the percentage of roles going to Hispanic actors actually declined from the previous year. But, pretty soon, the cast of "Friends" will need to find some amigos. Seeing as they live in New York City, and there's almost 2 million of us in the metropolitan area, this shouldn't prove too difficult. 6

Shifting to future tense ("will") marks these statements as predictions.

Face it: This is going to be a bilingual country. Back in 1849, the California Constitution was written in both Spanish and English, and we're headed that way again. If our children speak two languages instead of just one, how can that not be a benefit to us all? The re-Latinization of this country will pay off in other ways as well. I, for one, look forward to that pivotal moment in our history when all American men finally know how to dance. Latin music will no longer be found in record stores under "Foreign," and romance will bloom again. Our children will ask us what it was like to dance without a partner. 7

The paragraph begins with the word *dawn* and ends with *mañana* and *morning*.

"American food" will mean low-fat enchiladas and hamburgers served with rice and beans. As a result, the American standard of beauty will necessarily expand to include a female size 12, and anorexia will be found only in medical-history books. Finally, just in time for the baby boomers' senescence, living with extended family will become hip again. *Simpsons* fans of the next decade will see Grandpa moving back home. We'll all go back to church together. 8

At the dawn of a new millennium, America knows Latinos as entertainers and athletes. But, someday very soon, all American children can dream of growing up to be writers like Sandra Cisneros, astronauts like Ellen Ochoa, or judges like Jose Cabranes of the Second Circuit Court of Appeals. To put a Latin spin on a famous Anglo phrase: It is truly *mañana* in America. For those of you who don't know it (yet), that word doesn't just mean tomorrow; *mañana* also means morning. ■ 9

Reading for Better Writing

Working by yourself or with a group, answer these questions:

1. In one sentence, summarize the cause(s) and effect(s) of the changes described in this essay.

2. Writers must make their claims using words that convey an appropriate level of certainty. Is Haubegger's use of "will" (versus "may") appropriate in paragraphs 7 and 8? Why?

3. Review paragraph 9. What is the writer's point? Do you agree?

4. The writer published this essay in 1999. Cite examples showing that the changes she described are continuing.

Cause and Effect

Anna Quindlen's 1992 *New York Times* column "Public and Private" won the Pulitzer Prize for commentary. She now writes a regular column for *Newsweek* magazine, where the piece below was originally published in 2001.

Our Tired, Our Poor, Our Kids

As you read this essay, highlight passages that help advance Quindlen's cause-effect argument. In the margin, note why each passage is effective.

Six people live here, in a room the size of the master bedroom in a modest suburban house. Trundles, bunk beds, dressers side by side stacked with toys, clothes, boxes, in tidy claustrophobic clutter. One woman, five children. The baby was born in a shelter. The older kids can't wait to get out of this one. Everyone gets up at 6 a.m., the little ones to go to day care, the others to school. Their mother goes out to look for an apartment when she's not going to drug-treatment meetings. "For what they pay for me to stay in a shelter I could have lived in the Hamptons," Sharanda says.

Here is the parallel universe that has flourished while the more fortunate were rewarding themselves for the stock split with SUVs and home additions. There is a boom market in homelessness. But these are not the men on the streets of San Francisco holding out cardboard signs to the tourists. They are children, hundreds of thousands of them, twice as likely to repeat a grade or be hospitalized and four times as likely to go hungry as the kids with a roof over their heads. Twenty years ago New York City provided emergency shelter for just under a thousand families a day; last month it had to find spaces for 10,000 children on a given night. Not since the Great Depression have this many babies, toddlers, and kids had no place like home.

> *They are children, hundreds of thousands of them . . .*

Three mothers sit in the living room of a temporary residence called Casa Rita in the Bronx and speak of this in the argot of poverty. "The landlord don't call back when they hear you got EARP," says Rosie, EARP being the Emergency Assistance Rehousing Program. "You get priority for Section 8 if you're in a shelter," says Edna, which means federal housing programs will put you higher on the list. Edna has four kids, three in foster care; she arrived at Casa Rita, she says, "with two bags and a baby." Rosie has three, they share a bathroom down the hall with two other families. Sharanda's five range in age from thirteen to just over a year. Her eldest was put in the wrong grade when he changed schools. "He's humiliated, living here," his mother says.

All three women are anxious to move on, although they appreciate this place, where they can get shelter, get sober, and keep their kids at the same time. They remember the Emergency Assistance Unit, the city office that is the gateway to the system, where hundreds of families sit every day surrounded by their bags, where children sleep on benches until they are shuffled off dull-eyed for one night in a shelter or a motel, only to return as supplicants again the next day.

In another world, middle-class Americans have embraced new-home starts, the stock market, and the Gap. But in the world of these displaced families, problems ignored or fumbled or unforeseen during this great period of prosperity have dovetailed into an enormous subculture of children who think that only rich people have their own bedrooms. Twenty years ago, when the story of the homeless in America became a staple of news reporting, the solution was presented as a simple one: affordable housing. That's still true, now more than ever. Two years ago the National Low Income Housing Coalition calculated that the hourly income necessary to afford the average two-bedroom apartment was around $12. That's more than twice the minimum wage.   5

The result is that in many cities police officers and teachers cannot afford to live where they work, that in Las Vegas old motels provide housing for casino employees, that in shelters now there is a contingent of working poor who get up off their cots and go off to their jobs. The result is that if you are evicted for falling behind on your rent, if there is a bureaucratic foul-up in your welfare check, or the factory in which you work shuts down, the chances of finding another place to live are very small indeed. You're one understanding relative, one paycheck, one second chance from the street. And so are your kids.

> *[P]olice officers and teachers cannot afford to live where they work . . .*   6

So-called welfare reform, which emphasizes cutbacks and make-work, has played a part in all this. A study done in San Diego in 1998 found that a third of homeless families had recently had benefits terminated or reduced, and that most said that was how they had wound up on the street. Drugs, alcohol, and domestic abuse also land mothers with kids in the shelter system or lead them to hand their children over to relatives or foster homes. Today the average homeless woman is younger than ever before, may have been in foster care or in shelters herself, and so considers a chaotic childhood the norm. Many never finished high school, and have never held a job.   7

Ralph Nunez, who runs the organization Homes for the Homeless, says that all this calls for new attitudes. "People don't like to hear it, but shelters are going to be the low-income housing of the future," he says. "So how do we enrich the experience and use the system to provide job training and education?" Bonnie Stone of Women in Need, which has eight other residences along with Casa Rita, says, "We're pouring everything we've got into the nine months most of them are here—nutrition, treatment,   8 budgeting. By the time they leave, they have a subsidized apartment, day care and, hopefully, some life skills they didn't have before."

But these organizations are rafts in a rising river of need that has roared through this country without most of us ever even knowing. So now you know. There are hundreds of thousands of little nomads in America, sleeping in the back of cars, on floors in welfare offices, or in shelters five to a room. What would it mean, to spend your childhood drifting from one strange bed to another, waking in the morning to try to figure out where you'd landed today, without those things that confer security and happiness: a familiar picture on the wall, a certain slant of light through a curtained window? "Give me your tired, your poor," it says on the base of the Statue of Liberty, to welcome foreigners. Oh, but they are already here, the small refugees from the ruin of the American dream, even if you cannot see them. ■

9

Reading for Better Writing

Working by yourself or with a group, answer these questions:

1. In one sentence, state the cause/effect relationship that Quindlen outlines in "Our Tired, Our Poor, Our Kids."

2. In writing, an *allusion* is an indirect reference to another text. What allusions can you identify in this piece? Why does the writer use allusions in this essay?

3. Use a pencil or sticky notes to distinguish portions of the essay where Quindlen addresses the cause(s) and the effect(s) of the problem. What is the approximate ratio of space given to each? How are the cause-effect sections arranged? How do these factors affect the essay's message?

4. Notice that Quindlen occasionally begins sentences with conjunctions such as *but* or *and*. Where, and why? Where might this strategy be appropriate in your writing?

Model

Guidelines
Writing a Cause-Effect Essay

1. **Select a topic.** Look again at the list of facts, occurrences, or circumstances mentioned under "Topics to Consider" on page 184. Expand the list by jotting down additional items for each category, or listing new categories along with related items. From this finished list, choose a topic and prove its causes, its effects, or both.

   > **TIP:** If your professor approves, you could write an essay contradicting the logic in another writer's cause-effect essay. For an example, see "An Apology for the Life of Ms. Barbie D. Doll" on pages 277–278.

2. **Narrow and research the topic.** Write down or type your topic. Below it, brainstorm a list of related causes and effects in two columns. Next, do preliminary research to expand the list and distinguish primary causes and effects from secondary ones. Revise your topic as needed to address only primary causes and/or effects that research links to a specific phenomenon.

Cause/Effect Topic: _____

Causes (Because of)	Effects (this results)
1._____	1._____
2._____	2._____
3._____	3._____
4._____	4._____

3. **Draft and test your thesis.** Based on your preliminary research, draft a working thesis (you may revise it later) that introduces the topic, along with the causes and/or effects you intend to discuss. Limit your argument to only those points you can prove.

4. **Gather and analyze information.** Research your topic, looking for clear evidence that links specific causes to specific effects. At the same time, avoid arguments mistaking a coincidence for a cause-effect relationship. Use the list of logical fallacies (see pages 267–270) to weed out common errors in logic. For example, finding chemical pollutants in a stream running beside a chemical plant does not "prove" that the plant caused the pollutants.

5. **Get organized.** Develop an outline that lays out your thesis and argument in a clear pattern. Under each main point asserting a cause-effect connection, list details from your research that support the connection.

   Thesis: _____

Point 1	*Point 2*	*Point 3*
• Supporting details	• Supporting details	• Supporting details
• Supporting details	• Supporting details	• Supporting details
• Supporting details	• Supporting details	• Supporting details

6. **Use your outline to draft the essay.** Try to rough out the essay's overall argument before you attempt to revise it. As you write, show how each specific cause led to each specific effect, citing examples as needed. To show those cause-effect relationships, use transitional words like the following:

accordingly	for this purpose	since	therefore
as a result	for this reason	so	thus
because	hence	such as	to illustrate
consequently	just as	thereby	whereas

7. **Revise the essay.** Whether your essay presents causes, effects, or both, use the checklist below to trace and refine your argument.

    _____ The thesis and introduction clearly identify the causes and/or effects.

    _____ All major causes and/or effects are addressed.

    _____ Statements regarding the causes and/or effects are sufficiently limited and focused.

    _____ Supporting details are researched, relevant, and strong.

    _____ Links between causes and effects are clear and logical.

    _____ The conclusion restates the main argument and unifies the essay.

8. **Get feedback.** Ask a peer reviewer or someone from the college's writing center to read your essay for the following:

    -   An engaging opening
    -   A clear and logical thesis
    -   Clear and convincing reasoning that links specific causes to specific effects
    -   A closing that wraps up the argument, leaving no loose ends

9. **Edit the essay for clarity and correctness.** Check for the following:

    -   Precise, appropriate word choice
    -   Complete, smooth sentences
    -   Clear transitions between paragraphs
    -   Correct names, dates, and supporting details
    -   Correct mechanics, usage, and grammar

10. **Publish your essay.** Share your writing with others as follows:

    -   Submit it to your instructor.
    -   Post it on the class's or department's website.
    -   Submit the essay for presentation at an appropriate conference.
    -   Send it as a service to relevant nonprofit agencies.
    -   Share the essay with family and friends.

Writing Checklist

Use these seven traits to check the quality of your writing and revise as needed:

_____ The **ideas** explain the causes and/or effects of the topic in a clear, well-reasoned argument supported by credible information.

_____ The **organization** helps the reader understand the cause-effect relationship. The links between the main points and the supporting points are clear.

_____ The **voice** is informed, polite, and professional.

_____ The **words** are precise and clear. Technical or scientific terms are defined. Causes are linked to effects with transitional words and phrases such as *therefore*, *as a result*, and *for this reason*.

_____ The **sentences** are clear, varied in structure, and smooth.

_____ The **copy** is correct and clear.

_____ The **design** follows the assigned guidelines and format.

Interactive

Critical-Thinking and Writing Activities

As directed by your instructor, complete the following activities.

1. In "Life-Threatening Stress," the writer describes a health problem experienced by many college students. List their other common health problems, choose one, and write an essay proving its causes and/or effects.

2. Draft an essay in which you support your claim with cause-effect reasoning.

3. One way to instill coherence in an essay is to make direct or indirect connections between the opening and closing of the piece. Review Anna Quindlen's "Our Tired, Our Poor, Our Kids," noting the connections between the title and the concluding paragraph. Revise one of your essays by linking the language and ideas of the opening and closing sections.

4. Choose a phenomenon that is related to your program or major and that is discussed in the news media. Write an essay that analyzes and explains its causes, its effects, or both. Consider submitting the essay to your adviser, asking for feedback, and then polishing the piece for inclusion in your professional portfolio.

◀ VISUALLY SPEAKING

Review the photograph on the opening page of this chapter. What concepts or ideas does the picture convey? How might cause-effect reasoning be used to develop and advance these ideas? Explain.

COMPARISON AND CONTRAST

13

Audio

Video

In his plays, William Shakespeare creates characters, families, and even plot lines that mirror each other. As a result, we see Hamlet in relation to Laertes and the Montagues in relation to the Capulets. In the process, we do precisely what the writer wants us to do—we compare and contrast the subjects. The result is clarity and insight: By thinking about both subjects, we understand each one more clearly.

In this chapter, four writers use compare-and-contrast organization: one to analyze two literary characters, another to explain two views of a river, a third to assess two patterns of dress for Iranian women, and a fourth to describe ethnic groups. Elsewhere in this book, you will find writers working in the natural sciences, the social sciences, and the humanities—all comparing and contrasting two or more subjects with the goal of helping their readers understand the topics.

What's the point? Comparing and contrasting is a writing-and-thinking strategy used across the curriculum and in the workplace. You are about to write an essay using this strategy. What you learn in the process will help you succeed both in other courses and in your postcollege career.

Overview
Writing a Comparison-Contrast Essay

Writer's Goal

Your goal is to write an essay that (1) sets two or more subjects side by side, (2) shows the reader how they are similar and/or different, and (3) draws conclusions or makes some point based on what you have shown.

Keys for Success

Think about your readers. What do they know about the subject? What should they know? Why should they care? Answering these questions will help you understand both your readers and your purpose for writing.

Know your purpose. What do you want your essay to do? Inform? Explain? Persuade? Some combination of these? Knowing your purpose will help you decide what to include (and not include) in the essay, how to organize it, and how to help readers use the information.

Be logical. Comparing and contrasting is a logical process that helps you understand your subjects more fully and explain them more clearly. Begin by determining the basis of your comparison: How are the subjects related? Then decide whether to compare, to contrast, or both. When *comparing* subjects, show how they are similar. When *contrasting* them, show how they are different. When *comparing* and *contrasting* subjects, show how they are both similar and different. To choose which of the three patterns to follow, think about your purpose. Which pattern will help your essay accomplish what you want it to?

Topics to Consider

Choose subjects that are related in some important way. To get started, think about pairs of objects, events, places, processes, people, ideas, beliefs, and so on. For more inspiration, read the four models in this chapter and scan the models listed below. Each of these essays uses strategies to compare and contrast. List topics similar to those in the models.

- "Three Family Cancers," pages 217–219
- "Four Ways to Talk About Literature," pages 220–221
- "No Wonder They Call Me a Bitch," pages 222–225

> **Next Step** Read the model essays and perform the activities that follow. As you read, note whether the writer compares, contrasts, or both. Also note the pattern used to organize the essay: subject by subject, trait by trait, and so on.

Comparison

In this essay, Janae Sebranek compares the fate of two tragic literary characters, Bigger in *Native Son* and Alan in *Equus*. The student writer makes a trait-by-trait comparison, exploring how work, religion, and the media affect the characters.

Beyond Control

The writer introduces her topic, main points of comparison, and thesis.

Most children, no matter what their personal or family situation, lead more or less controlled lives. As they grow, they begin to sense the pressure of controlling factors in their lives, and start struggling to take control themselves. This can be a difficult process. In the works *Native Son* and *Equus*, Richard Wright and Peter Shaffer, respectively, create two characters who must deal with this struggle. Bigger in *Native Son* and Alan in *Equus* are both entering adulthood and have come to realize that they are controlled by work, religion, and the media. In the midst of these characters' efforts to gain control, each character falls into a tragic situation.

1

She describes one of the traits of the first character.

We find Alan experiencing the pressure of working as a clerk at Bryson's appliance store. The customers are demanding, and the many products and brand names are confusing. He finds that he cannot function in this work environment. Later, under hypnosis, he admits to Dr. Dysart that his "foes" are the myriad of brand names he is challenged to locate and explain to the customers—"The Hosts of Hoover. The Hosts of Philco. Those Hosts of Pifco. The House of Remington and all its tribe!" (73). However, by recognizing the demands of this job, Alan attempts to take some control over his life.

2

Alan exercises further control when he decides to look for another job. He likes being around horses, so he pursues and lands a job with Mr. Dalton, a stable owner. He enjoys his job and begins to deal more effectively with the whole concept of work.

3

She describes a parallel trait of the second character and then contrasts the traits.

Bigger must also struggle with the pressure and anxiety of his first job. Because of his family's desperate financial situation, he is forced to take the one job he is offered, coincidentally, by a Mr. Dalton. He works as a chauffeur for Mr. Dalton's wealthy suburban family. Bigger cannot relate to them. He sees himself as a foreigner, forced to live and work among the privileged. The Daltons tell him where, when, and even how to drive. Bigger struggles; but, like Alan, he cannot deal with the extreme discomfort he is feeling. He quits after only two days on the job. Unlike Alan, however, he does not have the option of getting a job that interests him.

4

Alan and Bigger also find religion to be a controlling factor in their lives. Alan's mother, Dora, "doses [religion] down the boy's throat" as she whispers "that Bible to him hour after hour, up there in his room" (33). Obviously, Alan's mother believes that he needs the controlling force of religion in his life, so she preaches to him every night. For a time, he is fascinated by the Bible's imagery and ideas. Eventually, though, this fascination begins to fade.

5

She notes a contrast.

Bigger's mother does not push the issue of religion to the extreme that 6
Alan's mother does. Instead, she tries to make her son see its value with
daily comments such as "You'll regret how you living someday" (13). She
offers her advice by singing religious songs from behind a curtain in their
one-room apartment. She tries to show Bigger that religion is a valid way of
dealing with a world out of control. But Bigger refuses to accept her religion,
and he is left with no spiritual footing or direction.

She introduces her last point of comparison.

Finally, we find the media playing a tormenting, controlling role in 7
both Alan's and Bigger's lives. Alan's father calls television a "dangerous
drug" (27) that can control the mind. Alan still manages to watch television,
but only because his mother "used to let him slip off in the afternoons to
a friend next door" (31) to watch. Later, while he is under psychiatric care,
he watches television every night and eventually finds himself becoming
controlled by the medium.

Bigger, in a more tragic way, is also controlled by the media. He reads 8
about himself in the newspapers and begins to believe certain things that
have no valid basis. He is referred to as a "Negro killer" who looks "as if
about to spring upon you at any moment" (260). The papers remark that
Bigger "seems a beast utterly untouched" (260) by and out of place in the
white man's world. Unfortunately, Bigger has no control over what is printed
or over what other people believe about him.

She summarizes her argument and restates the thesis.

Bigger's ultimate fate is clearly beyond his control. He is falsely accused 9
of raping and killing a woman, and he cannot convince anyone of the
truth. Bigger's identity is too closely linked with the descriptions given in
the newspapers. And this identity tragically leads to his death. Alan's fate is
different, although tragic in its own right. While in the psychiatric ward, he
gains a certain control with the help of therapy and medication. However,
he loses his passion for life: "Passion, you see, can be destroyed by a doctor.
It cannot be created" (108). This is Alan's personal tragedy.

Ultimately, both Alan and Bigger fail to gain real control over the 10
outside forces in their lives. Alan forfeits his interest in life, and Bigger
forfeits life itself. They, like so many people, become victims of the world in
which they live. ■

Note: The Works Cited page is not shown. For sample pages, see MLA (page
532–533) and APA (page **564**).

Reading for Better Writing

1. Do the opening paragraphs adequately introduce the topic and the
thesis? Why or why not?

2. This essay is organized trait by trait. Is this strategy used effectively?

3. Does the writer focus on similarities, differences, or both? Is her choice
effective?

Comparison and Contrast

Mark Twain is best known for his novels *The Adventures of Tom Sawyer* and *The Adventures of Huckleberry Finn*. In this excerpt from his 1883 memoir, *Life on the Mississippi,* Twain contrasts his mindset as an apprentice with his perspective as a steamboat pilot.

Two Views of the River

The writer starts the sentence with the contrasting conjunction *but*.

Now when I had mastered the language of this water, and had come to know every trifling feature that bordered the great river as familiarly as I knew the letters of the alphabet, I had made a valuable acquisition. But I had lost something, too. I had lost something which could never be restored to me while I lived. All the grace, the beauty, the poetry, had gone out of the majestic river! I still keep in mind a certain wonderful sunset which I witnessed when steamboating was new to me. A broad expanse of the river was turned to blood; in the middle distance the red hue brightened into gold, through which a solitary log came floating black and conspicuous; in one place a long, slanting mark lay sparkling upon the water; in another the surface was broken by boiling, tumbling rings that were as many-tinted as an opal; where the ruddy flush was faintest, was a smooth spot that was covered with graceful circles and radiating lines, ever so delicately traced; the shore on our left was densely wooded, and the somber shadow that fell from this forest was broken in one place by a long, ruffled trail that shone like silver; and high above the forest wall a clean-stemmed dead tree waved a single leafy bough that glowed like a flame in the unobstructed splendor that was flowing from the sun. There were graceful curves, reflected images, woody heights, soft distances; and over the whole scene, far and near, the dissolving lights drifted steadily, enriching it every passing moment with new marvels of coloring.

The sunset is described in a long, one-sentence list of sensory details.

Again a sentence begins with *but*.

I stood like one bewitched. I drank it in, in a speechless rapture. The world was new to me, and I had never seen anything like this at home. But as I have said, a day came when I began to cease from noting the glories and the charms which the moon and the sun and the twilight wrought upon the river's face; another day came when I ceased altogether to note them. Then, if that sunset scene had been repeated, I should have looked upon it without rapture, and should have commented upon it, inwardly, after this fashion: "This sun means that we are going to have wind tomorrow; that floating log means that the river is rising, small thanks to it; that slanting mark on the water refers to a bluff reef which is going to kill somebody's steamboat one of these nights, if it keeps on stretching out like that, those tumbling 'boils' show a dissolving bar and a changing channel there; the lines and circles in the slick water over yonder are a warning that that troublesome place

Another long, one-sentence list counters the earlier description of the river.

is shoaling up dangerously; that silver streak in the shadow of the forest is the 'break' from a new snag, and he has located himself in the very best place he could have found to fish for steamboats; that tall dead tree, with a single living branch, is not going to last long, and then how is a body ever going to get through this blind place at night without the friendly old landmark?"

No, the romance and beauty were all gone from the river. All the value any feature of it had for me now was the amount of usefulness it could furnish toward compassing the safe piloting of a steamboat. Since those days, I have pitied doctors from my heart. What does the lovely flush in a beauty's cheek mean to a doctor but a "break" that ripples above some deadly disease? Are not all her visible charms sown thick with what are to him the signs and symbols of hidden decay? Does he ever see her beauty at all, or doesn't he simply view her professionally, and comment upon her unwholesome condition all to himself? And doesn't he sometimes wonder whether he has gained most or lost most by learning his trade? ■

The paragraph ends with a series of interrelated questions.

Reading for Better Writing

Working by yourself or with a group, answer these questions:

1. The purpose for comparing and contrasting two things is to make a point. What two specific things is Twain comparing and contrasting, and what is the point he is making? How do you know?

2. Twain first describes one way of looking at the river, then another. How else might he have organized the ideas in this passage? Make an argument for the organizational pattern that you think is most effective.

3. At two points in the passage, Twain begins sentences with the conjunction *but*. Why doesn't he simply combine these sentences with those that precede them?

4. Find examples of short, average, and long sentences in this passage. Where are they located, and why does Twain vary his sentence length in this way?

5. This passage ends with a series of rhetorical questions—questions that are intended to provoke thought but not an expressed answer. What clues suggest that Twain is expecting thought rather than actual answers? Why might he use this strategy?

Comparison and Contrast

Gelareh Asayesh grew up in Iran before moving to Florida. She writes about her experiences in *Saffron Sky: A Life Between Iran and America.* The article below first appeared in the *New York Times* in November 2001.

Shrouded in Contradiction

Two contrasting scenes appear in the first sentence.

I grew up wearing the miniskirt to school, the veil to the mosque. In the Tehran of my childhood, women in bright sundresses shared the sidewalk with women swathed in black. The tension between the two ways of life was palpable. As a schoolgirl, I often cringed when my bare legs got leering or contemptuous glances. Yet, at times, I long for the days when I could walk the streets of my country with the wind in my hair. When clothes were clothes. In today's Iran, whatever I wear sends a message. If it's a chador, it embarrasses my Westernized relatives. If it's a skimpy scarf, I risk being accused of stepping on the blood of the martyrs who died in the war with Iraq. Each time I return to Tehran, I wait until the last possible moment, when my plane lands on the tarmac,

> *As a schoolgirl, I often cringed when my bare legs got leering or contemptuous glances.*

to don the scarf and long jacket that many Iranian women wear in lieu of a veil. To wear *hijab*—Islamic covering—is to invite contradiction. Sometimes I hate it. Sometimes I value it.

Italics distinguish *hijab* as a non-English word.

Most of the time, I don't even notice it. It's annoying, but so is wearing pantyhose to work. It ruins my hair, but so does the humidity in Florida, where I live. For many women, the veil is neither a symbol nor a statement. It's simply what they wear, as their mothers did before them. Something to dry your face with after your ablutions before prayer. A place for a toddler to hide when he's feeling shy. Even for a woman like me, who wears it with a hint of rebellion, *hijab* is just not that big a deal.

Notice the one-sentence paragraph.

Except when it is.

"Sister, what kind of get-up is this?" a woman in black, one of a pair, asks me one summer day on the Caspian shore. I am standing in line to ride a gondola up a mountain, where I'll savor some ice cream along with vistas of sea and forest. Women in chadors stand wilting in the heat, faces gleaming with sweat. Women in makeup and clunky heels wear knee-length jackets with pants, their hair daringly exposed beneath sheer scarves.

None have been more daring than I. I've wound my scarf into a turban, 5 leaving my neck bare to the breeze. The woman in black is a government employee paid to police public morals. "Fix your scarf at once!" she snaps.

"But I'm hot," I say. 6

"You're hot?" she exclaims. "Don't you think we all are?" 7

I start unwinding my makeshift turban. "The men aren't hot," 8 I mutter.

Her companion looks at me in shocked reproach. "Sister, this isn't 9 about men and women," she says, shaking her head. "This is about Islam."

> Contradictory feelings are pushed together in a compact list.

I want to argue. I feel like a child. Defiant, but powerless. Burning with 10 injustice, but also with a hint of shame. I do as I am told, feeling acutely conscious of the bare skin I am covering. In policing my sexuality, these women have made me more aware of it.

> The writer offers definitions of *passion* reflecting three different perspectives.

The veil masks erotic freedom, but its advocates believe *hijab* transcends the erotic— or expands it. In the West, we think of passion as a fever of the body, not the soul. In the East, Sufi poets used earthly passion as a metaphor; the beloved they celebrated was God. Where I come from, people are more likely to find delirious passion in the mosque than in the bedroom.

> *The veil masks erotic freedom, but its advocates believe "hijab" transcends the erotic—or expands it.* 11

There are times when I feel a hint of this passion. A few years after my 12 encounter on the Caspian, I go to the wake of a family friend. Sitting in a mosque in Mashhad, I grip a slippery black veil with one hand and a prayer book with the other. In the center of the hall, there's a stack of Koranic texts decorated with green-and-black calligraphy, a vase of white gladioluses and a large photograph of the dearly departed. Along the walls, women wait quietly.

From the men's side of the mosque, the mullah's voice rises in 13 lament. His voice is deep and plaintive, oddly compelling. I bow my head, sequestered in my veil while at my side a community of women pray and weep with increasing abandon. I remember from girlhood this sense of

The writer
uses terms
of limited
certainty,
such as
perhaps and
all I know.

being exquisitely alone in the company of others. Sometimes I have cried as well, free to weep without having to offer an explanation. Perhaps they are right, those mystics who believe that physical love is an obstacle to spiritual love; those architects of mosques who abstained from images of earthly life, decorating their work with geometric shapes that they believed freed the soul to slip from its worldly moorings. I do not aspire to such lofty sentiments. All I know is that such moments of passionate abandon, within the circle of invisibility created by the veil, offer an emotional catharsis every bit as potent as any sexual release.

The final line
summarizes
the
contradictions
described in
the passage.

Outside, the rain pours from a sullen sky. I make my farewells and walk toward the car, where my driver waits. My veil is wicking muddy water from the sidewalk. I gather up the wet and grimy folds with distaste, longing to be home, where I can cast off this curtain of cloth that gives with one hand, takes away with the other. ■ 14

Reading for Better Writing

Working by yourself or with a group, answer these questions:

1. Sometimes writers use comparison-contrast organization to take a position on an issue—in some cases to show that one side is better than the other, but in others, to show the difficulty of choosing one side over the other. What do you think is Asayesh's position on *hijab*, and why?

2. Find Asayesh's one-sentence paragraph (paragraph 3). Why might the writer have constructed the paragraph in this way? How would this excerpt differ if that sentence had been part of either the preceding or the following paragraph?

3. What contrasts are listed in paragraph 4? How does the writer use sentence structure and punctuation to mark the contrasts?

4. Why does Asayesh use words that indicate limited certainty, such as *perhaps* and *all I know*?

5. In what ways are the opening and closing sentences alike? How are these similarities significant for readers?

Comparison and Contrast

Author Gary Soto describes falling in love against his family's advice with a woman who is not Mexican. In doing so, he draws a number of comparisons.

In the text, highlight elements of comparison and contrast that you find interesting or engaging. Then in the margin, explain your response.

Like Mexicans

My grandmother gave me bad advice and good advice when I was in my early teens. For the bad advice, she said that I should become a barber because they made good money and listened to the radio all day. "Honey, they don't work como burros," she would say every time I visited her. She made the sound of donkeys braying. "Like that, Honey!" For good advice, she said that I should marry a Mexican girl. "No Okies, hijo"—she would say—"Look, my son. He marry one and they fight every day about I don't know what and I don't know what." For her, everyone who wasn't Mexican, black, or Asian was an Okie. The French were Okies, the Italians in suits were Okies. When I asked about Jews, whom I had read about, she asked for a picture. I rode home on my bicycle and returned with a calendar depicting the important races of the world. "Pues si, son Okies también!" she said, nodding her head. She waved the calendar away and we went to the living room, where she lectured me on the virtues of the Mexican girl: first, she could cook and, second, she acted like a woman, not a man, in her husband's home. She said she would tell me about a third when I got a little older.

I asked my mother about it—becoming a barber and marrying Mexican. She was in the kitchen. Steam curled from a pot of boiling beans, the radio was on, looking as squat as a loaf of bread. "Well, if you want to be a barber—they say they make good money." She slapped a round steak with a knife, her glasses slipping down with each strike. She stopped and looked up. "If you find a good Mexican girl, marry her, of course." She returned to slapping the meat, and I went to the backyard where my brother and David King were sitting on the lawn feeling the insides of their cheeks.

"This is what girls feel like," my brother said, rubbing the inside of his cheek. David put three fingers inside his mouth and scratched. I ignored them and climbed the back fence to see my best friend, Scott, a second-generation Okie. I had called him, and his mother pointed to the side of the house where his bedroom was, a small aluminum trailer, the kind you gawk at when they're flipped over on the freeway, wheels spinning in the air. I went around to find Scott pitching horseshoes.

I picked up a set of rusty ones and joined him. While we played, we talked about school and friends and record albums. The horseshoes scuffed up dirt, sometimes ringing the iron that threw out a meager shadow like a sundial. After three argued-over games we pulled two oranges apiece from his tree and started down the alley still talking school and friends and record albums. We pulled more oranges from the alley and talked about who we would marry. "No offense, Scott," I said with an orange slice in my mouth, "but I would never marry an Okie." We walked in step, almost touching, with a sled of shadows dragging behind us. "No offense, Gary," Scott said, "but I would *never* marry a Mexican." I looked at him: a fang of orange slice showed from his munching mouth. I didn't think anything of it. He had his girl and I had mine. But our seventh-grade vision was the same: to marry, get jobs, buy cars and maybe a house if we had money left over.

We talked about our future lives until, to our surprise, we were on   5
the downtown mall, two miles from home. We bought a bag of popcorn at Penneys and sat on a bench near the fountain watching Mexican and Okie girls pass. "That one's mine," I pointed with my chin when a girl with eyebrows arched into black rainbows ambled by. "She's cute," Scott said about a girl with yellow hair and mouthful of gum. We dreamed aloud, our chins busy pointing out girls. We agreed that we couldn't wait to become men and lift them onto our laps.

But the woman I married was not Mexican but Japanese. It was a   6
surprise to me. For years, I went about wide-eyed in my search for the brown girl in a white dress at a dance. I searched the playground at the baseball diamond. When the girls raced for grounders, their hair bounced like something that couldn't be caught. When they sat together in the lunchroom, heads pressed together, I knew they were talking about us Mexican guys. I saw them and dreamed them. I threw my face into my pillow, making up sentences that were as good as in the movies.

> *For years, I went about wide-eyed in my search for the brown girl in a white dress at a dance.*

But when I was twenty, I fell in love with   7
this other girl who worried my mother, who had my grandmother asking once again to see the calendar of the Important Races of the World. I told her I had thrown it away many years before. I took a much-glanced-at snapshot from my wallet. We looked at it together, in silence. Then Grandma reclined in her chair, lit a cigarette, and said, "Es pretty." She blew and asked with all her worry pushed up to her forehead: "Chinese?"

I was in love and there was no looking back. She was the one. I told   8
my mother, who was slapping hamburger into patties. "Well, sure, if you want to marry her," she said. But the more I talked, the more concerned she became. Later I began to worry. Was it all a mistake? "Marry a Mexican girl," I heard my mother say in my mind. I heard it at breakfast. I heard it over math problems, between Western Civilization and cultural geography. But then one afternoon while I was hitchhiking home from school, it struck me like a baseball in the back: My mother wanted me to marry someone of

my own social class—a poor girl. I considered my fiancee, Carolyn, and she didn't look poor, though I knew she came from a family of farm workers and pull-yourself-up-by-your-bootstraps ranchers. I asked my brother who was marrying Mexican poor that fall, if I should marry a poor girl. He screamed "Yeah" above this terrible guitar playing in his bedroom. I considered my sister, who had married Mexican. Cousins were dating Mexicans. Uncles were remarrying poor women. I asked Scott, who was still my best friend, and he said, "She's too good for you, so you better not."

I worried about it until Carolyn took me home to meet her parents. We drove in their Plymouth until the houses gave way to farms and ranches and finally her house fifty feet from the highway. We pulled into the drive; I panicked and begged Carolyn to make a U-turn and go back so we could talk about it over a soda. She pinched my cheek, calling me a "silly boy." I felt better, though, when I got out of the car and saw the house: the chipped paint, a cracked window, boards for a walk to the back door. There were rusting cars near the barn. A tractor with a net of spiderwebs under a mulberry. A field. A bale of barbed wire like children's scribbling leaning against an empty chicken coop. Carolyn took my hand and pulled me to my future mother-in-law, who was coming out to greet us. 9

She pinched my cheek, calling me a "silly boy."

We had lunch: sandwiches, potato chips, and iced tea. Carolyn and her mother talked mostly about neighbors and the congregation at the Japanese Methodist Church in West Fresno. Her father, who was in khaki work clothes, excused himself with a wave that was almost a salute and went outside. I heard a truck start, a dog bark, and then the truck rattle away. 10

Carolyn's mother offered another sandwich, but I declined with a shake of my head and a smile. I looked around when I could, when I was not saying over and over that I was a college student, hinting that I could take care of her daughter. I shifted my chair. I saw newspapers piled in corners, dusty cereal boxes and vinegar bottles in corners. The wallpaper was bubbled from rain that had come in from a bad roof. Dust. Dust lay on lamp shades and windowsills. These people are just like Mexicans, I thought. Poor people. 11

Carolyn's mother asked me through Carolyn if I would like a sushi. A plate of black and white things was held in front of me. I took one, wide-eyed, and turned it over like a foreign coin. I was biting into one when I saw a kitten crawl up the window screen over the sink. I chewed and the kitten opened its mouth of terror as she crawled higher, wanting to paw the leftovers from our plates. I looked at Carolyn, who said that the cat was just showing off. I looked up in time to see it fall. It crawled up, then fell again. 12

We talked for an hour and had apple pie and coffee, slowly. Finally, we
got up with Carolyn taking my hand. Slightly embarrassed, I tried to pull
away, but her grip held me. I let her have her way as she led me down the
hallway with her mother right behind me. When I opened the door, I was
startled by a kitten clinging to the screen door, its mouth screaming "cat
food, dog biscuits, *sushi* . . . . " I opened the door and the kitten, still holding
on, whined in the language of hungry animals. When I got into Carolyn's car,
I looked back: The cat was still clinging. I asked Carolyn if it were possibly
hungry, but she said the cat was being silly. She started the car, waved to her
mother, and bounced over the rain-poked drive, patting my thigh for being
her lover baby. Carolyn waved again. I looked back, waving, then gawking at
a window screen where there were now three kittens clawing and screaming
to get in. Like Mexicans, I thought. I remembered the Molinas and how the
cats clung to their screens—cats they shot down with squirt guns. On the
highway, I felt happy, pleased by it all. I patted Carolyn's thigh. Her people
were like Mexicans, only different. ■

13

Reading for Better Writing

1. Briefly explain what the title, "Like Mexicans," signifies.

2. List the items the writer either directly or indirectly compares (for
example, two kitchens, two mothers). Do these comparisons add to
or detract from the essay's main point? Explain your answer.

3. Explain how the essay is organized. Is the organization effective?
Why or why not?

4. The writer describes cats three times. How is the climbing of cats on
screens related to his main point?

Model

Guidelines
Writing a Comparison-Contrast Essay

1. **Select a topic.** List subjects that are similar and/or different in ways that you find interesting, perplexing, disgusting, infuriating, charming, or informing. Then choose two subjects whose comparison and/or contrast gives the reader some insight into who or what they are. For example, you could explain how two chemicals that appear to be similar are actually different—and how that difference makes one more explosive, poisonous, or edible.

2. **Get the big picture.** Using a computer or a paper and pen, create three columns as shown below. Brainstorm a list of traits under each heading. (Also see the Venn diagram on page **50**.)

    Traits of Subject 1   Shared Traits   Traits of Subject 2

3. **Gather information.** Review your list of traits, highlighting those that could provide insight into one or both subjects. Research the subjects, using hands-on analysis when possible. Consider writing your research notes in the three-column format shown above.

4. **Draft a working thesis.** Review your expanded list of traits and eliminate those that now seem unimportant. Write a sentence stating the core of what you learned about the subjects and whether you are comparing, contrasting, or both. If you're stuck, try completing the sentence below. (Switch around the terms "similar" and "different" if you wish to stress similarities.)

    While _____ and _____ seem similar, they are different in several ways, and the differences are important because _____.

5. **Get organized.** Decide how to organize your essay. Generally, *subject by subject* works best for short, simple comparisons. *Trait by trait* works best for longer, more complex comparisons.

6. **Draft the essay.** Review your outline and write your first draft in one sitting if possible. Check your outline for details and integrate them into the text.

Subject by Subject:	Trait by Trait:
Introduction	Introduction
Subject 1	Trait A
• Trait A	• Subject 1
• Trait B	• Subject 2
• Trait C	Trait B
Subject 2	• Subject 1
• Trait A	• Subject 2
• Trait B	Trait C
• Trait C	• Subject 1
	• Subject 2

Subject-by-subject pattern:

- **Opening**—get readers' attention and introduce the subjects and thesis.
- **Middle**—describe one "package" of traits representing the first subject and a parallel set of traits representing the second subject.
- **Conclusion**—point out similarities and/or differences, note their significance, and restate your main point.

Trait-by-trait pattern:

- **Opening**—get readers' attention and introduce the subjects and thesis.
- **Middle**—compare and/or contrast the two subjects trait by trait (include transitions that help readers look back and forth between the two subjects).
- **Conclusion**—summarize the key relationships, note their significance, and restate your main point.

7. **Revise the essay.** Check the essay for the following:
   - Balanced comparisons and contrasts of comparable traits
   - Complete and thoughtful treatment of each subject
   - Genuine and objective voice
   - Clear, smooth sentences with varied structure
   - Title and introduction that spark interest
   - Thoughtful, unifying conclusion

8. **Get feedback.** Ask a classmate or someone in the writing center to read your paper, looking for the following:
   - A clear, interesting thesis
   - An engaging and informative introduction
   - A middle that compares and/or contrasts significant, parallel traits
   - Ideas that offer insight into the subject
   - A conclusion that restates the main point and unifies the essay

9. **Edit your essay.** Look for the following:
   - Transitions that signal comparisons and link paragraphs: *on the other hand, in contrast, similarly, also, both, even though, in the same way*
   - Correct quotations and documentation
   - Correct spelling, punctuation, usage, and grammar

10. **Publish your essay.** Share your writing with others:
   - Submit it to your instructor.
   - Share it with other students or publish it on a website.

Writing Checklist

Use these seven traits to check the quality of your writing; then revise as needed:

_____ The **ideas** (points made or conclusions drawn from comparing and contrasting) provide insight into who or what both subjects are and why they are important. The basis for comparison is clear.

_____ The **organization** pattern (subject by subject, trait by trait) helps readers grasp the similarities and differences between the subjects.

_____ The **voice** is informed, involved, and genuine.

_____ The **words** are precise and clear. Technical or scientific terms are defined. Links between subjects are communicated with transitions such as these:

Although	Either one	In contrast	Neither
As a result	For this reason	In the same way	On the other hand
Both	However	Likewise	Therefore

_____ The **sentences** are clear, well reasoned, varied in structure, and smooth.

_____ The **copy** is correct and clean.

_____ The **design** includes proper formatting, and graphics such as photos or drawings are clear and well placed.

Interactive

Critical-Thinking and Writing Activities

As directed by your instructor, complete the following activities.

1. Review the way in which Mark Twain makes his point in "Two Views of the River" by comparing and contrasting two perspectives of the Mississippi River. Revise or draft a passage of your own in which you use comparison and contrast to emphasize a point.

2. Review Gelareh Asayesh's essay "Shrouded in Contradiction," noting how she uses comparison-contrast strategies so as to take a position. Draft or revise an essay in which you use comparison-contrast strategies to develop or support a position.

3. In "Like Mexicans," Gary Soto compares two ethnic groups who are part of his family. List related pairs that are part of your life (siblings, uncles, homes, family conflicts, educational experiences, teachers, neighbors, and so on). Write an essay in which you compare and/or contrast the subjects to share insight into your life.

◀ VISUALLY SPEAKING

Study the photograph on page **199**. What does the picture compare or contrast? What ideas or feelings does the comparison/contrast elicit? Could an essay addressing the same topic elicit the same response? Explain.

CLASSIFICATION

14

Audio

Video

Classification is an organizational strategy that helps writers make sense of large or complex sets of things. A writer who is using this strategy looks at a topic and then breaks it into components that can be sorted into clearly distinguishable subgroups. For example, if he or she is writing about the types of residents who live in assisted-care facilities, a nursing student might classify possible residents according to various physical and/or mental limitations.

By sorting the residents in this way, the writer can discuss them as individuals, as representatives of a subgroup, or as members of the group as a whole. By using an additional strategy such as compare/contrast, he or she can show both similarities and differences between one subgroup and another, or between individuals within a subgroup. By using classification, the writer helps readers understand both individual components of the topic and relationships among the components.

For help as you write a classification essay, read the instructions and models in this chapter.

Web Link

Overview
Writing a Classification Essay

Writer's Goal

Your goal is to divide a group of people, places, things, or concepts into subgroups, and then to write an essay that helps readers understand each component, the subgroups, and the topic as a whole.

Keys for Success

Choose classification criteria that fit the topic. Use classification criteria to distinguish one subgroup from another. For example, to explain her family's experience with cancer, student writer Kim Brouwer examines three types of cancer (*type* is a basis for classification). Because cancer is a complex illness, grouping by type fits her subject (see "Three Family Cancers," pages **217–219**).

Choose classification criteria that fit your purpose. Use criteria that help you achieve your goal. For example, Ann Hodgman wants to assess the quality of dog-food products (her purpose). To achieve this goal, she measures their color, texture, taste, smell, and nutritional value—suitable criteria for assessing levels of quality (see "No Wonder They Call . . . ," pages **222–225**).

Follow classification principles. Sort items into subgroups according to the following principles:

- **Consistency:** Use the same criteria in the same way when deciding which individual items to place in which subgroups. For example, Hodgman measures the quality of all dog-food products with the same criteria: color, taste, and so on.
- **Exclusivity:** Establish distinct subgroups so that each one differs from the others. For example, in "Three Family Cancers," the writer explains three distinct—or exclusive—types of cancer. Although the three types share some traits, each type is distinct.

Topics to Consider

To choose a topic, start by writing a half-dozen general headings like the academic headings below; then list two or three related topics under each heading. Finally, pick a topic that can best be explained by breaking it into subgroups.

Engineering	Biology	Social Work	Education
Machines	Whales	Child welfare	Learning styles
Bridges	Fruits	Organizations	Testing methods

Next Step Read the model essays and do the activities that follow. As you read, note how the classification strategy helps writers address complex topics.

Classification

Kim Brouwer's essay below is what professor Ken Macrorie calls an *I-search paper*—a piece that one writes "to find something he needs to know for his own life." Kim's conversational tone and use of personal pronouns are appropriate elements in such a document.

Audio

Three Family Cancers

The writer introduces the topic with an anecdote.

One day back in fourth grade, my teacher said, "Use your imagination and make an invention—something new and useful." I grumped all the way home from school. An invention? For what, I thought. What could I invent that we could use? "What about a cure for cancer?" Mom asked.   *1*

A few weeks earlier my family had learned that Grandpa DeRonde had cancer, so I went to work imagining my very own miracle cure. I drew a picture of a medicine bottle, similar to a bottle of cough syrup, with a drop of liquid coming out of it. I called my masterpiece, "The Cure for Cancer."   *2*

She gives her criterion for classifying ("different forms") and identifies subgroups.

I can remember those school days pretty well, but I can't say the same for three of my grandparents—Grandma and Grandpa DeRonde and Grandpa Vernooy. Before I could grow up and get to know them, their lives were invaded, taken over, and destroyed by different forms of cancer—multiple myeloma, prostate cancer, and lung cancer. Now, years later, I am a college freshman, faced with another assignment that gives me a chance to think about cancer: What is it, and what causes it? And what were these illnesses like for my grandparents? To get some answers, I researched cancer and talked with my mother.   *3*

She explains what all forms of cancer have in common.

Cancer, as my family learned firsthand, is a serious killer. In fact, it's the second leading cause of death in the United States. Each year, the disease kills about 500,000 Americans, and doctors discover more than one million new cases (Microsoft Encarta). Cancer is so powerful because it's not one illness, but rather many diseases attacking many parts of the body. All cancers are basically body cells gone crazy—cells that develop abnormally. These cells then clone themselves using an enzyme called telomerase. As they multiply like creatures in a sci-fi horror movie, the cells build into tumors, which are tissues that can "invade and destroy other tissues" (Microsoft Encarta).   *4*

The writer categorizes carcinogens.

Researchers aren't exactly sure what triggers these cancerous growths, but they think that 80 percent of cancers happen because people come into regular contact with carcinogens—cancer-causing agents. Carcinogens are classified into three groups: chemicals, radiation, and viruses (Compton's). People can be exposed to these carcinogens in many ways and situations. One study showed that 5 percent of cancers could be traced to environmental pollution, including carcinogens in the workplace. Radiation, for example, devastated the population of Chernobyl, Russia, after the nuclear power plant meltdown. But carcinogens don't cause cancer overnight—even from   *5* exposure in a terrible accident. The cancer may take thirty to forty years to develop (Compton's).

She describes the first subgroup.

I don't know what carcinogens attacked my Grandma DeRonde, but I do know the result: She developed multiple myeloma. For a multiple-myeloma patient, the average period of survival is twenty months to ten years (Madden 108). When I talked with my mother, she said that my family doesn't really know when Grandma came down with multiple myeloma, but she lived for two years after learning that she had it. For two years, she suffered through radiation and chemotherapy treatments, and life seemed measured by the spaces between appointments to check her white-blood cell count.

She gives distinguishing details.

What causes multiple myeloma remains a mystery, though its effects are well known. This cancer involves a malignant growth of cells in the bone marrow that makes holes in the skeleton. The holes develop mostly in the ribs, vertebrae, and pelvis. Because the holes make the bones brittle, the patient cannot do simple things like driving and cooking. In the end, patients fracture bones and die from infection and pneumonia (Madden 108). It was this weakening of the bones, along with the chemotherapy treatments, that made my grandmother suffer.

She describes the second subgroup.

My Grandpa DeRonde was diagnosed with prostate cancer several years after my grandma died. The doctors began radiation therapy right away, and my family was hopeful because the cancer was caught in its early stages. At first, the cancer seemed to go into remission, but cancer cells were actually invading other sites in his body. Because the cancer spread, the doctors couldn't treat all of it through radiation or surgery. Grandpa lived for only two years after learning he was ill, and during that time he had many chemotherapy treatments and spent a lot of time in the hospital. On his death certificate, the doctor wrote that Grandpa died of cardiac arrest and carcinoma of the lung, with metastasis.

She provides distinguishing details.

Like multiple myeloma, prostate cancer is a powerful killer. Even though many technological changes help doctors catch this cancer at an early stage, the number of deaths per year is still going up. Prostate cancer is the second most common cancer in the United States, and experts believe that it can be found in about 25 million men over the age of fifty (Fintor).

Prostate cancer is a tumor (called a carcinoma) lining the inside of the prostate gland. Many factors trigger this form of cancer: age, diet, environmental conditions, or maybe just having a cancer-prone family ("Prostate Cancer Trends" 183). A survey of more than 51,000 American men showed that eating a lot of fat, found mostly in red meat, can lead to advanced prostate cancer. On the other hand, researchers concluded that fats from vegetables, fish, and many dairy products are probably not linked to the growth of a carcinoma (Cowley 77).

She describes the third subgroup.

My second grandfather died from a different carcinoma—lung cancer. Doctors found a tumor in the lower lobe of Grandpa Vernooy's right lung, recommended surgery, and removed the lung. The next winter, he weakened, got pneumonia, and died. His doctors believed that his smoking habit caused the cancer. Smoking, in fact, remains the most important factor in developing lung cancer ("Family Ties" 109). The truth is that cigarette smoking causes almost half of all cancer cases, even though only one out of ten smokers actually comes down with this disease (Compton's).

She cites distinguishing details.

One study concluded that genetics may play a role in whether a person develops lung cancer. Research suggests that if a person is missing positive genes called tumor-suppressor genes, it's bad news. If these genes weren't inherited, or if smoking destroyed them, then cancer-related genes are free to do their damage (Edwards 358). Another study identified a special gene that is inherited from one or both parents and that metabolizes chemicals from cigarette smoke. In this case, if the gene is there, the cancer risk goes up, especially for smokers ("Family Ties" 109).

12

She closes by reviewing the subgroups and reflecting on the opening anecdote.

I still wish I could cure cancer with a magic miracle liquid in a medicine bottle. But today I understand that cancer is a complicated disease. My grandparents died from three types of the disease—multiple myeloma, prostate cancer, and lung cancer. If it hadn't been for cancerous tumors taking over their bodies, my grandparents might still be alive, and I'd have many more memories of them. Maybe I'd even be sharing with them stories about my first year at college. On the other hand, perhaps this paper is a cure of a different type—while it can't change what happened, it can help me understand it. ■

13

Note: The Works Cited page is not shown. For sample pages, see MLA (page 532–533) and APA (page 564).

Reading for Better Writing

Working by yourself or in a group, do the following:

1. The writer opens and closes the essay with a personal anecdote. Explain why this story does or does not strengthen the essay.

2. For each subgroup (type of cancer), the writer uses a grandparent as an example. Explain how her use of examples does or does not help clarify the subject.

3. Where in the essay does the writer compare and contrast different forms of cancer? Is the comparison and contrast effective? Why or why not?

4. Writing about a scientific topic like cancer nearly always requires technical terminology. Cite two such terms used in this essay, and explain how the writer clarifies each term's meaning.

Classification

In this essay John Van Rys, a college professor, classifies four basic approaches to literary criticism. His essay is intended to help college freshmen interpret literature.

Four Ways to Talk About Literature

The writer introduces the topic and criterion for creating four subgroups.

Have you ever been in a conversation in which you suddenly felt lost—out of the loop? Perhaps you feel that way in your literature class. You may think a poem or short story means one thing, and then your instructor suddenly pulls out the "hidden meaning." Joining the conversation about literature—in class or in an essay—may indeed seem daunting, but you can do it if you know what to look for and what to talk about. There are four main perspectives, or approaches, that you can use to converse about literature.

He describes the first subgroup and gives an example.

Text-centered approaches focus on the literary piece itself. Often called *formalist criticism,* such approaches claim that the structure of a work and the rules of its genre are crucial to its meaning. The formalist critic determines how various elements (plot, character, language, and so on) reinforce the meaning and unify the work. For example, the formalist may ask the following questions concerning Robert Browning's poem "My Last Duchess": How do the main elements in the poem—irony, symbolism, and verse form—help develop the main theme (deception)? How does Browning use the dramatic monologue genre in this poem?

He describes the second subgroup and gives an example.

Audience-centered approaches focus on the "transaction" between text and reader—the dynamic way the reader interacts with the text. Often called *rhetorical* or *reader-response criticism,* these approaches see the text not as an object to be analyzed, but as an activity that is different for each reader. A reader-response critic might ask these questions of "My Last Duchess": How does the reader become aware of the duke's true nature if it's never actually stated? Do men and women read the poem differently? Who were Browning's original readers?

He describes the third subgroup and gives examples.

Author-centered approaches focus on the origins of a text (the writer and the historical background). For example, an author-centered study examines the writer's life—showing connections, contrasts, and conflicts between his or her life and the writing. Broader historical studies explore social and intellectual currents, showing links between an author's work and the ideas, events, and institutions of that period. Finally, the literary historian may make connections between the text in question and earlier and later literary works. The author-centered critic might ask these questions of "My Last Duchess": What were Browning's views of marriage, men and women, art, class, and wealth? As an institution, what was marriage like in Victorian England (Browning's era) or Renaissance Italy (the duke's era)? Who was the historical Duke of Ferrara?

He describes the fourth approach and gives examples of each subgroup in it.

The fourth approach to criticism applies ideas outside of literature to literary works. Because literature mirrors life, argue these critics, disciplines that explore human life can help us understand literature. Some critics, for example, apply psychological theories to literary works by exploring dreams, symbolic meanings, and motivation. Myth or archetype criticism uses insights from psychology, cultural anthropology, and classical studies to explore a text's universal appeal. Moral criticism, rooted in religious studies and ethics, explores the moral dilemmas literary works raise. Marxist, feminist, and minority criticism are, broadly speaking, sociological approaches to interpretation. While the Marxist examines the themes of class struggle, economic power, and social justice in texts, the feminist critic explores the just and unjust treatment of women as well as the effect of gender on language, reading, and the literary canon. The critic interested in race and ethnic identity explores similar issues, with the focus shifted to a specific cultural group.

5

He cites sample questions.

Such ideological criticism might ask a wide variety of questions about "My Last Duchess": What does the poem reveal about the duke's psychological state and his personality? How does the reference to Neptune deepen the poem? What does the poem suggest about the nature of evil and injustice? In what ways are the duke's motives class-based and economic? How does the poem present the duke's power and the duchess's weakness? What is the status of women in this society?

6

The closing presents qualities shared by all four approaches.

If you look at the variety of questions critics might ask about "My Last Duchess," you see both the diversity of critical approaches and the common ground between them. In fact, interpretive methods actually share important characteristics: (1) a close attention to literary elements such as character, plot, symbolism, and metaphor; (2) a desire not to distort the work; and (3) a sincere concern for increasing interest and understanding in a text. In actual practice, critics may develop a hybrid approach to criticism, one that matches their individual questions and concerns about a text. Now that you're familiar with some of the questions defining literary criticism, exercise your own curiosity (and join the ongoing literary dialogue) by discussing a text that genuinely interests you. ∎

7

Reading for Better Writing

Working by yourself or with a group, do the following:

1. Explain how the writer introduces the subject and attempts to engage the reader. Is this strategy effective? Why or why not?

2. The writer uses one poem to illustrate how each of the four critical approaches works. Explain why this strategy is or is not effective.

3. Review the last paragraph and explain why it does or does not unify the essay.

Classification

This piece was first printed in *Spy* magazine, an engaging periodical that ceased publication in 1998. In its time, the magazine was known for pieces that were both humorous and research based. Ann Hodgman was a food editor for *Spy*.

Working with one or two classmates, read the article and note how Hodgman uses categories to organize her analysis of dog food. Then discuss how the categories help direct and clarify her study.

No Wonder They Call Me a Bitch

1   I've always wondered about dog food. Is a Gaines-burger really like a hamburger? Can you fry it? Does dog food "cheese" taste like real cheese? Does Gravy Train actually make gravy in the dog's bowl, or is that brown liquid just dissolved crumbs? And exactly what *are* by-products?

2   Having spent the better part of a week eating dog food, I'm sorry to say that I now know the answers to these questions. While my dachshund, Shortie, watched in agonies of yearning, I gagged my way through can after can of stinky, white-flecked mush and bag after bag of stinky, fat-drenched nuggets. And now I understand exactly why Shortie's breath is so bad.

3   Of course, Gaines-burgers are neither mush nor nuggets. They are, rather, a miracle of beauty and packaging—or at least that's what I thought when I was little. I used to beg my mother to get them for our dogs, but she always said they were too expensive. When I finally bought a box of cheese-flavored Gaines-burgers—after 20 years of longing—I felt deliciously wicked.

4   "Dogs love real beef," the back of the box proclaimed proudly. "That's why Gaines-burgers is the only beef burger for dogs with real beef and no meat by-products!" The copy was accurate: Meat by-products did not appear in the list of ingredients. Poultry by-products did, though—right there next to preserved animal fat.

5   One Purina spokesman told me that poultry by-products consist of necks, intestines, undeveloped eggs, and other "carcass remnants," but not feathers, heads, or feet. When I told him I'd been eating dog food, he said, "Oh, you're kidding! Oh no!" (I came to share his alarm when, weeks later, a second Purina spokesman said that Gaines-burgers *do* contain poultry heads and feet—but *not* undeveloped eggs).

6   Up close my Gaines-burger didn't much resemble chopped beef. Rather, it looked—and felt—like a single long, extruded piece of redness that had been chopped into segments and formed into a patty. You could make one at home if you had a Play-Doh Fun Factory.

7   I turned on the skillet. While I waited for it to heat up I pulled out a shred of cheese-colored material and palpated it. Again, like Play-Doh, it was quite malleable. I made a little cheese bird out of it; then I counted to three and ate the bird.

8   There was a horrifying rush of cheddar taste, followed immediately by the dull tang of soybean flour—the main ingredient in Gaines-burgers.

Next I tried a piece of red extrusion. The main difference between the meat-flavored and cheese-flavored extrusions is one of texture. The "cheese" chews like fresh Play-Doh, whereas the "meat" chews like Play-Doh that's been sitting out on a rug for a couple of hours.

Frying only turned the Gaines-burger black. There was no melting, no sizzling, no warm meat smells. A cherished childhood illusion was gone. I flipped the patty into the sink, where it immediately began leaking rivulets of red dye. 9

As alarming as the Gaines-burgers were, their soy meal began to seem like an old friend when the time came to try some *canned* dog foods. I decided to try the Cycle foods first. When I opened them, I thought about how rarely I use can openers these days, and I was suddenly visited by a long-forgotten sensation of can-opener distaste. *This* is the kind of unsavory place can openers spend their time when you're not watching! Every time you open a can of, say, Italian plum tomatoes, you infect them with invisible particles of by-product. 10

I had been expecting to see the usual homogeneous scrapple inside, but each can of Cycle was packed with smooth, round, oily nuggets. As if someone at Gaines had been tipped off that a human would be tasting the stuff, the four Cycles really were different from one another. Cycle-1, for puppies, is wet and soyish, Cycle-2, for adults, glistens nastily with fat, but it's passably edible—a lot like some canned Swedish meatballs I once got in a care package at college. Cycle-3, the "lite" one, for fatties, had no specific flavor, it just tasted like dog food. But at least it didn't make me fat. 11

Cycle-4, for senior dogs, had the smallest nuggets. Maybe old dogs can't open their mouths as wide. This kind was far sweeter than the other three Cycles—almost like baked beans. It was also the only one to contain "dried beef digest," a mysterious substance that the Purina spokesman defined as "enzymes" and my dictionary defined as "the products of digestion." 12

Next on the menu was a can of Kal-Kan Pedigree with Chunky Chicken. Chunky chicken? There were chunks in the can, certainly—big, purplish-brown chunks. I forked one chunk out (by now I was becoming more callous) and found that while it had no discernible chicken flavor, it wasn't bad except for its texture—like meat loaf with ground-up chicken bones. 13

In the world of canned dog food, a smooth consistency is a sign of low quality—lots of cereal. A lumpy, frightening, bloody, stringy horror is a sign of high quality—lots of meat. Nowhere in the world of wet dog foods was this demonstrated better than in the fanciest I tried—Kal Kan's Pedigree Select Dinners. These came not in a can but in a tiny foil packet with a picture of an imperious Yorkie. When I pulled open the container, juice spurted all over my hand, and the first chunk I speared was trailing a long gray vein. I shrieked and went instead for a plain chunk, which I was able to swallow only after taking a break to read some suddenly fascinating office 14 equipment catalogs. Once again, though, it tasted no more alarming than, say, canned hash.

Still, how pleasant it was to turn to *dry* dog food! Gravy Train was the first I tried, and I'm happy to report that it really does make a "thick, rich, real beef gravy" when you mix it with water. Thick and rich, anyway. Except for a lingering rancid-fat flavor, the gravy wasn't beefy, but since it tasted primarily like tap water, it wasn't nauseating either.   15

My poor dachshund just gets plain old Purina Dog Chow, but Purina also makes a dry food called Butcher's Blend that comes in Beef, Bacon & Chicken flavor. Here we see dog food's arcane semiotics at its best: a red triangle with a *T* stamped into it is supposed to suggest beef; a tan curl, chicken; and a brown *S*, a piece of bacon. Only dogs understand these messages. But Butcher's Blend does have an endearing slogan: "Great Meaty Tastes—without bothering the Butcher!" *You know, I wanted go buy some meat, but I just couldn't bring myself to bother the butcher. . . .*   16

Purina O.N.E. ("Optimum Nutritional Effectiveness") is targeted at people who are unlikely ever to worry about bothering a tradesperson. "We chose chicken as a primary ingredient in Purina O.N.E. for several reasonings," the long, long essay on the back of the bag announces. Chief among these reasonings, I'd guess, is the fact that chicken appeals to people who are—you know—*like us*. Although our dogs do nothing but spend 18-hour days alone in the apartment, we still want them to be *premium* dogs. We want them to cut down on red meat, too. We also want dog food that comes in a bag with an attractive design, a subtle typeface, and no kitschy pictures of slobbering golden retrievers.   17

Besides that, we want a list of the Nutritional Benefits of our dog food—and we get it on O.N.E. One thing I especially like about this list is its constant references to a dog's "hair coat," as in "Beef tallow is good for the dog's skin and hair coat." (On the other hand, beef tallow merely provides palatability, while the dried beef digest in Cycle provides palatability *enhancement*.)   18

I hate to say it, but O.N.E. was pretty palatable. Maybe that's because it has about 100 percent more fat than, say, Butcher's Blend. Or maybe I'd been duped by the packaging; that's been known to happen before.   19

As with people food, dog snacks taste much better than dog meals. They're better-looking, too. Take Milk-Bone Flavor Snacks. The loving-hands-at-home prose describing each flavor is colorful; the writers practically choke on their own exuberance. Of bacon they say, "It's so good, your dog will think it's hot off the frying pan." Of liver: "The only taste your dog wants more than liver—is even more liver!" Of poultry: "All those farm fresh flavors deliciously mixed in one biscuit. Your dog will bark with delight!" And of vegetable: "Gardens of taste! Specially blended to give your dog that vegetable flavor he wants—but can rarely get!"   20

Well, I may be a sucker, but advertising *this* emphatic just doesn't   *21*
convince me. I lined up all seven flavors of Milk-Bone Flavor Snacks on
the floor. Unless my dog's palate is a lot more sensitive than mine—and
considering that she steals dirty diapers out of the trash and eats them, I'm
loath to think it is—she doesn't detect any more difference in the seven
flavors than I did when I tried them.

I much preferred Bonz, the hard-baked, bone-shaped snack stuffed   *22*
with simulated marrow. I liked the bone part, that is; it tasted almost exactly
like the cornmeal it was made of. The mock-marrow inside was a bit more
problematic: in addition to looking like the sludge that collects in the treads
of my running shoes, it was bursting with tiny hairs.

I'm sure you have a few dog food questions of your own. To save us   *23*
time, I've answered them in advance.

Q. *Are those little cans of Mighty Dog actually branded with the sizzling*   *24*
word **BEEF**, *the way they show in the commercials?*

A. You should know by now that that kind of thing never happens.   *25*

Q. *Does chicken-flavored dog food taste like chicken-flavored cat food?*   *26*

A. To my surprise, chicken cat food was actually a little better—more   *27*
chickeny. It tasted like inferior canned pâté.

Q. *Was there any dog food that you just couldn't bring yourself to try?*   *28*

A. Alas, it was a can of Mighty Dog called Prime Entree with Bone   *29*
Marrow. The meat was dark, dark brown, and it was surrounded by gelatin
that was almost black. I knew I would die if I tasted it, so I put it outside
for the raccoons. ■

Reading for Better Writing

Working by yourself or with a group, answer these questions:

1. Why does Hodgman claim to taste-test dog food and then report on
her findings in writing? Can you think of other texts written for similar
purposes?

2. What criteria does Hodgman use to divide her subject into categories?
Where and how does she indicate that she is shifting her discussion
from one category to the next?

3. The title grabs our attention with the word *bitch*, a word rarely used in
titles. Does the word use serve additional purposes?

4. This piece is based on primary-source research. Review chapter 29,
"Conducting Primary and Library Research," especially the portion on
conducting primary research. What other research strategies could the
author have used to explore her topic? Which would be most effective
for her *Spy* audience? How would she need to change her tactics if her
audience were a scientific journal? A magazine for dog enthusiasts?

Guidelines
Writing a Classification Essay

1. **Select a topic.** Review the list of headings and topics that you developed in response to "Topics to Consider" on page 216. Choose a topic that you find interesting and can explain well using classification strategies. If you need more choices, develop a new list of headings and topics.

2. **Look at the big picture.** Conduct preliminary research to get an overview of your topic. Review your purpose (to explain, persuade, inform, and so on), and consider which classification criteria will help you divide the subject into distinct, understandable subgroups.

3. **Choose and test your criterion.** Choose a criterion for creating subgroups. Make sure it produces subgroups that are consistent (all members fit the criterion), exclusive (subgroups are distinct—no member of the group fits into more than one subgroup), and complete (each member fits into a subgroup with no member left over).

    > **TIP:** To better visualize how you are dividing your topic and classifying its members, take a few minutes to fill out a graphic organizer like the one shown below. (Also see the graphic organizer on page 50.)

4. **Gather and organize information.** Gather information from library and web resources, as well as interviews. To take notes and organize your information, consider using a classification grid like the one shown below. Set up the grid by listing the classification criteria down the left column and listing the subgroups in the top row of the columns. Then fill in the grid with appropriate details. (The following grid lists the classification criterion and subgroups used in "Four Ways to Talk About Literature," pages 220–221.)

Classification Criteria	Subgroup 1	Subgroup 2	Subgroup 3	Subgroup 4
	Text-centered approach	*Audience-centered approach*	*Author-centered approach*	*Ideas outside literature*
focus of the critical approach	• Trait 1 • Trait 2 • Trait 3	• Trait 1 • Trait 2 • Trait 3	• Trait 1 • Trait 2 • Trait 3	• Trait 1 • Trait 2 • Trait 3

Note: If you do not use a grid similar to this one, construct an outline to help organize your thoughts (see pages 48–49).

5. **Draft a thesis.** Draft a working thesis (you can revise it later as needed) that states your topic and main point. Include language introducing your criteria for classifying subgroups.

6. **Draft the essay.** Write your first draft, using either the organizational pattern in the classification grid or an outline.

   Opening: Get the readers' attention, introduce the subject and thesis, and give your criteria for dividing the subject into subgroups.

   Middle: Develop the thesis by discussing each subgroup, explaining its traits, and showing how it is distinct from the other subgroups. For example, in the middle section of "Four Ways to Talk About Literature," the writer first shows the unique focus of each of the four approaches to literary criticism, and then illustrates each approach by applying it to the same poem, "My Last Duchess."

   Closing: While the opening and the middle of the essay separate the subject into components and subgroups, the closing brings the components and subgroups back together. For example, in "Four Ways to Talk About Literature," the writer closes by identifying three characteristics that the four subgroups have in common (see pages 220–221).

7. **Get feedback.** Ask a classmate or someone from the writing center to read your essay, looking for the following:

   - An engaging opening that introduces the subject, thesis, and criteria for classification
   - A well-organized middle that distinguishes subgroups, shows why each subgroup is unique, and includes adequate details
   - A clear closing that reaches some sort of conclusion

8. **Revise the essay.** Check the essay for the following:

   - Subgroups that are consistent, exclusive, and complete
   - Organization that helps the reader understand the subject
   - Appropriate examples that clarify the nature and function of each subgroup
   - A unifying conclusion

9. **Edit the essay.** Check for the following:

   - An informed, reader-friendly voice
   - Clear, complete sentences
   - Unified paragraphs linked with appropriate transitions
   - Correct usage, grammar, punctuation, and spelling

10. **Publish the essay.** Share your writing by doing the following:

    - Offer copies to classmates and friends.
    - Publish it in a journal or on a website.
    - Place a copy in your professional portfolio.

Writing Checklist

Use these seven traits to check the quality of your writing; then revise as needed:

_____ The **ideas** in the classification criteria are logical and clear. The criteria result in subgroups that are consistent, exclusive, and complete.

_____ The **organization** of the essay helps the reader understand the components, the subgroups, and the subject as a whole. Paragraphs form cohesive units of thought.

_____ The **voice** is informed, courteous, and professional.

_____ The **words** are precise, descriptive, and appropriate for the subject. Terms used in classifications are employed in the same way throughout the essay.

_____ The **sentences** are complete, varied, and easy to read. Appropriate transitions link sentences and paragraphs.

_____ The **copy** has correct punctuation, grammar, and mechanics.

_____ The **design** follows assigned formatting instructions.

Interactive

Critical-Thinking and Writing Activities

As directed by your instructor, complete the following activities.

1. Kim Brouwer wrote "Three Family Cancers" to better understand a series of painful experiences in her family's life. List painful (or pleasant) experiences in your family's life, and select a topic that you can clarify by classifying. Write an essay using classification strategies that explain the topic.

2. "Four Ways to Talk About Literature" examines four approaches to reading and understanding a piece of literature. Identify a similar group of approaches to analysis or problem solving in your program or major. Write an essay in which you break your topic into subgroups, sort the subgroups, and explain the topic to the reader.

3. Review the ways in which Ann Hodgman incorporates primary-source research into her essay, "No Wonder They Call Me a Bitch." Employ this strategy in your draft or revision of an essay.

4. Develop a list of social, economic, or political topics in the news. Choose one, research it, classify its components, and then write an essay that explains the topic.

VISUALLY SPEAKING

Working with a classmate, look again at the photograph on page 215. Then discuss what the picture suggests about why one might classify things and what challenges are part of the process.

PROCESS WRITING

15

Process writing is practical writing that answers the kinds of questions we face every day at home, in college, or on the job: "How do I remove these ugly stains?" or "How does cancer spread?" or "How do I install this software?" Writing that answers these types of questions analyzes the process in which we're interested, breaks it down into steps, and shows how the process works.

The three basic forms of process writing include *describing* a process, *explaining* a process, and giving *instructions*. This chapter distinguishes these forms and shows how to write each. In addition, the chapter includes models showing how writers have used the forms to accomplish their writing goals.

Study this chapter for tips that will help you choose a topic, break it into steps, and explain it clearly in writing.

Audio

Video

Web Link

Overview
Writing About a Process

Writer's Goal

Your goal is to analyze a process, break it into specific steps, and write about it using one of the following forms: a *description* of a process, an *explanation* of the process, or *instructions* on how to carry out the process.

Keys for Success

Think logically. To write one of these forms, you must study the process until you understand it, and then write clearly about it. In other words, you must know—and show—how each step leads *logically* to the next, and how all the steps together complete the process.

Know your purpose and your audience. Decide what your writing should do and choose the form that fits your purpose and audience:

• To inform a broad audience how something happens, *describe* the process in an essay that tells how the process unfolds—for example, how cancer cells multiply (pages 231–232) or how interracial marriage has become common (pages 238–239).

• To help readers who want to know how something is done or made, *explain* the process in an essay that tells how someone would complete each step— for example, how to deal with campus racism (pages 234–237).

• To help readers who wish to perform the process themselves, provide how-to information in brief, clear *instructions*—for example, how to download photos onto your computer (page 233).

Note: While descriptions and explanations are usually formatted as essays, instructions are formatted somewhat differently. Instructions include a summary of the process, a list of materials and tools, and a numbered list of steps organized chronologically and stated using clear, imperative verbs.

Consider *all* of your readers. Regardless of the form that you choose, make your writing accessible to all of your readers by addressing the reader who knows the least about your topic. Include all the information that this person needs to have, and use language that everyone can understand.

Topics to Consider

• A course-related process
• A process that keeps you healthy
• A process that you've mastered

• A process in the news
• A process that helps you get a job
• A process in your planned occupation

> **Next Step** Read the model essays and perform the activities that follow. As you read, observe how each writer approaches the task of explaining, describing, or instructing.

Audio

Process: Description

Student writer Kerri Mertz wrote this essay to help nonscientists understand how cancer cells multiply and affect the body.

The writer uses the title and an analogy to introduce the topic.

She uses a simile to explain the analogy.

She describes the first step in the process and cites a potential cause.

She describes the next step and its result.

Wayward Cells

Imagine a room containing a large group of people all working hard toward the same goal. Each person knows his or her job, does it carefully, and cooperates with other group members. Together, they function efficiently and smoothly—like a well-oiled machine.

Then something goes wrong. One guy suddenly drops his task, steps into another person's workstation, grabs the material that she's working with, and begins something very different—he uses the material to make little reproductions of himself, thousands of them. These look-alikes imitate him—grabbing material and making reproductions of themselves. Soon the bunch gets so big that they spill into other people's workstations, getting in their way, and interrupting their work. As the number of look-alikes grows, the work group's activity slows, stutters, and finally stops.

A human body is like this room, and the body's cells are like these workers. If the body is healthy, each cell has a necessary job and does it correctly. For example, right now red blood cells are running throughout your body carrying oxygen to each body part. Other cells are digesting that steak sandwich that you had for lunch, and others are patching up that cut on your left hand. Each cell knows what to do because its genetic code—or DNA—tells it what to do. When a cell begins to function abnormally, it can initiate a process that results in cancer.

The problem starts when one cell "forgets" what it should do. Scientists call this "undifferentiating"—meaning that the cell loses its identity within the body (Pierce 75). Just like the guy in the group who decided to do his own thing, the cell forgets its job. Why this happens is somewhat unclear. The problem could be caused by a defect in the cell's DNA code or by something in the environment, such as cigarette smoke or asbestos (German 21). Causes from inside the body are called genetic, whereas causes from outside the body are called carcinogens, meaning "any substance that causes cancer" (Neufeldt and Sparks 90). In either case, an undifferentiated cell can disrupt the function of healthy cells in two ways: by not doing its job as specified in its DNA and by not reproducing at the rate noted in its DNA.

Most healthy cells reproduce rather quickly, but their reproduction rate is controlled. For example, your blood cells completely die off and replace themselves within a matter of weeks, but existing cells make only as many new cells as the body needs. The DNA codes in healthy cells tell them how many new cells to produce. However, cancer cells don't have this control, so they reproduce quickly with no stopping point, a characteristic

1

2

3

4

5

called "autonomy" (Braun 3). What's more, all their "offspring" have the same qualities as their messed-up parent, and the resulting overpopulation produces growths called tumors.

She describes the third step—how tumors damage the body.

Tumor cells can hurt the body in a number of ways. First, a tumor can grow so big that it takes up space needed by other organs. Second, some cells may detach from the original tumor and spread throughout the body, creating new tumors elsewhere. This happens with lymphatic cancer—a cancer that's hard to control because it spreads so quickly. A third way that tumor cells can hurt the body is by doing work not called for in their DNA. For example, a gland cell's DNA code may tell the cell to produce a necessary hormone in the endocrine system. However, if cancer damages or distorts that code, sick cells may produce more of the hormone than the body can use—or even tolerate (Braun 4). Cancer cells seem to have minds of their own, and this is why cancer is such a serious disease.   6

A transition signals a shift in focus from the illness to treatments.

Fortunately, there is hope. Scientific research is already helping doctors do amazing things for people with cancer. One treatment that has been used for some time is chemotherapy, or the use of chemicals to kill off all fast-growing cells, including cancer cells. (Unfortunately, chemotherapy can't distinguish between healthy and unhealthy cells, so it may cause negative side effects such as damaging fast-growing hair follicles, resulting in hair loss.) Another common treatment is radiation, or the use of light rays to kill cancer cells. One of the newest and most promising treatments is gene therapy—an effort to identify and treat chromosomes that carry a "wrong code" in their DNA. A treatment like gene therapy is promising because it treats the cause of cancer, not just the effect. Year by year, research is helping doctors better understand what cancer is and how to treat it.   7

The writer reuses the analogy to review main points.

Much of life involves dealing with problems like wayward workers, broken machines, or dysfunctional organizations. Dealing with wayward cells is just another problem. While the problem is painful and deadly, there is hope. Medical specialists and other scientists are making progress, and some day they will help win the battle against wayward cells. ■   8

Note: The Works Cited page is not shown. For sample pages, see MLA (pages **532–533**) and APA (page **564**).

Reading for Better Writing

1. Review the opening four-paragraph analogy used to introduce and describe the process. Explain why the analogy is or is not effective.

2. Review the three steps cited by the writer, and note the transitions used to lead into and out of each step. Are the transitions effective?

3. Review the guidelines on page **240** to identify and list traits of a *description* of a process. Explain why this essay does or does not exemplify these traits.

Process: Instructions

These instructions, like those for many technical devices, include both written and visual elements.

Downloading Photographs from the MC-150 Digital Camera

Note: MC-150 software must be loaded on your computer to download photographs from the camera.

1. Turn your computer on.

2. Plug the camera's USB cable into your computer.

3. Turn the camera's mode dial to the **data transfer setting** (Figure 1).

Figure 1: Data Transfer Setting

4. Open the camera's flash-card door and plug the other end of the USB cable into the **camera port** (Figure 2).

5. Select USB transfer from the camera screen menu. The MC-150 software will then launch on your computer.

6. Follow the instructions on the computer screen to download all of your photos or specific photos.

Figure 2: Camera Port

7. When your download is complete, turn the camera off and unplug the USB cable from the camera and the computer.

Note: If the MC-150 software doesn't launch, disconnect the camera (step 7), and then restart the computer and continue on from step 2. ■

Process: Explanation

Nikki Giovanni is an acclaimed poet and essayist; you can learn more about her work by visiting her webpage at http://nikki-giovanni.com/index.shtml. In this piece, first published in *Essence* in 1991, Giovanni advises African American students on how to succeed in colleges where the majority of students are white.

The title reminds us of the names of college courses.

The writer identifies problems that prompt her to write this essay.

The writer raises a question and then provides a list of answers.

The series of questions contributes to a conversational tone.

Campus Racism 101

There is a bumper sticker that reads: *TOO BAD IGNORANCE ISN'T PAINFUL.* I like that. But ignorance is. We just seldom attribute the pain to it or even recognize it when we see it. Like the postcard on my corkboard. It shows a young man in a very hip jacket smoking a cigarette. In the background is a high school with the American flag waving. The caption says: "Too cool for school. Yet too stupid for the real world." Out of the mouth of the young man is a bubble enclosing the words "Maybe I'll start a band." There could be a postcard showing a jock in a uniform saying, "I don't need school. I'm going to the NFL or NBA." Or one showing a young man or woman studying and a group of young people saying, "So you want to be white." Or something equally demeaning. We need to quit it.

> *Where can you go and what can you do that frees you from interacting with the white American mentality?*

I am a professor of English at Virginia Tech. I've been here for four years, though for only two years with academic rank. I am tenured, which means I have a teaching position for life, a rarity on a predominantly white campus. Whether from malice or ignorance, people who think I should be at a predominantly Black institution will ask, "Why are you at Tech?" Because it's here. And so are Black students. But even if Black students weren't here, it's painfully obvious that this nation and this world cannot allow white students to go through higher education without interacting with Blacks in authoritative positions. It is equally clear that predominantly Black colleges cannot accommodate the numbers of Black students who want and need an education.

Is it difficult to attend a predominantly white college? Compared with what? Being passed over for promotion because you lack credentials? Being turned down for jobs because you are not college-educated? Joining the armed forces or going to jail because you cannot find an alternative to the streets? Let's have a little perspective here. Where can you go and what can you do that frees you from interacting with the white American mentality?

You're going to interact; the only question is, will you be in some control of yourself and your actions, or will you be controlled by others? I'm going to recommend self-control.

What's the difference between prison and college? They both prescribe   4
your behavior for a given period of time. They both allow you to read books and develop your writing. They both give you time alone to think and time with your peers to talk about issues. But four years of prison doesn't give you a passport to greater opportunities. Most likely that time only gives you greater knowledge of how to get back in. Four years of college gives you an opportunity not only to lift yourself but to serve your people effectively. What's the difference when you are called nigger in college from when you are called nigger in prison? In college you can, though I admit with effort, follow procedures to have those students who called you nigger kicked out or suspended. You can bring issues to public attention without risking your life. But mostly, college is and always has been the future. We, neither less nor more than other people, need knowledge. There are discomforts attached to attending predominantly white colleges, though no more so than living in a racist world. Here are some rules to follow that may help:

Go to class. No matter how you feel. No matter how you think the   5
professor feels about you. It's important to have a consistent presence in the classroom. If nothing else, the professor will know you care enough and are serious enough to be there.

Meet your professors. Extend your hand (give a firm handshake) and   6
tell them your name. Ask them what you need to do to make an A. You may never make an A, but you have put them on notice that you are serious about getting good grades.

Do assignments on time. Typed or computer-generated. You have the   7
syllabus. Follow it, and turn those papers in. If for some reason you can't complete an assignment on time, let your professor know before it is due and work out a new due date—then meet it.

Go back to see your professor. Tell him or her your name again. If an   8
assignment received less than an A, ask why, and find out what you need to do to improve the next assignment.

Yes, your professor is busy. So are you. So are your parents who are   9
working to pay or help with your tuition. Ask early what you need to do if you feel you are starting to get into academic trouble. Do not wait until you are failing.

Understand that there will be professors who do not like you; there may   10
even be professors who are racist or sexist or both. You must discriminate among your professors to see who will give you the help you need. You may not simply say, "They are all against me." They aren't. They mostly don't

Repeated use of *you* also adds to the conversational feel.

After a paragraph addressed to *you*, the writer shifts to *we*.

Each rule is discussed in a new paragraph and is marked with italics.

The writer anticipates arguments and counters them.

care. Since you are the one who wants to be educated, find the people who want to help.

Don't defeat yourself. Cultivate your friends. Know your enemies. You cannot undo hundreds of years of prejudicial thinking. Think for yourself and speak up. Raise your hand in class. Say what you believe no matter how awkward you may think it sounds. You will improve in your articulation and confidence. *11*

Participate in some campus activity. Join the newspaper staff. Run for office. Join a dorm council. Do something that involves you on campus. You are going to be there for four years, so let your presence be known, if not felt. *12*

> *Cultivate your friends. Know your enemies.*

You will inevitably run into some white classmates who are troubling because they often say stupid things, ask stupid questions—and expect an answer. Here are some comebacks to some of the most common inquiries and comments: *13*

Q: What's it like to grow up in a ghetto? *14*

A: I don't know. *15*

Q (from the teacher): Can you give us the Black perspective on Toni Morrison, Huck Finn, slavery, Martin Luther King, Jr., and others? *16*

A: I can give you my perspective. (Do not take the burden of 22 million people on your shoulders. Remind everyone that you are an individual, and don't speak for the race or any other individual within it.) *17*

Q: Why do all the Black people sit together in the dining hall? *18*

A: Why do all the white students sit together? *19*

Q: Why should there be an African-American studies course? *20*

A: Because white Americans have not adequately studied the contributions of Africans and African-Americans. Both Black and white students need to know our total common history. *21*

Q: Why are there so many scholarships for "minority" students? *22*

A: Because they wouldn't give my great-grandparents their forty acres and the mule. *23*

Q: How can whites understand Black history, culture, literature, and so forth? *24*

A: The same way we understand white history, culture, literature, and so forth. That is why we're in school: to learn. *25*

Q: Should whites take African-American studies courses? *26*

A: Of course. We take white-studies courses, though the universities don't call them that. *27*

Comment: When I see groups of Black people on campus, it's really intimidating. *28*

The comebacks flip the intent of language from the original comments.

Comeback: I understand what you mean. I'm frightened when I see 29
white students congregating.

Comment: It's not fair. It's easier for you guys to get into college than 30
for other people.

Comeback: If it's so easy, why aren't there more of us? 31

Comment: It's not our fault that America is the way it is. 32

Comeback: It's not our fault, either, but both of us have a responsibility 33
to make changes.

The final line uses the positive word *chance*.

It's really very simple. Educational progress is a national concern; 34
education is a private one. Your job is not to educate white people; it is to
obtain an education. If you take the racial world on your shoulders, you will
not get the job done. Deal with yourself as an individual worthy of respect,
and make everyone else deal with you the same way. College is a little like
playing grown-up. Practice what you want to be. You have been telling your
parents you are grown. Now is your chance to act like it. ■

Reading for Better Writing

Working by yourself or with a group, answer these questions:

1. Summarize Giovanni's key points. What details suggest that this essay
was highly relevant when it was first published in 1991? Why might
textbook and anthology editors continue to republish this essay?

2. *Essence* magazine (in which this essay was first published) has been
described by its editors as the "preeminent lifestyle magazine for today's
African American woman." How does the *Essence* audience differ from
the target audience for texts such as *The College Writer?* In what ways
does Giovanni's essay speak to multiple audiences? In what ways might
the piece have relevance for you and your campus?

3. Comment on the essay's title: Why might Giovanni have chosen it?
How effective is it, and why?

4. Describe the tone of the essay. How does the writer achieve this tone,
and what is the effect for you as a reader? Imagine the piece with a tone
that contrasts starkly with the existing feel. How might this change the
effect of the piece, and when/where might such a tone be appropriate?

5. The writer gives direct instructions to readers through the final two-
thirds of the essay. Why isn't the last line an imperative or command?

Process Writing

Nicholas D. Kristof, a Pulitzer Prize-winning journalist, describes how interracial marriages have become common in the United States.

Love and Race

Highlight information indicating that interracial marriages are common and beneficial. In the margin, note whether the information is convincing.

In a world brimming with bad news, here's one of the happiest trends. *1* Instead of preying on people of different races, young Americans are falling in love with them.

Whites and blacks can be found strolling together as couples even at *2* the University of Mississippi, once a symbol of racial confrontation.

"I will say that they are always given a second glance," acknowledges *3* C. J. Rhodes, a black student at Ole Miss. He adds that there are still misgivings about interracial dating, particularly among black women and a formidable number of "white Southerners who view this race-mixing as abnormal, frozen by fear to see Sarah Beth bring home a brotha."

Mixed-race marriages in the U.S. now number 1.5 million and are *4* roughly doubling each decade. About 40 percent of Asian-Americans and 6 percent of blacks have married whites in recent years.

Still more striking, one survey found that 40 percent of Americans had *5* dated someone of another race.

In a country where racial divisions remain deep, all this love is an *6* enormously hopeful sign of progress in bridging barriers. Scientists who study the human genome say that race is mostly a bogus distinction reflecting very little genetic difference, perhaps one-hundredth of 1 percent of our DNA.

Skin color differences are recent, arising over only the last 100,000 *7* years or so, a twinkling of an evolutionary eye. That's too short a period for substantial genetic differences to emerge, and so there is perhaps 10 times more genetic differences within a race than there is between races. Thus we should welcome any trend that makes a superficial issue like color less central to how we categorize each other.

The rise in interracial marriage reflects a revolution in attitudes. As *8* recently as 1958, a white mother in Monroe, N.C., called the police after her little girl kissed a black playmate on the cheek; the boy, Hanover Thompson, 9, was then sentenced to 14 years in prison for attempted rape. (His appeals failed, but he was released later after an outcry.)

In 1963, 59 percent of Americans believed that marriage between *9* blacks and whites should be illegal. At one time or another 42 states banned interracial marriages, although the Supreme Court finally invalidated these laws in 1967.

Typically, the miscegenation laws voided any interracial marriages, *10* making the children illegitimate, and some states included penalties such

as enslavement, life imprisonment, and whippings. My wife is Chinese-American, and our relationship would once have been felonious.

At every juncture from the 19th century on, the segregationists warned   *11*
that granting rights to blacks would mean the start of a slippery slope, ending with black men marrying white women. The racists were prophetic.

"They were absolutely right," notes Randall Kennedy, the Harvard Law   *12*
School professor and author of a dazzling new book, *Interracial Intimacies*
. . . . "I do think [interracial marriage] is a good thing. It's a welcome sign of thoroughgoing desegregation. We talk about desegregation in the public sphere; here's desegregation in the most intimate sphere."

These days, interracial romance can be seen on the big screen, on TV   *13*
shows, and in the lives of some prominent Americans. Former Defense Secretary William Cohen has a black wife, as does Peter Norton, the software guru. The Supreme Court justice Clarence Thomas has a white wife.

I find the surge in intermarriage to be one of the most positive fronts   *14*
in American race relations today, building bridges and empathy. But it's still in its infancy.

I was excited to track down interracial couples at Ole Miss, thinking   *15*
they would be perfect to make my point about this hopeful trend: But none were willing to talk about the issue on record.

"Even if people wanted to marry [interracially], I think they'd keep it   *16*
kind of quiet," explained a minister on campus.

For centuries, racists warned that racial equality would lead to the   *17*
"mongrelization" of America. Perhaps they were right in a sense, for we're increasingly going to see a blurring of racial distinctions. But these distinctions acquired enormous social resonance without ever having much basis in biology. ■

Reading for Better Writing

Working by yourself or with a group, do the following:

1. Review the opening paragraph and explain why the passage does or does not effectively introduce the topic and focus the essay.

2. Kristof argues that the popularity of interracial marriages is a process that has developed over time. Cite key events or stages in that process and explain why they indicate progress.

3. "Love and Race" was written for a broad audience. How might the content and style of the essay be different if it were written as a research paper for a college course in sociology?

4. Review the last paragraph and explain why you do or do not find it a strong closing.

Model

Guidelines
Writing About a Process

1. **Select a topic.** Choose a topic from the list that you generated under "Topics to Consider" on page 230. If you're stuck, review your notes and textbooks to generate more course-related topics.

2. **Review the process.** Use your knowledge of the topic to fill out an organizer like the one on the right. List the subject at the top, each of the steps in chronological order, and the outcome at the bottom. Review the organizer to find issues you need to research.

PROCESS ANALYSIS
Subject:
• Step 1
• Step 2
• Step 3
Outcome:

3. **Research as needed.** Find information that spells out the process: what it is, what steps are required, what order the steps should follow, how to do the steps, what outcome the process should produce, and what safety precautions are needed. If possible, observe the process in action or perform it yourself. Carefully record correct names, materials, tools, and safety or legal issues.

4. **Organize information.** After conducting your research, revise the organizer by adding or reordering steps as needed. Then develop an outline, including steps listed in the organizer, as well as supporting details from your research.

5. **Draft the document.** Write the document using the guidelines below.

DESCRIBING A PROCESS	EXPLAINING A PROCESS	WRITING INSTRUCTIONS
Opening: Introduce the topic, stating its importance and giving an overview of the steps. **Middle:** Describe each step clearly (usually in separate paragraphs), and link steps with transitions like *first, second, next, finally,* and *while.* Describe the outcome and its importance. **Closing:** Describe the process as a whole and restate key points.	**Opening:** Introduce the topic and give an overview of the process. **Middle:** Explain what each step involves and how to do it (typically using a separate paragraph for each). Use transitions such as *first, second,* and *next* to link the steps. Explain the outcome. **Closing:** Explain follow-up activity and restate key points.	**Opening:** Name the process in the title; summarize the process and list any materials and tools needed. **Middle:** Present each step in a separate— usually one- or two-sentence—paragraph. Number the steps and state them as commands in parallel form (see page 100). **Closing:** In a short paragraph, explain any follow-up action.

6. **Revise the writing.** Check for the following and revise as needed:
   - A clear opening that identifies the process
   - Steps that are stated clearly and in the correct order
     For explanations and instructions:
     - Clear details explaining how to perform each step
     - A closing that includes necessary follow-up activity
     For instructions:
     - Clear and correct safety cautions in boldface type

7. **Test the writing.** Read the writing for organization and completeness. For *explanations* and *instructions,* perform the process yourself using the writing as a guide. For each step, do only *what* you're told to do and *how* you're told to do it. Note where the writing is incomplete, out of order, and/or lacking adequate safety precautions. Revise as needed.

8. **Get feedback.** Ask a classmate who is unfamiliar with the process to read the writing for clarity, completeness, and correctness. For *instructions,* have the person use the writing as a guide to perform the process, noting where details are incomplete or unclear, and noting where word choice is either imprecise or too technical. Use the feedback to guide further revision.

9. **Edit the writing by looking for the following:**
   - Word choice appropriate for your least-informed reader
   - Clear transitions between steps
   - Consistent verb tense in all steps
   - For *instructions*—verbs that give clear commands (imperative mood)
   - Correct, consistent terminology
   - Informed, respectful voice
   - Proper format (particularly for *instructions*—adequate white space)

10. **Publish the essay.** Share your writing with others:
    - Offer it to instructors or students working with the process.
    - Offer explanations and instructions to people on campus or at nonprofit agencies who can use the writing to do their work.
    - Post the writing on a suitable website.

INSIGHT: The *mood* of a verb indicates the tone or attitude of a sentence. For instructions, writers use the imperative mood (or command form) to communicate a firm, direct, and informed tone.

Writing Checklist

Use these seven traits to check your essay; then revise as needed:

_____ The **ideas** describe or explain the process clearly and completely.

_____ The **organization** sequence helps clarify the process. In explanations and instructions, the organization is chronological and helps the reader work through the process.

_____ The **voice** matches the writer's purpose. Cautions regarding safety or legal issues sound serious but are not alarming.

_____ The **words** are precise, and technical terms are defined.

_____ The **sentences** are smooth, varied in structure, and engaging. In instructions, sentences are shaped as clear, brief, no-nonsense commands stated in parallel form.

_____ The **copy** includes no errors in grammar, punctuation, and spelling.

_____ The page **design** and format are appropriate for an essay or a set of instructions.

Interactive

Critical-Thinking and Writing Activities

As directed by your instructor, complete the following activities.

1. Review the topics that you listed under "Topics to Consider" on page 230. Choose a topic and write about it, letting the writing take any one of these forms: *description, explanation,* or *instructions.*

2. Review the "Wayward Cells" and "Love and Race" models. List similar natural sciences or social sciences processes that interest you. Choose one and write about it as a *description.*

3. Review the process instructions titled "Downloading Photographs from the MC-150 Digital Camera," considering how the written and visual elements on the page work together. Draft or revise a piece in which visual elements are essential to effectively communicate your ideas. Integrate relevant, high-quality visuals (photos, illustrations, diagrams) that will help readers to better understand your ideas.

4. Using Giovanni's "Campus Racism 101" as a model, write a process essay based on your own experience in which you give advice about how to succeed in a difficult situation.

◖ VISUALLY SPEAKING

Study the photograph on page 229 and identify the ceremony taking place. Then select one person in the crowd and write a two-page essay describing the process that led him or her to participate. Create details as needed.

DEFINITION

16

Audio

Whether you're writing a persuasive essay, a lab report, or a project proposal, defining key terms helps you distinguish the boundaries of your subject.

In most writing situations, you will include short definitions of terms consisting of one or two sentences or one or two paragraphs. Although this chapter includes information (see pages **245–246** and **250**) that will enable you to write such brief definitions, its main purpose is to help you write longer, essay-length pieces sometimes called *extended definitions*.

When you write an extended definition, study this chapter, which will guide you through every step in the writing process—from choosing the term to refining the definition. When reading the model essays, look closely at the strategies that each writer uses "to peel the onion"—that is, to unfold and examine each layer of a word's meaning until finally reaching the core.

Web Link

Overview
Writing a Definition Essay

Writer's Goal

Your goal is to choose a word or phrase that interests you, explore what it means (and doesn't mean), and write an essay that helps readers better understand, appreciate, and use that term.

Keys for Success

Know your purpose. Decide what you want your writing to do: entertain, inform, explain, persuade readers to act, or a combination of these.

Choose appropriate writing strategies. Select strategies that help you accomplish your purpose. For example, the writers whose documents are included in this chapter make the following choices:

- In the excerpt from the research paper, "Economic Disparities Fuel Human Trafficking," Shon Bogar defines *human trafficking* in part by distinguishing it from related practices.
- To show readers how to treat patients with *dementia*, Sarah Anne Morelos defines the term using anecdotes and details gathered through both primary and library research.
- To entertain and instruct people listening to his radio program, David Schelhaas examines the word *deft* by first sharing a personal anecdote, and then comparing and contrasting the definitions and etymologies of *deft* and *daft*.
- To describe her mother and herself, Cynthia Ozick offers two distinct definitions of *excellence,* each clarified with precise, colorful details.

Present fresh information. Choose details that help readers understand the word's denotations (literal meanings) as well as its connotations (associated meanings). For example, one denotation of *cute* is *attractive*. Depending on the context, however, associations with this word may be positive or negative.

Topics to Consider

Beneath headings like the following, list words that you'd like to explore.

Words	Words	Words	Words	Words
that are related to an art or a sport	that are (or should be) in the news	that are over- used, unused, or abused	that make you chuckle, frown, or fret	that do— or do not— describe you

Next Step Read the model essays and notice the writing strategies these writers use; think about how you might use them in your own essays.

Definition

The excerpt below comes from a research paper by student writer Shon Bogar. The paper focuses on the problems of human trafficking and slavery as phenomena associated with current trends in globalization. After reviewing global economic trends since the end of the Cold War, Bogar defines the key terms that readers must understand if they are to appreciate the problem. (For more on research writing, see chapters 28–33.)

At the end of the introduction, the writer transitions to the extended definition.

An informal definition of the broader concept of slavery prefaces the extended definition.

The main term is distinguished from related terms using reliable source material.

Economic Disparities Fuel Human Trafficking

. . . . These great economic disparities, from extreme poverty to fabulous   *1* wealth, have helped fuel the international trade in human cargo, as those people with nothing seek a better life serving those with excess.

The buying, selling, and forced exploitation of people—slavery—is not   *2* a new phenomenon. Most nations and most cultures have, at one time or another, enslaved others and been themselves enslaved in turn. The pattern continues today; in fact, slavery exists far beyond the developing world and reaches into the comfortable First World of the United States, Europe, Japan, and Australia. However, examining current trends in the trade of human cargo shows that trafficking and slavery are extremely difficult to define and understand, and that they coexist with and are codependent upon each other. These problems, moreover, have a variety of complex causes and too few solutions that offer a realistic possibility of ending this global abomination.

Human trafficking, in particular, is a term that is difficult to define   *3* properly, but it must first be clarified if the problem itself is to be addressed. To begin, migration, human smuggling, and human trafficking are distinct but related phenomena, and incorrect definitions would put different groups of people in the wrong category, with potentially dire consequences. For example, the Trafficking Victims Prevention Act (TVPA), which came into law in 2000, requires the U.S. government to ensure that victims of trafficking are not jailed or "otherwise penalized solely for unlawful acts as a direct result of being trafficked" (U.S. Department of State, 2004), whereas illegal immigrants are still subject to deportation and criminal proceedings. The U.S. State Department recognizes the potentially "confusing" difference between smuggling and human trafficking, so it defines human smuggling as "the procurement or transport for profit of a person for illegal entry in a country" (2004). However, even if the smuggling involves "dangerous or degrading conditions," the act is still considered smuggling, not human trafficking, and so smuggling is considered an immigration matter, not necessarily a human rights issue (2004).

What distinguishes trafficking from smuggling is the element of   *4* exploitation, including but not limited to "fraud, force, or coercion" (U.S.

The writer offers a formal definition of the key term "human trafficking" by going to official sources.

Department of State, 2004). With this distinction in mind, the United Nations Convention Against Transnational Organized Crime has developed this standard definition of human trafficking: "the recruitment, transportation, transfer, harbouring or receipt of persons, by means of the threat or use of force or other forms of coercion, of abduction, of fraud, of deception, of the abuse of power, or of a position of vulnerability or of the giving or receiving of payments or benefits to achieve the consent of a person having control over another person, for the purpose of exploitation" (U.N. Resolution 25, 2001).

The writer restates a complex legal definition in terms readers will understand.

To unravel the U.N. legalese, human trafficking involves any use of force, coercion, fraud, or deception by those with power so as to exploit people, primarily by moving them into some form of slavery. Under this definition, smuggling can become trafficking if the smugglers have used any means of deception. Unfortunately, the requirement that the smuggler/trafficker be aware of the "victim's final circumstances" makes distinguishing between smuggling and trafficking an inexact science (U.S. Department of State, 2004), and it creates a new set of problems in combating trafficking apart from smuggling. Nevertheless, this definition of human trafficking is a helpful starting point from which the United Nations and governments around the globe can start to fight the trafficking and eventual enslavement of people.

While admitting a difficulty in the definition, the writer stresses the definition's usefulness.

All difficulties of definition aside, human trafficking and slavery are real problems—historical problems that have taken new shapes due to globalization. In fact, today human trafficking is linked to millions of people experiencing multiple forms of slavery, from traditional "chattel slavery" to sexual slavery to debt bondage. . . . ■ 5

Note: The Works Cited page is not shown. For sample pages, see MLA (pages **532–533**) and APA (page **564**).

Reading for Better Writing

Working by yourself or with a group, answer these questions:

1. Without looking back at the model, define "human trafficking" in a sentence or two.

2. Examine each of the three main paragraphs of Bogar's extended definition. What does each paragraph accomplish? How do the paragraphs build on each other?

3. Identify the strategies that the author uses to argue that the definition is necessary. Is the reasoning compelling? Why or why not?

4. Look again at the sources that the writer uses to develop the necessary definitions. Why are these sources appropriate for the terms in question? Which other types of sources might be useful?

5. Examine how the writer transitions into and out of the extended definition. Are these transitions effective? Why or why not?

Definition

In her sociology course, Sarah Anne Morelos was asked to use her personal experience and knowledge to write an essay that helps readers understand a health issue discussed in class. In response, she wrote the following essay that defines a class (or group) of illnesses known as dementia. (Note that Morelos's personal voice and use of personal pronouns are appropriate for her assignment.)

Understanding Dementia

The writer uses the title and an anecdote to introduce the topic.

"Hello, Jenny! It's Sarah . . . I'm going to clean your room." Saying her name assured her that I knew who she was and that I was friendly. As I made her bed, I asked, "How are you doing this morning, Jenny?" 1

"Oh, I'm good," she said. Then, after a pause, she added, "My husband, Charlie, died in this room, you know." 2

I looked in her face and saw the familiar tears. "I'm so sorry, Jenny," I answered. Then I held her hand and listened to the same details of Charlie's death that I had heard every week for the past year. Suddenly Jenny stopped her story, looked up, and asked, "Who are you?" She didn't even remember my entering her room. 3

She defines the word and distinguishes the class (dementia) from illnesses within that class.

Jenny has dementia, a disease that affects many people over eighty years old. When I first started work as a nursing-home housekeeper, the patients experiencing this illness frightened me. I didn't understand their words or behavior. Now that I understand more about the patients and their illness, I am better able to respond to them in a helpful way. 4

> *"You took it! You rotten thief!" she screamed.*

It is now estimated that more than half of the nursing-home residents in the United States have dementia. But what, exactly, is this disease? Dementia is a broad term that refers to a number of health problems, including Alzheimer's disease, brain tumors, and arteriosclerosis, the hardening of arteries to the heart. The outward symptoms of dementia are often disturbing, as this disease affects both the language skills and the behavior of the patient. 5

She describes symptoms.

The most common and noticeable symptom is memory loss. Patients in the early stages of dementia first experience short-term memory loss; as the illness advances, they also experience long-term memory loss. For example, Jenny demonstrated short-term loss. While she could remember countless details about Charlie's death, an event that had happened ten years earlier, she could not remember my name—or even that I had entered the room. Another sign of memory loss is repetitiveness: Patients like Jenny retell their stories over and over. 6

She uses
another
anecdote.

In addition to forgetting information and repeating stories, people ₇ with dementia may express strange beliefs or fears. At one point, a resident named Wilma accused me of stealing from her. "You took it! You rotten thief!" she screamed.

"What are you missing, Wilma?" I asked. She started to tell me, but ₈ then couldn't remember. Soon she had forgotten the episode altogether, although she was still flustered and very angry. This irrationality may be caused by bouts of schizophrenia.

Another symptom of dementia is diminished language skills. While ₉ adults with healthy minds easily recall thousands of vocabulary words, patients with dementia struggle to name even the most common things and most familiar people in their lives. For example, a woman in the middle stages of the illness may recognize her son, but not be able to recall his name. However, as the illness advances, she will lose the ability to recognize his face as well.

For each
symptom,
the writer
provides
examples
and/or
anecdotes.

Patients with dementia also show behavioral changes. One common change is forgetting how to do simple tasks like washing dishes. Another change is forgetting to do basic things like shutting off the stove. Other behavioral changes signal a shift in personality. For example, fifteen years ago,

"Get out of here!" she yells with arms flailing. ₁₀

Wilma was my friendly next-door neighbor who occasionally brought my family cookies. Today, Wilma is one of the dementia patients whom I take care of. As a neighbor, she was mild-mannered, but as a patient she gets very angry with anyone who enters her room. "Get out of here!" she yells with arms flailing. "You're not allowed in here!"

Not surprisingly, dementia can also leave people unable to care for ₁₁ themselves. They may have trouble dressing, bathing, or even using the bathroom. This level of neediness causes two problems. First, the individual cannot do the activity, and second, he or she often suffers from related depression.

A question
signals a
transition.

What's the solution to dementia? Sadly, there is no cure. While nursing- ₁₂ home staff can help patients with activities, and medication helps them cope with depression, nothing can stop the illness. Both the disease and its symptoms get worse.

The writer
gives
another
example.

Steve is a good example. When he entered the nursing home just ₁₃ six months ago, he was experiencing the early stages of dementia. Today, however, his illness is much more advanced. The stress of moving into this new environment and leaving his wife at home alone affected Steve deeply. When he first arrived, Steve often cried and begged to be taken home. "I'll give you $20—please just take me home," he'd plead.

Painfully, I would explain, "Steve, this is your home." After some time, *14* the situation got so bad that he would not sleep or eat. He was depressed, and he cried often, thinking that no one cared about him. Eventually, Steve was given stronger drugs to help with the depression. For a few months, the medication seemed to work—he laughed at jokes and occasionally told one himself. But then Steve's dementia advanced again. Soon he was asking his same sad questions: "Where am I?" and "Do you know what I'm doing here?"

So what is the best "medication" for people with dementia? While no *15* treatment can stop the illness, understanding the disease and its symptoms is the key to helping people cope. Doctors who understand the science of dementia can prescribe medicine. However, all of us who understand the heartbreaking symptoms and effects of the disease can provide another, possibly more effective treatment. We can respond to the victim of dementia with patience, kindness, and love. ■

> She closes by encouraging readers to show understanding and kindness.

Reading for Better Writing

Working by yourself or with a group, do the following:

1. Describe how the writer introduces the topic, and explain why the introduction is or is not effective.

2. Describe how the writer distinguishes the class (dementia) from specific illnesses within that class. How are illnesses within the class defined and explained?

3. The writer extends her definition by focusing largely on the symptoms of the disease. Examine her strategies for doing so, and explain whether you find them effective.

4. Review how the writer closes with an appeal to readers. Is the closing fitting? Why or why not?

5. The conversational voice and personal tone of this essay are appropriate for the writer's assignment described in the introduction to this essay. List ways in which the text and voice might be different if the assignment required writing that (a) was based on secondary sources (see page 448) and (b) followed the academic style described on pages 78–79.

Definition

Professor David Schelhaas delivered the following definition on his weekly radio program, *What's the Good Word?*

Deft or Daft

The writer introduces the topic with an anecdote.

The other day, my wife, watching our son-in-law with his large hands gracefully tie the shoelaces of his little daughter, remarked, "You really are deft." Ever the cynic, I remarked, "He's not only deft, he's daft." I talk that sort of nonsense frequently, but as I said this, I began to wonder. What if *deft* and *daft* come from the same root and once meant the same thing? A quick trip to the dictionary showed that, indeed, they did once mean the same thing (though my wife thought me daft when I first suggested it).

He describes the history of *daft*.

Let me see if I can explain the original meaning and also how *daft* and *deft* came to part company. *Daft* originally meant mild or gentle. The Middle English *dafte* comes from the Old English *gadaefte,* which has as its underlying sense *fit* or *suitable.* Quite likely, mild or gentle people were seen as behaving in a way that was fit and suitable.

Gradually, however, the mild, gentle meaning descended in connotation to mean crazy or foolish. First, animals were described as daft—that is, without reason—and eventually people also. The word *silly,* which once meant happy or blessed, slid down the same slope. So that explains where *daft* got its present meaning.

He compares and contrasts the two words.

But how does *deft,* meaning skillful or dexterous, fit into the picture? Again, if we start with the Old English meaning of *fit* or *suitable,* we can see a connection to skillful. In fact, the root of *gadaefte,* which is *dhabh,* to fit, carries with it the sense of a joiner or an artisan, someone who skillfully made the ends or corners of a cupboard or piece of furniture fit neatly together. From *fit* to *skillful* to *dexterous.* Thus we see how one root word meaning *fit* or *suitable* went in two different directions—one meaning crazy, the other meaning skillful.

He closes with a reflection and his usual sign-off.

These days it is usually considered much better to be deft than to be daft. But don't be too sure. It is good to remind ourselves that one person's deftness might very well appear as daftness to another.

This is David Schelhaas asking, "What's the Good Word?" ■

1
2
3
4
5
6

Reading for Better Writing

Working by yourself or with a group, answer these guidelines:

1. Explain how the opening attempts to engage the reader. In what ways does it succeed?

2. Describe how the writer shows that the meanings of the words have changed. Is his explanation clear? Why or why not?

3. Describe the writer's tone. Is it effective for a radio program? Explain.

Definition

Cynthia Ozick is an American writer known for her fiction, poetry, and essays on Jewish American life. In 2005, she was nominated for the Man Booker International Prize for lifetime achievement in literature.

> Working with classmates, read the essay and note how Ozick defines *excellence* in part by comparing and contrasting her mother's qualities with others' qualities. Highlight these passages in the text. Then discuss how each passage helps define *excellence*.

On *Excellence*

In my Depression childhood, whenever I had a new dress, my cousin Sarah would get suspicious. The nicer the dress was, and especially the more expensive it looked, the more suspicious she would get. Finally she would lift the hem and check the seams. This was to see if the dress had been bought or if my mother had sewed it. Sarah could always tell. My mother's sewing had elegant outsides, but there was something catch-as-catch-can about the insides. Sarah's sewing, by contrast, was as impeccably finished inside as out; not one stray thread dangled.

My uncle Jake built meticulous grandfather clocks out of rosewood; he was a perfectionist and sent to England for the clockworks. My mother built serviceable radiator covers and a serviceable cabinet, with hinged doors, for the pantry. She built a pair of bookcases for the living room. Once, after I was grown and in a house of my own, she fixed the sewer pipe. She painted ceilings, and also landscapes; she reupholstered chairs. One summer she planted a whole yard of tall corn. She thought herself capable of doing anything, and did everything she imagined. But nothing was perfect. There was always some clear flaw, never visible head-on. You had to look underneath where the seams were. The corn thrived, though not in rows. The stalks elbowed one another like gossips in a dense little village.

"Miss Brrrrooobaker," my mother used to mock, rolling her Russian *r*'s, whenever I crossed a *t* she had left uncrossed, or corrected a word she had misspelled, or became impatient with a *v* that had tangled itself up in a *w* in her speech. ("Vvventriloquist," I would say. "Vventriloquist," she would obediently repeat. And the next time it would come out "wiolinist.") Miss Brubaker was my high school English teacher, and my mother invoked her name as an emblem of raging finical obsession. "Miss Brrrrooobaker," my mother's voice hoots at me down the years, as I go on casting and recasting sentences in a tiny handwriting on monomaniacally uniform paper. The loops of my mother's handwriting—it was the Palmer Method—were as big as hoops, spilling generous splashy ebullience. She could pull off, at five minutes' notice, a satisfying dinner for ten concocted out of nothing more than originality and panache. But the napkin would be folded a little off-center, and the spoon might be on the wrong side of the knife. She was an optimist who ignored trifles; for her, God was not in the details but in the intent. And all these culinary and agricultural efflorescences were extracurricular, accomplished in the crevices and niches of a fourteen-hour business day. When she scribbled out her family memoirs, in heaps of dog-eared notebooks or on the backs of old bills or on the margins of last year's calendar, I would resist typing them; in the speed of the chase she often omitted words like "the," "and," "will." The same flashing and bountiful hand fashioned and fired ceramic pots, and painted brilliant autumn views and vases of imaginary flowers and ferns, and decorated ordinary Woolworth platters with lavish enameled gardens. But bits of the painted petals would chip away.

Lavish: my mother was as lavish as nature. She woke early and saturated the hours with work and inventiveness, and read late into the night. She was all profusion, abundance, fabrication. Angry at her children, she would run after us whirling the cord of the electric iron, like a lasso or a whip; but she never caught us. When, in the seventh grade, I was afraid of failing the Music Appreciation final exam because I could not tell the difference between "To a Wild Rose" and "Barcarolle," she got the idea of sending me to school with a gauze sling rigged up on my writing arm, and an explanatory note that was purest fiction. But the sling kept slipping off. My mother gave advice like mad—she boiled over with so much passion for the predicaments of strangers that they turned into permanent cronies. She told intimate stories about people I had never heard of.   *4*

Despite the gargantuan Palmer loops (or possibly because of them), I have always known that my mother's was a life of—intricately abashing word!—excellence: insofar as excellence means ripe generosity. She burgeoned, she proliferated; she was endlessly leafy and flowering. She wore red hats and called herself a gypsy. In her girlhood she marched with the suffragettes and for Margaret Sanger and called herself a Red. She made me laugh, she was so varied: like a tree on which lemons, pomegranates, and prickly pears absurdly all hang together. She had the comedy of prodigality.   *5*

My own way is a thousand times more confined. I am a pinched perfectionist, the ultimate fruition of Miss Brubaker; I attend to crabbed minutiae and am self-trammeled through taking pains. I am a kind of human snail, locked in and condemned by my own nature. The ancients believed that the moist track left by the snail as it crept was the snail's own essence, depleting its body little by little; the farther the snail toiled, the smaller it became, until it finally rubbed itself out. That is how perfectionists are. Say to us "Excellence," and we will show you how we use up our substance and wear ourselves away, while making scarcely any progress at all. The fact that I am an exacting perfectionist in a narrow strait only, and nowhere else, is hardly to the point, since nothing matters to me so much as a comely and muscular sentence. It is my narrow strait, this snail's road: the track of the sentence I am writing now; and when I have eked out the wet substance, ink or blood, that is its mark, I will begin the next sentence. Only in reading out sentences am I perfectionist; but then there is nothing else I know how to do, or take much interest in. I miter every pair of abutting sentences   *6* as scrupulously as Uncle Jake fitted one strip of rosewood against another. My mother's worldly and bountiful hand has escaped me. The sentence I am writing is my cabin and my shell, compact, self-sufficient. It is the burnished horizon—a merciless planet where flawlessness is the single standard, where even the inmost seams, however hidden from a laxer eye, must meet perfection. Here "excellence" is not strewn casually from a tipped cornucopia, here disorder does not account for charm, here trifles rule like tyrants.

I measure my life in sentences, and my sentences are superior to my   7
mother's, pressed out, line by line, like the lustrous ooze on the underside of the snail, the snail's secret open seam, its wound, leaking attar. My mother was too mettlesome to feel the force of a comma. She scorned minutiae. She measured her life according to what poured from the horn of plenty, which was her ample, cascading, elastic, susceptible, inexact heart. My narrower heart rides between the tiny horns of the snail, dwindling as it goes.

And out of this thinnest thread, this ink-wet line of words, must rise a   8
visionary fog, a mist, a smoke, forging cities, histories, sorrows, quagmires, entanglements, lives of sinners, even the life of my furnace-hearted mother: so much wilderness, waywardness, plentitude on the head of the precise and impeccable snail, between the horns. ■

Reading for Better Writing

Working by yourself or with a group, answer these questions:

1. What words and phrases does Ozick use to define *excellence?* How does contrasting her mother's life with her own enable Ozick to further define *excellence?* What point(s) is she making about *excellence?*

2. One way to write a definition is to use words and phrases that have similar meanings to the word you wish to define. What other techniques does Ozick use to define *excellence?* What additional strategies could be used to define a term?

3. Writing a good definition is challenging because it requires the use of precise words to shed light on the meaning of another word that has its own precise meaning(s). Find instances where Ozick lists one term or idea after another to build precision into a definition. How would her meaning change if she had used only one word from the list?

4. Find examples of words that have especially positive or negative connotations. How do these connotations help Ozick to make her main point(s)?

Model

Guidelines
Writing a Definition Essay

1. **Select a topic.** Review the words that you listed under "Topics to Consider" on page **244**, and choose one that you want to explore. If you're stuck, list words similar to those defined in the four models.

> **TIP:** The best topics are abstract nouns (*totalitarianism, individualism,* or *terrorism*), complex terms (*dementia, spousal abuse,* or *Italian opera*), or adjectives connected to a personal experience (like the words defined in the models—*human trafficking, excellence, deft* and *daft*).

2. **Identify what you know.** To discern what you already know about the topic, write freely about the word, letting your writing go where it chooses. Explore both your personal connections and your academic connections with the word.

3. **Gather information.** To find information about the word's history, usage, and grammatical form, use such strategies as the following:
   - Consult a general dictionary, including an unabridged dictionary; list both denotative (literal) and connotative (associated) meanings for the word.
   - Consult specialized dictionaries that define words from specific disciplines or occupations: music, literature, law, medicine, and so on.
   - When appropriate, interview experts or students on your topic.
   - Check reference books such as *Bartlett's Famous Quotations* to see how famous speakers and writers have used the word.
   - Research the word's etymology and usage by consulting appropriate web sources such as dictionary.com, m-w.com, or xrefer.com.
   - Do a general search on the web to see where the word pops up in titles of songs, books, or films; company names, products, and ads; nonprofit organizations; and news topics.
   - List synonyms (words meaning the same—or nearly the same) and antonyms (words meaning the opposite).

4. **Compress what you know.** Based on your freewriting and research, try writing a formal, one-sentence definition that satisfies the following equation:
   Equation: **Term = larger class + distinguishing characteristics**
   Examples: **Swedish pimple** = fishing lure + silver surface, tubular body, three hooks
   melodrama = stage play + flat characters, contrived plot, moralistic theme
   Alzheimer's = dementia + increasing loss of memory, hygiene, social skills

5. **Get organized.** To organize the information that you have, and to identify details that you may want to add, fill out a graphic organizer like the one on page 51.

> **TIP:** Although you can draft your essay directly from the organizer, you may save time by writing a traditional outline that lists your main points, subpoints, and supporting details.

6. **Draft the essay.** Review your outline as needed to write the first draft.

   Opening: Get the reader's attention and introduce the term. If you are organizing the essay from general to specific, consider using an anecdote, an illustration, or a quotation to set the context for what follows. If you are organizing it from specific to general, consider including an interesting detail from the word's history or usage. Wherever you use a dictionary definition, do so with a new slant and avoid the dusty phrase "According to *Webster's* . . . "

   Middle: Show your reader precisely what the word does or does not mean. Build the definition in unified paragraphs, each of which addresses distinct aspects of the word: common definitions, etymology, usage by professional writers, and so on. Link paragraphs so that the essay unfolds the word's meaning one layer after another.

   Closing: Review your main point and close your essay. (You might, for example, conclude by encouraging readers to use—or not use—the word.)

7. **Get feedback.** Ask a classmate or someone from the college's writing center to read your essay for the following:

   - **Engaging opening**—Does the introduction identify the word and set the context for what follows?
   - **Clarity**—Is each facet of the definition clear, showing precisely what the word does and does not mean?
   - **Continuity**—Is each paragraph unified, and is each one linked to the paragraphs that precede and follow it? Is the essay focused and unified?
   - **Completeness**—Is the definition complete, telling the reader all that she or he needs to know to understand and use the word?
   - **Fitting closing**—Does the conclusion wrap up the message and refocus on the word's core meaning?

8. **Revise and edit the essay.** Use the feedback to revise the essay. If necessary, do additional research to find information to answer your reader's questions. Edit the essay by looking for clear sentences; correct quotations; specific, appropriate words; and correct grammar, spelling, usage, and punctuation.

9. **Publish the essay.** Share your writing with interested readers, including friends, family, and classmates. Submit the essay to your instructor.

Writing Checklist

Use these seven traits to check your essay; then revise as needed:

_____ The **ideas** in the definition clearly distinguish what the word does and does not mean. Supporting details help strengthen main points.

_____ The **organizational** pattern is logical and appropriate for the definition's content. Paragraphs are unified and ordered to build a clear pattern of thought.

_____ The **voice** is informed, engaging, and courteous.

_____ The **words** are precise and appropriate, and complex or technical terms are defined. Transitional words and phrases link paragraphs smoothly and logically.

_____ The **sentences** are complete, clear, varied in structure, and readable.

_____ The **copy** includes no errors in spelling, punctuation, or grammar.

_____ The page **design** is attractive and properly formatted.

Interactive

Critical-Thinking and Writing Activities

As directed by your instructor, complete the following activities.

1. Review the definition excerpted from "Economic Disparities Fuel Human Trafficking," noting that at the end the writer transitions to a discussion of slavery. Research and draft an extended definition of "slavery" that would pick up where student writer Shon Bogar left off after defining "human trafficking." Tip: to gather your ideas, use the definition diagram on page 51.

2. Review "Deft or Daft" and choose a pair of words that similarly mirror each other's meaning. Research the words, and write an essay comparing and contrasting their etymologies and meanings.

3. Review "On *Excellence*" by Cynthia Ozick, concentrating on the way Ozick uses lists of words, phrases, and ideas to build precise definitions. Experiment with this strategy for definition in an essay that you draft or revise.

4. Write an essay defining a word or phrase that is understood by people in a particular field of study but not by "outsiders." Write for the audience of outsiders.

◆ Visually Speaking

Revisit the photograph on page 243. Then reflect on what the image might suggest about the nature of definitions and definition writing.

PERSUASIVE WRITING

"Convince me!" is the reader's cry that lies behind all persuasive writing. Whether you are taking a position on an issue (chapter 18), persuading readers to take action (chapter 19), or proposing a solution to a vexing problem (chapter 20), you are arguing a point in an attempt to persuade readers to accept your claims, with the result that they change their own thinking and perhaps even their actions. In other words, even though each of these forms has a distinctive rhetorical emphasis, all three rely on foundational strategies for argumentation and persuasion (chapter 17): from making and supporting claims effectively to avoiding logical fallacies.

Carefully study the four chapters in this section, noting the strategies discussed in each. Then, when you're writing a persuasive essay, use those strategies that best address your writing situation: your subject, audience, and purpose.

CONTENTS
Persuasive Writing

17 Strategies for Argumentation and Persuasion

Building Persuasive Arguments	260
Preparing Your Argument	261
Making and Qualifying Claims	262
Supporting Your Claims	264
Identifying Logical Fallacies	267
Engaging the Opposition	271
Using Appropriate Appeals	272
Critical-Thinking and Writing Activities	274

18 Taking a Position

Overview: Taking a Position	276
Student Model	277
Professional Models	279
Guidelines	292
Writing Checklist and Activities	294

19 Persuading Readers to Act

Overview: Persuading Readers to Act	296
Student Model	297
Professional Models	300
Guidelines	310
Writing Checklist and Activities	312

20 Proposing a Solution

Overview: Proposing a Solution	314
Student Model	315
Professional Models	318
Guidelines	326
Writing Checklist and Activities	328

STRATEGIES FOR ARGUMENTATION AND PERSUASION

17

"I wasn't convinced." "I just didn't buy it." Maybe you've said something similar while watching a political debate, viewing a TV ad, or discussing an issue in class or at work. You simply didn't find the argument logical, believable, or persuasive.

In a sense, college is a place where big issues get argued out. Your courses aim to strengthen your reasoning abilities so that you can construct persuasive arguments. Your goal as a persuasive writer is to reason effectively with your readers or listeners and to motivate them to believe, change, or act.

This chapter is a resource on reasoning. It explains the foundations of argumentation and persuasion, from making claims to using fitting appeals. The three chapters that follow introduce, explain, and model three related forms of argumentative writing: taking a position, persuading readers to act, and proposing a solution.

Web Link

Building Persuasive Arguments

What is an argument?

Formally, an *argument* is a series of statements arranged in a logical sequence, supported with sound evidence, and expressed powerfully so as to sway your reader or listener. Arguments appear in a variety of places:

- A research paper about e-mail surveillance by the FBI
- An analysis of "Good Country People" (short story) or *War of the Worlds* (film)
- A debate about the ethics of transferring copyrighted music over the Internet

How do you build a persuasive argument?

Step 1: Prepare your argument.

- **Identify your audience and purpose.** Who is your audience and what is your goal? Do you want to take a position, persuade readers to act, or offer a solution?
- **Generate ideas and gather solid evidence.** You can't base an argument on opinions. Find accurate, pertinent information about the issue and uncover all viewpoints on it.
- **Develop a line of reasoning.** To be effective, you need to link your ideas in a clear, logical sequence.

Step 2: Make and qualify your claim.

- **Draw reasonable conclusions from the evidence.** State your claim (a debatable idea) as the central point for which you will argue. For example, you might assert that something is true, has value, or should be done.
- **Add qualifiers.** Words such as "typically" and "sometimes" soften your claim, making it more reasonable and acceptable.

Step 3: Support your claim.

- **Support each point** in your claim with solid evidence.
- **Identify logical fallacies.** Test your thinking for errors in logic. (See pages 267–270.)

Step 4: Engage the opposition.

- **Make concessions,** if needed, by granting points to the opposition.
- **Develop rebuttals** that expose the weaknesses of the opposition's position, whenever possible.
- **Use appropriate appeals**—emotional "tugs" that ethically and logically help readers see your argument as convincing.

Preparing Your Argument

An argument is a reason or chain of reasons used to support a claim. To use argumentation well, you need to know how to draw logical conclusions from sound evidence. Preparing an effective argument involves a number of specific steps, starting with those discussed below.

Consider the situation.

- **Clearly identify your purpose and audience.** This step is essential for all writing, but especially true when building an argument. (See page **30**.)
- **Consider a range of ideas** to broaden your understanding of the issue and to help focus your thinking on a particular viewpoint. (See page **44**.)
- **Gather sound evidence** to support your viewpoint. (See pages **264–266**.)

Develop a line of reasoning.

Argumentative writing requires a clear line of reasoning with each point logically supporting your argument. Develop the line of reasoning as you study the issue, or use either of the following outlines as a guide.

SAMPLE ARGUMENTATIVE OUTLINES

Outline 1: **Present your supporting arguments, then address counterarguments, and conclude with the strongest argument.**
Introduction: question, concern, or claim
    1. Strong argument-supporting claim
      • Discussion and support
    2. Other argument-supporting claims
      • Discussion of and support for each argument
    3. Objections, concerns, and counterarguments
      • Discussion, concessions, answers, and rebuttals
    4. Strongest argument-supporting claim
      • Discussion and support
Conclusion: argument consolidated—claim reinforced

Outline 2: **Address the arguments and counterarguments point by point.**
Introduction: question, concern, or claim
    1. Strong argument-supporting claim
      • Discussion and support
      • Counterarguments, concessions, and rebuttals
    2. Other argument-supporting claims
      • For each argument, discussion and support
      • For each argument, counterarguments, concessions, and rebuttals
    3. Strongest argument-supporting claim
      • Discussion and support
      • Counterarguments, concessions, and rebuttals
Conclusion: argument consolidated—claim reinforced

Making and Qualifying Claims

An argument centers on a claim—a debatable statement. That claim is the thesis, or key point you wish to explain and defend so well that readers agree with it. A strong claim has the following traits:

- **It's clearly arguable**—it can be vigorously debated.
- **It's defendable**—it can be supported with sufficient arguments and evidence.
- **It's responsible**—it takes an ethically sound position.
- **It's understandable**—it uses clear terms and defines key words.
- **It's interesting**—it is challenging and worth discussing, not bland and easily accepted.

Distinguish claims from facts and opinions.

A claim is a conclusion drawn from logical thought and reliable evidence. A fact, in contrast, is a statement that can be checked for accuracy. An opinion is a personally held taste or attitude. A claim can be debated, but a fact or an opinion cannot.

Fact: *The Fellowship of the Ring* is the first book in J. R. R. Tolkien's trilogy *The Lord of the Rings.*

Opinion: I liked the movie almost as much as the book.

Claim: While the film version of *The Fellowship of the Ring* does not completely follow the novel's plot, the film does faithfully capture the spirit of Tolkien's novel.

Note: While the fact's accuracy can easily be checked, the opinion statement simply offers a personal feeling. Conversely, the claim states an idea that can be supported with reasoning and evidence.

Distinguish three types of claims.

Truth, value, and policy—these types of claims are made in an argument. The differences among them are important because each type has a distinct goal.

Claims of truth state that something is or is not the case. As a writer, you want readers to accept your claim as trustworthy.

- The Arctic ice cap will begin to disappear as early as 2050.
- The cholesterol in eggs is not as dangerous as previously feared.

Comment: Avoid statements that are (1) obviously true or (2) impossible to prove. Also, truth claims must be argued carefully because accepting them (or not) can have serious consequences.

Sample Essay: "An Apology for the Life of Ms. Barbie D. Doll," pages 277–278.

Claims of value state that something does or does not have worth. As a writer, you want readers to accept your judgment.

■ Volunteer reading tutors provide a valuable service.

■ Many music videos fail to present positive images of women.

> **Comment:** Claims of value must be supported by referring to a known standard or by establishing an agreed-upon standard. To avoid a bias, base your judgments on the known standard, not on your feelings.

Sample Essay: "Apostles of Hatred . . . , " pages 279–280

Claims of policy state that something ought or ought not to be done. As a writer, you want readers to approve your course of action.

■ Special taxes should be placed on gas-guzzling SUVs.

■ The developer should not be allowed to fill in the pond where the endangered tiger salamander lives.

> **Comment:** Policy claims focus on action. To arrive at them, you must often first establish certain truths and values; thus an argument over policy may include both truth and value claims.

Sample Essay: "Pornography," pages 281–286

Develop a supportable claim.

An effective claim balances confidence with common sense. Follow these tips:

Avoid all-or-nothing, extreme claims. Propositions using words that are overly positive or negative—such as *all, best, never,* and *worst*—may be difficult to support. Statements that leave no room for exceptions are easy to attack.

> **Extreme:** All people charged even once for DUI should never be allowed to drive again.

Make a truly meaningful claim. Avoid claims that are obvious, trivial, or unsupportable. None is worth the energy needed to argue the point.

> **Obvious:** College athletes sometimes receive special treatment.
>
> **Trivial:** The College Rec Center is a good place to get fit.
>
> **Unsupportable:** Athletics are irrelevant to college life.

Use qualifiers to temper your claims. Qualifiers are words or phrases that make claims more reasonable. Notice the difference between these two claims:

> **Unqualified:** Star athletes take far too many academic shortcuts.
>
> **Qualified:** Some star athletes take improper academic shortcuts.

Note: The "qualified" claim is easier to defend because it narrows the focus and leaves room for exceptions. Use qualifier words like these:

almost	many	often	tends to
frequently	maybe	probably	typically
likely	might	some	usually

Supporting Your Claims

A claim stands or falls on its support. It's not the popular strength of your claim that matters, but rather the strength of your reasoning and evidence. To develop strong support, consider how to select and use evidence.

Gather evidence.

Several types of evidence can support claims. To make good choices, review each type, as well as its strengths and weaknesses.

Observations and anecdotes share what people (including you) have seen, heard, smelled, touched, tasted, and experienced. Such evidence offers an "eyewitness" perspective shaped by the observer's viewpoint, which can be powerful but may also prove narrow and subjective.

- Most of us have closets full of clothes: jeans, sweaters, khakis, T-shirts, and shoes for every occasion.

Statistics offer concrete numbers about a topic. Numbers don't "speak for themselves," however. They need to be interpreted and compared properly—not slanted or taken out of context. They also need to be up-to-date, relevant, and accurate.

- Pennsylvania spends $30 million annually in deer-related costs.
- Wisconsin has an estimated annual loss of $37 million for crop damage alone.

Tests and experiments provide hard data developed through the scientific method, data that must nevertheless be carefully studied and properly interpreted.

- According to the two scientists, the rats with unlimited access to the functional running wheel ran each day and gradually increased the amount of running; in addition, they started to eat less.

Graphics provide information in visual form—from simple tables to more complex charts, maps, drawings, and photographs. When poorly done, however, graphics can distort the truth. See the line graph in the experiment report on page 345 and the photographs in "Downloading Photographs . . ." on page 233.

Analogies compare two things, creating clarity by drawing parallels. However, every analogy breaks down if pushed too far.

- It is obvious today that America has defaulted on this promissory note insofar as her citizens of color are concerned. Instead of honoring this sacred obligation, America has given the Negro people a bad check; a check which has come back marked "insufficient funds." But we refuse to believe that the bank of justice is bankrupt.

                                                                —Martin Luther King, Jr.

Expert testimony offers insights from an authority on the topic. Such testimony always has limits: Experts don't know it all, and they work from distinct perspectives, which means that they can disagree.

■ One specialist opposed to drilling is David Klein, a professor at the Institute of Arctic Biology at the University of Alaska–Fairbanks. Klein argues that if the oil industry opens up the ANWR for drilling, the number of caribou will likely decrease because the calving locations will change.

Illustrations, examples, and demonstrations support general claims with specific instances, making such statements seem concrete and observable. Of course, an example may not be your best support if it isn't familiar.

■ Think about how differently one can frame Rosa Parks' historic action. In prevailing myth, Parks—a holy innocent—acts almost on whim. . . . The real story is more empowering: It suggests that change is the product of deliberate, incremental action.

Analyses examine parts of a topic through thought patterns—cause/effect, compare/contrast, classification, process, or definition. Such analysis helps make sense of a topic's complexity, but muddles the topic when poorly done.

■ A girl's interest in romance is no more Barbie's fault than the fault of books like *On the Shores of Silver Lake.* Fashion magazines targeted at adolescents are the cause of far more anorexia cases than is Barbie.

Predictions offer insights into possible outcomes or consequences by forecasting what might happen under certain conditions. Like weather forecasting, predicting can be tricky. To be plausible, a prediction must be rooted in a logical analysis of present facts.

■ While agroterrorist diseases would have little direct effect on people's health, they would be devastating to the agricultural economy, in part because of the many different diseases that could be used in an attack.

Use evidence.

Finding evidence is one thing; using it well is another. To marshal evidence in support of your claim, follow three guidelines:

1. **Go for quality and variety, not just quantity.** More evidence is not necessarily better. Instead, support your points with sound evidence in different forms. Quality evidence is . . .
   - *accurate:* correct and verifiable in each detail.
   - *complete:* filled with pertinent facts.
   - *concrete:* filled with specifics.
   - *relevant:* clearly related to the claim.
   - *current:* reliably up-to-date.
   - *authoritative:* backed by expertise, training, and knowledge.
   - *appealing:* able to influence readers.

2. Use inductive and deductive patterns of logic. Depending on your purpose, use inductive or deductive reasoning. (See page **20**.)

Induction: Inductive reasoning works from the particular toward general conclusions. In a persuasive essay using induction, look at facts first, find a pattern in them, and then lead the reader to your conclusion.

For example, in "To Drill or Not to Drill," Rebecca Pasok first details specific threats to the environment before arriving at her claim that drilling for oil in an Alaskan wilderness refuge is not our best option. (See pages **297–299**.)

Deduction: Deductive reasoning—the opposite of inductive reasoning—starts from accepted truths and applies them to a new situation so as to reach a conclusion about it. For deduction to be sound, be sure the starting principles or facts are true, the new situation is accurately described, and the application is logical.

For example, Martin Luther King opened his 1963 "I Have a Dream" speech by noting that more than one hundred years earlier, the Emancipation Proclamation promised African Americans justice and freedom. He then described the continuing unjust treatment of African Americans, deducing that the promises in the Proclamation remained unfulfilled. (See pages **300–303**.)

3. Reason using valid warrants. To make sense, claims and their supporting reasons must have a logical connection. That connection is called the *warrant*— the often unspoken thinking used to relate the reasoning to the claim. If warrants are good, arguments hold water; if warrants are faulty, then arguments break down. In other words, beware of faulty assumptions.

Check the short argument outlined below. Which of the warrants seem reasonable and strong, and which seem weak? Where does the argument fail?

Reasoning: If current trends in water usage continue, the reservoir will be empty in two years.

Claim: Therefore, Emeryville should immediately shut down its public swimming pools.

Unstated Warrants or Assumptions:

- It is not good for the reservoir to be empty.
- The swimming pools draw significant amounts of water from the reservoir.
- Emptying the pools would help raise the level of the reservoir.
- No other action would better prevent the reservoir from emptying.
- It is worse to have an empty reservoir than an empty swimming pool.

INSIGHT: Because an argument is no stronger than its warrants, you must make sure that your reasoning clearly and logically supports your claims.

Identifying Logical Fallacies

Fallacies are false arguments—that is, bits of fuzzy, dishonest, or incomplete thinking. They may crop up in your own thinking, in your opposition's thinking, or in such public "arguments" as ads, political appeals, and talk shows. Because fallacies may sway an unsuspecting audience, they are dangerously persuasive. By learning to recognize fallacies, however, you may identify them in opposing arguments and eliminate them from your own writing. In this section, logical fallacies are grouped according to how they falsify an argument.

Distorting the Issue

The following fallacies falsify an argument by twisting the logical framework.

Bare Assertion The most basic way to distort an issue is to deny that it exists. This fallacy claims, "That's just how it is."

- The private ownership of handguns is a constitutional right. (*Objection:* The claim shuts off discussion of the U.S. Constitution or the reasons for regulation.)

Begging the Question Also known as circular reasoning, this fallacy arises from assuming in the basis of your argument the very point you need to prove.

- We don't need a useless film series when every third student owns a DVD player or VCR. (*Objection:* There may be uses for a public film series that private video viewing can't provide. The word "useless" begs the question.)

Oversimplification This fallacy reduces complexity to simplicity. Beware of phrases like "It's a simple question of." Serious issues are rarely simple.

- Capital punishment is a simple question of protecting society.

Either/Or Thinking Also known as black-and-white thinking, this fallacy reduces all options to two extremes. Frequently, it derives from a clear bias.

- Either this community develops light-rail transportation or the community will not grow in the future. (*Objection:* The claim ignores the possibility that growth may occur through other means.)

Complex Question Sometimes by phrasing a question a certain way, a person ignores or covers up a more basic question.

- Why can't we bring down the prices that corrupt gas stations are charging? (*Objection:* This question ignores a more basic question— "Are gas stations really corrupt?")

Straw Man In this fallacy, the writer argues against a claim that is easily refuted. Typically, such a claim exaggerates or misrepresents the opponents' position.

- Those who oppose euthanasia must believe that the terminally ill deserve to suffer.

Sabotaging the Argument

These fallacies falsify the argument by twisting it. They destroy reason and replace it with something hollow or misleading.

Red Herring This strange term comes from the practice of dragging a stinky fish across a trail to throw tracking dogs off the scent. When a person puts forth a volatile idea that pulls readers away from the real issue, readers become distracted. Suppose the argument addresses drilling for oil in the Arctic National Wildlife Refuge (ANWR) of Alaska, and the writer begins with this statement:

■ In 1989, the infamous oil spill of the *Exxon Valdez* led to massive animal deaths and enormous environmental degradation of the coastline. (*Objection:* Introducing this notorious oil spill distracts from the real issue—how oil drilling will affect the ANWR.)

Misuse of Humor Jokes, satire, and irony can lighten the mood and highlight a truth; when humor distracts or mocks, however, it undercuts the argument. What effect would the mocking tone of this statement have in an argument about tanning beds in health clubs?

■ People who use tanning beds will just turn into wrinkled old prunes or leathery sun-dried tomatoes!

Appeal to Pity This fallacy engages in a misleading tug on the heartstrings. Instead of using a measured emotional appeal, an appeal to pity seeks to manipulate the audience into agreement.

■ Affirmative action policies ruined this young man's life. Because of them, he was denied admission to Centerville College.

Use of Threats A simple but unethical way of sabotaging an argument is to threaten opponents. More often than not, a threat is merely implied: "If you don't accept my argument, you'll regret it."

■ If we don't immediately start drilling for oil in the ANWR, you will soon face hour-long lines at gas stations from New York to California.

Bandwagon Mentality Someone implies that a claim cannot be true because a majority of people are opposed to it, or it must be true because a majority support it. (History shows that people in the minority have often had the better argument.) At its worst, such an appeal manipulates people's desire to belong or be accepted.

■ It's obvious to intelligent people that cockroaches live only in the apartments of dirty people. (*Objection:* Based on popular opinion, the claim appeals to a kind of prejudice and ignores scientific evidence about cockroaches.)

Appeal to Popular Sentiment This fallacy consists of associating your position with something popularly loved: the American flag, baseball, apple pie. Appeals to popular sentiment sidestep thought to play on feelings.

■ Anyone who has seen *Bambi* could never condone hunting deer.

Drawing Faulty Conclusions from the Evidence

This group of fallacies falsifies the argument by short-circuiting proper logic in favor of assumptions or faulty thinking.

Appeal to Ignorance This fallacy suggests that because no one has proven a particular claim, it must be false; or, because no one has disproven a claim, it must be true. Appeals to ignorance unfairly shift the burden of proof onto someone else.

■ Flying saucers are real. No scientific explanation has ruled them out.

Hasty or Broad Generalization Such a claim is based on too little evidence or allows no exceptions. In jumping to a conclusion, the writer may use intensifiers such as *all, every,* or *never.*

■ Today's voters spend too little time reading and too much time being taken in by 30-second sound bites. (*Objection:* Quite a few voters may, in fact, spend too little time reading about the issues, but it is unfair to suggest that this is true of everyone.)

False Cause This well-known fallacy confuses sequence with causation: If *A* comes before *B, A* must have caused *B.* However, *A* may be one of several causes, or *A* and *B* may be only loosely related, or the connection between *A* and *B* may be entirely coincidental.

■ Since that new school opened, drug use among young people has skyrocketed. Better that the school had never been built.

Slippery Slope This fallacy argues that a single step will start an unstoppable chain of events. While such a slide may occur, the prediction lacks evidence.

■ If we legalize marijuana, it's only a matter of time before hard drugs follow and America becomes a nation of junkies and addicts.

Misusing Evidence

These fallacies falsify the argument by abusing or distorting the evidence.

Impressing with Numbers In this case, the writer drowns readers in statistics and numbers that overwhelm them into agreement. In addition, the numbers haven't been properly interpreted.

■ At 35 ppm, CO levels factory-wide are only 10 ppm above the OSHA recommendation, which is 25 ppm. Clearly, that 10 ppm is insignificant in the big picture, and the occasional readings in some areas of between 40 and 80 ppm are aberrations that can safely be ignored. (*Objection:* The 10 ppm may be significant, and higher readings may indicate real danger.)

Half-Truths A half-truth contains part of but not the whole truth. Because it leaves out "the rest of the story," it is both true and false simultaneously.

■ The new welfare bill is good because it will get people off the public dole. (*Objection:* This may be true, but the bill may also cause undue suffering for some truly needy individuals.)

Unreliable Testimonial An appeal to authority has force only if the authority is qualified in the proper field. If he or she is not, the testimony is irrelevant. Note that fame is not the same thing as authority.

■ On her talk show, Alberta Magnus recently claimed that most pork sold in the United States is tainted. (*Objection:* Although Magnus may be an articulate talk show host, she is not an expert on food safety.)

Attack Against the Person This fallacy directs attention to a person's character, lifestyle, or beliefs rather than to the issue.

■ Would you accept the opinion of a candidate who experimented with drugs in college?

Hypothesis Contrary to Fact This fallacy relies on "if only" thinking. It bases the claim on an assumption of what would have happened if something else had, or had not, happened. Being pure speculation, such a claim cannot be tested.

■ If only multiculturalists hadn't pushed through affirmative action, the United States would be a united nation.

False Analogy Sometimes a person will argue that *X* is good (or bad) because it is like *Y*. Such an analogy may be valid, but it weakens the argument if the grounds for the comparison are vague or unrelated.

■ Don't bother voting in this election; it's a stinking quagmire. (*Objection:* Comparing the election to a "stinking quagmire" is unclear and exaggerated.)

Misusing Language

Essentially, all logical fallacies misuse language. However, three fallacies falsify the argument, especially by the misleading use of words.

Obfuscation This fallacy involves using fuzzy terms like *throughput* and *downlink* to muddy the issue. These words may make simple ideas sound more profound than they really are, or they may make false ideas sound true.

■ Through the fully functional developmental process of a streamlined target-refractory system, the U.S. military will successfully reprioritize its data throughputs. (*Objection:* What does this sentence mean?)

Ambiguity Ambiguous statements can be interpreted in two or more opposite ways. Although ambiguity can result from unintentional careless thinking, writers sometimes use ambiguity to obscure a position.

■ Many women need to work to support their children through school, but they would be better off at home. (*Objection:* Does *they* refer to *children* or *women*? What does *better off* mean? These words and phrases can be interpreted in opposite ways.)

Slanted Language By choosing words with strong positive or negative connotations, a writer can draw readers away from the true logic of the argument. Here is an example of three synonyms for the word *stubborn* that the philosopher Bertrand Russell once used to illustrate the bias in slanted language:

■ I am firm. You are obstinate. He is pigheaded.

Engaging the Opposition

Think of an argument as an intelligent, lively dialogue with readers. Anticipate their questions, concerns, objections, and counterarguments. Then follow these guidelines.

Make concessions.

By offering concessions—recognizing points scored by the other side—you acknowledge your argument's limits and the truth of other positions. Paradoxically, such concessions strengthen your overall argument by making it seem more credible. Concede your points graciously, using words such as the following:

Admittedly	Granted	I agree that	I cannot argue with
It is true that	You're right	I accept	No doubt
Of course	I concede that	Perhaps	Certainly it's the case

- Granted, Barbie's physical appearance isn't realistic. As Motz explains . . .

Develop rebuttals.

Even when you concede a point, you can often answer that objection by rebutting it. A good rebuttal is a small, tactful argument aimed at a weak spot in the opposing argument. Try these strategies:

1. **Point out the counterargument's limits** by putting the opposing point in a larger context. Show that the counterargument leaves something important out of the picture.

2. **Tell the other side of the story.** Offer an opposing interpretation of the evidence, or counter with stronger, more reliable, more convincing evidence.

3. **Address logical fallacies** in the counterargument. Check for faulty reasoning or emotional manipulation. For example, if the counterargument forces the issue into an either/or straightjacket, show that other options exist.

   - Granted, Barbie's physical appearance isn't realistic. As Motz explains . . . I say, so what? While the only "real" version of Barbie's body would be a long-limbed 13-year-old with breast implants, who cares? Arguing that Barbie's body isn't realistic and that the lack of realism hurts girls' self-esteem is weak logic. Children have had dolls for ages. For example . . .

Consolidate your claim.

After making concessions and rebutting objections, you may need to regroup. Restate your claim so carefully that the weight of your whole argument can rest on it.

- Playing with Barbies need not be an unimaginative, antisocial activity that promotes conformity, materialism, and superficial ideals.

Using Appropriate Appeals

For your argument to be persuasive, it must not only be logical, but also "feel right." It must treat readers as real people by appealing to their common sense, hopes, pride, and notion of right and wrong. How do you appeal to all these concerns? Do the following: (1) build credibility, (2) make logical appeals, and (3) focus on readers' needs.

Build credibility.

A persuasive argument is credible—so trustworthy that readers can change their minds painlessly. To build credibility, observe these rules:

Be thoroughly honest. Demonstrate integrity toward the topic—don't falsify data, spin evidence, or ignore facts. Document your sources and cite them wherever appropriate.

Make realistic claims, projections, and promises. Avoid emotionally charged statements, pie-in-the-sky forecasts, and undeliverable deals.

Develop and maintain trust. From your first word to your last, develop trust—in your attitude toward the topic, your treatment of readers, and your respect for opposing viewpoints.

Make logical appeals.

Arguments stand or fall on their logical strength, but your readers' acceptance of those arguments is often affected more by the emotional appeal of your ideas and evidence. To avoid overly emotional appeals, follow these guidelines:

Engage readers positively. Appeal to their better natures—to their sense of honor, justice, social commitment, altruism, and enlightened self-interest. Avoid appeals geared toward ignorance, prejudice, selfishness, or fear.

Use a fitting tone. Use a tone that is appropriate for the topic, purpose, situation, and audience.

Aim to motivate, not manipulate, readers. While you do want them to accept your viewpoint, it's not a win-at-all-costs situation. Avoid bullying, guilt-tripping, and exaggerated tugs on heartstrings.

Don't trash-talk the opposition. Show tact, respect, and understanding. Focus on issues, not personalities.

Use arguments and evidence that readers can understand and appreciate. If readers find your thinking too complex, too simple, or too strange, you've lost them.

INSIGHT: Remember the adage: The best argument is so clear and convincing that it sounds like an explanation.

Focus on readers' needs.

Instead of playing on readers' emotions, connect your argument with readers' needs and values. Follow these guidelines:

Know your real readers. Who are they—peers, professors, or fellow citizens? What are their allegiances, their worries, their dreams?

Picture readers as resistant. Accept that your readers, including those inclined to agree with you, need convincing. Think of them as alert, cautious, and demanding—but also interested.

Use appeals that match needs and values. Your argument may support or challenge readers' needs and values. To understand those needs, study the table below, which is based loosely on the thinking of psychologist Abraham Maslow. Maslow's hierarchy ranks people's needs on a scale from the most basic to the most complex. The table begins at the bottom with *having necessities* (a basic need) and ends at the top with *helping others* (a more complex need). For example, if you're writing to argue for more affordable housing for the elderly, you'd argue differently to legislators (whose focus is on *helping others*) than to the elderly who need the housing (whose focus is on *having necessities*). Follow these guidelines:

- Use appeals that match the foremost needs and values of your readers.
- If appropriate, constructively challenge those needs and values.
- Whenever possible, phrase your appeals in positive terms.
- After analyzing your readers' needs, choose a persuasive theme for your argument—a positive benefit, advantage, or outcome that readers can expect if they accept your claim. Use this theme to help readers to care about your claims.

READER NEEDS . . .	USE PERSUASIVE APPEALS TO . . .
To make the world better by • *helping others*	values and social obligations
To achieve by • *being good at something* • *getting recognition*	self-fulfillment, status appreciation
To belong by • *being part of a group*	group identity, acceptance
To survive by • *avoiding threats* • *having necessities*	safety, security physical needs

Critical-Thinking and Writing Activities

As directed by your instructor, complete the following activities alone or with a group.

1. Select an essay from chapters 18–20, "Taking a Position," "Persuading Readers to Act," or "Proposing a Solution." Read the essay carefully. Then describe and evaluate the argumentative strategies used by the writer, answering the specific questions below:

   - *What is the writer's main claim? Is it a claim of truth, value, or policy?*
   - *Is the claim arguable—that is, is it supportable, appropriately qualified, and effectively phrased?*
   - *What arguments does the writer develop in support of the claim? Are these arguments logical?*
   - *What types of evidence does the writer provide to support her or his discussion? Is the evidence valid, sufficient, and accurate?*
   - *Does the writer effectively address questions, alternatives, objections, and counterarguments?*

2. Examine the essay that you read for the first activity, and then answer the following questions:

   - *Describe the writer's tone. Does it effectively engage readers?*
   - *Does the argument seem credible and authoritative? Explain.*
   - *Identify ways that the writer connects with readers' needs and values. How does he or she develop a persuasive theme that appeals to those needs and stresses reader benefits?*

3. Working with a classmate, examine an ad in a newspaper or magazine, on TV, or on the Internet. What kind of persuasive appeals (pages **272–273**) does the ad use? Are they used effectively and appropriately? For example, using the instructions on "Critical Thinking Through Viewing" (pages **12–17**), explain how the visuals aim to persuade viewers.

4. Find a letter to the editor on a current controversial issue. Examine the strengths and weaknesses of the writer's argument, and construct your own argument on this issue in the form of a letter to the same editor.

5. What are some of the key academic journals in your field of study? With help from a librarian or an instructor in your discipline, find a quality article in a respected journal. Read the article and then answer these questions: What forms of reasoning, appeals, and evidence does the author use? What forms does she or he avoid?

◀ VISUALLY SPEAKING ━━━━━━━━━━━━━━

Photographs are commonly used with writing to support an argument. How might you use the photograph on page **259** to make a point? Explain.

TAKING A POSITION

Audio

Video

Sometimes you just have to take a stand. An issue comes up that evokes strong feeling and challenges your thinking. In response, you say, "Okay, this is what I believe, and this is why I believe it."

Writing a position paper gives you the opportunity to take a stand. It's a chance, in other words, to refine what you think and feel, to clarify and deepen your perspective on an issue that you find meaningful—from scientific experiments on animals to regulating pornography. The list of debate-worthy issues is endless. In fact, each discipline in college has its own controversial issues that press scholars and students to test one another's positions.

Because a position paper articulates what you profess to believe about an issue, such writing requires commitment. Use the position paper, then, as an opportunity to take a stand, to debate those who hold different positions, and to explore what you are willing to risk.

Overview
Taking a Position

Writer's Goal

Your goal is to take a stand on a controversial issue. Aim to explain what you believe and why you believe it. Be thoughtful but bold, encouraging readers to respect and even adopt your position.

Keys for Success

Explore all positions. Before settling firmly on a position, study the pluses and minuses of all possible stands that could be taken on the issue.

Go beyond pure opinion. Opinions and positions are different. Whereas an opinion may be uninformed and inherited, you *think* your way into a position. A position carries weight because of tested reasoning and reliable evidence. The writing shows mature thinking—thinking that is lively and concrete, not clichéd.

Take a measured stance. Instead of taking a defend-at-all-costs approach, be reasonable. Concede points to your opponents, and address objections to your view. If necessary, soften your stance with qualifiers. Let the evidence weigh in favor of your position—not verbal aggression, bluster, or the fever of your feelings.

Topics to Consider

Which topics work well for a position paper? Debatable ones, of course—ideas about which thoughtful people can reasonably disagree.

- **Current Affairs:** Explore recent trends, new laws, major changes, and emerging controversies discussed in the news media, journals, or online discussion groups.
- **Burning Issues:** Which issues related to family, work, education, recreation, technology, the environment, or popular culture do you care about? Which issue do you want to confront?
- **Dividing Lines:** What dividing lines characterize the communities to which you belong—which issues set people against one another? Religion, gender, money, class, sports? Think about these broad subjects, and then identify a focused issue in one of them.
- **Fresh Fare:** Sometimes an unexpected topic, like barbed versus smooth fishing hooks, offers the most potential. Avoid tired issues unless you can revive them with a fresh perspective.

> **Next Step** Read the model essays and perform the activities that follow. As you read, think of similar issues on which you could take a stand. What position would you take, and how would you defend it?

Taking a Position

Rita Isakson was asked to use logic and her personal experience to critique an article in which the writer asserted that Barbie dolls harm young girls' development. In her essay below, Isakson analyzes the article and builds a counterargument.

An Apology for the Life of Ms. Barbie D. Doll

The writer states her opponent's arguments and disagrees with them.

Barbie's boobs and spacious mansion helped cause the decay of today's youth, supposed experts say. For example, in her article, "'I Want to Be a Barbie Doll When I Grow Up': The Cultural Significance of the Barbie Doll," Marilyn Ferris Motz argues the following: Barbie dolls encourage young girls to be conformists focused on "leisure activities, personal appearance, popularity, and the consumption of materials" (125). Barbie's skinny waist, huge bosom, and narrow hips entice girls into poor diets and eating disorders. Barbie-play trains girls to depend on Ken-figures (or other males) to achieve self-worth. Barbie's all-American-girl values teach conformity; and Barbie's racy cars, plush houses, and chic outfits cause materialism (128–132). But I don't buy Motz's "reasons." They sound fake—like the theories of somebody who lacks first-hand experience. I had Barbie dolls—twelve of them, in fact, and the Barbie Mansion and Soda Shop to boot—but I don't consider myself an anorexic, dependent, conforming, materialistic girl, at least no more than I would be had I foregone the Barbie experience.

Her tone is forceful and playful, but thoughtful.

She concedes a point but rebuts the argument.

Granted, Barbie's physical appearance isn't realistic. As Motz explains, "If Barbie stood five feet nine inches tall, her bust measurement would be 33 inches, her waist a meager 18 inches, and her hips only 28 1/2 inches" (128). In addition, Motz says, "Barbie's arms are extremely thin and her hands disproportionately small. Her legs are much too long . . ." (128–129). I say, so what? While the only "real" version of Barbie's body would be a long-limbed 13-year-old with breast implants, who cares? Arguing that Barbie's unrealistic body hurts girls' self-esteem is weak logic. Children have had dolls for ages. For example, in Pompeii, the preserved remains of a 3,000-year-old doll are displayed. That doll has an egghead, and a body that looks like a thick, shapeless rock. If Barbie's proportions hurt modern girls' self-esteem, I pity antiquity's girls, who had these lumps for models!

Her own experience adds support.

Motz says that the average age of girls who play with Barbie is six, and that girls this age imitate the doll's values, like her preoccupation with appearance (127). However, while I was about six when I played with Barbie, I didn't imitate her. At age seven, I had a bowl haircut that was constantly snarled because I wouldn't take time to brush it. I didn't care about my own appearance, while fixing Barbie's was fun. I didn't fuss over my own hair and weight until I was in high school, and fashion mags were scripture. In other words, Motz's theory—that girls' preoccupation with Barbie's appearance leads to later preoccupation with their own—simply doesn't reflect my experience. Nor does her theory reflect the experiences of many other girls, including my two roommates.

In response to Motz's idea that Barbies make girls dependent on males, I say, "Phooey." I played with Barbies until every last cow came home, and I am now a happy single girl. In fact, I have often been single, free from all romantic attachments. True, I've had boyfriends, but I never felt compelled to sacrifice my needs or identity to keep a boyfriend. And I am not an exception to Motz's rule! I know many girls whose primary concerns are their friends, family, and/or schoolwork. Admittedly, there is probably an equal number of girls who live only for their beaus; however, their behavior doesn't prove that Barbie causes female dependency. For example, my own interest in boys was prompted most by "good" TV shows and books—like Laura Ingalls Wilder's *On the Shores of Silver Lake.* It was stories like these— about teenage girls in love—that encouraged me to crave romance.

In other words, Motz uses Barbie as a scapegoat for problems that have complex causes. For example, a girl's interest in romance is no more Barbie's fault than the fault of books like *On the Shores of Silver Lake.* Fashion magazines targeted at adolescents are the cause of far more anorexia cases than is Barbie. Mothers who encourage daughters to find security in men teach female dependency, but Barbie doesn't. In fact, Motz herself points out that when "the Barbie doll was created, many parents hailed the doll as a model of wholesome teenage behavior and appearance" (130). I would add that today many parents still hail Barbie as a model for wholesome behavior. But it is more the manner in which parents give toys to their children—the parents' ideas and instructions about how to play—that determine whether Barbie-play is good or bad.

To Motz and similar "experts," I say this: Some of my finest childhood memories are of my best friend, Solara, coming over to my house with her pink carry-on suitcase stuffed with Barbies and their accoutrements. For hours we would play with them, giving haircuts, filling mixing bowls to make swimming pools, and creating small "campfires" so Barbie could make s'mores. Sometimes we dressed her in store-bought clothes, and sometimes we designed clothing for her. Other times we turned Barbie into the heroines in our books, and she helped us act out the plots. Playing with Barbies need not be an unimaginative, antisocial activity that promotes conformity, materialism, and superficial ideals. I played with Barbies and I'm fine. Take that, Motz! ■

Marginal notes:

The writer rebuts each point in turn, often quoting directly from the article.

She summarizes her disagreement and offers alternative explanations.

Speaking directly to the opposition, the writer shares an anecdote and restates her counterclaim.

Paragraph numbers: 4, 5, 6

Reading for Better Writing

Working by yourself or with a group, answer these questions:

1. The word *apology* can mean *defense,* as well as a statement of regret for wrongdoing. Is the use of the word fitting in the title? Why or why not?

2. This essay is a counterargument that relies heavily on logic and personal experience for support. How does the writer treat the original source? How do concessions and rebuttals function in the argument?

Taking a Position

Pulitzer Prize-winning political commentator Leonard Pitts, Jr., writes a syndicated column for the *Miami Herald*. This column was published in March 2005, shortly after news sources reported that a teen from Minnesota's Red Lake Reservation had posted messages to a neo-Nazi website before killing himself and nine others.

Apostles of Hatred Find It Easy to Spread Their Message

The phrase "I learned" introduces the ideas posted on the website.

The writer notes that his friend is white and implies that he is black.

The writer justifies giving attention to only one side of the issue.

I just visited the website that fascinated Jeff Weise, the 16-year-old who shot up his high school last week on the Red Lake Reservation in Minnesota. *1*

There, I learned that the tribes of humanity must be separated or risk destruction by assimilation. That Jews are a "fanatical religious-ethnic" group conspiring to control communications media. And that for all the dubious talk about a "Holocaust," you never hear about the good things Adolf Hitler did. *2*

I also read the posts that Weise left on the site's bulletin board. I was particularly interested in the one asking if the group would accept him, given that he was a Chippewa Indian. Weise was friendless, his father was dead, his mother in a nursing home, so there was something poignant and needy in the asking. *3*

In all, I spent half an hour on nazi.org. It gave me a headache. *4*

Used to be easier to laugh this stuff off. Once, when I was in college, a man in a "White Power" T-shirt came into the bookstore where I worked. My friend Cathy, who was white, promptly plopped herself in my lap, pecked me on the cheek, and asked loudly when I might be "home" for dinner. *5*

Mr. White Power glared at us, then beat a quick retreat. *6*

Thirty years later, it's harder to respond to the apostles of organized hatred. Not just because the Internet gives them a reach no guy in a T-shirt could match but because many have refined their message, made it slicker, given it a patina of reason. *7*

The people behind nazi.org, for instance, would want you to know they don't consider themselves white supremacists. To the contrary, they are open to anyone—black, Asian, Indian—who believes blacks, Asians, and Indians should confine themselves to their own countries—and that Jews are "vicious," "parasitic," "liars," and "hypocrites." *8*

I won't subject you to a treatise on why these people are abhorrent. If you don't already know, you need more help than anyone can give you in a few inches of newsprint. No, I am only here to note the sad incongruity of an American Indian boy asking admission to their ranks. *9*

A clarification is offered.

Perhaps when you heard that, you concluded that it spoke to the self-hatred that is sometimes inculcated among minority communities. But Weise's complaint wasn't that he hated Indians but, rather, that too many of his people were not "Indian" enough, that their culture was diluted by exposure to others. He was especially offended by those Native youth who are fans of hip-hop. He saw them as more black than Native.

It's a painful reminder that building a society where different cultures are welcomed and interaction valued is a difficult task. Some of us see it as the onerous burden of a politically correct era; others, as a clear and present danger to the status quo. The latter intuit, correctly, that when one culture is exposed to another, both are likely to be changed.

The words *us* and *we* show the writer identifying with his readers.

The difference between those people and the rest of us is that we aren't scared of change. We recognize that while change is a challenge, it is also a condition of life. The trick—difficult, to be sure, but also rewarding—is to hold on to what is good, yet incorporate what is new.

For some people, that's an accomplishment beyond achieving or even attempting.

We don't know what role Weise's Nazi beliefs played in his decision to kill nine people before taking his own life. But it seems obvious he needed what the Nazis provided—the illusion that culture can be made orderly and change put on hold.

The writer explains how quotations from the opposing view can be used to support his own claim.

Yet what did his Nazi friends have to say after the massacre? That they would not "wring hands" over a "tragedy," the last word in quotes to indicate that it wasn't tragic at all. Makes you sorrow for the boy even in the midst of your anger at him.

Weise wanted so badly to belong to something. Obviously, he never did. ■

Reading for Better Writing

Working by yourself or with a group, answer these questions:

1. On which issue is Pitts taking a position, and what is his view? In what ways is the topic controversial (or not), and how might this affect the ways in which various readers might respond to the piece?

2. In paragraph 2, Pitts states that he "learned" a number of things from the website. What do you think he means by his use of the word "learned," and why?

3. Writers are often encouraged to explore multiple views of an issue before taking a position. Why doesn't Pitts offer a detailed explanation about why he finds the nazi.org website "abhorrent"? What do you think about this choice?

4. Where does Pitts quote from the website in question, and why?

Taking a Position

Canadian author Margaret Atwood is well known for her ability to address feminist concerns in a wide range of genres. Her novels *The Handmaid's Tale* and *The Blind Assassin* (a winner of the 2000 Booker Prize) are especially well known. This essay was first published in 1983.

The topic is clearly stated in the title.

Pornography

When I was in Finland a few years ago for an international writers' conference, I had occasion to say a few paragraphs in public on the subject of pornography. The context was a discussion of political repression, and I was suggesting the possibility of a link between the two. The immediate result was that a male journalist took several large bites out of me. Prudery and pornography are two halves of the same coin, said he, and I was clearly a prude. What could you expect from an Anglo-Canadian? Afterward, a couple of pleasant Scandinavian men asked me what I had been so worked up about. All "pornography" means, they said, is graphic depictions of whores, and what was the harm in that?

The writer summarizes another person's comments about her to introduce and clarify her position.

Not until then did it strike me that the male journalist and I had two entirely different things in mind. By "pornography," he meant naked bodies and sex. I, on the other hand, had recently been doing the research for my novel *Bodily Harm*, and was still in a state of shock from some of the material I had seen, including the Ontario Board of Film Censors' "outtakes." By "pornography," I meant women getting their nipples snipped off with garden shears, having meat hooks stuck into their vaginas, being disemboweled; little girls being raped; men (yes, there are some men) being smashed to a pulp and forcibly sodomized. The cutting edge of pornography, as far as I could see, was no longer simple old copulation, hanging from the chandelier or otherwise: it was death, messy, explicit, and highly sadistic. I explained this to the nice Scandinavian men. "Oh, but that's just the United States," they said. "Everyone knows they're sick." In their country, they said, violent "pornography" of that kind was not permitted on television or in movies; indeed, excessive violence of any kind was not permitted. They had drawn a clear line between erotica, which earlier studies had shown did not incite men to more aggressive and brutal behavior toward women, and violence, which later studies indicated did.

She distinguishes between two terms: *erotica* and *violence*.

Some time after that I was in Saskatchewan, where, because of the scenes in *Bodily Harm*, I found myself on an open-line radio show answering questions about "pornography." Almost no one who phoned in was in favor of it, but again they weren't talking about the same stuff I was, because they hadn't seen it. Some of them were all set to stamp out bathing suits and negligees, and, if possible, any depictions of the female body whatsoever. God, it was implied, did not approve of female bodies, and sex of any kind, including that practiced by bumblebees, should be shoved back into the dark, where it belonged. I had more than a suspicion that *Lady Chatterley's*

Lover, Margaret Laurance's *The Diviners*, and indeed most books by most serious modern authors would have ended up as confetti if left in the hands of these callers.

For me, these two experiences illustrate the two poles of the emotionally heated debate that is now thundering around this issue. They also underline the desirability and even the necessity of defining the terms. "Pornography" is now one of those catchalls, like "Marxism" and "feminism," that have become so broad they can mean almost anything, ranging from certain verses in the Bible, ads for skin lotion, and sex texts for children to the contents of *Penthouse*, Naughty '90s postcards, and films with titles containing the word *Nazi* that show vicious scenes of torture and killing. It's easy to say that sensible people can tell the difference. Unfortunately, opinions on what constitutes a sensible person vary.

> *"Pornography" is now one of those catchalls . . .*

But even sensible people tend to lose their cool when they start talking about this subject. They soon stop talking and start yelling, and the name-calling begins. Those in favor of censorship (which may include groups not noticeably in agreement on other issues, such as some feminists and religious fundamentalists) accuse the others of exploiting women through the use of degrading images, contributing to the corruption of children, and adding to the general climate of violence and threat in which both women and children live in this society; or, though they may not give much of a hoot about actual women and children, they invoke moral standards and God's supposed aversion to "filth," "smut," and deviated *perversion*, which may mean ankles.

The camp in favor of total "freedom of expression" often comes out howling as loud as the Romans would have if told they could no longer have innocent fun watching the lions eat up Christians. It too may include segments of the population who are not natural bedfellows: those who proclaim their God-given right to freedom, including the freedom to tote guns, drive when drunk, drool over chicken porn, and get off on videotapes of women being raped and beaten, may be waving the same anticensorship banner as responsible liberals who fear the return of Mrs. Grundy, or gay groups for whom sexual emancipation involves the concept of "sexual theater." *Whatever turns you on* is a handy motto, as is *A man's home is his castle* (and if it includes a dungeon with beautiful maidens strung up in chains and bleeding from every pore, that's his business).

Meanwhile, theoreticians theorize and speculators speculate. Is today's pornography yet another indication of the hatred of the body, the deep mind–body split, which is supposed to pervade Western Christian society? Is it a backlash against the women's movement by men who are threatened by uppity female behavior in real life, and so like to fantasize

The writer acknowledges a range of views about how to define pornography.

A list illustrates a range of arguments that are made for censoring pornography.

Another list points to a range of people who may make arguments against censoring pornography.

Yet another list represents the questions that people raise about the causes and effects of pornography.

4

5

6

7

about women done up like outsize parcels, being turned into hamburger, kneeling at their feet in slavelike adoration, or sucking off guns? Is it a sign of collective impotence, of a generation of men who can't relate to real women at all but have to make do with bits of celluloid and paper? Is the current flood just a result of smart marketing and aggressive promotion by the money men in what has now become a multibillion-dollar industry?

If they were selling movies about men getting their testicles stuck full of knitting needles by women with swastikas on their sleeves, would they do as well, or is this penchant somehow peculiarly male? If so, why? Is pornography a power trip rather than a sex one? Some say that those ropes, chains, muzzles, and other restraining devices are an argument for the immense power female sexuality still wields

> *Is pornography a power trip rather than a sex one?*

in the male imagination: You don't put these things on dogs unless you're afraid of them. Others, more literary, wonder about the shift from the 19th-century Magic Woman or Femme Fatale image to the lollipoplicker, airhead, or turkey-carcass treatment of women in porn today.

[The writer labels two camps: proporners and antiporners.]

The proporners don't care much about theory: They merely demand product. The antiporners don't care about it in the final analysis either: There's dirt on the street, and they want it cleaned up, now.

[She cites an impasse.]

It seems to me that this conversation, with its *You're-a-prude/You're-a-pervert* dialectic, will never get anywhere as long as we continue to think of this material as just "entertainment." Possibly we're deluded by the packaging, the format: magazine, book, movie, theatrical presentation. We're used to thinking of these things as part of the "entertainment industry," and we're used to thinking of ourselves as free adult people who ought to be able to see any kind of "entertainment" we want to. That was what the First Choice pay-TV debate was all about. After all, it's only entertainment, right? Entertainment means fun, and only a killjoy would be antifun. What's the harm? 8

[The writer identifies a key point.]

This is obviously the central question: *What's the harm?* If there isn't any real harm to any real people, then the antiporners can tsk-tsk and/or throw up as much as they like, but they can't rightfully expect more legal controls or sanctions. However, the no-harm position is far from being proven. 9

(For instance, there's a clear-cut case for banning—as the federal government has proposed—movies, photos, and videos that depict children engaging in sex with adults: Real children are used to make the movies, and hardly anybody thinks this ethical. The possibilities for coercion are too great.) 10

[A transition sentence predicts the organization of ideas that will follow.]

To shift the viewpoint, I'd like to suggest three other models for looking at "pornography"—and here I mean the violent kind. 11

Those who find the idea of regulating pornographic materials repugnant *12* because they think it's Fascist or Communist or otherwise not in accordance with the principles of an open democratic society should consider that Canada has made it illegal to disseminate material that may lead to hatred toward any group because of race or religion. I suggest that if pornography of the violent kind depicted these acts being done predominantly to Chinese, to blacks, to Catholics, it would be off the market immediately, under the present laws. Why is hate literature illegal? Because whoever made the law thought that such material might incite real people to do real awful things to other real people. The human brain is to a certain extent a computer: garbage in, garbage out. We only hear about the extreme cases (like that of American multimurderer Ted Bundy) in which pornography has contributed to the death and/or mutilation of women and/or men. Although pornography is not the only factor involved in the creation of such deviance, it certainly has upped the ante by suggesting both a variety of techniques and the social acceptability of such actions. Nobody knows yet what effect this stuff is having on the less psychotic.

> *The human brain is to a certain extent a computer: garbage in, garbage out.*

The nature and effects of porn are compared to those of hate crimes.

Studies have shown that a large part of the market for all kinds of porn, *13* soft and hard, is drawn from the 16-to-21-year-old population of young men. Boys used to learn about sex on the street, or (in Italy, according to Fellini movies) from friendly whores, or, in more genteel surroundings, from girls, their parents, or, once upon a time, in school, more or less. Now porn has been added, and sex education in the schools is rapidly being phased out. The buck has been passed, and boys are being taught that all women secretly like to be raped and that real men get high on scooping out women's digestive tracts.

References to studies lend scientific authority to the argument.

Boys learn their concept of masculinity from other men: Is this what most *14* men want them to be learning? If word gets around that rapists are "normal" and even admirable men, will boys feel that in order to be normal, admirable, and masculine they will have to be rapists? Human beings are enormously flexible, and how they turn out depends a lot on how they're educated, by the society in which they're immersed as well as by their teachers. In a society that advertises and glorifies rape or even implicitly condones it, more women get raped. It becomes socially acceptable. And at a time when men and the traditional male role have taken a lot of flak and men are confused and casting around for an acceptable way of being male (and, in some cases, not getting much comfort from women on that score), this must be at times a pleasing thought.

It would be naïve to think of violent pornography as just harmless *15* entertainment. It's also an educational tool and a powerful propaganda

Two models are identified with labels.

device. What happens when boy educated on porn meets girl brought up on Harlequin romances? The clash of expectations can be heard around the block. She wants him to get down on his knees with a ring; he wants her to get down on all fours with a ring in her nose. Can this marriage be saved?

A comparison to regulated substances helps support an argument for regulating pornography.

Pornography has certain things in common with such addictive substances as alcohol and drugs: For some, though by no means for all, it induces chemical changes in the body, which the user finds exciting and pleasurable. It also appears to attract a "hard core" of habitual users and a penumbra of those who use it occasionally but aren't dependent on it in any way. There are also significant numbers of men who aren't much interested in it, not because they're undersexed but because real life is satisfying their needs, which may not require as many appliances as those of users. 16

For the "hard core," pornography may function as alcohol does for the alcoholic: Tolerance develops, and a little is no longer enough. This may account for the short viewing time and fast turnover in porn theatres. Mary Brown, chairwoman of the Ontario Board of Film Censors, estimates that for every one mainstream movie requesting entrance to Ontario, there is one porno flick. Not only the quantity consumed but the quality of explicitness must escalate, which may account for the growing violence: Once the big deal was breasts, then it was genitals, then copulation, then that was no longer enough and the hard users had to have more. The ultimate kick is death, and after that, as the Marquis de Sade so boringly demonstrated, multiple death. 17

> *The ultimate kick is death, and after that . . . multiple death.*

After outlining three alternative models, the writer reviews her main question.

The existence of alcoholism has not led us to ban social drinking. On the other hand, we do have laws about drinking and driving, excessive drunkenness, and other abuses of alcohol that may result in injury or death to others. 18

She proposes a direction for further study.

This leads us back to the key question: What's the harm? Nobody knows, but this society should find out fast, before the saturation point is reached. The Scandinavian studies that showed a connection between depictions of sexual violence and increased impulse toward it on the part of male viewers would be a starting point, but many more questions remain to be raised as well as answered. What, for instance, is the crucial difference between men who are users and men who are not? Does using affect a man's relationship with actual women, and, if so, adversely? Is there a clear line between erotica and violent pornography, or are they on an escalating continuum? Is this a "men versus women" issue, with all men secretly siding with the proporners and all women secretly siding against? (I think not; there *are* lots of men who don't think that running their true love through the Cuisinart is the best way they can think of to spend a Saturday night, 19 and they're just as nauseated by films of someone else doing it as women are.) Is pornography merely an expression of the sexual confusion of this age or an active contributor to it?

Nobody wants to go back to the age of official repression, when even piano legs were referred to as "limbs" and had to wear pantaloons to be decent. Neither do we want to end up in George Orwell's *1984*, in which pornography is turned out by the State to keep the proles in a state of torpor, sex itself is considered dirty and the approved practice it only for reproduction. But Rome under the emperors isn't such a good model either.   20

If all men and women respected each other, if sex were considered joyful and life-enhancing instead of a wallow in germ-filled glop, if everyone were in love all the time, if, in other words, many people's lives were more satisfactory for them than they appear to be now, pornography might just go away on its own. But since this is obviously not happening, we as a society are going to have to make some informed and responsible decisions about how to deal with it. ∎   21

The limits of the two extreme views are reviewed.

The writer states an ideal as well as a position grounded in reality.

Reading for Better Writing

Working by yourself or with a group, answer these questions:

1. What views on pornography does Atwood examine before detailing her own view?

2. Skilled writers often "make a space" for their arguments by demonstrating the limits or shortcomings of others' ideas and then showing how their own ideas fill the gaps. How (and where) does Atwood do this?

3. Atwood proposes three alternative models for thinking about pornography. What are they? How could the piece be edited to include signal words (such as headings or numbers) to make these three models more readily apparent?

4. Besides stating her opinion, what does the writer do to support her position?

5. In what ways does (or doesn't) Atwood succeed in taking a measured stance that may appeal to readers on both sides of the debate?

Taking a Position

In the essay below, David Blankenhorn argues that America is losing its understanding of and appreciation for fatherhood.

Blankenhorn builds his argument by making and supporting a series of bold claims. Working with one or two classmates, highlight key writing strategies and note in the margin how each strategy does or does not advance the thesis.

Fatherless America

The United States is becoming an increasingly fatherless society. A generation ago, an American child could reasonably expect to grow up with his or her father. Today, an American child can reasonably expect not to. Fatherlessness is now approaching a rough parity with fatherhood as a defining feature of American childhood. *1*

This astonishing fact is reflected in many statistics, but here are the two most important. Tonight, about 40 percent of American children will go to sleep in homes in which their fathers do not live. Before they reach the age of eighteen, more than half of our nation's children are likely to spend at least a significant portion of their childhoods living apart from their fathers. Never before in this country have so many children been voluntarily abandoned by their fathers. Never before have so many children grown up without knowing what it means to have a father. *2*

Fatherlessness is the most harmful demographic trend of this generation. It is the leading cause of declining child well-being in our society. It is also the engine driving our most urgent social problems, from crime to adolescent pregnancy to child abuse to domestic violence against women. Yet, despite its scale and social consequences, fatherlessness is a problem that is frequently ignored or denied. Especially within our elite discourse, it remains largely a problem with no name. *3*

If this trend continues, fatherlessness is likely to change the shape of our society. Consider this prediction. After the year 2000, as people born after 1970 emerge as a large proportion of our working-age adult population, the United States will be a nation divided into two groups, separate and unequal. The two groups will work in the same economy, speak a common language, and remember the same national history. But they will live fundamentally divergent lives. One group will receive basic benefits—psychological, social, economic, educational, and moral—that are denied to the other group. *4*

The primary fault line dividing the two groups will not be race, religion, class, education, or gender. It will be patrimony. One group will consist of those adults who grew up with the daily presence and provision of fathers. The other group will consist of those who did not. By the early years of the next [twenty-first] century, these two groups will be roughly the same size. *5*

Surely a crisis of this scale merits a response. At a minimum, it requires a serious debate. Why is fatherhood declining? What can be done about it? *6*

Can our society find ways to invigorate effective fatherhood as a norm of male behavior? Yet, to date, the public discussion on this topic has been remarkably weak and defeatist. There is a prevailing belief that not much can—or even should—be done to reverse the trend.

When the crime rate jumps, politicians promise to do something about it. When the unemployment rate rises, task forces assemble to address the problem. As random shootings increase, public health officials worry about the preponderance of guns. But when it comes to the mass defection of men from family life, not much happens. *7*

There is debate, even alarm, about specific social problems. Divorce. Out-of-wedlock childbearing. Children growing up in poverty. Youth violence. Unsafe neighborhoods. Domestic violence. The weakening of parental authority. But in these discussions, we seldom acknowledge the underlying phenomenon that binds together these otherwise disparate issues: the flight of males from their children's lives. In fact, we seem to go out of our way to avoid the connection between our most pressing social problems and the trend of fatherlessness. *8*

We avoid this connection because, as a society, we are changing our minds about the role of men in family life. As a cultural idea, our inherited understanding of fatherhood is under siege. Men in general, and fathers in particular, are increasingly viewed as superfluous to family life: either as expendable or as part of the problem. Masculinity itself, understood as anything other than a rejection of what it has traditionally meant to be male, is typically treated with suspicion and even hostility in our cultural discourse. Consequently, our society is now manifestly unable to sustain, or even find reason to believe in, fatherhood as a distinctive domain of male activity. *9*

The core question is simple: Does every child need a father? Increasingly, our society's answer is "no" or at least "not necessarily." Few idea shifts in this century are as consequential as this one. At stake is nothing less than what it means to be a man, who our children will be, and what kind of society we will become. *10*

This [essay] is a criticism not simply of fatherlessness but of a culture of fatherlessness. For, in addition to losing fathers, we are losing something larger: our idea of fatherhood. Unlike earlier periods of father absence in our history, we now face more than a physical loss affecting some homes. We face a cultural loss affecting every home. For this reason, the most important absence our society must confront is not the absence of fathers but the absence of our belief in fathers. *11*

In a larger sense, this [essay] is a *cultural* criticism because fatherhood, much more than motherhood, is a cultural invention. Its meaning for the *12* individual man is shaped less by biology than by cultural script or story—a societal code that guides, and at times pressures, him into certain ways of acting and of understanding himself as a man.

Like motherhood, fatherhood is made up of both a biological and a social dimension. Yet in societies across the world, mothers are far more successful than fathers at fusing these two dimensions into a coherent parental identity. Is the nursing mother playing a biological or social role? Is she feeding or bonding? We can hardly separate the two, so seamlessly are they woven together.   13

But fatherhood is a different matter. A father makes his sole biological contribution at the moment of conception—nine months before the infant enters the world. Because social paternity is only indirectly linked to biological paternity, the connection between the two cannot be assumed. The phrase "to father a child" usually refers only to the act of insemination, not to the responsibility for raising a child. What fathers contribute to their offspring after conception is largely a matter of cultural devising.   14

Moreover, despite their other virtues, men are not ideally suited to responsible fatherhood. Although they certainly have the capacity for fathering, men are inclined to sexual promiscuity and paternal waywardness. Anthropologically, human fatherhood constitutes what might be termed a necessary problem. It is necessary because, in all societies, child well-being and societal success hinge largely upon a high level of paternal investment: the willingness of adult males to devote energy and resources to the care of their offspring. It is a problem because adult males are frequently—indeed, increasingly—unwilling or unable to make that vital investment.   15

Because fatherhood is universally problematic in human societies, cultures must mobilize to devise and enforce the father role for men, coaxing and guiding them into fatherhood through a set of legal and extralegal pressures that require them to maintain a close alliance with their children's mother and to invest in their children. Because men do not volunteer for fatherhood as much as they are conscripted into it by the surrounding culture, only an authoritative cultural story of fatherhood can fuse biological and social paternity into a coherent male identity.   16

For exactly this reason, Margaret Mead and others have observed that the supreme test of any civilization is whether it can socialize men by teaching them to be fathers—creating a culture in which men acknowledge their paternity and willingly nurture their offspring. Indeed, if we can equate the essence of the antisocial male with violence, we can equate the essence of the socialized male with being a good father. Thus, at the center of our most important cultural imperative, we find the fatherhood script: the story that describes what it ought to mean for a man to have a child.   17

Just as the fatherhood script advances the social goal of harnessing male behavior to collective needs, it also reflects an individual purpose. That purpose, in a word, is happiness. Anthropologists have long understood that the genius of an effective culture is its capacity to reconcile individual happiness with collective well-being. By situating individual lives within a social narrative, culture endows private behavior with larger meaning. By linking the self to moral purposes larger than the self, an effective culture tells us a story in which individual fulfillment transcends selfishness, and personal satisfaction transcends narcissism. *18*

In this respect, our cultural script is not simply a set of imported moralisms, exterior to the individual and designed only to compel self-sacrifice. It is also a pathway—indeed, our only pathway—to what the founders of the American experiment called the pursuit of happiness. *19*

The stakes on this issue could hardly be higher. Our society's conspicuous failure to sustain or create compelling norms of fatherhood amounts to a social and personal disaster. Today's story of fatherhood features one-dimensional characters, an unbelievable plot, and an unhappy ending. It reveals in our society both a failure of collective memory and a collapse of moral imagination. It undermines families, neglects children, causes or aggravates our worst social problems, and makes individual adult happiness—both male and female—harder to achieve. *20*

Ultimately, this failure reflects nothing less than a culture gone awry: a culture increasingly unable to establish the boundaries, erect the sign-posts, and fashion the stories that can harmonize individual happiness with collective well-being. In short, it reflects a culture that increasingly fails to "enculture" individual men and women, mothers and fathers. *21*

In personal terms, the end result of this process, the final residue from what David Gutmann calls the "deculturation" of paternity, is narcissism: a me-first egotism that is hostile not only to any societal goal or larger moral purpose but also to any save the most puerile understanding of personal happiness. In social terms, the primary results of decultured paternity are a decline in children's well-being and a rise in male violence, especially against women. In a larger sense, the most significant result is our society's steady fragmentation into atomized individuals, isolated from one another and estranged from the aspirations and realities of common membership in a family, a community, a nation, bound by mutual commitment and shared memory. *22*

[A good father] is a cultural model, or what Max Weber calls an ideal social type—an anthropomorphized composite of cultural ideas about the meaning of paternity. I call him the Good Family Man. As described by one of the fathers [I] interviewed . . . , a good family man "puts his family first." *23*

A good society celebrates the ideal of the man who puts his family 24 first. Because our society is now lurching in the opposite direction, I see the Good Family Man as the principal casualty of today's weakening fatherhood script. And because I cannot imagine a good society without him, I offer him as the protagonist in the stronger script that I believe is both necessary and possible. ■

Reading for Better Writing

Working by yourself or with a group, answer these questions:

1. What is Blankenhorn's thesis, and how does he introduce that idea? Which key claims and supporting evidence develop the thesis?

2. Choose five paragraphs and analyze their structure (e.g., topic sentence, supporting details, sentence structure, and transitions linking paragraphs). Then explain how these elements do or do not help present a clear message.

3. Working with a classmate, choose seven logical fallacies explained on pages 267–270. Then discuss why you believe that Blankenhorn's argument does or does not include these fallacies. Share your ideas with the class.

4. In paragraph 9, Blankenhorn makes the following claim: "Masculinity itself, understood as anything other than a rejection of what it has traditionally meant to be male, is typically treated with suspicion and even hostility in our cultural discourse." Explain what he means and why you find it a strong or weak claim.

5. Analyze three passages in which the writer uses data to support a point. Then explain why that use of data is or is not effective.

6. In paragraph 17, Blankenhorn says, "Margaret Mead and others have observed that the supreme test of any civilization is whether it can socialize men by teaching them to be fathers—creating a culture in which men acknowledge their paternity and willingly nurture their offspring." Explain what the quotation means and why it does or does not support the writer's thesis.

7. In paragraph 22, the writer says, "In personal terms, the end result of this process, the final residue from what David Gutmann calls the 'deculturation' of paternity, is narcissism." Define *narcissism* and explain how Blankenhorn's use of the term does or does not develop his argument.

Model

Guidelines
Taking a Position

Note: For in-depth help on developing persuasive arguments, see pages 260–273.

1. **Select and narrow a topic.** Through reading, viewing, or surfing the Internet, explore current issues on which people can take different, well-reasoned positions. Select an issue that you care about, and identify one facet of the topic that you could address in an essay.

2. **Take stock.** Before you dig into your topic, assess your starting point. What is your current position on the topic? Why? What evidence do you have?

3. **Get inside the issue.** To take a defensible position, study the issue carefully. The following strategies will help you measure and develop what you know:
   - Investigate all possible positions on the issue. Through brainstorming and research, think through all arguments and issues on all sides.
   - Consider doing firsthand research that will help you speak with authority and passion.
   - Write your position at the top of a page. Below it, set up "Pro" and "Con" columns. List arguments in each column.
   - Develop a line of reasoning supporting your position. Then test that reasoning for two things:

     First, no logical fallacies, such as broad generalization, either/or thinking, oversimplification, or slanted language. (See pages 267–270.)

     Second, an effective range of support: statistics, observations, expert testimony, comparisons, experiences, and analysis. (See pages 264–266.)

4. **Refine your position.** By now, you may have sharpened or radically changed your starting position. Before you organize and draft your essay, clarify your position. If it helps, use this formula:

   I believe this to be true about _____ :

   _____ .

5. **Organize your development and support.** Now you've committed yourself to a position. Before drafting, review these organizational options:
   - **Traditional pattern:** Introduce the issue, state your position, support it, address and refute opposition, and restate your position.
   - **Blatant confession:** Place your position statement in the first sentence—boldly displayed for your reader to chew on.
   - **Delayed gratification:** In the first part of your essay, explore the various positions available on the topic; compare and contrast them, and then state and defend your position.

- **Changed mind:** If your research changed your mind on the topic, build that shift into the essay itself. Readers may respond well to such honesty.
- **Winning over:** If your readers may strongly oppose your position, then focus on that opposition. Defend your position by anticipating and answering each question, concern, and objection.

6. **Write your first draft.** If helpful, set aside your notes and get your position and support down on paper. If you prefer, work closely from your outline. Here are some possible strategies:

   Opening: Seize the reader's imagination. Raise concern for the issue with a dramatic story, a pointed example, a vivid picture, a thought-provoking question, or a personal confession. Supply background information that readers need to understand the issue.

   Development: Deepen, clarify, and support your position statement, using solid logic and reliable support. A clear, well-reasoned defense will help readers accept your position.

   Closing: End on a lively, thoughtful note that stresses your commitment. If appropriate, make a direct or indirect plea to readers to adopt your position.

   Title: Choose a bold title that offers a choice or stresses a stand.

7. **Share your position.** At this point, feedback from a peer or a tutor in the writing center might help. Does your reviewer accept your position? Why or why not?

8. **Revise your writing.** Consider your reviewer's comments and review the draft yourself. Cut, change, and/or add material with the following questions in mind:
   - Is the position clearly stated? Is it effectively qualified and refined?
   - Have you shown how your stand affects yourself and others?
   - Are the reasoning and support sound and complete?
   - Does the essay show awareness of questions, concerns, and other positions?
   - Do the ideas flow smoothly?
   - Is the tone confident and sincere, not bullying, cocky, or apologetic?

9. **Edit and proofread.** See pages 107 and 110 for guidelines, but check especially that your writing is free of slogans, clichés, platitudes, insults, and mystifying jargon. Make your language lively, concrete, and energetic.

10. **Prepare and publish your final essay.** Submit your position paper according to your instructor's requirements. In addition, seek a forum for your position—with peers in a discussion group, with relatives, or online.

Writing Checklist

Use these seven traits to check your essay; then revise as needed:

_____ The **ideas** establish and defend a stand on a debatable issue. The essay provides sound reasoning and support that help the reader understand and appreciate the position.

_____ The **organization** includes an engaging opening that raises the issue, a carefully sequenced development and defense of the position, and a reflective closing.

_____ The **voice** is thoughtful, measured, committed, convincing, and knowledgeable. The feelings expressed are appropriately strong.

_____ The **words** used are precise, concrete, and lively. Jargon, clichés, platitudes, and insults are avoided.

_____ The **sentences** flow smoothly. Their lengths are varied: Short sentences make snappy points and longer sentences develop thoughtful points.

_____ The **copy** follows rules of grammar, punctuation, and mechanics.

_____ The **design** and format are appropriate and attractive.

Interactive

Critical-Thinking and Writing Activities

As directed by your instructor, complete the following activities by yourself or with a group.

1. Take a position on a hot topic in your major. Check textbooks, talk to professors or other experts, and review journals in the field for controversial issues.

2. Review the column "Apostles of Hatred . . . ," noting how Leonard Pitts includes quotations that oppose his view and then presents counterarguments that support his own claim. Apply this strategy as you draft or revise a position statement on a controversial issue.

3. Review Margaret Atwood's essay "Pornography," paying special attention to the way that she "makes a space" for her argument by demonstrating the limits or shortcomings of others' ideas and then "fills the gaps" with her own. Draft or revise a position statement using these strategies.

4. Choose one of the essays in this chapter and consider how visuals might strengthen the writer's argument. Then find, develop, or describe one or more visuals that would add persuasive power to the piece.

◀ VISUALLY SPEAKING

Review the photograph on page 275. Then explain how publicly demonstrating on an issue is similar to or different from writing an essay on the issue.

PERSUADING READERS TO ACT

19

Persuasion is a challenging task, requiring that you convince readers to believe you, rethink their own perspectives, and take a concrete step. In the end, you want them to change their minds and their actions.

In an essay persuading readers to act, you seek to change readers' opinions on a debatable, complex, and timely issue about which you care deeply, such as wise energy policies or the problem of racism. In addition, your essay presses for the next logical step—motivating readers to act. You achieve that goal with sound logic, reliable support, and fitting appeals. In a sense, you say to readers, "Come, let us reason together."

What do you feel strongly about, and which actions do you want to influence? This chapter will help you write in a way that stirs people to action.

Audio

Video

Overview
Persuading Readers to Act

Writer's Goal

Your goal is to urge individual readers to change their behavior or to take action on an issue. To accomplish this goal, you need to change the minds of those who disagree with you, and give encouragement to those who do agree with you.

Keys for Success

Know your audience. When you seek to persuade, you assume that your reader will have some opposition or resistance to your viewpoint. To motivate resistant readers to act, you must know who they are—whether they are peers, professors, the college community, or your nation. Consider their knowledge of and attitudes toward the topic so that you can address their concerns.

Promote your cause—not a quarrel. Your goal is to motivate your readers to act, not to manipulate them so that you win an argument. Study the topic from all sides. Bottom line: Know your subject.

Be reasonable. Make logical claims about your topic, testing them to make sure that they can be supported with sufficient evidence. Review your thinking to identify any logical fallacies as well. Moreover, fine-tune the essay's voice until it is passionate, thoughtful, and sincere.

Topics to Consider

Choose a debate-worthy, timely issue that you care about. Consider topics in these categories:

- **Personal experiences:** Which personal experiences have raised questions or concerns for you?
- **Personal ideas:** Which issues often occupy your mind? What do you stew about or fear? What makes you say, "Something should be done"?
- **Community concerns:** Think about the different "communities" to which you belong—family, college, race, ethnic group, or gender. Which issues concern each group, and why?
- **National or international affairs:** Which national or global issues are discussed in your circle of friends, your college community, or the news?
- **"No comment" topics:** Consider issues about which you don't have an opinion. Would you like to develop a strong stance on one of those topics?

> **Next Step** Read the model essays and perform the activities that follow. As you read, think of parallel issues that interest you. Why do these issues intrigue you? How could you communicate that interest to readers and challenge them to take action?

Persuading Readers to Act

Rebecca Pasok is an environmental studies major who wrote this ecological essay to persuade readers to support lifestyle choices and energy policies that do not require drilling for oil in the Arctic National Wildlife Refuge.

To Drill or Not to Drill

The opening provides background information before raising the controversial position.

Known as "America's Last Frontier," the Arctic National Wildlife Refuge (ANWR) is located in the northeast corner of Alaska, right along the Beaufort Sea. President Dwight D. Eisenhower established the refuge in 1960, and today its 19 million acres make it one of the biggest refuges in the United States and home to a wide variety of wildlife such as eagles, wolves, moose, grizzly bears, polar bears, and caribou. During the last few years, however, the security of that home has been threatened by those who want to use one section of the ANWR to drill for oil. That section—named Area 1002—encompasses 1.5 million acres of pristine land near the coast.

The writer starts with a strong argument against drilling but then maps out why others support it.

One of the strongest arguments against oil drilling anywhere in the refuge is that the environmental impact of drilling conflicts with the very purpose of the ANWR. The primary mandate for the ANWR, as laid out by the U.S. Fish and Wildlife Service that administers the refuge, is "to protect the wildlife and habitats of the area for the benefit of people now and in the future." The question then is whether drilling for oil supports, or is in conflict with, this mandate. President George W. Bush and others argue that oil drilling does not conflict with the mandate because new oil-drilling techniques cause only minimal damage to the environment. These techniques include drilling fewer wells, placing wells closer together, and building pipelines above ground so as not to disturb the animals (McCarthy).

Some environmental experts support the argument that the new techniques will not hurt wildlife. While these individuals acknowledge that some land disturbance will result, they argue that animals such as caribou will not suffer. One expert taking this position is Pat Valkenberg, a research coordinator with the Alaska Department of Fish and Game; he maintains that the caribou population is thriving and should continue to thrive. To support this point, Valkenberg notes that between 1997 and 2000, the caribou population actually grew from 19,700 to 27,128 (*Petroleum News*).

She counters the position with expert testimony for the other side.

Other experts challenge those statistics with information about the caribou's birthing patterns. These experts point to herds like the porcupine caribou that live in the ANWR and move along the coast of the Beaufort Sea in the United States and also into Canada. A majority of the females in this herd wear radio collars that have been tracked to Area 1002 during calving season. Experts who argue against drilling note that the calves born on ANWR's coastal plain have a greater chance of surviving than those that are born in the foothills, where many of their predators live (*U.S. Fish and Wildlife*). This difference in survival ratios, argue antidrilling experts, may not be accounted for in the statistics used by prodrilling advocates like Valkenberg.

One specialist opposed to drilling is David Klein, a professor at the Institute of Arctic Biology at the University of Alaska Fairbanks. Klein argues that if the oil industry opens up the ANWR for drilling, the number of caribou will likely decrease because the calving locations would change. He points out that oil-industry work in the Prudhoe oil field (also in Alaska) has already split up the Central Arctic herd of caribou, so it is likely that drilling in Area 1002 will similarly affect the porcupine herd (McCarthy).

The writer strongly states her thesis— that she agrees with opponents of drilling.

But caribou are not the only wildlife that would be affected by drilling in Area 1002. Musk oxen, polar bears, and grizzly bears could be driven out of the refuge and possibly into regions where people live, thereby threatening both the animals' and people's safety. Clearly, the bottom line in this debate is that drilling in Area 1002 will destroy at least some of the ecological integrity that makes ANWR a natural treasure. Environmentalists say that "just as there is no way to be half-pregnant, there is no 'sensitive' way to drill in a wilderness" (McCarthy). They are right.

By looking at effects on people, the writer expands her opposition.

However, oil drilling in ANWR will hurt more than the environment and wildlife; the drilling also will hurt at least one of the two Inuit tribes living in Alaska—the Inupiat Eskimos and the Gwich'in Indians. The Inupiat is the larger group, and they favor drilling. Money generated by the oil industry, say the Inupiat, will help them improve a variety of tribal services such as education and health care. On the other hand, the Gwich'in tribe depends on the porcupine caribou for food. As a result, if oil drilling displaces such animals, the people will suffer. Not only do they need the caribou to survive, but they also need them to retain the tribe's dignity and way of life. In other words, while oil drilling in ANWR may give some residents more money, others clearly will pay a price.

A question serves as a transition to a key counter-argument.

So if oil drilling in ANWR would have so many negative effects, what is driving the argument for drilling? Unfortunately, nothing more than a shortsighted, ill-informed effort to satisfy America's excessive appetite for oil: To continue using too much, we want to produce more. But is drilling in the ANWR the answer to our consumption problem?

At best, getting more oil from Alaska is a shortsighted solution: ANWR's reserves are simply too small to provide a long-term solution. A 1998 study by the U.S. Geological Survey concluded that the total amount of accessible oil in the ANWR is 5.7 to 16 billion barrels, with an expected amount of 10.4 billion barrels (*Arctic Power*). While these figures are considered the official estimate, the National Resources Defense Council (a group of lawyers, scientists, and environmentalists) disagrees. It estimates the accessible amount to be 3.2 billion barrels—a resource the United States would use up in just six months! In the meantime, using the ANWR oil would do nothing to ease our dependence on Middle Eastern countries for oil. There has to be a better choice.

And there is. The question is not whether drilling should take place in the ANWR, but how to provide energy for everyone, now and in the future. A poll taken by the *Christian Science Monitor* shows that voters believe that the best option for Americans is to develop new technologies (Dillan). Finding new energy sources, they say, is more important than finding new oil reserves.

10

The writer redirects the discussion to the root of the problem.

There are two main problems with relying primarily on oil for our energy: Oil supplies are limited, and oil use pollutes. Democratic Representative Rosa DeLauro of Connecticut made this point well when she said the following:

11

> We need a serious energy policy in the United States. Drilling in the Arctic National Wildlife Refuge is not the solution. We should look to increase domestic production while balancing our desire for a cleaner environment. We must also look at ways to reduce our dependency on fossil fuels themselves, a smart and necessary step that will lead to a cleaner environment. (qtd. in Urban)

12

A closing quotation focuses and supports the writer's objections; the quotation is indented ten spaces.

While reducing our use of fossil fuels will not be easy, it is possible if we do two things: (1) develop energy-saving technologies, and (2) make lifestyle choices that conserve energy. Unlike the short-term (and shortsighted) solution of drilling in the ANWR, these strategies will help save the environment. In addition, the strategies will help people both now and in the future. ■

13

Note: The Works Cited page is not shown. For sample pages, see MLA (page **532–533**) and APA (page **564**).

Reading for Better Writing

Working by yourself or with a group, answer these questions:

1. The writer describes both positions on drilling before stating her opposition explicitly. Is this strategy effective?

2. The writer uses the testimony of experts extensively. Why?

3. What does the writer do to acknowledge, concede points to, and refute support for drilling?

4. Review pages **264–266** about types of support. Then trace the types of evidence provided in this essay. Evaluate the quality and completeness of the evidence.

5. Does the last paragraph offer an effective closing to the writer's argument? Why or why not?

Persuading Readers to Act

Dr. Martin Luther King, Jr., was a leader in the Civil Rights Movement during the 1950s and 1960s. On August 28, 1963, he delivered this persuasive speech to a crowd of 250,000 people gathered at the Lincoln Memorial in Washington, D.C.

I Have a Dream

King starts with a tragic contrast.

Five score years ago, a great American, in whose symbolic shadow we stand, signed the Emancipation Proclamation. This momentous decree came as a great beacon light of hope to millions of Negro slaves who had been seared in the flames of withering injustice. It came as a joyous daybreak to end the long night of captivity.

He uses figurative language to describe the present situation.

But one hundred years later, we must face the tragic fact that the Negro is still not free. One hundred years later, the life of the Negro is still sadly crippled by the manacles of segregation and the chains of discrimination. One hundred years later, the Negro lives on a lonely island of poverty in the midst of a vast ocean of material prosperity. One hundred years later, the Negro is still languishing in the corners of American society and finds himself an exile in his own land. So we have come here today to dramatize an appalling condition.

An analogy clarifies the problem.

In a sense we have come to our nation's Capitol to cash a check. When the architects of our republic wrote the magnificent words of the Constitution and the Declaration of Independence, they were signing a promissory note to which every American was to fall heir. This note was a promise that all men would be guaranteed the unalienable rights of life, liberty, and the pursuit of happiness.

It is obvious today that America has defaulted on this promissory note insofar as her citizens of color are concerned. Instead of honoring this sacred obligation, America has given the Negro people a bad check; a check which has come back marked "insufficient funds." But we refuse to believe that the bank of justice is bankrupt. We refuse to believe that there are insufficient funds in the great vaults of opportunity of this nation. So we have come to cash this check—a check that will give us upon demand the riches of freedom and the security of justice. We have also come to this hallowed spot to remind America of the fierce urgency of *now*. This is no time to engage in the luxury of cooling off or to take the tranquilizing drug of gradualism. *Now* is the time to make real the promises of Democracy. *Now* is the time to rise from the dark and desolate valley of segregation to the sunlit path of racial justice. *Now* is the time to open the doors of opportunity to all of God's children. *Now* is the time to lift our nation from the quicksands of racial injustice to the solid rock of brotherhood.

Repeated words and phrases create urgency.

It would be fatal for the nation to overlook the urgency of the moment and to underestimate the determination of the Negro. This sweltering summer of the Negro's legitimate discontent will not pass until there is an

1

2

3

4

5

invigorating autumn of freedom and equality. 1963 is not an end, but a beginning. Those who hope that the Negro needed to blow off steam and will now be content will have a rude awakening if the nation returns to business as usual. There will be neither rest nor tranquility in America until the Negro is granted his citizenship rights. The whirlwinds of revolt will continue to shake the foundations of our nation until the bright day of justice emerges.

King addresses specific audiences in turn.

But there is something I must say to my people who stand on the warm threshold which leads into the palace of justice. In the process of gaining our rightful place we must not be guilty of wrongful deeds. Let us not seek to satisfy our thirst for freedom by drinking from the cup of bitterness and hatred. We must forever conduct our struggle on the high plane of dignity and discipline. We must not allow our creative protest to degenerate into physical violence. Again and again we must rise to the majestic heights of meeting physical force with soul force. The marvelous new militancy which has engulfed the Negro community must not lead us to a distrust of all white people, for many of our white brothers, as evidenced by their presence here today, have come to realize that their destiny is tied up with our destiny and their freedom is inextricably bound to our freedom. We cannot walk alone. 6

He responds to the arguments of opponents.

And as we talk, we must make the pledge that we shall march ahead. We cannot turn back. There are those who are asking the devotees of civil rights, "When will you be satisfied?" We can never be satisfied as long as the Negro is the victim of the unspeakable horrors of police brutality. We can never be satisfied as long as our bodies, heaving with the fatigue of travel, cannot gain lodging in the motels of the highways and the hotels of the cities. We cannot be satisfied as long as the Negro's basic mobility is from a smaller ghetto to a larger one. We can never be satisfied as long as a Negro in Mississippi cannot vote and a Negro in New York believes he has nothing for which to vote. No, no, we are not satisfied, and we will not be satisfied until justice rolls down like waters and righteousness like a mighty stream. 7

Appropriate emotional appeals are used in the context of suffering.

I am not unmindful that some of you have come here out of great trials and tribulations. Some of you have come fresh from narrow jail cells. Some of you have come from areas where your quest for freedom left you battered by the storms of persecution and staggered by the winds of police brutality. You have been the veterans of creative suffering. Continue to work with the faith that unearned suffering is redemptive. 8

Go back to Mississippi, go back to Alabama, go back to South Carolina, go back to Georgia, go back to Louisiana, go back to the slums and ghettos of our northern cities, knowing that somehow this situation can and will be changed. Let us not wallow in the valley of despair. 9

I say to you today, my friends, that in spite of the difficulties and frustrations of the moment I still have a dream. It is a dream deeply rooted in the American dream. 10

I have a dream that one day this nation will rise up and live out the   *11*
true meaning of its creed: "We hold these truths to be self-evident; that all
men are created equal."

I have a dream that one day on the red hills of Georgia the sons of   *12*
former slaves and the sons of former slaveowners will be able to sit down
together at the table of brotherhood.

I have a dream that the state of Mississippi, a desert state sweltering   *13*
with the heat of injustice and oppression, will be transformed into an oasis
of freedom and justice.

I have a dream that my four little children will one day live in a nation   *14*
where they will not be judged by the color of their skin but by the content
of their character.

I have a dream today.   *15*

I have a dream that the state of Alabama, whose governor's lips are   *16*
presently dripping with the words of interposition and nullification, will
be transformed into a situation where little black boys and black girls will
be able to join hands with little white boys and girls and walk together as
sisters and brothers.

I have a dream today.   *17*

I have a dream that one day every valley shall be exalted, every hill   *18*
and mountain shall be made low, the rough places will be made plain, and .
the crooked places will be made straight, and the glory of the Lord shall be
revealed, and all flesh shall see it together.

This is our hope. This is the faith with which I return to the South.   *19*
With this faith we will be able to hew out of the mountain of despair a stone
of hope. With this faith we will be able to transform the jangling discords
of our nation into a beautiful symphony of brotherhood. With this faith we
will be able to work together, to pray together, to struggle together, to go to
jail together, to stand up for freedom together, knowing that we will be free
one day.

This will be the day when all God's children will be able to sing with   *20*
new meaning.

> *My country 'tis of thee*   *21*
> *Sweet land of liberty,*
> *Of thee I sing,*
> *Land where my fathers died,*
> *Land of the pilgrims' pride,*
> *From every mountainside*
> *Let freedom ring.*

And if America is to be a great nation this must become true. So let   *22*
freedom ring from the prodigious hilltops of New Hampshire. Let freedom
ring from the mighty mountains of New York. Let freedom ring from the
heightening Alleghenies of Pennsylvania!

The repetition of key phrases becomes a persuasive refrain.

King's vision offers hope and motivates readers to change society.

He appeals to ideals and to humanity's better nature, ending with a vision of a just society.

Let freedom ring from the snow-capped Rockies of Colorado!   *23*
Let freedom ring from the curvaceous peaks of California!   *24*
But not only that; let freedom ring from Stone Mountain of Georgia!   *25*
Let freedom ring from Lookout Mountain of Tennessee!   *26*
Let freedom ring from every hill and molehill of Mississippi! From   *27*
every mountainside, let freedom ring.

When we let freedom ring, when we let it ring from every village and   *28*
every hamlet, from every state and every city, we will be able to speed up
that day when all of God's children, black men and white men, Jews and
Gentiles, Protestants and Catholics, will be able to join hands and sing in
the words of the old Negro spiritual, "Free at last! Free at last! Thank God
almighty, we are free at last!" ■

> The closing urges readers to work for a better future.

Reading for Better Writing

Working by yourself or with a group, answer these questions:

1. King is actually speaking to several audiences at the same time. Who are these different audiences? How does King address each?

2. For what specific changes does King call? What does he want his listeners to do?

3. Explore the writer's style. How does he use religious imagery, comparisons, and analogies? How does repetition function as a persuasive technique?

4. In a sense, King's speech addresses a gap between reality and an ideal. How does he present this gap?

Persuading Readers to Act

This essay is by Jack G. Shaheen, Professor Emeritus of Mass Communication at Southern Illinois University at Carbondale, whose work on media portrayals of Arabs has earned recognition and awards. Some of his books include *Reel Bad Arabs* and *Arab and Muslim Stereotyping in American Pop Culture*.

The Media's Image of Arabs

The piece opens with a series of claims, moving from a broad statement to more specific claims.

America's bogyman is the Arab. Until the nightly news brought us TV pictures of Palestinian boys being punched and beaten, almost all portraits of Arabs seen in America were dangerously threatening. Arabs were either billionaires or bombers—rarely victims. They were hardly ever seen as ordinary people practicing law, driving taxis, singing lullabies, or healing the sick. Though TV news may portray them more sympathetically now, the absence of positive media images nurtures suspicion and stereotype. As an Arab-American, I have found that ugly caricatures have had an enduring impact on my family. 1

The writer gives background about his own history with the topic.

I was sheltered from prejudicial portraits at first. My parents came from Lebanon in the 1920s; they met and married in America. Our home in the steel city of Clairton, Pa., was a center for ethnic sharing—black, white, Jew, and gentile. There was only one major source of media images then, at the State movie theater where I was lucky enough to get a part-time job as an usher. But in the late 1940s, Westerns and war movies were popular, not Middle Eastern dramas. Memories of World War II were fresh, and the screen heavies were the Japanese and the Germans. True to the cliché of the times, the only good Indian was a dead Indian. But when I mimicked or mocked the bad guys, my mother cautioned me. She explained that stereotypes blur our vision and corrupt the imagination. "Have compassion for all people, Jackie," she said. "This way, you'll learn to experience the joy of accepting people as they are, and not as they appear in films. Stereotypes hurt." 2

This paragraph, like many others, begins with a short, simple sentence.

Mother was right. I can remember the Saturday afternoon when my son, Michael, who was seven, and my daughter, Michele, six, suddenly called out: "Daddy, Daddy, they've got some bad Arabs on TV." They were watching that great American morality play, TV wrestling. Akbar the Great, who liked to hear the cracking of bones, and Abdullah the Butcher, a dirty fighter who liked to inflict pain, were pinning their foes with "camel locks." From that day on, I knew I had to try to neutralize the media caricatures. 3

Quotation marks set apart others' words and phrases from those of the author.

It hasn't been easy. With my children, I have watched animated heroes Heckle and Jeckle pull the rug from under "Ali Boo-Boo, the Desert Rat," and Laverne and Shirley stop "Sheik Ha-Mean-Ie" from conquering "the U.S. and the world." I have read comic books like the *Fantastic Four* and *G.I. Combat* whose characters have sketched Arabs as "lowlifes" and "human hyenas." Negative stereotypes were everywhere. A dictionary informed my 4 youngsters that an Arab is a "vagabond, drifter, hobo, and vagrant." Whatever happened, my wife wondered, to Aladdin's good genie?

To a child, the world is simple: good versus evil. But my children and others with Arab roots grew up without ever having seen a humane Arab on the silver screen, someone to pattern their lives after. Is it easier for a camel to go through the eye of a needle than for a screen Arab to appear as a genuine human being?

Hollywood producers must have an instant Ali Baba kit that contains scimitars, veils, sunglasses, and such Arab clothing as *chadors* and *kufiyahs*. In the mythical "Ay-rabland," oil wells, tents, mosques, goats, and shepherds prevail. Between the sand dunes, the camera focuses on a mock-up of a palace from *Arabian Nights*—or a military air base. Recent movies suggest that Americans are at war with Arabs, forgetting the fact that out of 21 Arab nations, America is friendly with 19 of them. And in *Wanted Dead or Alive*, a movie that starred Gene Simmons, the leader of the rock group Kiss, the war comes home when an Arab terrorist comes to the United States dressed as a rabbi and, among other things, conspires with Arab Americans to poison the people of Los Angeles. The movie was released last year.

The Arab remains American culture's favorite whipping boy. In his memoirs, Terrel Bell, Ronald Reagan's first secretary of education, writes about an "apparent bias among mid-level, right-wing staffers at the White House" who dismissed Arabs as "sand niggers." Sadly, the racial slurs continue. At a recent teacher's conference, I met a woman from Sioux Falls, South Dakota, who told me about the persistence of discrimination. She was in the process of adopting a baby when an agency staffer warned her that the infant had a problem. When she asked whether the child was mentally ill, or physically handicapped, there was silence. Finally, the worker said: "The baby is Jordanian."

To me, the Arab demon of today is much like the Jewish demon of yesterday. We deplore the false portrait of Jews as a swarthy menace. Yet a similar portrait has been accepted and transferred to another group of Semites—the Arabs. Print and broadcast journalists have started to challenge this stereotype. They are now revealing more humane images of Palestinian Arabs, a people who traditionally suffered from the myth that Palestinian equals terrorist. Others could follow that lead and retire the stereotypical Arab to a media Valhalla.

> To me, the Arab demon of today is much like the Jewish demon of yesterday.

It would be a step in the right direction if movie and TV producers developed characters modeled after real-life Arab Americans. We could then see a White House correspondent like Helen Thomas, whose father came from Lebanon, in *The Golden Girls*, a heart surgeon patterned after

---

The writer makes claims related to his main thesis and then supports them with examples drawn from public and personal sources.

The writer compares the present situation with the past.

The writer states the actions that he wishes to persuade various groups to take.

Dr. Michael DeBakey on *St. Elsewhere,* or a Syrian-American playing tournament chess like Yasser Seirawan, the Seattle grandmaster.

Politicians, too, should speak out against the cardboard caricatures. *10* They should refer to Arabs as friends, not just as moderates. And religious leaders could state that Islam, like Christianity and Judaism, maintains that all mankind is one family in the care of God. When all imagemakers rightfully begin to treat Arabs and all other minorities with respect and dignity, we may begin to unlearn our prejudices. ■

Reading for Better Writing

Working by yourself or with a group, answer these questions:

1. Shaheen's essay was first published in 1988. To what extent is his argument still relevant? Give current examples that show how media images of Arabs have or have not changed.

2. Working with a classmate, review the section in chapter 17 about "Making and Qualifying Claims" (pages 262–263). Make notes in the margins of Shaheen's essay, labeling facts, opinions, and claims. For each claim that you identify, label the type of claim that is being made (for example, claims of truth, value, or policy). Look over your margin notes. What observations can you make about Shaheen's essay, and why are they significant?

3. Review the section in chapter 17 titled "Supporting Your Claims" (pages 264–266). Which kinds of evidence does Shaheen use to support his claims? Which types of evidence do you think are most or least effective in this piece? Why?

4. How might the meaning of paragraph 4 in this essay be changed if the author had omitted the quotation marks?

5. Part of Shaheen's style in this essay is to open many of his paragraphs with short, simple sentences. How does he vary the sentence length and structure throughout the remainder of each of these paragraphs? What is the effect of this variation for readers?

Persuading Readers to Act

Kofi A. Annan, the recent Secretary-General of the United Nations, wrote the essay below to urge readers worldwide to help address the suffering caused by AIDS and famine in Africa.

In Africa, AIDS Has a Woman's Face

Working with one or two classmates, note in the margin writing strategies that help the writer build a clear, forceful argument. Then assess why each strategy is or is not effective.

A combination of famine and AIDS is threatening the backbone of Africa—the women who keep African societies going and whose work makes up the economic foundation of rural communities. For decades, we have known that the best way for Africa to thrive is to ensure that its women have the freedom, power, and knowledge to make decisions affecting their own lives and those of their families and communities. At the United Nations, we have always understood that our work for development depends on building a successful partnership with the African farmer and her husband.

Study after study has shown that there is no effective development strategy in which women do not play a central role. When women are fully involved, the benefits can be seen immediately: Families are healthier; they are better fed; their income, savings, and reinvestment go up. And, what is true of families is true of communities and, eventually, of whole countries.

But today, millions of African women are threatened by two simultaneous catastrophes: famine and AIDS. More than 30 million people are now at risk of starvation in southern Africa and the Horn of Africa. All of these predominantly agricultural societies are also battling serious AIDS epidemics. This is no coincidence: AIDS and famine are directly linked.

> *But today, millions of African women are threatened by two simultaneous catastrophes: famine and AIDS.*

Because of AIDS, farming skills are being lost, agricultural development efforts are declining, rural livelihoods are disintegrating, productive capacity to work the land is dropping, and household earnings are shrinking—all while the cost of caring for the ill is rising exponentially. At the same time, H.I.V. infection and AIDS are spreading dramatically and disproportionately among women. A United Nations report released last month shows that women now make up 50 percent of those infected with H.I.V. worldwide—and in Africa that figure is now 59 percent. Today, AIDS has a woman's face.

AIDS has already caused immense suffering by killing almost 2.5 million   5
Africans this year alone. It has left 11 million African children orphaned
since the epidemic began. Now it is attacking the capacity of these countries
to resist famine by eroding those mechanisms that enable populations to
fight back—the coping abilities provided by women.

In famines before the AIDS crisis, women proved more resilient than   6
men. Their survival rate was higher, and their coping skills were stronger.
Women were the ones who found alternative foods that could sustain their
children in time of drought. Because droughts happened once a decade or
so, women who had experienced previous droughts were able to pass on
survival techniques to younger women. Women are the ones who nurture
social networks that can help spread the burden in times of famine.

But today, as AIDS is eroding the health of Africa's women, it is eroding   7
the skills, experience, and networks that keep their families and communities
going. Even before falling ill, a woman will often have to care for a sick
husband, thereby reducing the time she can devote to planting, harvesting,
and marketing crops. When her husband dies, she is often deprived of credit,
distribution networks, or land rights. When she dies, the household will risk
collapsing completely, leaving children to fend for themselves. The older
ones, especially girls, will be taken out of school to work in the home or
the farm. These girls, deprived of education and
opportunities, will be even less able to protect
themselves against AIDS.

Because this crisis is different from past   *Because*   8
famines, we must look beyond relief measures of   *this crisis is*
the past. Merely shipping in food is not enough.   *different from*
Our effort will have to combine food assistance   *past famines,*
and new approaches to farming with treatment   *we must look*
and prevention of H.I.V. and AIDS. It will require   *beyond relief*
creating early-warning and analysis systems that   *measures of*
monitor both H.I.V. infection rates and famine   *the past.*
indicators. It will require new agricultural
techniques, appropriate to a depleted work
force. It will require a renewed effort to wipe out H.I.V.-related stigma and
silence.

It will require innovative, large-scale ways to care for orphans, with   9
specific measures that enable children in AIDS-affected communities to stay
in school. Education and prevention are still the most powerful weapons
against the spread of H.I.V. Above all, this new international effort must put
women at the center of our strategy to fight AIDS.

Experience suggests that there is reason to hope. The recent United Nations report shows that H.I.V. infection rates in Uganda continue to decline. In South Africa, infection rates for women under 20 have started to decrease. In Zambia, H.I.V. rates show signs of dropping among women in urban areas and younger women in rural areas. In Ethiopia, infection levels have fallen among young women in the center of Addis Ababa. *10*

We can and must build on those successes and replicate them elsewhere. For that, we need leadership, partnership, and imagination from the international community and African governments. If we want to save Africa from two catastrophes, we would do well to focus on saving Africa's women. ■ *11*

Reading for Better Writing

Working by yourself or with a group, answer these questions:

1. How does Annan introduce the topic and focus the essay? Explain why these strategies are or are not effective.

2. Outline the essay by stating the writer's thesis and main supporting points. Then explain why you do or do not find the argument clear, well organized, and convincing.

3. Annan wants his readers to do something. What, precisely, does he ask them to do? Is his request sufficiently clear, complete, and doable? Explain.

4. Annan supports his argument with a variety of information, including data, historical details, anecdotes, examples, and emotional appeals. Choose a paragraph that you find convincing and explain why.

5. Review the logical fallacies explained on pages 267–270. Do you find any of these weaknesses in Annan's argument? Support your answer with details.

6. In the closing paragraph, the writer uses the pronoun "we" four times. Why does he do this? Replace each "we" with "you" and explain how the changes alter the tone and effectiveness of the writer's effort to convince readers to act.

Model

Guidelines
Persuading Readers to Act

Note: For in-depth help on developing persuasive arguments, see pages 260–273.

1. **Select a topic.** List issues about which you feel passionately, issues where you see a need for change. (See "Topics to Consider" on page 296.) Then choose a topic that meets these criteria: The topic is debatable, significant, current, and manageable.

Not Debatable	*Debatable*
Statistics on spending practices	The injustice of consumerism
The existence of racism	Solutions to racism

2. **Choose and analyze your audience.** Think about who your readers are. Make a list of words and phrases describing their perspectives on the issue.

3. **Narrow your focus and determine your purpose.** Consider what you can achieve within the assignment's constraints. Should you focus on one aspect of the issue or all of it? Which patterns of thinking and behavior can you try to change? With these readers, which actions can you call for?

4. **Generate ideas and support.** Use prewriting strategies like those below to develop your thinking and gather support:

   - Set up "opposing viewpoints" columns. In one column, take one side; in the other column, take the other side.
   - Construct a dialogue between two people—yourself and someone who doesn't support your position.
   - Talk to others about the issue. How do peers, friends, coworkers, and relatives respond to your ideas?
   - Research the issue to find current, reliable sources from a variety of perspectives. Consider interviewing an expert.
   - Consider what outcome or results you want.

5. **Organize your thinking.** Get your thoughts organized so that you can step confidently into your first draft. Consider the following strategies:

   - Make a sharp claim about the issue, a claim that points toward action. Try this basic pattern:

     On the issue of _____ , I believe _____ .

     Therefore, we must change _____ .

   - Review the evidence, and develop your line of reasoning by generating an outline or using a graphic organizer. (See pages 50–51.)

> *Simple Outline:*   **Introduction: claim**
>   Supporting point 1
>   Supporting point 2
>   Supporting point 3
>   **Conclusion: call to action**

6. **Write your first draft**. As you write, remember your persuasive goal and your specific readers. Here are some possible strategies:

    Opening: Gain the readers' attention, raise the issue, help the readers care about it, and state your claim.

    Development: Follow your outline but feel free to explore new ideas that arise. Decide where to place your most persuasive supporting argument: first or last. Anticipate readers' questions and objections, and use appropriate logical and emotional appeals to overcome their resistance.

    Closing: Do one or more of the following: Restate your claim, summarize your support, encourage readers to take the action you want.

    Title: Develop a thoughtful, energetic working title that stresses a vision or change. (For ideas, scan the titles of the sample essays in this chapter.)

7. **Share your essay**. Try out your thinking and persuasive appeals with a reader. Does he or she find your argument convincing? Why or why not?

8. **Revise your writing**. Think about your reviewer's comments, and then ask these questions of your draft:

    - Does your argument flow effectively? Consider shuffling points to make the sequence more persuasive. Add transitions if necessary.
    - Is the evidence credible and persuasive? Does your logic have gaps? Do you need to qualify some points and strengthen others?
    - Do images, examples, and analogies help readers understand and identify with your cause? Do these elements urge readers to act?
    - Is the voice fitting—energetic but controlled, confident but reasonable? Will your tone persuade readers or start a quarrel?

9. **Edit and proofread**. See pages 107–110 for guidelines, but check especially for appropriate word choice and clear sentences. Avoid clichés and jargon.

10. **Prepare and publish your final essay**. Submit your essay according to your instructor's format and documentation requirements. If appropriate, "publish" your essay and solicit feedback from your audience—perhaps on a website, in the school newspaper, or with an appropriate discussion group.

> **TIP:** Consider how one or more well-placed visuals (graph, photograph, and so on) might strengthen your argument. See pages 14–17 for more on visuals and pages 272–273 for more on appeals.

Writing Checklist

Use these seven traits to check the quality of your essay; then revise as needed:

_____ The **ideas** in your essay prompt readers to change their thinking and behavior. The essay has a clear opinion statement, effective reasoning, good support, and a clear call to action.

_____ The **organization** is logical and includes an engaging opening that raises the issue, a clearly sequenced argument, and a convincing conclusion focused on change and action.

_____ The **voice** is thoughtful, caring, and convincing.

_____ The **words** are precise, concrete, and easily understood (or defined as needed). The language is free of clichés and glib phrases.

_____ The **sentences** flow smoothly, with effective transitions and logical connections.

_____ The **copy** includes no errors in mechanics, usage, grammar, or punctuation.

_____ The **design** is correctly formatted and features the text, making reading easy.

Interactive

Critical-Thinking and Writing Activities

As directed by your instructor, complete the following activities.

1. The four essays in this chapter address significant social issues. List other significant social issues, choose one, and then write an essay that persuades readers to do something related to the issue.

2. If you are a natural sciences major, consider debatable issues that are central to studying and applying the sciences—environmental, medical, biotechnical, and agricultural issues, for example. If you are a social sciences or humanities major, do the same brainstorming in your area.

3. Consider the workplace. Which issues have come up in your job? Contemplate issues such as pay equity, equal opportunity, management policies, and unsafe work conditions. Then write a persuasive report to a decision maker or to fellow employees.

4. Review the discussion of critical viewing (pages **14–17**) and the principles of argumentation (pages **260–266**). Then explain how you could strengthen one of this chapter's essays by integrating one or more visuals.

◀ VISUALLY SPEAKING

Imagine that the woman pictured on page **295** is one of the women whom Kofi A. Annan describes in his essay on page **307**. Then write a two- or three-page paper describing who she is, what she is doing, and why. Create details as needed.

PROPOSING A SOLUTION

Audio

Video

Proposals are prescriptions for change. As such, they challenge readers to care about a problem, accept a solution, and act on it. A strong proposal offers a logical, practical, and creative argument that leads toward positive change, whether it's defending against terrorism, requiring both men and women to register for the military draft, or adding to the debate on cloning.

Proposal writers argue for such remedies in all areas of life. In your college courses, you'll be challenged to map out solutions to many difficult problems. In your community, you may participate in policy making and civic development. In the workplace, you may write proposals that justify expenditures, sell products, or troubleshoot problems. In each situation, you'll be challenged to clearly explain the problem, offer a solution, and argue for adopting that solution.

This chapter will walk you through the challenge of writing such proposals, from selecting a problem to submitting your plan.

Note: Some problem-solution writing can be explanatory rather than persuasive.

Overview
Proposing a Solution

Writer's Goal

Your goal is to argue for a positive change, convincing readers to accept and contribute to that change. To accomplish this goal, aim to describe a problem, analyze its causes and effects, argue for one solution among several options, defend that solution against objections, and prove the solution both feasible and desirable.

Keys for Success

Show passion for change. Proposal writing requires a willingness to challenge the status quo and a mind that is open to creative possibilities. Dare to ask, "What's really wrong here, and how can we fix it?"

Avoid cosmetic solutions. Whatever solution you choose, base it on a concrete and personal understanding of the problem and a bold exploration of all possible solutions. Choose the best solution only after weighing each option against sensible criteria for solving the problem, comparing and contrasting its strengths and weaknesses. Consider especially how well solutions attack root causes, bring about real benefits, and prove workable.

Know your readers. Who can bring about the change you envision—specific decision makers (the city council, college administrators, a department manager) or a broader community affected by the problem? What are their allegiances and alliances? Knowing your readers will help you speak convincingly to them, build a spirit of teamwork, and persuasively challenge readers to change.

Conduct quality research. Your proposal will stand or fall on the quality of both your reasoning and its support. To build that quality, conduct primary research (observations and interviews, for example), but also check journals, books, and Internet sources to understand the problem, explore possible solutions, and garner support for the solution you choose.

Problems to Consider

- **People problems:** Consider generations—your own or a relative's. What problems does this generation face?
- **College problems:** List the top ten problems faced by college students. In your major, which problems are experts trying to solve?
- **Social problems:** Which problems do our communities and country face? Where do you see suffering, injustice, waste, or harm?
- **Workplace problems:** What challenges do you encounter at work?

> **Next Step** Read the model essays and perform the activities that follow. As you read, consider the problems presented and the solutions offered. What similar problems do you care about?

Proposing a Solution

In this essay, student writer Brian Ley defines agroterrorism, predicts that it could become a serious problem, and proposes a multifaceted solution.

Audio

Preparing for Agroterror

The writer opens by illustrating the problem.

An al-Qaeda terrorist in Africa obtains a sample of fluid from a cow infected with foot-and-mouth disease, and he sends the fluid to an accomplice in a small, rural American town. This terrorist takes the sample around the country, stopping at several points to place small amounts of the fluid on objects that animals are likely to touch. When he is finished, he drives to the nearest airport and leaves the country unnoticed.   *1*

Cows, pigs, and sheep then come into contact with this highly contagious disease. Over the next few days, farmers see blisters on the feet and mouths of their animals. Thinking that the animals have a bacterial infection, the farmers administer antibiotics and wait for improvement. However, because antibiotics can't kill a virus, the animals get sicker. Meanwhile, the virus is spreading by means of wind and the movement of animals and humans. Within a few weeks, the virus is out of control.   *2*

While the story above is hypothetical, it is also very possible. People used to think of terrorists as men in ski masks blowing up embassies and taking hostages. But after the events of September 11, 2001, and the subsequent anthrax scares, it is clear that more kinds of terrorism are possible.   *3*

He defines the problem and presents expert testimony.

One type rarely considered is agroterrorism, which involves using diseases as weapons to attack a country's agriculture industry in order to attack the country itself. The agroterrorist's weapons of choice are those diseases that affect plants, animals, and even humans. Professor Peter Chalk of the RAND Corporation, an expert on transnational terrorism, believes that agroterrorism should be a huge concern for Americans because it has many advantages from a terrorist's point of view (37).   *4*

He analyzes why the problem could become serious.

First of all, an attack on the agricultural sector of the United States would be quite easy. The diseases needed to kill large populations of animals can be obtained with little difficulty; the most devastating ones are ready for use in their natural form. These samples pose little risk to the terrorist because many of the diseases are harmless to humans.   *5*

In addition, doing agroterrorism is less risky in terms of getting caught and getting punished. Agroterrorism is hard to trace, especially because Americans have assumed that all animal epidemics are natural in origin and that American livestock contract such diseases only by accident. Consequences for those caught inflicting a disease on animals are also less severe than for terrorists who harm humans. In fact, because agroterrorism first affects the health of plants and animals rather than humans, terrorists using this strategy can even escape some guilt for their actions.   *6*

However, while agroterrorist diseases would have little direct effect on people's health, they would be devastating to the agricultural economy, in part because of the many different diseases that could be used in an attack. One of the most devastating is foot-and-mouth disease. This illness hurts all infected animals by impeding their weight gain, and it hurts dairy cows in particular by decreasing their milk production. Because the disease is highly contagious, all infected animals, along with any cloven-hoofed animals within about 50 miles of the infection site, must be killed.

7

While foot-and-mouth disease is not dangerous to humans, other animal diseases are. One of these is bovine spongiform encephalopathy, better known as mad-cow disease ("Mad Cow"). This illness is not easily spread, but a few cases in the United States would send people into a panic. Meat consumption would drop sharply, and the agricultural economy would be deeply shaken.

8

Another disease that could be used as a weapon is West Nile encephalitis. This virus can be spread by insects and can even cross species, affecting horses, birds, pigs, and humans. It is a fatal illness without a vaccination or a cure. These diseases are likely candidates for use in an agroterrorist attack (Smith 249).

9

The agricultural community is particularly susceptible to a terrorist attack. Unlike "typical" terrorist targets in metropolitan areas, farms do not have sophisticated security systems to protect against intruders. The average farmer's security system includes a mean dog and a shotgun: the dog for humans and the gun for animal pests. If terrorists wanted to infect a dairy, swine operation, or even a large-scale cattle-finishing operation, they would encounter few obstacles. The terrorists merely have to place a piece of infected food in an area with livestock. This single action could start an epidemic.

10

Agroterrorism is a threat that demands a response. Several actions can be taken to discourage terrorism as well as to deal with its consequences. One of the first steps is convincing all citizens—farmers and nonfarmers alike—that agroterrorism could happen, and that it could cause horrific consequences. Farmers must realize that they are susceptible to an attack even though they may live far from large metropolitan areas. Nonfarmers must realize how an attack could affect them. If nonfarmers know that an attack could create panic, drive up food prices, and possibly eliminate food sources, they will look out for suspicious activity and report it.

11

Preventive action on farms is needed to ensure the safety of the food supply. For example, the South Dakota Animal Industry Board recently published a newsletter outlining several precautions that farmers can take. Farms should have better security, especially in areas where animals are kept. These security measures include allowing only authorized persons to have access to farm buildings and animals and keeping all key farm buildings locked ("Precautions").

12

Farmers also need training to detect the diseases that terrorists might *13* use and to know what actions can contain and decontaminate an infected area. For example, if a farmer discovers that cows have blisters on their tongues and noses, and that they are behaving abnormally, the owner should immediately call a veterinarian to assess the situation. Because the disease might be foot-and-mouth, no cattle should leave the farm until a diagnosis has been made.

In addition, public authorities need a plan for responding to an *14* identified agroterrorism attack. For example, thousands of animals may have to be killed and disposed of—an action with significant environmental concerns. Moreover, public money should be used for continued research of the diseases that may be spread by agroterrorists. Vaccines and treatments may be produced that would stop diseases or limit them from becoming epidemic.

The closing stresses the problem's seriousness and calls for action.

Agroterrorism has not yet been used on a large scale anywhere on the *15* globe. However, its use seems inevitable. The United States is a prime target for terrorism of this sort because the country has the largest, most efficiently raised food supply in the world. Destroying part of this supply would affect not only the United States but also all those countries with whom it trades. Because the United States is a prime target, it must act now to develop its defenses against agroterrorism. If the country waits until an attack happens, people may become ill, the overall economy could be damaged, and the agricultural economy may never recover. ■

Note: The Works Cited page is not shown. For sample pages, see MLA (page **532–533**) and APA (page **564**).

Reading for Better Writing

Working by yourself or with a group, answer these questions:

1. This essay predicts that a problem may develop. Is the writer's prediction persuasive? Why or why not?

2. What tactics does the writer use to get readers concerned about the problem? Are these strategies successful?

3. The solution proposed is multifaceted. Briefly list who must do what. Is this solution persuasive? Is it workable? Does it get at root causes?

4. A strong proposal provides convincing evidence about both the problem and the solution. Trace the evidence used in this essay. Are the types of evidence convincing? Do any gaps need to be filled?

Proposing a Solution

Anna Quindlen's *New York Times* column "Public and Private" won the 1992 Pulitzer Prize for commentary. She now writes a regular column for *Newsweek*, where "Uncle Sam and Aunt Samantha" was originally published in 2001.

Uncle Sam and Aunt Samantha

Each of the first five paragraphs is one sentence long.

One out of every five new recruits in the United States military is female.   *1*

The Marines gave the Combat Action Ribbon for service in the Persian Gulf to 23 women.   *2*

Two female soldiers were killed in the bombing of the *USS Cole*.   *3*

The Selective Service registers for the draft all male citizens between the ages of 18 and 25.   *4*

What's wrong with this picture?   *5*

The writer identifies the problem that she wants solved.

As Americans read and realize that the lives of most women in this country are as different from those of Afghan women as a Cunard cruise is from maximum-security lockdown, there has nonetheless been little attention paid to one persistent gender inequity in U.S. public policy. An astonishing anachronism, really: While women are represented today in virtually all fields, including the armed forces, only men are required to register for the military draft that would be used in the event of a national-security crisis.   *6*

She provides background about the source and history of the problem.

Since the nation is as close to such a crisis as it has been in more than sixty years, it's a good moment to consider how the draft wound up in this particular time warp. It's not the time warp of the Taliban, certainly, stuck in the worst part of the 13th century, forbidding women to attend school or hold jobs or even reveal their arms, forcing them into sex and marriage. Our own time warp is several decades old. The last time the draft was considered seriously was twenty years ago, when registration with the Selective Service was restored by Jimmy Carter after the Soviet invasion of, yep, Afghanistan. The president, as well as the Army chief of staff, asked at the time for the registration of women as well as men.   *7*

Amid a welter of arguments—women interfere with esprit de corps, women don't have the physical strength, women prisoners could be sexually assaulted, women soldiers would distract male soldiers from their mission—Congress shot down the notion of gender-blind registration. So did the Supreme Court, ruling that since women were forbidden to serve in combat positions and the purpose of the draft was to create a combat-ready force, it made sense not to register them.   *8*

But that was then, and this is now. Women have indeed served in combat positions, in the Balkans and the Middle East. More than 40,000 managed to serve in the Persian Gulf without destroying unit cohesion or failing because of upper-body strength. Some are even now taking out   *9* targets in Afghanistan from fighter jets, and apparently without any male soldier's falling prey to some predicted excess of chivalry or lust.

Talk about cognitive dissonance. All these military personnel, male and female alike, have come of age at a time when a significant level of parity was taken for granted. Yet they are supposed to accept that only males will be required to defend their country in a time of national emergency. This is insulting to men. And it is insulting to women. Caroline Forell, an expert on women's legal rights and a professor at the University of Oregon School of Law, puts it bluntly: "Failing to require this of women makes us lesser citizens."

> *Yet they are supposed to accept that only males will be required to defend their country . . .*

Neither the left nor the right has been particularly inclined to consider this issue judiciously. Many feminists came from the antiwar movement and have let their distaste for the military in general and the draft in particular mute their response. In 1980 NOW [National Organization for Women] released a resolution that buried support for the registration of women beneath opposition to the draft, despite the fact that the draft had been redesigned to eliminate the vexing inequities of Vietnam, when the sons of the working class served and the sons of the Ivy League did not. Conservatives, meanwhile, used an equal-opportunity draft as the linchpin of opposition to the Equal Rights Amendment, along with the terrifying specter of unisex bathrooms. (I have seen the urinal, and it is benign.) The legislative director of the right-wing group Concerned Women for America once defended the existing regulations by saying that most women "don't want to be included in the draft." All those young men who went to Canada during Vietnam and those who today register with fear and trembling in the face of the Trade Center devastation might be amazed to discover that lack of desire is an affirmative defense.

Parents face a series of unique new challenges in this more egalitarian world, not the least of which would be sending a daughter off to war. But parents all over this country are doing that right now, with daughters who enlisted; some have even expressed surprise that young women, in this day and age, are not required to register alongside their brothers and friends. While all involved in this debate over the years have invoked the assumed opposition of the people, even ten years ago more than half of all Americans polled believed women should be made eligible for the draft. Besides, this is not about comfort but about fairness. My son has to register with the Selective Service this year, and if his sister does not when she turns 18, it makes a mockery not only of the standards of this household but of the standards of this nation.

Margin notes:

A quotation helps to explain why the writer understands the situation to be a problem.

The writer anticipates and addresses counter-arguments to her position.

She supports her position with statistics as well as personal anecdotes and comparisons to other situations.

10

11

12

The writer appeals to the reader's logic and ethics.

It is possible in Afghanistan for women to be treated like little more than fecund pack animals precisely because gender fear and ignorance and hatred have been codified and permitted to hold sway. In this country, largely because of the concerted efforts of those allied with the women's movement over a century of struggle, much of that bigotry has been beaten back, even buried. Yet in improbable places the creaky old ways surface, the ways suggesting that we women were made of finer stuff. The finer stuff was usually porcelain, decorative and on the shelf, suitable for meals and show. Happily, the finer stuff has been transmuted into the right stuff. But with rights come responsibilities, as teachers like to tell their students. This is a responsibility that should fall equally upon all, male and female alike. If the empirical evidence is considered rationally, if the decision is divested of outmoded stereotypes, that's the only possible conclusion to be reached. ■

13

> *This is a responsibility that should fall equally upon all, male and female alike.*

Reading for Better Writing

Working by yourself or with a group, answer these questions:

1. Which problem(s) does Quindlen identify? Which solution(s) does she propose? To what extent would the proposed solution(s) solve the problem(s) Quindlen discusses?

2. Review the section in chapter 17 about "Identifying Logical Fallacies" (see pages 267–270). Quindlen's opponents might accuse her of "either/or thinking," pointing out that instead of addressing only two options, she could also have argued to end the draft for everyone. Which other logical fallacies might Quindlen's opponents accuse her of making? Would you agree with them? Why or why not?

3. Which strategies does Quindlen use to try to convince readers that the situation she describes is problematic?

4. Why does the writer acknowledge that there may be opposition to her description of the problem and to her proposed solution? How does she respond to these counterarguments? *she states their point and refutes it.*

5. Why does the essay open with a series of one-sentence paragraphs? How might the effect of the essay differ if these sentences had been combined into one paragraph?
It gives the essay more effect

Proposing a Solution

Leigh Turner worked at the Hastings Center, a nonprofit research institute in Garrison, New York. In the following essay, he explains why the current debate on cloning is a problem and he proposes a three-part solution.

Working with a classmate, read Leigh Turner's essay, noting how he first describes a problem and then proposes a three-part solution. In the margin, identify his key organizational strategies and explain how they do or do not clarify his argument.

The Media and the Ethics of Cloning

If the contemporary debate on cloning has a patron saint, surely it is Andy Warhol. Not only did Warhol assert that everyone would have fifteen minutes of fame—witness the lawyers, philosophers, theologians, and bioethicists who found their expertise in hot demand on the nightly morality plays of network television following Ian Wilmut's cloning of the sheep Dolly—but he also placed "clones," multiple copies of the same phenomenon, at the heart of popular culture. Instead of multiple images of Marilyn Monroe and Campbell's soup cans, we now have cloned sheep. Regrettably, it is Warhol's capacity for hyperbole rather than his intelligence and ironic vision that permeates the current debate on cloning. 1

It would be unfair to judge hastily written op-ed pieces, popular talk shows, and late-night radio programs by the same standards that one would apply to a sustained piece of philosophical or legal analysis. But the popular media could do more to foster thoughtful public debate on the legal, moral, political, medical, and scientific dimensions of the cloning of humans and nonhuman animals. 2

As did many of my colleagues at the Hastings Center, I participated in several interviews with the media following Ian Wilmut's announcement in *Nature* that he had succeeded in cloning Dolly from a mammary cell of an adult sheep. After clearly stating to one Los Angeles radio broadcaster before our interview that I was not a theologian and did not represent a religious organization, I was rather breathlessly asked during the taping what God's view on cloning is and whether cloning is "against creation." Predictably, the broadcaster didn't want to discuss how religious ethicists are contributing to the nascent public discourse about the ethics of cloning. Instead, he wanted me to provide a dramatic response that would get the radio station's phones ringing with calls from atheists, agnostics, and religious believers of all stripes. 3

> *Instead of multiple images of Marilyn Monroe and Campbell's soup cans, we now have cloned sheep.*

In addition to inundating the public with hyperbolic sound bites and their print equivalents, the media have overwhelmingly emphasized the issues involved in cloning humans, paying almost no attention to the moral 4 implications of cloning nonhuman animals. While the ethics of cloning humans clearly need to be debated, the cloning of nonhuman animals has already taken place and deserves to be treated as a meaningful moral concern.

Although I suspect that a compelling argument for the cloning of animals can be made, we should not ignore the difference between actually formulating such arguments and merely presuming that nonhuman cloning is altogether unproblematic. Admittedly, humans already consider nonhuman animals as commodities in many ways, including as a source of food. Yet perhaps cloning animals with the intent of using them as "pharmaceutical factories" to produce insulin and other substances to treat human illnesses should raise questions about how far such an attitude ought to extend. What moral obligations should extend to humans' use of other species? Do the potential medical benefits for humans outweigh the dangers of encouraging people to think of nonhuman animals as machines to be manipulated to fulfill human goals? These kinds of questions deserve to be part of the public discussion about cloning. Given some people's concerns about the use of traps to catch wild animals, the living conditions of farm animals, and the treatment of animals used in medical and pharmaceutical research, I find this gap in public discourse perplexing.

But perhaps the most significant problem with the media hyperbole concerning cloning is the easy assumption that humans simply are a product of their genes—a view usually called "genetic essentialism." Television hosts and radio personalities have asked whether it would be possible to stock an entire basketball team with clones of Michael Jordan. In response, philosophers, theologians, and other experts have reiterated wearily that, although human behavior undeniably has a genetic component, a host of other factors—including uterine environment, family dynamics, social setting, diet, and other personal history—play important roles in an individual's development. Consequently, a clone produced from the DNA of an outstanding athlete might not even be interested in sports.

While this more sophisticated message has received some media attention, we continue to see stories emphasizing that the wealthy might some day be able to produce copies of themselves, or that couples with a dying infant might create an identical copy of the child. The popular media seem to remain transfixed by what Dorothy Nelkin, the New York University sociologist of science, refers to as "DNA as destiny."

What's more, the cloning issue reveals the way in which the mass media foster attitudes of technological and scientific determinism by implying that scientific "progress" cannot be halted. Of course, many scientists share these attitudes, and, too often, they refuse to accept moral responsibility for their participation in research that may contribute to human suffering. But scientists should not merely ply their craft, leaving moral reasoning to others. They should participate in public debates about whether certain scientific projects are harmful and should not be allowed to continue because they have unjustifiable, dehumanizing implications. A good model is the outspoken criticism of nuclear weapons by many nuclear physicists, who have helped limit research intended to produce more effective nuclear devices.

Scientists are not riding a juggernaut capable of crushing everything in its path simply because mass cloning of animals, and possibly eventually humans, may be technically possible. There is no reason to think that scientific research has a mandate that somehow enables it to proceed outside the web of moral concerns that govern all other human endeavors; it does not exist above the law or outside the rest of society. To think otherwise is to succumb to a technological determinism that denies the responsibilities and obligations of citizenship.

Despite the media's oversimplifications, citizens have an obligation to scrutinize carefully all of the issues involved and, if necessary, to regulate cloning through laws, professional codes of behavior, and institutional policies. I want to suggest three ways that scholars, policy makers, and concerned citizens can, in fact, work to improve public debate about ethical issues related to new developments in science and technology.

Recognize Moral Implications

First, scientists and ethicists need a fuller understanding of each other's work. Scientists must recognize the moral implications of their research and address those implications when they discuss the research in public. The formal education of most scientists does not encourage them to consider ethical issues. Whereas courses in bioethics are now found in most schools of medicine and nursing, graduate students in such disciplines as human genetics, biochemistry, and animal physiology are not encouraged to grapple with the ethical aspects of their research. Similarly, most ethicists have very little knowledge of science, although many of them feel perfectly entitled to comment on the moral issues of new scientific discoveries.

This gap in understanding fosters an inaccurate, unrealistic conception of what the most pressing ethical issues are. For example, the real challenges for researchers today involve the cloning of nonhuman animals for use in developing pharmaceutical products. Sustained study of nonhuman clones will be needed before researchers can even begin to seriously consider research involving human subjects. Rather than encouraging the media's interest in cloning humans, ethicists more knowledgeable about the science involved might have been able to shift the public debate toward the moral questions raised by cloning sheep, pigs, and other animals, questions that need immediate public debate.

Thus, we need to include more courses in various scientific   *13*
departments on the ethics of contemporary scientific research; offer courses
for ethicists on the basics of human genetics, anatomy, and physiology;
and establish continuing-education courses and forums that bring together
scientists and scholars in the humanities.

Present Concerns of Ethicists

Second, ethicists need to do a better job of presenting their concerns in   *14*
the popular media. Scientific journals written for a popular audience—such
as *Scientific American, New Scientist, Discover,* and *The Sciences*—provide
excellent popular accounts of scientific research and technological
developments, but they rarely specifically address the moral implications
of the discoveries they report. Regrettably, most of the academic journals
that do address the ethical aspects of scientific topics—such as the *Hastings
Center Report,* the *Journal of Medical Ethics,* and the *Cambridge Quarterly
of Healthcare Ethics*—lack the broad readership of the popular-science
magazines. Right now, perhaps the best "popular" source of sustained
ethical analysis of science, medicine, and health care is the *New York Times
Magazine.*

If ethicists hope to reach larger audiences with more than trivial sound   *15*
bites, they need to establish and promote appropriate outlets for their
concerns. For example, Arthur Caplan, director of the Center for Bioethics
at the University of Pennsylvania, wrote a regular weekly newspaper column
for the *St. Paul Pioneer Press* when he directed a bioethics center at the
University of Minnesota. His column addressed the ethical implications
of medical and scientific research. Other scholars have yet to follow his
example—perhaps, in part, because many academics feel that writing for
the mass media is unworthy of their time. They are wrong.

One way of improving public debate on these important issues is for   *16*
universities to encourage their faculty members to write for newspapers,
popular magazines, and even community newsletters. Such forms of
communication should be viewed as an important complement to other
forms of published research. Leon Kass's writing on cloning in *The New
Republic* and Michael Walzer's and Michael Sandel's writing on assisted
suicide in the same publication should not be considered any less significant
simply because the work appears in a magazine intended for a wide
audience. After all, if universities are to retain their public support, they
must consistently be seen as important players in society, and one easy way
to do this is to encourage their faculty members to contribute regularly to
public discussion.

Expand Public Debate

Finally, we need to expand public debate about ethical issues in science   *17*
beyond the mass media. To complement the activities of the National

Bioethics Advisory Commission and the projects on ethics at universities and research centers, we should create forums at which academics and citizens from all walks of life could meet to debate the issues. Instead of merely providing a gathering place for scholars pursuing research projects, institutions such as the Hastings Center, Georgetown University's Kennedy Institute of Ethics, and the University of Pennsylvania's Center for Bioethics need to foster outreach programs and community-discussion groups that include nonspecialists. My experience suggests that members of civic organizations and community-health groups, such as the New York Citizens' Committee on Health Care Decisions, are quite eager to discuss the topic of cloning.

What we need are fewer commentaries by self-promoting experts   18
on network television, and more intelligent discussions by scholars and citizens in local media, including local public-television stations. We need creative alternatives to the onslaught of talking heads, all saying much the same thing (as though they themselves were clones) to docile, sheep-like audiences waiting for others to address the most pressing moral issues of the day. ■

Reading for Better Writing

Working by yourself or with a group, answer these questions:

1. The writer introduces the topic by using Andy Warhol as an analogy. Explain why the analogy is or is not effective.

2. Reread the first two pages, in which the writer states and explains the problem. Summarize what he says, and explain why his presentation is or is not clear.

3. Summarize the author's three-part solution, and explain why this part of the essay is or is not effective.

4. Reread the conclusion, and explain whether it effectively unifies the essay.

Model

Guidelines
Proposing a Solution

Note: For in-depth help on developing persuasive arguments, see pages 260–273.

1. **Select and narrow a topic.** Choose a problem from "Problems to Consider" on page 314, or search for one in periodicals, on news programs, or on the Internet. Then test your topic:
   - Is the problem real, serious, and fairly complex? Does it show brokenness, danger, or disadvantage? Does it predict future harm?
   - Do you care about this problem and believe that it must be solved?
   - Can you offer a workable solution? Should you narrow the focus to part of the problem or a local angle?

2. **Identify and analyze your audience.** Potentially, you could have three audiences: decision makers with the power to deliver change, people affected by the problem, and a public that needs to learn about the problem and get behind a solution. Once you've determined your audience, study them:
   - What do they know about the problem? What are their attitudes toward it, their likely questions, and their potential concerns?
   - Why might they accept or resist change? Would they prefer a specific solution?
   - Does the problem affect them directly or indirectly? What can and can't they do about the problem?
   - What arguments and evidence would convince them to agree that the problem exists, to care about it, and to take action?
   - What common ground do you and your readers share?

3. **Probe the problem.** If helpful, use the graphic organizer on page 51.
   - **Define the problem.** What is it, exactly? What are its parts or dimensions?
   - **Determine the problem's seriousness.** Why should it be fixed? Who is affected and how? What are its immediate, long-term, and potential effects?
   - **Analyze causes.** What are its root causes and contributing factors?
   - **Explore context.** What is the problem's background, history, and connection to other problems? What solutions have been tried in the past? Who, if anyone, benefits from the problem's existence?
   - **Think creatively.** Take a look at the problem from other perspectives —other states and countries, both genders, different races and ethnic groups, and other generations.

4. **Brainstorm possible solutions.** List all imaginable solutions—both modest and radical fixes. Then evaluate the alternatives:
   - List criteria that any solution should meet. (These measurements indicate a solution's effectiveness at resolving the problem: *The solution must . . .)*
   - Compare and contrast alternatives by examining strengths, weaknesses, and workability.

5. **Choose the best solution and map out support.** In a sentence, state the solution that best solves the problem—a workable plan that attacks causes and treats effects. Try this pattern for your thesis: "Given [the problem—its seriousness, effects, or causes], we must [the solution]." Next, identify support for your solution. Compared with alternatives, why is it preferable? Is it more thorough, beneficial, and practical?

6. **Outline your proposal and complete a first draft.** A proposal's structure is quite simple: Describe the problem, offer a solution, and defend the solution. However, what you do in each section can become complicated. Choose strategies that fit your purpose and audience.
   - **The problem:** Consider whether readers understand the problem and accept its seriousness. Inform and/or persuade them about the problem by using appropriate background information, cause/effect analysis, examples, analogies, parallel cases, visuals, and expert testimony.
   - **The solution:** If necessary, first argue against alternative solutions. Then present your solution. State clearly what should happen, who should be involved, and why. For a complex solution, lay out the different stages.
   - **The support:** Show how the solution solves the problem. Use facts and analysis to argue that your solution is feasible and to address objections. You may choose to accept some objections while refuting others.

7. **Get feedback and revise the draft.** Share your draft with a peer or a tutor in the writing center, getting answers to the following questions:
   - Does the solution fit the problem? Is the proposal precise, well reasoned, realistic, and complete? Does it address all objections?
   - Is the evidence credible, compelling, clear, and well documented?
   - Does the voice fit the problem and treat the opposition tactfully?
   - Is the opening engaging? Is the closing thoughtful, forceful, and clear?

8. **Edit and proofread.** Check for accurate word choice and helpful definitions; smooth, energetic sentences; and correct grammar, spelling, and format.

9. **Prepare and share your final essay.** Submit your proposal to your instructor, but also consider posting it on the web.

Writing Checklist

Use these seven traits to check your essay; then revise as needed:

_____ The **ideas** show a thorough understanding of the problem and present a workable solution. The proposal uses strong reasoning and well-researched evidence.

_____ The **organization** convincingly moves from problem to solution to support. Each part is effectively ordered using strategies such as cause/effect, compare/contrast, and process.

_____ The **voice** is positive, confident, objective, and sensitive to opposing viewpoints. The tone fits the seriousness of the problem.

_____ The **words** are precise and effectively defined.

_____ The **sentences** read and flow smoothly, with effective variations and logical transitions.

_____ The **copy** includes no errors in grammar, spelling, or punctuation.

_____ The **design** is attractive and features the text.

Interactive

Critical-Thinking and Writing Activities

As directed by your instructor, complete the following activities.

1. "Preparing for Agroterror" predicts that a problem may develop. Thinking about current conditions and trends, forecast a problem, and write a proposal explaining how to prepare for or prevent it.

2. Review the section in chapter 17 about "Engaging the Opposition" (page 271). Also review how Anna Quindlen engages her opposition in "Uncle Sam and Aunt Samantha." Then consider a persuasive piece that you are drafting or revising. How might you engage the opposition to your arguments? Revise your writing as needed.

3. Review the section in chapter 17 about "Identifying Logical Fallacies" (pages 267–270). Write a humorous essay in which you make an argument by relying on a number of obvious logical fallacies. A challenge: How effectively can you make serious points by combining these strategies?

4. What are some challenges facing the planet Earth and the human race in the foreseeable future? Find a focused challenge and write a proposal.

5. Select an essay from this chapter and find or develop visuals that support the writer's argument.

◀ VISUALLY SPEAKING

Explain why the "solution" pictured on page 313 is both creative and logical. Then explain which essay in this chapter proposes a solution that best illustrates the same qualities.

REPORT WRITING

It's tempting to suggest that the contents of reports include "just the facts." Whether they focus on interviews (chapter 21) or scientific research (chapter 22), reports at first glance seek only to share with readers the objective results of primary research. However, a more careful reading of reports reveals that they do much more. For example, the reports in this section not only describe their topics, but also use analytical strategies (such as cause/effect) to interpret or explain the activities that they describe.

As you read the various types of reports in this section, note both the research methods and organizational strategies used by each writer. Then, as you write your own report, choose research methods and writing strategies that fit your rhetorical situation: your audience, your purpose, and your subject.

CONTENTS

Report Writing

21 Interview Report ————————————————————————————

   Overview: Writing an Interview Report   **332**
      Student Model   **333**
   Guidelines   **336**
   Writing Checklist and Activities   **338**

22 Lab, Experiment, and Field Reports ——————————————————

   Overview: Writing Lab, Experiment, and Field Reports   **340**
      Student Models   **341**
      Professional Model   **347**
   Guidelines   **350**
   Writing Checklist and Activities   **352**

INTERVIEW REPORT

Audio

Video

The idea of an interview is simple. You talk with someone—an expert on a topic, a client, or a case-study subject—to gain insights into the topic and/or person. As a question-and-answer session, an interview can generate primary information to supplement other research, or it can provide the information and focus for an entire piece of writing such as an interview report.

The idea of an interview may be simple, but conducting a good interview and writing a good report can be challenging. A good interview must be carefully planned and executed to become a productive conversation. Planning gives you background information and helps you develop questions that produce solid data, vivid details, and lively quotations. Poor interviewing leads to flat facts, irrelevant tangents, and bland generalities.

This chapter focuses on developing meaningful interview reports. The overview, guidelines, and model that follow will help you carry out your interviews and write your reports.

Overview
Writing an Interview Report

Writer's Goal

Your goal is to gain insights by interviewing someone and then sharing those revelations with readers. Aim to ask the right questions, record answers accurately, and report results clearly.

Keys for Success

Plan carefully. An interview needs to be properly prepared, conducted, and processed. Give yourself enough time, and respect your interviewee by being on time, efficient, informed, and courteous.

Ask clear, relevant questions. Clear questions yield useful information—insights into the topic or person that peek below the factual surface. Getting quality information depends on the art of interviewing—planning relevant questions, listening well, following up with sensible responses, and being open to surprises.

Respect the interviewee's voice. Know the person's identity, story, and values. In the interview, listen much more than you talk. In the report, present the person's words and thoughts clearly and honestly. Consider sharing the report with the interview subject before you "go public."

Analyze and synthesize the results. Analysis helps you understand pieces of information, and synthesis helps you pull together separate facts to show relationships. To write an interview report, you must both analyze and synthesize the results of your interview to discover a meaningful theme. Shape the discussion so that the report hangs together, means something, and goes somewhere.

People to Consider

Choose an interviewee from one of the following categories:

- **The expert:** Who is an authority on your topic? Could you find such an expert in your college or community, through local organizations or businesses, or on the Internet?
- **The experienced:** Who has had unique, direct experiences with the topic? Who has participated in, witnessed, or been affected by the situation?
- **The person:** If your purpose is to focus on a person rather than a topic, choose someone intriguing—someone from a particular background, generation, ethnicity, nationality, or occupation.

> **Next Step** Read the model essay and perform the activities that follow. As you read, think about the interview subject chosen and the strategies used to report on the interview. Consider how to use similar strategies.

Audio

Interview Report

Because of a disturbing childhood experience, college student Benjamin Meyer toured a funeral home and interviewed the director. In the following essay, Benjamin reports on what he learned.

The Dead Business

The writer starts with background information that creates a personal theme.

"You're going to tour a what?" *1*

"A funeral home." *2*

My friends were shocked. They laughed while describing scenes from *3* *Night of the Living Dead* and *The Shining*.

But their stories didn't frighten me—I feared something else. When I *4* was ten, my grandmother died, and my family drove to the funeral home to view the body. As we entered the place, I noticed the funeral director standing in the corner, looking like a too-eager-to-please salesman who'd made a deal he didn't deserve. The guy's thin-lipped smile seemed unnatural—almost glib. Like a ghoul in a business suit, he didn't seem to care that a stroke had stopped my grandmother's beating heart midway through the doxology that concluded the Sunday-evening church service. He didn't seem to care that she and I would share no more cookies, no more coloring books, no more Rook games, no more laughing, no more. I was ten, very sad, and he didn't seem to care.

Freely using "I," the writer tells the story of his visit and interview.

Now a college student, I wanted to tour a different funeral home to *5* work through my earlier experience. While I no longer feared ghouls, I was still nervous while driving to the Vander Ploeg Furniture Store/Funeral Home. I remembered the thin-lipped smile.

I walked inside not knowing what to expect. Suddenly, a man *6* from behind a desk hopped out of his chair and said, "Hi, I'm Howard Beernink."

I looked at the tall, smiling guy, paused a moment, and glanced back *7* at the door. His partner had stepped in front of the exit while scribbling on tags that dangled from Lazy Boy rockers. I realized that this interview was something I had to do . . . like getting a tetanus shot.

He describes the setting.

Howard led me into a room full of furniture where he found a soft, *8* purple couch. We sat down, and he described how the business started.

He relates the early history of the business.

In 1892, pioneers established the town of Sioux Center, Iowa. Winter *9* storms and disease pummeled the tiny community, and soon residents needed someone to bury the dead. A funeral director wasn't available, but a furniture maker was. The furniture maker was the only person with the tools, hardwood, and knowledge to build coffins. As a result, the Vander Ploeg Furniture Store/Funeral Home was born.

The writer summarizes, paraphrases, and quotes from the interview.

Today, starting a funeral home isn't that easy. For example, a funeral home requires the services of an embalmer, and an embalmer must be certified by the state. To get a certificate, the person must complete two years of college, one year of embalming school, and one year of apprentice work. After that, the individual must pass a state exam every year to retain certification. *10*

"But why a funeral home director?" I was baffled. Why would anyone embalm dead bodies for a living? *11*

"Because it's a family business." Howard smiled as if he expected my question. "Vander Ploegs and Beerninks have run this place for generations. Today it's difficult to start a funeral home because there are so many of them with long histories and good reputations." *12*

After he answered the rest of my questions, Howard asked if I wanted to see the embalming room. *13*

He narrates what happened during the interview.

"Okay," I said, tentatively. *14*

He led me through doors, down hallways, up a staircase, and into a well-lighted display room containing several coffins. Finally, we entered a small, cold room containing a row of cupboards, a large ceramic table, and a small machine that resembled a bottled-water cooler. *15*

"We like to keep the room cold when we're not using it," Howard said. *16*

"What is all this stuff?" I asked. *17*

Howard described why embalming is done and what it involves. The purpose of embalming is to extend the period for viewing the body, and the process includes replacing body fluids with embalming fluid. He opened a cupboard, pulled out a bottle of fluid and said, "Here . . . smell." *18*

The writer shares surprises and what he learned.

"Smells like Pepto-Bismol," I replied. *19*

After he embalms the body, Howard applies makeup so the face appears "more natural." He gets his cosmetics (common powders and tints) from the local Avon lady. *20*

"But sometimes we also have to use this," Howard said, pulling out another bottle. *21*

"Tissue builder?" I asked, squinting at the label. *22*

"It's like silicon implants," he answered. "We inject it into sunken cheeks, like the cheeks of cancer victims." *23*

When the body is ready for burial, the funeral director must show a price list to the family of the deceased. The Funeral Rule, adopted in 1984 by the Federal Trade Commission, requires that a price list be shown to the family before they see caskets, cement boxes, and vaults. The purpose of the Funeral Rule is to prevent unethical funeral directors from manipulating customers with comments like, "But that's a pauper's casket; you don't want to bury your mother in that. Bury her in this beauty over here." *24*

Unfortunately, only a third of the country's 22,000 funeral homes abide by the Funeral Rule.

"After showing customers where the caskets are, I step away so they can talk among themselves," said Howard. "It's unethical to bother the family at this difficult time."   *25*

Before burying a casket, Howard and his partner place it in either a cement box or a vault. A cement box is a container that's neither sealed nor waterproofed, whereas a vault is both sealed and waterproofed. Howard explained, "Years ago, cemeteries began to sink and cave in on spots, so state authorities demanded containers. Containers make the cemetery look nicer."   *26*

After the tour, I asked Howard, "How has this job affected your life?"   *27*

He glanced at the ceiling, smiled, and said, "It's very fulfilling. My partner and I comfort people during a stressful time in their lives, and it strengthens our bond with them."   *28*

As I drove back to the college, I thought again about Howard's comment, and about my childhood fear. Howard was right. He doesn't exploit people. Instead, he comforts them and helps them move on. And while I still fear the pain of saying good-bye to someone I love, I don't fear funeral directors anymore. They're just people who provide services that a community needs. ■   *29*

> **He ends the report with a strong quotation and personal reflection.**

Reading for Better Writing

Working by yourself or with a group, answer these questions:

1. This report centers on the writer's own story, reflections, and needs. Discuss how these elements are woven into the report. Are they effective? Why or why not?

2. Examine the opening and the closing of the essay. Do they work well together? Do they effectively share a theme for the report? Explain.

3. Describe how the writer organizes the interview's results. Is the organization effective? Explain.

4. Look carefully at the writer's use of summary and paraphrase on the one hand and quotation on the other hand. Are the strategies effective? Explain.

Model

Guidelines
Writing an Interview Report

1. **Choose a person to interview.** Review "People to Consider" on page 332 to find an interviewee. Also consider a community or campus leader.

2. **Plan the interview.** As soon as possible, take care of the details:
    *   Determine your goal—what you want the interview to accomplish and what information and insights you want to gather.
    *   Choose a sensible recording method (pen and paper, recorder) and a medium (face-to-face, telephone, e-mail).
    *   Consider what you know about the topic and the interviewee. Then figure out what you must know to ask meaningful questions. If necessary, do some research on the interview subject.
    *   Contact the interviewee and politely request an interview. Explain who you are, why you need the interview, and how you will use it. Schedule a time and place convenient for the interviewee. If you wish to record the interview, ask permission.
    *   Gather and test tools and equipment: a notebook, pens, and perhaps recording equipment (tape, video, digital camera).

3. **Prepare questions.** Do the following to help you structure the interview:
    *   Consider types of questions to ask—the five *W*'s and *H* (*who, what, when, where, why,* and *how*).
    *   Understand open and closed questions. Closed questions ask for simple, factual answers; open questions ask for detailed explanations.
        Closed: How many months did you spend in Vietnam?
        Open: Can you describe your most vivid memory of Vietnam?
    *   Avoid slanted questions that pressure a person to give a specific answer.
        Slanted: Aren't you really angry that draft dodgers didn't do their duty?
        Neutral: How do you feel about those who avoided the draft?
    *   Think about specific topics to cover and write questions for each one. Start with a simple question that establishes rapport and groundwork. Plan target questions—ones that you must ask.
    *   Put questions on the left side of the page with room for notes on the right. Rehearse your questions, visualizing how the interview should go.

4. **Conduct the interview.** Arrive on time and be professional:
    *   Introduce yourself, reminding the interviewee why you've come.
    *   If you have permission to record the interview, set up equipment off to the side so that it doesn't interfere with the conversation. However, even if you're recording, take notes on key facts and quotations.

- Listen actively by including nods and eye contact. Pay attention to the interviewee's body language.
- Be flexible. If the person looks puzzled by a question, rephrase it or ask another. Ask one of these questions if an answer needs to be amplified:

    Clarifying: "Do you mean this or that?"
    Explanatory: "What do you mean by that?"
    Detailing: "What happened exactly? Can you describe that?"
    Analytical: "What were the causes? The outcomes?"
    Probing: "What do you think that meant?"
    Comparative: "Did that remind you of anything?"
    Contextual: "What else was going on then? Who else was involved?"
    Summarizing: "Overall, what was your response? What was the net effect?"

- Be tactful. If the person avoids a question, politely rephrase it. Don't react negatively or forcefully invade the interviewee's private territory.
- Listen "between the lines" for what the interviewee seems to want to say.
- Expect important points to come up late in the interview, and give the interviewee a chance to add any final thoughts.

5. **Follow up.** As soon as possible, review your notes and fill in the blanks. By phone or in writing, clarify points and thank the interviewee.

6. **Organize and draft the report.** Shape the opening to seize interest, the middle to sustain interest, and the closing to reward interest:
   - Analyze and interpret the interview results. Locate the heart or theme of your report, and then develop an outline supporting the theme.
   - Start with background, along with a point that grabs readers' interest.
   - Summarize and paraphrase material from the interview. (See pages 442–444.) Use quotations selectively to share the interviewee's character or stress a point.
   - If appropriate, weave your thoughts and reflections into the report.

7. **Get feedback and revise the report.** Ask someone to answer these questions: Does the report supply complete, satisfying insights? Is the organization effective, with an engaging opening and closing? Is the writing lively, fair, and respectful?

8. **Edit and proofread.** Review your report for precise word choice, smooth sentences, and correct grammar. In particular, make sure that quotations are integrated smoothly. (See page 487.)

9. **Prepare a final copy.** Submit a clean copy to your instructor (and perhaps the interviewee), but also look for ways to publish your report—as a webpage with digital photos and sound clips, or as a presentation for classmates.

Writing Checklist

Use these seven traits to check the quality of your writing; then revise as needed:

_____ The **ideas** share the heart of the interview—the interviewee's insights—through summary, paraphrase, and quotation.

_____ The **organization** centers on a theme and then creates, sustains, and rewards interest.

_____ The **voice** sounds genuine and interested. The interviewee's voice is understood and respected.

_____ The **words** are precise and understandable. Quotations reflect the interviewee's ideas and personality.

_____ The **sentences** are smooth, with quotations effectively integrated. Transitional words link sentences and sections.

_____ The **copy** has no errors in grammar, punctuation, usage, and spelling.

_____ The **design** is attractive, features the text, and uses photographs or graphics effectively.

Critical-Thinking and Writing Activities

As directed by your instructor, complete the following activities.

1. Generate a list of people who understand the challenges and opportunities related to the career you want to pursue. Then follow the guidelines for a personal interview on page **332** and write a report.

2. "The Dead Business" recounts the writer's exploration of a topic that caused him discomfort and sadness. What similar issues affect you? Would an interview help you work through the issue? Write your own reflective interview report.

3. Do you know someone who has led a fascinating life? Someone who on the surface seems to have led an ordinary life? Someone serving others in inspiring ways? Write that person's life story—an extended biography.

4. Is there a particular issue in your community that concerns you—a public debate, a college problem, a program being cut back? Who has insights into the issue? Who are people on different sides? Whose lives are affected? Who has the power to change things? Select one or more people to interview, and then write a report on the issue.

◀ VISUALLY SPEAKING

Award-winning CBS correspondent Ed Bradley is shown on page **331**. What does the picture suggest about his understanding of journalism and the interview process?

LAB, EXPERIMENT, AND FIELD REPORTS

22

Good science writing is rooted in good science—the careful study of phenomena through observation and experiment. Social scientists seek to understand human behavior and societies, whereas natural scientists investigate the physical world.

Audio

Video

As a student, you may be asked to conduct scientific research in a range of courses. In labs and in the field, you may perform experiments, gather data, and interpret results, and then share your insights with fellow students and members of the scientific community. Such experiences provide valuable preparation for a variety of careers in the sciences.

When you complete a scientific study, you share your research story. Whether you are studying the nature of hydrochloric acid or the factors affecting fermentation rates in ethanol, your report shares what you did, why you did it, and what you learned. This chapter will help you put your experiments and field research into writing—and your good writing into science.

Web Link

Overview
Writing Lab, Experiment, and Field Reports

Writer's Goal

Your goal is to accurately record and thoughtfully interpret the results of a scientific study or experiment so clearly that others could repeat your experiment.

Keys for Success

Follow the scientific method. Science focuses on measured observations aimed at understanding. Experiments are set up to test hypotheses about why things happen. However, experiments don't prove hypotheses correct: Experimental results can merely "agree with" or disprove a hypothesis. Overall, the method moves from observation to explanation as you do the following:

1. Observe something interesting (often while looking for something else).
2. Check whether other scientists have explained the same observation.
3. Summarize your observations and turn that generalization into a testable hypothesis—a working theory explaining the phenomenon.
4. Design research to test the hypothesis, paying attention to variables and controls.
5. Based on the results of your experiment, accept, reject, or modify your hypothesis.
6. Repeat steps 3 through 5 until you understand the phenomenon. Then write up your research so that others can respond to your work.

Follow the standard format. To model scientific thinking, lab and field reports include an introduction establishing the problem, a methods section detailing procedures, a results section providing the data, and a discussion that interprets the data.

Distinctions to Consider

Whatever your assignment, you need to understand these distinctions:

- **Distinguish facts from possibilities.** Facts are the data you collect. Possibilities are your interpretations of the data. Don't confuse the two.
- **Distinguish experiments from studies.** Experiments test hypotheses by manipulating variables. Studies observe what's there—by counting, measuring, sampling, and so on. In this chapter, the report on fermentation is an experiment, whereas the field report on cockroaches is a study.

> **Next Step** Read the model reports and perform the activities that follow. As you read, examine how the reports follow the scientific method so you can use that method in your own reports.

Lab Report

Student Coby Williams wrote the basic lab report below to describe a chemical compound and inform readers about its nature.

Audio

Working with Hydrochloric Acid

The writer identifies the chemical compound and states its nature.

Overview and Purpose   *1*

The goal in writing this report is to educate others on the dangers of using and storing hydrochloric acid in the lab (HCl) and in the home (muriatic acid). In addition, this report will list appropriate ways to protect against burns when using HCl as well as ways to dispose of it properly.

Characteristics   *2*

Hydrochloric acid (HCl), which is made from hydrogen gas and chlorine gas, is a clear, colorless to slightly yellow, fuming liquid with a sharp, irritating odor. HCl is a strong, highly corrosive acid, soluble in water and alcohol. Other characteristics include the following:

✔ The chemical reaction is: $H_2 + Cl_2 = 2HCl$.

✔ Its molecular weight is 36.45.

✔ Its boiling point is 85°C.

✔ Its specific gravity is 1.16.

Hydrochloric acid is commercially known as muriatic acid, a substance used to   *3*
manufacture dyes and plastics or to acidize (activate) petroleum wells. It is also used in the food processing of corn, syrup, and sodium glutamate, and is an ingredient in many household and industrial cleaners.

Safety Procedures   *4*

Hydrochloric acid is highly corrosive and can severely burn skin. Whenever HCl is used, it must be handled according to the following precautions:

Storage   *5*

• Keep hydrochloric acid in tightly capped bottles back from the edge of the shelf or table.

• Keep bottles away from metals. Contact will corrode metals and could release hydrogen gas, which is highly explosive.

He organizes details in distinct categories.

Protection   *6*

• Always wear safety glasses to protect your eyes.

• Wear latex gloves and old clothes when using concentrated HCl—not short-sleeved shirts, shorts, or sandals.

• Do not breathe the fumes, which can cause fainting.

• If acid spills on skin or splashes in someone's eyes, rinse the area with water for five minutes. Treat burns appropriately. In each case, get medical help immediately.

Usage   7

In the lab, hydrochloric acid is either diluted or titrated.

Information is accurate and terms are precise.

• When diluting, always pour the acid into the water. Doing the reverse can cause boiling, splashing, and burning.
• When titrating, carefully measure the HCl needed. Then react the HCl with a sample that has a base such as sodium hydroxide to get an accurate measurement of the base in the sample.

Disposal   8

• To dispose of HCl, neutralize it by mixing the acid with a sodium-hydroxide solution. Flush the neutralized solution down the drain.
• If you spill HCl, cover the spill with baking soda. After the fizzing stops, sweep up the soda and flush it down the drain. ■

Reading for Better Writing

Working by yourself or with a group, answer these questions:

1. Who would be the main audience for this type of report? What evidence can you point to that supports your analysis?

2. List the strategies used to organize the report. Are these strategies effective? Explain.

3. How does this report demonstrate scientific thinking?

Experiment Report

In this report, student writer Andrea Pizano shares the results of a lab experiment she completed to explore how different factors affect fermentation.

The Effects of Temperature and Inhibitors on the Fermentation Process for Ethanol

Andrea Pizano
January 29, 2008

Introduction

The opening creates context and explains concepts.

Alcoholic liquids were made and used for centuries before scientists   *1*
fully understood the process by which alcohol developed. An Egyptian papyrus dated 3500 B.C.E. mentions wine making, although production of alcoholic spirits like gin and brandy started only about a thousand years ago. From beverages such as beer and wine to fuel additives such as ethanol, alcohol has been used by people for recreation, religious rites, medical purposes, energy, and industry. Even today people are surprised to learn that it is ethanol—a by-product of yeast growth—that makes bread smell good. Studying the process by which alcohol is made can help make the process more efficient and successful.

Generally, alcohol can be made by fermenting different types of sugars,   *2*
including sucrose, glucose, and fructose. Fermentation is a process that creates heat and changes the properties of a substance through a leavening or fermenting agent. For the fermentation process to succeed, certain enzymes must function as catalysts. These enzymes are present in yeast, the fermenting agent. While useful as catalysts, these enzymes are sensitive to temperature changes and inhibitors.

The writer describes the experiment and states her hypotheses.

In this experiment, ethanol—a specific type of alcohol—was   *3*
synthesized from sucrose in the presence of yeast. The effects of extreme temperatures and of inhibitors on the rate of fermentation were tested quantitatively. The factors below were tested, and the outcomes below were anticipated. First, extremely high temperatures denature enzymes. Therefore, fermentation in the sample was expected to stop. Second, extremely cool temperatures reduce the kinetic energy of molecules. Therefore, the reaction rate in the sample was expected to drastically slow. Third, sodium fluoride can inhibit one of the enzymes needed in the fermentation process. Therefore, the presence of sodium fluoride was expected to effectively stop the reaction. Fourth, normal fermentation usually delivers a maximum of up to 15% ethanol. Through distillation, a 95% concentration of ethanol can be obtained. However, the presence of concentrated ethanol kills the yeast cells and also acts as a negative feedback

mechanism to the enzymes necessary for the fermentation process. Therefore, concentrated ethanol was expected to effectively stop the reaction.

Method

To test each of these hypotheses, the following procedure was followed in this experiment:

1. 200 mg of yeast were mixed with 1.25 mL of warm water in a 5-mL round-bottomed, long-necked flask. The mixture was shaken until the yeast was well distributed.

2. 9 mg of disodium hydrogen phosphate, 1.30 g sucrose, and 3.75 mL warm water were added to the flask. This mixture was left for 15 minutes—until the fermentation was proceeding at a vigorous rate.

3. The fermentation mixture was then divided equally into 5 reaction tubes.
   - To tube 1, 1.0 mL of water was added.
   - To tube 2, 1.0 mL of 95% ethanol was added.
   - To tube 3, 1.0 mL of 0.5 M sodium fluoride solution was added.
   - To each of tubes 4 and 5, 1.0 mL of water was added.

4. The bubbles produced in a reaction tube filled with water were counted. A septum was first fit over the neck of each reaction tube. Then some polyethylene tubing was connected from the septum to the water-filled reaction tube. In this way, the reaction rate could be quantitatively measured by counting the number of gas bubbles that were released into the water each minute for 5 minutes.

5. Test tube 4 was heated for 5 minutes in boiling water. Then it was cooled to room temperature, and the fermentation rate was measured as explained in step 4.

6. Test tube 5 was put on ice for 5 minutes, and then the fermentation rate was measured as explained in step 4, while the reaction tube was kept on ice to maintain the low temperature.

7. After the experiment was completed, the solutions were washed down the drain as waste.

She details the procedure using numbered steps and precise terms.

The writer uses passive voice to focus on the action and receiver—not the person doing the action.

Results

The reaction rates of the 5 reaction conditions are plotted on Figure   5
1 below.

The results are displayed in a line graph and then summarized.

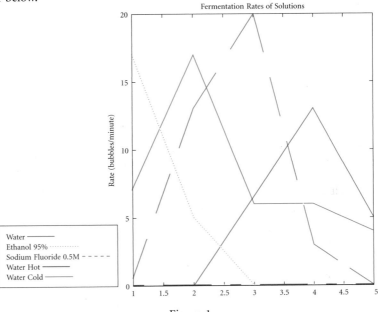

Figure 1

With the sample containing water at room temperature, the fermentation   6
rate peaked at 13 bubbles/minute at minute 4. The fermentation rate of
the sample with 95% ethanol started at 17 bubbles/minute, but within
2 minutes the rate quickly slowed to 5 bubbles/minute. By 3 minutes,
the rate was 0 bubbles/minute. In the sample with sodium fluoride, the
fermentation increased to 20 bubbles/minute after 3 minutes, but then
quickly reached 0 bubbles/minute after 5 minutes. In the sample that was
boiled, the fermentation rate was consistently 0 bubbles/minute. In the
sample placed on ice, the fermentation rate increased to 17 bubbles/minute
after 2 minutes, but then gradually slowed to 4 bubbles/minute after
5 minutes.

Discussion

The writer interprets the results for each hypothesis.

Many different factors affect fermentation rates. For example, when   7
ethanol concentration is very high, yeast usually dies. So when 95% ethanol
is added to a fermenting sugar and yeast mixture, one would expect the
fermentation rate to decline sharply. The experiment's data support this
hypothesis. After 3 minutes, the fermentation had completely stopped.

In addition, sodium fluoride inhibits the action of a specific enzyme   8
in yeast, an enzyme needed for the fermentation process. Therefore, when

sodium fluoride is added to a fermenting mixture, one would expect a halted fermentation rate. However, the reaction rate initially increased to 20 bubbles/minute when sodium fluoride was added. This increase may have occurred because not all of the enzymes were inhibited at first. Perhaps the fermentation rate declined to 0 bubbles/minute only when the sodium fluoride became evenly distributed. This measurement occurred after 5 minutes.

She explores possible explanations for unexpected results and suggests further research.

Temperature is a third factor affecting fermentation. On the one hand, high temperatures denature many enzymes; therefore, when a fermenting mixture is placed in boiling water for 5 minutes, one would expect the fermentation rate to stop because no enzymes are present at that point to carry out the fermentation process. This hypothesis is supported by the data, as no fermentation occurred in the hot mixture. On the other hand, cold temperatures reduce the kinetic energy of molecules. As a result, the speed decreases, and the likelihood of the enzymes making contact with the substrate decreases exponentially in relation to the temperature. One would expect that the reaction rate would slow down drastically after the mixture has been cooled. This hypothesis is somewhat supported by the data. After an initial increase in the reaction rate to 17 bubbles/minute, the reaction rate slowed to 4 bubbles/minute after 5 minutes. A repeat of the experiment would be needed to clarify this result. Moreover, because the measuring method was somewhat unsophisticated (as indicated by the spikes in the line graph), perhaps a new experiment could be designed to measure fermentation-rate changes more sensitively.

9

The closing summarizes the experiment's value.

This experiment helped quantify the effects that various factors such as temperature, inhibitors, and high ethanol concentration have on fermentation rates. Even though the measuring apparatus was fairly basic, the experiment largely supported the hypotheses. Such data are helpful for determining methods of efficient and successful fermentation. Further research testing other factors and other inhibitors would add to this knowledge. ■

10

Reading for Better Writing

Working by yourself or with a group, answer these questions:

1. Where does the writer discuss the experiment's purpose and value? Are her efforts convincing?

2. In the "Method" section, which strategies does the writer use to ensure that the experiment can be repeated?

3. In the "Results" section, what is the relationship between the line graph and the paragraph?

4. In the "Discussion" section, the writer addresses results that did and did not support the hypotheses. Are her interpretations and conclusions sound?

Field Report

In the following workplace report, a team of writers investigates the causes and effects of cockroach infestation in an apartment complex. In the study, they use their findings to recommend solutions.

SOMMERVILLE DEVELOPMENT CORPORATION

Date: September 20, 2008

To: Bert Richardson, VP of Tenant Relations

From: Hue Nguyen, Cherryhill Complex Manager
              Sandra Kao, Building Superintendent
              Roger Primgarr, Tenant Relations
              Juan Alexander, Tenant Representative

> The subject line functions as a title.

**Subject: Investigation of Cockroach Infestation at
5690 Cherryhill**

> The opening clarifies the study's purpose and goals.

During the month of July 2008, 26 tenants of the 400-unit building at 5690 Cherryhill informed the building superintendent that they had found cockroaches in their units. On August 8, the management-tenant committee authorized us to investigate these questions: *1*
1. How extensive is the cockroach infestation?
2. How can the cockroach population best be controlled?

We monitored this problem from August 9 to September 8, 2008. This report contains a summary, an overview of our research methods, and findings, conclusions, and recommendations.   *2*

SUMMARY

> The summary focuses on outcomes.

The 5690 Cherryhill building has a moderate infestation of German cockroaches. Only an integrated control program can manage this infestation. Pesticide fumigations address only the symptoms, not the causes. We recommend that Sommerville adopt a comprehensive program that includes (1) education, (2) cooperation, (3) habitat modification, (4) treatment, and (5) ongoing monitoring.   *3*

RESEARCH METHODS AND FINDINGS

Overview of Research

We researched the problem in the following ways: *4*

1. Contacted the Department of Agriculture, the Ecology Action Center, and Ecological Agriculture Projects.
2. Consulted three exterminators.
3. Inspected the 5690 Cherryhill building, from ground to roof.
4. Placed pheromone traps in all units to monitor the cockroach population.

Research methods are described.

The Cockroach Population

Pheromone traps revealed German cockroaches, a common variety. Of the   *5*
400 units, 112 units (28 percent) showed roaches. Based on the numbers, the infestation is rated as moderate.

Results are categorized logically.

The German Cockroach

Research shows that these roaches thrive in apartment buildings.   *6*

- Populations thrive when food, water, shelter, and migration routes are available. They prefer dark, humid conditions near food sources.
- The cockroach seeks shelter in spaces that allow its back and underside to remain in constant contact with a solid surface.

Methods of Control

Sources we consulted stressed the need for an integrated program of   *7*
cockroach control involving sanitation, habitat modification, and non-toxic treatments that attack causes. Here are the facts:

Findings are presented clearly and concisely.

- The German cockroach is immune to many chemicals.
- Roaches detect most pesticides before direct contact.
- Spot-spraying simply causes roaches to move to unsprayed units.
- Habitat modification through (1) eliminating food and water sources, (2) caulking cracks and crevices, (3) lowering humidity, and (4) increasing light and airflow makes life difficult for cockroaches.

CONCLUSIONS

Based on our findings, we conclude the following: *8*

1. A single method of treatment, especially chemical, will be ineffective.
2. A comprehensive program of sanitation, habitat modification, and nontoxic treatments will eliminate the German cockroach.

Conclusions follow logically from the findings.

RECOMMENDATIONS

Recommend-ations apply what was learned in the study.

We recommend that Sommerville Development adopt an Integrated Program of Cockroach Prevention and Control for its 5690 Cherryhill building. Management would assign the following tasks to appropriate personnel: *9*

Education: (1) Give tenants information on sanitation, prevention, and home remedies; and (2) hold tenant meetings to answer questions.   *10*

Habitat Modification: Revise the maintenance program and renovation schedule to give priority to the following: *11*

- Apply residual insecticides before sealing cracks.
- Caulk cracks and crevices (baseboards, cupboards, pipes, sinks). Insert steel wool in large cavities (plumbing, electrical columns).
- Repair leaking pipes and faucets. Insulate pipes to eliminate condensation.
- Schedule weekly cleaning of common garbage areas.

Treatment: In addition to improving sanitation and prevention through education, attack the roach population through these methods: *12*

- Use home remedies, traps, and hotels.
- Use borax or boric acid powder formulations as residual, relatively nontoxic pesticides.
- Use chemical controls on an emergency basis.
- Ensure safety by arranging for a Health Department representative to make unannounced visits to the building.

Monitoring: Monitor the cockroach population in the following ways: *13*
  1. Every six months, use traps to check on activity in all units.
  2. Keep good records on the degree of occurrence, population density, and control methods used.

The closing stresses the value and benefits of the study.

We believe that this comprehensive program will solve the cockroach problem. We recommend that Sommerville adopt this program for 5690 Cherryhill and consider implementing it in all its buildings.   *14*

Reading for Better Writing

Working by yourself or with a group, answer these questions:

1. Examine the report's format and organizational strategies. How is this workplace report similar to and different from the other lab and experiment reports in this chapter?

2. Describe the tone of the report. What does this tone accomplish?

3. This report depends extensively on cause/effect thinking. Where do the writers use cause/effect thinking, and how effective is it?

Model

Guidelines
Writing Lab, Experiment, and Field Reports

1. **Review the lab manual and any handouts.** In most science courses, studies and experiments are assigned through textbooks, manuals, and handouts. Study those materials to understand what you must do and why. Read background information on the topic in textbooks and other sources.

2. **Use a field or lab notebook.** Accurate, complete recordkeeping is crucial to doing good scientific research. Use the notebook to plan research, record what you do, collect data, make drawings, and reflect on results. For each notebook entry, record the date and your goal.

3. **Plan and complete your study or experiment.** For a productive study, do the following:
   - Develop your key research questions. If you are conducting an experiment (not just a study), then state your hypotheses and design procedures for testing them.
   - Gather the proper tools, equipment, and materials required to conduct your study.
   - Carefully conduct your tests and perform your observations.
   - Take copious notes, being especially careful to record data accurately, clearly, and completely. If helpful, use a data-collection sheet.

4. **Relying on your notebook, draft the report.** Wrestle with your data. What do they mean? Were results expected or unexpected? Which factors could explain those results? What further research might be necessary? Once you have conducted this analysis, draft parts of the report in the sequence outlined below:
   - **Methods:** Start by explaining what you did to study the topic or test the hypothesis. Supply essential details, factors, and explanations. Be so clear that someone else could repeat the steps you took.
   - **Results:** Using two strategies, present the data you collected. First, share data in graphical forms—as tables, line charts, bar graphs, photographs, and so on. While the correct design of graphics and the proper presentation of statistical data are beyond the scope of this book, follow this basic rule: Make your graphic independent of the written text by giving it a descriptive title, clear headings and labels, units of measurement, and footnotes. Readers should be able to study your graphics and see the "story" of your study. Second, draw attention to the major observations and key trends available in the data. However, do not interpret the data in your results or give your reactions to them.

- **Discussion:** Interpret the results by relating the data to your original questions and hypotheses, offering conclusions, and supporting each conclusion with details. Essentially, answer the question, "What does it all mean?" Explain which hypotheses were supported, and why. Also explore unexpected results, and suggest possible explanations. Conclude by reemphasizing the value of what you learned.

- **Introduction:** Once you have mapped out the methods, results, and discussion, write an introduction that creates a framework for the report. Explain why you undertook the study, provide background information and any needed definitions, and raise your key questions and/or hypotheses.

- **Summary or abstract:** If required, write a summary of your study's purpose, methods, results, and conclusions. An abstract is a one-paragraph summary that allows readers to (1) get the report in a nutshell and (2) determine whether or not to read the study.

- **Title:** Develop a precise title that captures the "story" of your study. Worry less about the length of the title and more about its clarity.

- **Front and end matter:** If so required, add a title page, references page, and appendixes.

5. **Share and revise the draft.** Once you have roughed out the report, show it to a peer or a tutor in the writing center. Ask these questions:
   - Are the report's purpose, hypotheses, conclusions, and support clear and complete?
   - Is the traditional structure of a lab or field report followed effectively?
   - Is the voice objective, curious, and informed?

6. **Edit and proofread.** Carefully examine the style of your report, checking for these conventions of science writing:
   - **Measured use of passive voice:** Generally, use the passive voice only when needed—usually to keep the focus on the action and the receiver, not the actor. (See page 80.)
   - **Past and present tenses of verbs:** Generally, use the past tense in your report. However, present tense may be appropriate when discussing published work, established theories, and your conclusions.
   - **Objectivity:** Make sure that your writing is precise (not ambiguous), specific (not vague), and concise (not wordy).
   - **Mechanics:** Follow the conventions in the discipline with respect to capitalization, abbreviations, numbers, and symbols.

7. **Prepare and share your report.** Following the format and documentation conventions of the discipline, submit a polished report to your instructor. Also find ways to share your study with the scientific community.

Writing Checklist

Use these seven traits to check your report; then revise as needed:

_____ The **ideas** provide scientifically sound conclusions about accurate data.

_____ The **organization** effectively follows the standard structure: introduction, methods, results, and discussion.

_____ The **voice** demonstrates interest and curiosity, yet remains objective.

_____ The **words** are used accurately. The language of the specific discipline is used precisely.

_____ The **sentences** flow smoothly from point to point. Passive voice constructions are used only when necessary.

_____ The **copy** has no errors in grammar, punctuation, usage, and spelling.

_____ The **design's** use of headings, white space, and graphics feature or clarify the message.

Critical-Thinking and Writing Activities

As directed by your instructor, complete the following activities.

1. The report on hydrochloric acid describes a chemical compound. In your discipline, what are the main objects of study? Write a report that introduces that topic to students new to the discipline.

2. The lab experiment report on fermentation describes careful research that should be repeatable. With appropriate supervision, repeat the lab experiment and compare your results with the student writer's results.

3. The field report objectively researches the problem of cockroach infestation. Which campus or community problems could you research in a similar manner? Develop a research plan, get approval from your instructor, and complete your study.

4. Which issues, problems, or puzzles exist in your area of study? With help from an instructor in your major, write a proposal to conduct a lab experiment or field research.

◄ VISUALLY SPEAKING

Study the graph on page **345** and explain how it clarifies the report's message. Then review the field report on pages **347–349** and suggest visual elements (e.g., graphs, photographs) that might help communicate its message.

SPECIAL FORMS OF WRITING

Chapters 23 through 27 focus on special writing occasions—or rhetorical situations. These chapters explain how to develop a variety of writing forms: a literary analysis, an essay test, a resumé, a webpage, and an oral presentation.

As you read the model pieces, note each writer's strategies for organizing and presenting her or his message. Analyze how and why those strategies are (or are not) effective for the writer's audience, purpose, and subject. Then consider how you might address a similar writing situation.

CONTENTS

Special Forms of Writing

23 Writing About Literature and the Arts

Overview: Writing About Literature and the Arts	356
Student Models	357
Guidelines	366
Literary Terms	368
Poetry Terms	371
Writing Checklist and Activities	372

24 Taking Essay Tests

Reviewing for Tests	374
Forming a Study Group	375
Using Mnemonics and Other Memory Guides	376
Taking the Essay Test	377
Writing Under Pressure: The Essay Test Quick Guide	382
Taking an Objective Test	383

25 Writing for the Workplace

Writing the Business Letter	386
Writing Memos and E-mail	388
Applying for a Job	390
Preparing a Resumé	394

26 Writing and Designing for the Web

Webpage Elements and Functions	398
Developing a Website and Webpages	400
Writing for Different Internet Environments	407
Writing Checklist and Activities	408

27 Preparing Oral Presentations

Organizing Your Presentation	410
Writing Your Presentation	413
Student Model	414
Developing Computer Presentations	417
Checklist: Overcoming Stage Fright	418

WRITING ABOUT LITERATURE AND THE ARTS

23

In one way or another, people respond to the arts. Audiences may applaud a dancer, gripe about a film or play, or give a standing ovation to a musician. Often writers are moved to respond even more precisely, by analyzing one actor's portrayal while criticizing another's performance, or by praising a film's script but questioning camera angles or lighting.

Audio

Video

Because the arts are complex, writing about them requires careful listening, reading, and/or viewing. For example, you might analyze a film or play in terms of the acting, the casting, or the directing. Similarly, you might analyze a poem or story by looking at its form, its diction, or the insights it provides. In other words, to write effectively about the arts, you need a good ear, a keen eye, and an open mind.

This chapter includes model essays, guidelines, literary terms, and assignments to help you evaluate a variety of art forms.

Web Link

Overview
Writing About Literature and the Arts

Writer's Goal

Your goal is to experience an artwork or a performance, understand its elements, and then write an essay analyzing and perhaps evaluating the work.

Keys for Success

Know your subject. Read the poem, view the film or painting, or listen to the concert more than once, if possible. Be sure you understand what the artist/ writer is trying to do, noting specific choices and their effects.

Analyze the work's key elements. In works of fiction, for example, consider issues of point of view, plot, character, setting, and theme. (See the list of literary terms on pages 368–370 for other elements to think about.)

Compare it. If this work of art reminds you of some other piece, review the second work and note similarities and differences.

Form your own insights and opinions. If others have written about this work of art, do not read what they wrote until you have experienced the work yourself and developed your own insights and opinions.

Topics to Consider

Choose a piece of literature, a film, a concert, or a play that has meaning for you or has aroused your curiosity.

- **Poems:** You could choose one of thousands of great poems from literature or poetry anthologies. Poems from literary magazines, college classmates, relatives, or a website may also be analyzed if they merit your time and your readers' attention.
- **Short stories:** Like poems, short stories from literature anthologies, literary or popular magazines, or websites are easy to access.
- **Films:** While you could write about a current big-name film, consider analyzing a classic film or a film never shown in your area theaters. Choosing a film on video will enable you to replay the entire film or just specific scenes.
- **Concerts:** You could write about a major concert in your city or on campus, but consider analyzing the music played by lesser-known artists performing in student recitals or backstreet theaters.
- **Plays:** Any play may invite an analysis (big-name touring shows, for instance), but consider writing about campus productions or plays staged in your community. You might also analyze a play based on your reading of it.

Next Step Read the model essays and perform the activities that follow, noting strategies that help you understand an artwork and write about it.

Writing About a Short Story

In the essay below, student writer Anya Terekhina analyzes the characters and ideas in Flannery O'Connor's short story "Good Country People."

"Good Country People": Broken Body, Broken Soul

The writer provides background for understanding the characters in O'Connor's stories.

Flannery O'Connor's short stories are filled with characters who are bizarre, freakish, devious, and sometimes even murderous. Every short story, according to O'Connor in *Mystery and Manners: Occasional Prose*, should be "long in depth" and meaning (94). To achieve this, O'Connor develops characters with heavily symbolic attributes and flaws, and "it is clearly evident that boldly outlined inner compulsions are reinforced dramatically by a mutilated exterior self" (Muller 22). In "Good Country People," Joy-Hulga is a typical O'Connor character—grotesque yet real. Her realness comes from her many flaws and, ironically, her flaws are a self-constructed set of illusions. Throughout the story, O'Connor carefully links Joy-Hulga's physical impairments with deeper handicaps of the soul; then, at the closing, she strips Hulga of these physical flaws while helping her realize that her corresponding beliefs are flawed as well.

O'Connor first introduces her character as Joy Hopewell, a name of optimism. However, we soon understand that her chosen name, Hulga, is more fitting. The new name distresses her mother, Mrs. Hopewell, who is "certain that she [Joy] had thought and thought until she had hit upon the ugliest name in any language" (O'Connor 1943). Hulga has connotations of "hull = hulk = huge = ugly" (Grimshaw 51), and all of these are accurate descriptions of her. Far from having a sweet temperament, Hulga stomps and sulks around the farm, "constant outrage . . . [purging] every expression from her face" (1942).

Although Hulga's demeanor could be blamed on her physical impairments, she devises her own rationalizations for behaving as she does. Ironically, each rationale is symbolized by one of her physical disabilities, yet she doesn't recognize the handicaps for what they imply.

The writer begins listing the protagonist's physical disabilities and explains how each one symbolizes a deeper problem in her soul.

One of Hulga's many ailments is her weak heart, which will likely limit her life span. Hulga blames this affliction for keeping her on the Hopewell farm, making it plain that "if it had not been for this condition, she would be far from these red hills and good country people" (1944). Having a Ph.D. in philosophy, Hulga claims to want work as a university professor, lecturing to people at her intellectual level. Hulga's weak heart functions as more than a dream-crusher; it "symbolizes her emotional detachment—and inability to love anyone or anything" (Oliver 233). She exhibits no compassion or love for anything, not even "dogs or cats or birds or flowers or nature or nice young men" (1944–45).

Hulga also suffers from poor vision. Without her eyeglasses, she is   5
helpless. Strangely though, her icy blue eyes have a "look of someone who
has achieved blindness by an act of will and means to keep it" (1942). Her
self-induced blindness symbolizes her blindness to reality. She is indeed
intelligent, but she has packed her brain full of ideas and thoughts that
only obscure common sense, let alone truth. Because of Hulga's extensive
education and her focus on philosophical reasoning, she considers herself
superior to everyone around her. For example, she yells at her mother,
"Woman! . . . Do you ever look inside and see what you are not? God!"
(1944).

Hulga's last and most noticeable physical impairment is her missing leg,   6
which was "literally blasted off" (1944) in a hunting accident when she was
ten years old. In *Mystery and Manners,* O'Connor stresses that the wooden
leg operates interdependently at a literal and a symbolic level, which means
"the wooden leg continues to accumulate meaning" throughout the story
(99). Hulga's biggest physical handicap symbolizes her deepest affliction:
her belief in nothing.

> **She points out the root of the protagonist's problems: her lack of belief in anything.**

Hulga's philosophical studies did focus   7
on the study of nothing, particularly on the
arguments of the French philosopher Nicolas
Malebranche. O'Connor describes Hulga as
believing "in nothing but her own belief in
nothing" (*Mystery* 99). Over time, Hulga's
belief in nothing develops into more than just
academic study. Her nihilism becomes her
religion—suitable for a woman who considers
herself superior and despises platitudes. As she
explains to Manley Pointer, "We are all damned
. . . but some of us have taken off our blindfolds
and see that there's nothing to see. It's a kind
of salvation" (1952). Hulga's religious terms
suggest that she uses faith in nothingness to
find the meaning that she can't find elsewhere.

Her nihilism becomes her religion—suitable for a woman who considers herself superior and despises platitudes.

Hulga's nihilism is symbolized by her wooden leg, which is the only   8
thing she tends to with care: "She took care of it as someone else would
his soul, in private and almost with her own eyes turned away" (1953).
This limb is wooden and corresponds to Hulga's wooden soul. Whereas she
believes she worships Nothing, what she actually worships is an "artificial
leg and an artificial belief" (Oliver 235).

> **The writer demonstrates how the protagonist's flaws lead her to make distorted judgments.**

Not realizing that her false leg and false religion cripple her both   9
physically and spiritually, Hulga considers seducing Manley Pointer, the
Bible salesman. She delightfully imagines that she will have to help him deal
with his subsequent remorse, and then she will instruct him into a "deeper
understanding of life" (1950). Of course, her intellectual blindness keeps

her from realizing that her superiority is only an illusion. Instead, she views Manley as "a vulnerable innocent, a naïve Fundamentalist, and she wishes to seduce him to prove that her sophisticated textbook nihilism is superior to his simpleminded faith" (Di Renzo 76).

In classic O'Connor fashion, the characters and situation reverse *10* dramatically at the end of the story. Hulga and Manley are alone in a hayloft and begin embracing. At first, Hulga is pleased with her reaction to kissing as it aligns well with Malebranche's teachings: "it was an unexceptional experience and all a matter of the mind's control" (1951). Soon, however, she realizes that she is enjoying the first human connection of her life. At this point, the *innocent* Bible salesman has already stripped Hulga of her first physical impairment: her weak heart.

> **She revisits the protagonist's physical disabilities, showing how the Bible salesman exploits each one.**

Hulga hardly notices when Manley takes advantage of her next impairment: "when her glasses got in his way, he took them off of her and slipped them into his pocket" (1952). With her heart opened and her intellectual perspective fuzzy, Hulga swiftly descends into what she despises—platitudes. Hulga and Manley exchange clichéd mumblings of love, and this leads Manley to ask if he can remove her artificial leg. After brief hesitation, Hulga agrees because she feels he has touched and understood a central truth inside her. She considers it a complete surrender, "like losing her own life and finding it again, miraculously, in his" (1953).

> *With her heart opened and her intellectual perspective fuzzy, Hulga swiftly descends into what she despises— platitudes.*

11

As soon as the artificial leg is off, Manley *12* whips out one of his Bibles, which is hollow. Inside are whiskey, obscene playing cards, and contraceptives. In only moments, Hulga loses control: As each of her physical handicaps is exploited, pieces of her world view crumble, leaving her confused and weak.

> **The writer reflects on the change in both characters.**

In an ironic reversal, Hulga becomes the naïf and Manley becomes the *13* cynic. Hulga pleads in disbelief, "Aren't you . . . just good country people?" (1954). She knows that she has reverted to her mother's platitudes: "If the language is more sophisticated than any at Mrs. Hopewell's command, it is no less trite, and the smug self-deception underlying it . . . is, if anything, greater" (Asals 105). Manley assumes a startling, haughty air, exclaiming, "'I hope you don't think . . . that I believe in that crap! I may sell Bibles but I know which end is up and I wasn't born yesterday and I know where I'm going!'" (1954). Although they exchange roles, both characters use clichés to express their immature, yet authentic, worldviews.

Manley runs off with Hulga's wooden leg, leaving her vulnerable and   *14*
dependent, two things she previously despised. But "Hulga's artificial self—
her mental fantasy of her own perfection—has gone out the door with her
artificial limb. She is stuck in the hayloft with her actual self, her body, her
physical and emotional incompleteness" (Di Renzo 79).   *15*

In one brief morning of delusional seduction, Hulga learns more about
herself and her world than she learned in all her years of university. Forced
to acknowledge her physical, emotional, and spiritual disabilities, Hulga
begins to realize what she is not—neither a wise intellectual for whom there
is *hope*, nor "good country people" who merely *hope well*. ◼

> The closing explains how Hulga finally acknowledges the truth about herself.

Note: The Works Cited page is not shown. For sample pages, see MLA (pages
532–533) and APA (page **564**).

Reading for Better Writing

Working by yourself or with a group, answer these questions:

1. In her opening paragraph, Terekhina cites Flannery O'Connor's view
that every short story should be "long in depth" and meaning. Does
Terekhina adequately explore that depth and meaning? Why?

2. In her second paragraph, Terekhina analyzes Hulga Hopewell's first
name; in the last paragraph, she comments on the last name. Does
Terekhina's attention to names help you understand Hulga's character
and the story's themes? How?

3. A writer's thesis is a type of "contract" that he or she makes with
readers, spelling out what the essay will do. Review Terekhina's thesis
(last sentence, first paragraph) and assess how effectively she fulfills that
contract. Cite supporting details.

4. Flannery O'Connor has received strong acclaim for her clearly
developed, complex characters. Does Terekhina adequately explore that
complexity? Explain.

5. Many praise O'Connor for the challenging philosophical or ethical
questions raised in her fiction. What questions does Terekhina identify
in "Good Country People," and does she effectively discuss them?

6. What does Terekhina say about the story's plot, symbols, and diction?
Does she effectively analyze these elements? Why?

Audio

Writing About a Poem

In the essay on the following two pages, student writer Sherry Van Egdom analyzes the form and meaning of the poem below, "Let Evening Come," by American poet Jane Kenyon. Born in 1947 and raised on a farm near Ann Arbor, Michigan, Kenyon settled in New Hampshire at Eagle Pond Farm after she married fellow poet Donald Hall. During her life, Kenyon struggled with her faith, with depression, and with cancer. At the time of her death in 1995 from leukemia, she was the poet laureate of New Hampshire.

Before you read the student writer's analysis, read the poem aloud to enjoy its sounds, rhythm, images, diction, and comparisons. Then read the piece again to grasp more fully how the poem is structured, what it expresses, and how its ideas might relate to your life. Finally, read Van Egdom's analysis and answer the questions that follow it.

Let Evening Come

Let the light of late afternoon
Shine through chinks in the barn, moving
up the bales as the sun moves down.

Let the crickets take up chafing
as a woman takes up her needles
and her yarn. Let evening come.

Let dew collect on the hoe abandoned
in long grass. Let the stars appear
and the moon disclose her silver horn.

Let the fox go back to its sandy den.
Let the wind die down. Let the shed
go black inside. Let evening come.

To the bottle in the ditch, to the scoop
in the oats, to air in the lung
let evening come.

Let it come, as it will, and don't
be afraid. God does not leave us
comfortless, so let evening come.

"Let Evening Come":
An Invitation to the Inevitable

by Sherry Van Egdom

The work of American poet Jane Kenyon is influenced primarily by the circumstances and experiences of her own life. She writes carefully crafted, deceptively simple poems that connect both to her own life and to the lives of her readers. Growing out of her rural roots and her struggles with illness, Kenyon's poetry speaks in a still voice of the ordinary things in life in order to wrestle with issues of faith and mortality (Timmerman 163). One of these poems is "Let Evening Come." In this poem, the poet takes the reader on a journey into the night, but she points to hope in the face of that darkness.

That movement toward darkness is captured in the stanza form and in the progression of stanzas. Each three-line stanza offers a self-contained moment in the progress of transition from day to night. The first stanza positions the reader in a simple farm setting. Late afternoon fades into evening without the rumble of highways or the gleam of city lights to distract one's senses from nature, the peace emphasized by the alliteration of "l" in "Let the light of late afternoon." As the sun sinks lower on the horizon, light seeps through cracks in the barn wall, moving up the bales of hay. In the second stanza, the crickets get busy with their nighttime noises. Next, a forgotten farm hoe becomes covered with dew drops, and the silvery stars and moon appear in the sky. In the fourth stanza, complete blackness arrives as a fox returns to its empty den and the silent wind rests at close of day. The alliteration of "d" in "den" and "die down" gives a sinking, settling feeling (Timmerman 176). In the fifth stanza, a bottle and scoop keep still, untouched in their respective places, while sleep comes upon the human body. In the final stanza, Kenyon encourages readers to meet this emerging world of darkness without fear.

Within this stanza progression, the journey into the night is intensified by strong images, figures of speech, and symbols. The natural rhythm of work and rest on the farm is symbolized by the light that rises and falls in the first stanza (Timmerman 175). The simile comparing the crickets taking up their song to a woman picking up her knitting suggests a homespun energy and conviction. The moon revealing her "silver horn" implies that the moon does not instantly appear with brightness and beauty but rather reveals her majesty slowly as the night comes on. The den, the wind, and the shed in stanza four stress a kind of internal, hidden darkness. Then stanza five focuses on connected objects: the thoughtlessly discarded bottle resting in the ditch, oats and the scoop for feeding, human lungs and the air that fills them. Kenyon mentions the air in the lung *after* the bottle, ditch, scoop, and oats in order to picture humanity taking its position among the established natural rhythm of the farm (Harris 31).

The refrain, "let evening come," is a powerful part of the poem's journey toward darkness, though critics interpret the line differently. Judith Harris suggests that it symbolizes an acceptance of the inevitable: Darkness will envelop the world, and night will surely come, just as mortality will certainly take its toll in time. This acceptance, in turn, acts as a release from the confinement of one's pain and trials in life. Rather than wrestle with something that cannot be beaten or worry about things that must be left undone, Kenyon advises herself and her readers to let go (31). Night intrudes upon the work and events of the day, perhaps leaving them undone just as death might cut a life short and leave it seemingly unfinished.

> The writer compares possible interpretations of a central, repeated statement in the poem.

By contrast, John Timmerman argues that "let" is used twelve times in a supplicatory, prayer-like manner (176). The final two lines, in turn, act as a benediction upon the supplications. The comfort of God is as inevitable as the evening, so cling to faith and hope and let evening come. Although the Comforter is mentioned only in the last two lines, that statement of faith encourages readers to find a spiritual comfort in spite of the coming of the night.

> In her conclusion, the writer offers the poet's explanation of the poem's origin and then expands on the thesis.

When asked how she came to write "Let Evening Come," Jane Kenyon replied that it was a redemptive poem given to her by the Holy Ghost. When there could be *nothing*—a great darkness and despair, there is a great *mystery* of love, kindness, and beauty (Moyers 238). In the poem's calm journey into the night, Kenyon confronts darkness and suffering with a certain enduring beauty and hope (Timmerman 161). Death will come, but there remains divine comfort. "Let Evening Come" encourages readers to release their grip on the temporary and pay attention to the Comforter who reveals Himself both day *and* night. ■

Note: The Works Cited page is not shown. For sample pages, see MLA (pages **532–533**) and APA (page **564**).

Reading for Better Writing

Working by yourself or with a group, answer these questions:

1. Review the opening and closing paragraphs of the essay. How do they create a framework for the writer's analysis of the poem?

2. On which elements of the poem does the writer focus? Does this approach make sense for her analysis? Explain.

3. In her essay, the writer refers to the poet's life and to ideas from secondary sources. Do these references work well with her analysis? Why or why not?

4. Read the essay "Four Ways to Talk About Literature" on pages **220–221**. Which approach does the student writer use to analyze Kenyon's poem? Does this approach make sense? How might another approach interpret the poem differently?

Writing About a Performance

In the essay below, student writer Annie Moore reviews the performance of a rock music group, Sigur Ros. She praises several qualities of their experimental music.

Sigur Ros, *Agaetis Byrjun*

The writer states the accomplish-ments of the group.

Sigur Ros, an experimental noise quartet hailing from Reykjavik, is the   *1*
biggest thing since Bjork. Those Icelandic folk must know something we don't. Never before has a rock/pop album captured the beauty and quiet strength that pervades *Agaetis Byrjun,* the band's sophomore release.

She describes the quality of their sound.

The album flows seamlessly as a single stream of consciousness. Jonsi   *2*
Birgisson's ethereal vocals are divine as his falsetto effortlessly rides the sweeping melodies. Tension builds from the delicate intros, gathers fury, and then explodes in a burst of percussion and crashing guitars hammered by violin bow. The storm ends, a quiet lull follows, and then the cycle begins again. Added pianos, muted horns, and the strings of the Icelandic Symphony Orchestra give the songs of *Agaetis Byrjun* the essence of a twentieth-century classic.

She describes their effect on the audience.

Although the lyrics are impossibly cryptic, written entirely in Icelandic,   *3*
they are sung with an emotion and urgency so intense they are not merely perceived, but *felt.* The full force of the music resonates deep in the souls of listeners. It is exactly this "inarticulate speech of the heart," of which Van Morrison once spoke, that gives *Agaetis Byrjun* its heart-wrenching sense of sincerity.

With impeccable musicianship and a skillful mix of the traditional   *4*
and innovative, Sigur Ros will change the world of music. Or perhaps they already have. ∎

Reading for Better Writing

Working by yourself or with a group, answer these questions:

1. Which characteristics of the vocalists does the writer cite? Why?

2. Which other instrumental sounds does she cite?

3. Why does she tell us of the effect on the audience?

Writing About a Film

In the film review below, David Schaap analyzes Stephen Spielberg's film *War of the Worlds* by asking key questions about the filmmaker's strategies and their effects.

Terror on the Silver Screen: Who Are the Aliens?

The writer introduces the filmmaker and film; he then describes a pivotal scene.

In Steven Spielberg's 2005 movie, *War of the Worlds,* Ray Ferrier and his two children flee their New Jersey home in a stolen minivan. To escape outer-space aliens who are destroying houses and killing people from their enormous three-legged machines, this father, son, and daughter lurch through scene after scene of 9/11-type destruction. At one point, the daughter surveys the violence, panics, and shrieks, "Is it the terrorists?"

1

He cites an important quotation and explores its significance.

The girl's question nudges the audience to ask the same question, "Are the aliens terrorists?" That would make sense. Often filmmakers will play off members of the audience's real-life emotions to give them a sensational imaginary experience as well as a glimpse at their real world. In this case, by suggesting that the aliens' imaginary attack resembles Al Qaeda's 9/11 attack, Spielberg could be doing two things: (1) heightening fear of the alien characters and (2) suggesting a political theme.

2

Two questions focus the writer's analysis.

But is Spielberg's *War of the Worlds* this type of film? First, does the film inspire fear by suggesting that the aliens' attack is similar to Al Qaeda's attack? And second, does the film's alien attack represent a future terrorist invasion of the United States?

3

He answers the first question and offers supporting details.

The answer to the first question is *yes.* Spielberg inspires fear of his outer-space aliens by emphasizing their resemblance to 9/11 terrorists. In a series of scenes, he shows a crashed airliner like the ones used on 9/11, a wall covered with posters of missing loved ones, and mobs of ash- and dust-covered characters like those escaping the collapsing World Trade Center. Because the film takes place in the United States, viewers subconsciously further fear the aliens' violence.

4

He answers the second question by explaining the film's focus.

However, do the aliens invading the United States represent Al Qaeda fighters? Not really. The aliens are Spielberg's universal stand-in for whatever strikes fear into viewers' hearts. This film does not examine the political, psychological, or cultural roots of any problem. The film's focus is on the *effect* of violence, not the *identity* of the perpetrators. *War of the Worlds* is about *terror,* not *terrorists.* ■

5

Model

Guidelines
Writing About Literature and the Arts

1. **Select a topic.** Choose an art form or a type of performance with which you are familiar or you are willing to learn about. For ideas, review "Topics to Consider" on page **356**.

2. **Understand the work.** Experience it thoughtfully (two or three times, if possible), looking carefully at its content, form, and overall effect.
    *   For plays and films, examine the plot, setting, characters, dialogue, lighting, costumes, sound effects, music, acting, and directing.
    *   For novels and short stories, focus on point of view, plot, setting, characters, style, diction, and theme. (See pages **368–370**.)
    *   For poems, examine diction, simile, tone, sound, figures of speech, symbolism, irony, form, and theme. (See page **371**.)
    *   For music, focus on harmonic and rhythmic qualities, dynamics, melodic lines, lyrics, and interpretation.

3. **Gather information.** Take notes on what you experience, using the list above to guide your thoughts. Seek to understand the whole work before you analyze the parts. Consider freewriting briefly on one or more aspects of the work to explore your response and to dig more deeply into the work. If you are analyzing a written text, annotate it.

4. **Organize your thoughts.** Review the notes that you took as you analyzed the work. What key insight about the work has your analysis led you to see? Make that insight or judgment your thesis, and then organize supporting points logically in a scratch or full outline.

5. **Write the first draft.**
    Opening: Use ideas like the following to gain your readers' attention, identify your topic, narrow the focus, and state your thesis:
    *   Summarize your subject briefly. Include the title, the author, and the literary form or performance.
        Example: In her poem **"Let Evening Come,"** Jane Kenyon points to hope in the face of death.
    *   Start with a quotation from the film, story, or poem and then comment on its importance.
    *   Explain the artist's purpose and how well she or he achieves it.
    *   Open with a general statement about the artist's style or aesthetic process. (See page **362**.)
        Example: The work of American poet Jane Kenyon is influenced primarily by the circumstances and experiences of her own life.

- Begin with a general statement about the plot or performance. (See page 365.)

    Example: In Stephen Spielberg's movie *War of the Worlds,* Ray Ferrier and his two children flee from their New Jersey home in a stolen minivan.

- Assert your thesis. State the key insight about the work that your analysis has revealed—the insight your essay will seek to support.

Middle: Develop or support your focus by following this pattern:

- State the main points, relating them clearly to the focus of your essay.
- Support each main point with specific details or direct quotations.
- Explain how these details prove your point.

Conclusion: Tie key points together to focus your analysis. Assert your thesis or evaluation in a fresh way, leaving readers with a sense of the larger significance of your analysis.

6. **Review and revise.** Once you have a first draft written, relax for a time, and then reread your essay for its logic and completeness. Check whether you have supported each of your observations with evidence from the poem, story, film, or other artwork. Test your analysis with questions like these:

   - Did you fully understand the performance, the reasons for the acting or costuming, the lyrics of the song, or whatever is central to the work?
   - Did you explore the ironies, if present, or any important images, vocal nuances, dramatic action, shift in setting, or symbolism?
   - Did you bring your analysis to a clear conclusion?

7. **Get feedback.** Ask a knowledgeable classmate, friend, or tutor to read your essay, looking for the following:

   _____ An analytical thesis statement supported by evidence

   _____ Key insights into both content or meaning on the one hand and form or style on the other hand

   _____ Clear transitions between sentences and paragraphs

   _____ A tone that is respectful and honest

8. **Edit and proofread.** Once you have revised your essay, clarified your transitions, and checked your evidence, polish the phrasing and diction. Make certain your paper is free of awkward syntax or errors in usage, punctuation, spelling, or grammar. In particular, check that you have used the special terms of the literary genre or art form clearly and accurately.

9. **Publish your essay.**

   - Share your essay with friends and family.
   - Publish it in a journal or on a website.
   - Place a copy in your personal or professional portfolio.

Literary Terms

Your analysis of novels, poems, plays, and films will be deeper and more sophisticated if you understand the most common literary terms.

Allusion is a reference to a person, a place, or an event in history or literature.

Analogy is a comparison of two or more similar objects, suggesting that if they are alike in certain respects, they will probably be alike in other ways, too.

Anecdote is a short summary of an interesting or humorous, often biographical incident or event.

Antagonist is the person or thing actively working against the protagonist, or hero, of the work.

Climax is the turning point, an intense moment characterized by a key event.

Conflict is the problem or struggle in a story that triggers the action. There are five basic types of conflict:

Person versus person: One character in a story is in conflict with one or more of the other characters.

Person versus society: A character is in conflict with some element of society: the school, the law, the accepted way of doing things, and so on.

Person versus self: A character faces conflicting inner choices.

Person versus nature: A character is in conflict with some natural happening: a snowstorm, an avalanche, the bitter cold, or any other element of nature.

Person versus fate: A character must battle what seems to be an uncontrollable problem. Whenever the conflict is a strange or unbelievable coincidence, the conflict can be attributed to fate.

Denouement is the outcome of a play or story. See **Resolution**.

Diction is an author's choice of words based on their correctness or effectiveness.

Archaic words are old-fashioned and no longer sound natural when used, such as "I believe thee not" for "I don't believe you."

Colloquialism is an expression that is usually accepted in informal situations and certain locations, as in "He really grinds my beans."

Heightened language uses vocabulary and sentence constructions that produce a stylized effect unlike that of standard speech or writing, as in much poetry and poetic prose.

Profanity is language that shows disrespect for someone or something regarded as holy or sacred.

Slang is the everyday language used by group members amongst themselves.

Trite expressions lack depth or originality, or are overworked or not worth mentioning in the first place.

Vulgarity is language that is generally considered common, crude, gross, and, at times, offensive. It is sometimes used in fiction, plays, and films to add realism.

Exposition is the introductory section of a story or play. Typically, the setting, main characters, and themes are introduced, and the action is initiated.

Falling action is the action of a play or story that follows the climax and shows the characters dealing with the climactic event or decision.

Figure of speech is a literary device used to create a special effect or to describe something in a fresh way. The most common types are *antithesis, hyperbole, metaphor, metonymy, personification, simile,* and *understatement.*

> **Antithesis** is an opposition, or contrast, of ideas.
> "It was the best of times, it was the worst of times, it was the age of wisdom, it was the age of foolishness . . ."
> — Charles Dickens, *A Tale of Two Cities*

> **Hyperbole** (hi-pur´ ba-lee) is an extreme exaggeration or overstatement.
> "I have seen this river so wide it had only one bank."
> —Mark Twain, *Life on the Mississippi*

> **Metaphor** is a comparison of two unlike things in which no word of comparison (*as* or *like*) is used: "Life is a banquet."

> **Metonymy** (ma-ton´a-mee) is the substituting of one term for another that is closely related to it, but not a literal restatement.
> "Friends, Romans, countrymen, lend me your ears." (The request is for the *attention* of those assembled, not literally their *ears.*)

> **Personification** is a device in which the author speaks of or describes an animal, object, or idea as if it were a person: "The rock stubbornly refused to move."

> **Simile** is a comparison of two unlike things in which *like* or *as* is used.
> "She stood in front of the altar, shaking like a freshly caught trout."
> —Maya Angelou, *I Know Why the Caged Bird Sings*

> **Understatement** is stating an idea with restraint, often for humorous effect.
> Mark Twain described Aunt Polly as being "prejudiced against snakes." (Because she hated snakes, this way of saying so is *understatement.*)

Genre refers to a category or type of literature based on its style, form, and content. The mystery novel is a literary *genre.*

Imagery refers to words or phrases that a writer uses to appeal to the reader's senses.
> "The sky was dark and gloomy, the air was damp and raw, the streets were wet and sloppy."
> —Charles Dickens, *The Pickwick Papers*

Irony is a deliberate discrepancy in meaning or in the way something is understood. There are three kinds of irony:

> **Dramatic irony,** in which the reader or the audience sees a character's mistakes or misunderstandings, but the character does not.

> **Verbal irony,** in which the writer says one thing and means another ("The best substitute for experience is being sixteen").

> **Irony of situation,** in which there is a great difference between the purpose of a particular action and the result.

Mood is the feeling that a piece of literature arouses in the reader: *happiness, sadness, peacefulness, anxiety,* and so forth.

Paradox is a statement that seems contrary to common sense yet may, in fact, be true: "The coach considered this a good loss."

Plot is the action or sequence of events in a story. It is usually a series of related incidents that build upon one another as the story develops. There are five basic elements in a plot line: *exposition, rising action, climax, falling action,* and *resolution.*

Point of view is the vantage point from which the story unfolds.
In the **first-person** point of view, the story is told by one of the characters: "I stepped into the darkened room and felt myself go cold."
In the **third-person** point of view, the story is told by someone outside the story: "He stepped into the darkened room and felt himself go cold."
Third-person narrations can be *omniscient,* meaning that the narrator has access to the thoughts of all the characters, or *limited,* meaning that the narrator focuses on the inner life of one central character.

Protagonist is the main character or hero of the story.

Resolution (or denouement) is the portion of the play or story in which the problem is solved. The resolution comes after the climax and falling action and is intended to bring the story to a satisfactory end.

Rising action is the series of conflicts or struggles that build a story or play toward a fulfilling climax.

Satire is a literary tone used to ridicule or make fun of human vice or weakness, often with the intent of correcting, or changing, the subject of the satiric attack.

Setting is the time and place in which the action of a literary work occurs.

Structure is the form or organization a writer uses for her or his literary work. A great number of possible forms are used regularly in literature: parable, fable, romance, satire, farce, slapstick, and so on.

Style refers to how the author uses words, phrases, and sentences to form his or her ideas. Style is also thought of as the qualities and characteristics that distinguish one writer's work from the work of others.

Symbol is a person, a place, a thing, or an event used to represent something else. For example, the dove is a symbol of peace.

Theme is the statement about life that a particular work shares with readers. In stories written for children, the theme is often spelled out clearly at the end. In more complex literature, the theme will often be more complex and will be implied, not stated.

Tone is the overall feeling, or effect, created by a writer's use of words. This feeling may be serious, mock-serious, humorous, satiric, and so on.

Poetry Terms

Alliteration is the repetition of initial consonant sounds in words such as "rough and ready." An example of alliteration is underlined below:
> "Our gang paces the pier like an old myth . . . "
> —Anne-Marie Oomen, "Runaway Warning"

Assonance is the repetition of vowel sounds without the repetition of consonants.
> "My words like silent rain drops fell . . . "—Paul Simon, "Sounds of Silence"

Blank verse is an unrhymed form of poetry. Each line normally consists of ten syllables in which every other syllable, beginning with the second, is stressed. As blank verse is often used in very long poems, it may depart from the strict pattern from time to time.

Consonance is the repetition of consonant sounds. Although it is very similar to alliteration, consonance is not limited to the first letters of words:
> " . . . and high school girls with clear-skin smiles . . . "
> —Janis Ian, "At Seventeen"

Foot is the smallest repeated pattern of stressed and unstressed syllables in a poetic line. (See **Verse.**)
Iambic: an unstressed followed by a stressed syllable (re-peat´)
Anapestic: two unstressed followed by a stressed syllable (in-ter-rupt´)
Trochaic: a stressed followed by an unstressed syllable (old´-er)
Dactylic: a stressed followed by two unstressed syllables (o´-pen-ly)
Spondaic: two stressed syllables (heart´-break´)
Pyrrhic: two unstressed syllables (Pyrrhic seldom appears by itself.)

Onomatopoeia is the use of a word whose sound suggests its meaning, as in *clang, buzz,* and *twang.*

Refrain is the repetition of a line or phrase of a poem at regular intervals, especially at the end of each stanza. A song's refrain may be called the *chorus.*

Rhythm is the ordered or free occurrences of sound in poetry. Ordered or regular rhythm is called *meter.* Free occurrence of sound is called *free verse.*

Stanza is a division of poetry named for the number of lines it contains:

Couplet: two-line stanza	**Sestet:** six-line stanza
Triplet: three-line stanza	**Septet:** seven-line stanza
Quatrain: four-line stanza	**Octave:** eight-line stanza
Quintet: five-line stanza	

Verse is a metric line of poetry. It is named according to the kind and number of feet composing it: *iambic pentameter, anapestic tetrameter,* and so on. (See **Foot.**)

Monometer: one foot	**Pentameter:** five feet
Dimeter: two feet	**Hexameter:** six feet
Trimeter: three feet	**Heptameter:** seven feet
Tetrameter: four feet	**Octometer:** eight feet

Writing Checklist

Use these seven traits to check your writing; then revise as needed:

_____ The **ideas** offer insight into what the literature or art means and how it communicates.

_____ The **organization** of the essay flows logically and provides an easy-to-follow pattern.

_____ The **voice** is positive, confident, objective, and sensitive to opposing viewpoints. The tone fits the literature or art being discussed.

_____ The **words** are precise and effectively defined.

_____ The **sentences** read and flow smoothly, with effective variations and logical transitions.

_____ The **copy** has no errors in spelling, punctuation, mechanics, or grammar.

_____ The page **design** is attractive and follows appropriate formatting rules.

Critical-Thinking and Writing Activities

As directed by your instructor, complete the following activities.

1. Get a copy of "Good Country People," read the story, write your own analysis, and share the essay with your class.

2. Choose a poem or film that you find meaningful and write an essay in which you analyze how and why the work is strong.

3. Attend a concert. Respond to the style of the music, to the performance of the singer or group, and to the content of the lyrics. Note also the age of the audience, its response, and the way in which the performance is or is not affected by that response. Explain your own response as well.

4. Visit an art gallery. Find an exhibit that engages you. Explain what in this exhibit you find appealing or intriguing. Also explain what value this exhibit might have to society or to you personally, and why.

◀ VISUALLY SPEAKING

The short story, film, and poem reviewed in this chapter all include these literary elements: setting, mood, plot, and characters. Does the photograph on page **355** also include these elements? Explain.

TAKING ESSAY TESTS

There is nothing more disheartening than sitting down to take a test for which you're not prepared. The results are predictable—and they're not pretty. Conversely, there is nothing more exhilarating than walking out of a classroom after nailing a test. This is especially true in a college setting, where tests count for so much and second chances and extra credit are rare.

Many of the writing skills that you've already developed should serve you well in taking essay tests. Read the instructions for an essay test carefully, and you'll find requests for describing, analyzing, classifying, persuading, and more.

This chapter will help you write better essay answers. As a bonus, it suggests a variety of other helpful ways to improve your test-taking skills.

Audio

Video

Reviewing for Tests

Do you consider yourself a "bad" test taker? Do you know the material, yet somehow perform poorly on tests? Do you feel overwhelmed by all the information you have to cover when studying for a test? Does even the thought of studying so much material make you nervous? What you need is a positive mental attitude—and good study habits. Together they can make the difference between "spacing" during a test and "acing" an exam.

Perform daily reviews.

Why daily? Begin your reviews on the first day of class; if you miss a day, dust yourself off and keep going. Daily reviews are especially good because you tend to forget new information rapidly. Reviewing while the material is fresh in your mind helps to move it from your short-term memory into your long-term memory.

How much time? Even spending five or ten minutes on your review before or after each class will pay big dividends. Depending on the day's class, you may read through (or talk through) your notes, look over the headings in a reading assignment, skim any summaries you have, or put information into graphic organizers.

What to Do

- Put "Daily review of . . ." on your "To Do" list, calendar, or date book.
- Use the buddy system. Make a pact with a classmate and review together.
- Put your subconscious to work by reviewing material before you go to sleep.

Perform weekly reviews.

Why weekly? More than anything else, repetition helps anchor memory. You can cram a lot of data into your brain the night before an exam, but a day or two later you won't remember much of anything. And when final exam time comes, you'll have to learn the material all over again.

How much time? Plan to spend about one hour per week for each class. (This review can take place either by yourself or with a study group.) Remember that repetition is the single most important factor in learning anything.

What to Do

- Make mind maps and flash cards of important information.
- Practice answering review questions by saying them aloud and by writing out short answers.
- Test your understanding of a subject by teaching or explaining it to someone else.
- Organize a study group. (See page 375.)
- Create mnemonics. (See page 376.)

Forming a Study Group

A study group can keep you interested in a subject, force you to keep up with classwork, and increase your retention of study material. Group energy can be more powerful than individual energy. You will hear other points of view and other ways to approach a subject that you may never have thought of on your own. If you use a chat room, you can meet via a computer. To get started, follow these guidelines.

1. **Find five to six people.**
   - Consider people who seem highly motivated and collaborative.
   - Ask your instructor to inform the class about the opportunity.

2. **Consider a chat room.**
   - Check first with your instructor and student services about the availability of chat rooms on your campus network.
   - Go to any search engine (Yahoo!, Google, Excite, and so on) and enter the term "chat room." For example, Yahoo! provides both private and public chat rooms ("clubs") free of charge.

3. **Arrange a time and place.**
   - Plan one session. (It may become obvious at the first meeting that your group won't work out.)
   - Agree on a time limit for the initial session.
   - Choose somebody in the group to keep everyone on task (or rotate this duty) and agree to accept any prodding and nudging with good humor.

4. **Set realistic goals and decide on a plan of action.**
   - Discuss what the group needs to accomplish and what your goals are.
   - Agree to practice "people skills" (listening, observing, cooperating, responding, and clarifying).
   - Decide which parts of the coursework you will review (lectures? labs? texts? exam questions?).

5. **Evaluate at the end of the first session.**
   - Honestly and tactfully discuss any problems that arose.
   - Ask who wants to continue.
   - Choose a time (and place) for your next session.
   - Determine an agenda for the next session.
   - Exchange necessary information such as phone numbers, e-mail addresses, chat room passwords, and so forth.

Using Mnemonics and Other Memory Guides

Mnemonics is the art of improving memory by using key words, formulas, or other aids to create "file tabs" in your brain that help you pull out hard-to-remember information.

Acronyms Use the first letter in each word to form a new word. Everyone learns a few acronyms during their school years, but feel free to make up your own.

> HOMES (the Great Lakes—Huron, Ontario, Michigan, Erie, Superior)

Acrostics Form a phrase or silly sentence in which the first letter of each word helps you remember the items in a series.

> **Z**oe **C**ooks **C**howder **I**n **P**ink **P**ots **I**n **M**iami. (essential minerals—**z**inc, **c**alcium, **c**hromium, **i**ron, **p**otassium, **p**hosphorus, **i**odine, **m**agnesium)

Categories Organize your information into categories for easier recall.

> Types of joints in body
>
> immovable: skull sutures, teeth in sockets . . .
> slightly movable: between vertebrae, junction at front of pelvis . . .
> freely movable: shoulder, elbow, hip, knee, ankle . . .

Peg words Create a chain of associations with objects in a room, a sequence of events, or a pattern with which you are familiar (such as the player positions on a baseball diamond).

> To remember a sequence of Civil War battles, you might "peg" them to the positions on a baseball field—for example, Shiloh to home plate (think of the "high" and "low" balls); the Battle of Bull Run to the pitcher's mound (think of the pitcher's battle for no runs); and so on.

Rhymes Make up rhymes or puns.

> *Brown v. Board of Education* / ended public-school segregation.

TIPS to improve your memory

- **Intend to remember.** Scientists say that our brains never forget anything: It's our recall that is at fault. Who forgets that they have tickets to a concert? We remember the things that are important to us.
- **Link new information** to things you already know.
- **Organize your material.** Understand the big picture and then divide the information you need to know into smaller, more manageable categories.
- **Review new material as soon as possible.** The sooner you review, the more likely you'll remember.

Taking the Essay Test

Your teachers expect you to include all the right information, and they expect you to organize it in a clear, well-thought-out way. In addition, they expect you to evaluate, synthesize, predict, analyze, and write a worthwhile answer.

Look for key words.

Key words help you define your task. Pay special attention to them when you read questions. Key words tell you how to present all the information you'll need to write an essay answer.

Following is a list of key terms, along with a definition and an example of how each is used. Studying these terms carefully is the first step in writing worthwhile answers to essay questions.

Analyze To analyze is to break down a larger problem or situation into separate parts of relationships.

> Analyze the major difficulties found at urban housing projects.

Classify To classify is to place persons or things (especially animals and plants) together in a group because they share similar characteristics. Science uses a special classification or group order: phylum, class, order, family, genus, species, and variety.

> Classify three kinds of trees found in the rainforests of Costa Rica.

Compare To compare is to use examples to show how things are similar and different, placing the greater emphasis on similarities.

> Compare the vegetation in the rainforests of Puerto Rico with the vegetation in the rainforests of Costa Rica.

Contrast To contrast is to use examples to show how things are different in one or more important ways.

> Contrast the views of George Washington and Harry S Truman regarding the involvement of the United States in world affairs.

Compare and contrast To compare and contrast is to use examples that show the major similarities and differences between two things (or people, events, ideas, and so forth). In other words, two things are used to clarify each other.

> Compare and contrast people-centered leadership with task-centered leadership.

Define To define is to give the meaning for a term. Generally, defining involves identifying the class to which a term belongs and explaining how it differs from other things in that class.

> Define the term "emotional intelligence" as it pertains to humans.

Describe To describe is to give a detailed sketch or impression of a topic.
> Describe how the Euro tunnel (the Chunnel) was built.

Diagram To diagram is to explain with lines or pictures—a flowchart, map, or other graphic device. Generally, a diagram will label the important points or parts.
> Diagram the parts of a DNA molecule.

Discuss To discuss is to review an issue from all sides. A discussion answer must be carefully organized to stay on track.
> Discuss how Rosa Parks's refusal to move to the back of the bus affected the civil rights movement.

Evaluate To evaluate is to make a value judgment by giving the pluses and minuses along with supporting evidence.
> Evaluate the efforts of midsized cities to improve public transportation services.

Explain To explain is to bring out into the open, to make clear, and to analyze. This term is similar to *discuss* but places more emphasis on cause/effect relationships or step-by-step sequences.
> Explain the effects of global warming on a coastal city like New Orleans.

Justify To justify is to tell why a position or point of view is good or right. A justification should be mostly positive—that is, the advantages are stressed over the disadvantages.
> Justify the use of antilock brakes in automobiles.

Outline To outline is to organize a set of facts or ideas by listing main points and subpoints. A good outline shows at a glance how topics or ideas fit together or relate to one another.
> Outline the events that caused the United States to enter World War II.

Prove To prove is to bring out the truth by giving evidence to back up a point.
> Prove that Atticus Finch in *To Kill a Mockingbird* provided an adequate defense for his client.

Review To review is to reexamine or to summarize the key characteristics or major points of the topic. Generally speaking, a review presents material in the order in which it happened or in decreasing order of importance.
> Review the events since 1976 that have led to the current hip-hop culture.

State To state is to present a concise statement of a position, fact, or point of view.
> State your reasons for voting in the last national election.

Summarize To summarize is to present the main points of an issue in a shortened form. Details, illustrations, and examples are usually omitted.
> Summarize the primary responsibilities of a school in a democracy.

Trace To trace is to present—in a step-by-step sequence—a series of facts that are somehow related. Usually the facts are presented in chronological order.
> Trace the events that led to the fall of the Union of Soviet Socialist Republics.

Plan and write the essay-test answer.

In addition to a basic understanding of the key words, you must understand the process of writing the essay answer.

1. **Reread the question several times.** (Pay special attention to any key words used in the question.)

2. **Rephrase the question into a topic sentence/thesis statement** with a clear point.

> **Question:** Explain why public housing was built in Chicago in the 1960s.

> **Thesis statement:** Public housing was built in Chicago because of the Great Migration, the name given to the movement of African Americans from the South to the North.

3. **Outline the main points you plan to cover in your answer.** Time will probably not allow you to include all supporting details in your outline.

4. **Write your essay (or paragraph).** Begin with your thesis statement (or topic sentence). Add whatever background information may be needed, and then follow your outline, writing as clearly as possible.

One-Paragraph Answer

If you feel that only one paragraph is needed to answer the question, use the main points of your outline as supporting details for your thesis statement.

Question: Explain why public housing was built in Chicago in the 1960s.

Topic sentence ----- Public housing was built in Chicago because of the Great Migration, the name given to the movement of African Americans from the South to the North. The mechanical cotton picker, introduced in the 1920s, replaced field hands in the cotton fields of the South. At that time Chicago's factories and stockyards were hiring workers. In addition, Jim Crow laws caused hardships and provided reasons for African Americans to move north. Finally, some African Americans had family and relatives in Chicago who had migrated earlier and who, it was thought, could provide a home base for the new migrants until they could get work and housing. According to the U.S. Census **Supporting details** Reports, there were 109,000 African Americans in Chicago in 1920. By 1960, there were more than 800,000. However, this increase in population could have been handled except that the public wanted to keep the African Americans in the Black Belt, an area in South Chicago. Reluctant lending agencies and realtors made it possible for speculators to operate. Speculators increased the **Conclusion** cost of houses by 75 percent. All of these factors led to a housing shortage for African Americans, which public housing filled.

Multiparagraph Answer

If the question is too complex to be handled in one paragraph, your opening paragraph should include your thesis statement and any essential background information. Begin your second paragraph by rephrasing one of the main points from your outline into a suitable topic sentence. Support this topic sentence with examples, reasons, or other appropriate details. Handle additional paragraphs in the same manner. If time permits, add a summary or concluding paragraph to bring all of your thoughts to a logical close.

Question: Explain the advantages and disadvantages of wind energy.

Thesis: Wind energy has an equal number of advantages and disadvantages.

Outline
I. Advantages of wind energy
    A. Renewable
    B. Economical
    C. Nonpolluting
II. Disadvantages of wind energy
    A. Intermittent
    B. Unsightly
    C. A danger to some wildlife

The introductory paragraph sets up the essay's organization.

Wind energy has an equal number of advantages and disadvantages. [1] It is renewable, economical, and nonpolluting; but it is also intermittent, unsightly, and a danger to the bird population.

Wind energy is renewable. No matter how much wind energy is used [2] today, there will still be a supply tomorrow. As evidence indicates that wind energy was used to propel boats along the Nile River about 5000 B.C.E., it can be said that wind is an eternal, renewable resource.

Wind energy is economical. The fuel (wind) is free, but the initial cost [3] for wind turbines is higher than for fossil-fueled generators. However, wind energy costs do not include fuel purchases and only minimal operating expenses. Wind power reduces the amount of foreign oil the United States imports and reduces health and environmental costs caused by pollution. Is it possible to sell excess power? The Public Utilities Regulatory Policy Act of 1978 (PURPA) states that a local electric company must buy any excess power produced by a qualifying individual. This act encourages the use of wind power.

Each paragraph follows a point in the outline.

Wind energy does not pollute. Whether one wind turbine is used by an [4] individual or a wind farm supplies energy to many people, no air pollutants or greenhouse gases are emitted. California reports that 2.5 billion pounds of carbon dioxide and 15 million pounds of other pollutants have *not* entered the air thanks to wind energy.

How unfortunate is it that wind energy is intermittent? If a wind does not blow, there is little or no electrical power. One way to resolve this dilemma is to store the energy that wind produces in batteries. The word *intermittent* also refers to the fact that wind power is not always available at the places where it is most needed. Often the sites that offer the greatest winds are located in remote locations far from the cities that demand great electrical power.

Specific details explain the main point.

Are wind turbines unsightly? A home-sized wind machine rises about 30 feet with rotors between 8 and 25 feet in diameter. The largest machine in Hawaii stands about 20 stories high with rotors a little longer than the length of a football field. This machine supplies electricity to 1,400 homes. Does a single wind turbine upset the aesthetics of a community as much as a wind farm? The old adage "Beauty is in the eye of the beholder" holds up wherever wind turbines rotate. If ongoing electrical costs are almost nil, that wind turbine may look beautiful.

Questions help the reader understand the issue.

How serious is the issue of bird safety? The main questions are these: (1) Why do birds come near wind turbines? (2) What, if any, are the effects of wind development on bird populations? (3) What can be done to lessen the problem? If even one bird of a protected species is killed, the Endangered Species Act has been violated. If wind turbines kill migratory birds, the Migratory Bird Treaty Act has been violated. As a result, many countries and agencies are studying the problem carefully.

The ending makes a final conclusion.

The advantages of wind energy seem to outweigh the disadvantages. The wind-energy industry has been growing steadily in the United States and around the world. The new wind turbines are reliable and efficient. People's attitudes toward wind energy are mostly positive. Many manufacturers and government agencies are now cooperating to expand wind energy, making it the fastest-growing source of electricity in the world. ■

Reading for Better Writing

Working by yourself or with a group, answer these questions:

1. How does the writer provide a clear focus and logical organization in the essay answer? How soon are the focus and organization provided? What advantages does this approach offer the writer? The reader?

2. How do the sentences used to introduce the advantages differ from the sentences used to introduce the disadvantages? How does this technique aid the reader?

3. Why must the paragraphs in the body contain specific facts and examples? Which facts and examples does this writer use?

QUICK GUIDE
▬ Writing Under Pressure: The Essay Test ▬

▬ **Make sure you are ready for the test both mentally and physically.**

- **Carefully listen to or read the instructions.**
  1. How much time do you have to complete the test?
  2. Do all the essay questions count equally?
  3. Can you use any aids, such as a dictionary or handbook?
  4. Are there any corrections, changes, or additions to the test?

- **Begin the test immediately and watch the time.** Don't spend so much time answering one question that you run out of time before answering the others.

- **Read all the essay questions carefullly,** paying special attention to the key words. (See pages **377–378**.)

- **Ask the instructor for clarification** if you don't understand something.

- **Rephrase each question into a controlling idea for your essay answer.** (This idea becomes your thesis statement.)

- **Think before you write.** Jot down all the important information and work it into a brief outline. Do this on the back of the test sheet or on a piece of scrap paper.

- **Use a logical pattern of organization and a strong topic sentence for each paragraph.** Tie points together with clear, logical transitions.

- **Write concisely,** but don't use abbreviations or nonstandard language.

- **Be efficient.** Write about those areas of the subject of which you are most certain first; then work on other areas as time permits.

- **Keep your test paper neat and use reasonable margins.** Neatness is always important, and readability is a must, especially on an essay exam.

- **Revise and proofread.** Read through your essay as carefully and completely as time permits.

Note: Also see "Tips for coping with test anxiety," page **384**.

Taking an Objective Test

Even though objective tests are generally straightforward and clear, following some tips can help you avoid making foolish mistakes.

True/False Test

- Read the entire question before answering. Often the first half of a statement will be true or false, while the second half is just the opposite. For an answer to be true, the entire statement must be true.

- Read each word and number. Pay special attention to names, dates, and numbers that are similar and could be easily confused.

- Beware of true/false statements that contain words such as *all, every, always,* and *never.* Very often these statements will be false.

- Watch for statements that contain more than one negative word. Remember: Two negatives make a positive. (*Example:* It is unlikely ice will not melt when the temperature rises above 32 degrees F.)

Matching Test

- Read through both lists quickly before you begin answering. Note any descriptions that are similar and pay special attention to the differences.

- When matching a word to a word, determine the part of speech of each word. If the word is a verb, for example, match it with another verb.

- When matching a word to a phrase, read the phrase first and look for the word it describes.

- Cross out each answer as you find it—unless you are told that the answer can be used more than once.

- Use capital letters rather than lowercase letters because they are less likely to be misread by the person correcting the test.

Multiple-Choice Test

- Read the directions to determine whether you are looking for the correct answer or the best answer. Also, check whether some questions can have two (or more) correct answers.

- Read the first part of the question, checking for negative words such as *not, never, except,* and *unless.*

- Try to answer the question in your mind before looking at the choices.

- Read all the choices before selecting your answer. This step is especially important on tests in which you must select the best answer, or on tests where one of your choices is a combination of two or more answers. (*Example:* d. Both a and b / e. All of the above / f. None of the above)

TIPS for coping with test anxiety

Consider the following advice:

- **Study smart.** Use a variety of study and memory techniques to help you see your coursework from several different angles.

- **Review with others.** Join a study group and prepare with the members. Also, ask a classmate or family member to put you to the test.

- **Prepare yourself both physically and mentally.** Get a good night's sleep and eat a healthful, light meal before the test (doughnuts and coffee are *not* a healthful, light meal).

- **Get some exercise.** Aerobic exercise (running, swimming, walking, aerobics) is a great way to relieve stress, and exercise has been proven to help you think more quickly and more clearly.

- **Hit the shower.** Hot water is relaxing, cold water is stimulating, and warm water is soothing. Take your pick.

- **Get to class early . . . but not too early!** Hurrying increases anxiety, but so does waiting.

- **Relax.** Take a few deep breaths, close your eyes, and think positive thoughts. The more relaxed you are, the better your memory will serve you.

- **Glance through the entire test.** Then plan your time, and pace yourself accordingly. You don't want to discover with only 5 minutes of class time left that the last question is an essay that counts for 50 percent of your grade.

- **Begin by filling in all the answers you know.** This process relieves anxiety and helps to trigger answers for other questions that you may not know immediately. Also, jot down important facts and formulas that you know you will need later on.

- **Don't panic.** If other people start handing in their papers long before you are finished, don't worry. They may have given up or rushed through the exam. The best students often finish last.

Bottom Line

The better you prepare for a test—mentally and physically—the less likely you'll be to suffer serious test anxiety.

WRITING FOR THE WORKPLACE

Audio

One thing you already know about writing in college is that you have to do a lot of it—and it has to be good. Nothing does more to help you make a good impression than writing well. You also know that college is very much like real life, in that you have to take care of business in and out of class. There are bills to pay, letters to write, memos to fax, and messages to e-mail. It's your personal responsibility to get each of these jobs done clearly, concisely, and on time.

This chapter should aid you in taking care of the business at hand. Sample letters and memos will help you communicate effectively with people ranging from the registrar to scholarship committees. The sample applications and resumés will help you make a favorable impression when you apply for a job or an internship. There's even a special set of guidelines to help you master e-mail messages so that you can "take care of business," no matter where in the world it may be.

Writing the Business Letter

Business letters do many things—for example, share ideas, promote products, or ask for help. Putting a message in writing gives you time to think about, organize, and edit what you want to say. In addition, a written message serves as a record of important details for both the sender and the recipient.

Parts of the Business Letter

1. Heading The heading gives the writer's complete address, either in the letterhead (company stationery) or typed out, followed by the date.

2. Inside Address The inside address gives the reader's name and address.
   - If you're not sure which person to address or how to spell someone's name, you could call the company or check their website for the information.
   - If the person's title is a single word, place it after the name and a comma (Mary Johnson, President). A longer title goes on a separate line.

3. Salutation The salutation begins with *Dear* and ends with a colon, not a comma.
   - Use *Mr.* or *Ms.* plus the person's last name, unless you are well acquainted. Do not guess at *Miss* or *Mrs.*
   - If you can't get the person's name, replace the salutation with *Dear* or *Attention* followed by the title of an appropriate reader.

   (*Examples:* Dear Dean of Students: or Attention: Personnel Manager)

   Note: See pages 104–106 for a complete list of "unbiased" ways to refer to an individual or a particular group.

4. Body The body should consist of single-spaced paragraphs with double-spacing between paragraphs. (Do not indent the paragraphs.)
   - If the body goes to a second page, put the reader's name at the top left, the number 2 in the center, and the date at the right margin.

5. Complimentary Closing For the complimentary closing, use *Sincerely, Yours sincerely,* or *Yours truly* followed by a comma; use *Best wishes* if you know the person well.

6. Signature The signature includes the writer's name both handwritten and typed.

7. Initials When someone types the letter for the writer, that person's initials appear (in lowercase) after the writer's initials (in capitals) and a colon.

8. Enclosure If a document (brochure, form, copy, or other form) is enclosed with the letter, the word *Enclosure* or *Encl.* appears below the initials.

9. Copies If a copy of the letter is sent elsewhere, type *cc:* beneath the enclosure line, followed by the person's or department's name.

Model Letter

Heading

Box 143
Balliole College
Eugene, OR 97440-5125
August 29, 2008

Four to Seven Spaces

Inside Address

Ms. Ada Overlie
Ogg Hall, Room 222
Balliole College
Eugene, OR 97440-0222

Double Space

Salutation

Dear Ms. Overlie:

Double Space

As the president of the Earth Care Club, I welcome you to Balliole Community College. I hope the year will be a great learning experience both inside and outside the classroom.

Double Space

That learning experience is the reason I'm writing—to encourage you to join the Earth Care Club. As a member, you could participate in the educational and action-oriented mission of the club. The club has most recently been involved in the following:

Body

- Organizing a reduce, reuse, recycle program on campus
- Promoting cloth rather than plastic bag use among students
- Giving input to the college administration on landscaping, renovating, and building for energy efficiency
- Putting together the annual Earth Day celebration

Double Space

Which environmental concerns and activities would you like to focus on? Bring them with you to the Earth Care Club. Simply complete the enclosed form and return it by September 8. Then watch the campus news for details on our first meeting.

Double Space

Complimentary Closing and Signature

Yours sincerely,

Four Spaces

Dave Wetland

Dave Wetland
President

Double Space

Initials Enclosure Copies

DW:kr
Encl. membership form
cc: Esther du Toit, membership committee

Writing Memos and E-mail

A memorandum is a written message sent from one person to one or more other people within the same organization. As such, it is less formal than a letter. A memo can vary in length from a sentence or two to a four- or five-page report. It can be delivered in person, dropped in a mailbox, or sent via e-mail.

Memos are written to create a flow of information within an organization—asking and answering questions, describing procedures and policies, or reminding people about appointments and meetings. Here are some guidelines:

- Write memos only when necessary, and only to those people who need them.
- Distribute them through the appropriate media—mail, fax, bulletin boards, kiosk, intranet, or e-mail.
- Make your subject line precise so that the topic is clear and the memo is easy to file.
- Get to the point: (1) state the subject, (2) give necessary details, and (3) state the response you want.

Date: September 26, 2008

To: All Users of the Bascom Hill Writing Lab

The subject line clarifies the memo's purpose.

From: Kerri Kelley, Coordinator

Subject: New Hours/New Equipment

The main point is stated immediately.

Beginning October 3, the Bascom Hill Writing Lab will expand its weekend hours as follows: Fridays, 7:00 A.M.–11:00 P.M.; Saturdays, 8:00 A.M.–11:00 P.M.

Also, six additional computers will be installed next week, making it easier to get computer time. We hope these changes will help meet the increased demand for time and assistance we've experienced this fall. Remember, it's still a good idea to sign up in advance. To reserve time, call the lab at 462-7722 or leave your request at bhill@madwis.edu.

Readers are asked to take note of a few final facts.

Finally, long-range planners, mark your calendars. The lab will be closed on Thanksgiving Day morning and open from 1:00 P.M. to 11:00 P.M. We will also be closed on Christmas and New Year's Day. We will post our semester-break hours sometime next month.

Sending E-mail

With e-mail, people can correspond through computer networks around the globe. E-mail allows you to do the following:

- Send, forward, and receive many messages quickly and efficiently, making it ideal for group projects and other forms of collaboration
- Set up mailing lists (specific groups of e-mail addresses) so that you can easily send the same message to several people at the same time
- Organize messages in "folders" for later reference, and reply to messages

---

TIPS for e-mail

- **Revise and edit messages for clarity and correctness before sending them.** Confusing sentences, grammatical errors, and typos limit your ability to communicate on a computer screen just as they do on paper.
- **Use e-mail responsibly.** Sooner or later you will send e-mail to the wrong person, or a reader will forward your message to another person without your permission. Keep these possibilities in mind at all times, and never write anything that would embarrass you if the wrong party received it.
- **Make messages easy to read and understand.** (1) Provide a clear subject line so readers will scan it and decide whether to read or delete the message. (2) Type short paragraphs.

From:	"Sherry West" SWEST@stgeorge.edu
To:	outreach@stgeorge.edu
Date sent:	Mon, 22 Sept 2008 14:13:06 CST
Subject:	Agenda for Student Outreach Committee Meeting

Please remember that our next meeting is this Wednesday, Sept. 24, at 8:00 p.m. in SUB Room 201. We'll discuss the following agenda items:

1. The minutes of our Sept. 10 meeting
2. A proposal from SADD about Alcohol Awareness Week
3. A progress report on the Habitat for Humanity project

Before the meeting, please review the minutes and the SADD proposal attached to this message.

Applying for a Job

When you apply for some jobs, you have to do nothing more than fill out an application form. With other jobs, it's a different story. You may be required to write a letter of application, gather letters of recommendation, write an application essay, and put together a resume. The following pages provide models to fit nearly every occasion.

Web Link

The Letter of Application

Your letter of application (or cover letter) introduces you to an employer and often highlights information on an accompanying resume. Your goal in writing this letter is to convince the employer to invite you for an interview.

Ogg Hall, Room 222
Balliole College
Eugene, OR 97440-0222
April 17, 2008

Address a specific person, if possible.

Professor Edward Mahaffy
Greenhouse Coordinator
Balliole College
Eugene, OR 97440-0316

Dear Professor Mahaffy:

State the desired position and your chief qualification.

I recently talked with Ms. Sierra Arbor in the Financial Aid Office about work-study jobs for 2008–2009. She told me about the Greenhouse Assistant position and gave me a job description. As a full-time Balliole student, I'm writing to apply for this position. I believe that my experience qualifies me for the job.

Focus on how your skills meet the reader's needs.

As you can see from my resume, I spent two summers working in a raspberry operation, doing basic plant care and carrying out quality-control lab tests on the fruit. Also, as I was growing up, I learned a great deal by helping with a large farm garden. In high school and college, I studied botany. Because of my interest in this field, I'm enrolled in the Environmental Studies program at Balliole.

Request an interview and thank the reader.

I am available for an interview. You may phone me any time at 341-3611 (and leave a message on my machine) or e-mail me at dvrl@balliole.edu. Thank you for considering my application.

Yours sincerely,

Ada Overlie

Ada Overlie

Encl. resume

The Recommendation Request Letter

When you apply for a job or program, it helps to present references or recommendations to show your fitness for the position. To get the support you need from people familiar with your work (instructors and employers), you need to ask for that support. You can do so in person or by phone, but a courteous and clear letter or e-mail message makes your request official and helps the person complete the recommendation effectively. Here is a suggested outline:

Situation: Remind the reader of your relationship to him or her; then ask the person to write a recommendation or to serve as a reference for you.

Explanation: Describe the work you did for the reader and the type of job, position, or program for which you are applying.

Action: Explain what form the recommendation should take, to whom it should be addressed, and where and when it needs to be sent.

2456 Charles Street
Lexington, KY 40588-8321
March 21, 2008

Dr. Rosa Perez
271 University Boulevard
University of Kentucky
Lexington, KY 40506-1440

Dear Dr. Perez:

The situation

As we discussed on the phone, I would appreciate your writing a recommendation letter for me. You know the quality of my academic work, my qualities as a person, and my potential for working in the medical field.

The explanation

As my professor for Biology 201 and 202, you are familiar with my grades and work habits. As my adviser, you know my career plans and should have a good sense of whether I have the qualities needed to succeed in the medical profession. I am asking you for your recommendation because I am applying for summer employment with the Lexington Ambulance Service. I recently received my Emergency Medical Technician (Basic) license to prepare for such work.

The action

Please send your letter to Rick Falk, EMT Coordinator, at the University Placement Office by April 8. Thank you for your help. Let me know if you need any other information (phone 231-6700; e-mail jnwllms@ukentucky.edu).

Yours sincerely,

Jon Williams

Jon Williams

The Application Essay

For some applications, you may be asked to submit an essay, a personal statement, or a response paper. For example, you might be applying for admission to an academic program (social work, engineering, optometry school) or for an internship, a scholarship, or a research grant. Whatever the situation, what you write and how well you write it will be important factors in the success of your application.

On the facing page is a model application essay. Jessy Jezowski wrote this essay as part of her application to a college social work program.

TIPS for an application essay

- Understand what you are being asked to write and why. How does the essay fit into the entire application? Who will read your essay? What will they look for?

- Focus on the instructions for writing the essay. What type of question is it? What topics are you asked to write about? What hints do the directions give about possible organization, emphasis, style, length, and method of submitting the essay?

- Be honest with yourself and your readers. Don't try to write only what you think readers want to hear.

- Think about your purpose and audience:
  - What do you want to gain (internship, scholarship, job interview), and how could your writing help you gain it?
  - Who are your readers? What do they know about you? What should they know?

- Develop your essay using the following organization (if the instructions allow for it):
  - An introduction with a fresh, interesting opening statement and a clear focus or theme
  - A body that develops the focus or theme clearly and concisely—with some details and examples—in a way appropriate to the instructions
  - A conclusion that stresses a positive point and looks forward to participating in the program, internship, organization, or position

- Write in a style that is personal but professional. Use words that fit the subject and the readers. Avoid clichés, and balance generalizations with concrete examples and details.

- Refine your first draft into a polished piece. First, get feedback from another student or, if appropriate, a professor, and revise the essay. Second, edit the final version thoroughly: You don't want typos and grammar errors to derail your application.

Model Application Essay

Audio

February 28, 2008
Jessy Jezowski

Personal Statement

The opening provides a clear focus for the essay.

While growing up in Chicago, I would see people hanging out on street corners, by grocery stores, and in parks—with no home and barely any belongings. Poverty and its related problems are all around us, and yet most people walk by them with blinders on. I have found myself quick to assume that someone else will help the poor man on the corner, the woman trapped in an abusive relationship, or the teenager struggling with an eating disorder. But I know in my heart that all members of society are responsible to and for each other. Social welfare issues affect every member of society—including me.   *1*

The writer demonstrates knowledge of the field and explains what she hopes to learn.

Because these issues are serious and difficult to solve, I wish to major in social work and eventually become a social worker. In the major, I want to gain the knowledge, skills, and attitudes that will make me part of the solution, not part of the problem. By studying social work institutions, the practices of social work, and the theory and history behind social work, I hope to learn how to help people help themselves. When that pregnant teenager comes to me, I want to have strong, practical advice—and be part of an effective social work agency that can help implement that advice.   *2*

Two concrete examples help back up her general statements.

I am especially interested at this point in working with families and teenagers, in either a community counseling or school setting. Two experiences have created this interest. First, a woman in my church who works for an adoption agency, Ms. Lesage, has modeled for me what it means to care for individuals and families within a community and around the world. Second, I was involved in a peer counseling program in high school. As counselors, we received training in interpersonal relationships and the nature of helping. In a concrete way, I experienced the complex challenges of helping others.   *3*

The conclusion summarizes her goals for the future.

I believe strongly in the value of all people and am interested in the well-being of others. As a social worker, I would strive to make society better (for individuals, families, and communities) by serving those in need, whatever their problems.   *4*

Preparing a Resumé

A strong resumé isn't generic—a ho-hum fill-in-the-blanker. Rather, it's a vivid word picture of your skills, knowledge, and past responsibilities. It says exactly who you are by providing the kind of information listed below.

Personal Data: name, address, phone number, e-mail address (enough for the reader to identify you and reach you easily).

Job Objective: the type of position you want and the type of organization for which you want to work.

Skills Summary: the key qualities and skills you bring to a position, listed with supporting details. Here are some skill areas that you might consider for your own resumé:

- Communication
- Organization
- Problem solving
- Computer

- Management (people, money, other resources)
- Working with people, counseling, training
- Sales, marketing, public relations
- Languages

Experience: positions you've held (where and when), and your specific duties and your accomplishments.

Education: degrees, courses, and special projects.

Other Experiences: volunteer work, awards, achievements, tutoring jobs, extra-curricular activities (related to your job objective), licenses, and certifications.

TIPS for resumé writing

- Design each resumé to fit the particular job.
- Be specific—use numbers, dates, and names.
- Present information first that is the most impressive and/or most important to the job for which you are applying. This guideline will help you determine whether to put your experience or your education first.
- Use everyday language and short, concise phrases.
- Be parallel—list similar items using similar structures.
- Use boldface type, underlining, white space, and indentations to make your resumé more readable.
- Get someone else's reaction; then revise and proofread.

Sample Resumé

Present contact information and employment objectives.

Ada Overlie

Home
451 Wiser Lake Road
Ferndale, WA 98248-8941
(360) 354-5916

School
Ogg Hall, Room 222
Balliole College
Eugene, OR 97440-0222
Phone: (503) 341-3611
E-mail: dvrl@balliole.edu

Job Objective: Part-time assistant in a nursery or greenhouse.

Skills Summary:
Horticultural Skills: Familiar with garden planting, care, and
    harvesting practices—planning, timing, companion planting,
    fertilizing.

Lab Skills: Familiar with procedures for taking fruit
    samples, pureeing them, checking for foreign objects, and
    testing sugar content.

Feature skills with appropriate headings and lists.

Experience:
Summers 2007 and 2008: Lab Technician.
    Mayberry Farms and Processing Plant, Ferndale, WA.
    Worked in Quality Control testing raspberries to make sure
    they met company standards.

Summers 2005 and 2006: Camp Counselor.
    Emerald Lake Summer Camp, Hillsboro, WA.
    Supervised 12-year-olds in many camp activities, including
    nature hikes in which we identified plants and trees.

List work and education chronologically, from most to least current.

Education:
August 2008 to present: Balliole College, Eugene, OR.
    Environmental Studies and Communication major.
    Courses completed and in progress include environmental
    studies and general botany. First semester GPA 3.7.

August 2004 to June 2008: Ferndale High School, Ferndale, WA.
    Courses included biology, agriculture, U.S. government, and
    economics.

    Special Projects: Completed research papers on
    clean-water legislation and organic farming practices.

Format for paper only: boldface, underlining, bulleted or indented lists, two columns.

References available upon request.

Offer references.

Sample Electronic Resumé

To find employees, companies often use computer programs to search electronic resumés for keywords (especially nouns) found in job descriptions or ads. Anticipating such a search, Jonathan Greenlind identified keywords and inserted them into his job description and resumé.

Present contact information and employment objective.

Jonathan L. Greenlind
806 5th Avenue
Waterloo, Iowa 50701
Telephone: 319.268.6955
E-mail: grnlnd@aol.com

OBJECTIVE
Position as hydraulics supervisor that calls for hydraulics expertise, technical skills, mechanical knowledge, reliability, and enthusiasm

List skills, experiences, and education using many keywords.

SKILLS
Operation and repair specialist in main and auxiliary power systems, subsystems, landing gears, brakes and pneumatic systems, hydraulic motors, reservoirs, actuators, pumps and cylinders from six types of hydraulic systems

Dependable, resourceful, strong leader, team worker

EXPERIENCE
Aviation Hydraulics Technician
United States Navy (2003–present)
* Repair, test, and maintain basic hydraulics, distribution systems, and aircraft structural hydraulics systems
* Manufacture low-, medium-, and high-pressure rubber and Teflon hydraulic hoses, and aluminum stainless-steel tubing
* Perform preflight, postflight, and other periodic aircraft inspections
* Operate ground-support equipment
* Supervise personnel
Aircraft Mechanic
Sioux Falls International Airport (2001–2003)
Sioux Falls, South Dakota
* Performed fueling, engine overhauls, minor repairs, and tire and oil changes of various aircraft

Format for e-mail:
•one column
•asterisks as bullets
•simple sans serif typeface
•flush-left margin
•no italics, boldface, or underlining
•ASCII or RTF text (readable by all computers)

EDUCATION
* United States Navy (2003–2007)
* Certificate in Hydraulic Technical School "A", GPA 3.8/4.0
* Certificate in Hydraulic, Pneumatic Test Stand School, GPA 3.9/4.0
* Courses in Corrosion Control, Hydraulic Tube Bender, Aviation Structural Mechanics
* Equivalent of 10 semester hours in Hydraulic Systems Maintenance and Structural Repair

Offer references.

References available upon request.

WRITING AND DESIGNING FOR THE WEB

26

A strong website depends on well-written, well-organized, and well-designed content. Above all, web content should be concise, focused, and visually appealing. After all, people don't read websites so much as they scan them, so information should be presented in short chunks of text. Webpages should be brief, designed to minimize scrolling and maximize the use of available screen space. Moreover, because online readers can be impatient, the writing must quickly and clearly address its intended purpose, audience, and topic. The chapter addresses the rhetorical fundamentals of creating a strong website and developing strong webpages.

Audio

Video

.01
.02
.03

Webpage Elements and Functions

To design an effective website and develop dynamic webpages, you need to start with a basic understanding of webpage elements and functions. Because webpages use the same elements as printed pages, many of the same design principles apply. However, unlike printed pages, webpages are fluid (flowing their contents to match screen and browser settings), and they can include both elements and functions, as shown and discussed below and on the pages that follow.

Page Elements

On the web, page elements are defined primarily by purpose—headings, body text, image, and so forth. Before designing a webpage, it helps to understand the purpose of those elements.

1. **Headings** (also called headers) come in six levels and are used to separate different sections and subsections of web documents. Heading 1 is the largest; heading 6 is the smallest. All are bold black serif font by default.

2. **Body text** is organized into chunks, called paragraphs, which are separated by white space. Unlike printed text, paragraphs on the web do not generally have a first-line indentation. By default, body text is a black serif font roughly the same size as a heading level 4 (though not bold).

3. **Preformatted text** is "monospaced"; it displays all characters at the same width, like typewriter font. It is used primarily to show mathematical formulas, computer code, and the like.

4. **Lists** can be formatted in three types: Ordered lists are numbered, unordered lists are bulleted, and definition lists present pairs of information—usually terms alongside their definitions, which are indented. Because readers can scan them quickly, lists are an efficient way to present information.

5. **Images** can include photographs, clip art, graphs, line drawings, cartoon figures, icons, and animations. These can make a page much slower to display, so use them judiciously. Always be sure you have the legal right to use any images that you include in your pages. (See "Copyright violations," page **481**.)

6. **Background color** for a webpage is white by default (medium gray in older browsers), which makes the standard headings and text easily legible.

7. **Tables** are a common tool for webpage layout. Simply put, tables are grids made up of rows and columns. By creating a table with no visible borders, a web designer can gain some control over where elements appear on a page.

Sample Webpage

Clear title —

Major sections —

Concise text —

Feature graphic —

Topic heading —

Feature heading —

Concise text —

Plain background for legibility —

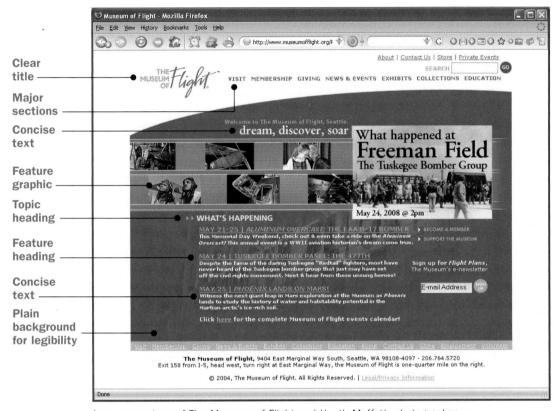

Images courtesy of The Museum of Flight and Heath Moffett, photographer.

As seen above, not all webpages have black serif font on a white background. However, because web browsers are designed to flow content to suit each computer screen, changing the default styles can be problematic. It helps to keep the following tips in mind:

- **Simple is best.** Simple pages display the fastest and have the least chance of breaking. The more graphics you add, the longer a page takes to load. The more you change the default font settings, the more complicated the code becomes and the greater the chance of computer error.
- **Different computers display things differently.** Not every computer has the same font styles installed, and colors look different on different monitors. Always check your work on many different systems.
- **The user is king (or queen).** No matter which font style and size you choose, the reader can change how things display on her or his machine. So focus on useful content and clear organization instead of struggling to control graphic design.

Page Functions

Webpage functions set electronic pages apart from printed pages. On the web, readers can browse pages in almost any order, send and receive e-mail, send messages and files, post messages, and join live "chat" sessions. In short, readers can interact with webpages in ways they cannot with printed pages. Like webpage elements, webpage functions should serve your site's purpose.

1. **Hyperlinks** are strings of specially formatted text that enable readers to jump to another spot on the web. Internal hyperlinks (links for short) take you to another section of the same webpage or to another page on the same site. External links lead to pages on other websites. "Mail to" links allow readers to address e-mail to recipients, such as a professor or a classmate.

2. **Menus** offer structured lists of links that operate like a website's table of contents. Menus are typically presented in a column or row at the edge of a webpage. Good websites include a standard site menu on every page so readers don't get lost.

3. **Forms** enable the host of a website to interact with the site's readers. Web forms can be used for questionnaires, surveys, complaints and service requests, job applications, or suggestion boxes.

Developing a Website and Webpages

Regardless of the purpose, topic, and audience of your website, you can develop it by following the steps outlined on the next four pages.

Get focused.

Create an overview of the project—the purpose, the audience, and the topic. The questions below will help you get focused and develop fitting content for the site.

1. **What is the primary purpose of the website?** Am I creating a library of documents that my audience will reference? Am I going to present information and announcements about myself or my organization? Am I trying to promote a specific product or service?

2. **Who is the site's audience?** Which people will seek out this site? Why? What do they need? How often will they visit the site, and how often should it be updated? How comfortable is my audience with using computers and websites? What level of formality is appropriate for the language? Which graphics, colors, and design will appeal to them?

3. **What is the site's central topic?** What do I already know about the topic? What do I need to learn, and where can I find the information? How will I demonstrate that the information is credible and reliable? What will my audience want to know about the topic? How can I divide the information into brief segments? What visual elements would help present my message? Which other websites address this topic? Should my website link to them?

Establish your central message.

After you've made decisions about your purpose, audience, and topic, write out the main idea you want to communicate. You might call this the theme or "mission statement" of your website.

> The purpose of this website is to inform fellow students and the general public about current research into hybrid-vehicle transportation.

To help you stay on target with your project, post this mission statement in plain sight. Note, too, that you might modify your goal as the site develops, or add secondary goals for the site.

Create a site map.

As you gather content for your site, create a site map. Websites can be as simple as an elementary school bulletin board or as complex as a United States federal government site. Here are four principles to keep in mind:

1. **No one will read your entire site.** People curl up with books, not websites. If your audience is not asking for content, don't provide it.

2. **Your site will have many small audiences**—not one big audience. A site's audience may include anyone with a computer, an Internet connection, and an interest in your site's topic. Keep all potential readers in mind.

3. **Websites are not linear.** A single "home page" or "splash page" introduces the site, which branches out like tree limbs into pages with varied content. Websites "conclude" whenever the reader quits reading.

4. **You may need to build the site in phases.** You can add pages to a website after it has been published, so be careful that your site's organization does not limit future additions.

Sample Site Map

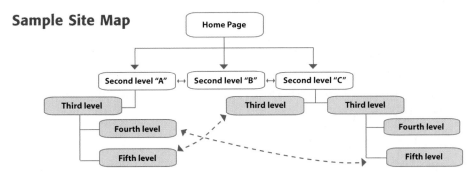

A map for a simple site might include only four items—a home page, page "A," page "B," and page "C" (as shown in white on the diagram). Users can "jump" between any of the secondary-level pages or back to the home page.

A more complex website typically needs more levels (as shown in green on the diagram). Likewise, its menu will offer more navigation choices. Related pages might be connected with links (as represented by the dotted lines).

Study similar sites.

Learn from successful sites, especially sites that serve a similar purpose—a campus club site, a department site, a personal job-search site. How do similar sites use elements: headings, body text, preformatted text, background color, lists, images, and tables? How do the sites use functions—links, menus, and forms? The seven traits (see pages 140–142) can also supply helpful benchmarks for evaluating sites.

1. **Ideas:** Does the site present clear ideas and information?

2. **Organization:** Is the content carefully and clearly structured?

3. **Voice:** Is the tone fitting for the audience?

4. **Words:** Is the language understandable? Is the wording concise?

5. **Sentences:** Are the sentences easy to read and generally short?

6. **Correctness:** Does the site avoid distracting errors?

7. **Design:** Are the pages user friendly? Is the site easy to navigate?

Gather and prioritize content.

Brainstorm and research the actual content, with the goal of creating an outline for your site. How many topics will the site address? How wide will your coverage of a topic be? How deep? Your outline can also be used to create the website's table of contents. Based on your research, discussions with others, and the deadlines for the project, select the content, features, and functions your site will offer.

Think about support materials.

List the documents (brochures, artworks, instructions, poems, reports) that will be presented on your site and note whether they will be displayed as webpages, made available for readers to download, or both. Construct a grid to keep track of how documents will be used.

List graphics that could make your pages more visual and informative and could help readers grasp the meaning of complex data or processes. Photographs may help "put a face" on your organization. Logos and icons will help brand your pages. Review the list below for electronic files that may be appropriate to your topic, audience, and purpose. (Remember: Use only graphics that are legally available. See the discussion of copyright on page 481.)

Images	Audio	Video
charts	music	animations
drawings	sound effects	film clips
graphs	spoken text	presentations
photographs		webcasts

Design and develop individual pages.

When you create individual pages for your site, consider both the design and the content—specifically, how to make the two work well together.

Design Principles

Most webpages—and the pages of most other publications—are designed on grids. Look at any newspaper or magazine page, and you should be able to draw horizontal and vertical lines denoting columns and rows of content. Some rows may span multiple columns, and some columns may overrun several rows.

Another fundamental design concept is balance. You might balance light elements with dark ones, text with images, and so forth. The balance of your page design should be driven by the purpose of your website, its audience, and its topic.

Websites may contain a variety of pages—each tailored to different purposes, audiences, and topics—to present some combination of informational and promotional content. Use each page's purpose to guide decisions about which elements and functions to include.

Webpage design should follow fundamental document-design principles, including strategies for using color effectively. For more information, visit **www.thecollegewriter.com/3e.**

Drafting Principles

1. **Identify the site.** Working from your mission statement, write a brief introduction informing visitors about the site's purpose.

2. **Provide clear links.** Create links for your pages, using clear descriptors such as "Original Poetry." (Avoid phrases such as "Click here for poetry.") If necessary, add a descriptive sentence to further identify the link. Let visitors know precisely where each link will take them.

3. **Introduce each page.** Search sites may deliver some visitors to a page other than your home page. Give each page a brief introduction that clearly identifies it. Also, remember to provide a link back to your home page.

4. **Title each page.** Atop the browser window is a title bar where the current page should be identified. This title is used in browser bookmarks, search engine listings, and the like, so be sure to give every page on your website a descriptive title.

5. **Keep pages uncluttered.** Dense text is even more difficult to read on screen than on paper, so use short paragraphs when you can. Add headings to identify sections, and include visuals to help break up the text.

6. **Save the page as HTML.** To be viewed in a web browser, your pages must be formatted in Hypertext Markup Language (HTML). Your word processor may have a "Save as HTML" or "Save as Webpage" option. Many HTML editing programs are also available on the web.

Test, refine, and post your site.

Most websites are developed through the combined efforts of writers, graphic designers, and programmers. In such an environment, many content and layout ideas might be considered, rejected, and reformulated to produce and launch the site. Of course, the audience ultimately decides a website's success or failure. For that reason, test and refine your site before posting it.

1. **Check the site yourself.** Open your home page from your web browser. Does the site make sense? Can you navigate it easily?

2. **Get peer review.** Ask classmates—both experienced and inexperienced with the website's topic and with Internet searching—to use your site. Watch them navigate it, and take notes about any confusion they have.

3. **Check the text.** Reread all the text on your site. Trim wherever possible (the shorter, the better online), and check all spelling and punctuation.

4. **Check the graphics.** Do images load properly? Do they load quickly? Are menus and page headings in the same place on every page?

5. **Provide a feedback link.** Provide your e-mail address on the site, inviting visitors to contact you with any comments after the site goes "live."

6. **Post the site.** Upload the site to your hosting space. (Check your host's instructions for doing so.) Add the posting date to each page, and update it each time you change a page.

7. **Check for universality.** View the site on several different types of computers, using different browsers. Does the layout display well on all of them? Make any needed changes.

8. **Announce the site.** Advertise your site in e-mails. Submit it to search sites. Consider joining a "web ring" of similar sites to draw more traffic. Let your professors, classmates, friends, and family know about your site.

9. **Monitor the site.** After a site has been launched, its success may be measured by the amount of traffic it receives, feedback submitted by users, and any use of resources or services. (Check with your host for ways to measure traffic.)

10. **Make adjustments and updates.** A website should be a living thing. Update the content when possible to keep it fresh, and make any adjustments needed to adapt to changing technologies.

INSIGHT: Avoid using any features and functions that do not support your overall purpose for writing. If you find yourself distracted by the many bells and whistles of the web, remember that it's better to have a simple website that presents information clearly and effectively than a complex site that does not.

Sample Webpages

On the next two pages, you'll find sample pages from student and academic websites. Study each model for insights about what makes for strong web content and design.

For further analysis of webpages, including nonprofit and business sites, go to **www.thecollegewriter.com/3e.** There you'll also find tutorials on analyzing and evaluating websites.

Student-Designed Website

The following website was developed by undergraduate students from a Southwestern U.S. university who were studying abroad. Southwest Sojourners is a multiuser site with blogs and chat rooms that allow students to keep in touch with one another and with friends and family back home.

Purpose: This site is a gathering place for undergraduate students studying abroad. It describes itself as a "home away from home" for such students. The tone is light, conversational, and inviting, as befitting the purpose of connecting these students to one another and to the important people in their lives.

Audience: The site is meant for students, friends, and family members. By providing straight news, individualized blogs, and chat rooms and e-mail options, the site allows users to be as passive or as active as they wish. Membership is required for active participation, and members must "sign" a user's agreement before posting material.

Format: The golden background and sun icon visually convey the Southwestern theme, while the minimalist format makes the site easy to navigate. A large four-item toolbar on the left directs users to the linked pages, and brief text on the right gives a clear indication of what lies at the end of each link.

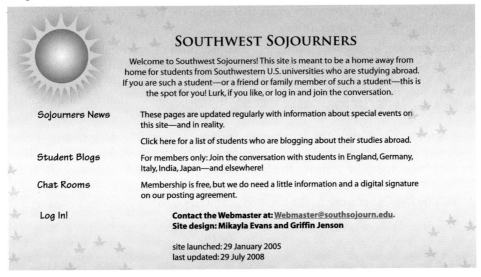

Academic Website

The Massachusetts Institute of Technology's Space Nanotechnology Laboratory website is an academic research site. It contains information about a specialized laboratory in the MIT Kavli Institute for Astrophysics and Space Research.

Courtesy of Space Nanotechnology Laboratory, Massachusetts Institute of Technology.

Purpose: This site aims to inform a very specific audience about a team of professors, graduate research assistants, and staff and their work to develop nanotechnology for space exploration. The site features the laboratory's creation of the "MIT Nanoruler," a device capable of measuring to the billionth of a meter. The site also provides pages that outline the laboratory's mission, history, people, projects, and facilities.

Audience: This website addresses "a consortium of microfabrication facilities with shared interests." In addition to providing articles of interest to this group, the site includes a list of available positions for professionals and students who may wish to join the laboratory. A sponsors page shows that the audience also includes funding agencies such as NASA and the National Science Foundation.

Format: The top of the home page announces the site and university, using iconic images of waveforms and a satellite to convey its central focus. Beneath this masthead, the page features the laboratory's current great achievement: "Home of the MIT Nanoruler" and "Read more about the Nanoruler." A selection of photos highlights work in the lab, and to the left, a list of pages makes navigation transparent.

Writing for Different Internet Environments

The Internet is a complex construct made up of much more than webpages. Other writing venues on the Net are described below, with writing tips for each.

OWLs Your university or college probably has a writing lab where you can seek help with your writing assignments. It might also have a web-based OWL (online writing lab) where you can access help. OWLs post answers to questions you may have about writing, and they often allow you to e-mail or send an instant message (see below) to a writing tutor. Before contacting an OWL tutor, carefully read any instructions posted on the site. *Example:* Purdue University OWL, owl.english.purdue.edu

Web Link

MUDs, MOOs, and MUSHes Some instructors hold classes or deliver lectures online in a MUD (multiuser dimension), a text-based "world" that people can share. (MOOs and MUSHes are variants of MUDs.) MUDs have virtual rooms to explore and virtual objects to examine and handle. To use a MUD, you must learn the text commands for interacting with it. Most MUDs require software for a telnet connection, but some are accessible via telnet-enabled webpages. *Example:* Diversity University MOO, www.marshall.edu/commdis/moo

Web Link

Message Boards Many websites have forms that allow visitors to post messages for public display. The messages and any replies are usually listed together so that readers can follow the message "thread."

Web Link

Mailing Lists Mailing lists allow users to send and receive text messages within a specific group of people interested in a particular subject. The software that maintains a mailing list is called a "list server." Some mailing lists are excellent resources of specialized information. *Example:* **QUANTUMTEACHING-NMC <MTEACHING-NMC@LISTS.MAINE.EDU>**

Web Link

Chat Servers A chat server provides a place on the Net where you can type a message that other people will see instantly. Those people can then respond with text messages of their own. Some teachers and tutors may use a chat room to confer with students or to hold a class discussion online. Although some chat servers require special software, many are available as webpages. *Example:* Yahoo! Chat, chat.yahoo.com

Web Link

Instant Messaging Services Instant messaging (IM) services allow you to send a text message instantaneously to friends and colleagues who use the same software. Most IMs also allow users to send computer files to one another. (Just be careful not to pass on a computer virus this way.) *Example:* ICQ, web.icq.com

Web Link

Blogs A blog (short for "weblog") is basically just an online journal posted to a webpage. In effect, it is a one-person message board (see above). For many people, blogging is more convenient than creating a webpage of their own, because it involves no design issues and requires no uploading of files.

Web Link

Writing Checklist

Use this checklist to review and revise your site and its pages:

_____ The purpose of the website is presented—or evident—on the home page and elsewhere on the site.

_____ The page elements—headlines, body text, preformatted text, background colors, lists, images, and tables—work together and are suited to the page's audience, topic, and purpose.

_____ The page functions, including navigation menus, are logically presented and enable readers to find what they need quickly.

_____ The content collected for the site (from brochures to reports) and support materials (images, audio, and video) are available, approved, accurate, and in the correct format for presentation or download.

_____ The site plan allows information to be presented and cross-referenced in logical and efficient pathways.

_____ The page design incorporates the design principles described on pages 403–404.

_____ The informational and promotional aspects of the site are appropriate to the audience, topic, and purpose.

Critical-Thinking and Writing Activities

As directed by your instructor, complete the following activities.

1. Research and study the content, style, and design of websites related to your particular major, field, or discipline. Then develop a report on those sites, incorporating three or four screen shots for analysis.

2. Go to the home page of your college or university and review the page elements and functions. Team up with a classmate to discuss how well the page addresses its purpose(s), audience(s), and topic(s). Then imagine you have been hired to revise and refine the page. Print out a copy and mark it up with your changes. Create a "mockup" of a new and improved home page. Draft a one-page overview that explains how your revision is better than the original.

3. Working with classmates, brainstorm a list of campus clubs and associations that currently do not have websites (or at least not quality websites). Using the guidelines from this chapter, develop a website for one of them. As another option, consider a nonprofit organization in your area. Collaborate and conduct research as needed.

◀ VISUALLY SPEAKING

Examine the photograph on page **397** and explain what it suggests about web design and web use.

PREPARING ORAL PRESENTATIONS 27

Throughout your career (including your college years), you will give many oral presentations—from brief introductions to lengthy reports. In each situation, the following basic steps will help you develop a strong message.

Audio

Video

State your purpose.

- Am I trying to persuade, inspire, inform, or teach?

Identify your audience.

- What are my listeners' ages, interests, and knowledge of the topic?
- What will their attitude be toward the topic and toward me?

Select and research your topic.

- Which topics will fulfill my assignment and achieve my purpose?
- Where can I find information about my topic?
- Which support materials would help me present my message?

Organizing Your Presentation

After you've gathered your information, you must organize and develop the message. How? Start by thinking about your presentation as having three distinct parts: (1) an introduction, (2) a body, and (3) a conclusion. The guidelines on this page and the following two pages will help you integrate, organize, and refine all the parts so they communicate the message and achieve your purpose.

Prepare an introduction.

For any speaking situation, you should develop an introduction that does the following things:

- Greets the audience and grabs their attention
- Communicates your interest in them
- Introduces your topic and main idea
- Shows that you have something worthwhile to say
- Establishes an appropriate tone

You may greet the audience in many ways, including introducing yourself or making appropriate comments about the occasion, the individuals present, or the setting. Following these comments, introduce your topic and main idea as quickly and as clearly as you can. For example, you could open with one of these attention-grabbing strategies:

- A little-known fact or statistic
- A series of questions
- A humorous story or anecdote
- An appropriate quotation
- A description of a serious problem
- A cartoon, picture, or drawing
- A short demonstration
- A statement about the topic's importance
- An eye-catching prop or display
- A video or an audio clip

Tip: As a matter of courtesy, audiences will generally give you their attention—but only for about thirty seconds. After that, you must *earn* it by presenting information that they believe is worth hearing.

Develop the body.

The body of your presentation should deliver the message—and supporting points—so clearly that the audience understands the presentation after hearing it only once. The key to developing such a clear message is choosing an organizational pattern that fits your purpose.

Before you outline the body, take a moment to review what you want your presentation to do: Explain a problem? Promote an idea? Teach a process? Be sure the organizational pattern will help you do that. For example, if you want to teach a process, the outline should list the process steps in chronological order. If your outline is clear, you may begin to write.

Organizational Patterns

Organizational patterns for explaining a process and other purposes are listed below.

- **Chronological order:** Arrange information according to the time order in which events (or steps in a process) take place.
- **Order of importance:** Arrange information according to its importance—greatest to least or least to greatest.
- **Comparison/contrast:** Give information about subjects by comparing and contrasting them.
- **Cause/effect:** Give information about a situation or problem by showing the causes and the effects.
- **Order of location:** Arrange information about subjects according to where things are located in relation to each other.
- **Problem/solution:** Describe a problem and then present a solution for it.

Writing an Outline or a Manuscript

After deciding how to organize your message, write it out in either outline or manuscript form. For help, see the tips below and the model on pages 414–415.

Body-Building Tips

- Build your presentation around several key ideas. (Don't try to cover too much ground.)
- Write with a personal, natural voice.
- Support your main points with reliable facts and clear examples.
- Present your information in short, easy-to-follow segments.
- Use positive, respectful language. (Avoid jargon.)
- Use graphic aids and handouts.

Come to a conclusion.

A strong introduction and conclusion work like bookends supporting the body of the presentation. The introduction gets the audience's attention, sets the tone, states the main idea, and identifies the key points of the message. Almost in reverse, the conclusion reviews those points, restates the main idea, reinforces the tone, and refocuses the audience on what it should think about or do. Together, those bookends emphasize and clarify the message so that listeners will understand and remember it.

Concluding Strategies

Here are some strategies—which you can use alone or in combination—for concluding a presentation:

- Review your main idea and key points.
- Issue a personal challenge.
- Come "full circle." (State those arguments or details that back up your original point.)
- Recommend a plan of action.
- Suggest additional sources of information.
- Thank the audience and ask for questions.

Hold a Q & A session.

After your presentation, you may want to invite your audience to ask questions. Very often, a Q & A session is the real payoff for participants. They can ask for clarification of points or inquire about how your message applies to their personal situations. Audience members may even offer their own insights or solutions to problems mentioned in the presentation.

Q & A Tips

The following suggestions will help you lead a good Q & A session:

- Listen carefully and think about each part of the question.
- Repeat or paraphrase questions for the benefit of the entire group.
- Answer the questions concisely and clearly.
- Respond honestly when you don't know the answer, and offer to find one.
- Ask for a follow-up question if someone seems confused after your answer.
- Look directly at the group when you answer.
- Be prepared to pose an important question or two if no one asks a question.
- Conclude by thanking the audience for their participation.

Writing Your Presentation

How much of your presentation you actually write out depends on your topic, audience, purpose, and—of course—personal style. The three most common forms to use when making a presentation are a list, an outline, and a manuscript.

List: Use a list for a short, informal speech such as an after-dinner introduction. Think about your purpose and then list the following:

- Your opening sentence (or two)
- A summary phrase for each of your main points
- Your closing sentence

Outline: Use an outline for a more complex or formal topic. You can organize your material in greater detail without tying yourself to a word-for-word presentation. Here's one way you can do it:

- Opening (complete sentences)
- All main points (sentences)
- Supporting points (phrases)
  quotations (written out)
  all supporting technical details,
  statistics, and sources (listed)
- Closing (complete sentences)

Wherever appropriate, include notes on visual aids (in caps or boldface).

Manuscript: Use the guidelines below if you plan to write out your presentation word for word:

- Double-space and number pages (or cards).
- Use complete sentences on a page (do not run sentences from one page to another).
- Mark difficult words for pronunciation.
- Mark the script for interpretation using symbols such as boldface or italics to signal emphasis or vocal color.

List

1. Opening sentence or two
2. Phrase 1
   Phrase 2
   Phrase 3
3. Closing sentence

Outline

I. Opening statement
   A. Point with support
   B. Point (purpose or goal) [VISUAL 1]
II. Body (with 3-5 main points)
   A. Main point
      1. Supporting details
      2. Supporting details
   B. Main point
      1. Supporting details
      2. Supporting details
   C. Main point
      1. Supporting details
      2. Supporting details
III. Closing statement
   A. Point, including restatement of purpose
   B. Point, possibly a call to action [VISUAL 2]

Student Model

In her formal presentation below, student Burnette Sawyer argues that college students must begin a retirement savings plan today. Notice that she uses italics to mark words needing vocal color and boldface to mark words needing emphasis. She places all visual aid cues in color.

Save Now or Pay Later

The speaker begins with an anecdote.

Imagine that you've finished school, gotten a job, worked hard all week, and this dollar bill represents your whole paycheck. [hold up dollar bill] As your employer, I'm about to hand you the check when I stop, tear off about 20 percent like this, give it to Uncle Sam, and say, "Here's my employee's income tax." Then I tear off another 30 percent like this, give that to Uncle Sam too, and say, "And here's her Medicare and Social Security tax."   *1*

She tears the dollar for emphasis.

Finally, I give you this half and say, "Here, hard worker, this is what's left of your *whole paycheck.*"   *2*

Does that sound like science fiction?   *3*

Senator Alan Simpson doesn't think so. In the magazine *Modern Maturity,* he says that unless legislation changes the Social Security system, *our generation* will have to pay 20 percent [SLIDE 1] of our paychecks as income tax, and 30 percent [SLIDE 2] as Social Security tax. That means we can keep just **50 percent** [SLIDE 3] of what we earn.   *4*

But the news gets **worse.** Remember this 30 percent that we paid to Social Security? [hold up piece of dollar bill] Well, that won't be enough money for retired people to live on in the year 2043. Remember that year, 2043—we'll come back to that soon.   *5*

The speaker asks questions to involve the audience.

What's the problem? The Social Security system can't ensure our savings for retirement.   *6*

What's the solution? We have to start our own savings plans, and the earlier, the better.   *7*

Throughout the speech, she uses 11 slides to give her listeners a clear understanding of the main points.

Ever since the Social Security system started back in 1935 [SLIDE 4], it has never been secure. While the system has been "fixed" a number of times, these fix-it jobs haven't solved the problem. For example, writer Keith Carlson points out that in 1983 [SLIDE 5] Congress raised payroll taxes, extended the retirement age, and said that the system would be in good financial shape until 2056.   *8*

But then, says Carlson, *just nine years later,* a report came out saying that Congress had been **wrong.** The report [SLIDE 6] said in 1992 that Social Security money wouldn't even last that long—it would run out by 2043. *Remember that year, 2043?* That's before many of us are supposed *to retire at age 67!*   *9*

Do you think this news is bad? The AARP Bulletin reported on the Bipartisan Commission on Entitlement and Tax Reform. This commission warned that entitlement programs like Social Security [SLIDE 7] are   *10* growing so fast they could "bankrupt the country" by the year 2029—long before we retire!

So what should we do? This fall many of us will vote in a presidential election for the first time. Both Democrats and Republicans say they have a plan to fix Social Security. What if we all vote for the presidential candidate with the best plan? Will that save our retirement funds? **Don't count on it!** As the track record for Social Security shows, one more fix-it job won't fix the system. We have to start *our own* retirement plans—and do it early in our careers. *11*

In fact, in his book *Retirement 101,* Willard Enteman says that we should start a personal savings plan the day we get our first paychecks. In sociology class last week, Mr. Christians made the same point. He gave us this bar graph [SLIDE 8] showing that if our goal is to save $500,000 by age 67, we had better *start early* before saving gets too expensive. *12*

As you can see from the graph, if we start saving when we're 25, we can reach $500,000 by saving just $121 a month. [SLIDE 9] If we wait until we're 35, we'll have to save $282 a month. [SLIDE 10] If we wait until we're 45, we'll have to put away $698 a month. [SLIDE 11] And if we wait until we're 55, we'll need $2,079 a month. *13*

Look at the difference. To reach $500,000 by age 67 would cost $121 a month if we start at 25, and $2,079 a month if we start at 55. *14*

What's my point? The Social Security system *can't promise us* financial security when we retire in 2050. *15*

What's the solution? We have to start our own savings plans; and the *earlier* we start, the *easier* it will be to reach our goals. ■ *16*

> The closing paragraphs help listeners reflect on the subject.

Note: Sample slides for this presentation are shown on page **416**.

Marking Your Presentation

As you rehearse your presentation, decide which words or phrases to emphasize, where to pause, and where to add visual aids. Then use the symbols and text enhancements below to mark the copy of your presentation.

Italic or boldface. . . . . for additional feeling or emotion
Underlining . . . . for greater volume or emphasis
Dash, diagonal, ellipsis. . . . . for a pause—or / a break in the flow
Brackets . . . . for actions or [visual aids]

Use visual aids.

While constructing your presentation, think about visual aids that would grab the audience's attention and help them understand the message. For example, in her speech, Burnette Sawyer used the computer-generated graphics below. (See pages 414–415.)

Sample Graphics

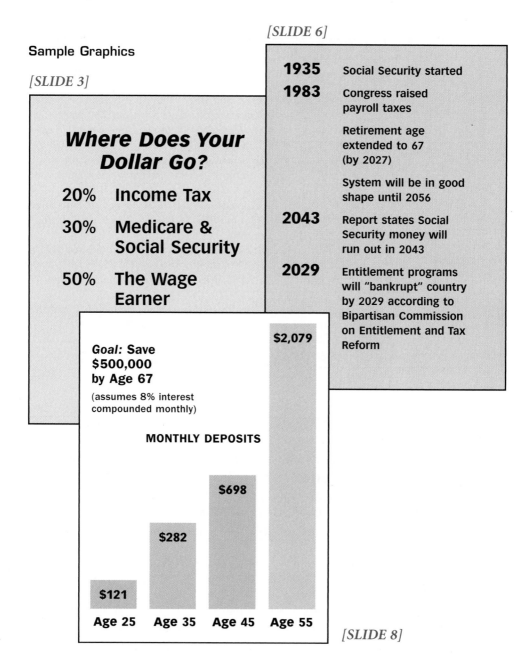

[SLIDE 3]

Where Does Your Dollar Go?

20% **Income Tax**

30% **Medicare & Social Security**

50% **The Wage Earner**

[SLIDE 6]

1935 Social Security started

1983 Congress raised payroll taxes

Retirement age extended to 67 (by 2027)

System will be in good shape until 2056

2043 Report states Social Security money will run out in 2043

2029 Entitlement programs will "bankrupt" country by 2029 according to Bipartisan Commission on Entitlement and Tax Reform

Goal: **Save $500,000 by Age 67**

(assumes 8% interest compounded monthly)

MONTHLY DEPOSITS

$2,079

$698

$282

$121

Age 25 **Age 35** **Age 45** **Age 55**

[SLIDE 8]

Developing Computer Presentations

To help you use presentation software effectively, follow the guidelines below.

1. **Develop a design.** Be sure your graphic design fits your topic and your audience—polished for a serious topic, casual for an informal topic.

2. **Create pages.** If a main idea has several parts, present each one on its own page. Each click of the mouse button (or computer key) should reveal a new detail.

3. **Use transitions.** Dissolves, fades, wipes, and other transitional effects refine a computer presentation and keep the audience's attention (as long as the devices don't detract from the message).

4. **Add sound.** Just as graphics and animation can enhance a presentation, so, too, can sound. Music can serve as an introduction or backdrop, and sound effects can add emphasis. Voice recording can add authority and help drive home key points.

TIP for speakers: Text can be animated to appear from off-screen at just the right moment. Graphics can be made to appear one element at a time, and illustrations can change before the viewer's eyes. Remember to use special effects—especially animation—wisely.

5. **Fine-tune your presentation.** Practice delivering your presentation while clicking through your pages. Try it with an audience of fellow students, if possible, and ask for their input.

6. **Check for word choice and style.** Make sure that the words on the screen are key words. Use these words as talking points—don't try to cover any point word for word. Also, check that transitions, animations, and sounds are smooth and not disruptive.

7. **Edit the final version.** Check spelling, punctuation, usage, and other mechanics. Remember: On-screen errors are glaringly obvious to everyone.

8. **Rehearse.** Perform your presentation for a friend or family member. Practice running the equipment until you can use it with confidence.

9. **Make a backup copy.** Protect all the effort you invested in your presentation.

TIP: Choose an easy-to-read font and type-size. In most situations, 36-point headings and 24-point text work well. However, the type-size needed depends on a number of variables, including the screen size, lens type, and audience's distance from the screen.

Overcoming Stage Fright Checklist

While it's okay to feel a little nervous before a presentation (the emotion keeps you alert), stage fright can limit your ability to communicate. The remedy for stage fright is confidence—confidence in what to say and how to say it. To develop that confidence, do the following:

Personal Preparation

_____ Know your subject well.

_____ Rehearse the presentation thoroughly, including the use of visuals.

_____ Schedule your time carefully, making sure to arrive early.

_____ Try to relax before the presentation by stretching or doing a deep-breathing exercise, remembering that your presentation can be successful without being perfect.

The Room and Equipment

_____ See that the room is clean, comfortable, and well lit.

_____ Make sure tables and chairs are set up and arranged correctly.

_____ Check that AV equipment is in place and working.

_____ Test the microphone volume.

_____ Position the screen and displays for good visibility.

Personal Details

_____ Check your clothing and hair.

_____ Arrange for drinking water to be available.

_____ Put your script and handouts in place.

Speaking Strategies

_____ Be confident, positive, and energetic.

_____ Maintain eye contact when speaking or listening.

_____ Use gestures naturally—don't force them.

_____ Provide for audience participation; survey the audience: "How many of you . . . ?"

_____ Maintain a comfortable, erect posture.

_____ Speak up and speak clearly—don't rush.

_____ Reword and clarify when necessary.

_____ After the presentation, ask for questions and answer them clearly.

_____ Thank the audience.

III

RESEARCH
AND WRITING

CONTENTS
Research and Writing

28 Getting Started: From Planning Research to Evaluating Sources

Papers with Documented Research
Quick Guide   **422**
The Research Process: A Flowchart   **423**
Getting Started: Getting Focused   **424**
Developing a Research Plan   **426**
Exploring Possible Information
Resources and Sites   **428**
Conducting Effective Keyword Searches   **430**
Engaging and Evaluating Sources   **432**
Creating a Working Bibliography   **436**
Developing a Note-Taking System   **438**
Summarizing, Paraphrasing, and
Quoting Source Material   **442**
Avoiding Unintentional Plagiarism   **445**
Checklist and Writing Activities   **446**

29 Conducting Primary and Library Research

Primary and Secondary Sources   **448**
Conducting Primary Research   **449**
Using the Library   **455**
Using Books in Research   **458**
Finding Periodical Articles   **460**
Checklist and Writing Activities   **464**

30 Conducting Research on the Internet

Understanding Internet Basics: A Primer   **466**
Locating Reliable Information   **468**
Checklist and Writing Activities   **474**

31 Drafting a Paper with Documented Research

Avoiding Plagiarism   **476**
Avoiding Other Source Abuses   **480**
Organizing and Synthesizing
Your Findings   **482**
Developing Your First Draft   **484**
Using Source Material in Your Writing   **486**
Checklist and Writing Activities   **490**

GETTING STARTED: FROM PLANNING RESEARCH TO EVALUATING SOURCES

Audio

At first glance, research looks like a dry-as-dust business carried out by obsessed scholars in dim libraries and mad scientists in cluttered laboratories. Research couldn't be further from the reality of your life.

But is it? Consider car tires. Before these were mounted, scientists researched which materials would resist wear and which adhesives would keep treads on steel belts. Sloppy research could cause blowouts; good research builds safe tires.

You want to do such good research in your college research assignments, which may be your toughest projects. They may take weeks to complete, including hours spent on the trail of facts, figures, and ideas. These projects demand that you organize your tasks carefully and digest the thinking of others while discovering your own perspective. However, the rewards of research projects can be great—new insights into a subject that really interests you, a deepened understanding of your major or profession, reliable knowledge to share with others, and sharpened thinking skills.

QUICK GUIDE

Papers with Documented Research

Web Link

When you work on a research project, you ask important questions, look systematically for answers, and share your conclusions with readers. In other words, it's all about curiosity, discovery, and dialogue.

Starting Point: The assignment usually relates to a course concept, so consider what your instructor wants you to learn and how your project will be evaluated. Then take ownership of the project by looking for an angle that makes the writing relevant for you.

Purpose: The project requires you to conduct research and share results. Your main goal is to discover the complex truth about a topic and clarify that discovery for others.

Form: The traditional research paper is a fairly long essay (5 to 15 pages) complete with thesis, supporting paragraphs, integrated sources, and careful documentation. However, you may be asked to shape your research into a field report, a website, or a multimedia presentation.

Audience: Traditionally, research writing addresses "the academic community," a group made up mainly of instructors and students. However, your actual audience may be more specific: addicted smokers, all Floridians, fellow immigrants, and so on.

Voice: The tone is usually formal or semiformal, but check your instructor's expectations. In any research writing, maintain a thoughtful, confidently measured tone. After all, your research has made you somewhat of an authority on the topic.

Point of View: Generally, research writers avoid the pronouns "I" and "you" in an effort to remain properly objective and academic sounding. Unfortunately, this practice can result in an overuse of both the pronoun "one" and the passive voice. Some instructors encourage students to connect research with experience, meaning that you may use the pronouns "I" and "you" occasionally. Be careful, however, to keep the focus where it belongs— on the topic. Bottom line: Follow your instructor's requirements concerning pronoun use. For more on developing a strong academic style for your research writing, see pages **78–79**.

INSIGHT: The best research writing centers on *your* ideas—ideas you develop through thoughtful engagement with sources. In poor research papers, the sources dominate, and the writer's perspective disappears.

The Research Process: A Flowchart

The research process involves getting started, planning, conducting the research, and organizing the results. This process is flexible enough to be adapted to diverse research projects. In fact, real research is typically dynamic: You might think during the planning phase that you've nailed down your topic, only to discover a surprising topical detour while conducting research. Generally, however, the research process maps out as shown below. When you get your assignment—whether to write a five-page paper on pasteurization or to develop a website on Middle Eastern political conflicts—review the process and tailor it to the task.

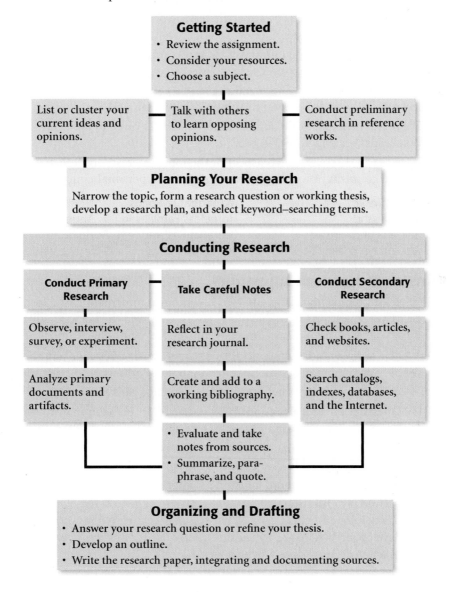

Getting Started
- Review the assignment.
- Consider your resources.
- Choose a subject.

List or cluster your current ideas and opinions.

Talk with others to learn opposing opinions.

Conduct preliminary research in reference works.

Planning Your Research
Narrow the topic, form a research question or working thesis, develop a research plan, and select keyword–searching terms.

Conducting Research

Conduct Primary Research

Take Careful Notes

Conduct Secondary Research

Observe, interview, survey, or experiment.

Reflect in your research journal.

Check books, articles, and websites.

Analyze primary documents and artifacts.

Create and add to a working bibliography.

Search catalogs, indexes, databases, and the Internet.

- Evaluate and take notes from sources.
- Summarize, paraphrase, and quote.

Organizing and Drafting
- Answer your research question or refine your thesis.
- Develop an outline.
- Write the research paper, integrating and documenting sources.

Video

Getting Started: Getting Focused

Early in your project, get focused by narrowing your topic, brainstorming research questions, and developing a working thesis. For help understanding assignments and selecting topics, as well as other prewriting strategies, see pages **30–31**.

Establish a narrow, manageable topic.

To do good research, you need an engaging, manageable topic. Once you have a broad topic, narrow your focus to a specific feature or angle that allows for in-depth research. Try these strategies:

Video

- Check your topic in the Library of Congress subject headings, available in your library. Note "narrower terms" listed (see page **430**).
- Read about your topic. By consulting specialized reference works, explore background that directs you to subtopics (see page **461**).
- Check the Internet. For example, follow a subject directory to see where your topic leads (see pages **469–473**).
- Freewrite to discover which aspect of the topic interests you most: a local angle, a connection with a group of people, or a personal concern.

Broad Topic	Manageable Focus
Homelessness	Homeless Families in Los Angeles
Bacteria and Viruses	Bacterial Resistance to Antibiotics
Alternative Energy Sources	Development of Hybrid-Electric Vehicles

Brainstorm research questions.

Good research questions help you find meaningful information and ideas about your topic. These questions sharpen your research goal, and the answers will become the focus of your writing. Brainstorm questions by following these guidelines:

List both simple and substantial questions. Basic questions aim for factual answers. More complex questions get at analysis, synthesis, and evaluation.

- **Question of fact:** When did Saddam Hussein gain power in Iraq?
- **Question of interpretation:** How did Saddam Hussein maintain power?

List main and secondary questions. Ask a primary question about your topic—the main issue that you want to get at. Then brainstorm secondary questions that you need to research to answer your primary question.

- **Main Question:** Should consumers embrace hybrid cars?
- **Secondary Questions** (*Who, What, When, Where, Why, How*): Who has developed hybrid cars? What is a hybrid car? When were hybrids developed? Where are hybrids currently used? Why are hybrids being developed? How does a hybrid work?

Testing Your Main Research Question

_____ Is the question so broad that I can't answer it in the project's time and page limits?

_____ Is the question so narrow that I won't be able to find sources?

_____ Is the question so simple that it will be too easy to answer?

_____ Will the question lead to significant sources and intellectual challenge?

_____ Am I committed to answering this question? Does it interest me?

_____ Will the question and answers interest my readers?

Develop a working thesis.

A working thesis offers a preliminary answer to your main research question. As your initial perspective on the topic, a good working thesis keeps you focused during research, helping you decide whether to carefully read a particular book or just skim it, fully explore a website or quickly surf through it. Make your working thesis a statement that demands "Prove it!" Don't settle for a simple statement of fact about your topic; instead, choose a working thesis that seems debatable or that requires some explanation. Try this formula:

Formula: Working Thesis =
        limited topic + _tentative claim, statement, or hypothesis_

Examples: **E-communication technologies** _are eroding real communication skills._

   Downtown revitalization _will have distinct economic, environmental, and social benefits._

   Internet dating _is weakening long-term relationships._

Working Thesis Checklist

_____ Does my working thesis focus on a single, limited topic?

_____ Is my working thesis stated in a clear, direct sentence?

_____ Does my working thesis convey my initial perspective about the topic?

_____ Do I have access to enough good information to support this working thesis?

_____ Does my working thesis direct me to write a paper that meets all assignment requirements?

INSIGHT: Your working thesis is written in sand, not stone. It may change as you research the topic because sources may push you in new directions. In fact, such change shows that you are engaging your sources and growing in your thinking.

Video

Developing a Research Plan

It pays to plan your research. In fact, minutes spent planning research can save hours doing research. With your limited topic, main research question, and working thesis in front of you, plan your project more fully.

Choose research methods.

Consider these questions: What do you already know about the topic? What do you need to know? Which resources will help you answer your research question? Which resources does the assignment require? Based on your answers, map out a research plan that draws resources from fitting categories.

Background research: To find information about your topic's context, central concepts, and key terms, take these steps:

- Use the Library of Congress subject headings to find keywords for searching the library catalog, periodical databases, and the Internet (see page **430**).
- Conduct a preliminary search of the library catalog, journal databases, and the Internet to confirm that good resources on your topic exist.
- Use specialized reference works to find background information, definitions, facts, and statistics (see page **461**).

Field or primary research: If appropriate for your project, conduct field research:

- Use interviews (page **454**) or surveys (page **450–451**) to get key information from experts or others.
- Conduct observations or experiments (page **449**) to obtain hard data.
- Analyze key documents or artifacts (pages **452–453**).

Library research: Select important library resources:

- Use scholarly books to get in-depth, reliable material (pages **458–459**).
- Use periodical articles (print or electronic) to get current, reliable information (pages **460–462**). Select from news sources, popular magazines, scholarly journals, and trade journals.
- Consider other library resources, such as a documentary, recorded interview, pamphlet, marketing study, or government publication.

Internet research: Plan effective Internet searches using the following:

- Search engines and subject guides: Choose tools that will lead you to quality resources (pages **472–473**).
- Expert guidance: Select reputable websites that librarians or other experts recommend (pages **468–471**).
- Evaluation: Test all web resources for reliability (pages **432–435**).
- Limitations: How many web resources are you allowed to use, if any?

Get organized to do research.

An organized approach to doing your research will save you time, help you work efficiently, and prevent frustration. Get organized by addressing these issues:

Establishing Priorities for Resources, Time, and Effort

- How much research material do you need?
- What range of resources will give you quality, reliable information?
- Which types of research does the assignment specify? Are you limited, for example, in the number of Internet sources you can use?
- What are the project's priorities: What must you do? Which tasks are secondary in nature?
- What weight does the project carry in the course? How should you match your time and effort with that weight?

INSIGHT: Gather more information than you could ever use in your paper. That richness gives you choices and allows you to sift for crucial information.

Selecting Research Methods and Systems

- Given the resources and technologies available, select methods that help you do research efficiently: signing out hard-copy library holdings or using interlibrary loan; photocopying book sections and journal articles; printing, saving, downloading, bookmarking, or e-mailing digital materials.
- Develop a note-taking system. Choose from the note-card, double-entry notebook, copy-and-annotate, and research-log methods (pages **438–441**). In addition, set up a working bibliography (pages **436–437**).
- Choose and review a documentation system. It's likely that your instructor will designate a system such as MLA (pages **493–534**) or APA (pages **535–566**). If he or she doesn't do so, then use a method that suits the subject matter and discipline. Review the system's basic rules and strategies.

Establishing a Schedule

Generally, you should spend about half your time on research and half on writing. Sketch out tentative deadlines for completing each phase of your work.

Web Link: A sample schedule is at **www.thecollegewriter.com/3e.**

Developing a Research Proposal

For some research projects (e.g., individual studies, field research, a senior thesis paper), you may have to formalize your plan by writing a research proposal. Such a proposal aims to show that the research is both valid and valuable; to communicate your enthusiasm for the project; to show that your plan is workable within the constraints of the assignment; and to gain your instructor's feedback and approval.

Web Link: A sample proposal is at **www.thecollegewriter.com/3e.**

Exploring Possible Information Resources and Sites

To conduct thorough, creative, but efficient research, you need a sense of which types of resources are available for your project and where to find them. Check the tables that follow.

Consider different information resources.

Examine the range of resources available: Which will give you the best information for your project? While one project (for example, a sociological report on airport behaviors) might require personal, direct sources, another project (for example, the effects of the September 11, 2001, terrorist attacks on the air transportation industry) might depend on government reports, business publications, and journal articles. Generally, a well-rounded research paper relies on a range of quality resources; in particular, it avoids relying on insubstantial web information.

Type of Resource	Examples
Personal, direct resources	Memories, diaries, journals, logs, experiments, tests, observations, interviews, surveys
Reference works (print and electronic)	Dictionaries, thesauruses, encyclopedias, almanacs, yearbooks, atlases, directories, guides, handbooks, indexes, abstracts, catalogs, bibliographies
Books (print and electronic)	Nonfiction, how-to, biographies, fiction, trade books, scholarly and scientific studies
Periodicals and news sources	Print newspapers, magazines, and journals; broadcast news and news magazines; online magazines, news sources, and discussion groups
Audiovisual, digital, and multimedia resources	Graphics (tables, graphs, charts, maps, drawings, photos), audiotapes, CDs, videos, DVDs, webpages, online databases
Government publications	Guides, programs, forms, legislation, regulations, reports, records, statistics
Business and nonprofit publications	Correspondence, reports, newsletters, pamphlets, brochures, ads, catalogs, instructions, handbooks, manuals, policies and procedures, seminar and training materials

Consider different information sites.

Where do you go to find the resources that you need? Consider the information "sites" listed below, remembering that many resources may be available in different forms in different locations. For example, a journal article may be available in library holdings or in an electronic database.

Information Location	Specific "Sites"
People	Experts (knowledge area, skill, occupation) Population segments or individuals (with representative or unusual experiences)
Libraries	General: public, college, online Specialized: legal, medical, government, business
Computer resources	Computers: software, CD-ROMs Networks: Internet and other online services (e-mail, limited-access databases, discussion groups, MUDs, chat rooms, websites, blogs, YouTube, image banks, wikis); intranets
Mass media	Radio (AM and FM) Television (network, public, cable, satellite) Print (newspapers, magazines, journals)
Testing, training, meeting, and observation sites	Plants, facilities, field sites, laboratories Research centers, universities, think tanks Conventions, conferences, seminars Museums, galleries, historical sites
Municipal, state, and federal government offices	Elected officials, representatives Offices and agencies, Government Printing Office Websites (GPO, www.gpoaccess.gov)
Business and nonprofit publications	Computer databases, company files Desktop reference materials Bulletin boards (physical and electronic) Company and department websites Departments and offices Associations, professional organizations Consulting, training, and business information services

Web Link

Conducting Effective Keyword Searches

Keyword searching can help you find information in electronic library catalogs, online databases that index periodical articles (for example, Lexis-Nexis, EBSCOhost), print indexes to periodical publications (for example, *Business Periodicals Index*), Internet resources, print books, and e-books.

Choose keywords carefully.

Keywords give you "compass points" for navigating through a sea of information. That's why choosing the best keywords is crucial. Consider these tips:

1. **Brainstorm a list of possible keywords**—topics, titles, and names—based on your current knowledge and/or background reading.

2. **Consult the Library of Congress subject headings.** These books contain the keywords librarians use when classifying materials. For example, if you looked up *immigrants,* you would find the entry below, indicating keywords to use, along with narrower, related, and broader terms. When you are conducting subject searches of catalogs and databases, these are the terms that will get you the best results.

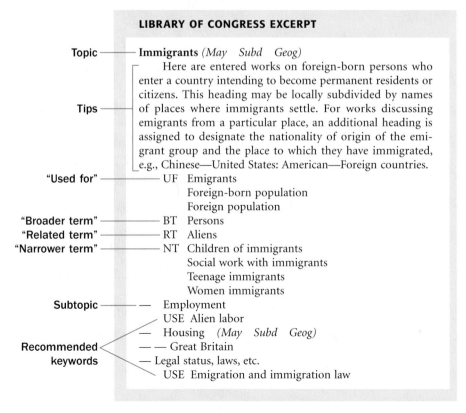

LIBRARY OF CONGRESS EXCERPT

Topic — **Immigrants** *(May Subd Geog)*

Tips — Here are entered works on foreign-born persons who enter a country intending to become permanent residents or citizens. This heading may be locally subdivided by names of places where immigrants settle. For works discussing emigrants from a particular place, an additional heading is assigned to designate the nationality of origin of the emigrant group and the place to which they have immigrated, e.g., Chinese—United States: American—Foreign countries.

"Used for" — UF Emigrants
Foreign-born population
Foreign population

"Broader term" — BT Persons
"Related term" — RT Aliens
"Narrower term" — NT Children of immigrants
Social work with immigrants
Teenage immigrants
Women immigrants

Subtopic — — Employment
USE Alien labor
— Housing *(May Subd Geog)*
Recommended — — Great Britain
keywords — Legal status, laws, etc.
USE Emigration and immigration law

Use keyword strategies.

The goal of a keyword search is to find quality research sources. To ensure that you identify the best resources available, follow these strategies:

Get to know the database. Look for answers to these questions:

- What material does the database contain? What time frames?
- What are you searching—authors, titles, subjects, full text?
- What are the search rules? How can you narrow the search?

Use a shotgun approach. Start with the most likely keyword. If you have no "hits," choose a related term. Once you get some hits, check the citations for clues regarding which words to use as you continue searching.

Use Boolean operators to refine your search. When you combine keywords with Boolean operators—such as those below—you will obtain better results.

Boolean Operators

Narrowing a Search
And, +, not, –
Use when one term gives you too many hits, especially irrelevant ones

And, +, not, – Use when one term gives you too many hits, especially irrelevant ones	buffalo and bison or **buffalo + bison**	Searches for citations containing both keywords
	buffalo not water +**buffalo –water**	Searches for "buffalo" but not "water," so that you eliminate material on water buffalo

Expanding a Search
Or Combine a term providing few hits with a related word	**buffalo or bison**	Searches for citations containing either term

Specifying a Phrase
Quotation marks Indicate that you wish to search for the exact phrase enclosed	"reclamation project"	Searches for the exact phrase "reclamation project"

Sequencing Operations
Parentheses Indicate that the operation should be performed before other operations in the search string	(buffalo or bison) and ranching	Searches first for citations containing either "buffalo" or "bison" before checking the resulting citations for "ranching"

Finding Variations
Wild card symbols Depending on the database, symbols such as $, ?, or # can find variations of a word	ethic# ethic$	Searches for terms like *ethics* and *ethical*

Engaging and Evaluating Sources

Using reliable benchmarks, you should test all sources before you rely on them in your writing. After all, credible sources help your own credibility; sources that aren't credible destroy it. The benchmarks on the next four pages will help you test your sources' usefulness and reliability.

Engage your sources.

Engaged reading is the opposite of passive reading—treating all sources equally, swallowing whole what's in the material, or looking only for information that supports your opinion. Full engagement involves these practices:

Test each source to see if it's worth reading. When reviewing source citations and generating a working bibliography, study titles, descriptions, lengths, and publication dates, asking these questions:

- How closely related to my topic is this source?
- Is this source too basic, overly complex, or just right?
- What could this source add to my overall balance of sources?

If you were writing about NASA's space shuttle program, for example, you might find a ten-page article in *Scientific American* more valuable and insightful than a brief news article on a specific flight or a *Star Trek* fan's blog on the topic.

INSIGHT: Don't reject a source simply because it disagrees with your perspective. Good research engages rather than ignores opposing points of view.

Skim sources before reading in-depth. Consider marking key pages or passages with sticky notes, tabs, or a digital bookmark.

- Review the author biography, preface, and/or introduction to discover the perspective, approach, scope, and research methods.
- Using your keywords, review any outline, abstract, table of contents, index, or home page to get a sense of coverage.

Read with an open but not an empty mind. Carry on a dialogue with the source, asking questions like "Why?" and "So what?"

- Note the purpose and audience. Was the piece written to inform or persuade? Is it aimed at the public, specialists, supporters, or opponents?
- Read to understand the source: What's clear and what's confusing?
- Relate the source to your research question: How does the source affirm or challenge your ideas? Synthesize what you read with what you know.
- Record your reactions to it—what it makes you think, feel, believe.
- Consider how you might use this source in your writing—key facts, important ideas, opposing perspectives, or examples.
- Check footnotes, references, appendices, and links for further leads.

Rate source reliability and depth.

You should judge each source on its own merit. Generally, however, types of sources can be rated for depth and reliability, as shown in the table below, based on their authorship, length, topic treatment, documentation, publication method, review process, distance from primary sources, allegiances, stability, and so on. Use the table to

1. Target sources that fit your project's goals,

2. Assess the approximate quality of the sources you're gathering, and

3. Build a strong bibliography that readers will respect.

DEEP, RELIABLE, CREDIBLE SOURCES

Scholarly Books and Articles: largely based on careful research; written by experts for experts; address topics in depth; involve peer review and careful editing; offer stable discussion of topic

Trade Books and Journal Articles: largely based on careful research; written by experts for educated general audience. *Sample periodicals: Atlantic Monthly, Scientific American, Nature, Orion*

Government Resources: books, reports, webpages, guides, statistics developed by experts at government agencies; provided as service to citizens; relatively objective. *Sample source: Statistical Abstract of the United States*

Reviewed Official Online Documents: Internet resources posted by legitimate institutions—colleges and universities, research institutes, service organizations; although offering a particular perspective, sources tend to be balanced

Reference Works and Textbooks: provide general and specialized information; carefully researched, reviewed, and edited; lack depth for focused research (e.g., general encyclopedia entry)

News and Topical Stories from Quality Sources: provide current affairs coverage (print and online), introduction-level articles of interest to general public; may lack depth and length. *Sample sources:* the *Washington Post,* the *New York Times; Time, Psychology Today;* NPR's *All Things Considered*

Popular Magazine Stories: short, introductory articles often distant from primary sources and without documentation; heavy advertising. *Sample sources: Glamour, Seventeen, Reader's Digest*

Business and Nonprofit Publications: pamphlets, reports, news releases, brochures, manuals; range from informative to sales-focused

List Server Discussions, Usenet Postings, Blog Articles, Talk Radio Discussions: highly open, fluid, undocumented, untested exchanges and publications; unstable resource

SHALLOW, UNRELIABLE, NOT CREDIBLE SOURCES

Unregulated Web Material: personal sites, joke sites, chat rooms, special-interest sites, advertising and junk e-mail (spam); no review process, little accountability, biased presentation

Tabloid Articles (print and web): contain exaggerated and untrue stories written to titillate and exploit. *Sample source:* the *National Enquirer,* the *Weekly World News*

Evaluate print and online sources.

As you work with a source, you need to test its reliability. The benchmarks that follow apply to both print and online sources; note, however, the additional tests offered for web sources.

Credible author An expert is an authority—someone who has mastered a subject area. Is the author an expert on this topic? What are her or his credentials, and can you confirm them? For example, an automotive engineer would be an expert on hybrid-vehicle technology, whereas a celebrity in a commercial would not.

> *Web test:* Is an author indicated? If so, are the author's credentials noted and contact information offered (for example, an e-mail address)?

Reliable publication Has the source been published by a scholarly press, a peer-reviewed professional journal, a quality trade-book publisher, or a trusted news source? Did you find this resource through a reliable search tool (for example, a library catalog or database)?

> *Web test:* Which individual or group posted this page? Is the site rated by a subject directory or library organization? How stable is the site—has it been around for a while and does material remain available, or is the site "fly-by-night"? Check the site's home page, and read "About Us" pages and mission statements, looking for evidence of the organization's perspective, history, and trustworthiness.

Unbiased discussion While all sources come from a specific perspective and represent specific commitments, a biased source may be pushing an agenda in an unfair, unbalanced, incomplete manner. Watch for bias toward a certain region, country, political party, industry, gender, race, ethnic group, or religion. Be alert to connections among authors, financial backers, and the points of view shared. For example, if an author has functioned as a consultant to or a lobbyist for a particular industry or group (oil, animal rights), his or her allegiances may lead to a biased presentation of an issue.

> *Web test:* Is the online document one-sided? Is the site nonprofit (.org), government (.gov), commercial (.com), educational (.edu), business (.biz), informational (.info), network-related (.net), or military (.mil)? Is the site U.S. or international? Is this organization pushing a cause, product, service, or belief? How do advertising or special interests affect the site? You might suspect, for example, the scientific claims of a site sponsored by a pro-smoking organization.

Web Link: Beware especially of masquerade sites—those that appear to be legitimate but are joke sites or, worse, propaganda lures. Check, for example, www.dhmo.org.

Current information A five-year-old book on computers may be outdated, but a forty-year-old book on Abraham Lincoln could still be the best source. Given what you need, is this source's discussion up-to-date?

Web test: When was the material originally posted and last updated? Are links live or dead?

Accurate information Bad research design, poor reporting, and sloppy documentation can lead to inaccurate information. Check the source for factual errors, statistical flaws, and conclusions that don't add up.

Web test: Is the site information-rich or -poor—filled with helpful, factual materials or fluffy with thin, unsubstantiated opinions? Can you trace and confirm sources by following links or conducting your own search?

Full, logical support Is the discussion of the topic reasonable, balanced, and complete? Are claims backed up with quality evidence? Does the source avoid faulty assumptions, twisted statistical analysis, logical fallacies, and unfair persuasion tactics? (See pages 267–270, for help.)

Web test: Does the webpage offer well-supported claims and helpful links to additional information?

Quality writing and design Is the source well written? Is it free of sarcasm, derogatory terms, clichés, catch phrases, mindless slogans, grammar slips, and spelling errors? Generally, poor writing correlates with sloppy thinking.

Web test: Are words neutral ("conservative perspective") or emotionally charged ("fascist agenda")? Are pages well designed—with clear rather than flashy, distracting multimedia elements? Is the site easy to navigate?

Positive relationship with other sources Does the source disagree with other sources? If yes, is the disagreement about the facts themselves or about how to interpret the facts? Which source seems more credible?

Web test: Is the site's information logically consistent with print sources? Do other reputable sites offer links to this site?

INSIGHT: Engage and evaluate visual resources as thoroughly as verbal materials. For example, ask yourself what tables, graphs, and photos really "say":

- Is the graphic informative or merely decorative?
- Does the graphic create a valid or manipulative central idea? For example, does the image seek to bypass logic by appealing to sexual impulses or to crude stereotypes?
- What does the graphic include and exclude in terms of information?
- Is the graphic well designed and easy to understand, or is it cluttered and distorted?
- Is a reliable source provided?

For more instruction on critical viewing, see pages 12–13.

Creating a Working Bibliography

A working bibliography lists sources you have used and intend to use. It helps you track your research, develop your final bibliography, and avoid plagiarism. Here's what to do:

Choose an orderly method.

Select an efficient approach for your project:

- **Paper note cards:** Use 3 × 5 inch cards, and record one source per card.
- **Paper notebook:** Use a small, spiral-bound book to record sources.
- **Computer program:** Record source information electronically, either by capturing citation details from online searches or by recording bibliographic information using word-processing software or research software such as TakeNote, EndNote Plus, or Bookends Pro.

Including Identifying Information for Sources

Start by giving each source a code number or letter: Doing so will help you when drafting and documenting your paper. Then include specific details for each kind of source listed below, shown on the facing page.

- A. **Books:** author, title and subtitle, publication details (place, publisher, date)
- B. **Periodicals:** author, article title, journal name, publication information (volume, number, date), page numbers
- C. **Online sources:** author (if available), document title, site sponsor, database name, publication or posting date, access date, other publication information, URL
- D. **Primary or field research:** date conducted, name and/or descriptive title of person interviewed, place observed, survey conducted, document analyzed

INSIGHT: Consider recording bibliographic details in the format of the documentation system you are using—MLA (pages 493–534) or APA (pages 535–566), for example. Doing so now will save time later. In addition, some research software allows you to record bibliographic information and then format it according to a specific system.

Adding Locating Information

Because you may need to retrace your research footsteps, include details about your research path:

- A. **Books:** Include the Library of Congress or Dewey call number.
- B. **Articles:** Note where and how you accessed them (stacks, current periodicals, microfilm, database)
- C. **Webpages:** Record the complete URL, not just the broader site address.
- D. **Field research:** Include a telephone number or e-mail address.

Annotating the Source

Add a note about the source's content, focus, reliability, and usefulness.

Sample Working Bibliography Entries

A. BOOK SOURCE NOTE:

> #2
>
> Howells, Coral Ann. Alice Munro.
> Contemporary World Writers. Manchester and New York:
> Manchester UP, 1998.
>
> PS 8576.U57 Z7 1998
>
> Book provides good introduction to Alice Munro's fiction,
> chapters arranged by Munro's works; contains intro,
> conclusion, and bibliography; 1998 date means author
> doesn't cover Munro's recent fiction

B. PERIODICAL SOURCE NOTE:

> #5
>
> Valdes, Marcela. "Some Stories Have to Be Told by
> Me: A Literary History of Alice Munro." Virginia
> Quarterly Review 82.3 (Summer 2006): 82-90.
>
> EBSCOhost Academic Search Premier http://web.
> ebscohost.com
>
> Article offers good introduction to Munro's life, her roots
> in Ontario, her writing career, and the key features of her
> stories

C. INTERNET SOURCE NOTE:

> #3
>
> "Alice Munro." Athabasca University Centre for Language
> and Literature: Canadian Writers. Updated 31 January
> 2008. Accessed 17 April 2008.
>
> http://www.athabascau.ca/writers/munro.html
> site offers good introduction to Munro's writing, along
> with links to bibliography and other resources

D. INTERVIEW SOURCE NOTE:

> #4
>
> Thacker, Robert. E-Mail interview. 7 March 2008.
>
> rthacker@mdu.edu
>
> author of critical biography on Munro, Alice Munro:
> Writing Her Lives, offered really helpful insights into her
> creative process, especially useful for story "Carried Away"

Developing a Note-Taking System

Accurate, thoughtful notes create a foundation for your research writing. The trick is to practice some sensible strategies and choose an efficient method.

Develop note-taking strategies.

What are you trying to do when you take notes on sources? What you are not doing is (a) collecting quotations to plunk in your project, (b) piling isolated grains of data into a large stack of disconnected facts, or (c) intensively reading and taking notes on every source you find. Instead, use these strategies:

Be selective. Guided by your research questions and working thesis, focus on sources that are central to your project. From these sources, record information clearly related to your limited topic, but also take notes on what surprises or puzzles you. Be selective, avoiding notes that are either too meager or too extensive. Suppose, for example, that you were writing a paper on the engineering problems facing NASA's space shuttle. If you were reading an article on the history and the future of this program, you might take careful notes on material describing the shuttle's technical details, but not on the astronauts' biographies.

Develop accurate, complete records. Your notes should . . .

- Accurately summarize, paraphrase, and quote sources (pages 442–444).
- Clearly show where you got your information.
- Cover all the research you've done—primary research (e.g., interviews, observations), books and periodical articles, and online sources.

Engage your sources. Evaluate what you are reading and develop your own responses. (See pages 4–11.) For example, with an article about NASA's space shuttle, you might test the author's biases, credentials, and logic; and you might respond with knowledge you have gained about other space programs.

INSIGHT: Take good notes on graphics in sources—tables, line graphs, photographs, maps, and so on. Such graphics are typically packed with information and powerfully convey ideas. (See "Critical Thinking Through Viewing," pages 12–17.)

Note-Taking Systems

A good note-taking system should help you do the following:

- Avoid unintentional plagiarism by developing accurate records, distinguishing among sources, and separating source material from your own ideas.
- Work efficiently at gathering what you need for the project.
- Work flexibly with a wide range of resources—primary and secondary, print and electronic, verbal and visual.
- Engage sources through creative and critical reflection.
- Record summaries, paraphrases, and quotations correctly.

- Be accurate and complete so that you need not reread sources.
- Efficiently develop your paper's outline and first draft.

INSIGHT: Different disciplines use different note-taking practices. In your major, learn these practices through courses that introduce you to the subject matter. Here are two examples:

- In literature studies, students conduct literary analyses by annotating print texts. Students may also take notes through keyword searches of e-books (for example, a Shakespeare play) and reviews of literary criticism.
- In environmental studies, students conduct research by (a) taking notes on published research to develop literature reviews, and (b) using a standard field notebook to collect data, make drawings, and reflect on results.

Four note-taking systems are outlined on the pages that follow. Choose the system that works best for your project, or combine elements to develop your own.

System 1: Paper or electronic note cards. Using paper note cards is the traditional method of note taking; however, note-taking software is now available with most word-processing programs and special programs like TakeNote, EndNote Plus, and Bookends Pro. Here's how a note-card system works:

1. Establish one set of cards (3 × 5 inches, if paper) for your bibliography.

2. On a second set of cards (4 × 6 inches, if paper), take notes on sources:
   - Record one point from one source per card.
   - Clarify the source: List the author's last name, a shortened title, or a code from the matching bibliography card. Include a page number.
   - Provide a topic or heading: Called a slug, the topic helps you categorize and order information.
   - Label the note as a summary, paraphrase, or quotation of the original.
   - Distinguish between the source's information and your own thoughts.

	1
Slug ———————————	PROBLEMS WITH INTERNAL-COMBUSTION CARS
Quotation ———————————	"In one year, the average gas-powered car produces five tons of carbon dioxide, which as it slowly builds up in the atmosphere causes global warming." (p. 43)
Page Number ———————————	
	-helpful fact about the extent of pollution caused by the traditional i-c engine
Comments ———————————	-how does this number compare with what a hybrid produces?
Source ———————————	#7

Upside: Note cards are highly systematic, helping you categorize material and organize it for an outline and a first draft.

Downside: The method can be initially tedious and time-consuming.

System 2: Copy (or save) and annotate. The copy-and-annotate method involves working with photocopies, print versions, or digital texts of sources:

1. Selectively photocopy, print, and/or save important sources. Copy carefully, making sure you have full pages, including the page numbers.

2. As needed, add identifying information on the copy—author, publication details, and date. Each page should be easy to identify and trace. When working with books, simply copy the title and copyright pages and keep them with the rest of your notes.

3. As you read, mark up the copy and highlight key statements. In the margins or digital file, record your ideas:
   - Ask questions. Insert a "?" in the margin, or write out the question.
   - Make connections. Draw arrows to link ideas, or make notes like "see page 36."
   - Add asides. Record what you think and feel while reading.
   - Define terms. Note important words that you need to understand.
   - Create a marginal index. Write keywords to identify themes and main parts.

   Upside: Copying, printing, and/or saving helps you record sources accurately; annotating encourages careful reading and thinking.

   Downside: Organizing material for drafting is inconvenient; when done poorly, annotating and highlighting involve skimming, not critical thinking.

 For a sample of annotation in action, see page **7**.

System 3: The computer notebook or research log. The computer notebook or research log method involves taking notes on a computer or on sheets of paper. Here's how it works:

1. Establish a central location for your notes—a notebook, a file folder, a binder, or an electronic folder.

2. Take notes one source at a time, making sure to identify the source fully. Number your note pages.

3. Using your initials or some other symbol, distinguish your own thoughts from source material.

4. Use codes in your notes to identify which information in the notes relates to which topic in your outline. Then, under each topic in the outline, write the page number in your notes where that information is recorded. With a notebook or log, you may be able to rearrange your notes into an outline by using copy and paste—but don't lose source information in the process!

   Upside: Taking notes feels natural without being overly systematic.
   Downside: Outlining and drafting may require time-consuming paper shuffling.

System 4: The double-entry notebook. The double-entry notebook involves parallel note taking—notes from sources beside your own brainstorming, reaction, and reflection. Using a notebook or the columns feature of your word-processing program, do the following:

1. Divide pages in half vertically.
2. In the left column, record bibliographic information and take notes on sources.
3. In the right column, write your responses. Think about what the source is saying, why the point is important, whether you agree with it, and how the point relates to other ideas and other sources.

Upside: This method creates accurate source records while encouraging thoughtful responses; also, it can be done on a computer.

Downside: Organizing material for drafting may be a challenge.

Cudworth, Erika. Environment and Society. Routledge Introductions to Environment Series. London and New York: Routledge, 2003.	
Ch. 6 "Society, 'Culture' and 'Nature'—Human Relations with Animals"	*I've actually had a fair bit of personal experience with animals—the horses, ducks, dogs, and cats on our hobby farm. Will this chapter make trouble for my thinking?*
chapter looks at how social scientists have understood historically the relationship between people and animals (158)	
the word animal is itself a problem when we remember that people too are animals but the distinction is often sharply made by people themselves (159)	*Yes, what really are the connections and differences between people and animals? Is it a different level of intelligence? Is there something more basic or fundamental? Are we afraid to see ourselves as animals, as creatures?*
"In everyday life, people interact with animals continually." (159) – author gives many common examples	*Many examples—pets, food, TV programs, zoos—apply to me. Hadn't thought about how much my life is integrated with animal life! What does that integration look like? What does it mean for me, for the animals?*

Summarizing, Paraphrasing, and Quoting Source Material

As you work with sources, you must decide what to put in your notes and how to record it—as a summary, a paraphrase, or a quotation. Use these guidelines:

- How relevant is the passage to your research question or working thesis?
- How strong and important is the information offered?
- How unique or memorable is the thinking or phrasing?

The more relevant, the stronger, and the more memorable the material is, the more likely you should note it.

The passage below comes from an article on GM's development of fuel-cell technology. Review the passage; study how the researcher summarizes, paraphrases, and quotes from the source; and then practice these same strategies as you take notes on sources.

INSIGHT: Whenever possible, include a page number, paragraph number, or other locating detail with your paraphrase, summary, or quotation. Such identification at this stage is crucial to avoiding plagiarism down the road (see pages **486–489**).

From Burns, L. D., McCormick, J. B., and Borroni-Bird, C. E. "Vehicle of Change." *Scientific American* **287:4 (October 2002): 10 pp.**

When Karl Benz rolled his Patent Motorcar out of the barn in 1886, he literally set the wheels of change in motion. The advent of the automobile led to dramatic alterations in people's way of life as well as the global economy—transformations that no one expected at the time. The ever increasing availability of economical personal transportation remade the world into a more accessible place while spawning a complex industrial infrastructure that shaped modern society.

Now another revolution could be sparked by automotive technology: one fueled by hydrogen rather than petroleum. Fuel cells—which cleave hydrogen atoms into protons and electrons that drive electric motors while emitting nothing worse than water vapor—could make the automobile much more environmentally friendly. Not only could cars become cleaner, they could also become safer, more comfortable, more personalized—and even perhaps less expensive. Further, these fuel-cell vehicles could be instrumental in motivating a shift toward a "greener" energy economy based on hydrogen. As that occurs, energy use and production could change significantly. Thus, hydrogen fuel-cell cars and trucks could help ensure a future in which personal mobility—the freedom to travel independently—could be sustained indefinitely, without compromising the environment or depleting the earth's natural resources.

A confluence of factors makes the big change seem increasingly likely. For one, the petroleum-fueled internal-combustion engine (ICE), as highly refined, reliable and economical as it is, is finally reaching its limits. Despite steady improvements, today's ICE vehicles are only 20 to 25 percent efficient in converting the energy content of fuels into drive-wheel power. And although the U.S. auto industry has cut exhaust emissions substantially since the unregulated 1960s—hydrocarbons dropped by 99 percent, carbon monoxide by 96 percent and nitrogen oxides by 95 percent—the continued production of carbon dioxide causes concern because of its potential to change the planet's climate.

Summarize useful passages.

Summarizing condenses in your own words the main points in a passage. Summarize when the source provides relevant ideas and information on your topic.

1. Reread the passage, jotting down a few key words.

2. State the main point in your own words. Add key supporting points, leaving out examples, details, and long explanations. Be objective: Don't mix your reactions with the summary.

3. Check your summary against the original, making sure that you use quotation marks around any exact phrases you borrow.

Sample Summary:

While the introduction of the car in the late nineteenth century has led to dramatic changes in society and world economics, another dramatic change is now taking place in the shift from gas engines to hydrogen technologies. Fuel cells may make the car "greener," and perhaps even safer, cheaper, and more comfortable. These automotive changes will affect the energy industry by making it more environmentally friendly; as a result, people will continue to enjoy mobility while transportation moves to renewable energy. One factor leading to this technological shift is that the internal-combustion engine has reached the limits of its efficiency, potential, and development—while remaining problematic with respect to emissions, climate change, and health.

Paraphrase key passages.

Paraphrasing puts a whole passage in your own words. Paraphrase passages that present important points, explanations, or arguments but that don't contain memorable or straightforward wording. Follow these steps:

1. Quickly review the passage to get a sense of the whole, and then go through the passage carefully, sentence by sentence.
   - State the ideas in your own words, defining words as needed.
   - If necessary, edit for clarity, but don't change the meaning.
   - If you borrow phrases directly, put them in quotation marks.

2. Check your paraphrase against the original for accurate tone and meaning.

Sample Paraphrase of the Second Paragraph in the Passage:

Automobile technology may lead to another radical economic and social change through the shift from gasoline to hydrogen fuel. By breaking hydrogen into protons and electrons so that the electrons run an electric motor with only the by-product of water vapor, fuel cells could make the car a "green" machine. But this technology could also increase the automobile's safety, comfort, personal tailoring, and affordability. Moreover, this shift to fuel-cell engines in automobiles could lead to drastic, environmentally friendly changes in the broader energy industry, one that will be now tied to hydrogen rather than fossil fuels. The result from this shift will be radical changes in the way we use and produce energy. In other words, the shift to hydrogen-powered vehicles could promise to maintain society's valued mobility, while the clean technology would preserve the environment and its natural resources.

Web Link

Quote crucial phrases, sentences, and passages.

Quoting records statements or phrases in the original source word for word. Quote nuggets only—statements that are well phrased or authoritative:

1. Note the quotation's context—how it fits in the author's discussion.

2. Copy the passage word for word, enclosing it in quotation marks and checking its accuracy.

3. If you omit words, note that omission with an ellipsis. If you change any word for grammatical reasons, put changes in brackets. (See page 489).

Sample Quotations:

"[H]ydrogen fuel-cell cars and trucks could help ensure a future in which personal mobility . . . could be sustained indefinitely, without compromising the environment or depleting the earth's natural resources."

Note: This sentence captures the authors' main claim about the benefits and future of fuel-cell technology.

"[T]he petroleum-fueled internal-combustion engine (ICE), as highly refined, reliable and economical as it is, is finally reaching its limits."

Note: This quotation offers a well-phrased statement about the essential problem.

INSIGHT: Whether you are summarizing, paraphrasing, or quoting, aim to be true to the source by respecting the context and spirit of the original. Avoid shifting the focus or ripping material out of its context and forcing it into your own. For example, in the sample passage the authors discuss the limits of the internal-combustion engine. If you were to claim that these authors are arguing that the internal-combustion engine was an enormous engineering and environmental mistake, you would be twisting their comments to serve your own writing agenda.

For instruction on effectively integrating quotations, paraphrases, and summaries into your writing, see pages 486–489.

Avoiding Unintentional Plagiarism

Careful note taking helps prevent unintentional plagiarism. Plagiarism—using source material without giving credit—is treated more fully elsewhere (pages 476–479); essentially, however, unintentional plagiarism happens when you accidentally use a source's ideas, phrases, or information without documenting that material. At the planning stage of your project, you can prevent this problem from happening by adhering to principles of ethical research and following some practical guidelines.

Practice the principles of ethical research.

Because of the nature of information and the many challenges of working with it, conducting ethical research can be very complex and involved. To start with, however, commit to these principles of ethical research:

- Do the research and write the paper yourself.
- Adhere to the research practices approved in your discipline.
- Follow school- and discipline-related guidelines for working with people, resources, and technology.
- Avoid one-sided research that ignores or conceals opposition.
- Present real, accurate data and results—not "fudged" or twisted facts.
- Treat source material fairly in your writing.

Practices That Prevent Unintentional Plagiarism

The principles of ethical research above find expression when you prevent unintentional plagiarism. Do so by following these practices:

- Maintain an accurate working bibliography (pages 436–437).
- When taking notes, distinguish source material from your own reflection by using quotation marks, codes, and/or separate columns or note cards.
- When you draft your paper, transfer source material carefully by coding material that you integrate into your discussion, using quotation marks, double-checking your typing, or using copy and paste to ensure accuracy.
- Take time to do the project right—both research and writing. Avoid pulling an all-nighter during which you can't properly work with sources.

Practices That Prevent Internet Plagiarism

An especially thorny area related to unintentional plagiarism centers on the Internet. As with traditional print sources, Internet sources must be properly credited; in other words, web material cannot simply be transferred to your paper without acknowledgement. So treat web sources like print sources. And if you copy and paste digital material while taking notes and drafting, always track its origins with codes, abbreviations, or separate columns.

Checklist for Research

Use the checklist below to test how well you have gotten started on any given research project.

_____ I have clarified my assignment: the purpose, readers, and resources.

_____ I have selected an appropriate topic, conducted preliminary research, narrowed my focus, and developed a key research question or a clear working thesis.

_____ I have chosen research methods and gotten organized to do my research effectively.

_____ I have considered the range of resources and possible research sites available for my project.

_____ I have established and used a note-taking system that effectively keeps track of research resources, helps me gather key ideas and information from these sources, and encourages me to do my own thinking.

_____ I have carefully engaged and evaluated all my sources.

_____ I have sensibly summarized, paraphrased, and quoted useful sources.

_____ I have taken careful notes to prevent unintentional plagiarism.

Critical-Thinking and Writing Activities

As directed by your instructor, complete the following activities.

1. Write a research report about your major area of study. Discuss the types of knowledge the major explores and the professions to which it leads. Address the paper to students considering this major.

2. For a current research project, find and list fifteen to twenty available sources on your topic. Visit libraries to locate books, articles, and so forth. Use a search engine and locate sources on the web. Finally, list any interviews, observations, surveys, and questionnaires that you might set up.

3. Test the reliability of one of your Internet sources for a current research project. Refer to the "web test" questions on pages 434–435, and see if you can answer all of them. Based on your answers, decide whether the source is credible enough to strengthen your paper.

4. Choose a short article or a passage from one of your longer sources. Restate (paraphrase) what you have read using your own words. Put quotation marks around key words and phrases that you take directly from the text. Next, use the same materials to create a summary. Reduce what you just read to a few clear and important points using your own words.

◀ VISUALLY SPEAKING

Study the photograph at the beginning of this chapter (page 421). What does the collection of tools suggest about research and getting started on a research project?

CONDUCTING PRIMARY AND LIBRARY RESEARCH

Audio

Today, conducting research is both easy and difficult. It's easy because research technology is powerful and many research methods are available. It's difficult because that technology and those methods provide access to so much information—the good, the bad, and the ugly.

How do you meet this challenge and conduct quality research? First, consider whether your project would benefit from primary research. When you engage in primary research, you gather information firsthand by observing sites, interviewing people, and analyzing documents. Second, learn how to use an expert resource—your college library. The library is your gateway to print and electronic materials.

Primary and Secondary Sources

Information sources for your research project can be either primary or secondary. Depending on your assignment, you may be expected to use one or both kinds of sources.

Consider primary sources.

A primary source is an original source, which gives firsthand information on a topic. This source (such as a diary, a person, or an event) informs you directly about the topic, rather than through another person's explanation or interpretation. The most common forms of primary research are observations, interviews, surveys, experiments, and analyses of original documents and artifacts.

Consider secondary sources.

Secondary sources present secondhand information on your topic—information at least once removed from the original. This information has been compiled, summarized, analyzed, synthesized, interpreted, or evaluated by someone studying primary sources. Journal articles, encyclopedia entries, documentaries, and nonfiction books are typical examples of such secondary sources.

Example: Below are possible primary and secondary sources for a research project exploring hybrid car technology and its viability. Note: Whether a source is primary or secondary depends on what you are studying. For example, if you were studying U.S. attitudes toward hybrid cars (and not hybrid car technology itself), the newspaper editorial and TV roundtable would be primary sources.

Primary Sources	Secondary Sources
E-mail interview with automotive engineer	Journal article discussing the development of hybrid car technology
Fuel-efficiency legislation	Newspaper editorial on fossil fuels
Visit and test-drive a car at a dealership	TV news roundtable discussion of hybrid car advantages and disadvantages
Published statistics about hybrid car sales	Promotional literature for a specific hybrid car

INSIGHT: Some resources are tertiary—that is, thirdhand. They are essentially reports of reports of research and, therefore, are distant from the original information. Examples of tertiary sources would include some articles in popular magazines and entries in Wikipedia. Aside from giving you ideas for focusing your topic, tertiary sources should generally not be used in college research projects and should not appear in works-cited or references lists.

Conducting Primary Research

When published sources can't give you the information that you need, consider conducting primary research. However, you must first weigh all its advantages and disadvantages.

Upside of Primary Research

- It produces information precisely tailored to your research needs.
- It gives you direct, hands-on access to your topic.

Downside of Primary Research

- It can take a lot of time and many resources to complete.
- It can require special skills, such as designing surveys and analyzing statistics and original documents.

Conduct primary research.

You need to choose the method of primary research that best suits your project. For help, review the following descriptions:

1. **Surveys and questionnaires** gather written responses you can review, tabulate, and analyze. These research tools pull together varied information—from simple facts to personal opinions and attitudes. See "Conduct surveys" on pages **450–451**.

2. **Interviews** involve consulting two types of people. First, you can interview experts for their insights on your topic. Second, you can interview people whose direct experiences with the topic give you their personal insights. See "Conduct interviews," page **454**, and "Interview Report," pages **331–338**.

3. **Observations, inspections, and field research** require you to examine and analyze people, places, events, and so on. Whether you rely simply on your five senses or use scientific techniques, observing provides insights into the present state of your subject. For help with observation, field research, and writing reports based on this work, go to **www.thecollegewriter.com/3e**.

4. **Experiments** test hypotheses—predictions about why things do what they do—to arrive at conclusions that can be accepted and acted upon. Such testing often explores cause/effect relationships. See "Lab, Experiment, and Field Reports" on pages **339–352**.

5. **Analysis of documents and artifacts** involves studying original reports, statistics, legislation, literature, artwork, and historical records. Such analysis provides unique, close-up interpretations of your topic. See "Analyze texts, documents, records, and artifacts" on pages **452–453**, as well as "Writing About Literature and the Arts" on pages **355–372**.

Conduct surveys.

One source of primary information that you can use for research projects is a survey or questionnaire. Surveys can collect facts and opinions from a wide range of people about virtually any topic. To get valid information, follow these guidelines:

1. **Find a focus.**
   - Limit the purpose of your survey.
   - Target a specific audience.

2. **Ask clear questions.**
   - Phrase questions so they can be easily understood.
   - Use words that are objective (not biased or slanted).

3. **Match your questions to your purpose.**
   - Closed questions give respondents easy-answer options, and the answers are easy to tabulate. Closed questions can provide two choices (*yes* or *no, true* or *false*), multiple choices, a rating scale (*poor 1 2 3 excellent*), or a blank to fill.
   - Open-ended questions bring in a wide variety of responses and more complex information, but they take time to complete, and the answers can be difficult to summarize.

4. **Organize your survey so that it's easy to complete.**
   - In the introduction, state who you are and why you need the information. Explain how to complete the survey and when and where to return it.
   - Guide readers by providing numbers, instructions, and headings.
   - Begin with basic questions and end with any complex, open-ended questions that are necessary. Move in a logical order from one topic to the next.

5. **Test your survey before using it.**
   - Ask a friend or classmate to read your survey and help you revise it, if necessary, before printing it.
   - Try out your survey with a small test group.

6. **Conduct your survey.**
   - Distribute the survey to a clearly defined group that won't prejudice the sampling (random or cross section).
   - Get responses from a good sample of your target group (10 percent if at all possible).
   - Tabulate responses carefully and objectively.
     Note: To develop statistically valid results, you may need expert help. Check with your instructor.

Sample Survey

The introduction includes the essential information about the survey.

Confidential Survey

My name is Cho Lang, and I'm conducting research about the use of training supplements. I'd like to hear from you, Alfred University's athletes. Please answer the questions below by circling or writing out your responses. Return your survey to me, care of the Dept. of Psychology, through campus mail by Friday, April 5. Your responses will remain confidential.

The survey begins with clear, basic questions.

1. Circle your gender.   **Male   Female**

2. Circle your year.
   Freshman   Sophomore   Junior   Senior

3. List the sports that you play.

4. Are you presently using a training supplement?
   Yes   No
   Note: If you circled "no," you may turn in your survey at this point.

The survey asks an open-ended question.

5. Describe your supplement use (type, amount, and frequency).

6. Who supervises your use of this training supplement?
   Coach   Trainer   Self   Others

7. How long have you used it?
   Less than 1 month   1–12 months
   12+ months

The survey covers the topic thoroughly.

8. How many pounds have you gained while using this supplement?

9. How much has your athletic performance improved?
   None   1   2   3   4   5   Greatly

10. Circle any side effects you've experienced.
    Dehydration   Nausea   Diarrhea

Analyze texts, documents, records, and artifacts.

An original document or record is one that relates directly to the event, issue, object, or phenomenon you are researching. Examining original documents and artifacts can involve studying letters, e-mail exchanges, case notes, literary texts, sales records, legislation, and material objects such as tools, sculptures, buildings, and tombs. As you analyze such documents and records, you examine evidence in an effort to understand a topic, arrive at a coherent conclusion about it, and support that judgment. How do you work with such diverse documents, records, and artifacts? Here are some guidelines:

Choose evidence close to your topic. Which texts, documents, records, and artifacts originated from or grew out of the topic you are researching? The closer to the topic, the more primary the source. Select materials that are directly related to your research questions and/or working thesis.

Example: If you were studying English labor riots of the 1830s, you could investigate these primary sources:

- To understand what rioters were demanding, copies of speeches given at demonstrations
- To know who the rioters were, names from police reports or union membership lists
- To learn the political response to the riots, political speeches or legislation
- To get at the attitudes of people from that time, newspaper reports, works of art, or novels from the period
- To find people's personal stories and private opinions related to the riots, personal letters, diaries, family albums, gravestones, and funeral eulogies

Frame your examination with questions. To make sense of the text, document, record, or artifact, understand what you are looking for and why. List the secondary questions that you want to answer in relation to the main question behind your research project.

Example: To study the legislative background behind the development of cleaner cars, such as the hybrid-fuel vehicle, you could access various documents on the Clean Air Act of 1990 (for example, *The Plain English Guide to the Clean Air Act,* an EPA publication). As you study this legislation, you could frame your reading with these additional questions:

- What are the requirements of the Clean Air Act?
- Specifically, how do those requirements affect automotive technology?
- Which private and public research projects will likely influence these requirements?
- Are schedules for change or deadlines written into the Clean Air Act?

Put the document or artifact in context. So that the material takes on meaning, clarify its external and internal natures. First, consider its external context—the five W's and H: What exactly is it? Who made it, when, where, why, and how? Second, consider its internal nature—what the document means, based on what it can and cannot show you: What does the language mean or refer to? What is the document's structure? What are the artifact's composition and style?

Example: If you were examining Mary Wollstonecraft's *A Vindication of the Rights of Woman* in a history or women's studies course, you would consider the following:

- **External Context:** who Mary Wollstonecraft was; when and why she wrote *A Vindication* and under what conditions; for whom she wrote it and their response; the type of document it is
- **Internal Context:** Wollstonecraft's essential argument and evidence; the nature of her views, their relationship to her times, and their relevance today

Draw coherent conclusions about meaning. Make sense of the source in relation to your research questions. What connections does the source reveal? What important changes or developments? What cause/effect relationships? What themes?

Example: A study of the Clean Air Act might lead you to a variety of conclusions regarding how environmental legislation relates to the development of hybrid technology—for example, that the United States must produce cleaner cars if it hopes to gain improved air quality.

INSIGHT: Studying primary documents and artifacts is central to many disciplines—history, literature, theology, philosophy, political studies, and archaeology, for example. Good analysis depends on asking research questions appropriate for the discipline. With the English labor riots of the 1830s again as an example, here's what three disciplines might ask:

- **Political science:** What role did political theories, structures, and processes play in the riots—both in causing and in responding to them?
- **Art:** How were the concerns of the rioters embodied in the new "realist" style of the mid-1800s? Did artists sympathize with and address an alienated working-class audience? How did art comment on the social structures of the time?
- **Sociology:** What type and quality of education did most workers have in the 1830s? How did that education affect their economic status and employment opportunities? Did issues related to the riots prompt changes in the English educational system? What changes and why?

With these examples in mind, consider your own major: What questions would this discipline ask of the English labor riots, of Mary Wollstonecraft's *A Vindication of the Rights of Woman,* or of the Clean Air Act of 1990?

Conduct interviews.

The purpose of an interview is simple: To get information, you talk with someone who has significant experience or someone who is an expert on your topic. Use the guidelines below whenever you conduct an interview. (See also pages **331–338**.)

1. **Before the interview,** do your homework about the topic and the person you are planning to interview.

    *   Arrange the interview in a thoughtful way. Explain to the interviewee your purpose and the topics to be covered.
    *   Think about the specific ideas you want to cover in the interview and write questions for each. Addressing the 5 W's and H (*Who? What? Where? When? Why?* and *How?*) is important for good coverage.
    *   Organize your questions in a logical order so the interview moves smoothly from one subject to the next.
    *   Write the questions on the left side of a page. Leave room for quotations, information, and impressions on the right side.

2. **During the interview,** try to relax so that your conversation is natural and sincere.

    Based on the interviewee's responses, ask follow-up questions, and don't limit yourself to your planned questions only.

    *   Provide some background information about yourself, your project, and your plans for using the interview information.
    *   Use recording equipment only with the interviewee's permission.
    *   Jot down key facts and quotations.
    *   Listen actively. Show that you're listening through your body language—eye contact, nods, smiles. Pay attention not only to what the person says, but also to how he or she says it.
    *   Be flexible. If the person looks puzzled by a question, rephrase it. If the discussion gets off track, redirect it. Based on the interviewee's responses, ask follow-up questions, and don't limit yourself to your planned questions only.

3. **After the interview,** do the appropriate follow-up work.

    *   As soon as possible, review your notes. Fill in responses you remember but couldn't record at the time.
    *   Thank the interviewee with a note, an e-mail, or a phone call.
    *   If necessary, ask the interviewee to check whether your information and quotations are accurate.
    *   Offer to send the interviewee a copy of your writing.

Using the Library

The library door is your gateway to information. Inside, the college library holds a wide range of research resources, from books to periodicals, from reference librarians to electronic databases.

Become familiar with the library.

To improve your ability to succeed at all your research assignments, become familiar with your college library system. Take advantage of tours and orientation sessions to learn its physical layout, resources, and services. Check your library's website for policies, tutorials, and research tools. The college library offers a variety of resources for your research projects.

Librarians: Librarians are information experts:

- Librarians manage the library's materials and guide you to resources.
- They help you perform online searches.

Collections: The library collects and houses a variety of materials:

- **Books and electronic materials**—CD-ROMs, CDs, and DVDs
- **Periodicals**—journals, magazines, and newspapers (print or microform)
- **Reference materials**—directories, indexes, handbooks, encyclopedias, and almanacs
- **Special collections**—government publications, historical documents, and original artifacts

Research tools: The library contains many tools that direct you to materials:

- The online catalog allows you to search everything in the library.
- Print indexes and subscription databases (Lexis-Nexis, EBSCOhost, ProQuest Direct) point you to abstracts and full-text articles.
- Internet access connects you with other library catalogs and online references.

Special services: Special services may also help you to complete research:

- Interlibrary loan allows you to obtain books and articles not available in your library.
- "Hold" allows you to request a book that is currently signed out.
- "Reserve" materials give you access to materials recommended by your instructors or heavily in demand.
- The reference desk can help you find information quickly, point you to the right resources, and help you with a search.
- Photocopiers, CD burners, scanners, and presentation software help you perform and share your research.

Search the catalog.

Library materials are catalogued so they are easy to find. In most college libraries, books, videos, and other holdings are catalogued in an electronic database. To find material, use book titles, author names, and related keyword searching. (See also pages **430–431**.)

SAMPLE ELECTRONIC CATALOG

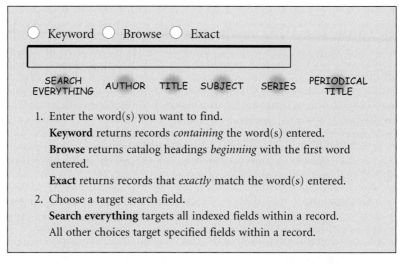

○ Keyword ○ Browse ○ Exact

SEARCH EVERYTHING   AUTHOR   TITLE   SUBJECT   SERIES   PERIODICAL TITLE

1. Enter the word(s) you want to find.
   Keyword returns records *containing* the word(s) entered.
   Browse returns catalog headings *beginning* with the first word entered.
   Exact returns records that *exactly* match the word(s) entered.
2. Choose a target search field.
   Search everything targets all indexed fields within a record.
   All other choices target specified fields within a record.

When you find a citation for a book or other resource, the result will provide some or all of the following information. Use that information to determine whether the resource is worth exploring further and to figure out other avenues of research. Note that a number of items appearing in blue, underlined type provide links to related books and other resources in the catalog.

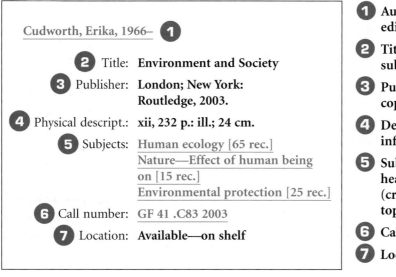

Cudworth, Erika, 1966– **1**

2 Title: **Environment and Society**

3 Publisher: **London; New York: Routledge, 2003.**

4 Physical descript.: **xii, 232 p.: ill.; 24 cm.**

5 Subjects: Human ecology [65 rec.]
Nature—Effect of human being on [15 rec.]
Environmental protection [25 rec.]

6 Call number: GF 41 .C83 2003

7 Location: **Available—on shelf**

1 Author or editor's name

2 Title and subtitle

3 Publisher and copyright date

4 Descriptive information

5 Subject headings (crucial list of topics)

6 Call number

7 Location

Web Link

Locating Resources by Call Numbers

Library of Congress (LC) call numbers combine letters and numbers to specify a resource's broad subject area, topic, and authorship or title. Finding a book, DVD, or other item involves combining both the alphabetical and the numerical order. Here is a sample call number for *Arctic Refuge: A Vanishing Wilderness?*:

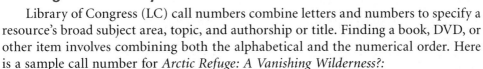

VIDEO QH84.1.A72 1990

subject area (**QH**) topic number (**84**) subtopic number (**1**) cutter number (**A72**)

To find this resource in the library, first note the tab VIDEO. Although not part of the call number, this locator may send you to a specific area of the library. Once there, follow the parts of the call number one at a time:

1. Find the library section on natural history containing videos with the "QH" designation.

2. Follow the numbers until you reach "84."

3. Within the "84" items, find those with the subtopic "1."

4. Use the cutter "A72" to locate the resource alphabetically with "A," and numerically with "72."

Note: In the LC system, pay careful attention to the arrangement of subject area letters, topic numbers, and subtopic numbers: Q98 comes before QH84; QH84 before QH8245; QH84.A72 before QH84.1.A72.

Classification Systems

The LC classification system combines letters and numbers. The Dewey decimal system, which is used in some libraries, uses numbers only. Here is a list of the subject classes for both the LC and Dewey systems.

THE LIBRARY OF CONGRESS AND DEWEY DECIMAL SYSTEMS

LC Category		Dewey Decimal	LC Category		Dewey Decimal
A	General Works	000–999	K	Law	340–349
B	Philosophy	100–199	L	Education	370–379
	Psychology	150–159	M	Music	780–789
	Religion	200–299	N	Fine Arts	700–799
C	History: Auxiliary Sciences	910–929	P	Language	800–899
D	History: General and			Literature	400–499
	Old World	930–999	Q	Science	500–599
E–F	History: American	970–979	R	Medicine	610–619
G	Geography	910–919	S	Agriculture	630–639
	Anthropology	571–573	T	Technology	600–699
	Recreation	700–799	U	Military Science	355–359, 623
H	Social Sciences	300–399	V	Naval Science	359, 623
J	Political Science	320–329	Z	Bibliography and	010–0199
				Library Science	020–029

Using Books in Research

Your college library contains a whole range of books for you to use, from scholarly studies and reference works to trade books and biographies. Unfortunately, for most research projects you simply don't have time to read an entire book, and rarely do the entire contents relate to your topic. Instead, use the strategy outlined below to refine your research effort.

Approach the book systematically.

1. **Check out front and back information.**

   The title and copyright pages give the book's full title and subtitle; the author's name; and publication information, including publication date and Library of Congress subject headings. The back may contain a note on the author's credentials and other publications.

2. **Scan the table of contents.**

   Examine the contents page to see what the book covers and how it is organized. Ask yourself which chapters are relevant to your project.

3. **Using key words, search the index.**

   Check the index for coverage and page locations of the topics most closely related to your project. Are there plenty of pages, or just a few? Are these pages concentrated or scattered throughout the book?

4. **Skim the preface, foreword, or introduction.**

   Skimming the opening materials will often indicate the book's perspective, explain its origin, and preview its contents.

5. **Check appendices, glossaries, or bibliographies.**

   These special sections may be a good source of tables, graphics, definitions, statistics, and clues for further research.

6. **Carefully read appropriate chapters and sections.**

   Think through the material you've read and take good notes. (See pages **438–441**.) Follow references to authors and other works to do further research on the topic. Study footnotes and endnotes for insights and leads.

Consider these options for working productively with books:

- When you find a helpful book, browse nearby shelves for more books.
- To confirm a book's quality, check the Internet, a periodical database, or *Book Review Digest* for a review.
- If your library subscribes to an e-book service such as NetLibrary, you have access to thousands of books in electronic form. You can conduct electronic searches, browse or check out promising books, and read them online.

Check reference works that supply information.

Encyclopedias supply facts and overviews for topics arranged alphabetically.

- General encyclopedias cover many fields of knowledge: *Encyclopedia Britannica, Collier's Encyclopedia.*
- Specialized encyclopedias focus on a single topic: *McGraw-Hill Encyclopedia of Science and Technology, Encyclopedia of American Film Comedy.*

Almanacs, yearbooks, and statistical resources, normally published annually, contain diverse facts.

- *The World Almanac and Book of Facts* presents information on politics, history, religion, business, social programs, education, and sports.
- *Statistical Abstract of the United States* provides data on population, geography, politics, employment, business, science, and industry.

Vocabulary resources supply information on languages.

- General dictionaries, such as *The American Heritage College Dictionary,* supply definitions and histories for a whole range of words.
- Specialized dictionaries define words common to a field, topic, or group: *Dictionary of Engineering, The New Harvard Dictionary of Music.*
- Bilingual dictionaries translate words from one language to another.

Biographical resources supply information about people. General biographies cover a broad range of people. Other biographies focus on people from a specific group. ***Examples:*** *Who's Who in America, Dictionary of Scientific Biography, World Artists 1980–1990.*

Directories supply contact information for people, groups, and organizations. ***Examples:*** *The National Directory of Addresses and Telephone Numbers, USPS ZIP Code Lookup and Address Information* (online), *Official Congressional Directory.*

Check reference works that are research tools.

Guides and handbooks help readers explore specific topics: *The Handbook of North American Indians, A Guide to Prairie Fauna.*

Indexes point you to useful resources. Some indexes are general, such as *Readers' Guide to Periodical Literature;* others are specific, such as *Environment Index* or *Business Periodicals Index.* (Many are now available online in databases your library subscribes to.)

Bibliographies list resources on a specific topic. A good, current bibliography can be used as an example when you compile your own bibliography on a topic.

Abstracts, like indexes, direct you to articles on a particular topic. But abstracts also summarize those materials so you learn whether a resource is relevant before you invest time in locating and reading it. Abstracts are usually organized into subject areas: Computer Abstracts, Environmental Abstracts, Social Work Abstracts. They are incorporated in many online subscription databases.

Finding Periodical Articles

Periodicals are publications or broadcasts produced at regular intervals (daily, weekly, monthly, quarterly). Although some periodicals are broad in their subject matter and audience, as a rule they focus on a narrow range of topics geared toward a particular audience.

- **Daily newspapers and newscasts** provide up-to-date information on current events, opinions, and trends—from politics to natural disasters (*Wall Street Journal, USA Today, The NewsHour*).
- **Weekly and monthly magazines** generally provide more in-depth information on a wide range of topics (*Time, Newsweek, 60 Minutes*).
- **Journals,** generally published quarterly, provide specialized scholarly information for a narrowly focused audience (*English Journal*).

With thousands of periodicals available, how do you find helpful articles? Learn (a) which search tools your library offers, (b) which periodicals it has available in which forms, and (c) how to gain access to those periodicals.

Search online databases.

If your library subscribes to EBSCOhost, Lexis-Nexis, or another database service, use keyword searching (see pages 430–431) to find citations on your topic. You might start with the general version of such databases, such as EBSCOhost's Academic Search Elite, which provides access to more than 4,100 scholarly publications covering all disciplines.

Basic Search: The example below shows an EBSCOhost search screen for a search on hybrid electric cars. Notice how limiters, expanders, and other advanced features help you find the highest-quality materials.

Database list

Keyword field

Limiters available

Expanders available

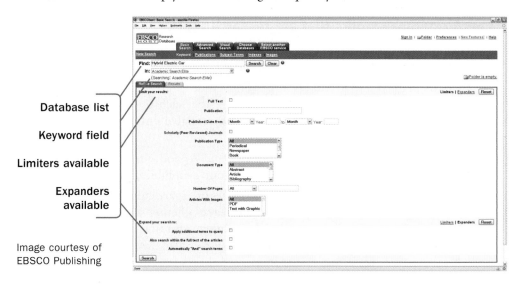

Image courtesy of EBSCO Publishing

Advanced Search: A more focused research strategy would involve turning to specialized databases, which are available for virtually every discipline and are often an option within search services such as EBSCOhost (for example, Business Source Elite, PsycINFO, ERIC) and Lexis-Nexis (for example, Legal, Medical, and Business databases). If a basic search turns up little, turn to specialized databases, seeking help from a librarian if necessary. For a list of specialized databases, see page 463.

Particularly if you need articles published before 1985, you may need to go to the *Readers' Guide to Periodical Literature* or another print index. While databases are converting pre-1985 articles to digital form (for example, the JSTOR database), many excellent periodical articles are available only in print. To use the *Readers' Guide,* consult a librarian.

Generate citation lists of promising articles.

Your database search should generate lists of citations, brief descriptions of articles that were flagged through keywords in titles, subject terms, abstracts, and so on. For example, a search focused on hybrid electric cars leads to the results shown below. At this point, study the results and do the following:

- Refine the search by narrowing or expanding it.
- Mark specific citations for "capture" or further study.
- Re-sort the results.
- Follow links in a specific citation to further information.

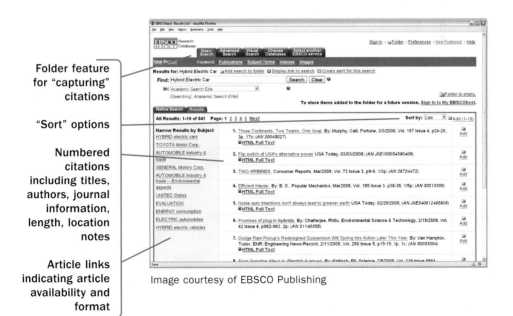

Folder feature for "capturing" citations

"Sort" options

Numbered citations including titles, authors, journal information, length, location notes

Article links indicating article availability and format

Image courtesy of EBSCO Publishing

Study citations and capture identifying information.

By studying citations (especially abstracts), you can determine three things:

- Is this article relevant to your research?
- Is an electronic, full-text version available?
- If not, does the library have this periodical?

To develop your working bibliography (see pages **436–437**), you should also "capture" the article's identifying details by using the save, print, or e-mail function, or by recording the periodical's title, the issue and date, and the article's title and page numbers. These functions are shown in the EBSCOhost citation below.

Save options

Source link for more details or full text

Subject links for further research

Summary with keywords highlighted

Image courtesy of EBSCO Publishing

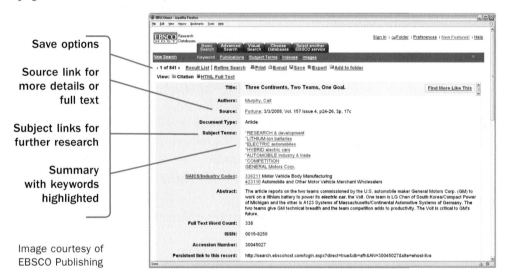

Find and retrieve the full text of the article.

When citations indicate that you have promising articles, access those articles efficiently, preferably through a direct link in the citation to an electronic copy. From there you can print, save, or e-mail the article. If the article is not available electronically, track down a print version:

- Check the online citation to see if your library has the article. If necessary, check your library's inventory of periodicals held; this list should be available online and/or in print. Examine especially closely the issues and dates available, the form (print or microfilm), and the location (bound or current shelves).
- To get the article, follow your library's procedure. You may have to submit a request slip so that a librarian can get the periodical, or you may be able to get it yourself in the current, bound, or microfilm collection. If the article is not available online or in your library, use interlibrary loan.

Databases for Disciplines

Most libraries offer access to databases from a wide range of disciplines. Check your library's website for access to databases like these:

Agricola offers citations from the National Agricultural Library group—with materials focused on issues from animal science to food and nutrition.

ARTbibliographies Modern abstracts articles, books, catalogs, and other resources on modern and contemporary art.

CAIRSS for Music offers bibliographic citations for articles on music-related topics, from music education to music therapy.

Communication & Mass Media Complete offers access to resources on topics like public speaking and TV broadcasting.

Engineering E-journal Search Engine offers free, full-text access to more than 150 online engineering journals.

ERIC offers citations, abstracts, and digests for more than 980 journals in the education field.

First Search, a fee-based information service, offers access to more than 30 scholarly databases in a range of disciplines.

GPO, the Government Printing Office, offers access to records for U.S. government documents (e.g., reports, hearings, judicial rules, addresses, and so on).

Health Source offers access to abstracts, indexing, and full-text material on health-related topics, from nutrition to sports medicine.

Ingenta offers citations for more than 25,000 journals, most in the sciences.

JSTOR offers full-text access to scholarly articles in a full range of disciplines, articles once available only in print.

Math Database offers article citations for international mathematics research.

Medline offers access to journals in medicine and medicine-related disciplines through references, citations, and abstracts.

MLA Bibliography provides bibliographic citations for articles addressing a range of modern-language and literature-related topics.

National Environmental Publications Internet Site (NEPIS) offers access to more than 6,000 EPA documents (full text, online).

PsycINFO offers access to materials in psychology and psychology-related fields (for example, social work, criminology, organizational behavior).

Scirus indexes science resources, citing article titles and authors, source publication information, and lines of text indicating the article's content.

Vocation and Career Collection offers full-text access to more than 400 trade- and industry-related periodicals.

Worldwide Political Science Abstracts offers bibliographic citations in politics-related fields, from public policy to international law.

Checklist for Research

Use the following checklist to monitor your primary and library research.

_____ I have chosen methods of primary research that fit the assignment.

_____ I have systematically, carefully, and ethically gathered and analyzed primary information.

_____ I have become familiar with my library's resources and services.

_____ Using solid keyword searching strategies, I have effectively searched the library's holdings for books and other items relevant to my topic.

_____ I have tapped print and electronic reference works for information.

_____ I have used my library's print and electronic periodical search tools and holdings to find relevant articles on my topic.

Critical-Thinking and Writing Activities

As directed by your instructor, complete the following activities.

1. Think about a research project that you have done or are doing now. How might primary research and library research (scholarly books and journals) strengthen your writing? Why not do all your research on the Free Web (see page **466**) using Google and resources like Wikipedia?

2. For the subject "Gender Differences in Toy Preferences," indicate whether the following sources would be considered primary or secondary (P or S):

_____ a. Observing children in a day-care setting

_____ b. Journal article about gender-based differences in the brain

_____ c. Magazine article about a hot new toy

_____ d. Survey of day-care workers

_____ e. *Boys' Toys of the Fifties and Sixties* (a book)

_____ f. Interviews with parents

3. By working with your library's website and its orientation tools, identify where you can physically and/or electronically locate books, reference resources, and journals.

4. Indicate which section of the library would house the following items:

_____ a. *JAMA (Journal of the American Medical Association)*

_____ b. *Places Rated Almanac*

_____ c. *Principles of Corporate Finance* (book)

◄ VISUALLY SPEAKING ━━━━━━━━━━━━━━━━━━━━━━

Review the photograph on page **447**. What does the image suggest about doing research today? How does the image relate to your own research practices?

CONDUCTING RESEARCH ON THE INTERNET

Audio

For researchers, the Internet can be a great resource or a great waste of time. Consider the Internet's benefits and drawbacks:

Benefits

- The Internet contains a wealth of textual, audio, and video information.
- Information can be searched, copied, saved, and sent.

Drawbacks

- Finding useful information requires careful digging and evaluation.
- The Internet lacks quality control.
- Surfing can encourage shallow research practices and plagiarism.
- The Net changes rapidly—information vanishes or changes.

Understanding Internet Basics: A Primer

If you're familiar with the Internet, you already understand the basics of searching this medium. However, the following questions and answers may help you do quality research on the Net.

What is the Internet?

The Internet is a worldwide network of connected local computers and computer networks that allows computers to share information with one another. Your college's network likely gives you access to the library, local resources, and the Internet.

What is the World Wide Web?

The **web** provides access to much of the material on the Internet. Millions of webpages are available because of **hypertext links** that connect them. These links appear as clickable icons or highlighted web addresses. A **website** is a group of related webpages posted by the same sponsor or organization. A **home page** is a website's "entry" page. A **web browser** such as Safari, Internet Explorer, or Firefox gives you access to web resources through a variety of tools, such as directories and search engines. (**Directories** and **search engines** are special websites that provide a searchable listing of many services on the web.)

Sample
Webpage:

Title bar

Navigation bar

Graphic link

Text links

Status bar

Reprinted by permission of CNN ImageSource.

INSIGHT: Distinguish between the Deep Web and the Free Web. The Deep Web includes material not generally accessible with popular search engines, such as all the scholarly research available through your library's subscription databases. The Free Web offers less reliable information.

What does an Internet address mean?

An Internet address is called a Uniform Resource Locator (URL). The address includes the protocol indicating how the computer file should be accessed—often *http:* or *ftp:* (followed by a double slash); a domain name—often beginning with *www;* and additional path information (following a single slash) to access other pages within a site.

http://www.nrcs.usda.gov/news/index.html#csp_watershed2

The domain name is a key part of the address because it indicates what type of organization created the site and gives you clues about its goal or purpose. Does the site aim to educate, inform, persuade, sell, and/or entertain? Most sites combine a primary purpose with secondary ones.

.com   a commercial organization or business
.gov   a government organization—federal, state, or local
.edu   an educational institution
.org   a nonprofit organization
.net   an organization that is part of the Internet's infrastructure
.mil   a military site
.biz   a business site
.info   any site primarily providing information

INSIGHT: International addresses generally include national abbreviations (for example, Canada = .ca). This clue helps you determine the origin of the information and communicate more sensitively on the Internet.

How can you save Internet information?

Accurately saving Internet addresses and material is an essential part of good research. Moreover, you may want to revisit sites and embed URLs in your research writing. Save Internet information through these methods:

Bookmark: Your browser can save a site's address through a "bookmark" or "favorites" function on your menu bar.

Printout: If a document looks promising, print a hard copy of it. Remember to write down all details needed for citing the source. (Although many details will automatically print with the document, some could be missing.)

Save or download: To keep an electronic copy of material, save the document to a specific drive on your computer. Beware of large files with many graphics: They take up a lot of space. To save just the text, highlight it, copy it, and then paste it into a word-processing program.

E-mail: If you're not at your own computer, you can e-mail the document's URL to your e-mail address through copy and paste.

For instructions on writing for the web, see pages 397–408.

Locating Reliable Information

Because the Internet contains so much information of varying reliability, you need to become familiar with search tools that locate information you can trust. The key is knowing which search tool to use in which research situation.

Proceed with caution.

When it comes to doing Internet research, proceed with caution:

- Adhere to your assignment's restrictions on using websites (number and type). In fact, some instructors may not allow web resources for specific projects, limiting you to print sources and scholarly articles available in subscription databases.

- When you are using web resources, make sure the sites are sponsored by legitimate, recognizable organizations: government agencies, nonprofit groups, and educational institutions. For most projects, avoid relying on personal, commercial, and special-interest sites, as well as chat rooms, blogs, and news groups. Test the quality and reliability of online information by using the benchmarks outlined on pages **432–435**.

- Avoid developing your paper based on copying and pasting together chunks of webpages. By doing so, not only do you fail to engage your sources meaningfully, but you also commit plagiarism. For more on plagiarism, see pages **476–479**.

Use your library's website.

Your library may sponsor a website that gives you access to quality Internet resources. For example, it may provide the following assistance:

- Tutorials on using the Internet
- Guides to Internet resources in different disciplines
- Links to online document collections (Project Gutenberg, Etext Archives, New Bartleby Digital Library, and so on)
- Connections to virtual libraries, subscription databases, search engines, directories, government documents, and online reference works

Example: Your library may give you access to WorldCat, a global catalog. If you click on the "Internet" limiter, you'll be able to search specifically for websites and other Internet information recommended by librarians.

> **TIP:** If you need help doing electronic research, consider these options:
> - Ask a librarian for instructions.
> - Attend one of the library's training sessions on using library resources and conducting research.
> - Request instructions or a tutorial from your college writing center.

Work with URLs.

Finding useful Internet resources can be as easy as typing in a URL. If you don't have the exact URL, sometimes you can guess it, especially for an organization (company, government agency, or nonprofit group). Try the organization's name or a logical abbreviation to get the home page.

Follow helpful links.

Locating information on the Net can involve "surfing" leads:

- If you come across a helpful link (often highlighted in blue), click on the link to visit that new page. Note that the link may take you to another site.
- Your browser keeps a record of the pages you visit. Click the back arrow to go back one page or the forward arrow to move ahead again. Clicking the right mouse button on these arrows shows a list of recently visited pages.

INSIGHT: Note that "sponsored links" listed at a website are a form of advertising. Their purpose is primarily commercial, though they may contain useful information.

Follow the branches of a "subject tree."

Web Link

A *subject tree*, sometimes called a *subject guide* or *directory*, lists websites that have been organized into categories by experts who have reviewed those sites. Use subject trees or directories for the following reasons:

- You need to narrow down a broad topic.
- You want sites that have been evaluated, or you desire quality over quantity.

How does a subject tree work? Essentially, it allows you to select from a broad range of subjects or "branches." With each topic choice, you narrow down your selection until you arrive at a list of websites, or you can keyword-search a limited number of websites.

Check whether your library subscribes to a service such as NetFirst, a database in which subject experts have catalogued Internet resources by topic. Here are some other common subject directories that you can likely access at your library:

WWW Virtual Library	http://vlib.org/Overview.html
Argus	http://www.clearinghouse.net
Librarians' Index to the Internet	http://www.lii.org
Google Directory	http://www.google.com/dirhp
LookSmart	http://looksmart.com

A sample subject tree search is outlined on the pages that follow. Study the search, and then try one yourself with the subject trees available through your library.

TIP: To get the best results from your search, avoid these problems: misspelling keywords; using vague or broad keywords (*education* or *business*); incorrectly combining Boolean operators; or shortening keywords too much.

Step 1: Select an appropriate broad category. Study the subject tree below provided by the Librarians' Index to the Internet (Lii). To find reviewed websites containing information on hybrid electric cars, you could select from this start page a range of categories, depending on the angle you want to explore: Arts & Humanities, Business, Computers, and so on. Each of these starting points will lead to a different listing of relevant sites. Another option would be to use the keyword search feature shown. *Hybrid cars* would likely appear under Science.

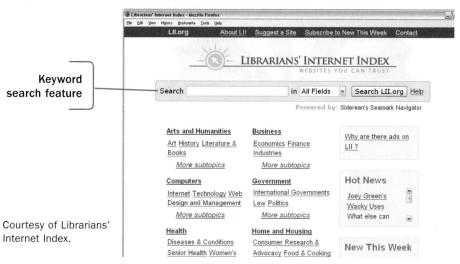

Courtesy of Librarians' Internet Index.

Step 2: Choose a fitting subcategory. If you chose Science, the subcategories shown below would appear. At this point, you would again have several choices: (1) to select Environment, (2) to follow Transportation, or (3) to do a keyword search of this now more limited grouping of websites. Each choice might lead to a distinct set of websites. In fact, your research may benefit by trying all three options.

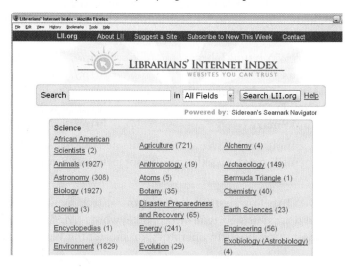

Courtesy of Librarians' Internet Index.

Step 3: Work toward a listing of websites. As you work down through narrower branches of the tree, you will arrive at a listing of relevant websites. Such sites, remember, have all been reviewed in terms of quality, though you still need to evaluate what you find. In the citation for a site, study the site title, the description of information available, site sponsorship, and the web address (particularly the domain name). Use that information to determine the site's relevance to your research. At this point, you can save the results (see page **467**) and/or click on the site's web address and proceed to research the site.

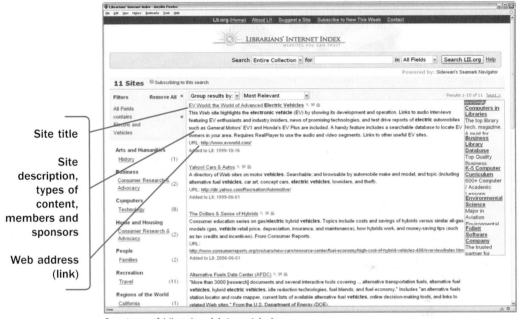

Courtesy of Librarians' Internet Index.

Step 4: Visit, explore, and evaluate recommended sites. Once you have identified a promising site from the citation list, follow the links provided. Study and evaluate the site by asking questions such as these:

1. Who authored or sponsored the site? What is the author's or sponsor's perspective on the topic? Why did the author post these pages? What can you find out about the author through a broader Internet search?

2. What content does the site offer? What depth of information is available?

3. Does the website function as a primary, secondary, or tertiary source?

4. What external links does the site offer? Might these links take you to additional resources that are relevant and reliable?

INSIGHT: Careful investigation and evaluation of websites is even more important when you use search engines, like those discussed on the next pages. Use the resource evaluation guidelines on pages **434–435** for webpages that you find through either subject directories or search engines. Always proceed with caution, making sure that your research writing does not rely on unstable, shallow webpages.

Web Link

Use search engines and metasearch tools.

Unlike a subject directory, which is constructed with human input, a search engine is a program that automatically scours a large amount of Internet material for keywords that you submit. A search engine is useful in the following circumstances:

- You have a very narrow topic in mind.
- You have a specific word or phrase to use in your search.
- You want a large number of results.
- You are looking for a specific type of Internet file.
- You have the time to sort through the material for reliability.

Be aware that not all search engines are the same. Some search citations of Internet materials, whereas others conduct full-text searches. Choose a search engine that covers a large portion of the Internet, offers quality indexing, and provides high-powered search capabilities. Here's an overview of some popular search engines.

Basic Search Engines: Search millions of webpages gathered automatically.

Alta Vista	http://www.altavista.com
AllTheWeb	http://www.alltheweb.com
Google	http://www.google.com
HotBot	http://www.hotbot.com
Vivísimo	http://www.vivisimo.com

Metasearch Tools: Search several basic search engines at once, saving you the time and effort of checking more than one search engine.

Ask	http://www.ask.com
Dog Pile	http://www.dogpile.com
Ixquick	http://www.ixquick.com
Northern Light	http://www.northernlight.com

"Deep Web" Tools: Check Internet databases and other sources not accessible to basic search engines.

Complete Planet	http://www.completeplanet.com

INSIGHT: One key to successfully using search engines lies in effective keyword searching (see pages 430–431). To ensure successful searches, it's best to become familiar with a few search engines—which areas of the Internet they search, whether they can access full text, and what rules you must follow.

A sample search: What would a search look like? If you were interested in information specifically on the Toyota hybrid-electric vehicles (a fairly narrow search term), you could conduct a search using the metasearch engine Ask Jeeves, following these steps:

Step 1: Begin your search with precise, narrow terms. Using Boolean operators and quotation marks, you might begin with the search terms "Toyota" and "hybrid electric vehicles." The more precise and narrow your terms are, the better your results will be.

Step 2: Study the results and refine your search as needed. The results of the initial search are shown below. At this point, you have several choices:

- Narrow or broaden your search by using the drop-down menus in the box.
- Follow the links (on the right) to related topics.
- Search the "Sponsored Web Results"—essentially advertising sites, such as Toyota's own website for the Prius.
- Search "Web Results"—sites that generally go beyond advertising into more in-depth information, although the site sponsorship is still important.
- Explore a related search of other topics and of other Internet resources.

For example, you might choose to check Toyota's pages on the Prius, to view Toyota's North America Environmental Report at its website, or to examine the "Honda Insight / Toyota Prius" comparison, which comes from an educational site (.edu). The key is to use sound judgment about where the information comes from, which sites provide the most reliable information, how the information relates to your research question, and what web graphics offer as potential resources for your research writing.

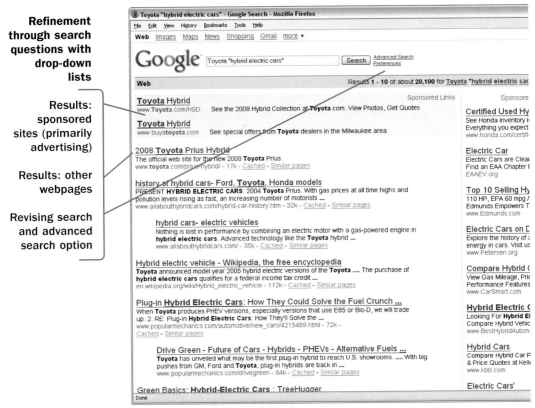

Reprinted by permission of Google.

Checklist for Internet Research

As you conduct Internet research, use the following checklist to remind yourself of key principles to follow.

_____ I have avoided an over-reliance on free-web resources at the expense of more scholarly sources.

_____ By studying sites and their URLs, I understand where the information is coming from.

_____ I have used Internet search tools intelligently—from URL addresses to subject trees to search engines—to find quality, reliable information.

_____ I have carefully saved Internet information through bookmarking, printing, saving, or e-mailing.

_____ When copying and pasting material from Internet sources, I have carefully tracked that material so as to avoid plagiarism.

_____ I have carefully evaluated each Internet source for credible authorship, reliable sponsorship, lack of bias, currency, accuracy, logical support, and quality design. (See page 468 for more details on evaluating web resources.)

Critical-Thinking and Writing Activities

As directed by your instructor, complete the following activities.

1. Explore your library's handouts and website for information about Internet research. What services, support, and access does the library provide? Explore the various resources with your own major in mind, and draft an informal report to share with your instructor and classmates about web resources available in your discipline.

2. With a current research project in one of your classes as the focus, use one of the subject trees on page 469 to investigate and evaluate potential websites. After saving useful information in an appropriate fashion, conduct a search for this project using a search engine listed on page 472. Compare and contrast these two processes for finding Internet information.

3. Using the variety of methods outlined in this chapter, work with some classmates to search the Internet for information on a controversial topic, event, person, or place. Carefully analyze and evaluate the range of web information you find—the quality, perspective, depth, and reliability. Create a report on your findings for the rest of the class.

◀ VISUALLY SPEAKING

Study the photo montage on page 465 and explain what the image suggests about using the Internet for quality research.

DRAFTING A PAPER WITH DOCUMENTED RESEARCH

31

"That's incredible!" is normally a positive exclamation of amazement. But maybe it's an exclamation you *don't* want to hear about your writing, if incredible means unbelievable. Think about it:

- **A poor paper** reads like a recitation of unconnected facts, a set of unsupported opinions, or a string of undigested quotations. Sources are absent, or sources dominate and the writer disappears. At its worst, such writing is plagiarism.

- **A strong paper** centers on the writer's ideas, ideas advanced through thoughtful engagement with and crediting of sources.

Obviously, you want to draft a strongly documented paper—a credible discussion of your carefully researched topic. This chapter will help you achieve that goal.

Web Link

Video

Avoiding Plagiarism

The road to plagiarism may be paved with the best intentions—or the worst. Either way, the result is still a serious academic offense. As you write your research paper, do everything you can to stay off that road! Start by studying your school's and your instructor's guidelines on plagiarism and other academic offenses. Then study the following pages.

What is plagiarism?

Plagiarism is using someone else's words, ideas, or images (what's called intellectual property) so they appear to be your own. When you plagiarize, you use source material—whether published in print or online—without acknowledging the source. In this sense, plagiarism refers to a range of thefts:

- Submitting a paper you didn't write yourself.
- Pasting large chunks of a source into your paper and passing it off as your own work.
- Using summaries, paraphrases, or quotations without documentation.
- Using the exact phrasing of a source without quotation marks.
- Mixing up source material and your own ideas—failing to distinguish between the two.

Plagiarism refers to more than "word theft." Because plagiarism is really about failing to credit ideas and information, the rules also apply to visual images, tables, graphs, charts, maps, music, videos, and so on.

In other words, plagiarism refers to a range of source abuses. What exactly do these violations look like? Read the passage below, and then review the five types of plagiarism that follow, noting how each misuses the source.

ORIGINAL ARTICLE

The passage below is from page 87 of "Some Stories Have to Be Told by Me: A Literary History of Alice Munro," by Marcela Valdes, published in the *Virginia Quarterly Review* 82.3 (Summer 2006).

What makes Munro's characters so enthralling is their inconsistency; like real people, at one moment they declare they will cover the house in new siding, at the next, they vomit on their way to the hospital. They fight against and seek refuge in the people they love. The technique that Munro has forged to get at such contradictions is a sort of pointillism, the setting of one bright scene against another, with little regard for chronology.

Submitting Another Writer's Paper

The most blatant plagiarism is taking an entire piece of writing and claiming it as your own work. Examples:

- Downloading, reformatting, and submitting an article as your own work.
- Buying a paper from a "paper mill" or taking a "free" paper off the Internet.
- Turning in another student's work as your own (see "Falstaffing" on page 481).

 Just as it's easy to plagiarize using the Internet, it's easy for your professors to recognize and track down plagiarism using Internet tools.

Using Copy and Paste

It is unethical to take chunks of material from another source and splice them into your paper without acknowledgment. In the example below, the writer pastes in a sentence from the original article (boldfaced) without using quotation marks or a citation. Even if the writer changed some words, it would still be plagiarism.

> Life typically unfolds mysteriously for Munro's characters, with unexplained events and choices. **Like real people, at one moment they declare they will cover the house in new siding, at the next, they vomit on their way to the hospital.**

Failing to Cite a Source

Borrowed material must be documented. Even if you use information accurately and fairly, don't neglect to cite the source. Below, the writer correctly summarizes the passage's idea but offers no citation.

> For the reader, the characters in Munro's stories are interesting because they are so changeable. Munro shows these changes by using a method of placing scenes side by side for contrast, without worrying about the chronological connections.

Neglecting Necessary Quotation Marks

Whether it's a paragraph or a phrase, if you use the exact wording of a source, that material must be enclosed in quotation marks. In the example below, the writer cites the source but doesn't use quotation marks around a phrase taken from the original (boldfaced).

> What makes Munro's characters so typically human is that they **fight against and seek refuge in the people they love** (Valdes 87).

Confusing Borrowed Material with Your Own Ideas

Through carelessness (often in note taking), you may confuse source material with your own thinking. Below, the writer indicates that he borrowed material in the first sentence, but fails to indicate that he also borrowed the next sentence.

> As Marcela Valdes explains, "[w]hat makes Munro's characters so enthralling is their inconsistency" (87). To achieve this sense of inconsistency, Munro places brightly lit scenes beside each other in a kind of pointillist technique.

Why is plagiarism serious?

Perhaps the answer is obvious. But some people operate with the notion that material on the Internet (whether text, graphics, or sound) is "free" and, therefore, fair game for research writing. After all, a lot of stuff on the web doesn't even list an author, so what's the harm? Here's some food for thought:

Academic Dishonesty

At its heart, plagiarism is cheating—stealing intellectual property and passing it off as one's own work. Colleges take such dishonesty seriously. Plagiarism, whether intentional or unintentional, will likely be punished in one or more ways:

- A failing grade for the assignment
- A failing grade for the course
- A note on your academic transcript (often seen by potential employers) that failure resulted from academic dishonesty
- Expulsion from college

Theft from the Academic Community

The research paper represents your dialogue with other members of the academic community—classmates, the instructor, others in your major, others who have researched the topics, and so on. When you plagiarize, you short-circuit the dialogue:

- You gain an unfair advantage over your classmates who follow the rules and earn their grades.
- You disrespect other writers, researchers, and scholars.
- You disrespect your readers by passing off others' ideas as your own.
- You insult your instructor, a person whose respect you need.
- You harm your college by risking its reputation and its academic integrity.

Now and in the Future

Because research projects help you master course-related concepts and writing skills, plagiarism robs you of an opportunity to learn either. Moreover, you rob yourself of your integrity and reputation. After all, as a student you are seeking to build your credibility within the broader academic community, your major, and your future profession.

In addition, research projects often train you for your future work in terms of research, thinking, and writing skills—skills that you will need to succeed in the workplace. If you do not learn the skills now, you will enter the workplace without them—a situation that your employer will, at some point, find out.

 One tool to deter plagiarism is Turnitin.com. Students submit their papers for comparison against millions of webpages and other student papers. Students and instructors get reports about originality and matching text. For more on this tool, visit **www.thecollegewriter.com/3e.**

How do I avoid plagiarism?

Preventing plagiarism begins the moment you get an assignment. Essentially, prevention requires your commitment and diligence throughout the project.

Resist temptation. With the Internet, plagiarism is a mouse click away. Avoid last-minute all-nighters that make you desperate; start research projects early. *Note:* It's better to ask for an extension or accept a penalty for lateness than to plagiarize.

Play by the rules. Become familiar with your college's definition, guidelines, and policies regarding plagiarism so that you don't unknowingly violate them. When in doubt, ask your instructor for clarification.

Take orderly, accurate notes. From the start, carefully keep track of source material and distinguish it from your own thinking. Specifically, do the following:

- Maintain an accurate working bibliography (pages **436–437**).
- Adopt a decent note-taking system (pages **438–441**).
- Accurately summarize, paraphrase, and quote sources in your notes (pages **442–444**).

Document borrowed material. Credit information that you have summarized, paraphrased, or quoted from any source, whether that information is statistics, facts, graphics, phrases, or ideas. Readers can then see what's borrowed and what's yours, understand your support, and do their own follow-up research.

Common Knowledge Exception: Common knowledge is information—a basic fact, for instance—that is generally known to readers or easily found in several sources, particularly reference works. Such knowledge need *not* be cited. However, when you go beyond common knowledge into research findings, interpretations of the facts, theories, explanations, claims, arguments, and graphics, you *must* document the source. Study the examples below, but whenever you are in doubt, document.

Examples:
- The fact that automakers are developing hybrid-electric cars is common knowledge, whereas the details of GM's AUTOnomy project are not.
- The fact that Shakespeare wrote *Hamlet* is common knowledge, whereas the details of his sources are not.

Work carefully with source material in your paper. See pages **486–489** for more on integrating and documenting sources, but here, briefly, are your responsibilities:

- Distinguish borrowed material from your own thinking by signaling where source material begins and ends.
- Indicate the source's origin with an attributive phrase and a citation (parenthetical reference or footnote).
- Provide full source information in a works-cited or references page.

Avoiding Other Source Abuses

Plagiarism, though the most serious offense, is not the only source abuse to avoid when writing a paper with documented research. Consider these pitfalls, which refer again to the sample passage on page **476**.

Using Sources Inaccurately

When you get a quotation wrong, botch a summary, paraphrase poorly, or misstate a statistic, you misrepresent the original. *Example:* In this quotation, the writer carelessly uses several wrong words that change the meaning, as well as adding two words that are not in the original.

> As Marcela Valdes explains, "[w]hat makes Munro's characters so **appalling** is their **consistency**. . . . They fight against and seek **refuse** in the people **they say** they love" (87).

Using Source Material Out of Context

By ripping a statement out of its context and forcing it into yours, you can make a source seem to say something that it didn't really say. *Example:* This writer uses part of a statement to say the opposite of the original.

> According to Marcela Valdes, while Munro's characters are interesting, Munro's weakness as a fiction writer is that she shows "little regard for chronology" (87).

Overusing Source Material

When your paper reads like a string of references, especially quotations, your own thinking disappears. *Example:* The writer takes the source passage, chops it up, and splices it together.

> Anyone who has read her stories knows that "[w]hat makes Munro's characters so enthralling is their inconsistency." That is to say, "like real people, at one moment they declare they will cover the house in new siding, at the next, they vomit on their way to the hospital." Moreover, "[t]hey fight against and seek refuge in the people they love." This method "that Munro has forged to get at such contradictions is a sort of pointillism," meaning "the setting of one bright scene against another, with little regard for chronology" (Valdes 87)

"Plunking" Quotations

When you "plunk" quotations into your paper by failing to prepare the reader for them and follow them up, the discussion becomes choppy and disconnected. *Example:* The writer interrupts the flow of ideas with a quotation "out of the blue." In addition, the quotation hangs at the end of a paragraph with no follow-up.

> Typically, characters such as Del Jordan, Louisa Doud, and Almeda Roth experience a crisis through contact with particular men. "They fight against and seek refuge in the people they love" (Valdes 87).

Using "Blanket" Citations

Your reader shouldn't have to guess where borrowed material begins and ends. For example, if you place a parenthetical citation at the end of a paragraph, does that citation cover the whole paragraph or just the final sentence?

Relying Heavily on One Source

If your writing is dominated by one source, readers may doubt the depth and integrity of your research. Instead, your writing should show your reliance on a balanced diversity of sources.

Failing to Match In-Text Citations to Bibliographic Entries

All in-text citations must clearly refer to accurate entries in the works-cited, references, or endnotes page. Mismatching occurs in the following circumstances:

- An in-text citation refers to a source that is not listed in the bibliography.
- A bibliographic resource is never actually referenced anywhere in the paper.

Related Academic Offenses

Beyond plagiarism and related source abuses, steer clear of these academic offenses:

Double-dipping: When you submit one paper in two different classes without permission from both instructors, you take double credit for one project.

Falstaffing: This practice refers to a particular type of plagiarism in which one student submits another student's work. Know that you are guilty of Falstaffing if you let another student submit your paper.

Copyright violations: When you copy, distribute, and/or post in whole or in part any intellectual property without permission from or payment to the copyright holder, you commit a copyright infringement, especially when you profit from this use. To avoid copyright violations in your research projects, do the following:

- **Observe *fair use* guidelines:** Quote small portions of a document for limited purposes, such as education or research. Avoid copying large portions for your own gain.
- **Understand what's in the *public domain*:** You need not obtain permission to copy and use public domain materials—primarily documents created by the government, but also some material posted on the Internet as part of the "copy left" movement.
- **Observe *intellectual property and copyright laws*:** First, know your college's policies on copying documents. Second, realize that copyright protects the expression of ideas in a range of materials—writings, videos, songs, photographs, drawings, computer software, and so on. Always obtain permission to copy and distribute copyrighted materials.
- **Avoid changing a source** (e.g., a photo) without permission of the creator or copyright holder.

Organizing and Synthesizing Your Findings

Your research may generate a mass of notes, printouts, photocopies, electronic files, and more. The challenge is to move from this mass to a coherent structure for the paper you need to write. If you have systematically taken good notes (see pages **438–441**), you are well on the way. In addition, the tips below and on the next page will help you move toward order.

Develop your ideas.

Good thinking is foundational to good research writing. To develop ideas for your research project, follow these steps:

Refocus on your research questions and working thesis. Has research changed your perspective and position?

Study the evidence. Review your materials once, twice, or more—as long as it takes for ideas to percolate and information to make sense. Consider these questions:

- Is the information complete or at least sufficient for the project?
- Does the information seem reliable and accurate?
- How does the information relate to the topic?
- What connections exist among different pieces of evidence?
- Does the information gathered fall naturally into patterns?

Develop sound conclusions through analysis and synthesis. Practice these strategies (and check pages **18–25** for more on sound thinking):

- Work against personal biases that create blind spots to what the evidence is saying. Be open to different angles provided by *all* the evidence. Think through both pros and cons.
- Practice logic in your analysis, but also tap into your intuition, creativity, and imagination.
- Interpret statistical data carefully and correctly.
- Logically distinguish between causes and effects; carefully link them.
- If you are comparing, make sure that the items can logically be compared, and make sure that you think through both similarities and differences.
- Avoid either/or and black-and-white thinking, as well as circular arguments, slippery slope claims, and sweeping generalizations. (See logical fallacies at pages **267–270**.)
- Check your conclusions against counterarguments, your experience, and common sense. For example, what are the limits of hybrid-vehicle technology? What does your experience with cars and with culture tell you about how technological changes happen and get accepted?

Develop a structure for delivering research results.

Using your research questions and conclusions as guides, sift through and order your information. Consider these strategies:

Follow assignment recommendations. A pattern for your paper may be built into the assignment. For example, you may be asked to write a comparison/contrast paper. Shape your outline within that framework.

Clump and split. Using key ideas as main headings, arrange support and evidence under the most fitting heading. Depending on the note-taking system you used, separate and pile note cards, sketch out the structure on paper, use a graphic organizer (see pages 50–51), use a code system, copy and paste material electronically, or cut up your note pages. After categorizing information, decide how best to sequence the key ideas.

Rely on tested patterns. The patterns below offer sound methods for developing your thinking. Each choice offers a basic structure for your paper, but several patterns may be useful within your paper's body.

- **Argumentation** asserts and supports a claim, counters any opposition, and then reasserts the claim (perhaps in a modified form). See pages 259–312.
- **Cause/effect** can (1) explore the factors that led to an event or (2) explore the consequences of a specific event. See pages 183–198.
- **Chronological order** puts items in a sequence (order of events, steps in a process). See pages 229–242.
- **Classification** groups details based on their common traits or qualities. See pages 215–228.
- **Comparison/contrast** shows similarities and/or differences between specific elements of a topic. See pages 199–214.
- **Description** orders details in terms of spatial relationships, color, form, texture, and so on. See pages 145–180.
- **Explanation** clarifies how something works by breaking the object or phenomenon into parts or phases and then showing how they work together. See pages 229–242.
- **Order of importance** arranges items from most to least important, or least to most.
- **Partitioning** breaks down an object, a space, or a location into ordered parts, or a process into steps or phases.
- **Problem/solution** states a problem, explores its causes and effects, and presents solutions. See pages 313–328.
- **Question/answer** moves back and forth from questions to answers in a sequence that logically clarifies a topic

 For more help developing a structure, see pages 48–51.

Video

Developing Your First Draft

As you write your paper, your first goal is to develop and support your ideas—referring to sources, not being dominated by them. The discussion that follows will help you achieve this goal. Your second goal is to respect sources by integrating them naturally and providing correct documentation; that goal is addressed on pages **486–489**.

Choose a drafting method.

Before starting your draft, choose a drafting method that makes sense for your project and your writing style. Consider these two options or something in between:

Writing Systematically

1. Develop a detailed outline, including supporting evidence.

2. Arrange your notes in precise order.

3. Write methodically, following your thesis, outline, and notes.

4. Cite your sources as you write.

Writing Freely

1. Review your working thesis and notes. Then set them aside.

2. If you need to, jot down a brief outline.

3. Write away—get all your research-based thinking down on paper.

4. Going back to your notes, develop your draft further and integrate citations.

Shape your first draft.

Develop the following parts in any order.

Draft an introduction. The introduction should do three things: First, it should say something interesting or surprising to gain your readers' attention. Second, the introduction should focus in on your topic by establishing some common ground. Third, your introduction should identify the issue or challenge related to your topic, and then offer your thesis. Consider these options:

- Begin with a revealing story or quotation.
- Give important background information.
- Offer a series of interesting or surprising facts.
- Cite details showing the topic's relevance.
- Provide important definitions.
- Introduce a problem issue, challenge, puzzle, or confusion about your topic.
- Identify the purpose and scope of your research.
- Identify your focus or thesis.
- Forecast how you will develop and support your thesis.

Draft the body. How do you develop a complete and insightful research paper? How do you add dimension and depth to your writing? For starters, you make sure that you have carefully explored and reflected on your specific topic. You also make sure that you have gathered plenty of compelling evidence to support your thesis.

It's in the main part of your paper—in the body—that you develop your thesis. The process usually works in this way: You present each main point supporting your thesis, expand on the points logically, include solid evidence such as facts or examples, and then offer additional analysis or documentation as needed.

Another way to approach your writing is to envision it as a series of paragraph clusters—one cluster of paragraphs for each main point. As you write, you imagine yourself conversing with your readers, telling them what they need to know, and communicating it as clearly and interestingly as you can.

Draft a conclusion. An effective closing adds to the reader's understanding of a research paper. The first part of the closing usually reviews (or ties together) important points in the paper, reinforces or reasserts the thesis, and/or draws a conclusion. The closing's final lines may expand the scope of the text by making a connection between the paper and the reader's experience, or between the paper and life in general.

Create a working title. At any point in the writing process, jot down possible titles that capture your paper's focused topic, research discoveries, and spirit. Consider key words and phrases that hint at your paper's thesis. For some papers, you may want to create a main title and a subtitle, separated by a colon.

TIPS for research writing
- As you draft your paper, keep the focus on your own thoughts. You don't want your paper to read like a strung-together series of references to other sources.
- Present your own ideas honestly and clearly. Although you will be considering the research of others, be sure to analyze this information yourself and relate your sources to one another. Work at offering your personal perspective on the topic.
- Your instructor may want your thesis in a specific location (perhaps in the last sentence of your first paragraph). Follow her or his wishes.
- Don't try to cram everything you've learned into your draft. Select material that is truly needed to develop your thesis.
- Avoid overusing one particular source; also avoid using too many direct quotations.
- To avoid accidental plagiarism, indicate the sources of all borrowed facts as you write your draft. (See "Avoiding Plagiarism," pages 476–479.)

Using Source Material in Your Writing

After you've found good sources and taken good notes on them, you want to use that research effectively in your writing. Specifically, you want to show (1) what information you are borrowing and (2) where you got it. By doing so, you create credibility. This section shows you how to develop credibility by integrating and documenting sources so as to avoid plagiarism and other abuses. *Note:* For a full treatment of documentation, see chapter 32 (MLA) and chapter 33 (APA).

Integrate source material carefully.

Source material—whether a summary, a paraphrase, or a quotation—should be integrated smoothly into your discussion. Follow these strategies:

The Right Reasons

Focus on what you want to say, not on all the source material you've collected. Use sources to do the following:

- Deepen and develop your point with the reasoning offered by a source.
- Support your point and your thinking about it with evidence—with facts, statistics, details, and so on.
- Give credibility to your point with an expert's supporting statement.
- Bring your point to life with an example, an observation, a case study, an anecdote, or an illustration.
- Address a counterargument or an alternative.

Quotation Restraint

In most research documents, restrict your quoting to nuggets:

- Key statements by authorities (e.g., the main point that a respected Shakespeare scholar makes about the role of Ophelia in *Hamlet*)
- Well-phrased claims and conclusions (e.g., a powerful conclusion by an ethicist about the problem with the media's coverage of cloning debates and technological developments)
- Passages where careful word-by-word analysis and interpretation are important to your argument (e.g., an excerpt from a speech made by a politician about the future of the NASA space shuttle program—a passage that requires a careful analysis for the between-the-lines message)

Quotations, especially long ones, must pull their weight, so generally paraphrase or summarize source material instead.

Primary Document Exception: When a primary text (a novel, a piece of legislation, a speech) is a key piece of evidence or the actual focus of your project, careful analysis of quoted excerpts is required. See pages **452–453** for more.

Smooth Integration

When you use quotations, work them into your writing as smoothly as possible. To do so, you need to pay attention to style, punctuation, and syntax. (See pages 488–489.)

Use enough of the quotation to make your point without changing the meaning of the original. Use quotation marks around key phrases taken from the source.

Example: Ogden, Williams, and Larson also conclude that the hydrogen fuel-cell vehicle is "a strong candidate for becoming the Car of the Future," given the trend toward "tighter environmental constraints" and the "intense efforts underway" by automakers to develop commercially viable versions of such vehicles (25).

Integrate all sources thoughtfully. Fold source material into your discussion by relating it to your own thinking. Let your ideas guide the way, not your sources, by using this pattern:

1. State and explain your idea, creating a context for the source.

2. Identify and introduce the source, linking it to your discussion.

3. Summarize, paraphrase, or quote the source, providing a citation in an appropriate spot.

4. Use the source by explaining, expanding, or refuting it.

5. When appropriate, refer back to a source to further develop the ideas it contains.

Sample Passage: Note the integration of sources in the paragraph below.

Writer's ideas

Attributive phrase

Paraphrase, quotation, or summary

Citation

Commentary

Conclusion

The motivation and urgency to create and improve hybrid-electric technology comes from a range of complex forces. Some of these forces are economic, others environmental, and still others social. In "Societal Lifestyle Costs of Cars with Alternative Fuels/Engines," Joan Ogden, Robert Williams, and Eric Larson argue that "[c]ontinued reliance on current transportation fuels and technologies poses serious oil supply insecurity, climate change, and urban air pollution risks" (7). Because of the nonrenewable nature of fossil fuels as well as their negative side effects, the transportation industry is confronted with making the most radical changes since the introduction of the internal-combustion automobile more than 100 years ago. Hybrid-electric vehicles are one response to this pressure.

Effectively document your sources.

Just as you need to integrate source material carefully into your writing, so you must also carefully document where that source material comes from. Readers should recognize which material is yours and which material is not.

Identify clearly where source material begins. Your discussion must offer a smooth transition to source material. Follow the guidelines below:

- For first references to a source, use an attributive statement that indicates some of the following: author's name and credentials, title of the source, nature of the study or research, and helpful background.

  Example: **Joan Ogden, Robert Williams, and Eric Larson, members of the Princeton Environmental Institute, explain** that modest improvements in energy efficiency and emissions reductions will not be enough over the next century because of anticipated transportation increases (7).

- For subsequent references to a source, use a simplified attributive phrase, such as the author's last name or a shortened version of the title.

  Example: **Ogden, Williams, and Larson go on to argue** that "[e]ffectively addressing environmental and oil supply concerns will probably require radical changes in automotive engine/fuel technologies" (7).

- In some situations, such as quoting straightforward facts, simply skip the attributive phrase. The parenthetical citation supplies sufficient attribution.

  Example: Various types of transportation are by far the main consumers of oil (three fourths of world oil imports); moreover, these same technologies are responsible for one fourth of all greenhouse gas sources (Ogden, Williams, and Larson 7).

- The verb you use to introduce source material is key. Use fitting verbs, such as those in the table below. Normally, use the present tense. Use the past tense only to stress the "pastness" of a source.

  Example: In their 2004 study, "Societal Lifecycle Costs of Cars with Alternative Fuels/Engines," Ogden, Williams, and Larson **present** a method for comparing and contrasting alternatives to internal-combustion engines. Earlier, these authors **made** preliminary steps . . .

accepts	considers	explains	rejects	acknowledges
contradicts	highlights	reminds	adds	contrasts
identifies	responds	affirms	criticizes	insists
shares	argues	declares	interprets	shows
asserts	defends	lists	states	believes
denies	maintains	stresses	cautions	describes
outlines	suggests	claims	disagrees	points out
supports	compares	discusses	praises	urges
concludes	emphasizes	proposes	verifies	confirms
enumerates	refutes	warns		

Indicate where source material ends. Closing quotation marks and a citation, as shown below, indicate the end of a source quotation. Generally, place the citation immediately after any quotation, paraphrase, or summary. However, you may also place the citation early in the sentence or at the end if the parenthetical note is obviously obtrusive. When you discuss several details from a page in a source, use an attributive phrase at the beginning of your discussion and a single citation at the end.

> *Example:* As the "Lifestyle Costs" study concludes, when greenhouse gases, air pollution, and oil insecurity are factored into the analysis, alternative-fuel vehicles "offer lower LCCs than typical new cars" (Ogden, Williams, and Larson 25).

Set off longer quotations. If a quotation is longer than four typed lines, set it off from the main text. Generally, introduce the quotation with a complete sentence and a colon. Indent the quotation one inch (10 spaces) and double-space it, but don't put quotation marks around it. Put the citation outside the final punctuation mark.

> *Example:* Toward the end of the study, Ogden, Williams, and Larson argue that changes to the fuel delivery system must be factored into planning:
>
> > In charting a course to the Car of the Future, societal LCC comparisons should be complemented by considerations of fuel infrastructure requirements. Because fuel infrastructure changes are costly, the number of major changes made over time should be minimized. The bifurcated strategy advanced here—of focusing on the H_2 FCV for the long term and advanced liquid hydrocarbon-fueled ICEVs and ICE/HEVs for the near term—would reduce the number of such infrastructure change to one (an eventual shift to H_2). (25)

Marking Changes to Quotations

You may shorten or change a quotation so that it fits more smoothly into your sentence—but don't alter the original meaning. Use an ellipsis within square brackets to indicate that you have omitted words from the original. An ellipsis is three periods with a space before and after each period.

> *Example:* In their projections of where fuel-cell vehicles are heading, Ogden, Williams, and Larson discuss GM's AUTOnomy vehicle, with its "radical redesign of the entire car. [. . .] In these cars, steering, braking, and other vehicle systems are controlled electronically rather than mechanically" (24).

Use square brackets to indicate a clarification or to change a pronoun or verb tense or to switch around uppercase and lowercase.

> *Example:* As Ogden, Williams, and Larson explain, "[e]ven if such barriers [the high cost of fuel cells and the lack of an H_2 fuel infrastructure] can be overcome, decades would be required before this embryonic technology could make major contributions in reducing the major externalities that characterize today's cars" (25).

 Chapters 2–7 contain additional tips. See pages **27–42** (beginning the writing process), pages **43–54** (planning), pages **55–70** (drafting), pages **71–110** (revising, editing), and pages **111–116** (submitting/portfolio work).

Writing Checklist

Use the seven-traits checklist below to review documented research.

Ideas

_____ The thesis is clear and sharp; the support strong and balanced.

_____ Researched data are accurate, complete, and properly credited.

Organization

_____ The writing offers a structured chain of ideas built on evidence.

_____ The opening presents the purpose and scope of the research, the middle provides complete discussion, and the closing focuses on conclusions.

Voice

_____ The tone is confident but also sincere, measured, and objective.

_____ "I" and "you" are avoided unless allowed by the instructor.

Words

_____ Precise, clear phrasing is used throughout the paper.

_____ Terms are defined as needed.

Sentences

_____ The prose contains a good blend of sentence lengths and patterns.

_____ Source material is carefully integrated.

Copy

_____ Grammar, punctuation, mechanics, usage, and spelling are correct.

_____ Documentation is complete, correct, and consistent.

Design

_____ The format, page layout, and typography are all reader friendly.

_____ Data are effectively presented in discussion, lists, tables, graphs.

Critical-Thinking and Writing Activities

1. With some classmates, debate the seriousness of plagiarism and the use of tools such as Turnitin.com.

2. Closely examine one of your most recent research papers. Have you followed this chapter's guidelines? Where do you need to improve?

◀ VISUALLY SPEAKING

Review the photograph at the beginning of this chapter (page **475**). What does the image suggest about research writing? How does the image relate to your research?

DOCUMENTATION AND FORMAT STYLES

Research-based writing—whether it is done in the humanities, social sciences, or natural and applied sciences—is assigned not only *to show* learning, but also *to share* learning. Careful and correct documentation of sources helps you do both. First, such documentation is a type of road map that *shows* your professor where you have gone and what you have done to learn about your topic and develop your thesis. Second, careful documentation *shares* your research results with all readers, enabling them to retrace your research steps, track the logic of your argument, and possibly study your sources for themselves.

The two chapters that follow will help you document your sources clearly and correctly. Chapter 32 explains how to document sources in accordance with the Modern Language Association's (MLA) style, outlined in the *MLA Handbook for Writers of Research Papers*, Seventh Edition (2009). The chapter includes "An American Hybrid," Katie Hughey's paper illustrating MLA formatting. Chapter 33 explains how to document sources in the American Psychological Association's (APA) style. This chapter includes "Our Roots Go Back to Roanoke . . . ," Renee Danielle Singh's paper illustrating APA formatting.

CONTENTS

Documentation and Format Styles

32 MLA Documentation Format ────────────────────────────

MLA Research Paper Guidelines   **494**
Guidelines for In-Text Citations   **496**
Sample In-Text Citations   **498**
MLA Works Cited Quick Guide   **504**
Books and Other Documents   **505**
Print Periodical Articles   **511**
Online Sources   **514**
Other Sources   **520**
Sample MLA Paper   **522**
Checklist and Writing Activities   **534**

33 APA Documentation Format ────────────────────────────

APA Research Paper Guidelines   **536**
Guidelines for In-Text Citations   **538**
Sample In-Text Citations   **538**
APA References Quick Guide   **542**
Books and Other Documents   **543**
Print Periodical Articles   **546**
Online Sources   **548**
Other Sources   **551**
Sample APA Paper   **553**
Checklist and Writing Activities   **565**
Research Paper Abbreviations   **566**

MLA
DOCUMENTATION FORMAT

Audio

In research papers, it is commonly said, "You are commanded to borrow but forbidden to steal." To borrow ideas while avoiding plagiarism (see pages 476–479), you must not only mention the sources you borrow from but also document them completely and accurately. You must follow to the last dot the documentation conventions for papers written in your general subject area.

If you are composing a research paper in the humanities, your instructor will most likely require you to follow the conventions established in the style manual of the Modern Language Association (MLA). This chapter provides you with explanations and examples for citing sources in MLA format. An excellent way to learn MLA documentation is to see it in use, so turn to the sample paper demonstrating MLA form on pages 522–533. Additional information and MLA updates can be found on the website for this book: **www.thecollegewriter .com/3e**.

Video

MLA Research Paper Guidelines

Questions & Answers

IS A SEPARATE TITLE PAGE REQUIRED?

No. (unless your instructor requires one, in which case you would format it according to his or her instructions). On the first page of a research paper, type your name, your instructor's name, the course name and number, and the date, one below the other. The title comes next, centered. Then simply begin the text on the next line.

IS THE RESEARCH PAPER DOUBLE-SPACED?

Yes. Double-space everything, even tables, captions, long quotations, or works-cited entries.

WHAT ABOUT LONGER QUOTATIONS?

Verse quotations of more than three lines should be indented one inch (ten spaces) and double-spaced. Do not add quotation marks. Each line of a poem or play begins a new line of the quotation; do not run the lines together. When you are quoting prose that needs more than four typed lines, indent each line of the quotation one inch (ten spaces) from the left margin and double-space it; do not add quotation marks.

To quote two or more paragraphs—in addition to the one inch that you are already indenting for the lengthy quotation—you should indent the first line of each paragraph an extra quarter-inch (three spaces). However, if the first sentence quoted does not begin a paragraph in the source, do not include the additional indent. Indent only the first lines of the successive paragraphs.

ARE PAGE NUMBERS REQUIRED?

Yes. Pages should be numbered consecutively in the upper-right corner, one-half inch from the top and flush with the right margin (one inch). Your last name should precede the page number, and no abbreviations or other symbols should be included.

IS AN APPENDIX REQUIRED?

No. In MLA style, tables and illustrations are placed as close as possible to the related text.

IS AN ABSTRACT REQUIRED?	*No.* An abstract, or summary of your research paper, is not an MLA requirement.
HOW WIDE SHOULD THE MARGINS BE?	Top, bottom, left, and right margins should be one inch (except for page numbering). The first word in a paragraph should be indented one-half inch (five spaces). Longer quotations should be set off one inch (ten spaces) from the left margin (see page **494**).
ARE REFERENCES PLACED IN THE TEXT?	*Yes.* Indicate only page numbers parenthetically if you identify the author in your text. Give the author's last name in a parenthetical reference if it is not mentioned in the text.
IS A LIST OF SOURCES USED IN THE PAPER REQUIRED?	*Yes.* Full citations for all sources used (e.g., books, periodicals) are placed in an alphabetized list labeled "Works Cited" at the end of the paper. Whereas in-text parenthetical references generally indicate just the author's last name and a page number for the source material, the works-cited entry provides full publication details.
WHAT ABOUT HEADINGS?	MLA style does not specify a particular format for headings within the text; normally, headings are used only for separate sections of the paper ("Works Cited" or "Notes," for example).
HOW DO I INCORPORATE REFERENCE MARKERS IF I SUBMIT MY PAPER ELECTRONICALLY?	Numbering paragraphs is common in electronic publications. Place the paragraph number in brackets. Follow with a space and begin the paragraph. (For other electronic formatting guidelines, check with your instructor.)
ANY OTHER SPECIAL INSTRUCTIONS?	Always ask whether your school, department, or instructor has special requirements that may take precedence over those listed here.

Web Link: For additional questions and answers about MLA format, see the MLA Q&A page at http://www.mla.org/handbook_faq.

Web Link

Guidelines for In-Text Citations

The *MLA Handbook for Writers of Research Papers*, Seventh Edition (2009), suggests giving credit for your sources of information in the body of your research paper. One way to do so is by indicating the author and/or title in the text of your essay, and then putting a page reference in parentheses after the summary, paraphrase, or quotation, as needed. The simplest way to do so is to insert the appropriate information (usually the author and page number) in parentheses after the words or ideas taken from the source. To avoid disrupting your writing, place citations where a pause would naturally occur (usually at the end of a sentence but sometimes within a sentence, before internal punctuation such as a comma or semicolon). These in-text citations (often called "parenthetical references") refer to sources listed on the "Works Cited" page at the end of your paper. (See pages 532–533 for a sample works-cited list.)

General Guidelines for In-Text Citations

As you integrate citations into your paper, follow the guidelines below, referring to the sample citation as needed.

Sample In-Text Citation

> As James Cuno, director of the Harvard University Art Museums, points out, the public, which subsidizes museums either directly through donations or indirectly via their status as tax-free nonprofit organizations, expects them to "carry out their duties professionally on its behalf" (164).

- Make sure each in-text citation clearly points to an entry in your list of works cited. The identifying information provided (usually the author's last name) must be the word or words by which the entry is alphabetized in that list.

- Keep citations brief, and integrate them smoothly into your writing.

- When paraphrasing or summarizing rather than quoting, make it clear where your borrowing begins and ends. Use stylistic cues to distinguish the source's thoughts ("Kalmbach points out . . . ," "Some critics argue . . .") from your own ("I believe . . . ," "It seems obvious, however"). See pages 486–487 for more on integrating sources.

- When using a shortened title of a work, begin with the word by which the work is alphabetized in your list of works cited (e.g., "Egyptian, Classical," not "Middle Eastern Art," for "Egyptian, Classical, and Middle Eastern Art").

- For inclusive page numbers larger than ninety-nine, give only the two digits of the second number (113–14, not 113–114).

- When including a parenthetical citation at the end of a sentence, place it before the end punctuation. (Citations for long, indented quotations are an exception. See pages 489, 494, 502, and 503.)

Special Guidelines for Sources Without Traditional Authorship and/or Pagination

Today many sources, especially electronic ones, have no stated authors and/or no pagination. For such sources, use these in-text citation strategies:

Source Without a Stated Author: In a signal phrase or in the parenthetical reference, identify the source as precisely as possible by indicating the sponsoring agency, the type of document, or the title (shortened in the parenthetical reference). See pages 499–500.

> While the Brooklyn Museum may be best known for the recent
> controversy over the Sensation exhibition, it does contain a strong
> collection of contemporary if less controversial art, "ranging from
> representational to abstract to conceptual" ("Contemporary Art").

Source with No Pagination: If no pagination exists within the document, use paragraph numbers (with the abbreviation *par.*), if the document provides them. If the document includes neither page nor paragraph numbers, cite the entire work. Do not create your own numbering system.

> The Museum's collection of Art of the Americas includes extensive
> holdings of works by the aboriginal peoples of North, Central, and
> South America, many of these gathered by archaeologist Herbert
> Spinden during at least seven expeditions between 1929 and 1950
> ("Art of the Americas" par. 3).

Note: Because parenthetical notations are used to signal the end of an attribution, sources with no pagination or paragraph numbers offer a special challenge. When no parenthetical notation is possible, signal a shift back to your own discussion with a source-reflective statement indicating your thinking about the source.

> . . . indicated by his recording the audio tour of the exhibit, his supporting
> the show financially, and his promoting Sensation at his website.
> As Welland's discussion of David Bowie's participation indicates, the
> controversy over the Brooklyn Museum of Art's Sensation exhibit . . .

INSIGHT:

- Stable pagination for many electronic resources is available when you use the ".pdf" rather than the ".html" version of the source.
- For instruction on smoothly integrating source material into your paper, see pages 486–489.
- For cautions about sources without identified authors, see pages 499, 500, 506, and 512.

Sample In-Text Citations

The following entries illustrate the most common in-text citations.

Video

One Author: A Complete Work

You do not need an in-text citation if you identify the author in your text. (See the first entry below.) However, you must give the author's last name in an in-text citation if it is not mentioned in the text. (See the second entry.) When a source is listed in your works-cited page with an editor, a translator, a speaker, or an artist instead of the author, use that person's name in your citation.

With Author in Text: (This is the preferred way of citing a complete work.)

> In *No Need for Hunger*, Robert Spitzer recommends that the U.S. government develop a new foreign policy to help Third World countries overcome poverty and hunger.

Without Author in Text:

> *No Need for Hunger* recommends that the U.S. government develop a new foreign policy to help Third World countries overcome poverty and hunger (Spitzer).

Note: Do not offer page numbers when citing complete works, articles in alphabetized encyclopedias, one-page articles, and unpaginated sources.

One Author: Part of a Work

List the necessary page numbers in parentheses if you borrow words or ideas from a particular source. Leave a space between the author's last name and the page reference. No abbreviation or punctuation is needed.

With Author in Text:

> Bullough writes that genetic engineering was dubbed "eugenics" by a cousin of Darwin's, Sir Francis Galton, in 1885 (5).

Without Author in Text:

> Genetic engineering was dubbed "eugenics" by a cousin of Darwin's, Sir Francis Galton, in 1885 (Bullough 5).

A Work by Two or Three Authors

Give the last names of every author in the same order that they appear in the works-cited section. (The correct order of the authors' names can be found on the title page of the book.)

> Students learned more than a full year's Spanish in ten days using the complete supermemory method (Ostrander and Schroeder 51).

A Work by Four or More Authors

Give the first author's last name as it appears in the works-cited section followed by *et al.* (meaning "and others").

> Communication on the job is more than talking; it is "inseparable from your total behavior" (Culligan et al. 111).

Note: You may instead choose to list all of the authors' last names.

Two or More Works by the Same Author(s)

In addition to the author's last name(s) and page number(s), include a shortened version of the work's title when you cite two or more works by the same author(s).

> With Author in Text:
>
> Wallerstein and Blakeslee claim that divorce creates an enduring identity for children of the marriage (*Unexpected Legacy* 62).
>
> Without Author in Text:
>
> They are intensely lonely despite active social lives (Wallerstein and Blakeslee, *Second Chances* 51).

Note: When including both author(s) and title in a parenthetical reference, separate them with a comma, as shown above, but do not put a comma between the title and the page number.

Works by Authors with the Same Last Name

When citing different sources by authors with the same last name, it is best to use the authors' full names in the text to avoid confusion. However, if circumstances call for parenthetical references, add each author's first initial. If first initials are the same, use each author's full name.

> Some critics think *Titus Andronicus* too abysmally melodramatic to be a work of Shakespeare (A. Parker 73). Others suggest that Shakespeare meant it as black comedy (D. Parker 486).

A Work Authored by an Agency, a Committee, or an Organization

If a book or other work was written by an organization such as an agency, a committee, or a task force, it is said to have a corporate author. (See also page 506.) If the corporate name is long, include it in the text (rather than in parentheses) to avoid disrupting the flow of your writing. After the full name has been used at least once, use a shortened form of the name (common abbreviations are acceptable) in subsequent references. For example, *Task Force* may be used for *Task Force on Education for Economic Growth*.

> The thesis of the Task Force's report is that economic success depends on our ability to improve large-scale education and training as quickly as possible (113–14).

An Anonymous Work

When there is no author listed, give the title or a shortened version of the title as it appears in the works-cited section. (See page 506.)

> Statistics indicate that drinking water can make up 20 percent of
> a person's total exposure to lead (*Information* 572).

Two or More Works Included in One Citation

To cite multiple works within a single parenthetical reference, separate the references with a semicolon.

> In Medieval Europe, Latin translations of the works of Rhazes, a
> Persian scholar, were a primary source of medical knowledge
> (Albala 22; Lewis 266).

A Series of Citations from a Single Work

If no confusion is possible, it is not necessary to name a source repeatedly when making multiple parenthetical references to that source in a single paragraph. If all references are to the same page, identify that page in a parenthetical note after the last reference. If the references are to different pages within the same work, you need identify the work only once, and then use a parenthetical note with page number alone for the subsequent references.

> Domesticating science meant not only spreading scientific knowledge,
> but also promoting it as a topic of public conversation (Heilbron 2). One
> way to enhance its charm was by depicting cherubic putti as "angelic
> research assistants" in book illustrations (5).

A Work Referred to in Another Work

If you must cite an indirect source—that is, information from a source that is quoted from another source—use the abbreviation *qtd. in* (quoted in) before the indirect source in your reference.

> Paton improved the conditions in Diepkloof (a prison) by "removing all
> the more obvious aids to detention. The dormitories [were] open at
> night: the great barred gate [was] gone" (qtd. in Callan xviii).

A Work Without Page Numbers

If a work has no page numbers or paragraph numbers, treat it as you would a complete work. (See page 497.) This is commonly the case with electronic resources, for example. Do not count pages to create reference numbers of your own.

> Antibiotics become ineffective against such organisms through two natural
> processes: first, genetic mutation; and second, the subsequent transfer of this
> mutated genetic material to other organisms (Davies par. 5).